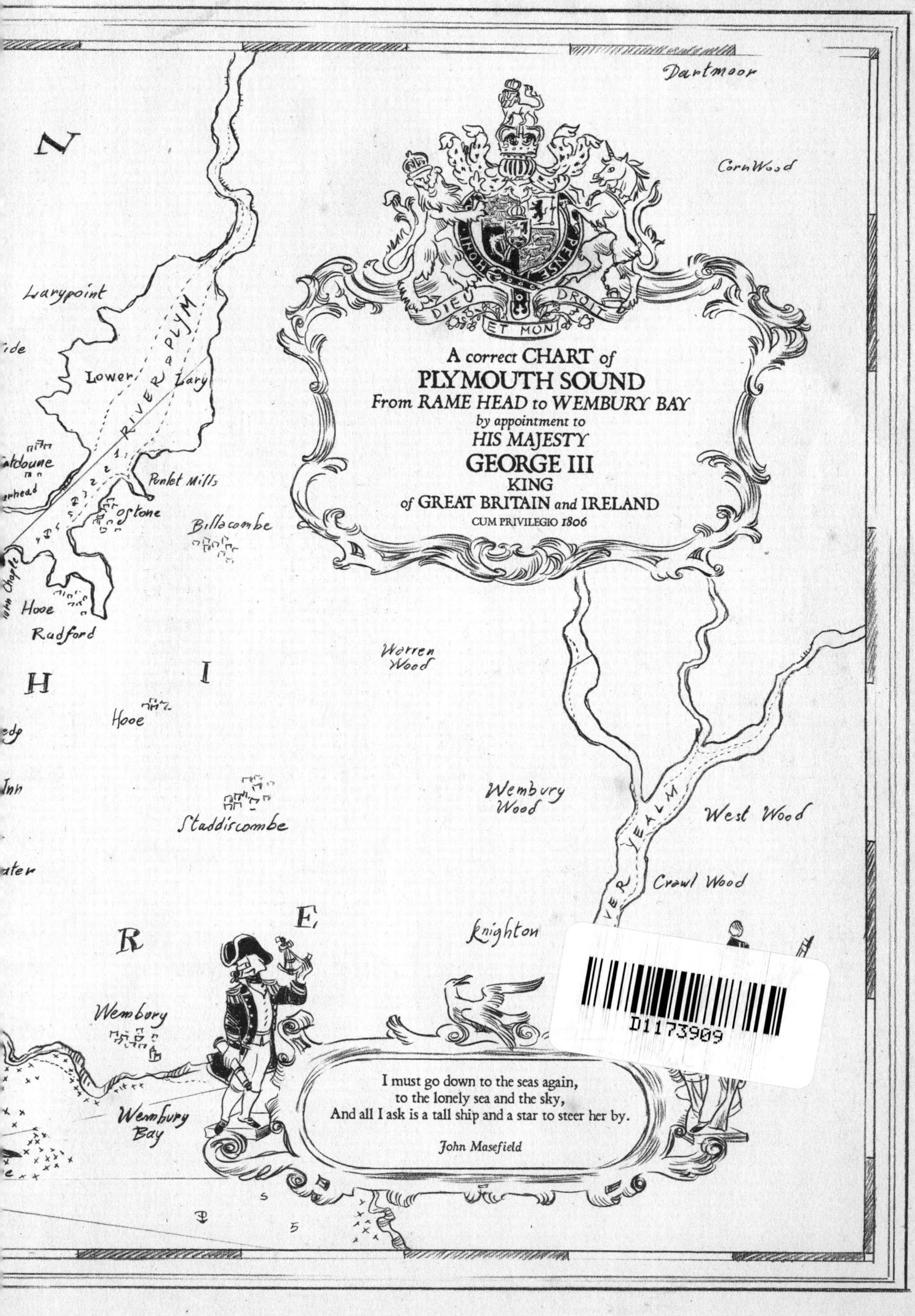

N

Dartmoor

CornWood

Larypoint

ide

Lower Lary

RIVER PLYM

A correct CHART of
PLYMOUTH SOUND
From RAME HEAD to WEMBURY BAY
by appointment to
HIS MAJESTY
GEORGE III
KING
of GREAT BRITAIN and IRELAND
CUM PRIVILEGIO *1806*

atdoune

head

Punlet Mills

Frostone

Billacombe

rn Chaple

Hooe
Radford

Warren
Wood

H

I

Hooe

edg

Jnn

Wembury
Wood

West Wood

ater

Staddiscombe

RIVER YEALM

Crawl Wood

R

E

knighton

Wembory

Wembury
Bay

I must go down to the seas again,
to the lonely sea and the sky,
And all I ask is a tall ship and a star to steer her by.

John Masefield

S

5

Teresa Radice   Stefano Turconi

THE
FORBIDDEN
HARBOR

nbm GRAPHIC
NOVELS
Nantier · Beall · Minoustchine
NEW YORK

T   H   A   N   K - Y   O   U

To Caterina and Michele, for believing in this crazy mission and making such great ship owners.

To Viola Nenne and Mickey Cuorcontento, for the candid enthusiasm with which
they faced English wanderings, nautical tales and sea shanties at the dinner table.

To grandparents Raffi and grandparents Lu, for providing mess
and warm bunks for the little'uns, as their oldies were on a mission.

To Sister Angela who, during the high school years, unwittingly traced the course
that brought us here with her passion for English Romanticism.

To the ever so reserved Captain McLeod of Catalone, Cape Breton, Nova Scotia who,
behind an anonymous apron and a hearty breakfast, disclosed the secrets
of buried treasures and recovered wreckages.

To Izumi and Michele, Ale and Ciskije — friends, and sailing companions — who, like us, climb up
those ropes every single day, unafraid of heights, in the constant search for new horizons.

To Anthony De Mello, Antonia Pozzi, Bjorn Larsson, Derek Walcott, Edgar Lee Masters,
Emily Dickinson, Eugenio Montale, Geoff Hunt, George Gordon Lord Byron, Jane Austen,
Joseph Conrad, Kahlil Gibran, Luigi Pirandello, Mario Luzi, Nicholas Pocock, Pablo Neruda,
Par Lagerkvist, Patrick O'Brian, Peter Weir, Rabindranath Tagore, Robert Louis Stevenson,
Samuel Taylor Coleridge, Sant'Agostino, William Beechey, William Blake, William Shakespeare,
William Turner, William Wordsworth, for two years unwitting crew of the
House With No North and constant "compass of inspiration".

To Odri and the Baoboys for their smiley welcome.

To those who have known us in the company of ducks, mice and sorceresses and
never stopped following us, sharing with us night-watches and patrolling shifts.

To those who made it possible for us to enjoy good winds and favourable seas,
so that this story could get to shore safe and sound.

To Father Federico, for the "caress from God".

Last but not least, thank you to those that are willing to forgive us our mistakes and nautical inaccuracies: we travelled around books and locations, we became charmed by the story and its protagonists, building possibilities and scale models... However, the vessels whose decks we had the honour of treading, sailed — with us on board — just the waves of our imagination. At least, until now.

TERESA RADICE
STEFANO TURCONI

THE
FORBIDDEN
HARBOR

GRAPHIC NOVEL
in four acts

LONDON
1811

ISBN 9781681122328
© 2015 - BAO PUBLISHING - RADICE E TURCONI
Library of Congress Control Number: 2019940466
Translation: Carla Roncalli di Montorio, Nanette McGuiness
Lettering: Sara Bottaini, Vanessa Nascimbene, Ortho
Original title: Il porto proibito
Originally published in Italy by BAO PUBLISHING in 2015.
All rights reserved.
www.baopublishing.it

Printed in India

Also available wherever ebooks are sold.

CURTAIN

Well, gentlemen,
I speak to you as we once spoke to the pilgrims:
Loosen your shoes and lay down your staff.
You reached your destination.
I have been waiting years for people like you
To revive other ghosts I have in mind.

LUIGI PIRANDELLO
The Mountain Giants

ACT I
HMS EXPLORER

Once more upon the waters! Yet once more!
And the waves bound beneath me as a steed
That knows his rider. Welcome to their roar!
Swift be their guidance, wheresoe'er it lead!
Though the strained mast should quiver as a reed,
And the rent canvass fluttering strew the gale,
Still must I on; for I am as a weed,
Flung from the rock on Ocean's foam, to sail
Where'er the surge may sweep, the tempest's breath prevail.

GEORGE GORDON LORD BYRON
Childe Harold's Pilgrimage

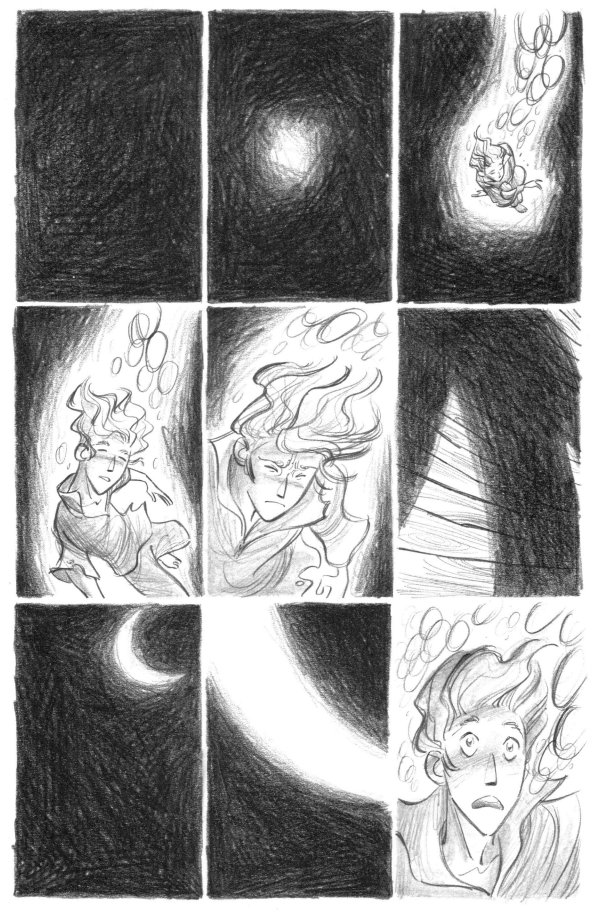

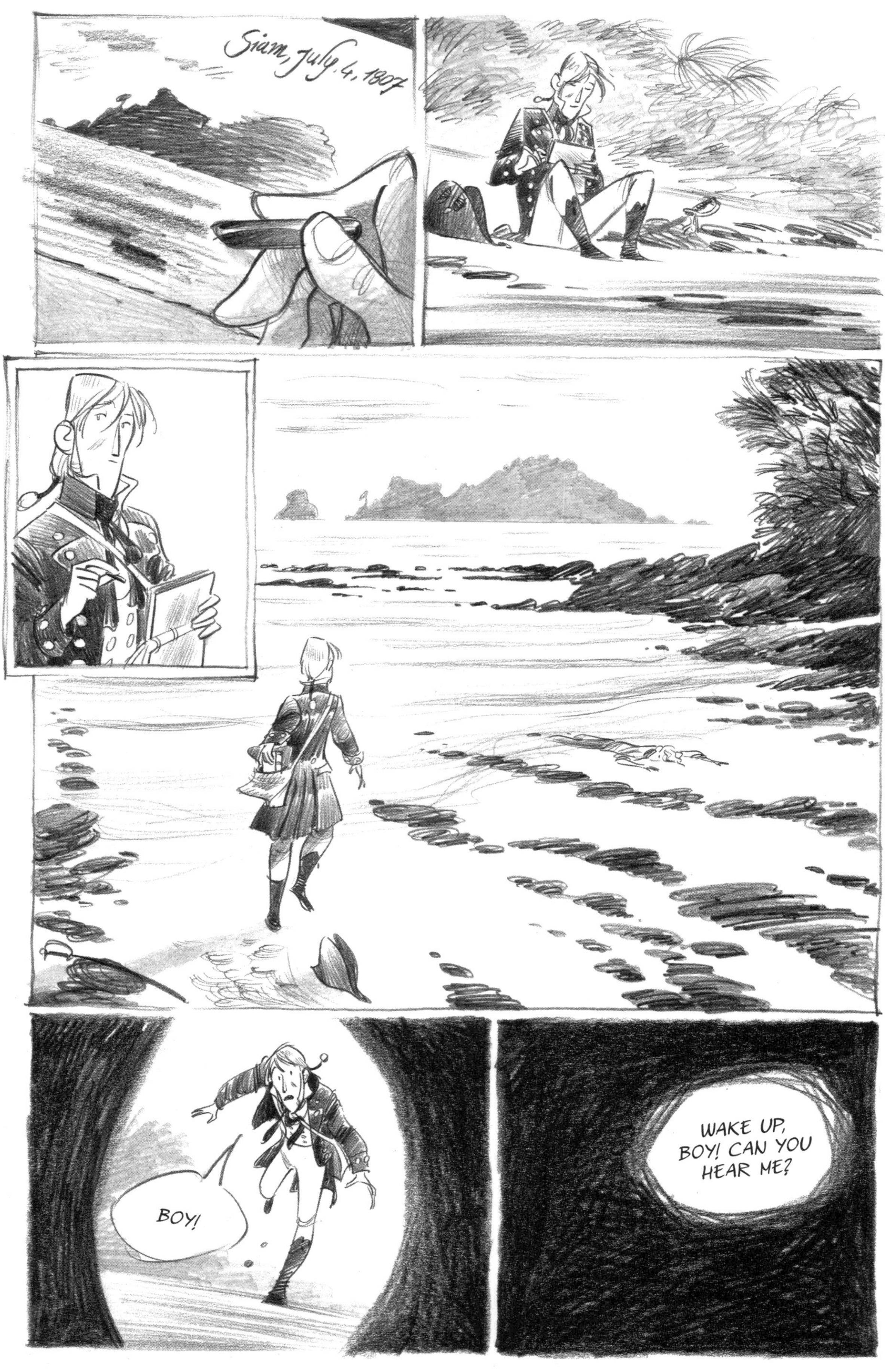
Siam, July 4, 1807
BOY!
WAKE UP, BOY! CAN YOU HEAR ME?

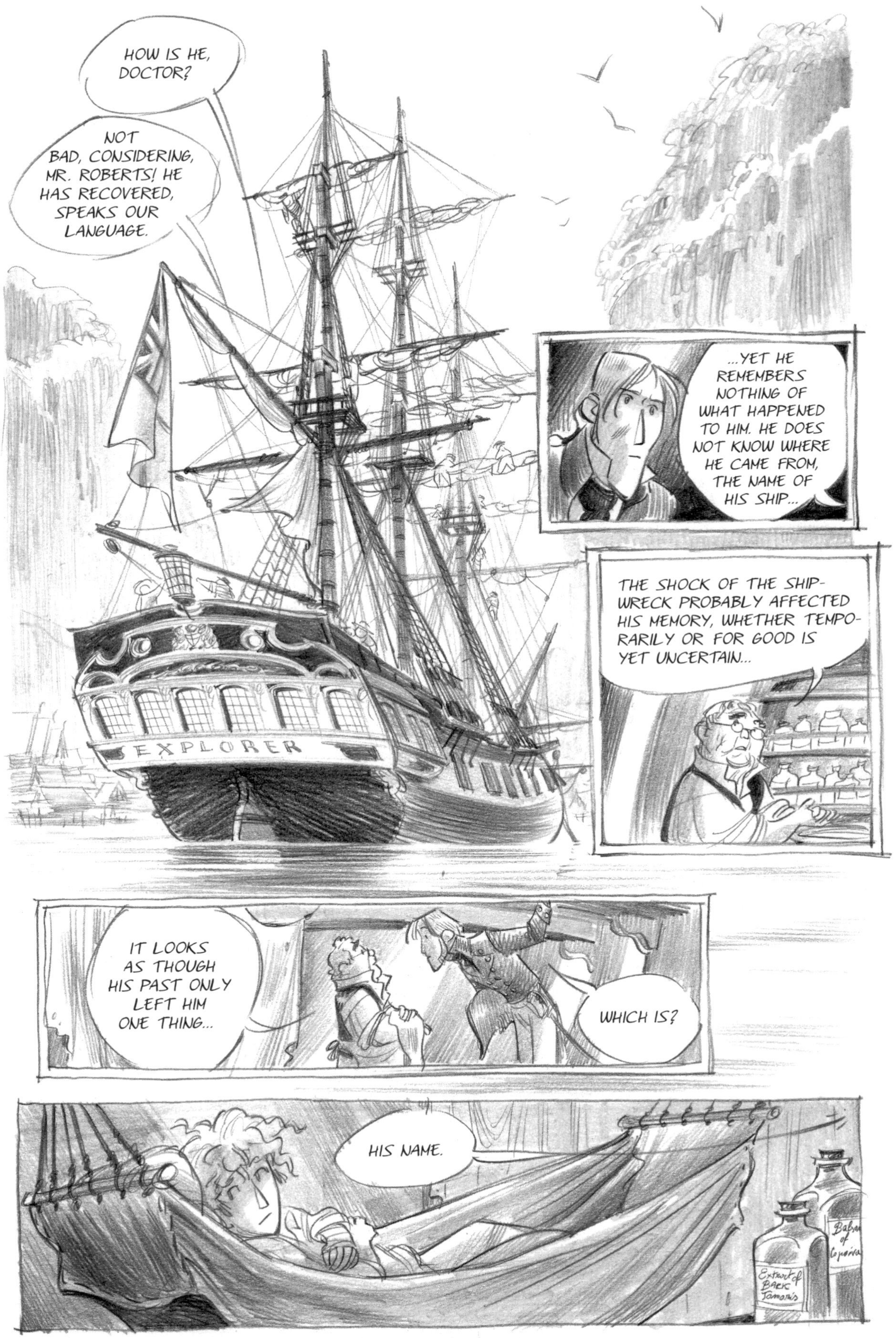
HOW IS HE, DOCTOR?
NOT BAD, CONSIDERING, MR. ROBERTS! HE HAS RECOVERED, SPEAKS OUR LANGUAGE.
EXPLORER
...YET HE REMEMBERS NOTHING OF WHAT HAPPENED TO HIM. HE DOES NOT KNOW WHERE HE CAME FROM, THE NAME OF HIS SHIP...
THE SHOCK OF THE SHIP-WRECK PROBABLY AFFECTED HIS MEMORY, WHETHER TEMPO-RARILY OR FOR GOOD IS YET UNCERTAIN...
IT LOOKS AS THOUGH HIS PAST ONLY LEFT HIM ONE THING...
WHICH IS?
HIS NAME.

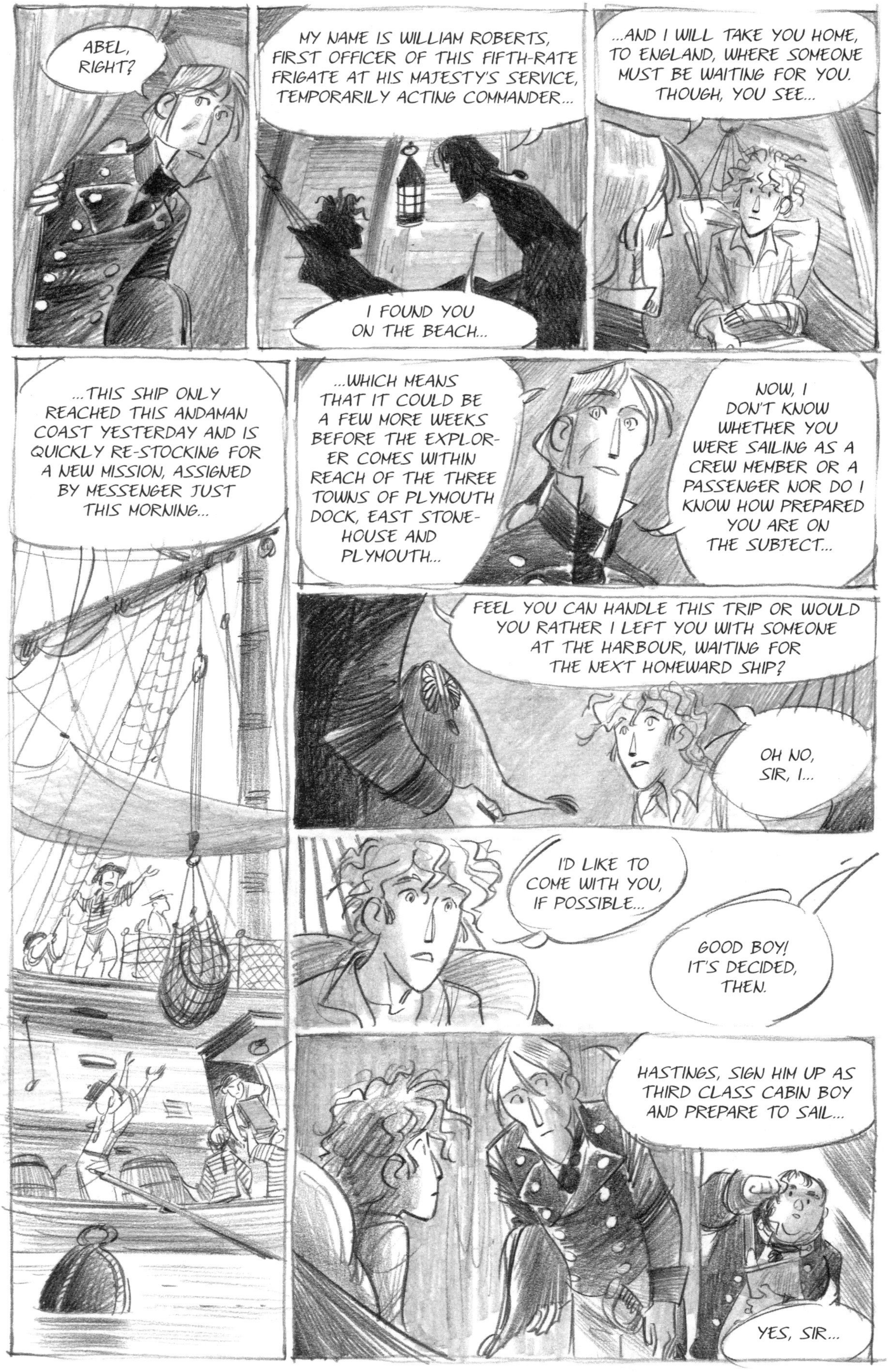
ABEL, RIGHT?
MY NAME IS WILLIAM ROBERTS, FIRST OFFICER OF THIS FIFTH-RATE FRIGATE AT HIS MAJESTY'S SERVICE, TEMPORARILY ACTING COMMANDER...
I FOUND YOU ON THE BEACH...
...AND I WILL TAKE YOU HOME, TO ENGLAND, WHERE SOMEONE MUST BE WAITING FOR YOU. THOUGH, YOU SEE...
...THIS SHIP ONLY REACHED THIS ANDAMAN COAST YESTERDAY AND IS QUICKLY RE-STOCKING FOR A NEW MISSION, ASSIGNED BY MESSENGER JUST THIS MORNING...
...WHICH MEANS THAT IT COULD BE A FEW MORE WEEKS BEFORE THE EXPLOR-ER COMES WITHIN REACH OF THE THREE TOWNS OF PLYMOUTH DOCK, EAST STONE-HOUSE AND PLYMOUTH...
NOW, I DON'T KNOW WHETHER YOU WERE SAILING AS A CREW MEMBER OR A PASSENGER NOR DO I KNOW HOW PREPARED YOU ARE ON THE SUBJECT...
FEEL YOU CAN HANDLE THIS TRIP OR WOULD YOU RATHER I LEFT YOU WITH SOMEONE AT THE HARBOUR, WAITING FOR THE NEXT HOMEWARD SHIP?
OH NO, SIR, I...
I'D LIKE TO COME WITH YOU, IF POSSIBLE...
GOOD BOY! IT'S DECIDED, THEN.
HASTINGS, SIGN HIM UP AS THIRD CLASS CABIN BOY AND PREPARE TO SAIL...
YES, SIR...

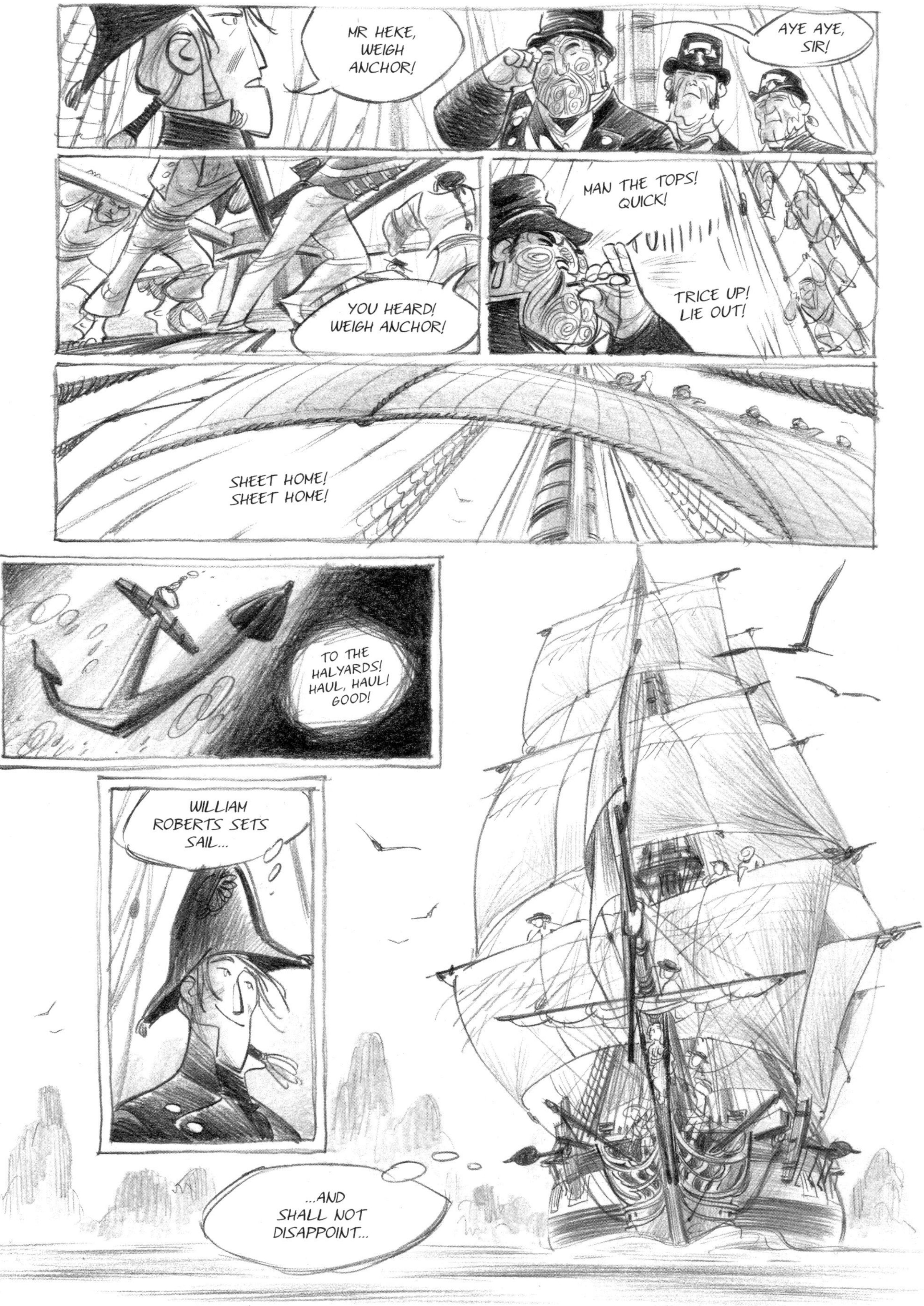
MR HEKE, WEIGH ANCHOR!
AYE AYE, SIR!
YOU HEARD! WEIGH ANCHOR!
MAN THE TOPS! QUICK!
TUI
TRICE UP! LIE OUT!
SHEET HOME! SHEET HOME!
TO THE HALYARDS! HAUL, HAUL! GOOD!
WILLIAM ROBERTS SETS SAIL...
...AND SHALL NOT DISAPPOINT...

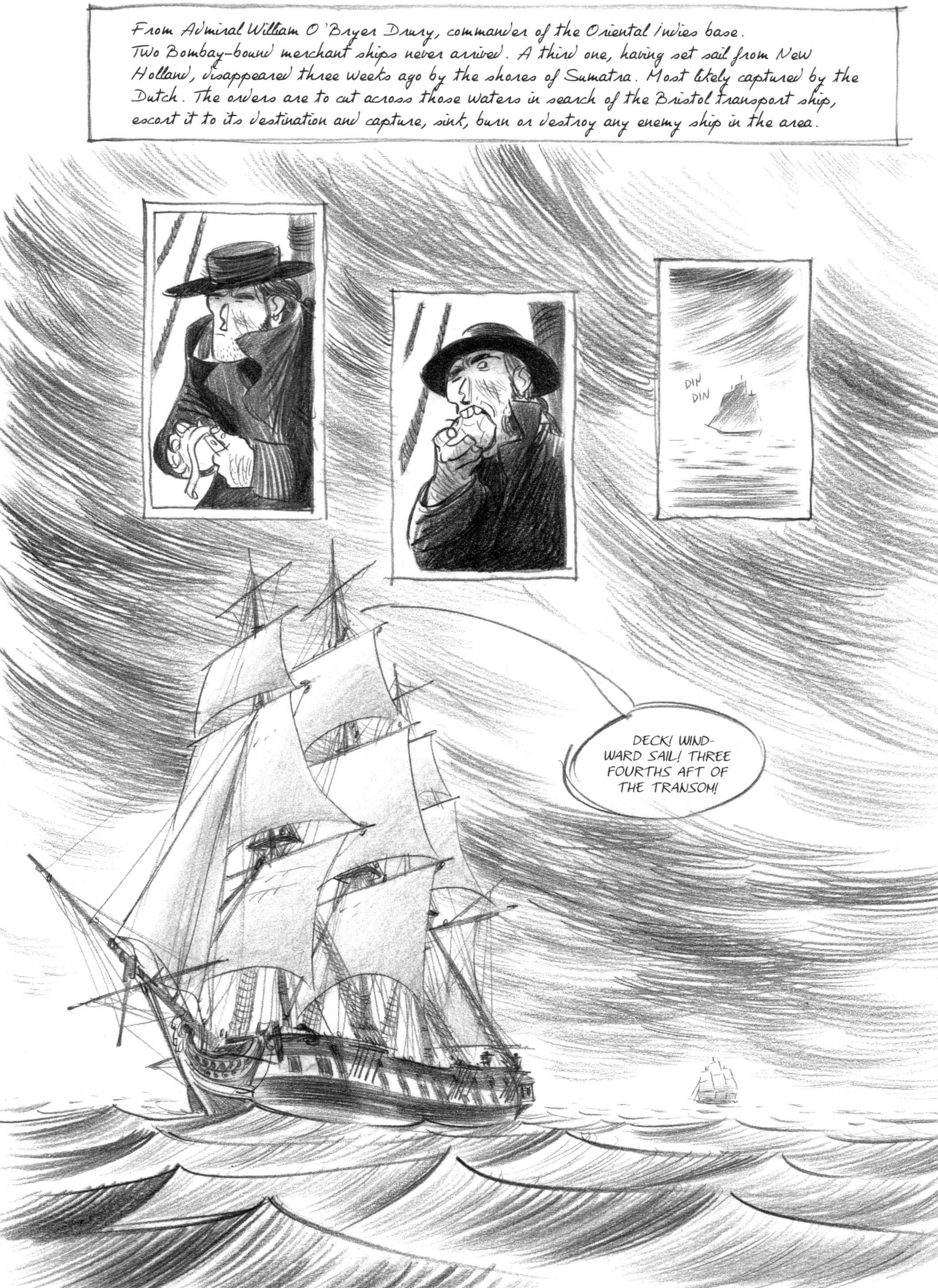
From Admiral William O'Bryer Drury, commander of the Oriental Indies base.
Two Bombay-bound merchant ships never arrived. A third one, having set sail from New Holland, disappeared three weeks ago by the shores of Sumatra. Most likely captured by the Dutch. The orders are to cut across those waters in search of the Bristol transport ship, escort it to its destination and capture, sink, burn or destroy any enemy ship in the area.
DIN DIN
DECK! WINDWARD SAIL! THREE FOURTHS AFT OF THE TRANSOM!

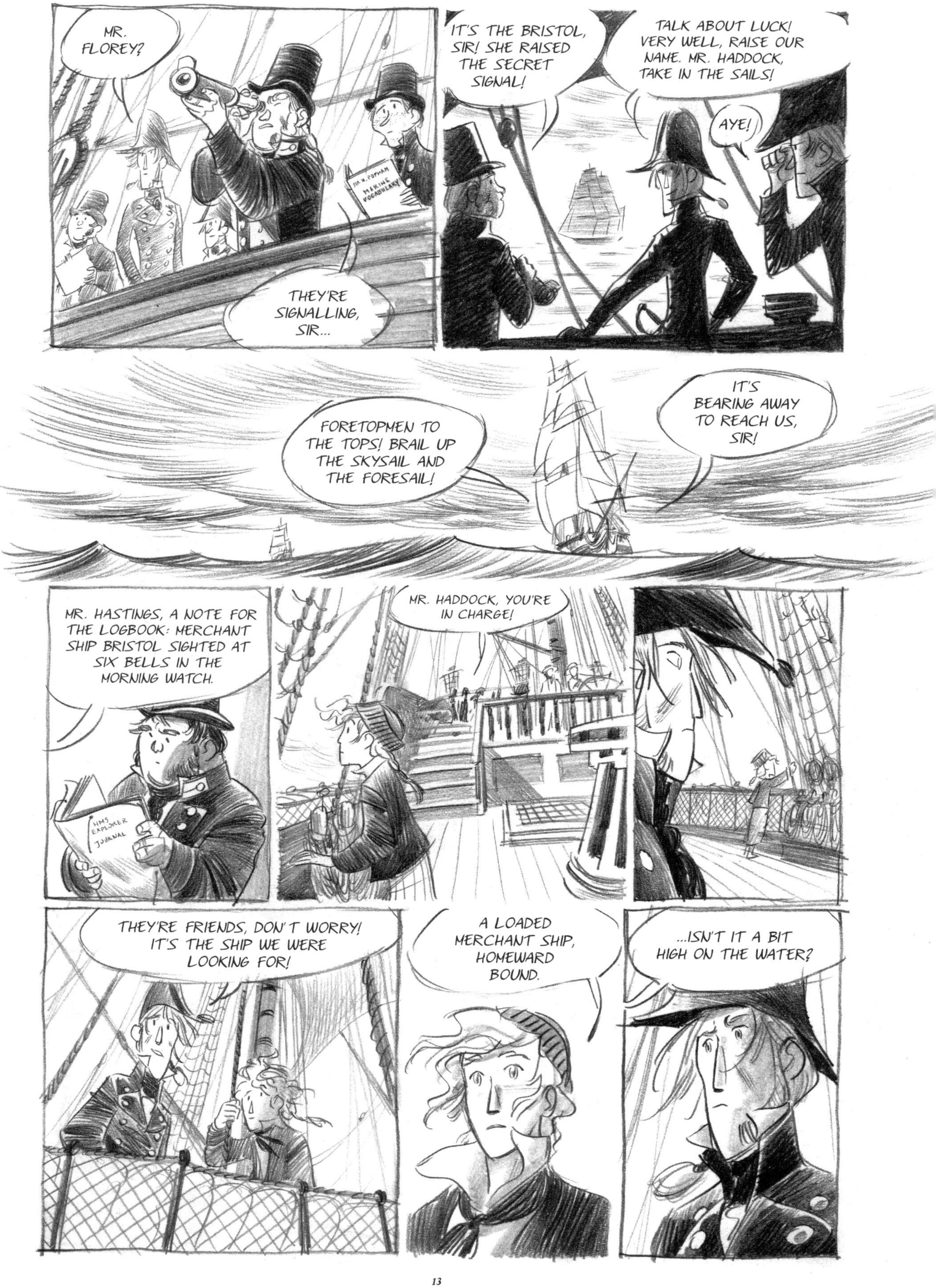
MR. FLOREY?
THEY'RE SIGNALLING, SIR...
SIR H. POPHAM MARINE VOCABULARY
IT'S THE BRISTOL, SIR! SHE RAISED THE SECRET SIGNAL!
TALK ABOUT LUCK! VERY WELL, RAISE OUR NAME. MR. HADDOCK, TAKE IN THE SAILS!
AYE!
FORETOPMEN TO THE TOPS! BRAIL UP THE SKYSAIL AND THE FORESAIL!
IT'S BEARING AWAY TO REACH US, SIR!
MR. HASTINGS, A NOTE FOR THE LOGBOOK: MERCHANT SHIP BRISTOL SIGHTED AT SIX BELLS IN THE MORNING WATCH.
HMS EXPLORER JOURNAL
MR. HADDOCK, YOU'RE IN CHARGE!
THEY'RE FRIENDS, DON'T WORRY! IT'S THE SHIP WE WERE LOOKING FOR!
A LOADED MERCHANT SHIP, HOMEWARD BOUND.
...ISN'T IT A BIT HIGH ON THE WATER?

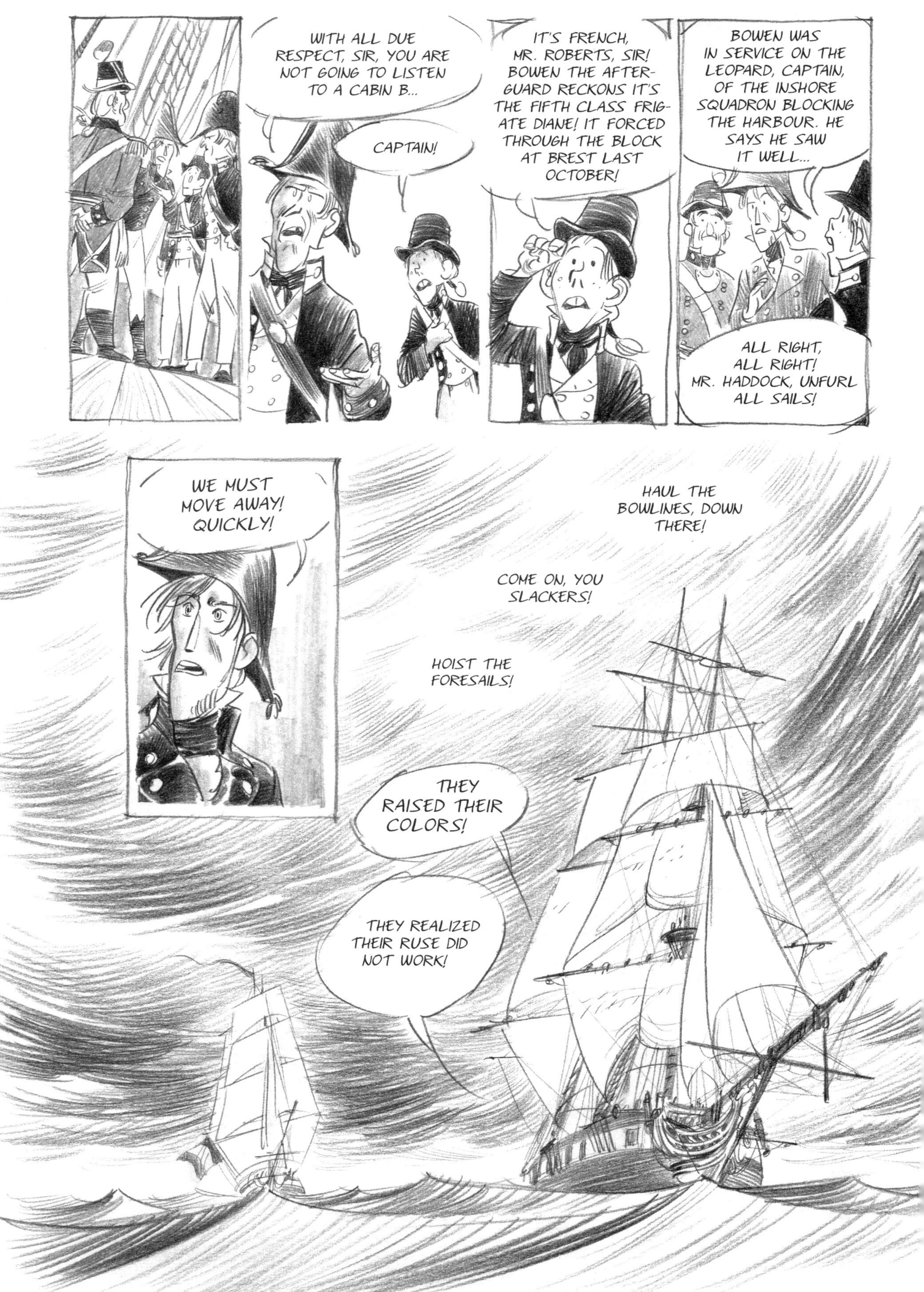

WITH ALL DUE RESPECT, SIR, YOU ARE NOT GOING TO LISTEN TO A CABIN B...
CAPTAIN!
IT'S FRENCH, MR. ROBERTS, SIR! BOWEN THE AFTER-GUARD RECKONS IT'S THE FIFTH CLASS FRIG-ATE DIANE! IT FORCED THROUGH THE BLOCK AT BREST LAST OCTOBER!
BOWEN WAS IN SERVICE ON THE LEOPARD, CAPTAIN, OF THE INSHORE SQUADRON BLOCKING THE HARBOUR. HE SAYS HE SAW IT WELL...
ALL RIGHT, ALL RIGHT! MR. HADDOCK, UNFURL ALL SAILS!
WE MUST MOVE AWAY! QUICKLY!
HAUL THE BOWLINES, DOWN THERE!
COME ON, YOU SLACKERS!
HOIST THE FORESAILS!
THEY RAISED THEIR COLORS!
THEY REALIZED THEIR RUSE DID NOT WORK!

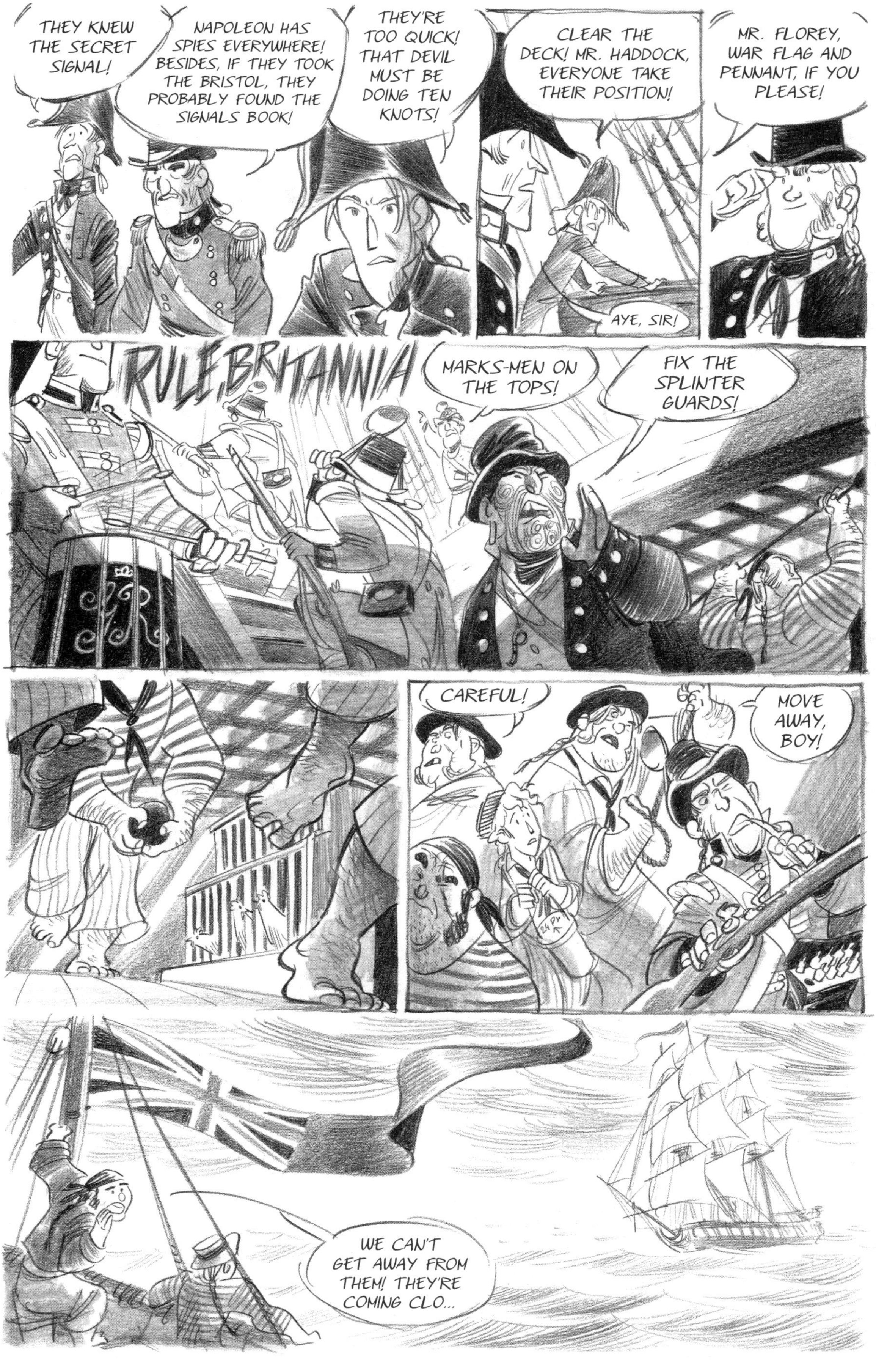
THEY KNEW THE SECRET SIGNAL!
NAPOLEON HAS SPIES EVERYWHERE! BESIDES, IF THEY TOOK THE BRISTOL, THEY PROBABLY FOUND THE SIGNALS BOOK!
THEY'RE TOO QUICK! THAT DEVIL MUST BE DOING TEN KNOTS!
CLEAR THE DECK! MR. HADDOCK, EVERYONE TAKE THEIR POSITION!
AYE, SIR!
MR. FLOREY, WAR FLAG AND PENNANT, IF YOU PLEASE!
RULE, BRITANNIA
MARKS-MEN ON THE TOPS!
FIX THE SPLINTER GUARDS!
CAREFUL!
MOVE AWAY, BOY!
WE CAN'T GET AWAY FROM THEM! THEY'RE COMING CLO...

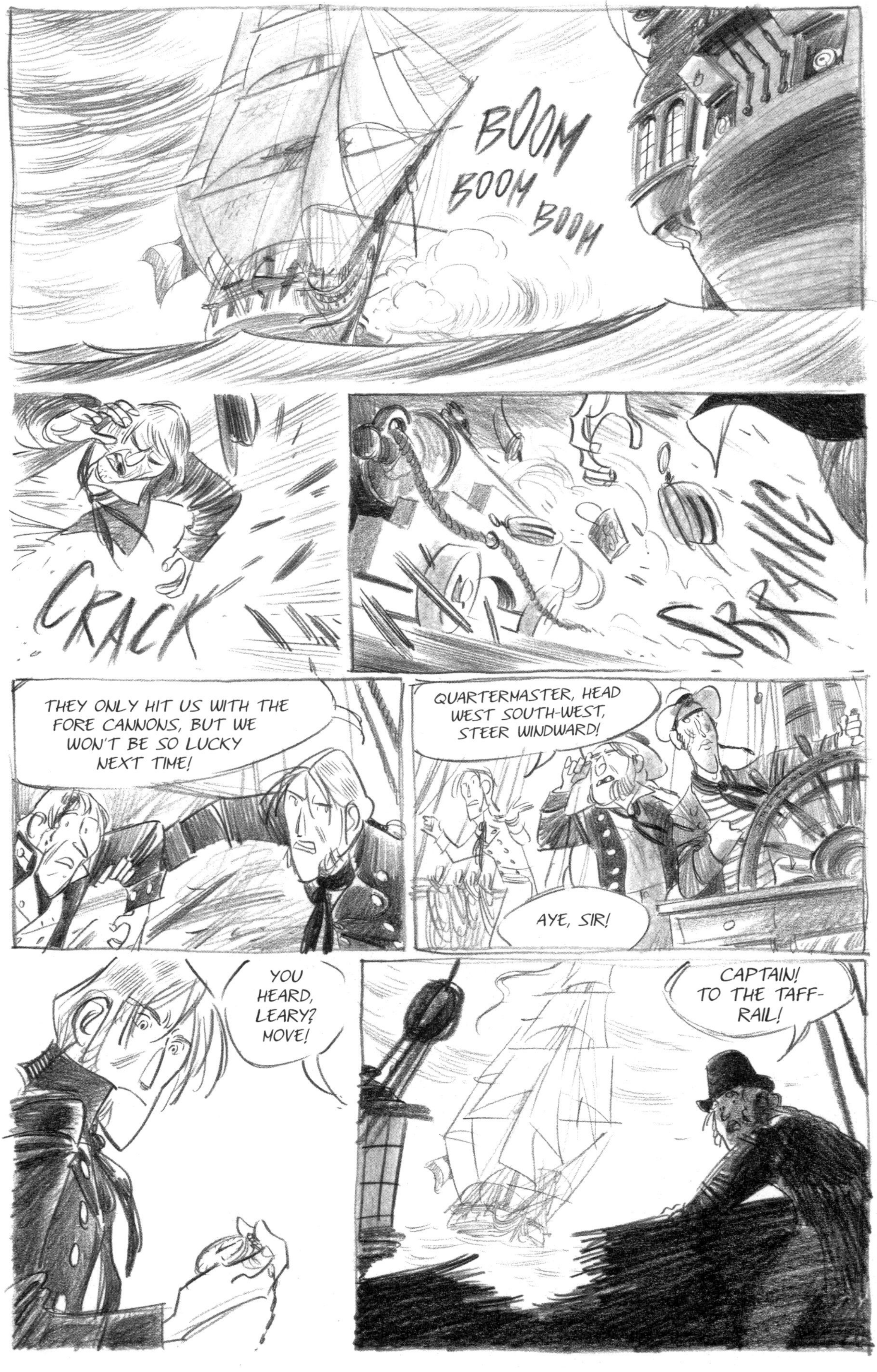
BOOM
BOOM
BOOM
CRACK
SBRANG
THEY ONLY HIT US WITH THE FORE CANNONS, BUT WE WON'T BE SO LUCKY NEXT TIME!
QUARTERMASTER, HEAD WEST SOUTH-WEST, STEER WINDWARD!
AYE, SIR!
YOU HEARD, LEARY? MOVE!
CAPTAIN! TO THE TAFF-RAIL!

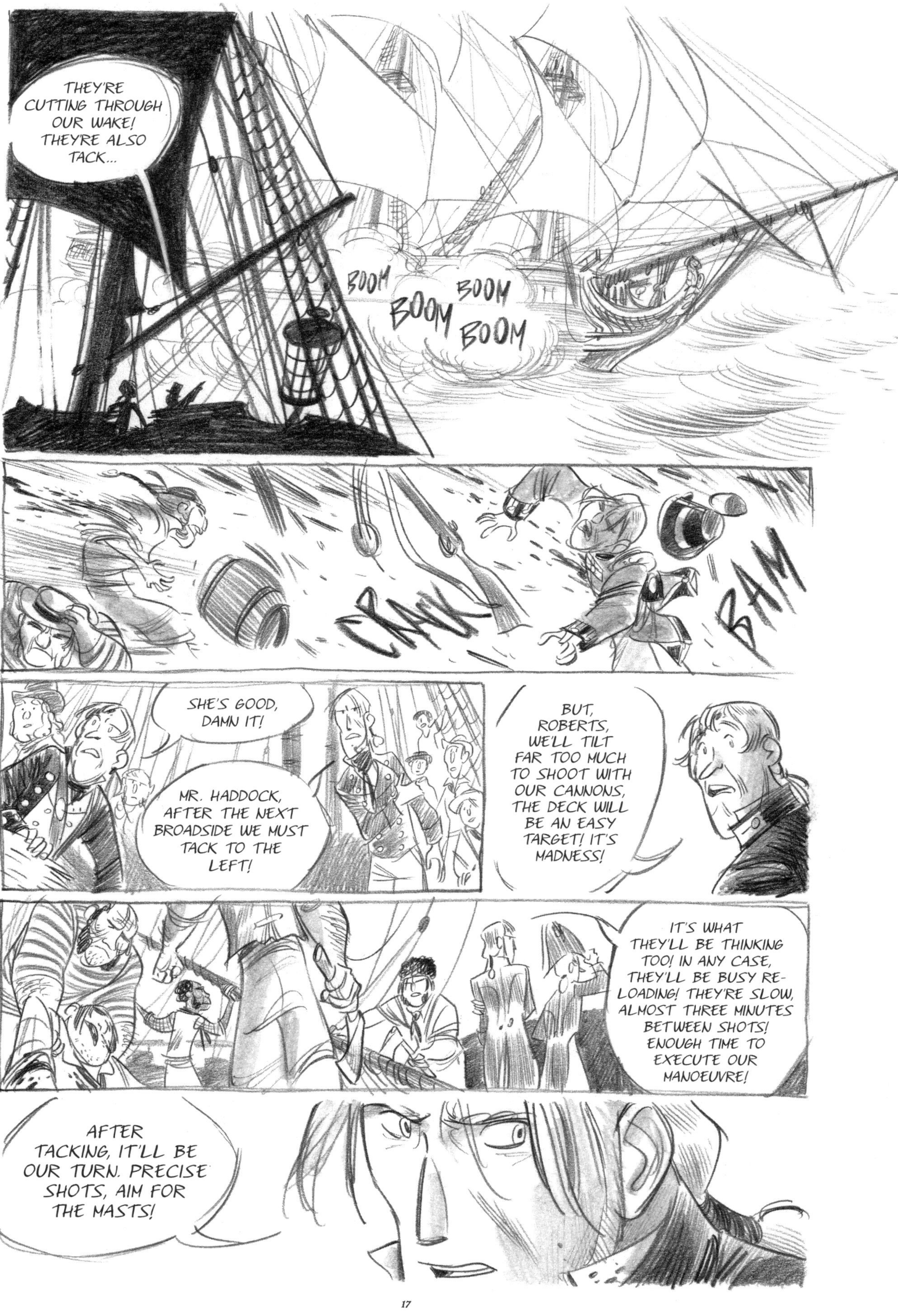
THEY'RE CUTTING THROUGH OUR WAKE! THEY'RE ALSO TACK...
BOOM
BOOM
BOOM
BOOM
CRAK
BAM
SHE'S GOOD, DAMN IT!
MR. HADDOCK, AFTER THE NEXT BROADSIDE WE MUST TACK TO THE LEFT!
BUT, ROBERTS, WE'LL TILT FAR TOO MUCH TO SHOOT WITH OUR CANNONS, THE DECK WILL BE AN EASY TARGET! IT'S MADNESS!
IT'S WHAT THEY'LL BE THINKING TOO! IN ANY CASE, THEY'LL BE BUSY RE-LOADING! THEY'RE SLOW, ALMOST THREE MINUTES BETWEEN SHOTS! ENOUGH TIME TO EXECUTE OUR MANOEUVRE!
AFTER TACKING, IT'LL BE OUR TURN. PRECISE SHOTS, AIM FOR THE MASTS!

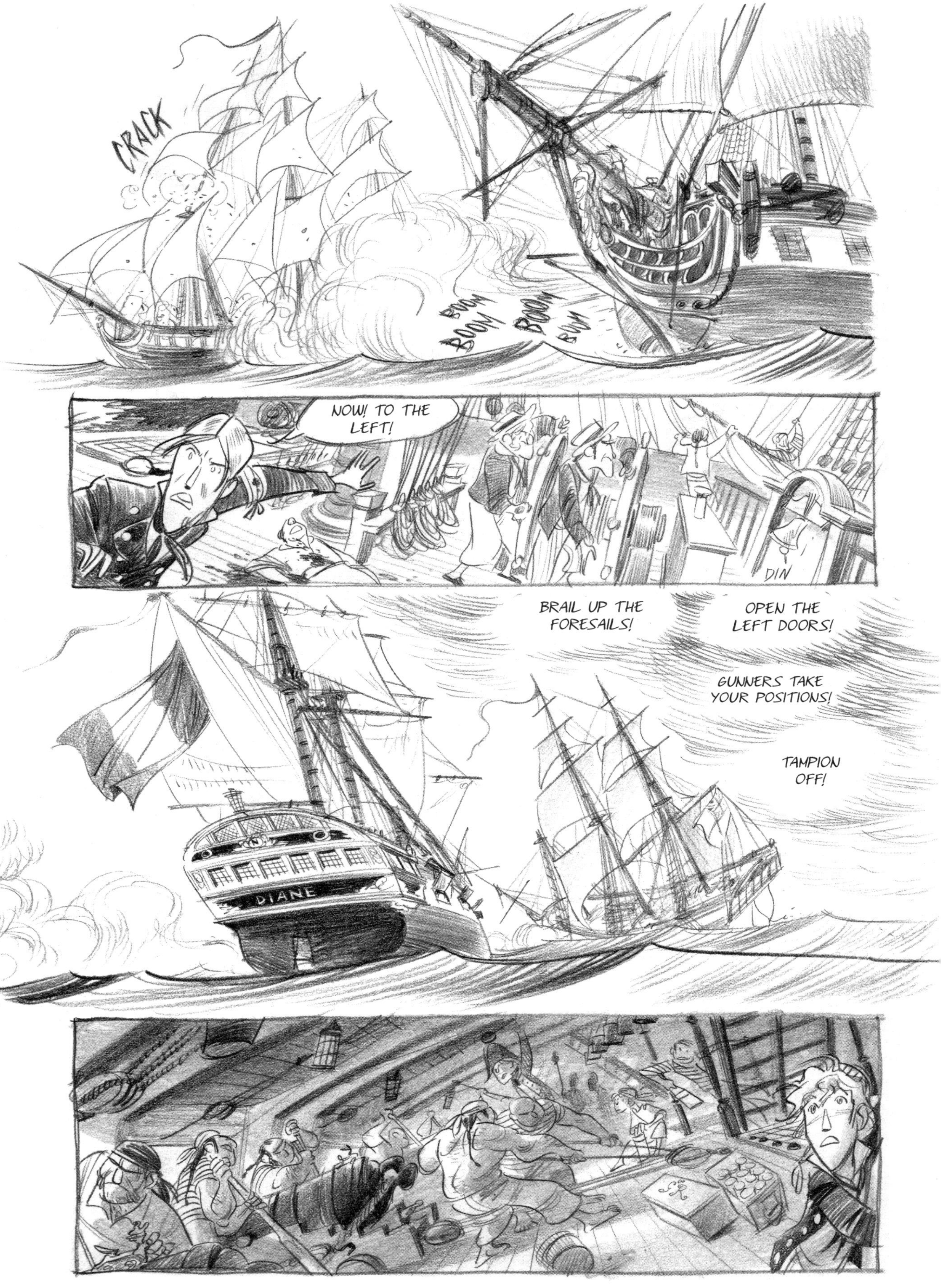
CRACK
BOOM BOOM BOOM BUM
NOW! TO THE LEFT!
DIN
BRAIL UP THE FORESAILS!
OPEN THE LEFT DOORS!
GUNNERS TAKE YOUR POSITIONS!
TAMPION OFF!
DIANE

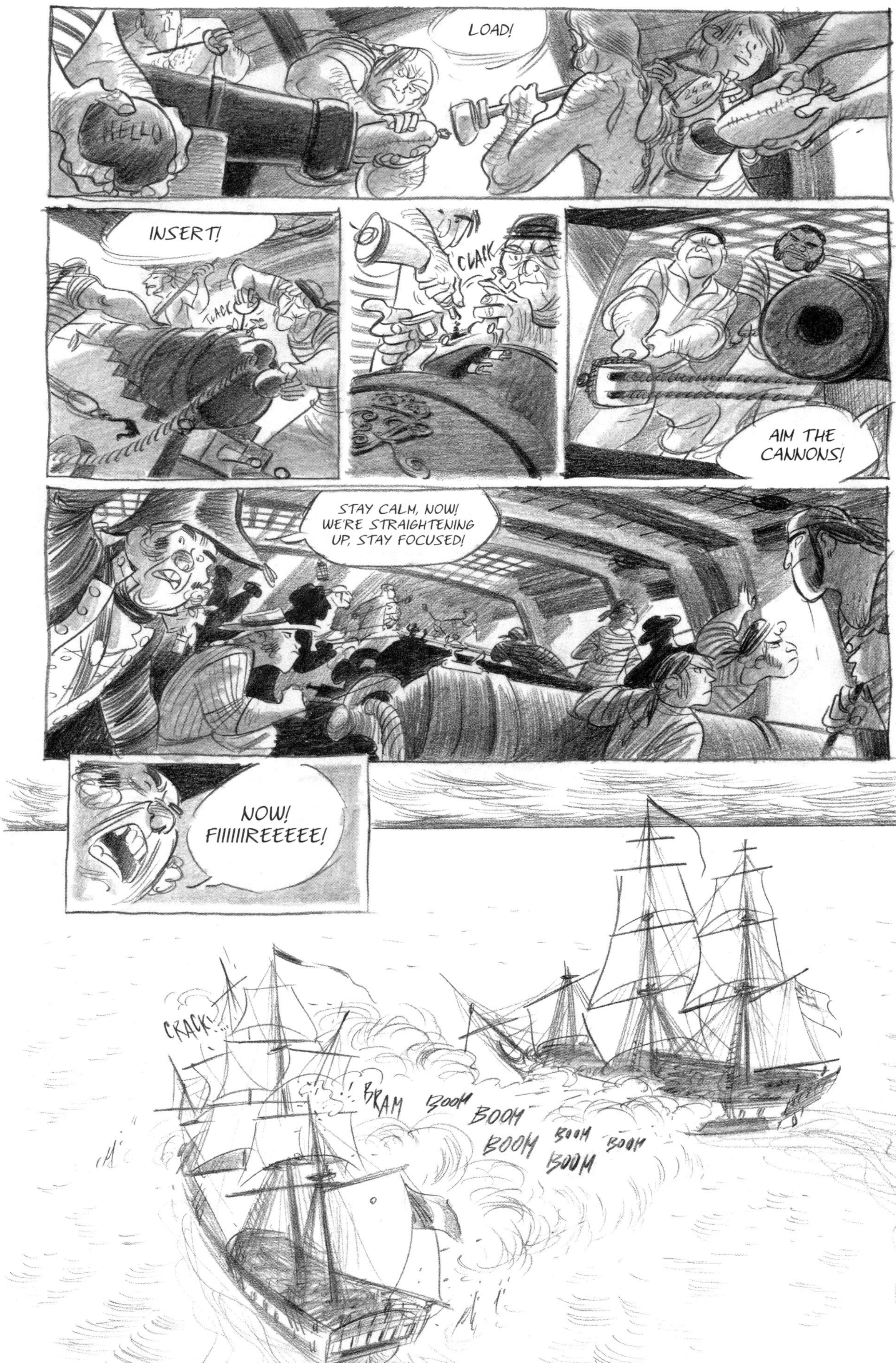
LOAD!
HELLO
INSERT!
TCLACK
CLACK
AIM THE CANNONS!
STAY CALM, NOW! WE'RE STRAIGHTENING UP, STAY FOCUSED!
NOW! FIIIIIREEEEEE!
CRACK!...
BRAM
BOOM
BOOM
BOOM
BOOM
BOOM
BOOM
BOOM

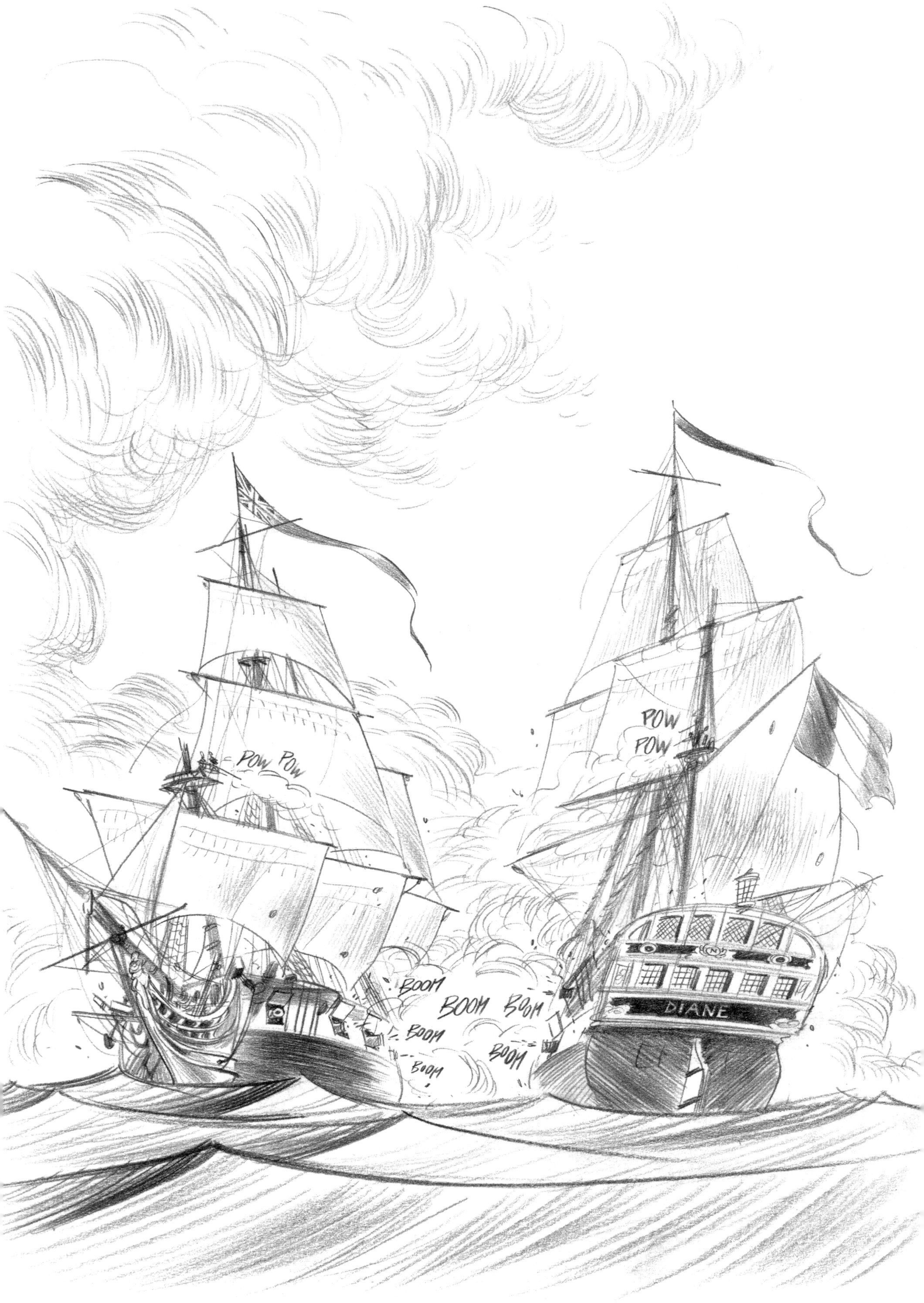
POW POW
POW
POW
BOOM
BOOM
BOOM
BOOM
BOOM
BOOM
DIANE

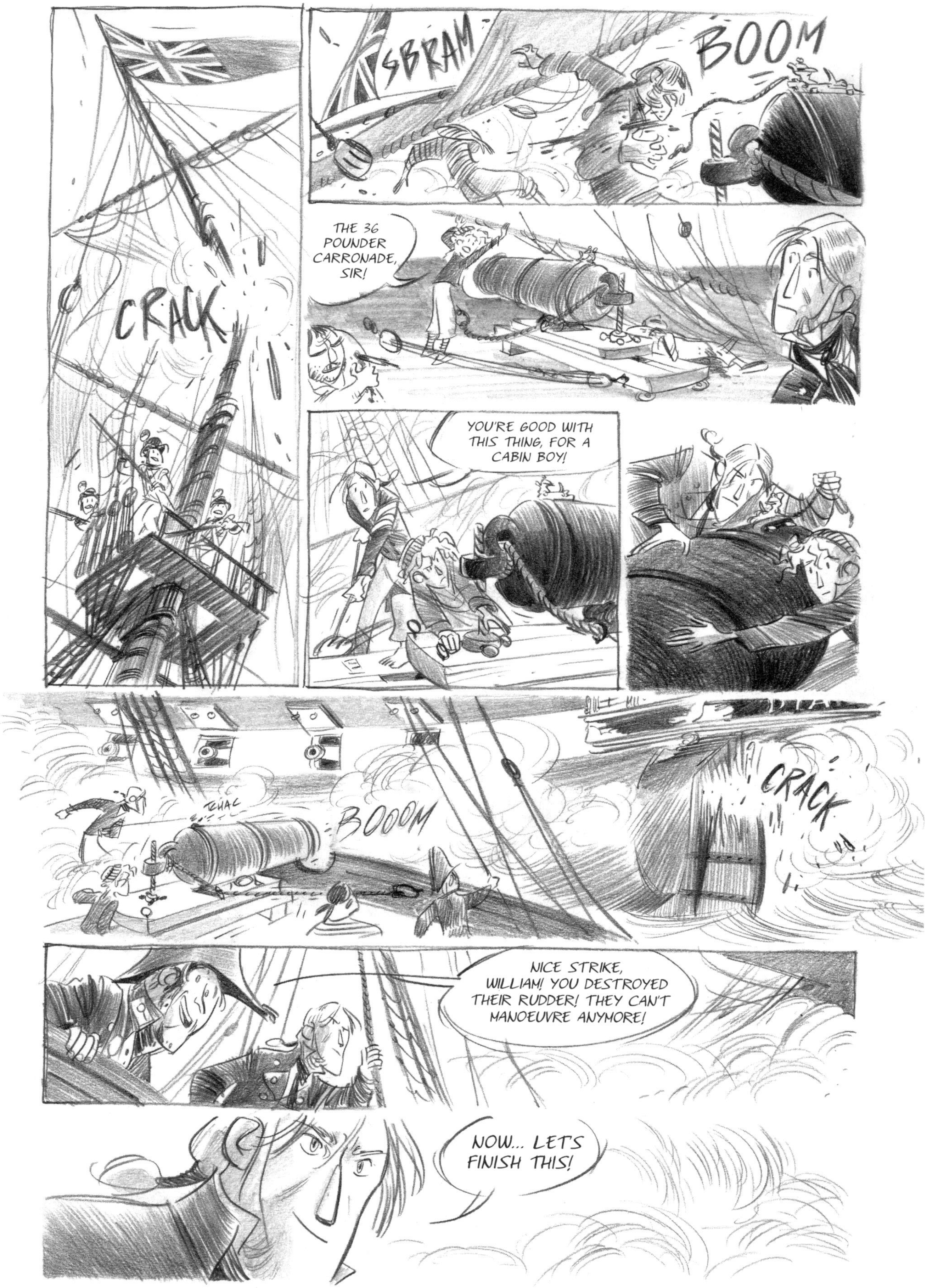
CRACK
SBRAM
BOOM
THE 36 POUNDER CARRONADE, SIR!
YOU'RE GOOD WITH THIS THING, FOR A CABIN BOY!
TCHAC
BOOOM
CRACK
NICE STRIKE, WILLIAM! YOU DESTROYED THEIR RUDDER! THEY CAN'T MANOEUVRE ANYMORE!
NOW... LET'S FINISH THIS!

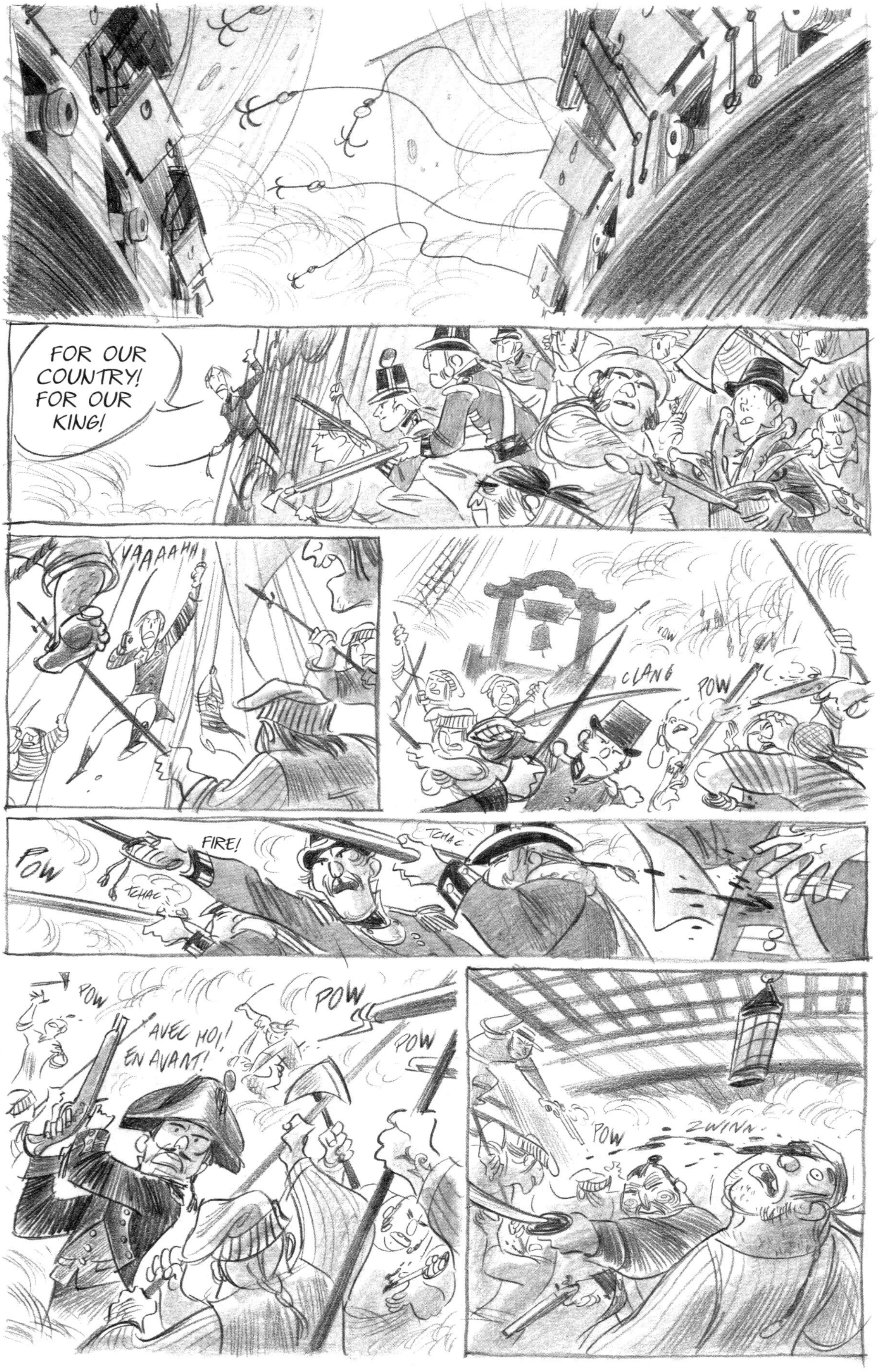
FOR OUR COUNTRY! FOR OUR KING!
YAAAAHH
POW
CLANG
POW
POW
FIRE!
TCHAC
TCHAC
POW
POW
AVEC MOI! EN AVANT!
POW
POW
ZWINN

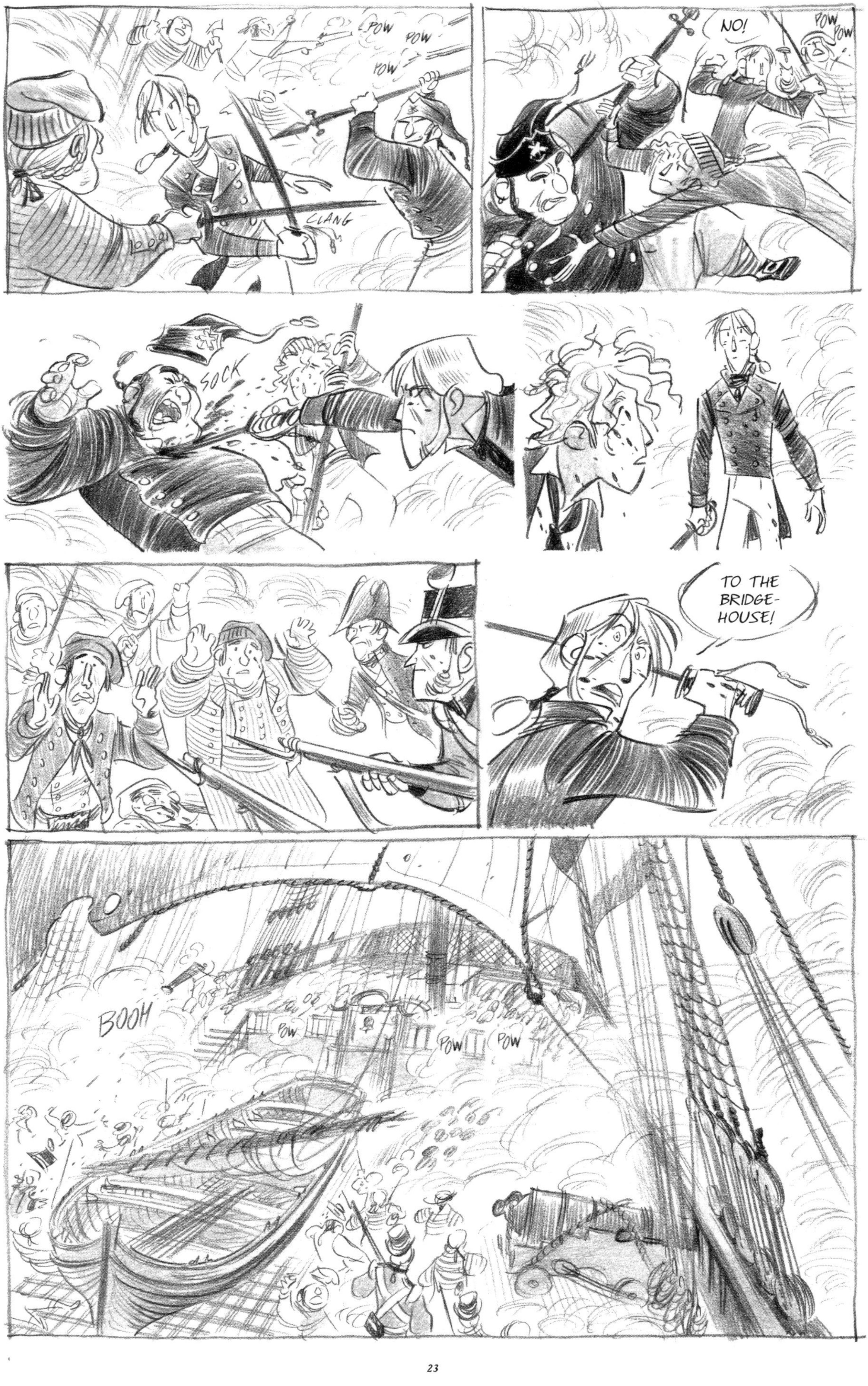
POW
POW
POW
CLANG
NO!
POW
POW
SOCK
TO THE BRIDGE-HOUSE!
BOOM
POW
POW
POW

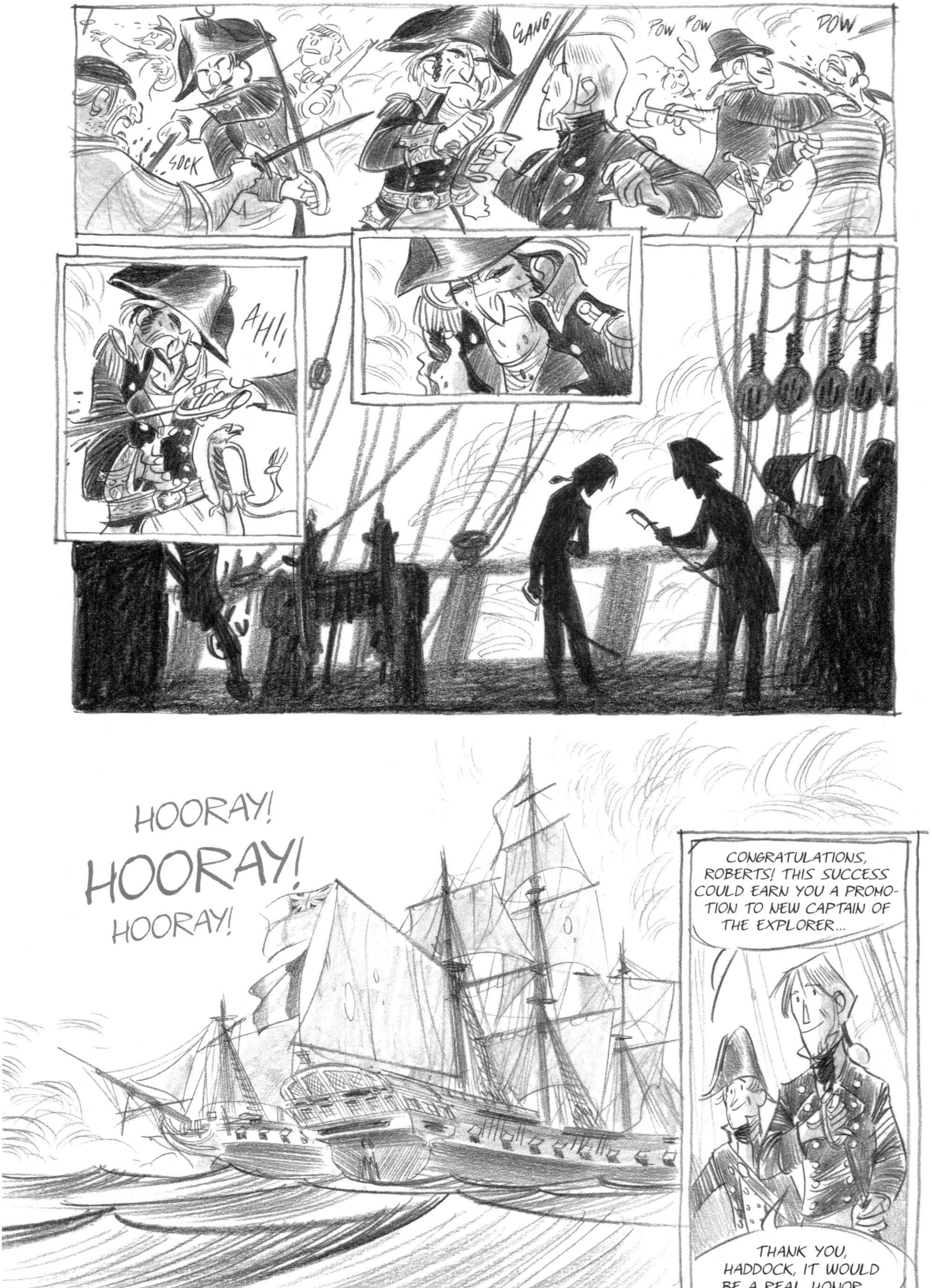
SOCK
CLANG
POW POW
DOW
AH!!
HOORAY!
HOORAY!
HOORAY!
CONGRATULATIONS, ROBERTS! THIS SUCCESS COULD EARN YOU A PROMOTION TO NEW CAPTAIN OF THE EXPLORER...
THANK YOU, HADDOCK, IT WOULD BE A REAL HONOR...

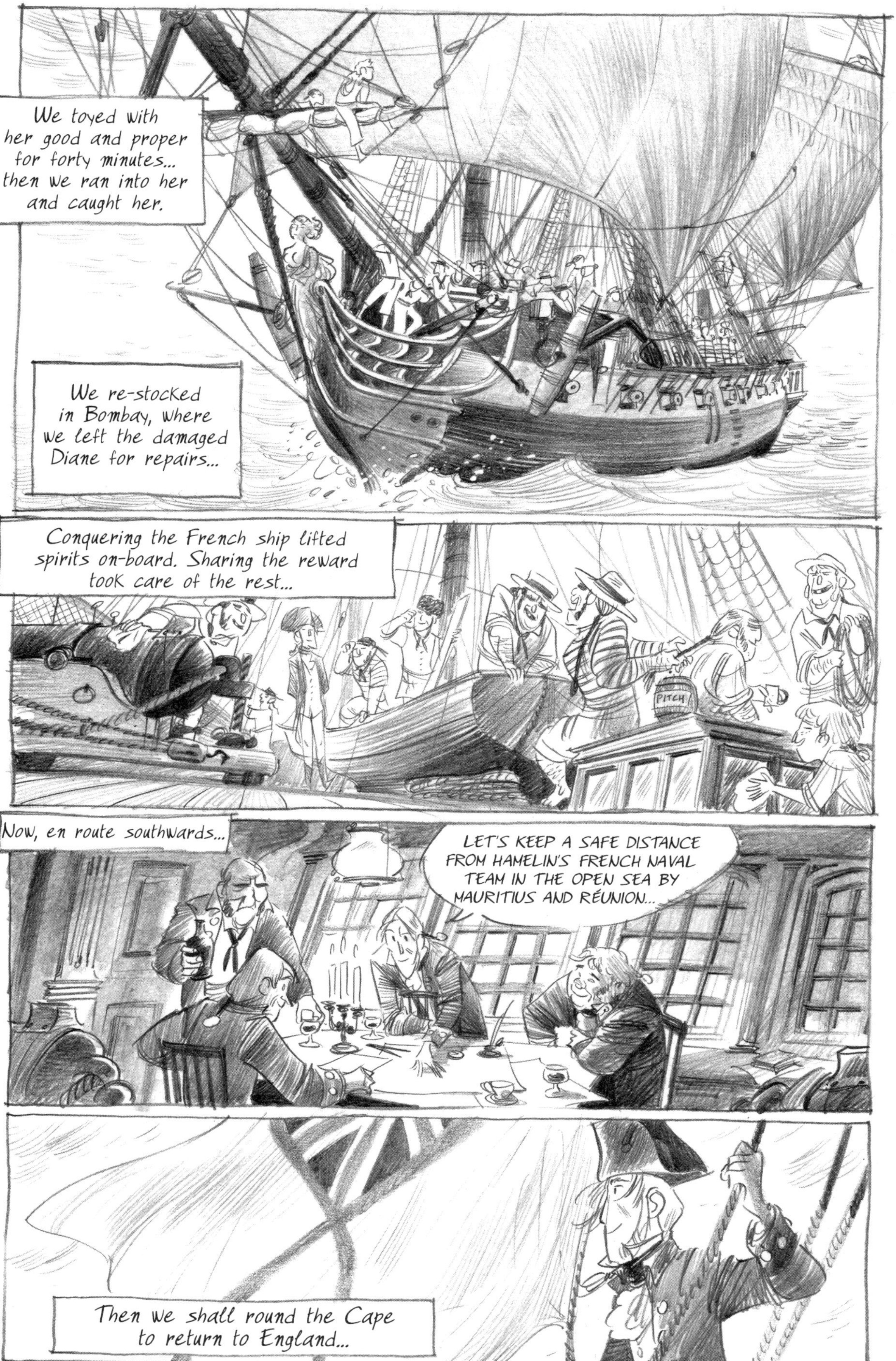
We toyed with her good and proper for forty minutes... then we ran into her and caught her.
We re-stocked in Bombay, where we left the damaged Diane for repairs...
Conquering the French ship lifted spirits on-board. Sharing the reward took care of the rest...
PITCH
Now, en route southwards...
LET'S KEEP A SAFE DISTANCE FROM HAMELIN'S FRENCH NAVAL TEAM IN THE OPEN SEA BY MAURITIUS AND RÉUNION...
Then we shall round the Cape to return to England...

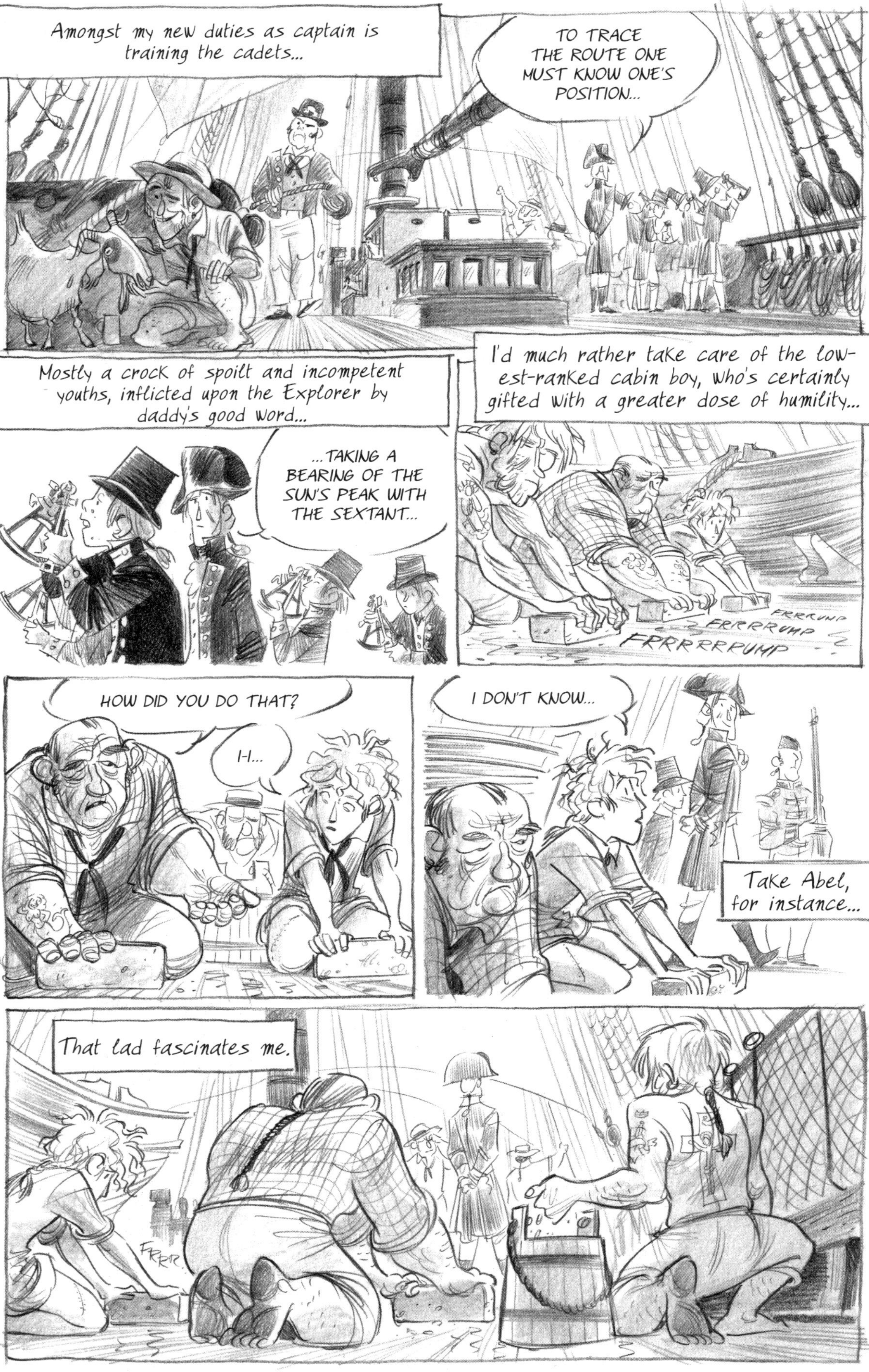
Amongst my new duties as captain is training the cadets...
TO TRACE THE ROUTE ONE MUST KNOW ONE'S POSITION...
Mostly a crock of spoilt and incompetent youths, inflicted upon the Explorer by daddy's good word...
...TAKING A BEARING OF THE SUN'S PEAK WITH THE SEXTANT...
I'd much rather take care of the lowest-ranked cabin boy, who's certainly gifted with a greater dose of humility...
FRRRUMP
FRRRRUMP
FRRRRRRUMP
HOW DID YOU DO THAT?
I-I...
I DON'T KNOW...
Take Abel, for instance...
That lad fascinates me.
FRRR.

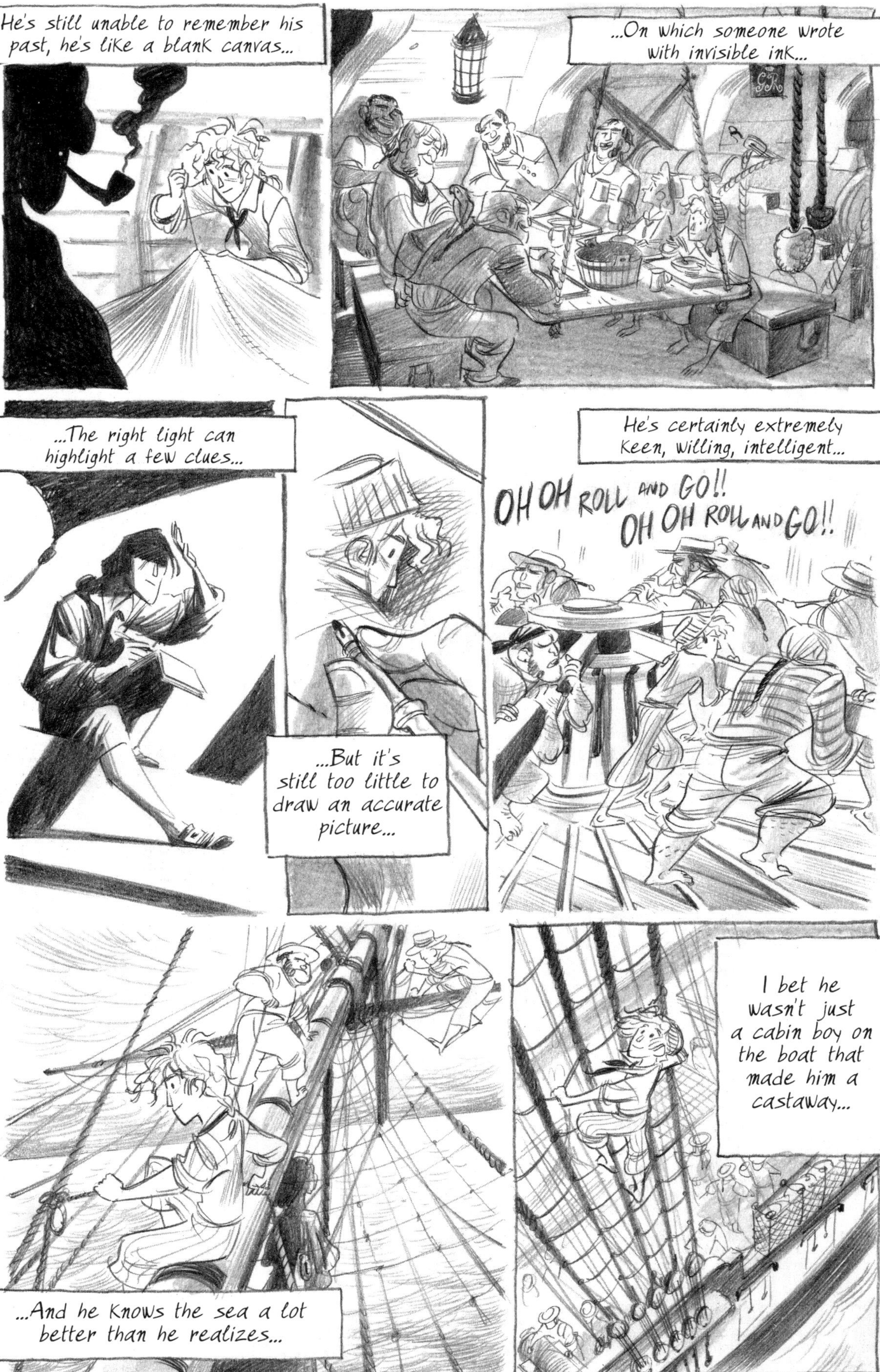
He's still unable to remember his past, he's like a blank canvas...
...On which someone wrote with invisible ink...
...The right light can highlight a few clues...
...But it's still too little to draw an accurate picture...
He's certainly extremely keen, willing, intelligent...
OH OH ROLL AND GO!!
OH OH ROLL AND GO!!
...And he knows the sea a lot better than he realizes...
I bet he wasn't just a cabin boy on the boat that made him a castaway...

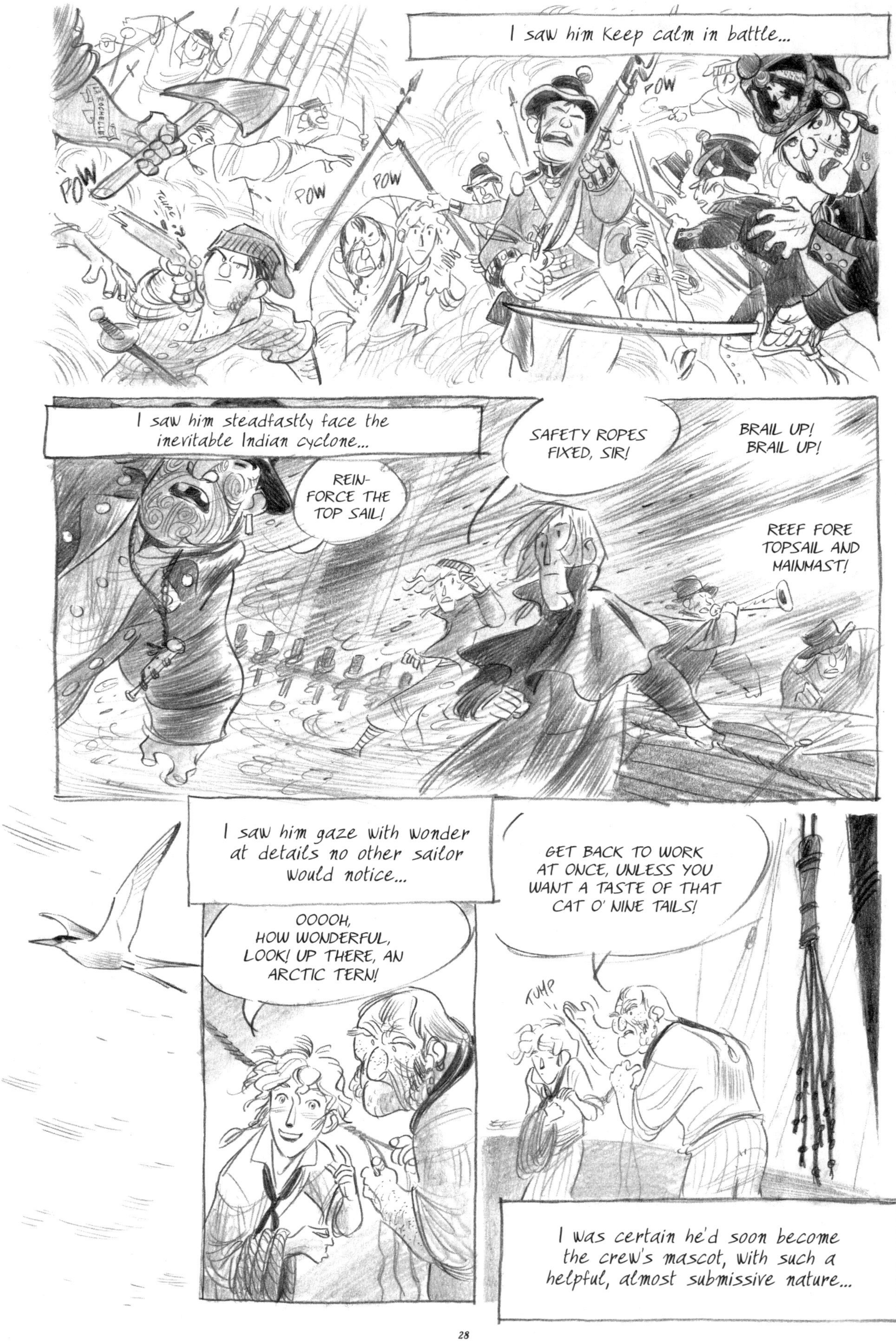

I saw him keep calm in battle...
POW
THAP
POW
POW
POW
I saw him steadfastly face the inevitable Indian cyclone...
REIN-FORCE THE TOP SAIL!
SAFETY ROPES FIXED, SIR!
BRAIL UP! BRAIL UP!
REEF FORE TOPSAIL AND MAINMAST!
I saw him gaze with wonder at details no other sailor would notice...
OOOOH, HOW WONDERFUL, LOOK! UP THERE, AN ARCTIC TERN!
GET BACK TO WORK AT ONCE, UNLESS YOU WANT A TASTE OF THAT CAT O' NINE TAILS!
TUMP
I was certain he'd soon become the crew's mascot, with such a helpful, almost submissive nature...

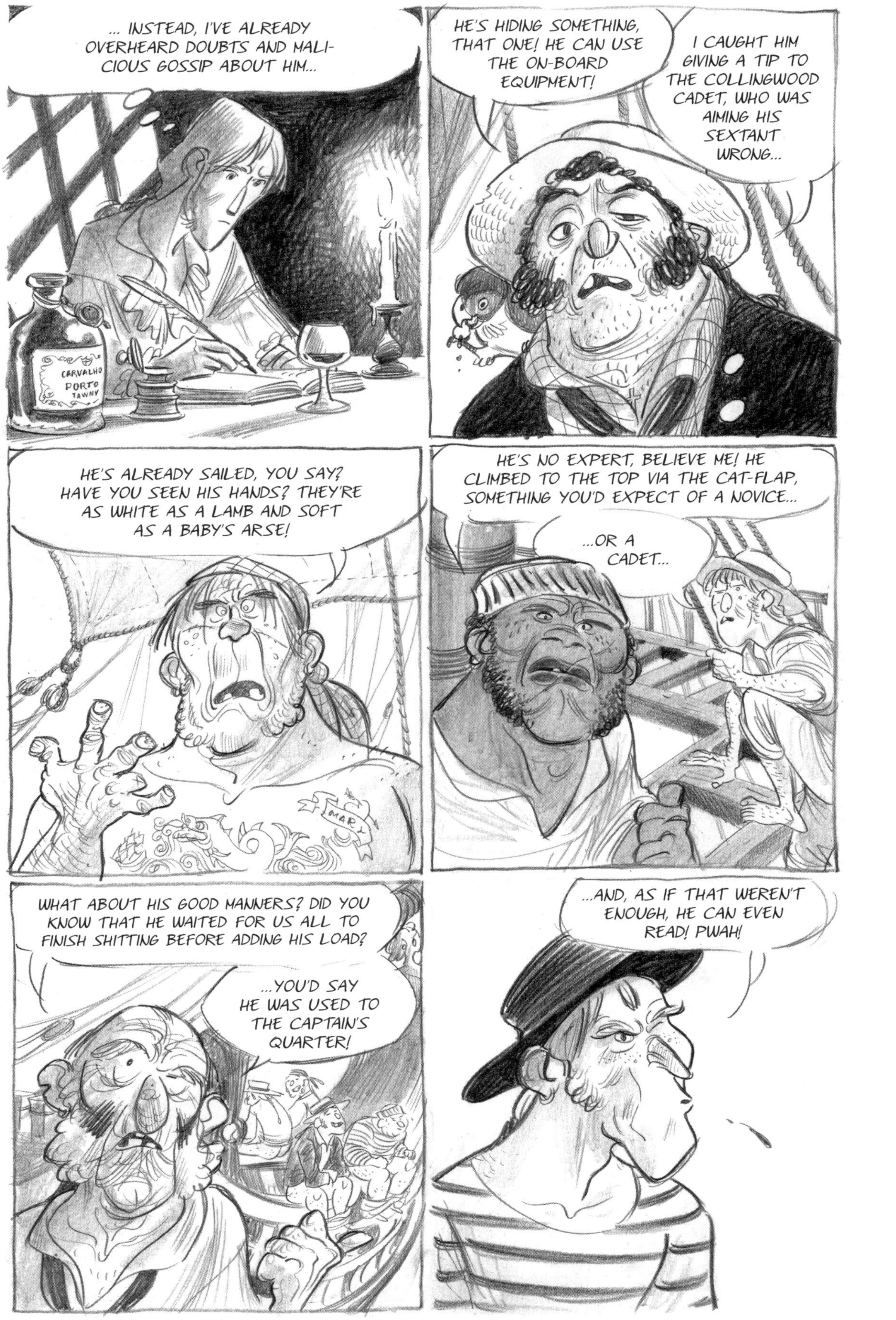
... INSTEAD, I'VE ALREADY OVERHEARD DOUBTS AND MALICIOUS GOSSIP ABOUT HIM...
CARVALHO PORTO TAWNY
HE'S HIDING SOMETHING, THAT ONE! HE CAN USE THE ON-BOARD EQUIPMENT!
I CAUGHT HIM GIVING A TIP TO THE COLLINGWOOD CADET, WHO WAS AIMING HIS SEXTANT WRONG...
HE'S ALREADY SAILED, YOU SAY? HAVE YOU SEEN HIS HANDS? THEY'RE AS WHITE AS A LAMB AND SOFT AS A BABY'S ARSE!
HE'S NO EXPERT, BELIEVE ME! HE CLIMBED TO THE TOP VIA THE CAT-FLAP, SOMETHING YOU'D EXPECT OF A NOVICE...
...OR A CADET...
WHAT ABOUT HIS GOOD MANNERS? DID YOU KNOW THAT HE WAITED FOR US ALL TO FINISH SHITTING BEFORE ADDING HIS LOAD?
...YOU'D SAY HE WAS USED TO THE CAPTAIN'S QUARTER!
...AND, AS IF THAT WEREN'T ENOUGH, HE CAN EVEN READ! PWAH!

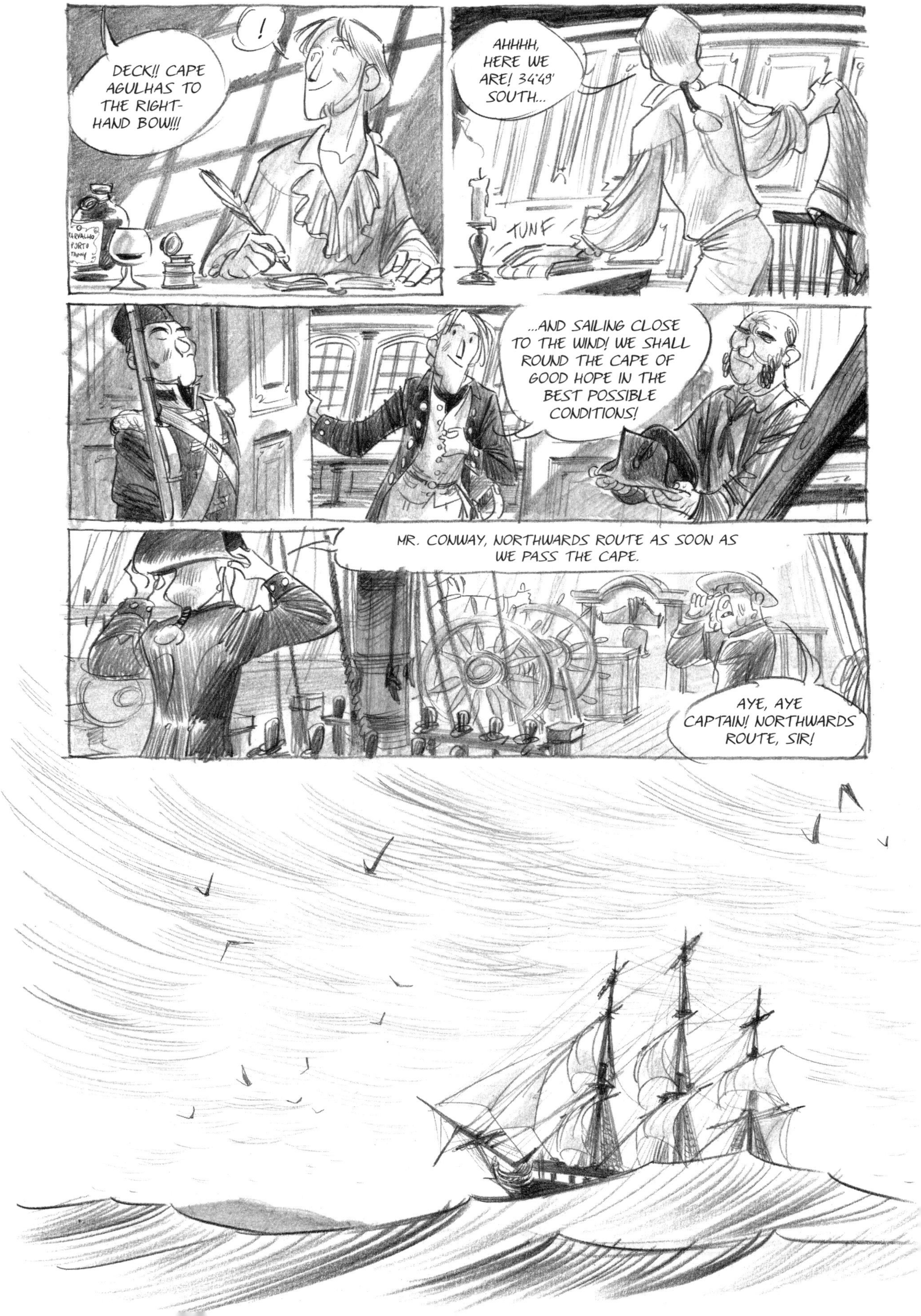
DECK!! CAPE AGULHAS TO THE RIGHT-HAND BOW!!!
!
AHHHH, HERE WE ARE! 34°49' SOUTH...
TUNF
...AND SAILING CLOSE TO THE WIND! WE SHALL ROUND THE CAPE OF GOOD HOPE IN THE BEST POSSIBLE CONDITIONS!
MR. CONWAY, NORTHWARDS ROUTE AS SOON AS WE PASS THE CAPE.
AYE, AYE CAPTAIN! NORTHWARDS ROUTE, SIR!

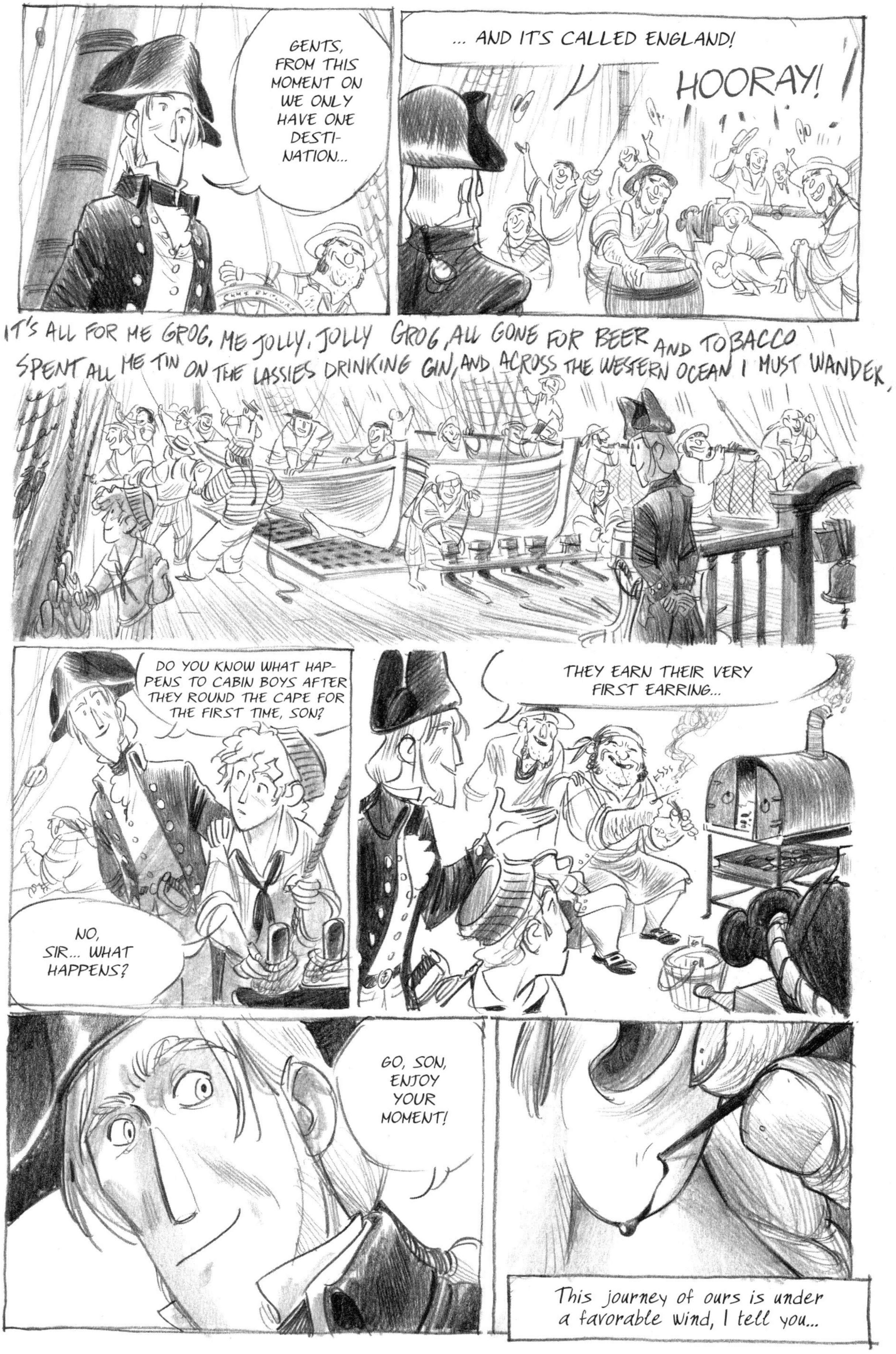

GENTS, FROM THIS MOMENT ON WE ONLY HAVE ONE DESTI- NATION...
... AND IT'S CALLED ENGLAND!
HOORAY!
IT'S ALL FOR ME GROG, ME JOLLY, JOLLY GROG, ALL GONE FOR BEER AND TOBACCO
SPENT ALL ME TIN ON THE LASSIES DRINKING GIN, AND ACROSS THE WESTERN OCEAN I MUST WANDER...
DO YOU KNOW WHAT HAP- PENS TO CABIN BOYS AFTER THEY ROUND THE CAPE FOR THE FIRST TIME, SON?
NO, SIR... WHAT HAPPENS?
THEY EARN THEIR VERY FIRST EARRING...
GO, SON, ENJOY YOUR MOMENT!
This journey of ours is under a favorable wind, I tell you...

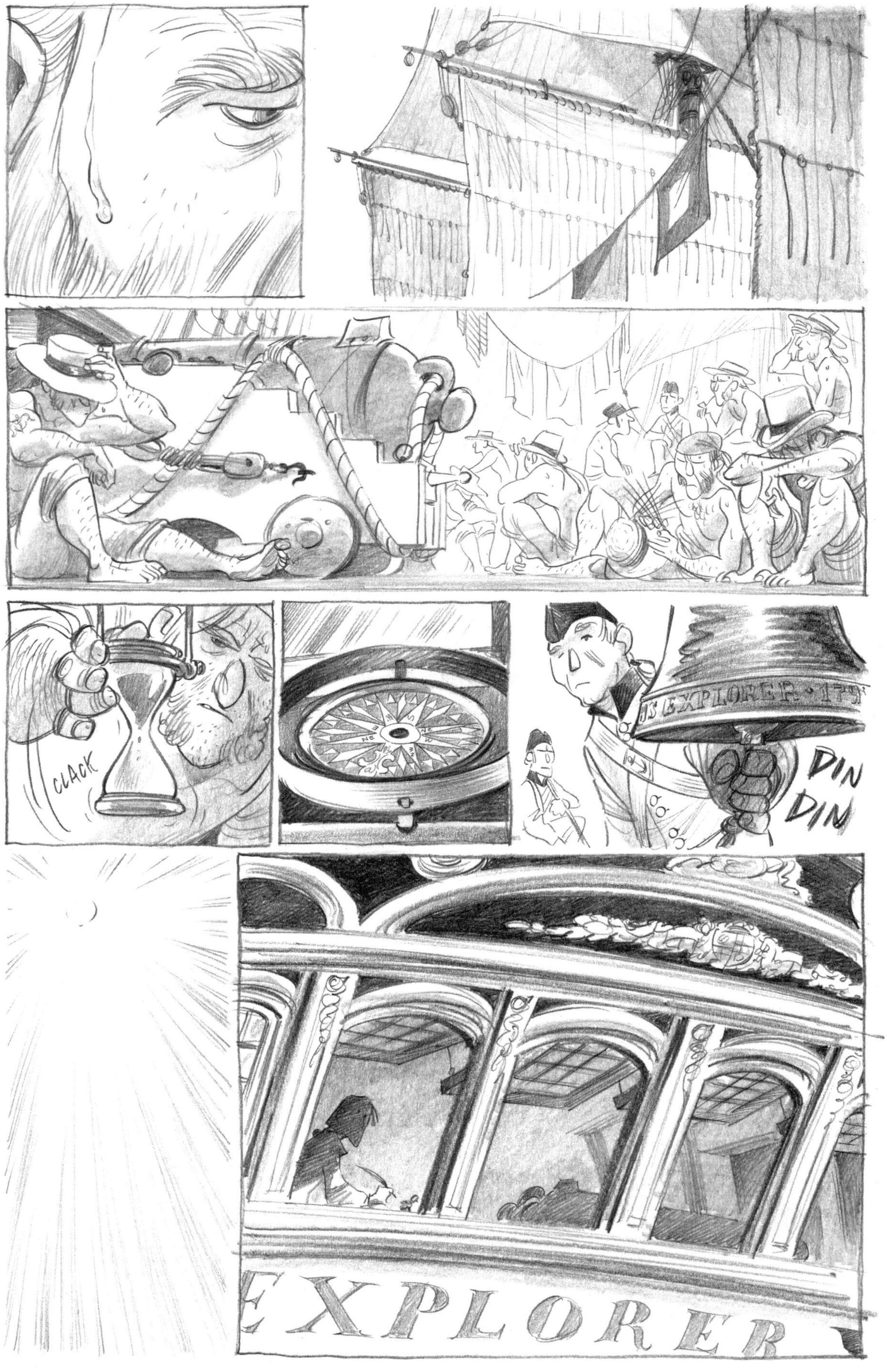
CLACK
US EXPLORER • 179
DIN
DIN
EXPLORER

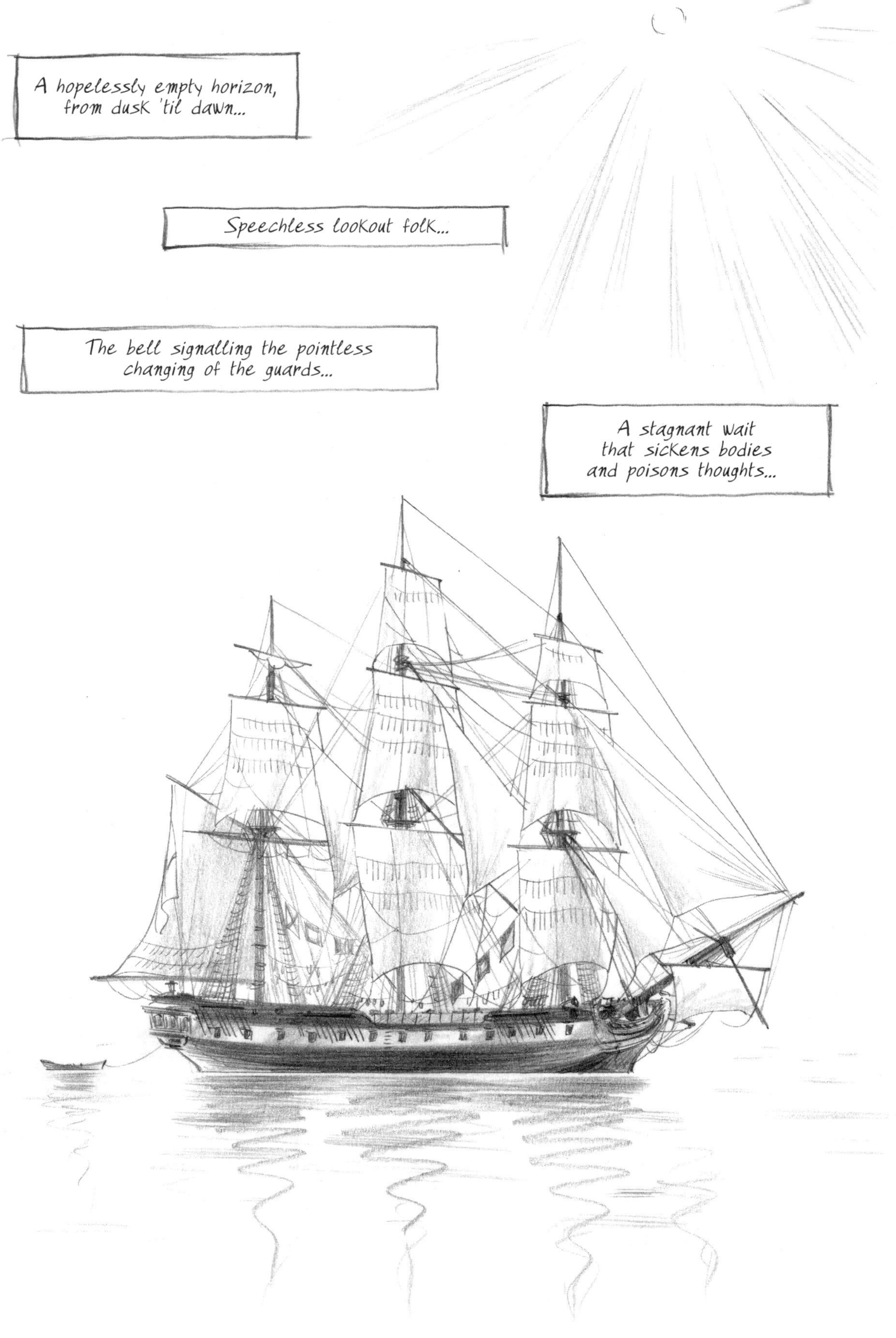
A hopelessly empty horizon, from dusk 'til dawn...
Speechless lookout folk...
The bell signalling the pointless changing of the guards...
A stagnant wait that sickens bodies and poisons thoughts...

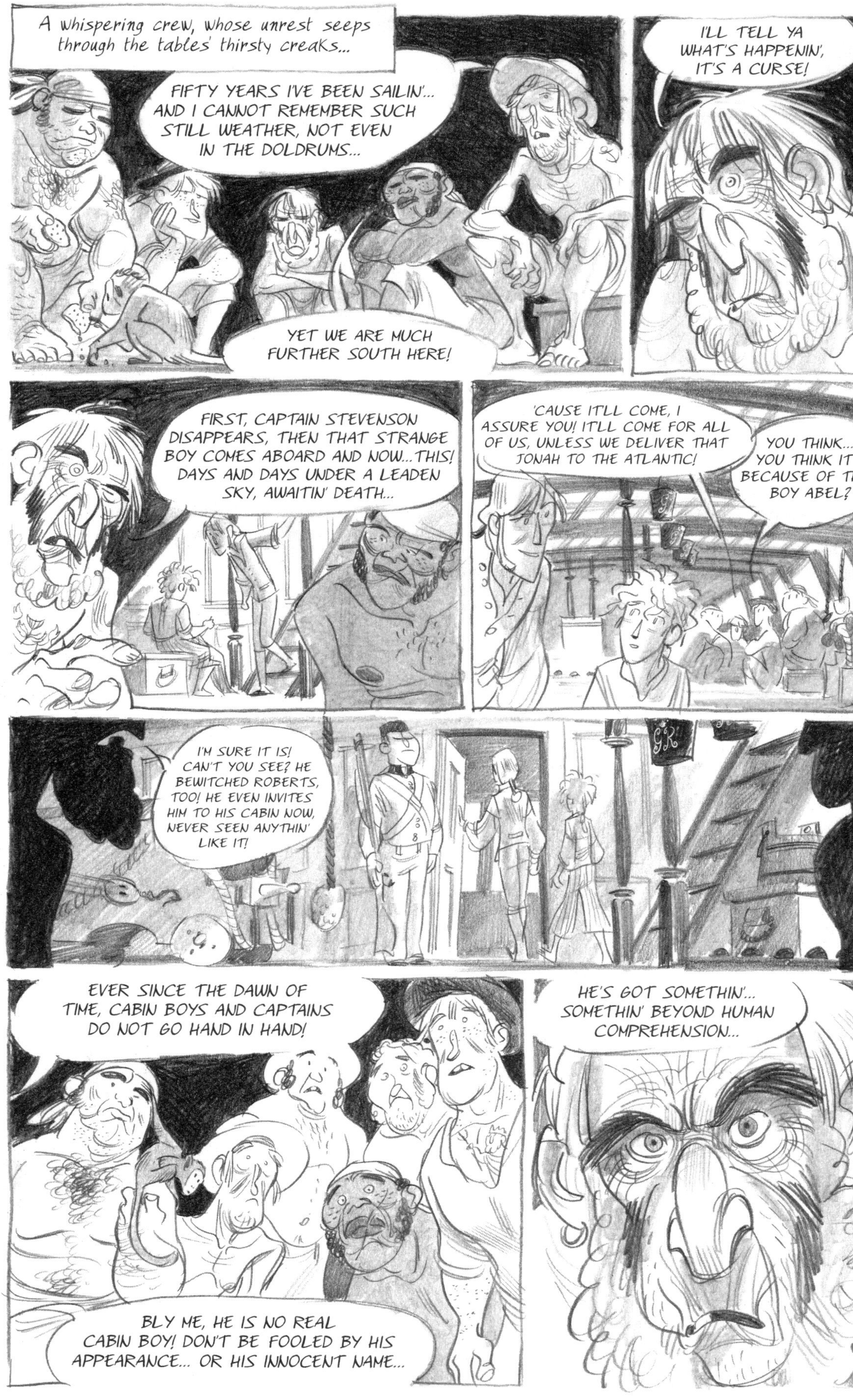
A whispering crew, whose unrest seeps through the tables' thirsty creaks...
FIFTY YEARS I'VE BEEN SAILIN'... AND I CANNOT REMEMBER SUCH STILL WEATHER, NOT EVEN IN THE DOLDRUMS...
YET WE ARE MUCH FURTHER SOUTH HERE!
I'LL TELL YA WHAT'S HAPPENIN', IT'S A CURSE!
FIRST, CAPTAIN STEVENSON DISAPPEARS, THEN THAT STRANGE BOY COMES ABOARD AND NOW...THIS! DAYS AND DAYS UNDER A LEADEN SKY, AWAITIN' DEATH...
'CAUSE IT'LL COME, I ASSURE YOU! IT'LL COME FOR ALL OF US, UNLESS WE DELIVER THAT JONAH TO THE ATLANTIC!
YOU THINK... YOU THINK IT'S BECAUSE OF THAT BOY ABEL?
I'M SURE IT IS! CAN'T YOU SEE? HE BEWITCHED ROBERTS, TOO! HE EVEN INVITES HIM TO HIS CABIN NOW, NEVER SEEN ANYTHIN' LIKE IT!
EVER SINCE THE DAWN OF TIME, CABIN BOYS AND CAPTAINS DO NOT GO HAND IN HAND!
BLY ME, HE IS NO REAL CABIN BOY! DON'T BE FOOLED BY HIS APPEARANCE... OR HIS INNOCENT NAME...
HE'S GOT SOMETHIN'... SOMETHIN' BEYOND HUMAN COMPREHENSION...

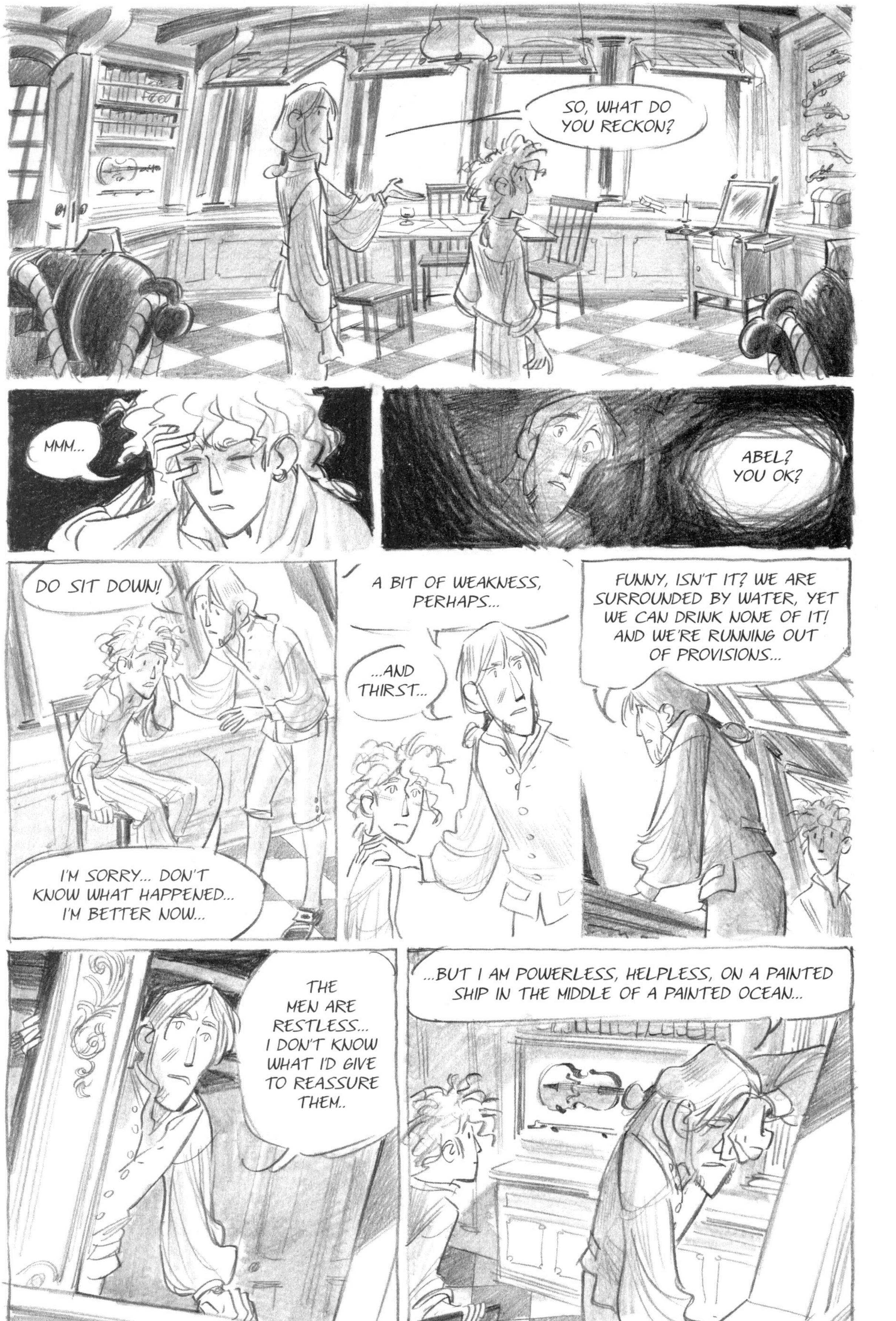
SO, WHAT DO YOU RECKON?
MMM...
ABEL? YOU OK?
DO SIT DOWN!
I'M SORRY... DON'T KNOW WHAT HAPPENED... I'M BETTER NOW...
A BIT OF WEAKNESS, PERHAPS...
...AND THIRST...
FUNNY, ISN'T IT? WE ARE SURROUNDED BY WATER, YET WE CAN DRINK NONE OF IT! AND WE'RE RUNNING OUT OF PROVISIONS...
THE MEN ARE RESTLESS... I DON'T KNOW WHAT I'D GIVE TO REASSURE THEM..
...BUT I AM POWERLESS, HELPLESS, ON A PAINTED SHIP IN THE MIDDLE OF A PAINTED OCEAN...

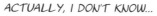

CAN YOU PLAY?

WELL...

ACTUALLY, I DON'T KNOW...

IT WAS CAPTAIN STEVENSON'S, A GREAT FIDDLER! I CAN'T EVEN GET HALF AN OFF-KEY NOTE OUT OF IT...

YOU CAN BORROW IT, IF YOU LIKE! TAKE GOOD CARE OF IT, MIND, I'LL HAVE TO RETURN IT TO THE FAMILY, ONCE HOME...

IF WE EVER GET TO RETURN HOME...

SHOCKING! HE GAVE HIM THE CAPTAIN'S FIDDLE!

MONROE WAS RIGHT. ROBERTS' LOST HIS MIND!

WE MUST GET RID OF THAT BRAT, BEFORE THE CAPTAIN LANDS US ALL INTO MORE CRAZY TROUBLE AND...

OH, DO SHUT YOUR TRAP, KEATING!

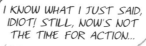

WHAT DO YOU MEAN? YOU JUST SAID...

I KNOW WHAT I JUST SAID, IDIOT! STILL, NOW'S NOT THE TIME FOR ACTION...

LET HIM PLAY HIS FUNERAL SONG, FIRST...

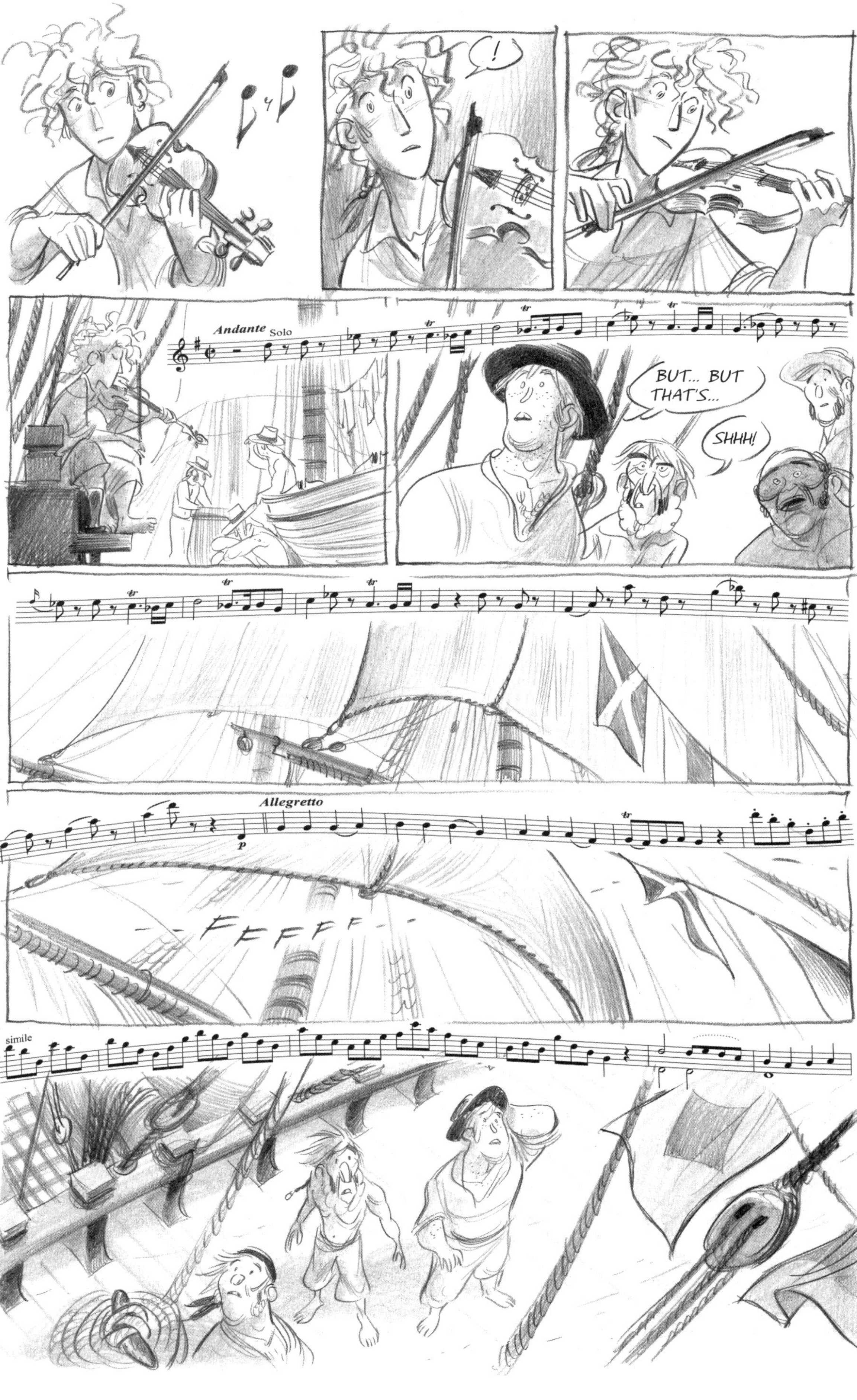

!
Andante
Solo
BUT... BUT THAT'S...
SHHH!
Allegretto
FFFFF
simile

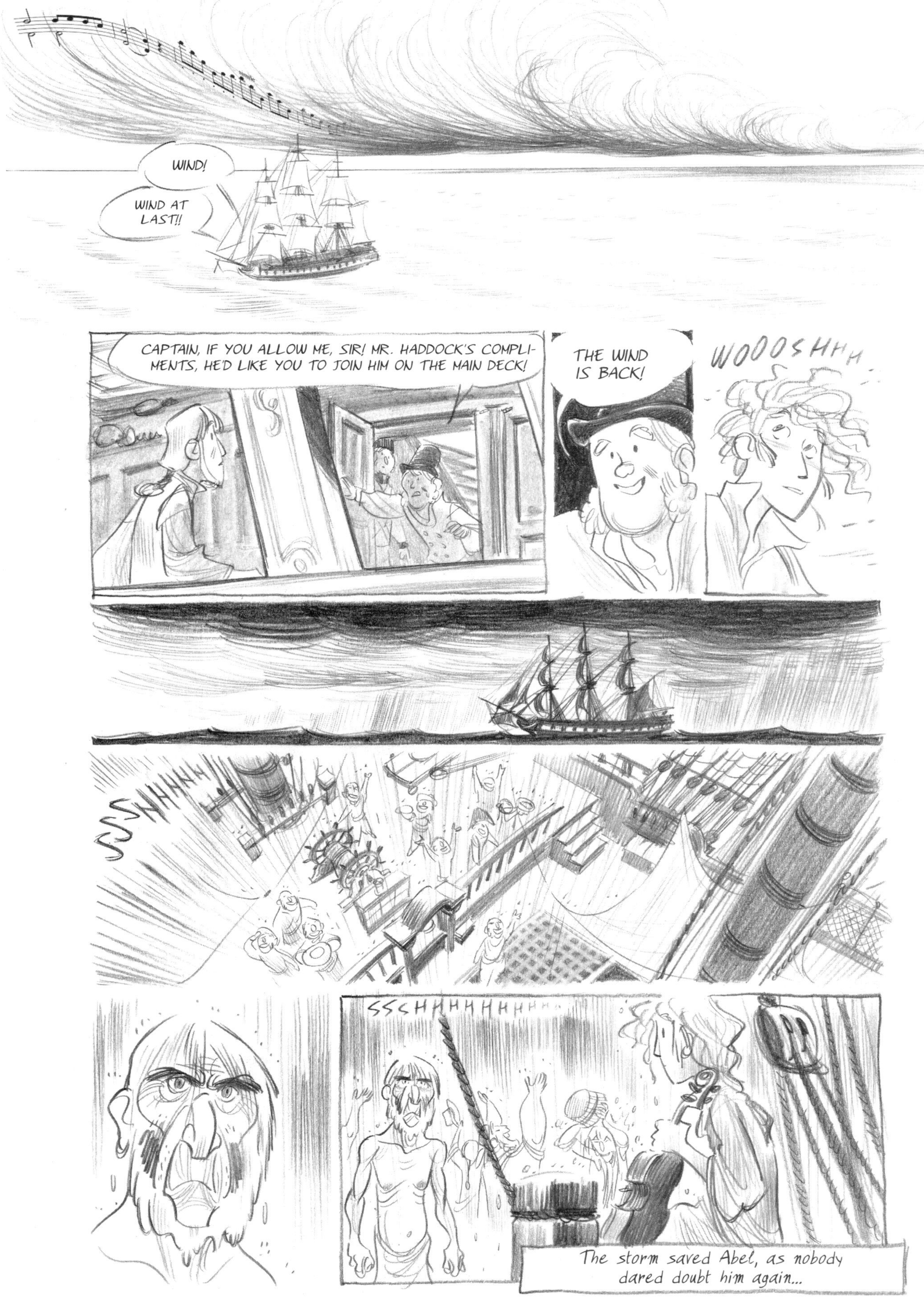
WIND!
WIND AT LAST!!
CAPTAIN, IF YOU ALLOW ME, SIR! MR. HADDOCK'S COMPLIMENTS, HE'D LIKE YOU TO JOIN HIM ON THE MAIN DECK!
THE WIND IS BACK!
WOOOSHHH
SSSHHHHH
SSCHHHHHHHHH
The storm saved Abel, as nobody dared doubt him again...

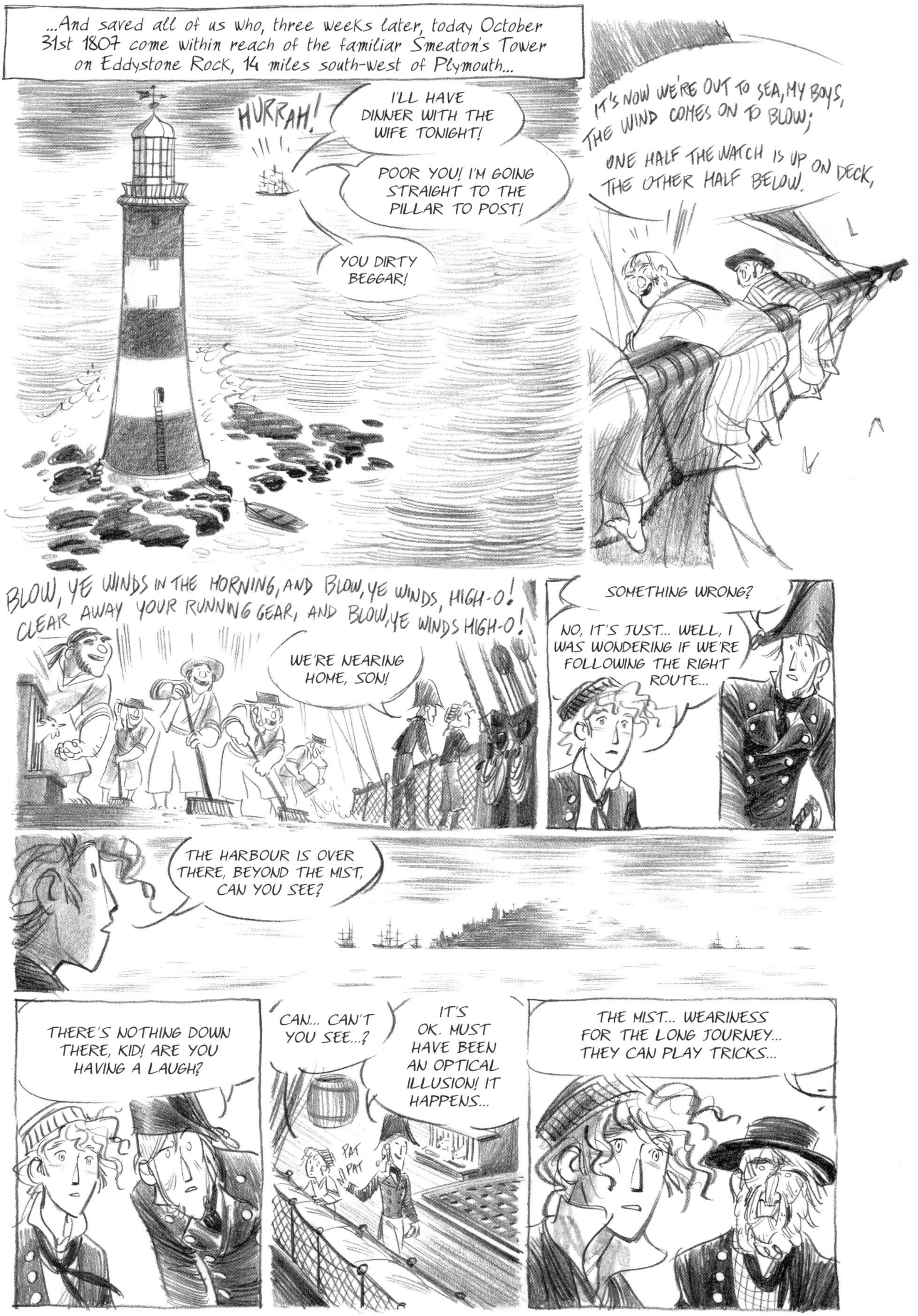
...And saved all of us who, three weeks later, today October 31st 1807 come within reach of the familiar Smeaton's Tower on Eddystone Rock, 14 miles south-west of Plymouth...
HURRAH!
I'LL HAVE DINNER WITH THE WIFE TONIGHT!
POOR YOU! I'M GOING STRAIGHT TO THE PILLAR TO POST!
YOU DIRTY BEGGAR!
IT'S NOW WE'RE OUT TO SEA, MY BOYS, THE WIND COMES ON TO BLOW;
ONE HALF THE WATCH IS UP ON DECK, THE OTHER HALF BELOW.
BLOW, YE WINDS IN THE MORNING, AND BLOW, YE WINDS, HIGH-O!
CLEAR AWAY YOUR RUNNING GEAR, AND BLOW, YE WINDS HIGH-O!
WE'RE NEARING HOME, SON!
SOMETHING WRONG?
NO, IT'S JUST... WELL, I WAS WONDERING IF WE'RE FOLLOWING THE RIGHT ROUTE...
THE HARBOUR IS OVER THERE, BEYOND THE MIST, CAN YOU SEE?
THERE'S NOTHING DOWN THERE, KID! ARE YOU HAVING A LAUGH?
CAN... CAN'T YOU SEE...?
IT'S OK. MUST HAVE BEEN AN OPTICAL ILLUSION! IT HAPPENS...
PAT PAT
THE MIST... WEARINESS FOR THE LONG JOURNEY... THEY CAN PLAY TRICKS...

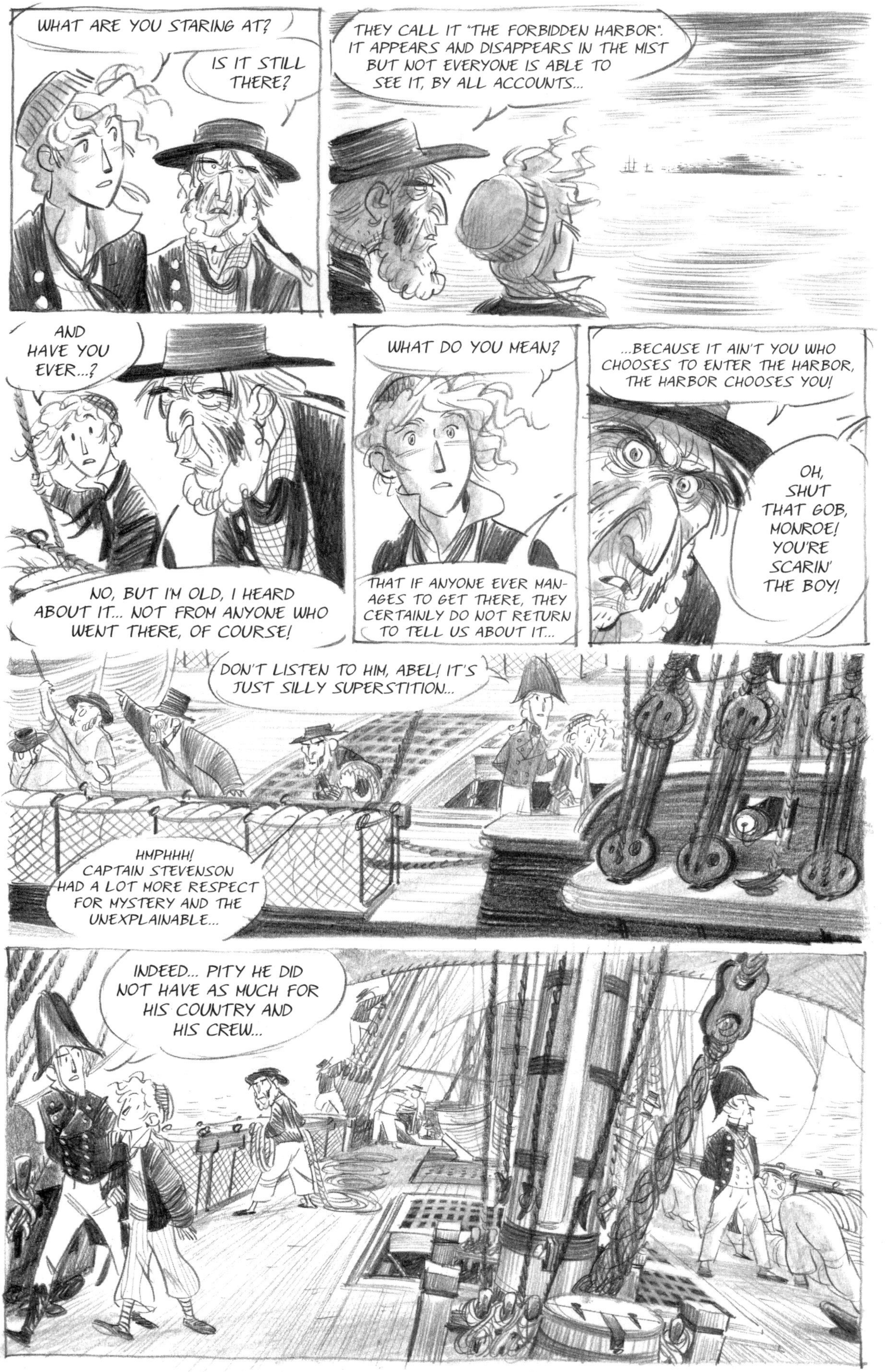
WHAT ARE YOU STARING AT?
IS IT STILL THERE?
THEY CALL IT "THE FORBIDDEN HARBOR". IT APPEARS AND DISAPPEARS IN THE MIST BUT NOT EVERYONE IS ABLE TO SEE IT, BY ALL ACCOUNTS...
AND HAVE YOU EVER...?
NO, BUT I'M OLD, I HEARD ABOUT IT... NOT FROM ANYONE WHO WENT THERE, OF COURSE!
WHAT DO YOU MEAN?
THAT IF ANYONE EVER MANAGES TO GET THERE, THEY CERTAINLY DO NOT RETURN TO TELL US ABOUT IT...
...BECAUSE IT AIN'T YOU WHO CHOOSES TO ENTER THE HARBOR, THE HARBOR CHOOSES YOU!
OH, SHUT THAT GOB, MONROE! YOU'RE SCARIN' THE BOY!
DON'T LISTEN TO HIM, ABEL! IT'S JUST SILLY SUPERSTITION...
HMPHHH! CAPTAIN STEVENSON HAD A LOT MORE RESPECT FOR MYSTERY AND THE UNEXPLAINABLE...
INDEED... PITY HE DID NOT HAVE AS MUCH FOR HIS COUNTRY AND HIS CREW...

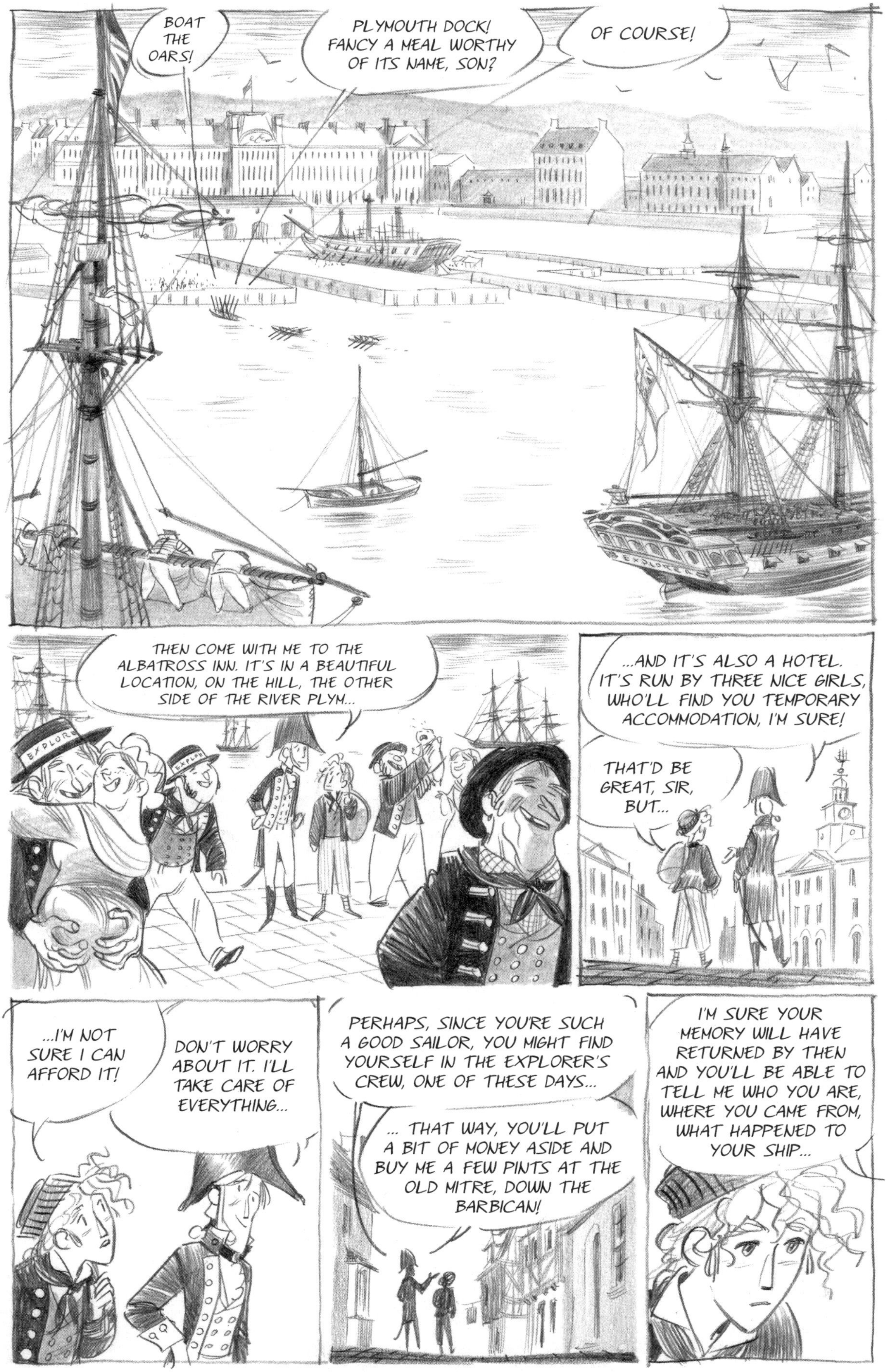
BOAT THE OARS!
PLYMOUTH DOCK! FANCY A MEAL WORTHY OF ITS NAME, SON?
OF COURSE!
THEN COME WITH ME TO THE ALBATROSS INN. IT'S IN A BEAUTIFUL LOCATION, ON THE HILL, THE OTHER SIDE OF THE RIVER PLYM...
...AND IT'S ALSO A HOTEL. IT'S RUN BY THREE NICE GIRLS, WHO'LL FIND YOU TEMPORARY ACCOMMODATION, I'M SURE!
THAT'D BE GREAT, SIR, BUT...
...I'M NOT SURE I CAN AFFORD IT!
DON'T WORRY ABOUT IT. I'LL TAKE CARE OF EVERYTHING...
PERHAPS, SINCE YOU'RE SUCH A GOOD SAILOR, YOU MIGHT FIND YOURSELF IN THE EXPLORER'S CREW, ONE OF THESE DAYS...
... THAT WAY, YOU'LL PUT A BIT OF MONEY ASIDE AND BUY ME A FEW PINTS AT THE OLD MITRE, DOWN THE BARBICAN!
I'M SURE YOUR MEMORY WILL HAVE RETURNED BY THEN AND YOU'LL BE ABLE TO TELL ME WHO YOU ARE, WHERE YOU CAME FROM, WHAT HAPPENED TO YOUR SHIP...

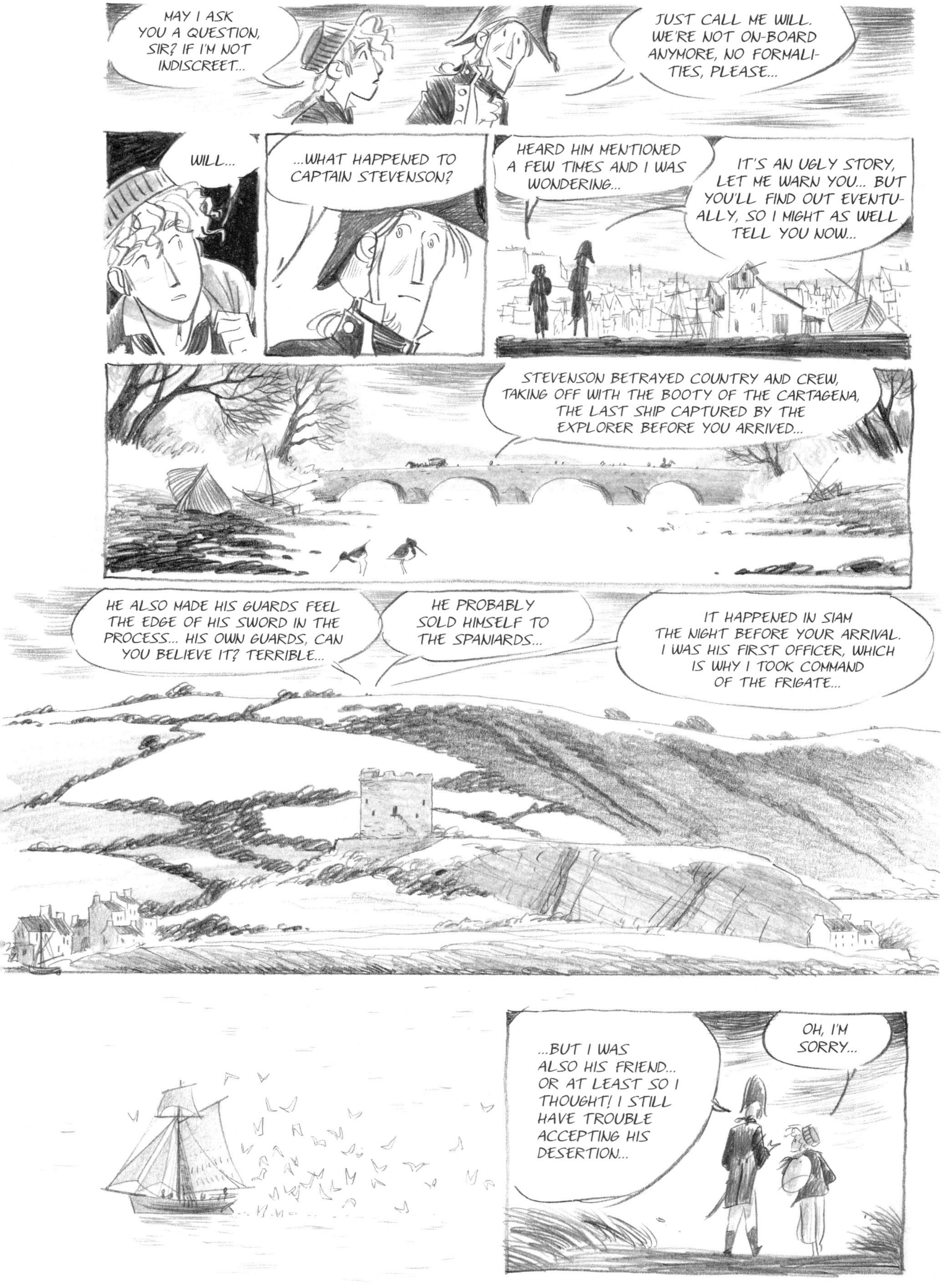
MAY I ASK YOU A QUESTION, SIR? IF I'M NOT INDISCREET...
JUST CALL ME WILL. WE'RE NOT ON-BOARD ANYMORE, NO FORMALITIES, PLEASE...
WILL...
...WHAT HAPPENED TO CAPTAIN STEVENSON?
HEARD HIM MENTIONED A FEW TIMES AND I WAS WONDERING...
IT'S AN UGLY STORY, LET ME WARN YOU... BUT YOU'LL FIND OUT EVENTUALLY, SO I MIGHT AS WELL TELL YOU NOW...
STEVENSON BETRAYED COUNTRY AND CREW, TAKING OFF WITH THE BOOTY OF THE CARTAGENA, THE LAST SHIP CAPTURED BY THE EXPLORER BEFORE YOU ARRIVED...
HE ALSO MADE HIS GUARDS FEEL THE EDGE OF HIS SWORD IN THE PROCESS... HIS OWN GUARDS, CAN YOU BELIEVE IT? TERRIBLE...
HE PROBABLY SOLD HIMSELF TO THE SPANIARDS...
IT HAPPENED IN SIAM THE NIGHT BEFORE YOUR ARRIVAL. I WAS HIS FIRST OFFICER, WHICH IS WHY I TOOK COMMAND OF THE FRIGATE...
...BUT I WAS ALSO HIS FRIEND... OR AT LEAST SO I THOUGHT! I STILL HAVE TROUBLE ACCEPTING HIS DESERTION...
OH, I'M SORRY...

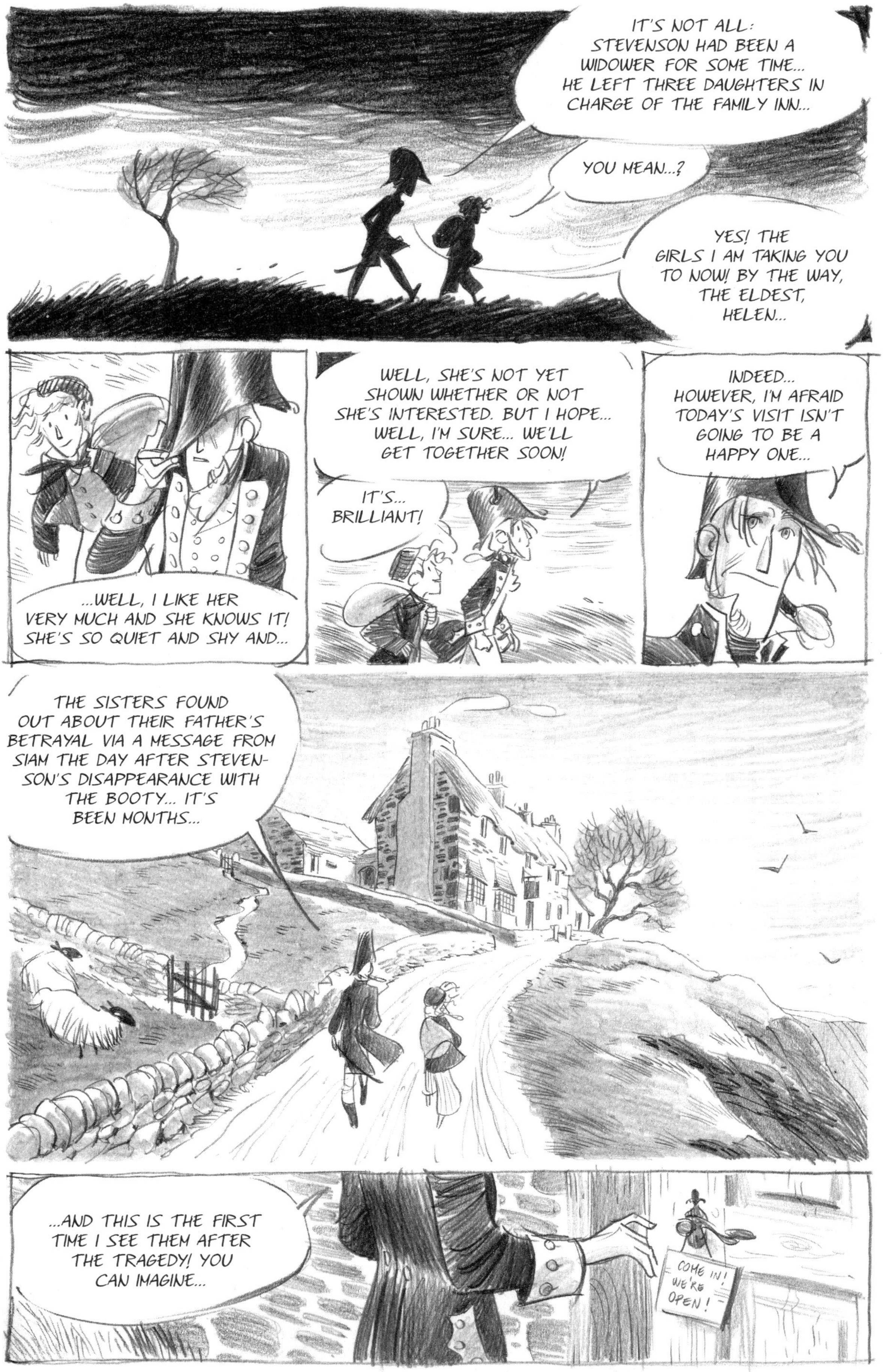
IT'S NOT ALL: STEVENSON HAD BEEN A WIDOWER FOR SOME TIME... HE LEFT THREE DAUGHTERS IN CHARGE OF THE FAMILY INN...
YOU MEAN...?
YES! THE GIRLS I AM TAKING YOU TO NOW! BY THE WAY, THE ELDEST, HELEN...
...WELL, I LIKE HER VERY MUCH AND SHE KNOWS IT! SHE'S SO QUIET AND SHY AND...
WELL, SHE'S NOT YET SHOWN WHETHER OR NOT SHE'S INTERESTED. BUT I HOPE... WELL, I'M SURE... WE'LL GET TOGETHER SOON!
IT'S... BRILLIANT!
INDEED... HOWEVER, I'M AFRAID TODAY'S VISIT ISN'T GOING TO BE A HAPPY ONE...
THE SISTERS FOUND OUT ABOUT THEIR FATHER'S BETRAYAL VIA A MESSAGE FROM SIAM THE DAY AFTER STEVENSON'S DISAPPEARANCE WITH THE BOOTY... IT'S BEEN MONTHS...
...AND THIS IS THE FIRST TIME I SEE THEM AFTER THE TRAGEDY! YOU CAN IMAGINE...
COME IN! WE'RE OPEN!

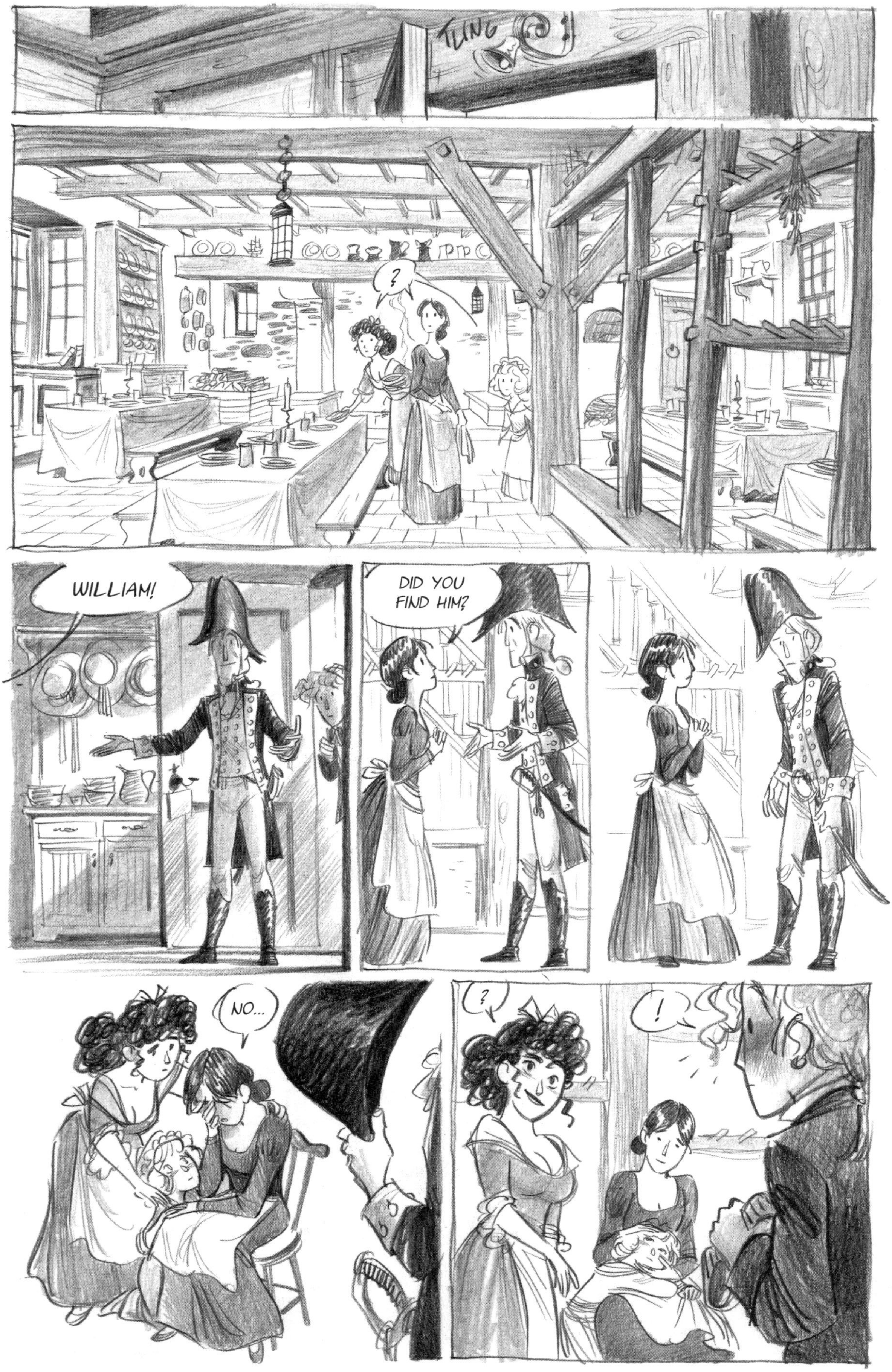
TLING
?
WILLIAM!
DID YOU FIND HIM?
NO...
?
!

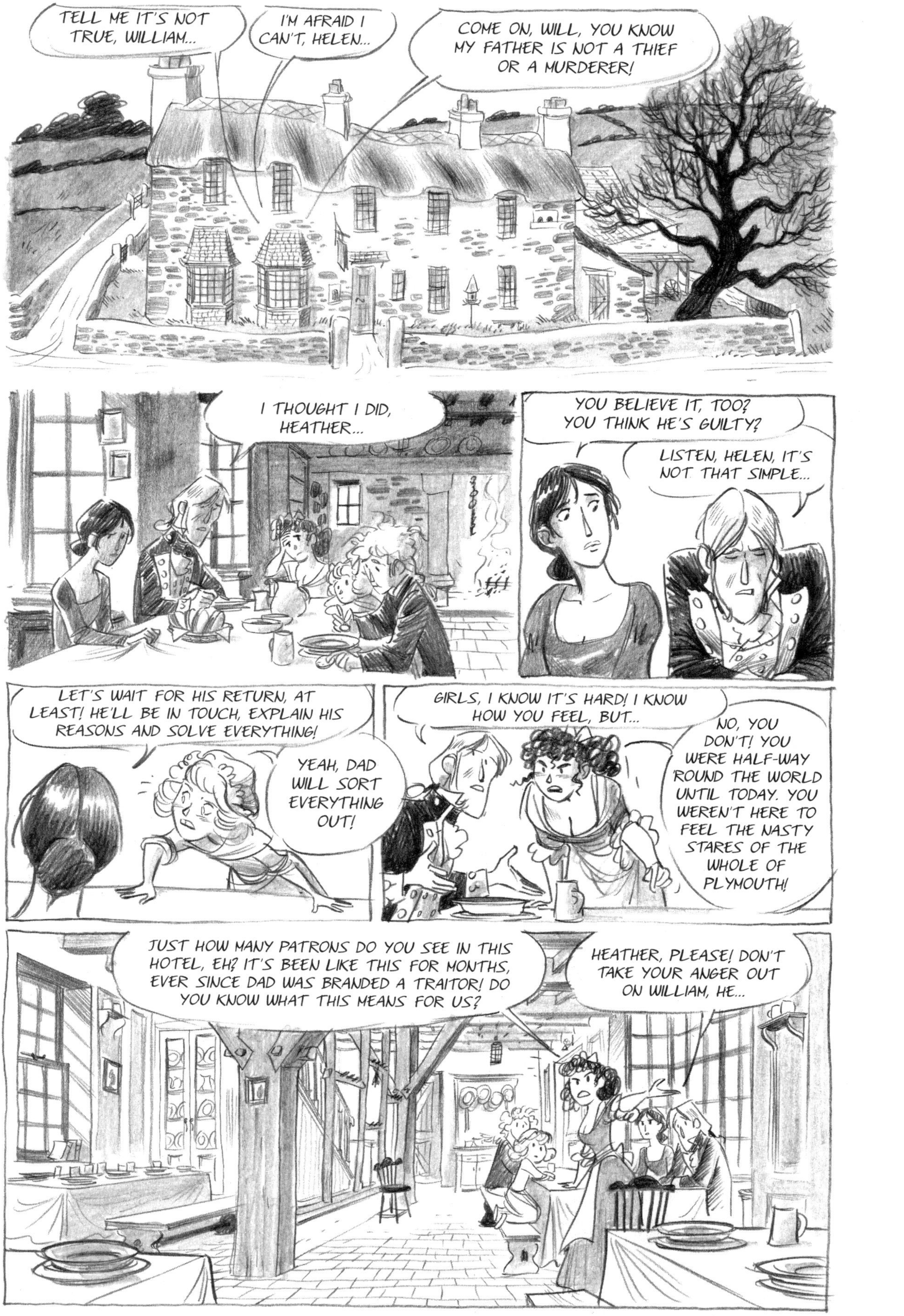
TELL ME IT'S NOT TRUE, WILLIAM...
I'M AFRAID I CAN'T, HELEN...
COME ON, WILL, YOU KNOW MY FATHER IS NOT A THIEF OR A MURDERER!
I THOUGHT I DID, HEATHER...
YOU BELIEVE IT, TOO? YOU THINK HE'S GUILTY?
LISTEN, HELEN, IT'S NOT THAT SIMPLE...
LET'S WAIT FOR HIS RETURN, AT LEAST! HE'LL BE IN TOUCH, EXPLAIN HIS REASONS AND SOLVE EVERYTHING!
YEAH, DAD WILL SORT EVERYTHING OUT!
GIRLS, I KNOW IT'S HARD! I KNOW HOW YOU FEEL, BUT...
NO, YOU DON'T! YOU WERE HALF-WAY ROUND THE WORLD UNTIL TODAY. YOU WEREN'T HERE TO FEEL THE NASTY STARES OF THE WHOLE OF PLYMOUTH!
JUST HOW MANY PATRONS DO YOU SEE IN THIS HOTEL, EH? IT'S BEEN LIKE THIS FOR MONTHS, EVER SINCE DAD WAS BRANDED A TRAITOR! DO YOU KNOW WHAT THIS MEANS FOR US?
HEATHER, PLEASE! DON'T TAKE YOUR ANGER OUT ON WILLIAM, HE...

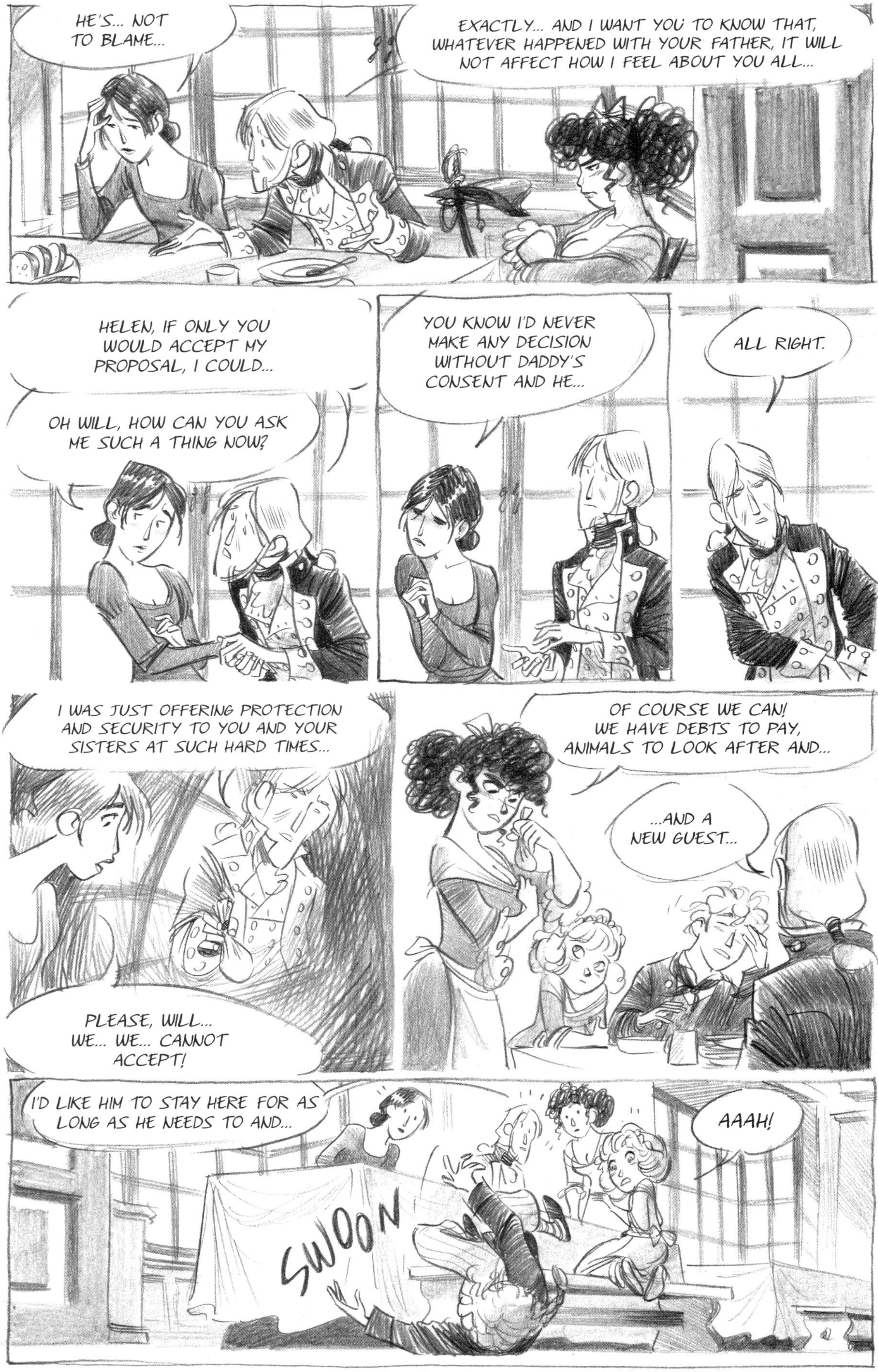
HE'S... NOT TO BLAME...
EXACTLY... AND I WANT YOU TO KNOW THAT, WHATEVER HAPPENED WITH YOUR FATHER, IT WILL NOT AFFECT HOW I FEEL ABOUT YOU ALL...
HELEN, IF ONLY YOU WOULD ACCEPT MY PROPOSAL, I COULD...
OH WILL, HOW CAN YOU ASK ME SUCH A THING NOW?
YOU KNOW I'D NEVER MAKE ANY DECISION WITHOUT DADDY'S CONSENT AND HE...
ALL RIGHT.
I WAS JUST OFFERING PROTECTION AND SECURITY TO YOU AND YOUR SISTERS AT SUCH HARD TIMES...
PLEASE, WILL... WE... WE... CANNOT ACCEPT!
OF COURSE WE CAN! WE HAVE DEBTS TO PAY, ANIMALS TO LOOK AFTER AND...
...AND A NEW GUEST...
I'D LIKE HIM TO STAY HERE FOR AS LONG AS HE NEEDS TO AND...
AAAH!
SWOON

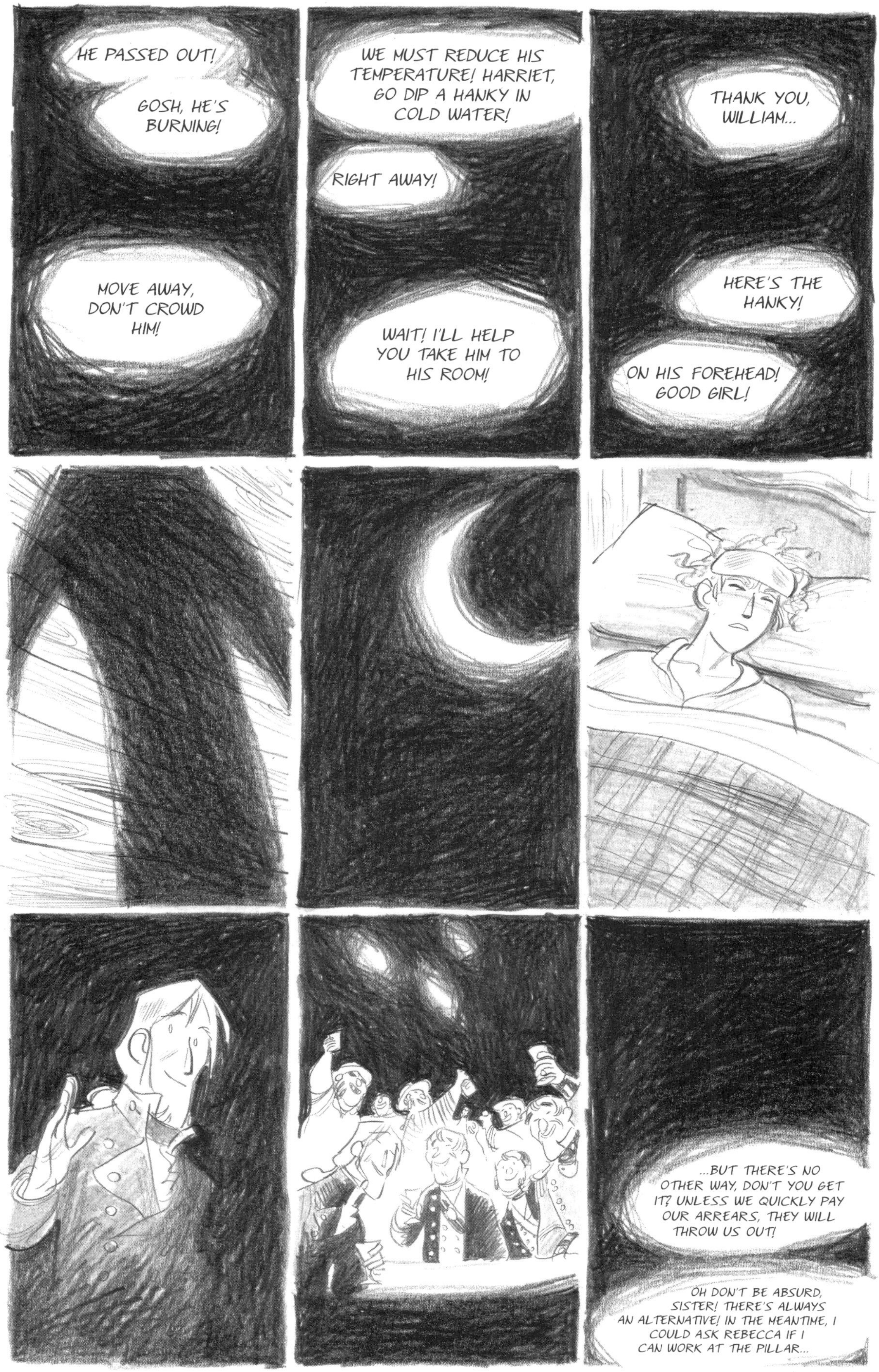
HE PASSED OUT!
GOSH, HE'S BURNING!
MOVE AWAY, DON'T CROWD HIM!
WE MUST REDUCE HIS TEMPERATURE! HARRIET, GO DIP A HANKY IN COLD WATER!
RIGHT AWAY!
WAIT! I'LL HELP YOU TAKE HIM TO HIS ROOM!
THANK YOU, WILLIAM...
HERE'S THE HANKY!
ON HIS FOREHEAD! GOOD GIRL!
...BUT THERE'S NO OTHER WAY, DON'T YOU GET IT? UNLESS WE QUICKLY PAY OUR ARREARS, THEY WILL THROW US OUT!
OH DON'T BE ABSURD, SISTER! THERE'S ALWAYS AN ALTERNATIVE! IN THE MEANTIME, I COULD ASK REBECCA IF I CAN WORK AT THE PILLAR...

FOR HEAVEN'S SAKE, HEATHER! IF DADDY COULD HEAR YOU! THIS IS NO TIME FOR JOKES!

I WASN'T JOKING AT ALL! DON'T YOU THINK MY GRACES WOULD BE APPRECIATED?

WHAT GRACES?

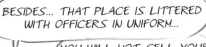

BESIDES... THAT PLACE IS LITTERED WITH OFFICERS IN UNIFORM...

YOU WILL NOT SELL YOUR MORALS IN A HOUSE OF ILL REPUTE!

WHOSE HOUSE?

AND YOU WILL NOT SELL YOUR FUTURE TO THAT SPINELESS DANDY!

SPINE? DO WE REALLY HAVE ONE? LIKE FISH? WHERE IS IT, EH? WHERE?

HARRIET...

YES?

WOULD YOU MIND LOOKING IN ON OUR GUEST?

MAYBE DAMPEN HIS HANKY... SEE IF HE NEEDS ANYTHING!

OF COURSE!

MAYBE I COULD BRING HIM SOME WATER, YES? IF HE'S THIRSTY...

AND... A BUNCH OF FLOWERS TO BRIGHTEN UP HIS ROOM! WILL ANY HAVE SURVIVED, IN THE GARDEN?

YOU DON'T LOVE HIM, HELEN.

NO, IT'S TRUE... BUT PERHAPS I COULD LEARN...

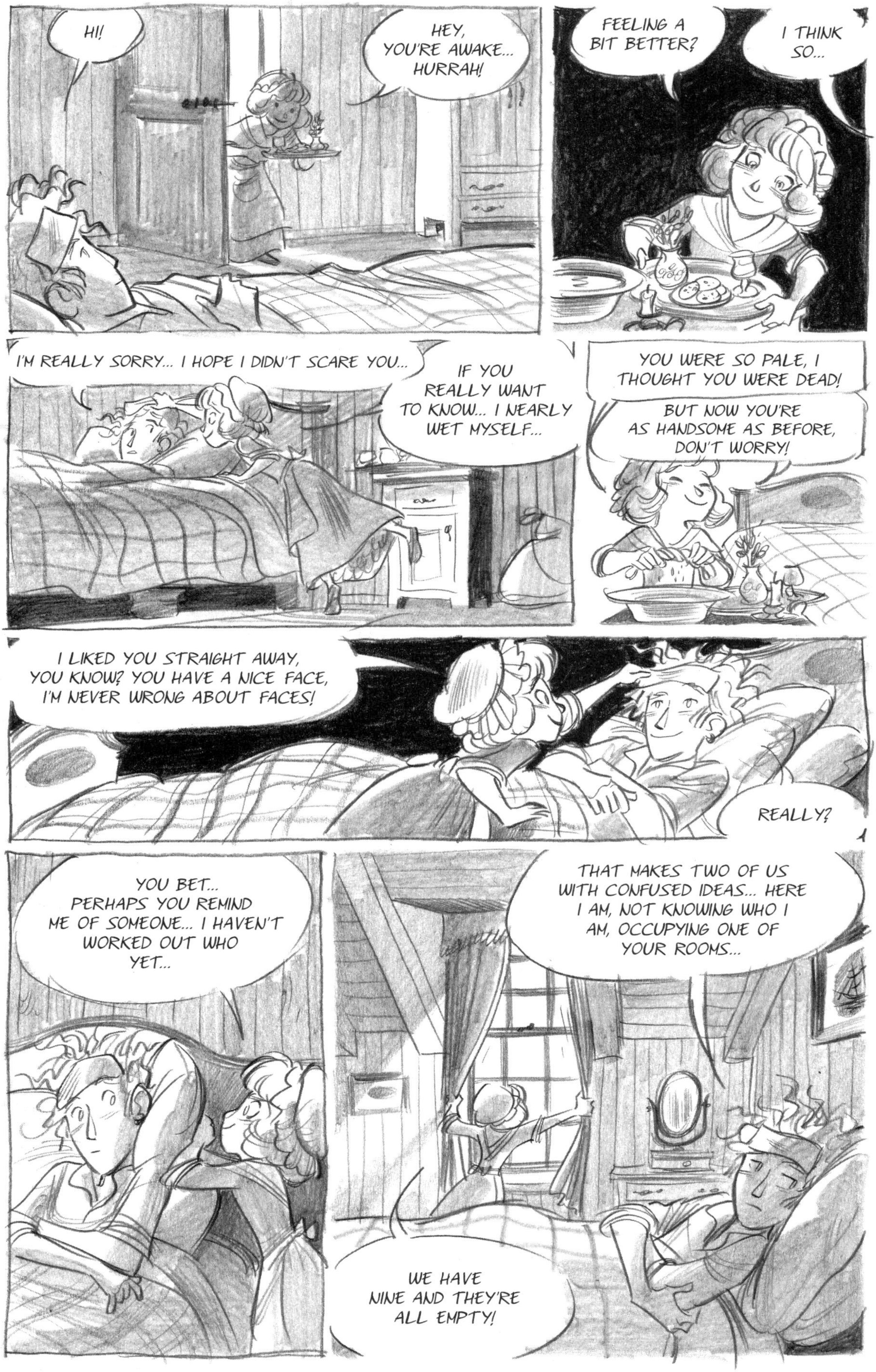
HI!
HEY, YOU'RE AWAKE... HURRAH!
FEELING A BIT BETTER?
I THINK SO...
I'M REALLY SORRY... I HOPE I DIDN'T SCARE YOU...
IF YOU REALLY WANT TO KNOW... I NEARLY WET MYSELF...
YOU WERE SO PALE, I THOUGHT YOU WERE DEAD!
BUT NOW YOU'RE AS HANDSOME AS BEFORE, DON'T WORRY!
I LIKED YOU STRAIGHT AWAY, YOU KNOW? YOU HAVE A NICE FACE, I'M NEVER WRONG ABOUT FACES!
REALLY?
YOU BET... PERHAPS YOU REMIND ME OF SOMEONE... I HAVEN'T WORKED OUT WHO YET...
THAT MAKES TWO OF US WITH CONFUSED IDEAS... HERE I AM, NOT KNOWING WHO I AM, OCCUPYING ONE OF YOUR ROOMS...
WE HAVE NINE AND THEY'RE ALL EMPTY!

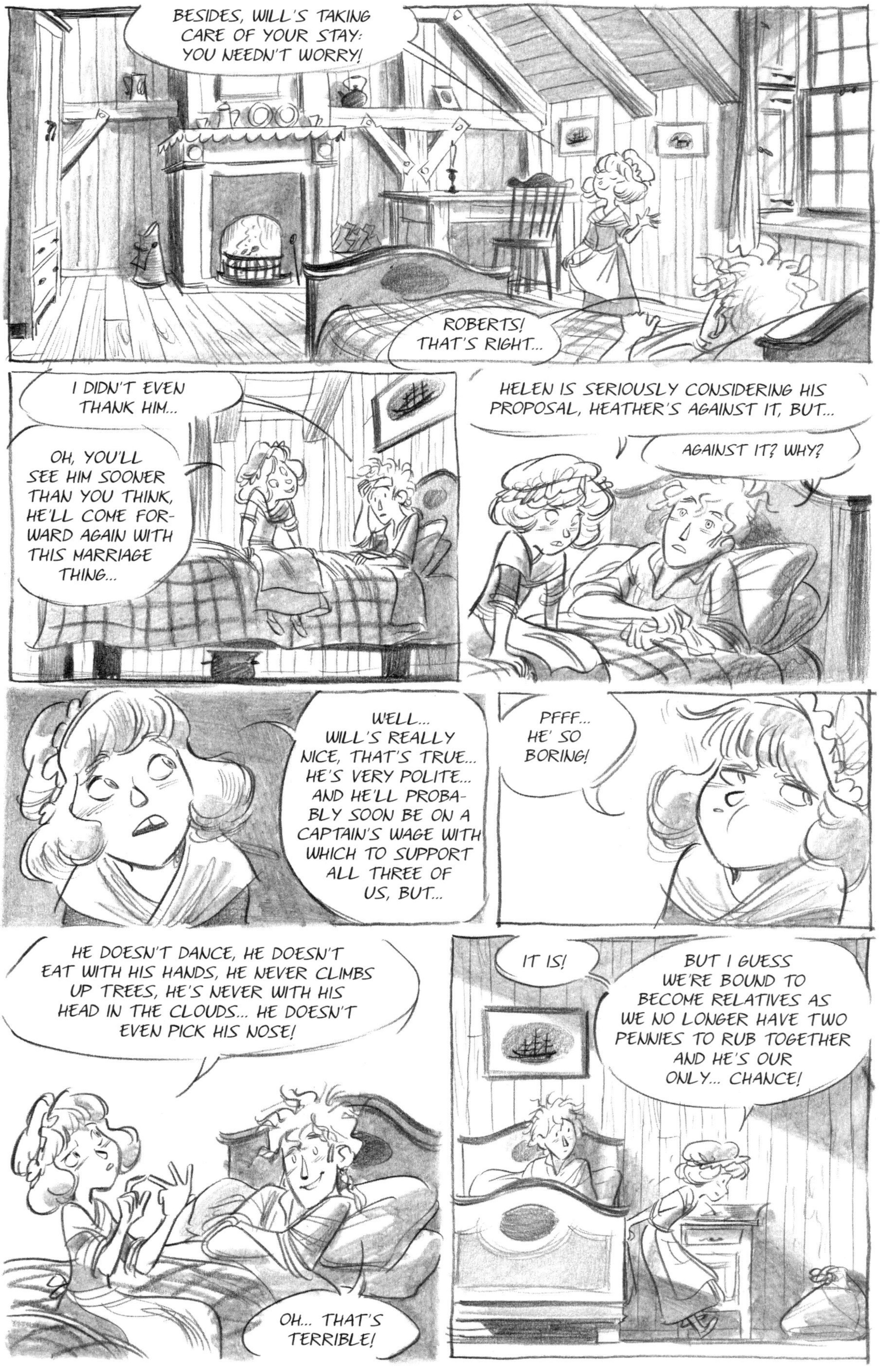
BESIDES, WILL'S TAKING CARE OF YOUR STAY: YOU NEEDN'T WORRY!
ROBERTS! THAT'S RIGHT...
I DIDN'T EVEN THANK HIM...
OH, YOU'LL SEE HIM SOONER THAN YOU THINK, HE'LL COME FOR-WARD AGAIN WITH THIS MARRIAGE THING...
HELEN IS SERIOUSLY CONSIDERING HIS PROPOSAL, HEATHER'S AGAINST IT, BUT...
AGAINST IT? WHY?
WELL... WILL'S REALLY NICE, THAT'S TRUE... HE'S VERY POLITE... AND HE'LL PROBA-BLY SOON BE ON A CAPTAIN'S WAGE WITH WHICH TO SUPPORT ALL THREE OF US, BUT...
PFFF... HE' SO BORING!
HE DOESN'T DANCE, HE DOESN'T EAT WITH HIS HANDS, HE NEVER CLIMBS UP TREES, HE'S NEVER WITH HIS HEAD IN THE CLOUDS... HE DOESN'T EVEN PICK HIS NOSE!
OH... THAT'S TERRIBLE!
IT IS!
BUT I GUESS WE'RE BOUND TO BECOME RELATIVES AS WE NO LONGER HAVE TWO PENNIES TO RUB TOGETHER AND HE'S OUR ONLY... CHANCE!

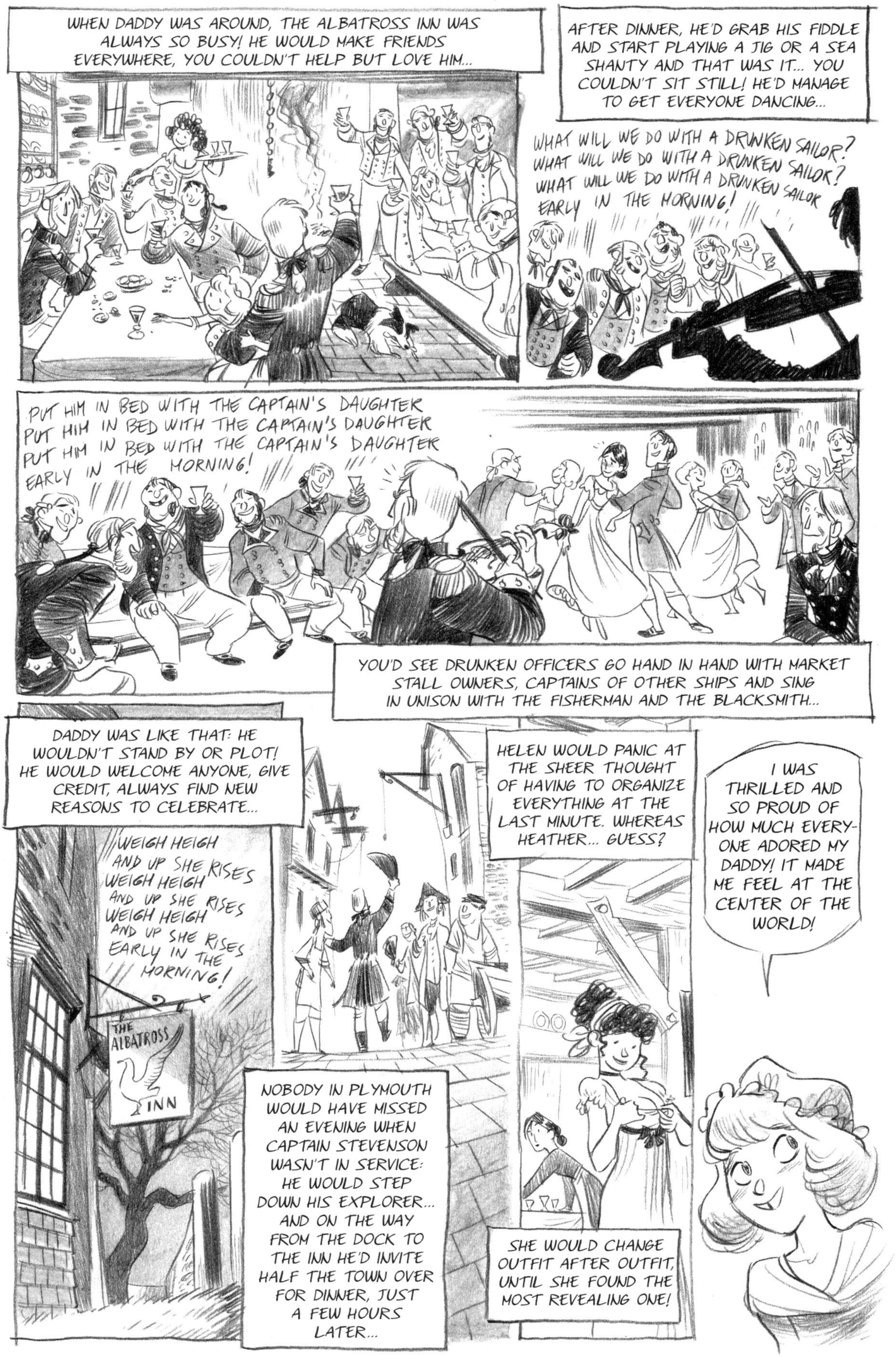

WHEN DADDY WAS AROUND, THE ALBATROSS INN WAS ALWAYS SO BUSY! HE WOULD MAKE FRIENDS EVERYWHERE, YOU COULDN'T HELP BUT LOVE HIM...
AFTER DINNER, HE'D GRAB HIS FIDDLE AND START PLAYING A JIG OR A SEA SHANTY AND THAT WAS IT... YOU COULDN'T SIT STILL! HE'D MANAGE TO GET EVERYONE DANCING...
WHAT WILL WE DO WITH A DRUNKEN SAILOR? WHAT WILL WE DO WITH A DRUNKEN SAILOR? WHAT WILL WE DO WITH A DRUNKEN SAILOR EARLY IN THE MORNING!
PUT HIM IN BED WITH THE CAPTAIN'S DAUGHTER PUT HIM IN BED WITH THE CAPTAIN'S DAUGHTER PUT HIM IN BED WITH THE CAPTAIN'S DAUGHTER EARLY IN THE MORNING!
YOU'D SEE DRUNKEN OFFICERS GO HAND IN HAND WITH MARKET STALL OWNERS, CAPTAINS OF OTHER SHIPS AND SING IN UNISON WITH THE FISHERMAN AND THE BLACKSMITH...
DADDY WAS LIKE THAT: HE WOULDN'T STAND BY OR PLOT! HE WOULD WELCOME ANYONE, GIVE CREDIT, ALWAYS FIND NEW REASONS TO CELEBRATE...
WEIGH HEIGH AND UP SHE RISES WEIGH HEIGH AND UP SHE RISES WEIGH HEIGH AND UP SHE RISES EARLY IN THE MORNING!
THE ALBATROSS INN
NOBODY IN PLYMOUTH WOULD HAVE MISSED AN EVENING WHEN CAPTAIN STEVENSON WASN'T IN SERVICE: HE WOULD STEP DOWN HIS EXPLORER... AND ON THE WAY FROM THE DOCK TO THE INN HE'D INVITE HALF THE TOWN OVER FOR DINNER, JUST A FEW HOURS LATER...
HELEN WOULD PANIC AT THE SHEER THOUGHT OF HAVING TO ORGANIZE EVERYTHING AT THE LAST MINUTE. WHEREAS HEATHER... GUESS?
SHE WOULD CHANGE OUTFIT AFTER OUTFIT, UNTIL SHE FOUND THE MOST REVEALING ONE!
I WAS THRILLED AND SO PROUD OF HOW MUCH EVERY-ONE ADORED MY DADDY! IT MADE ME FEEL AT THE CENTER OF THE WORLD!

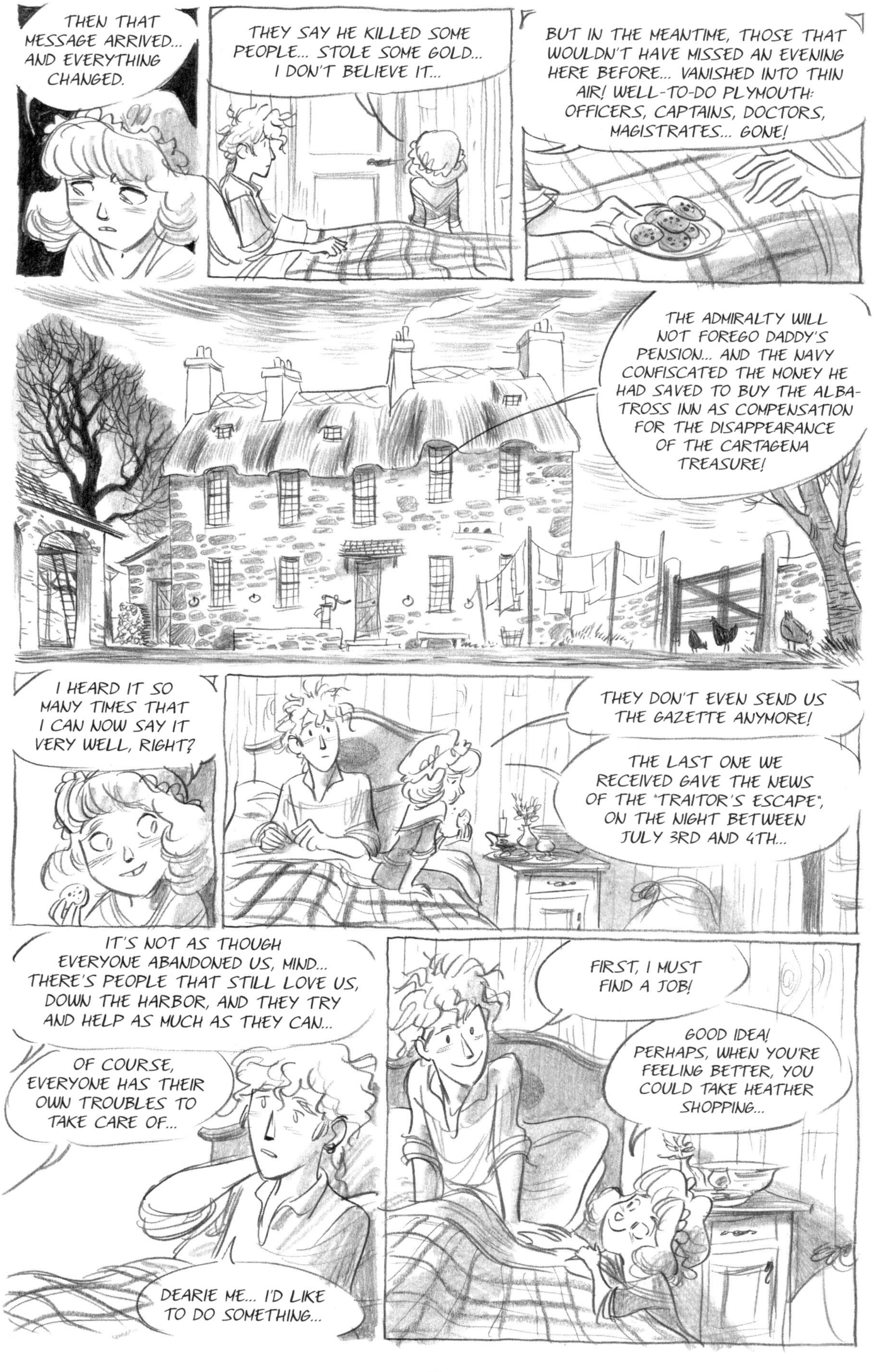
THEN THAT MESSAGE ARRIVED... AND EVERYTHING CHANGED.
THEY SAY HE KILLED SOME PEOPLE... STOLE SOME GOLD... I DON'T BELIEVE IT...
BUT IN THE MEANTIME, THOSE THAT WOULDN'T HAVE MISSED AN EVENING HERE BEFORE... VANISHED INTO THIN AIR! WELL-TO-DO PLYMOUTH: OFFICERS, CAPTAINS, DOCTORS, MAGISTRATES... GONE!
THE ADMIRALTY WILL NOT FOREGO DADDY'S PENSION... AND THE NAVY CONFISCATED THE MONEY HE HAD SAVED TO BUY THE ALBA-TROSS INN AS COMPENSATION FOR THE DISAPPEARANCE OF THE CARTAGENA TREASURE!
I HEARD IT SO MANY TIMES THAT I CAN NOW SAY IT VERY WELL, RIGHT?
THEY DON'T EVEN SEND US THE GAZETTE ANYMORE!
THE LAST ONE WE RECEIVED GAVE THE NEWS OF THE "TRAITOR'S ESCAPE", ON THE NIGHT BETWEEN JULY 3RD AND 4TH...
IT'S NOT AS THOUGH EVERYONE ABANDONED US, MIND... THERE'S PEOPLE THAT STILL LOVE US, DOWN THE HARBOR, AND THEY TRY AND HELP AS MUCH AS THEY CAN...
OF COURSE, EVERYONE HAS THEIR OWN TROUBLES TO TAKE CARE OF...
DEARIE ME... I'D LIKE TO DO SOMETHING...
FIRST, I MUST FIND A JOB!
GOOD IDEA! PERHAPS, WHEN YOU'RE FEELING BETTER, YOU COULD TAKE HEATHER SHOPPING...

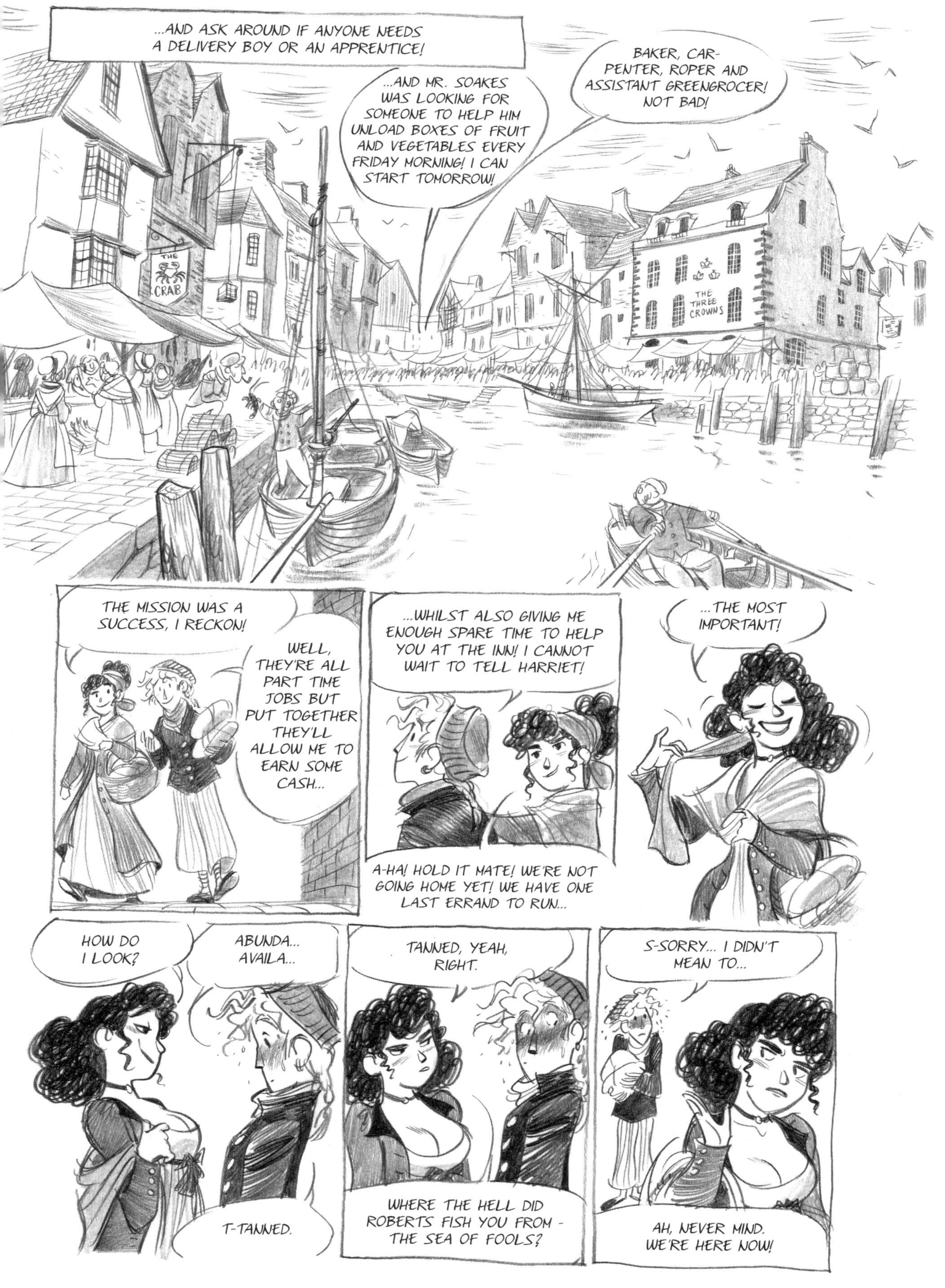
...AND ASK AROUND IF ANYONE NEEDS A DELIVERY BOY OR AN APPRENTICE!
...AND MR. SOAKES WAS LOOKING FOR SOMEONE TO HELP HIM UNLOAD BOXES OF FRUIT AND VEGETABLES EVERY FRIDAY MORNING! I CAN START TOMORROW!
BAKER, CARPENTER, ROPER AND ASSISTANT GREENGROCER! NOT BAD!
THE CRAB
THE THREE CROWNS
THE MISSION WAS A SUCCESS, I RECKON!
WELL, THEY'RE ALL PART TIME JOBS BUT PUT TOGETHER THEY'LL ALLOW ME TO EARN SOME CASH...
...WHILST ALSO GIVING ME ENOUGH SPARE TIME TO HELP YOU AT THE INN! I CANNOT WAIT TO TELL HARRIET!
A-HA! HOLD IT MATE! WE'RE NOT GOING HOME YET! WE HAVE ONE LAST ERRAND TO RUN...
...THE MOST IMPORTANT!
HOW DO I LOOK?
ABUNDA... AVAILA...
T-TANNED.
TANNED, YEAH, RIGHT.
WHERE THE HELL DID ROBERTS FISH YOU FROM - THE SEA OF FOOLS?
S-SORRY... I DIDN'T MEAN TO...
AH, NEVER MIND. WE'RE HERE NOW!

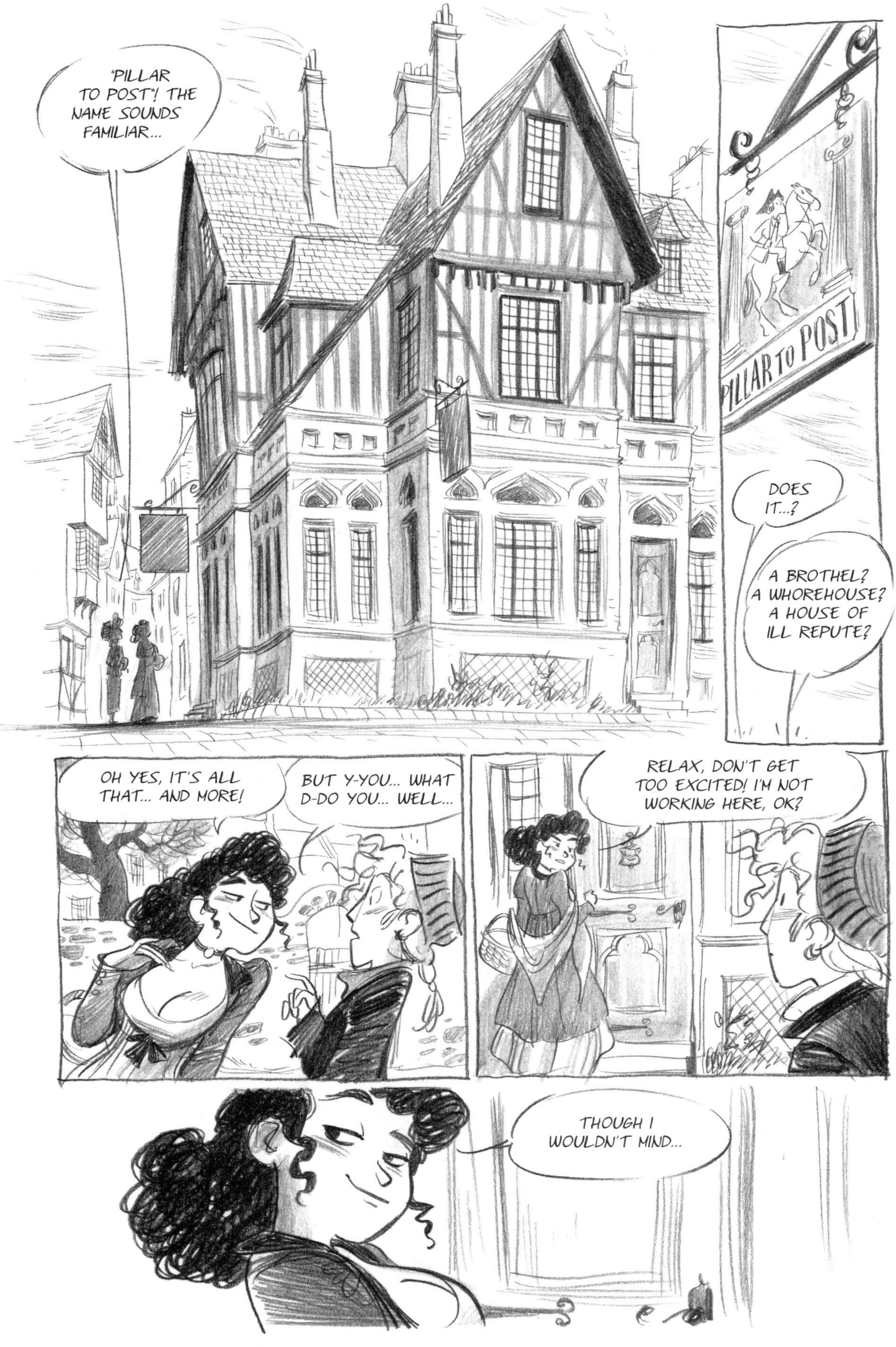

"PILLAR TO POST"! THE NAME SOUNDS FAMILIAR...
PILLAR TO POST
DOES IT...?
A BROTHEL? A WHOREHOUSE? A HOUSE OF ILL REPUTE?
OH YES, IT'S ALL THAT... AND MORE!
BUT Y-YOU... WHAT D-DO YOU... WELL...
RELAX, DON'T GET TOO EXCITED! I'M NOT WORKING HERE, OK?
THOUGH I WOULDN'T MIND...

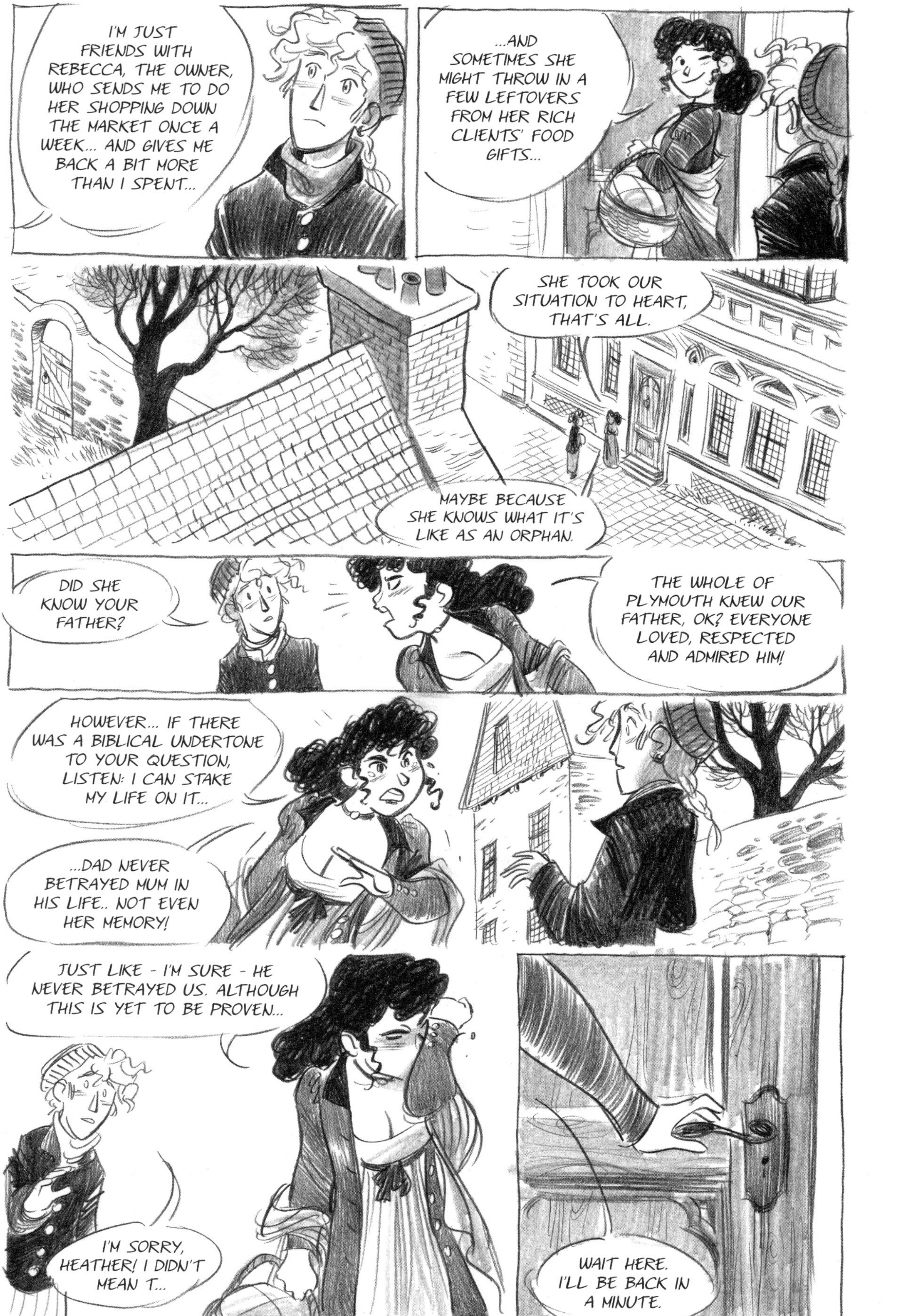
I'M JUST FRIENDS WITH REBECCA, THE OWNER, WHO SENDS ME TO DO HER SHOPPING DOWN THE MARKET ONCE A WEEK... AND GIVES ME BACK A BIT MORE THAN I SPENT...
...AND SOMETIMES SHE MIGHT THROW IN A FEW LEFTOVERS FROM HER RICH CLIENTS' FOOD GIFTS...
SHE TOOK OUR SITUATION TO HEART, THAT'S ALL.
MAYBE BECAUSE SHE KNOWS WHAT IT'S LIKE AS AN ORPHAN.
DID SHE KNOW YOUR FATHER?
THE WHOLE OF PLYMOUTH KNEW OUR FATHER, OK? EVERYONE LOVED, RESPECTED AND ADMIRED HIM!
HOWEVER... IF THERE WAS A BIBLICAL UNDERTONE TO YOUR QUESTION, LISTEN: I CAN STAKE MY LIFE ON IT...
...DAD NEVER BETRAYED MUM IN HIS LIFE.. NOT EVEN HER MEMORY!
JUST LIKE - I'M SURE - HE NEVER BETRAYED US. ALTHOUGH THIS IS YET TO BE PROVEN...
I'M SORRY, HEATHER! I DIDN'T MEAN T...
WAIT HERE. I'LL BE BACK IN A MINUTE.

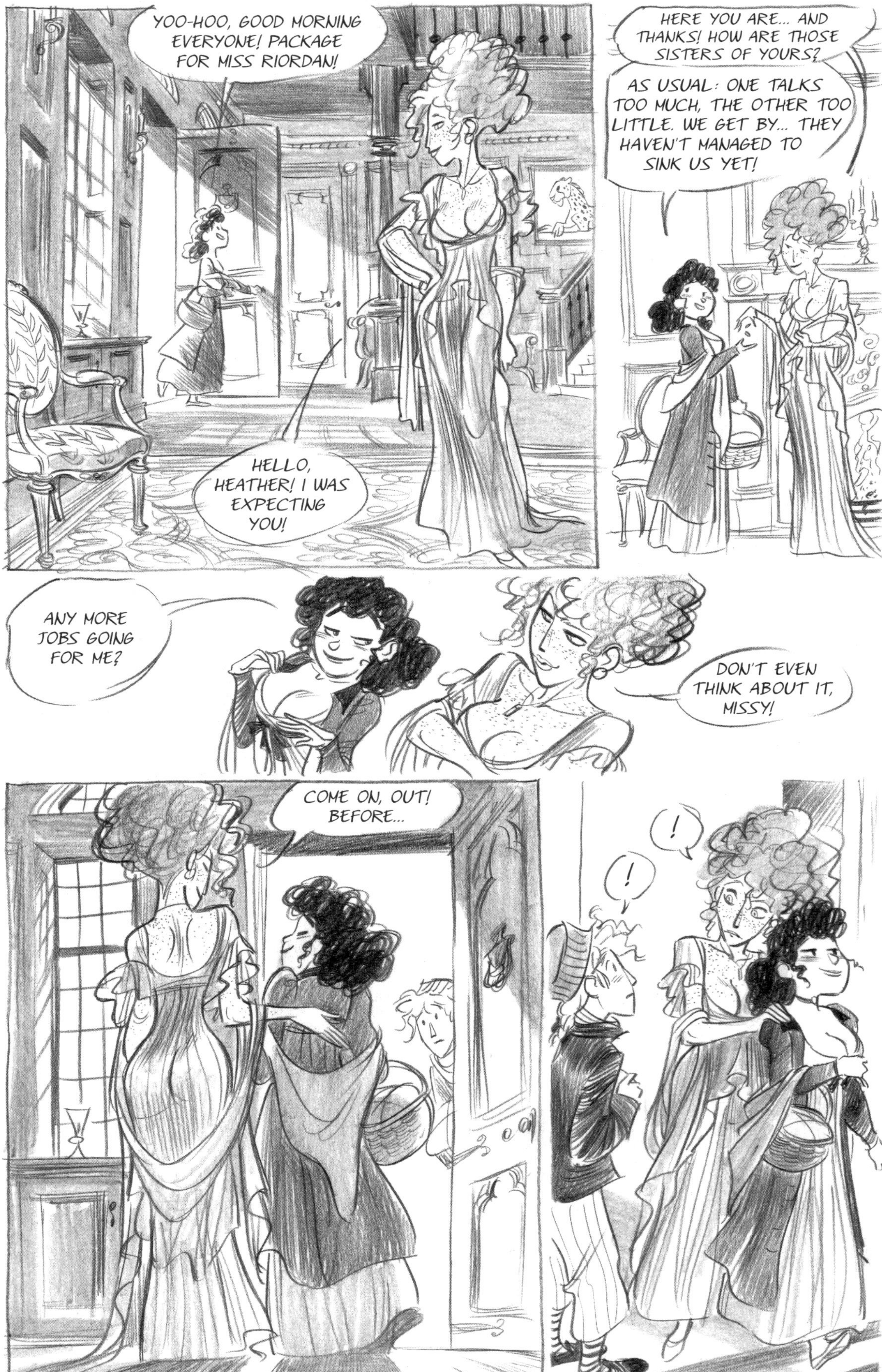
YOO-HOO, GOOD MORNING EVERYONE! PACKAGE FOR MISS RIORDAN!
HELLO, HEATHER! I WAS EXPECTING YOU!
HERE YOU ARE... AND THANKS! HOW ARE THOSE SISTERS OF YOURS?
AS USUAL: ONE TALKS TOO MUCH, THE OTHER TOO LITTLE. WE GET BY... THEY HAVEN'T MANAGED TO SINK US YET!
ANY MORE JOBS GOING FOR ME?
DON'T EVEN THINK ABOUT IT, MISSY!
COME ON, OUT! BEFORE...
!
!

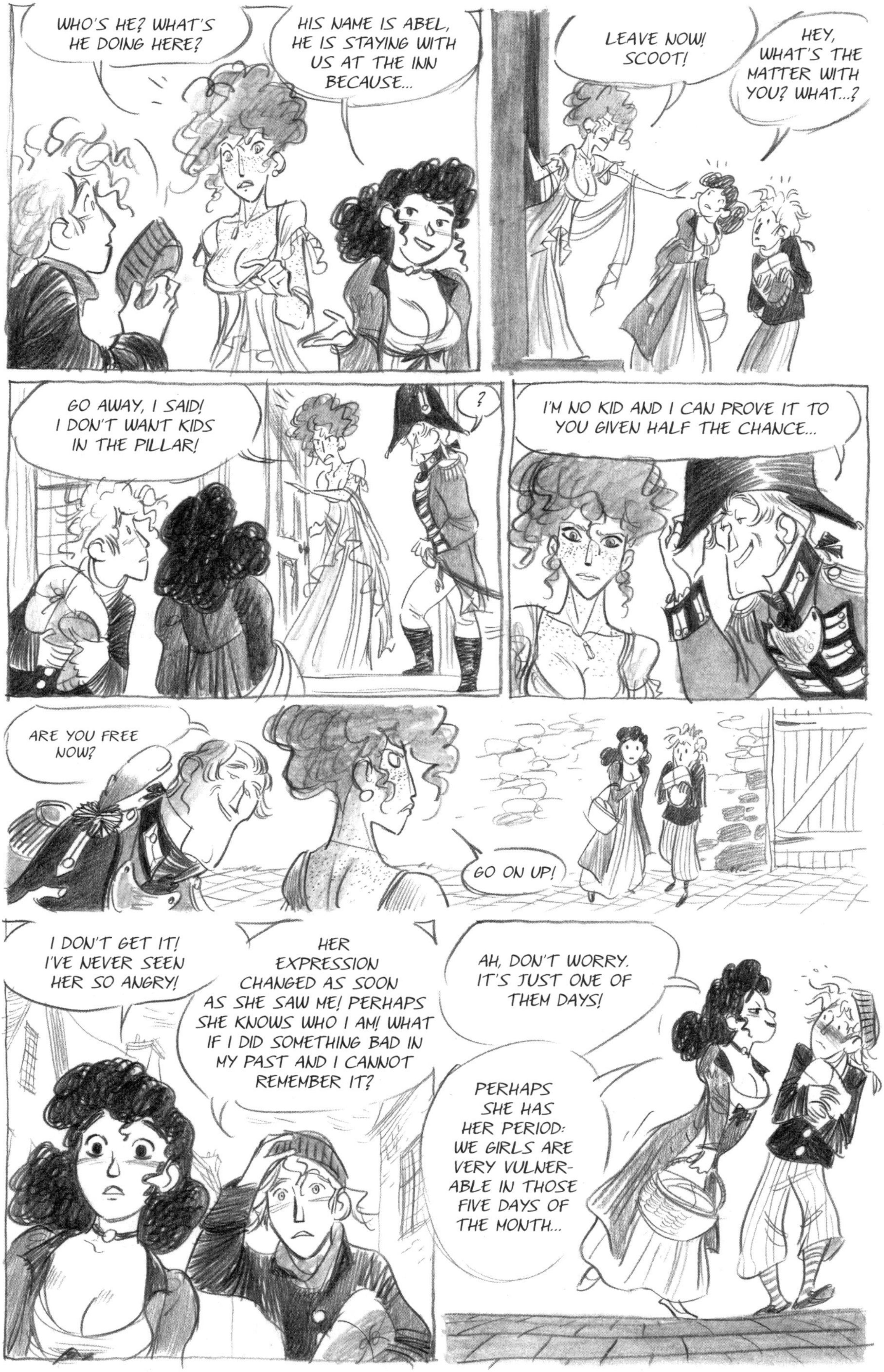
WHO'S HE? WHAT'S HE DOING HERE?
HIS NAME IS ABEL, HE IS STAYING WITH US AT THE INN BECAUSE...
LEAVE NOW! SCOOT!
HEY, WHAT'S THE MATTER WITH YOU? WHAT...?
GO AWAY, I SAID! I DON'T WANT KIDS IN THE PILLAR!
?
I'M NO KID AND I CAN PROVE IT TO YOU GIVEN HALF THE CHANCE...
ARE YOU FREE NOW?
GO ON UP!
I DON'T GET IT! I'VE NEVER SEEN HER SO ANGRY!
HER EXPRESSION CHANGED AS SOON AS SHE SAW ME! PERHAPS SHE KNOWS WHO I AM! WHAT IF I DID SOMETHING BAD IN MY PAST AND I CANNOT REMEMBER IT?
AH, DON'T WORRY. IT'S JUST ONE OF THEM DAYS!
PERHAPS SHE HAS HER PERIOD: WE GIRLS ARE VERY VULNER-ABLE IN THOSE FIVE DAYS OF THE MONTH...

ANYWAY, I BET HER MOOD WILL IMPROVE IN A MINUTE...

WHAT DO YOU MEAN?

YOU SEE THAT BIG FELLOW GOING IN? HIS NAME'S NATHAN MACLEOD AND HE CAPTAINS THE SHIP OF AN INDIAN COMPANY...

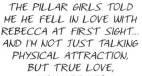

THE PILLAR GIRLS TOLD ME HE FELL IN LOVE WITH REBECCA AT FIRST SIGHT... AND I'M NOT JUST TALKING PHYSICAL ATTRACTION, BUT TRUE LOVE, YOU GET ME?

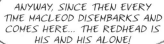

ANYWAY, SINCE THEN EVERY TIME MACLEOD DISEMBARKS AND COMES HERE... THE REDHEAD IS HIS AND HIS ALONE!

WHAT DID I TELL YOU? I THINK REBECCA HAS A SOFT SPOT FOR HIM TOO... THOUGH IT IS ALWAYS SO DIFFICULT TO IMAGINE WHAT GOES ON IN HER HEAD!

SOMETIMES SHE'S UTTERLY SWEET, OTHERS MORE ABRUPT BUT... SHE'S A REALLY NICE PERSON, I ASSURE YOU. BESIDES...

...ISN'T SHE PRETTY MUCH THE MOST FASCINATING WOMAN YOU HAVE EVER SEEN? I HEARD SHE RECENTLY TURNED 35... BUT YOU'D NEVER TELL SHE WAS THAT OLD, WOULD YOU?

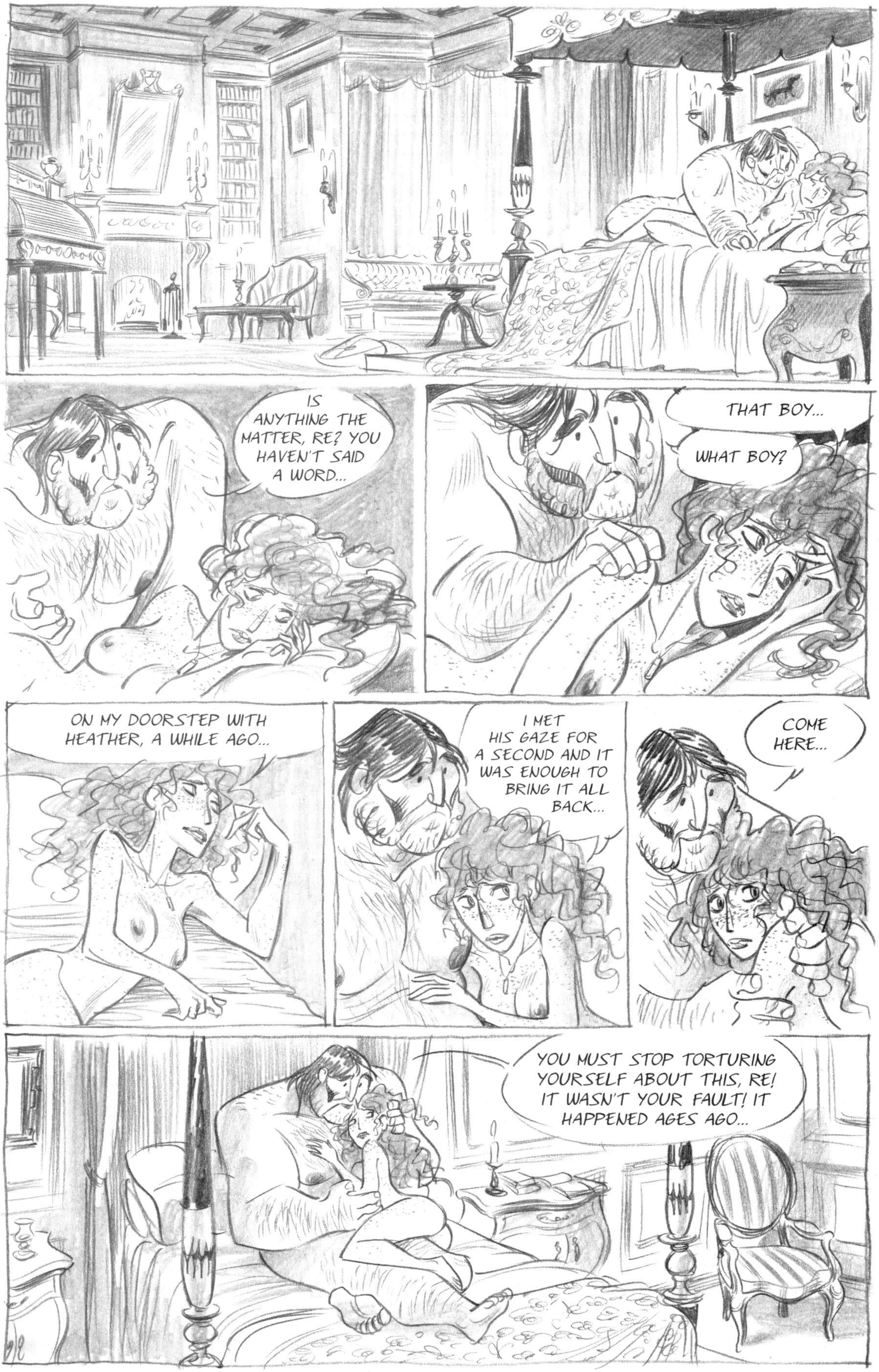

IS ANYTHING THE MATTER, RE? YOU HAVEN'T SAID A WORD...
THAT BOY...
WHAT BOY?
ON MY DOORSTEP WITH HEATHER, A WHILE AGO...
I MET HIS GAZE FOR A SECOND AND IT WAS ENOUGH TO BRING IT ALL BACK...
COME HERE...
YOU MUST STOP TORTURING YOURSELF ABOUT THIS, RE! IT WASN'T YOUR FAULT! IT HAPPENED AGES AGO...

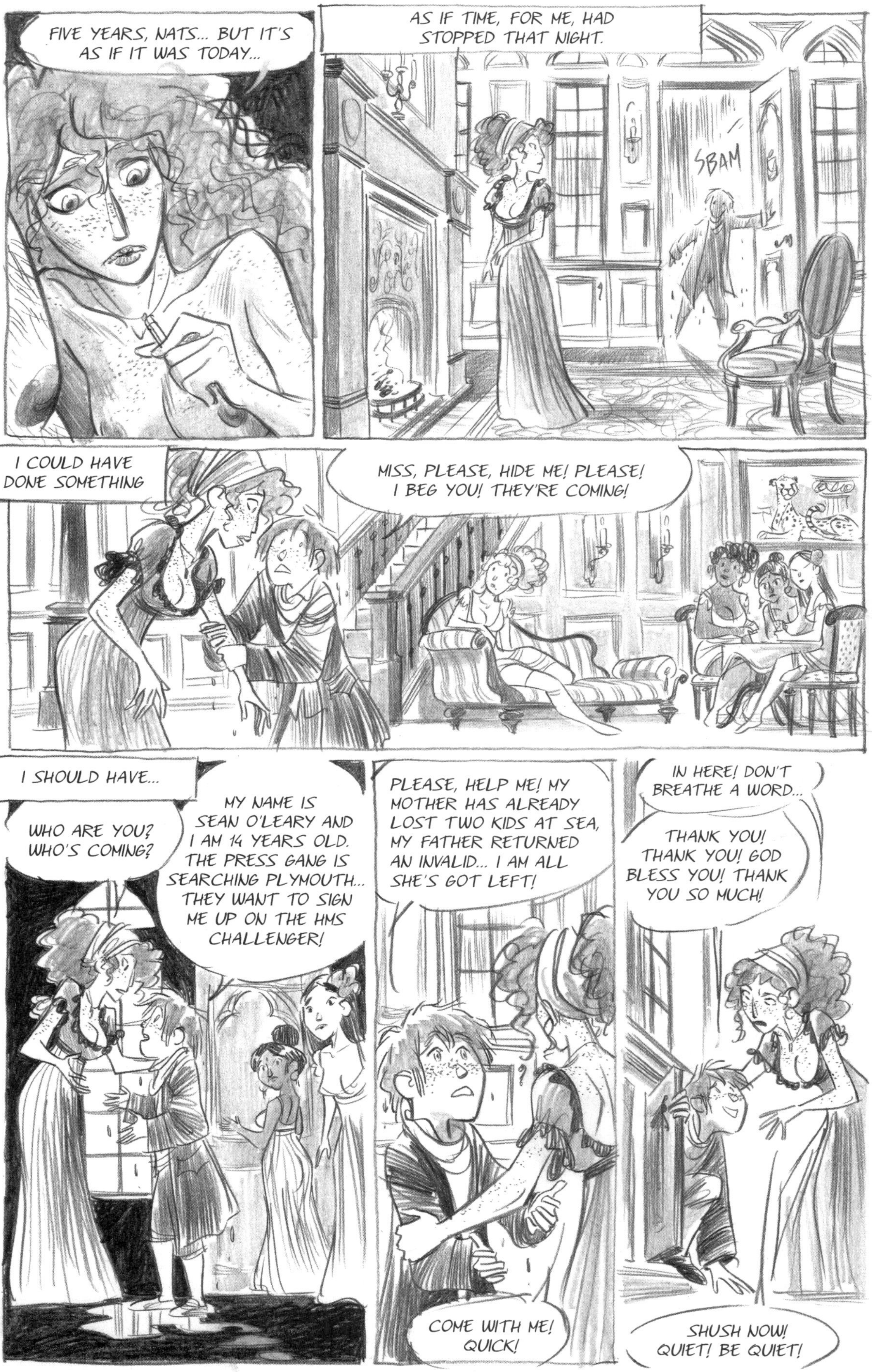
FIVE YEARS, NATS... BUT IT'S AS IF IT WAS TODAY...
AS IF TIME, FOR ME, HAD STOPPED THAT NIGHT.
SBAM
I COULD HAVE DONE SOMETHING
MISS, PLEASE, HIDE ME! PLEASE! I BEG YOU! THEY'RE COMING!
I SHOULD HAVE...
WHO ARE YOU? WHO'S COMING?
MY NAME IS SEAN O'LEARY AND I AM 14 YEARS OLD. THE PRESS GANG IS SEARCHING PLYMOUTH... THEY WANT TO SIGN ME UP ON THE HMS CHALLENGER!
PLEASE, HELP ME! MY MOTHER HAS ALREADY LOST TWO KIDS AT SEA, MY FATHER RETURNED AN INVALID... I AM ALL SHE'S GOT LEFT!
COME WITH ME! QUICK!
IN HERE! DON'T BREATHE A WORD...
THANK YOU! THANK YOU! GOD BLESS YOU! THANK YOU SO MUCH!
SHUSH NOW! QUIET! BE QUIET!

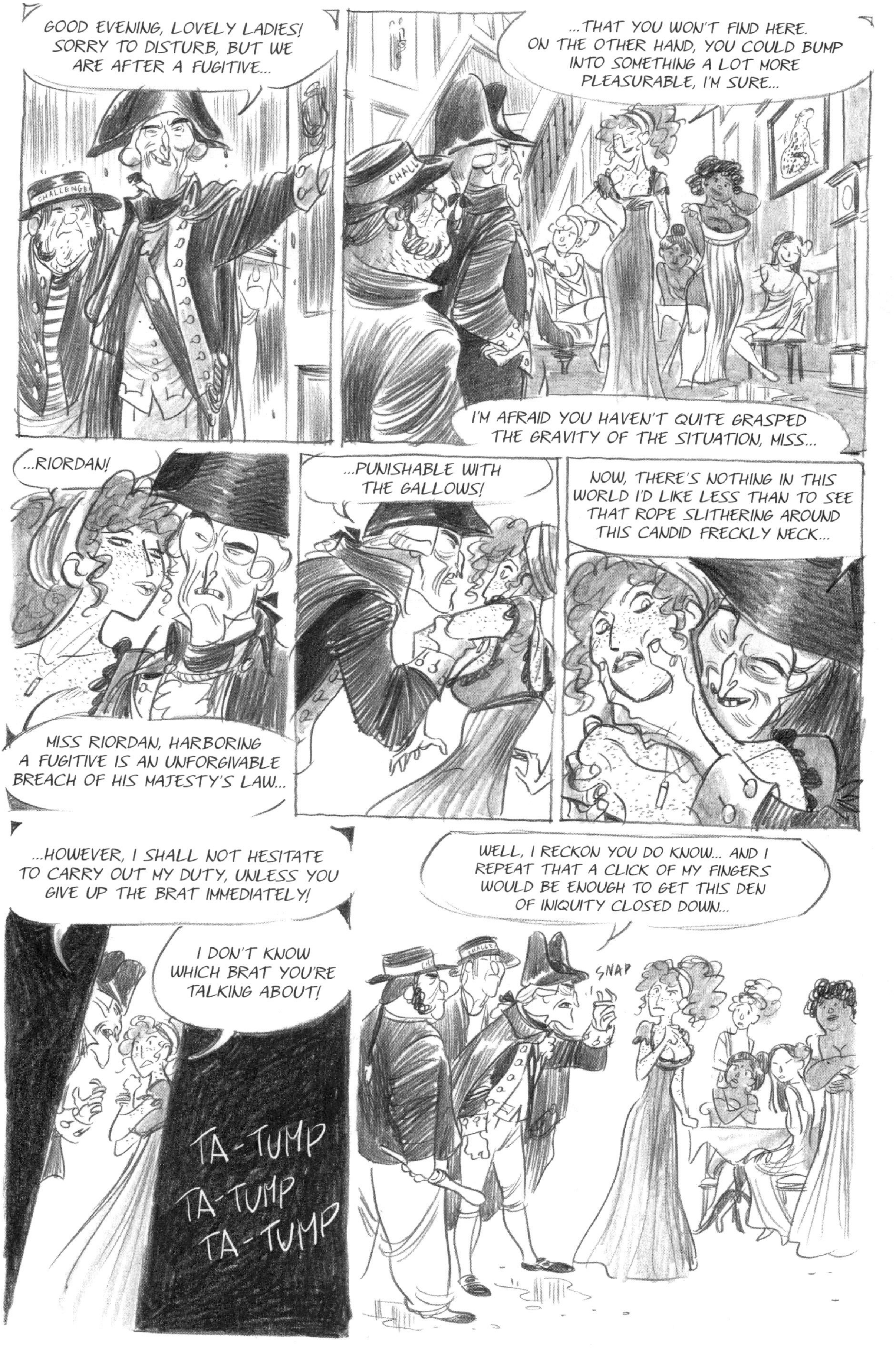
GOOD EVENING, LOVELY LADIES! SORRY TO DISTURB, BUT WE ARE AFTER A FUGITIVE...
CHALLENGER
...THAT YOU WON'T FIND HERE. ON THE OTHER HAND, YOU COULD BUMP INTO SOMETHING A LOT MORE PLEASURABLE, I'M SURE...
I'M AFRAID YOU HAVEN'T QUITE GRASPED THE GRAVITY OF THE SITUATION, MISS...
...RIORDAN!
MISS RIORDAN, HARBORING A FUGITIVE IS AN UNFORGIVABLE BREACH OF HIS MAJESTY'S LAW...
...PUNISHABLE WITH THE GALLOWS!
NOW, THERE'S NOTHING IN THIS WORLD I'D LIKE LESS THAN TO SEE THAT ROPE SLITHERING AROUND THIS CANDID FRECKLY NECK...
...HOWEVER, I SHALL NOT HESITATE TO CARRY OUT MY DUTY, UNLESS YOU GIVE UP THE BRAT IMMEDIATELY!
I DON'T KNOW WHICH BRAT YOU'RE TALKING ABOUT!
TA-TUMP
TA-TUMP
TA-TUMP
WELL, I RECKON YOU DO KNOW... AND I REPEAT THAT A CLICK OF MY FINGERS WOULD BE ENOUGH TO GET THIS DEN OF INIQUITY CLOSED DOWN...
SNAP

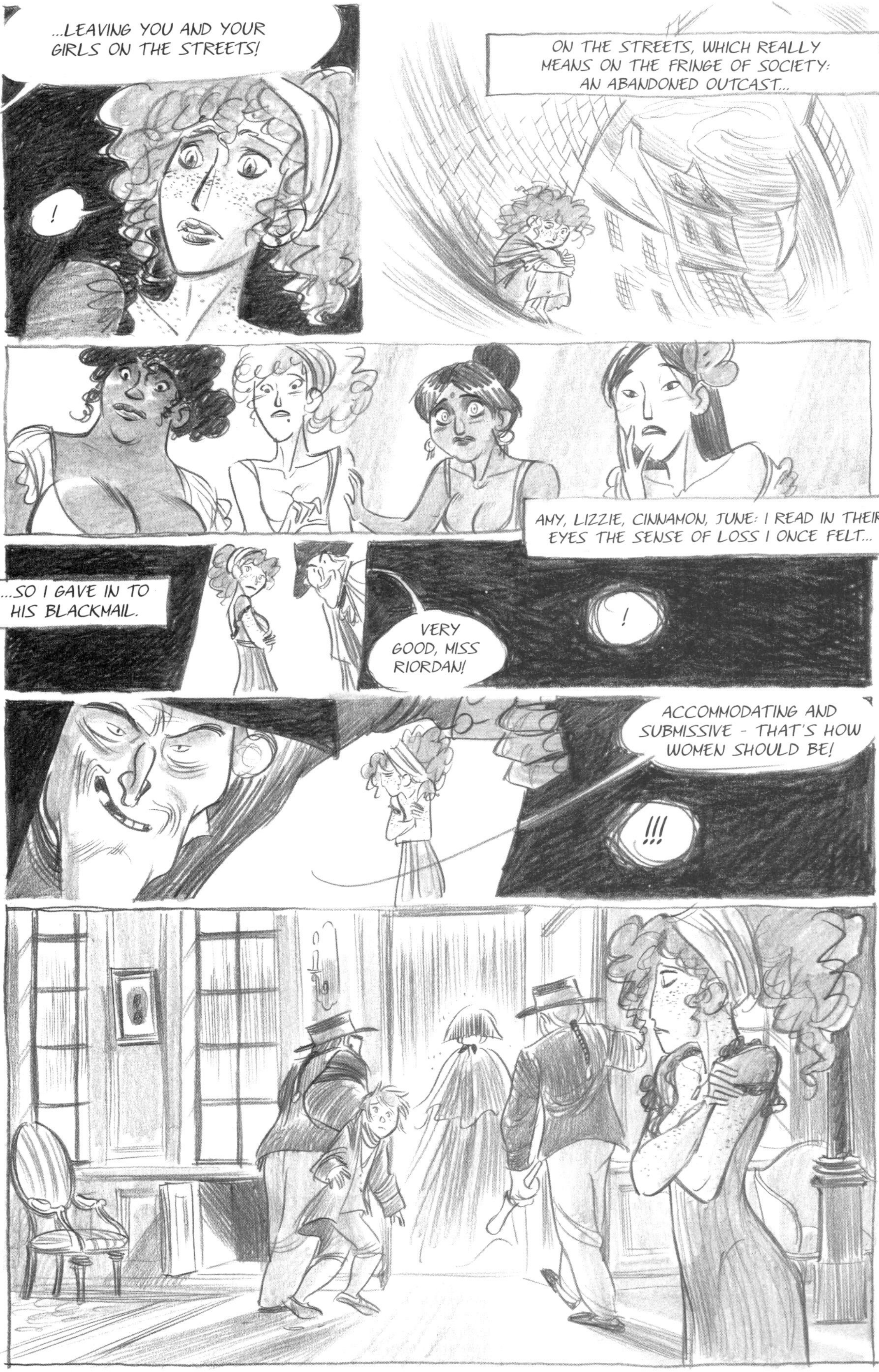
...LEAVING YOU AND YOUR GIRLS ON THE STREETS!
!
ON THE STREETS, WHICH REALLY MEANS ON THE FRINGE OF SOCIETY: AN ABANDONED OUTCAST...
AMY, LIZZIE, CINNAMON, JUNE: I READ IN THEIR EYES THE SENSE OF LOSS I ONCE FELT...
...SO I GAVE IN TO HIS BLACKMAIL.
VERY GOOD, MISS RIORDAN!
!
ACCOMMODATING AND SUBMISSIVE - THAT'S HOW WOMEN SHOULD BE!
!!!

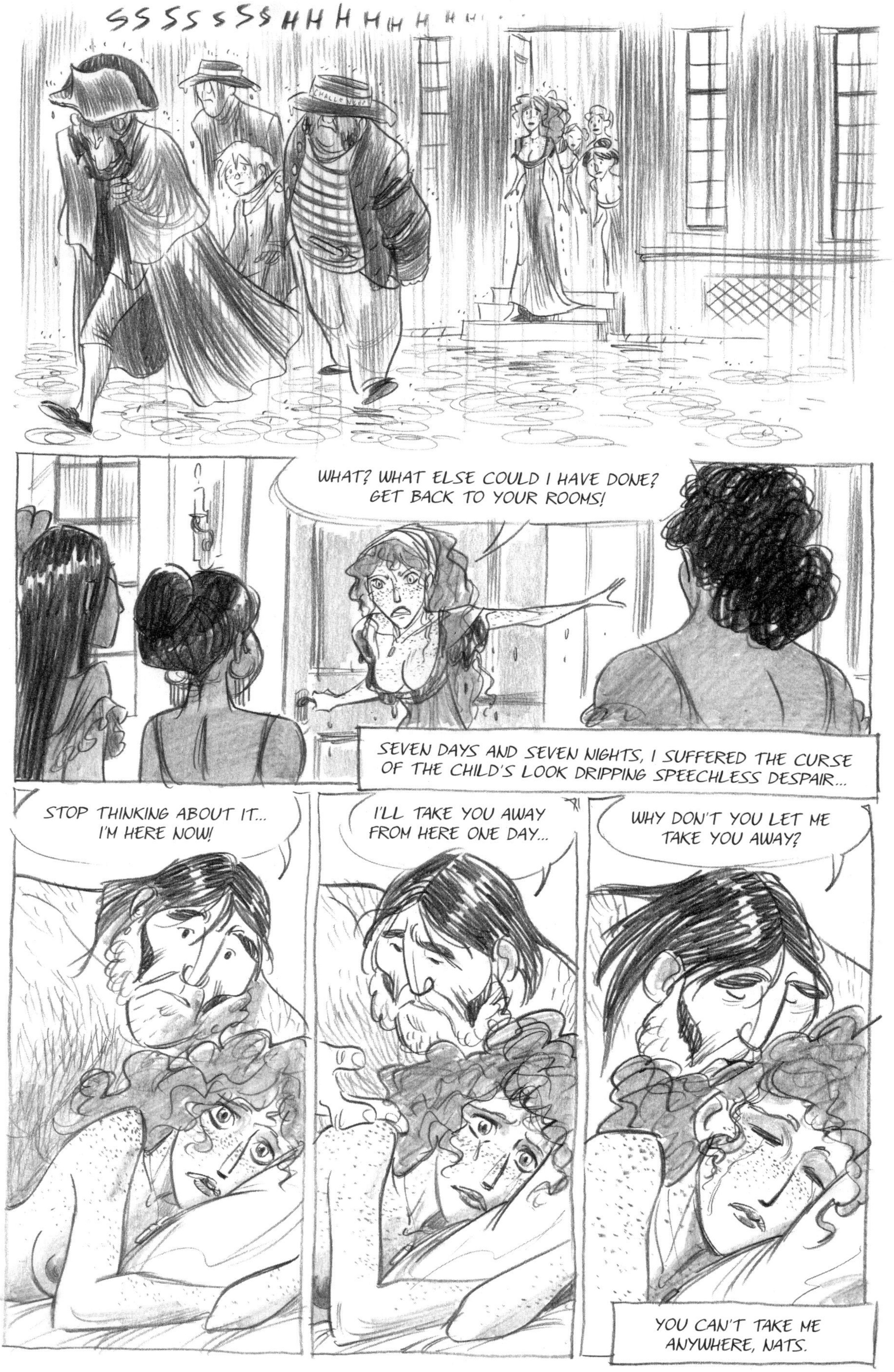
SSSSSSSHHHHHHHH
WHAT? WHAT ELSE COULD I HAVE DONE? GET BACK TO YOUR ROOMS!
SEVEN DAYS AND SEVEN NIGHTS, I SUFFERED THE CURSE OF THE CHILD'S LOOK DRIPPING SPEECHLESS DESPAIR...
STOP THINKING ABOUT IT... I'M HERE NOW!
I'LL TAKE YOU AWAY FROM HERE ONE DAY...
WHY DON'T YOU LET ME TAKE YOU AWAY?
YOU CAN'T TAKE ME ANYWHERE, NATS.

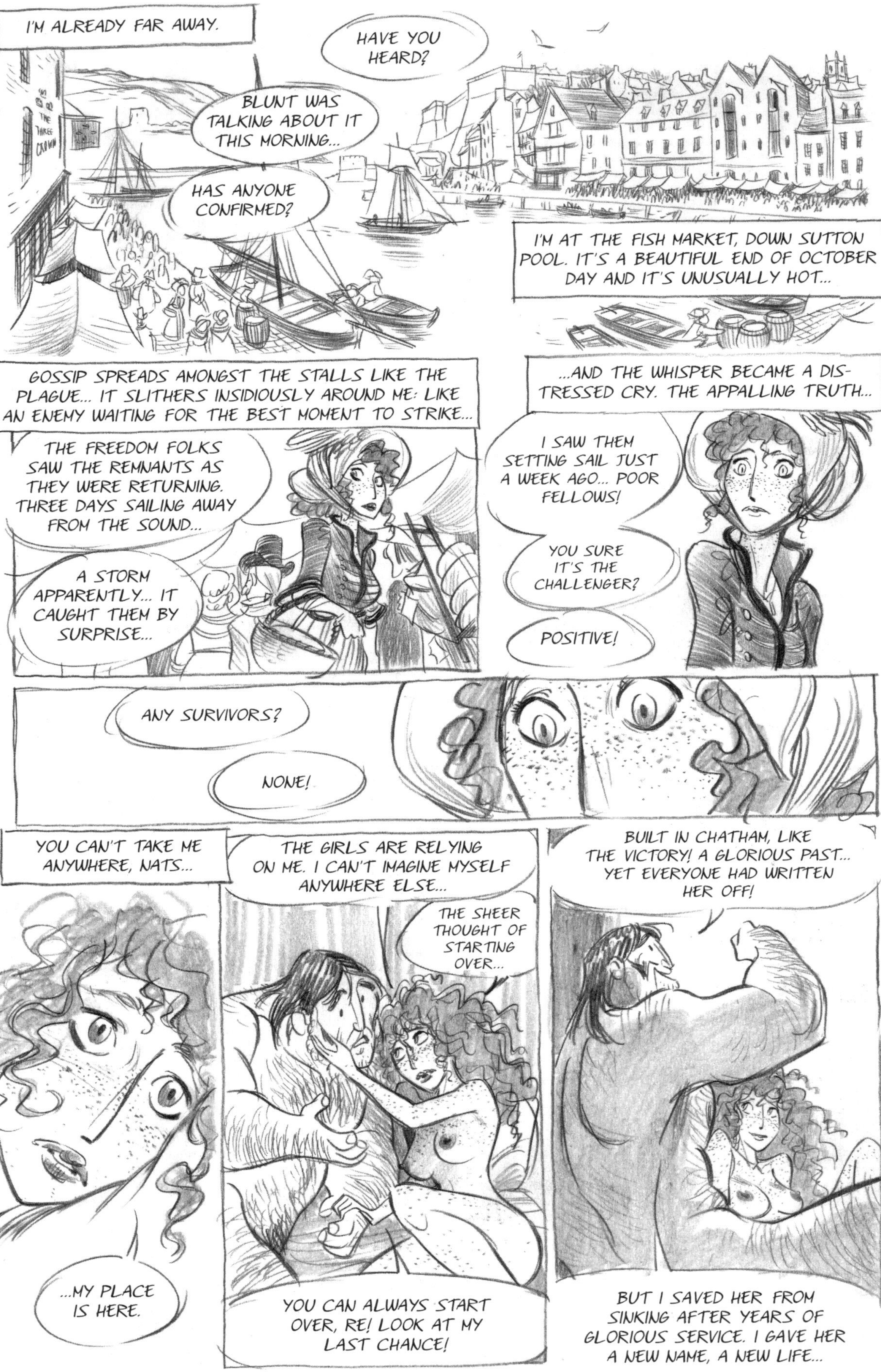

I'M ALREADY FAR AWAY.
HAVE YOU HEARD?
BLUNT WAS TALKING ABOUT IT THIS MORNING...
HAS ANYONE CONFIRMED?
I'M AT THE FISH MARKET, DOWN SUTTON POOL. IT'S A BEAUTIFUL END OF OCTOBER DAY AND IT'S UNUSUALLY HOT...
GOSSIP SPREADS AMONGST THE STALLS LIKE THE PLAGUE... IT SLITHERS INSIDIOUSLY AROUND ME: LIKE AN ENEMY WAITING FOR THE BEST MOMENT TO STRIKE...
THE FREEDOM FOLKS SAW THE REMNANTS AS THEY WERE RETURNING. THREE DAYS SAILING AWAY FROM THE SOUND...
A STORM APPARENTLY... IT CAUGHT THEM BY SURPRISE...
...AND THE WHISPER BECAME A DISTRESSED CRY. THE APPALLING TRUTH...
I SAW THEM SETTING SAIL JUST A WEEK AGO... POOR FELLOWS!
YOU SURE IT'S THE CHALLENGER?
POSITIVE!
ANY SURVIVORS?
NONE!
YOU CAN'T TAKE ME ANYWHERE, NATS...
...MY PLACE IS HERE.
THE GIRLS ARE RELYING ON ME. I CAN'T IMAGINE MYSELF ANYWHERE ELSE...
THE SHEER THOUGHT OF STARTING OVER...
YOU CAN ALWAYS START OVER, RE! LOOK AT MY LAST CHANCE!
BUILT IN CHATHAM, LIKE THE VICTORY! A GLORIOUS PAST... YET EVERYONE HAD WRITTEN HER OFF!
BUT I SAVED HER FROM SINKING AFTER YEARS OF GLORIOUS SERVICE. I GAVE HER A NEW NAME, A NEW LIFE...

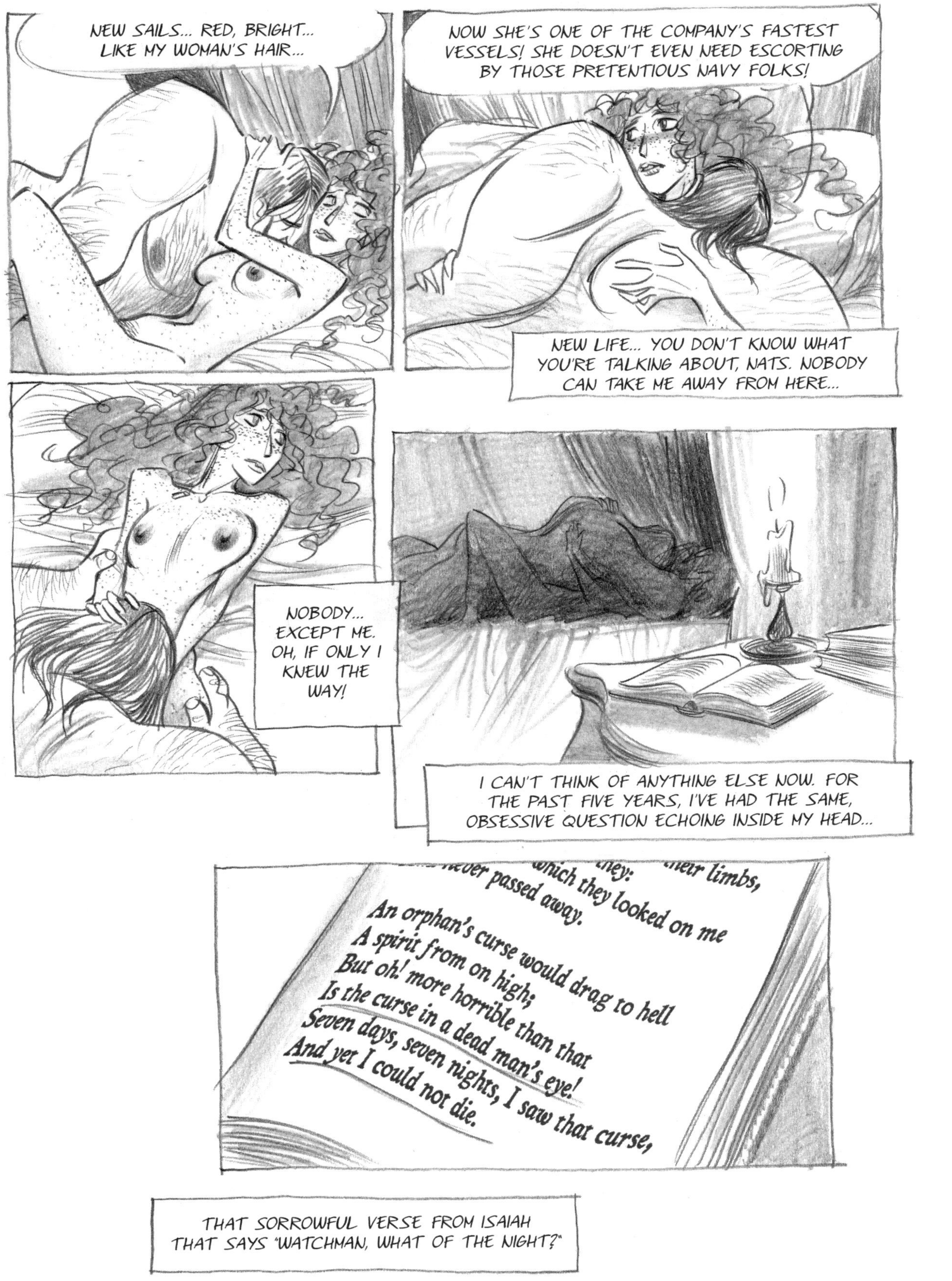
NEW SAILS... RED, BRIGHT... LIKE MY WOMAN'S HAIR...
NOW SHE'S ONE OF THE COMPANY'S FASTEST VESSELS! SHE DOESN'T EVEN NEED ESCORTING BY THOSE PRETENTIOUS NAVY FOLKS!
NEW LIFE... YOU DON'T KNOW WHAT YOU'RE TALKING ABOUT, NATS. NOBODY CAN TAKE ME AWAY FROM HERE...
NOBODY... EXCEPT ME. OH, IF ONLY I KNEW THE WAY!
I CAN'T THINK OF ANYTHING ELSE NOW. FOR THE PAST FIVE YEARS, I'VE HAD THE SAME, OBSESSIVE QUESTION ECHOING INSIDE MY HEAD...
which they looked on me
never passed away.
An orphan's curse would drag to hell
A spirit from on high;
But oh! more horrible than that
Is the curse in a dead man's eye!
Seven days, seven nights, I saw that curse,
And yet I could not die.
THAT SORROWFUL VERSE FROM ISAIAH THAT SAYS "WATCHMAN, WHAT OF THE NIGHT?"

ACT II

PILLAR TO POST

I have studied many times
The marble which was chiseled for me—
A boat with a furled sail at rest in a harbor.
In truth it pictures not my destination
But my life.
For love was offered me and I shrank from its disillusionment;
Sorrow knocked at my door, but I was afraid;
Ambition called to me, but I dreaded the chances.
Yet all the while I hungered for meaning in my life.
And now I know that we must lift the sail
And catch the winds of destiny
Wherever they drive the boat.
To put meaning in one's life may end in madness,
But life without meaning is the torture
Of restlessness and vague desire—
It is a boat longing for the sea and yet afraid.

EDGAR LEE MASTERS

George Gray
(Spoon River Anthology)

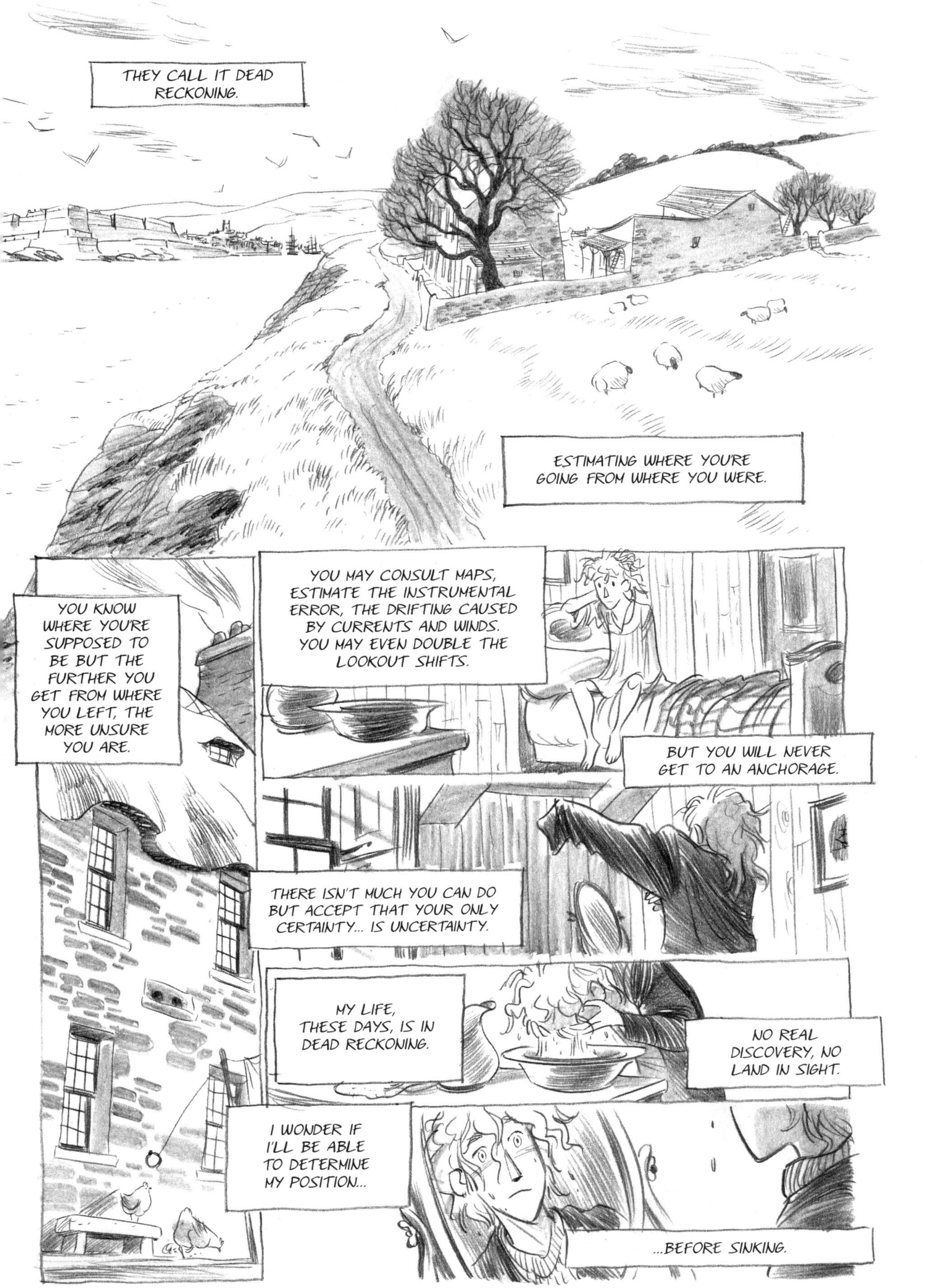
THEY CALL IT DEAD RECKONING.
ESTIMATING WHERE YOU'RE GOING FROM WHERE YOU WERE.
YOU KNOW WHERE YOU'RE SUPPOSED TO BE BUT THE FURTHER YOU GET FROM WHERE YOU LEFT, THE MORE UNSURE YOU ARE.
YOU MAY CONSULT MAPS, ESTIMATE THE INSTRUMENTAL ERROR, THE DRIFTING CAUSED BY CURRENTS AND WINDS. YOU MAY EVEN DOUBLE THE LOOKOUT SHIFTS.
BUT YOU WILL NEVER GET TO AN ANCHORAGE.
THERE ISN'T MUCH YOU CAN DO BUT ACCEPT THAT YOUR ONLY CERTAINTY... IS UNCERTAINTY.
MY LIFE, THESE DAYS, IS IN DEAD RECKONING.
NO REAL DISCOVERY, NO LAND IN SIGHT.
I WONDER IF I'LL BE ABLE TO DETERMINE MY POSITION...
...BEFORE SINKING.

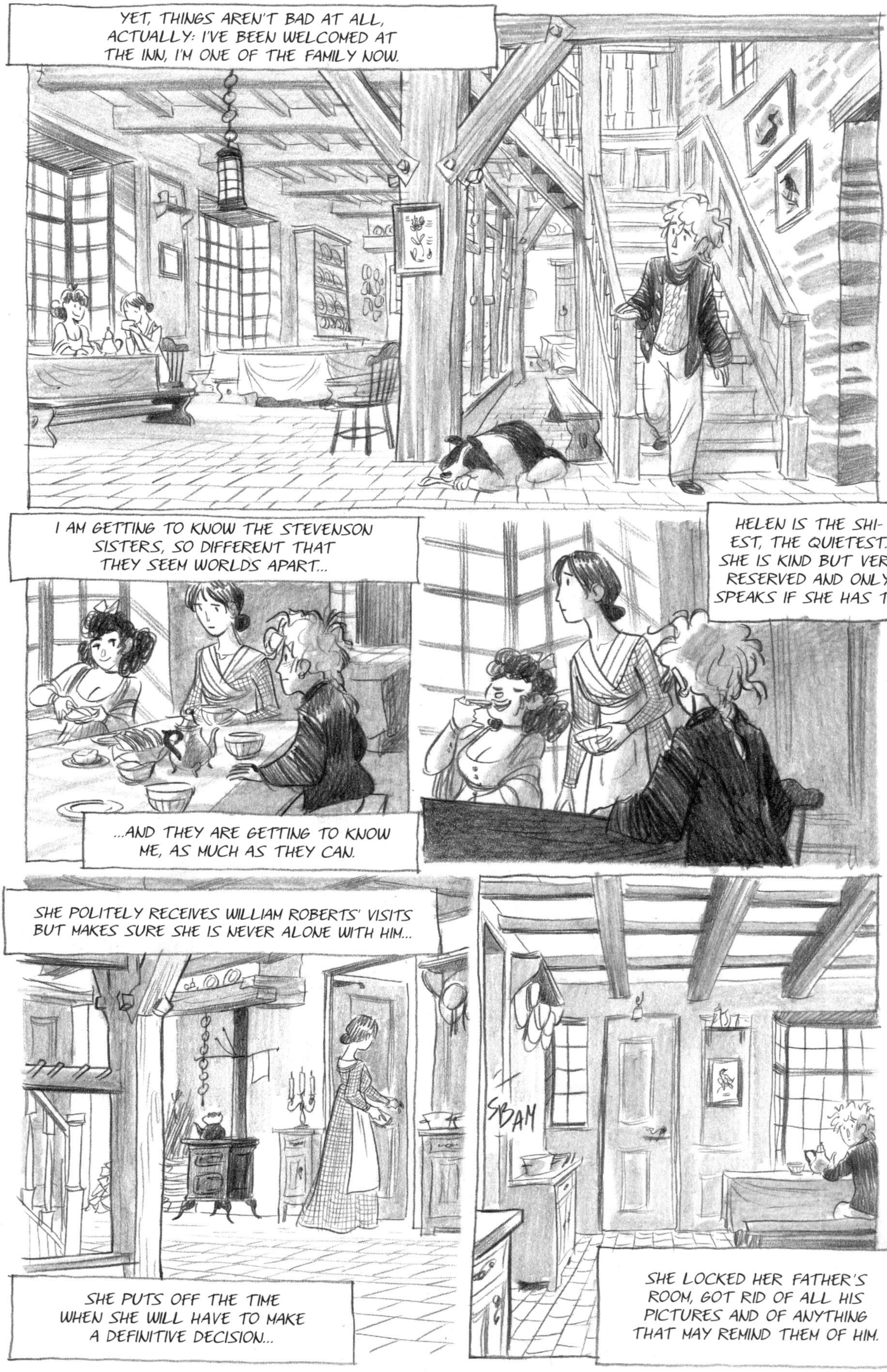
YET, THINGS AREN'T BAD AT ALL, ACTUALLY: I'VE BEEN WELCOMED AT THE INN, I'M ONE OF THE FAMILY NOW.
I AM GETTING TO KNOW THE STEVENSON SISTERS, SO DIFFERENT THAT THEY SEEM WORLDS APART...
...AND THEY ARE GETTING TO KNOW ME, AS MUCH AS THEY CAN.
HELEN IS THE SHI-EST, THE QUIETEST. SHE IS KIND BUT VERY RESERVED AND ONLY SPEAKS IF SHE HAS TO.
SHE POLITELY RECEIVES WILLIAM ROBERTS' VISITS BUT MAKES SURE SHE IS NEVER ALONE WITH HIM...
SHE PUTS OFF THE TIME WHEN SHE WILL HAVE TO MAKE A DEFINITIVE DECISION...
SBAM
SHE LOCKED HER FATHER'S ROOM, GOT RID OF ALL HIS PICTURES AND OF ANYTHING THAT MAY REMIND THEM OF HIM.

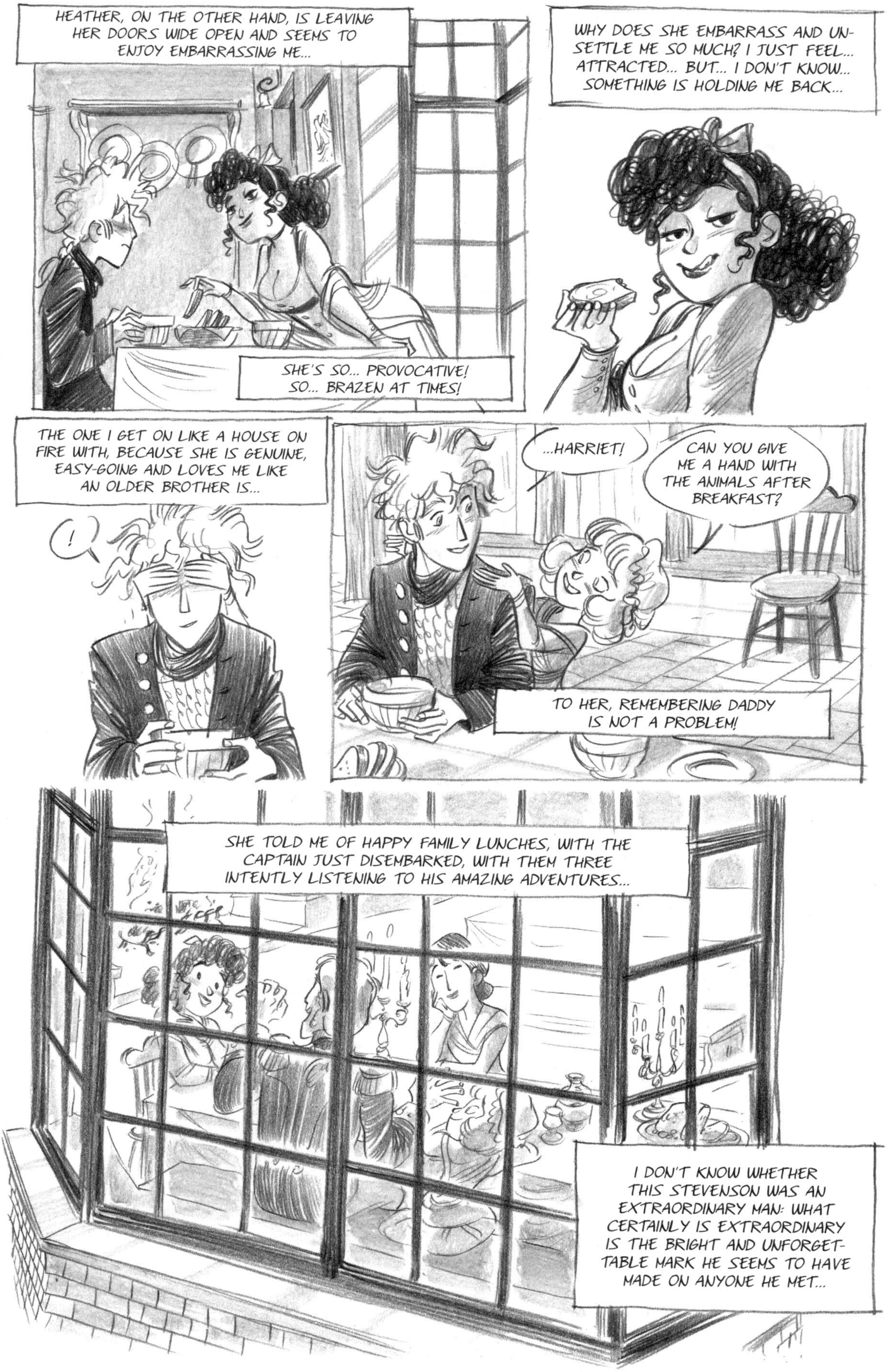
HEATHER, ON THE OTHER HAND, IS LEAVING HER DOORS WIDE OPEN AND SEEMS TO ENJOY EMBARRASSING ME...
SHE'S SO... PROVOCATIVE! SO... BRAZEN AT TIMES!
WHY DOES SHE EMBARRASS AND UN-SETTLE ME SO MUCH? I JUST FEEL... ATTRACTED... BUT... I DON'T KNOW... SOMETHING IS HOLDING ME BACK...
THE ONE I GET ON LIKE A HOUSE ON FIRE WITH, BECAUSE SHE IS GENUINE, EASY-GOING AND LOVES ME LIKE AN OLDER BROTHER IS...
!
...HARRIET!
CAN YOU GIVE ME A HAND WITH THE ANIMALS AFTER BREAKFAST?
TO HER, REMEMBERING DADDY IS NOT A PROBLEM!
SHE TOLD ME OF HAPPY FAMILY LUNCHES, WITH THE CAPTAIN JUST DISEMBARKED, WITH THEM THREE INTENTLY LISTENING TO HIS AMAZING ADVENTURES...
I DON'T KNOW WHETHER THIS STEVENSON WAS AN EXTRAORDINARY MAN: WHAT CERTAINLY IS EXTRAORDINARY IS THE BRIGHT AND UNFORGET-TABLE MARK HE SEEMS TO HAVE MADE ON ANYONE HE MET...

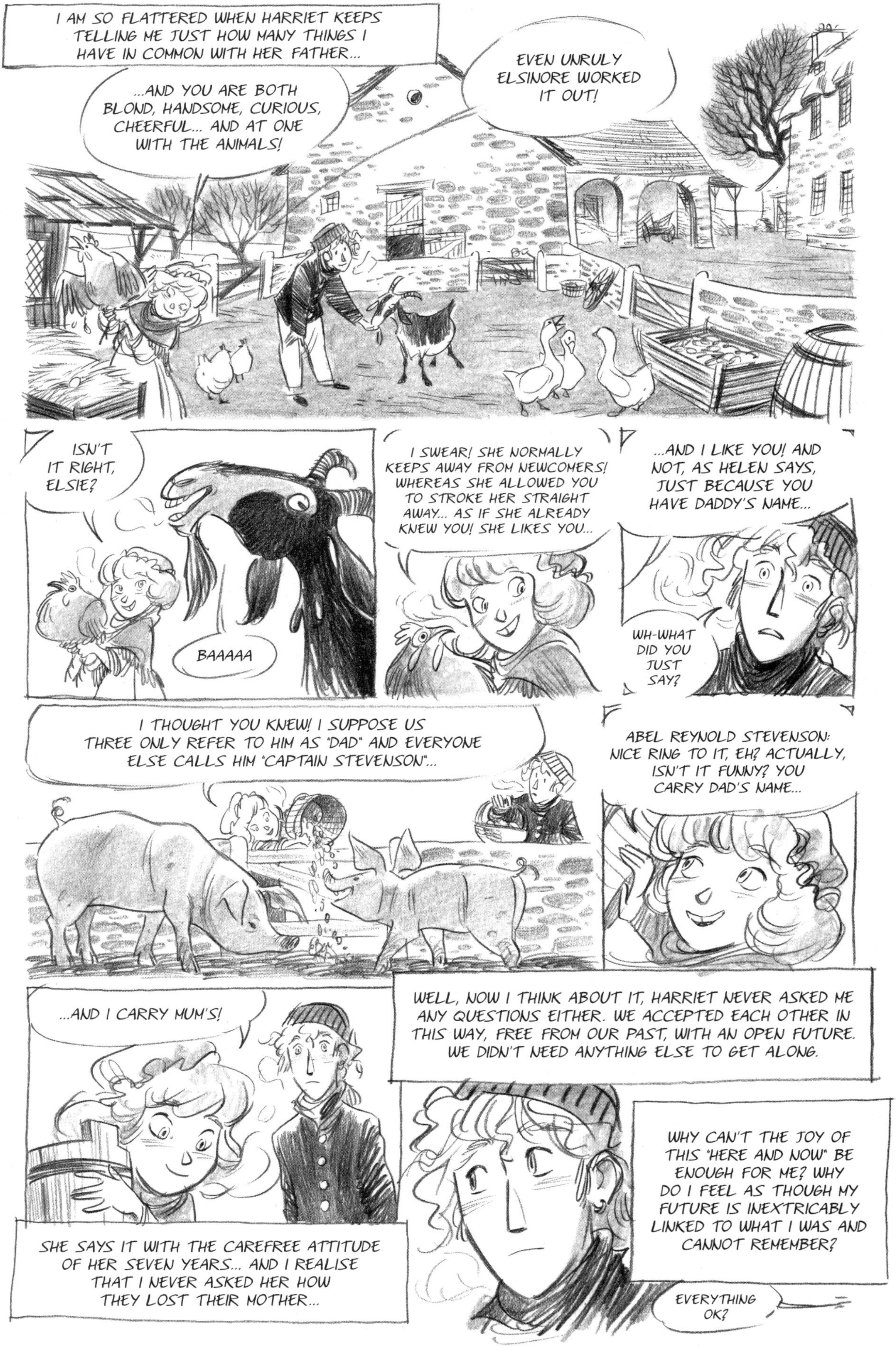

I AM SO FLATTERED WHEN HARRIET KEEPS TELLING ME JUST HOW MANY THINGS I HAVE IN COMMON WITH HER FATHER...
...AND YOU ARE BOTH BLOND, HANDSOME, CURIOUS, CHEERFUL... AND AT ONE WITH THE ANIMALS!
EVEN UNRULY ELSINORE WORKED IT OUT!
ISN'T IT RIGHT, ELSIE?
BAAAAA
I SWEAR! SHE NORMALLY KEEPS AWAY FROM NEWCOMERS! WHEREAS SHE ALLOWED YOU TO STROKE HER STRAIGHT AWAY... AS IF SHE ALREADY KNEW YOU! SHE LIKES YOU...
...AND I LIKE YOU! AND NOT, AS HELEN SAYS, JUST BECAUSE YOU HAVE DADDY'S NAME...
WH-WHAT DID YOU JUST SAY?
I THOUGHT YOU KNEW! I SUPPOSE US THREE ONLY REFER TO HIM AS "DAD" AND EVERYONE ELSE CALLS HIM "CAPTAIN STEVENSON"...
ABEL REYNOLD STEVENSON: NICE RING TO IT, EH? ACTUALLY, ISN'T IT FUNNY? YOU CARRY DAD'S NAME...
...AND I CARRY MUM'S!
WELL, NOW I THINK ABOUT IT, HARRIET NEVER ASKED ME ANY QUESTIONS EITHER. WE ACCEPTED EACH OTHER IN THIS WAY, FREE FROM OUR PAST, WITH AN OPEN FUTURE. WE DIDN'T NEED ANYTHING ELSE TO GET ALONG.
SHE SAYS IT WITH THE CAREFREE ATTITUDE OF HER SEVEN YEARS... AND I REALISE THAT I NEVER ASKED HER HOW THEY LOST THEIR MOTHER...
WHY CAN'T THE JOY OF THIS "HERE AND NOW" BE ENOUGH FOR ME? WHY DO I FEEL AS THOUGH MY FUTURE IS INEXTRICABLY LINKED TO WHAT I WAS AND CANNOT REMEMBER?
EVERYTHING OK?

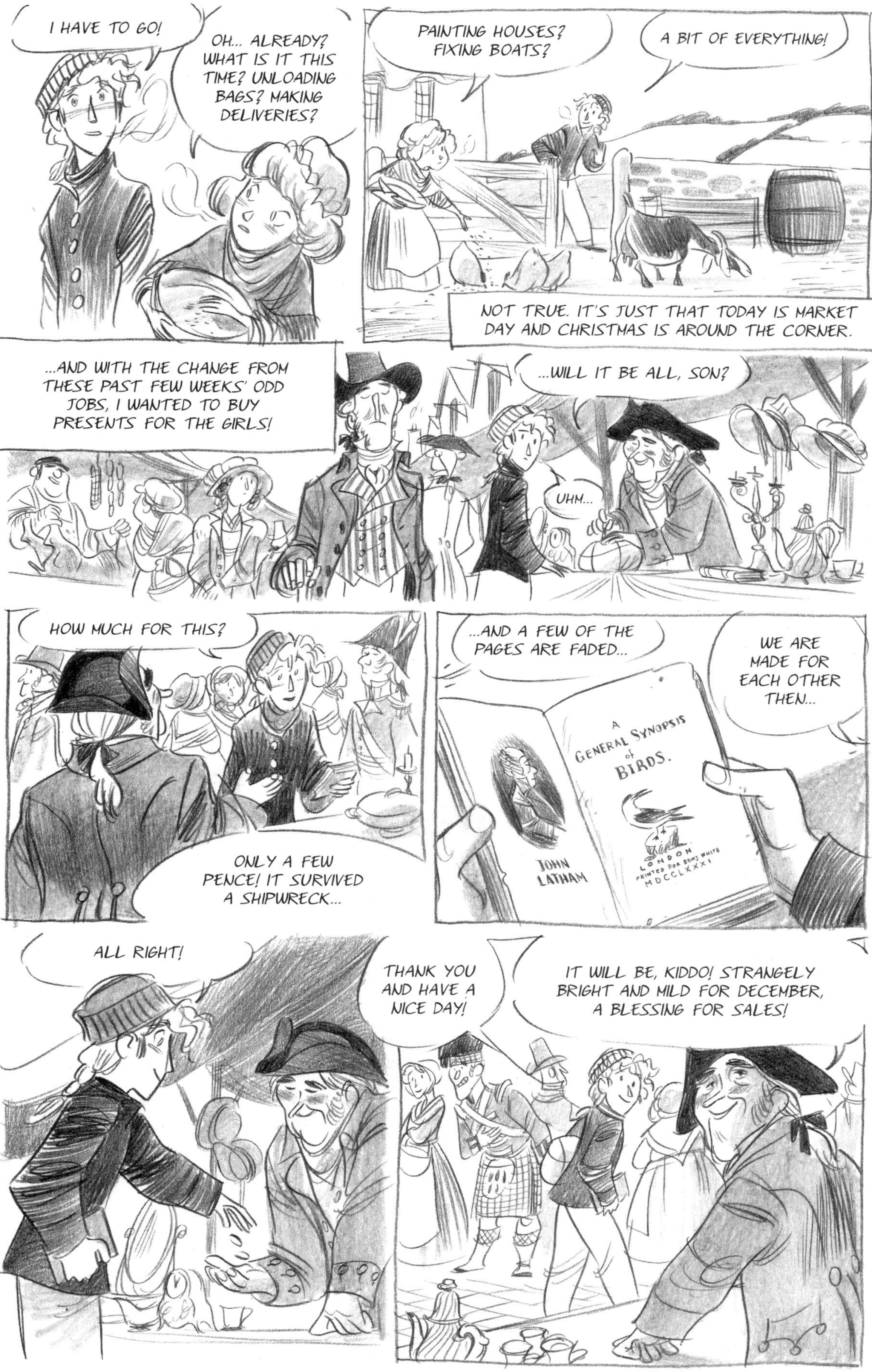
I HAVE TO GO!
OH... ALREADY? WHAT IS IT THIS TIME? UNLOADING BAGS? MAKING DELIVERIES?
PAINTING HOUSES? FIXING BOATS?
A BIT OF EVERYTHING!
NOT TRUE. IT'S JUST THAT TODAY IS MARKET DAY AND CHRISTMAS IS AROUND THE CORNER.
...AND WITH THE CHANGE FROM THESE PAST FEW WEEKS' ODD JOBS, I WANTED TO BUY PRESENTS FOR THE GIRLS!
...WILL IT BE ALL, SON?
UHM...
HOW MUCH FOR THIS?
ONLY A FEW PENCE! IT SURVIVED A SHIPWRECK...
...AND A FEW OF THE PAGES ARE FADED...
WE ARE MADE FOR EACH OTHER THEN...
A GENERAL SYNOPSIS of BIRDS.
JOHN LATHAM
LONDON PRINTED FOR BENJ WHITE MDCCLXXXI
ALL RIGHT!
THANK YOU AND HAVE A NICE DAY!
IT WILL BE, KIDDO! STRANGELY BRIGHT AND MILD FOR DECEMBER, A BLESSING FOR SALES!

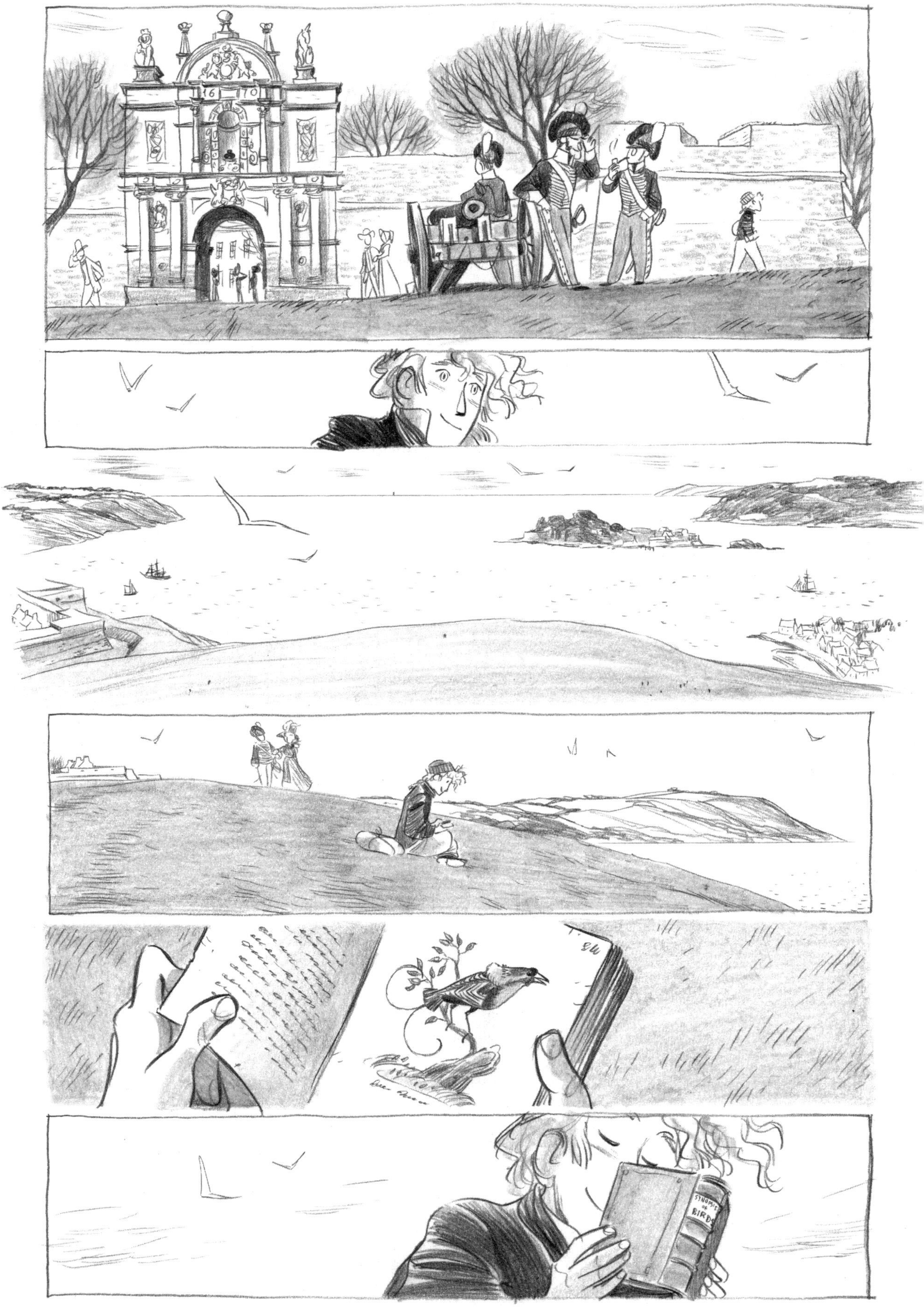
16 70
SYNOPSIS OF BIRDS

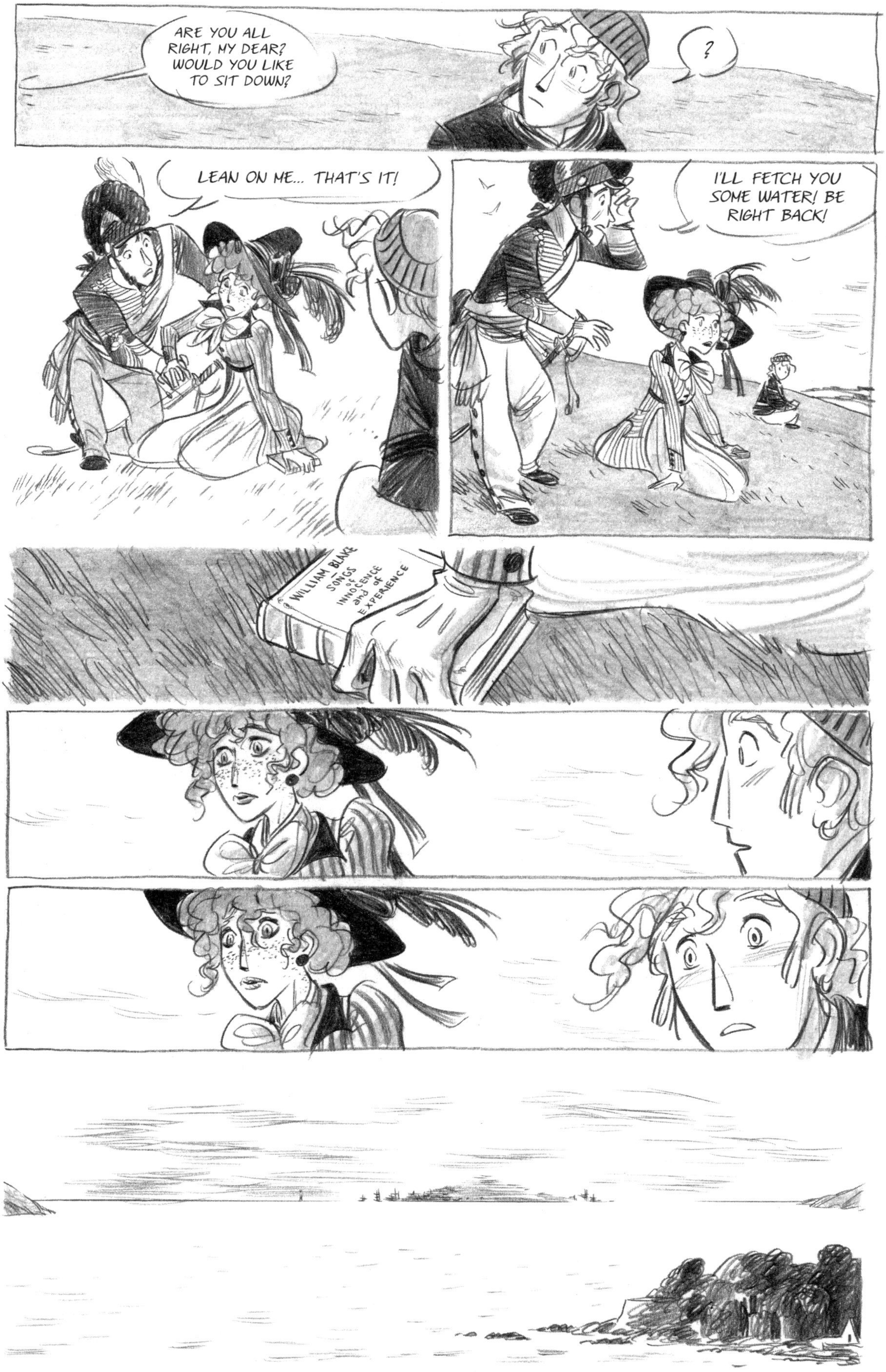
ARE YOU ALL RIGHT, MY DEAR? WOULD YOU LIKE TO SIT DOWN?
?
LEAN ON ME... THAT'S IT!
I'LL FETCH YOU SOME WATER! BE RIGHT BACK!
WILLIAM BLAKE SONGS of INNOCENCE and of EXPERIENCE

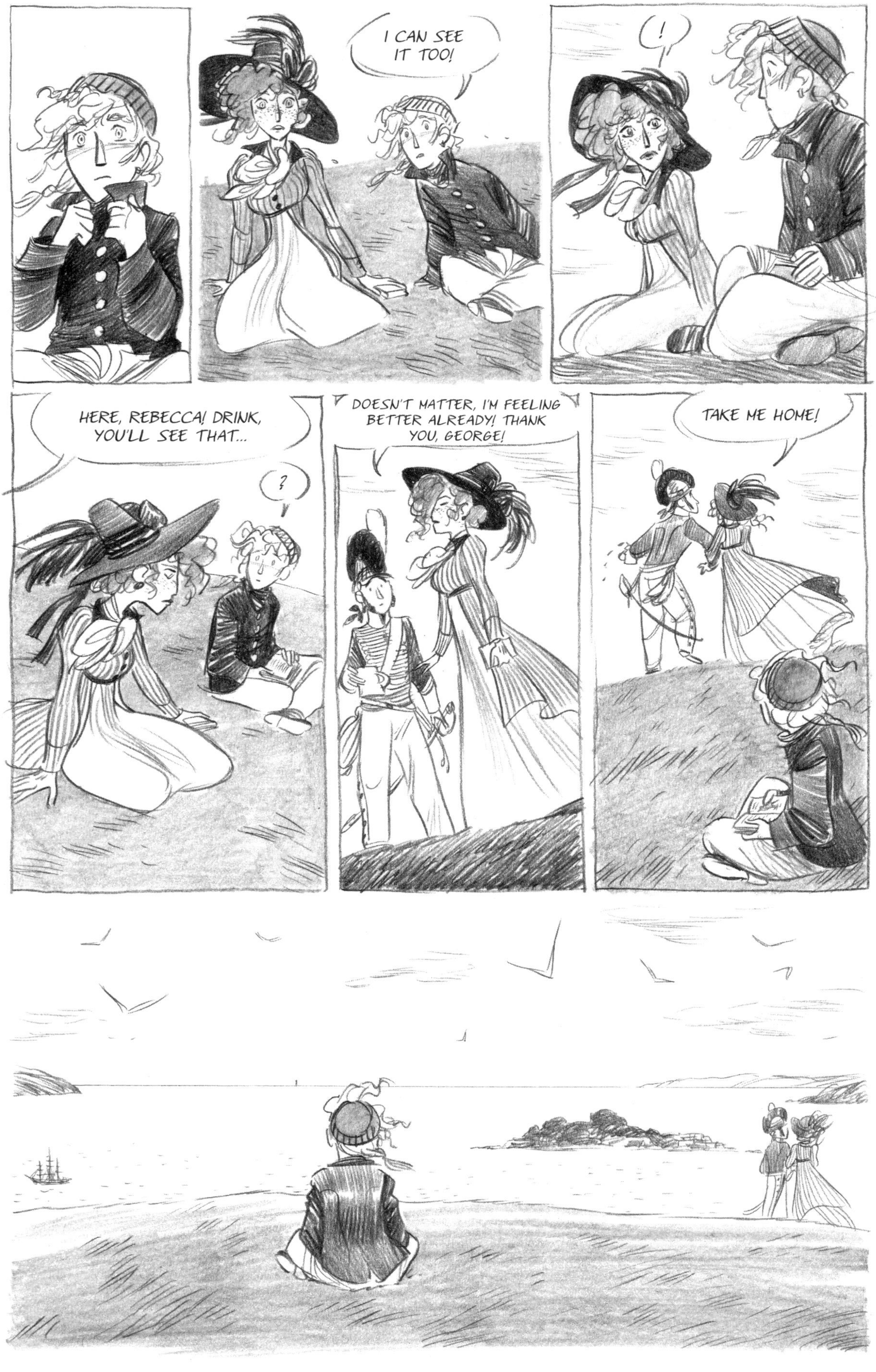
I CAN SEE IT TOO!
!
HERE, REBECCA! DRINK, YOU'LL SEE THAT...
?
DOESN'T MATTER, I'M FEELING BETTER ALREADY! THANK YOU, GEORGE!
TAKE ME HOME!

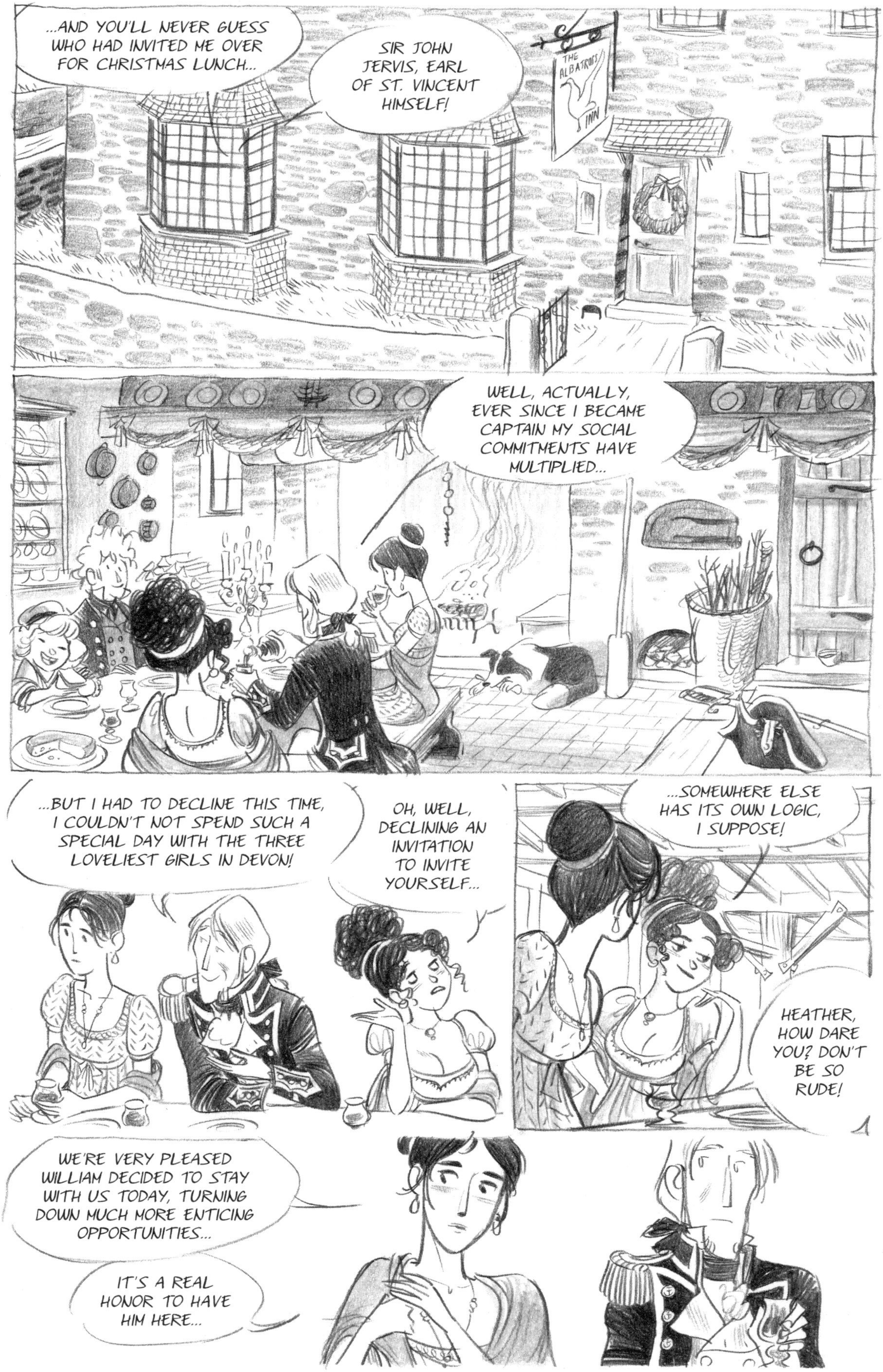

...AND YOU'LL NEVER GUESS WHO HAD INVITED ME OVER FOR CHRISTMAS LUNCH...
SIR JOHN JERVIS, EARL OF ST. VINCENT HIMSELF!
THE ALBATROSS INN
WELL, ACTUALLY, EVER SINCE I BECAME CAPTAIN MY SOCIAL COMMITMENTS HAVE MULTIPLIED...
...BUT I HAD TO DECLINE THIS TIME, I COULDN'T NOT SPEND SUCH A SPECIAL DAY WITH THE THREE LOVELIEST GIRLS IN DEVON!
OH, WELL, DECLINING AN INVITATION TO INVITE YOURSELF...
...SOMEWHERE ELSE HAS ITS OWN LOGIC, I SUPPOSE!
HEATHER, HOW DARE YOU? DON'T BE SO RUDE!
WE'RE VERY PLEASED WILLIAM DECIDED TO STAY WITH US TODAY, TURNING DOWN MUCH MORE ENTICING OPPORTUNITIES...
IT'S A REAL HONOR TO HAVE HIM HERE...

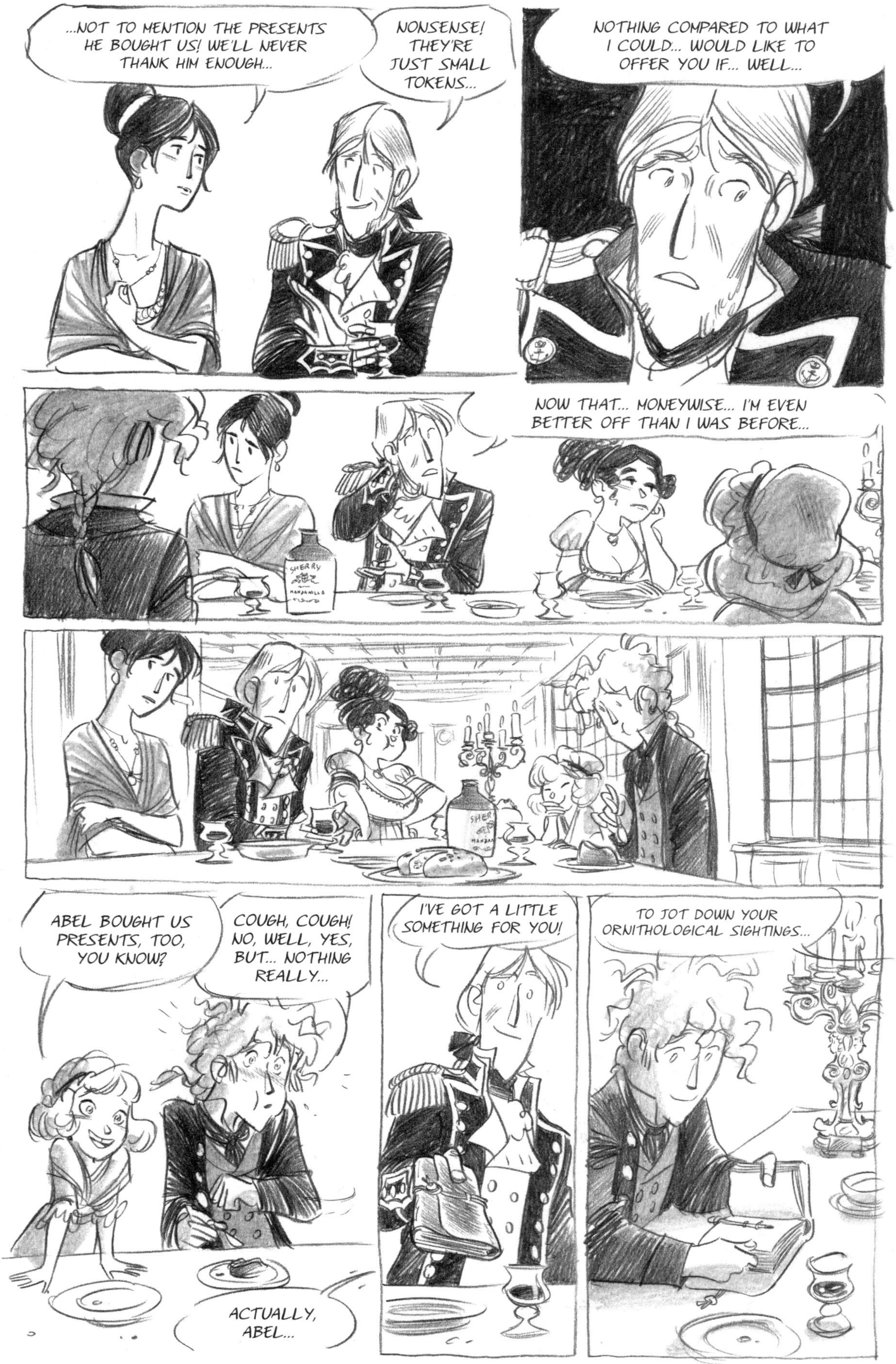
...NOT TO MENTION THE PRESENTS HE BOUGHT US! WE'LL NEVER THANK HIM ENOUGH...
NONSENSE! THEY'RE JUST SMALL TOKENS...
NOTHING COMPARED TO WHAT I COULD... WOULD LIKE TO OFFER YOU IF... WELL...
NOW THAT... MONEYWISE... I'M EVEN BETTER OFF THAN I WAS BEFORE...
SHERRY
ABEL BOUGHT US PRESENTS, TOO, YOU KNOW?
COUGH, COUGH! NO, WELL, YES, BUT... NOTHING REALLY...
ACTUALLY, ABEL...
I'VE GOT A LITTLE SOMETHING FOR YOU!
TO JOT DOWN YOUR ORNITHOLOGICAL SIGHTINGS...

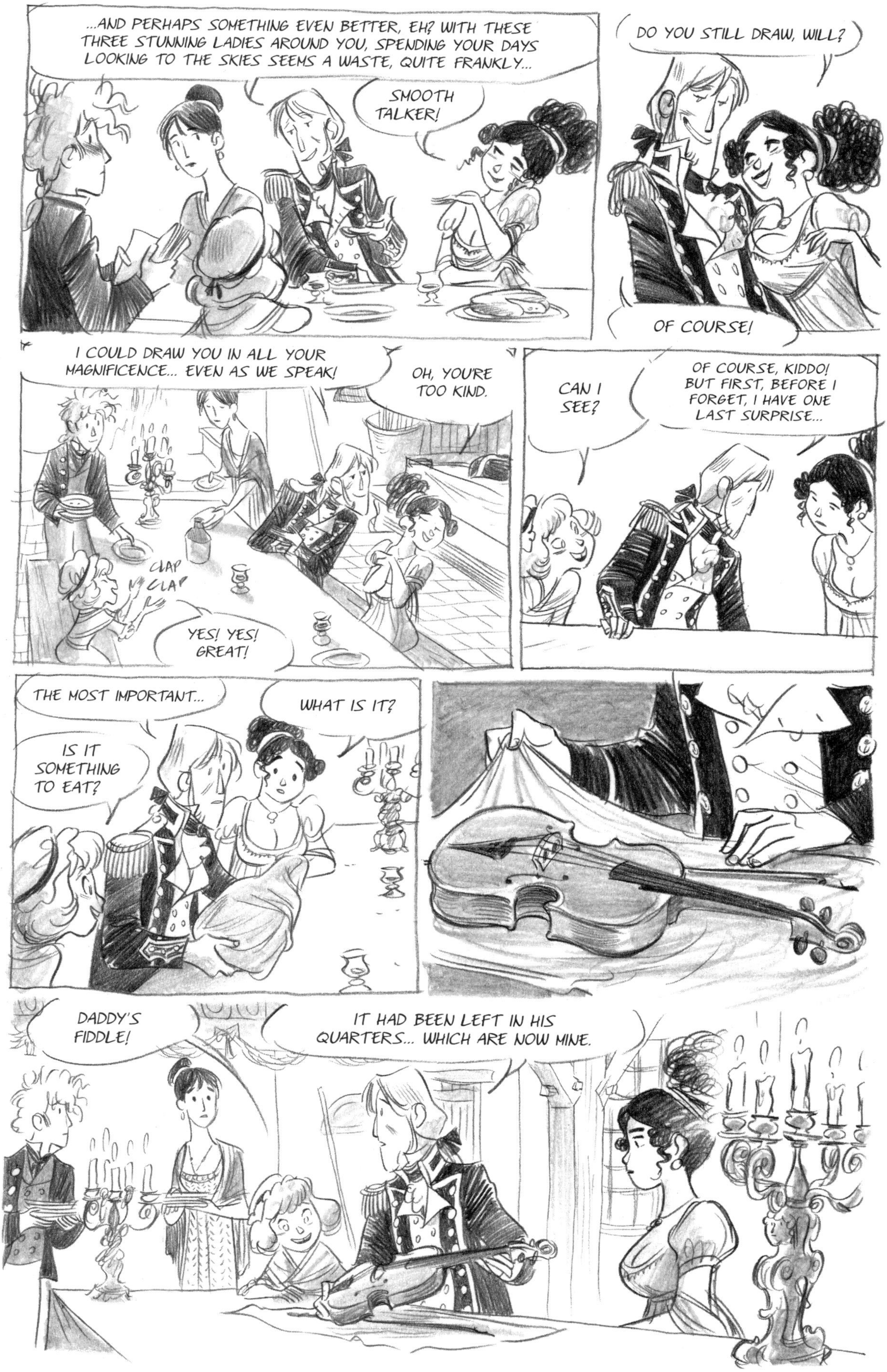
...AND PERHAPS SOMETHING EVEN BETTER, EH? WITH THESE THREE STUNNING LADIES AROUND YOU, SPENDING YOUR DAYS LOOKING TO THE SKIES SEEMS A WASTE, QUITE FRANKLY...
SMOOTH TALKER!
DO YOU STILL DRAW, WILL?
OF COURSE!
I COULD DRAW YOU IN ALL YOUR MAGNIFICENCE... EVEN AS WE SPEAK!
OH, YOU'RE TOO KIND.
CLAP CLAP
YES! YES! GREAT!
CAN I SEE?
OF COURSE, KIDDO! BUT FIRST, BEFORE I FORGET, I HAVE ONE LAST SURPRISE...
THE MOST IMPORTANT...
WHAT IS IT?
IS IT SOMETHING TO EAT?
DADDY'S FIDDLE!
IT HAD BEEN LEFT IN HIS QUARTERS... WHICH ARE NOW MINE.

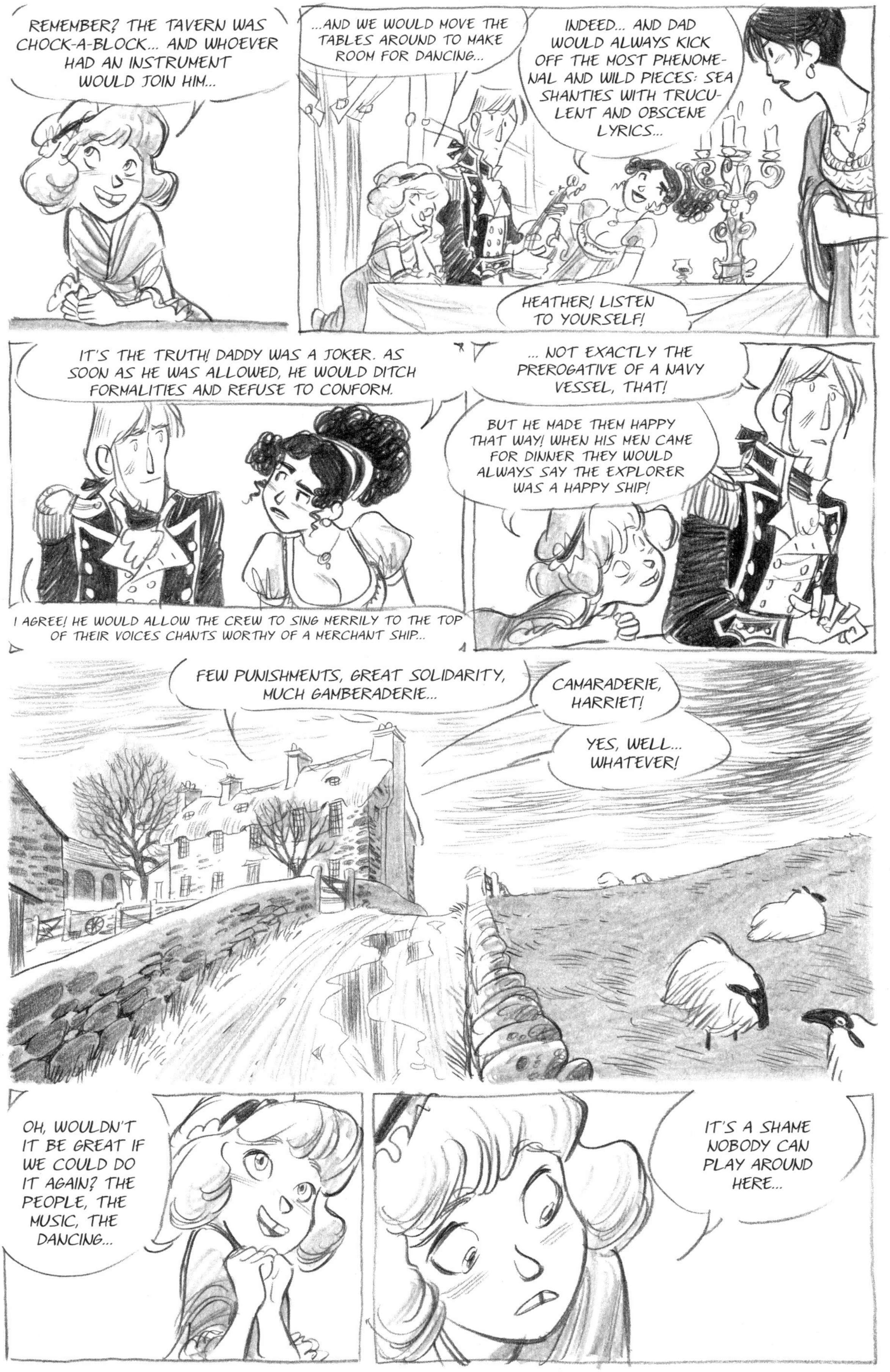
REMEMBER? THE TAVERN WAS CHOCK-A-BLOCK... AND WHOEVER HAD AN INSTRUMENT WOULD JOIN HIM...
...AND WE WOULD MOVE THE TABLES AROUND TO MAKE ROOM FOR DANCING...
INDEED... AND DAD WOULD ALWAYS KICK OFF THE MOST PHENOMENAL AND WILD PIECES: SEA SHANTIES WITH TRUCULENT AND OBSCENE LYRICS...
HEATHER! LISTEN TO YOURSELF!
IT'S THE TRUTH! DADDY WAS A JOKER. AS SOON AS HE WAS ALLOWED, HE WOULD DITCH FORMALITIES AND REFUSE TO CONFORM.
I AGREE! HE WOULD ALLOW THE CREW TO SING MERRILY TO THE TOP OF THEIR VOICES CHANTS WORTHY OF A MERCHANT SHIP...
... NOT EXACTLY THE PREROGATIVE OF A NAVY VESSEL, THAT!
BUT HE MADE THEM HAPPY THAT WAY! WHEN HIS MEN CAME FOR DINNER THEY WOULD ALWAYS SAY THE EXPLORER WAS A HAPPY SHIP!
FEW PUNISHMENTS, GREAT SOLIDARITY, MUCH GAMBERADERIE...
CAMARADERIE, HARRIET!
YES, WELL... WHATEVER!
OH, WOULDN'T IT BE GREAT IF WE COULD DO IT AGAIN? THE PEOPLE, THE MUSIC, THE DANCING...
IT'S A SHAME NOBODY CAN PLAY AROUND HERE...

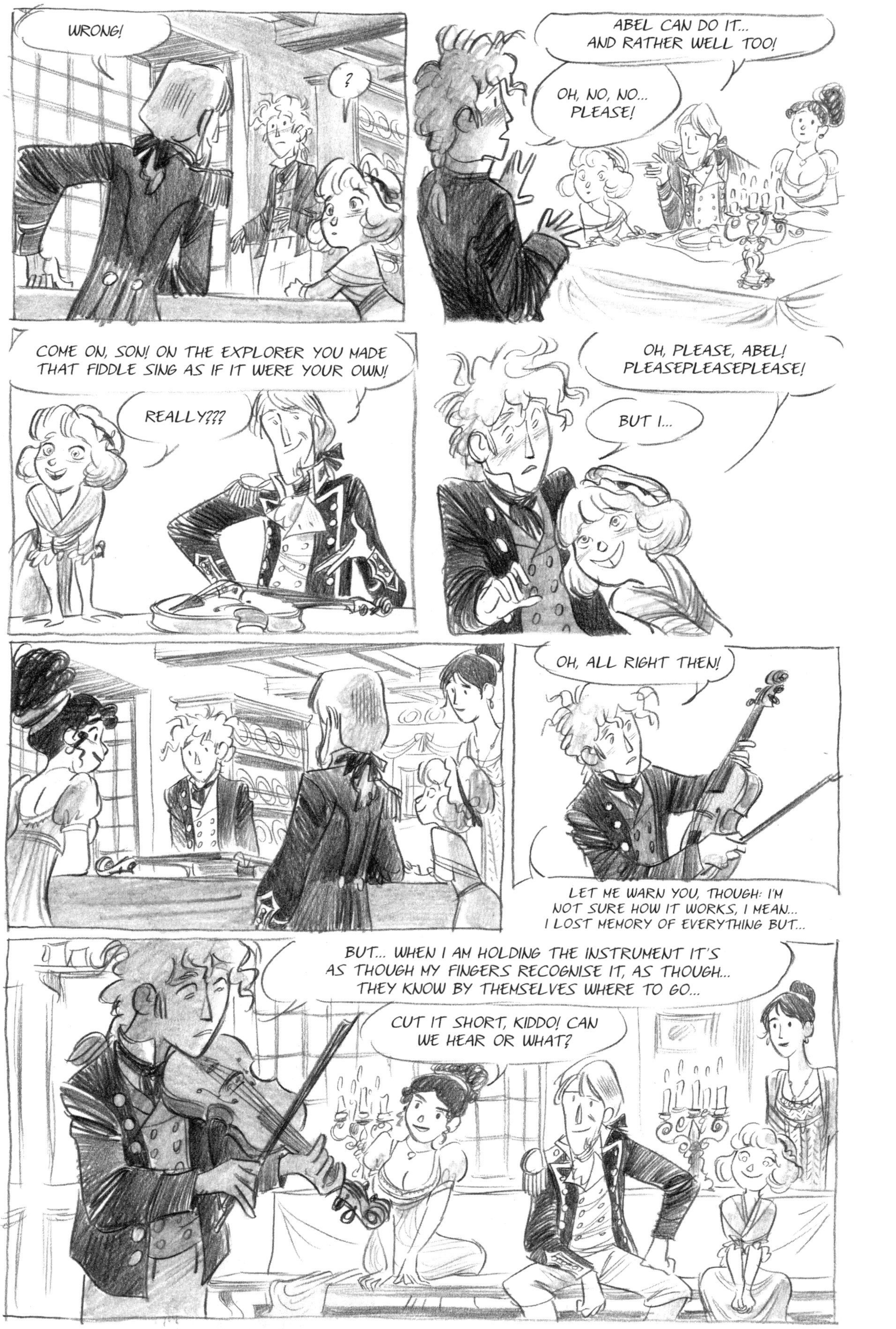
WRONG!
?
ABEL CAN DO IT... AND RATHER WELL TOO!
OH, NO, NO... PLEASE!
COME ON, SON! ON THE EXPLORER YOU MADE THAT FIDDLE SING AS IF IT WERE YOUR OWN!
REALLY???
OH, PLEASE, ABEL! PLEASEPLEASEPLEASE!
BUT I...
OH, ALL RIGHT THEN!
LET ME WARN YOU, THOUGH: I'M NOT SURE HOW IT WORKS, I MEAN... I LOST MEMORY OF EVERYTHING BUT...
BUT... WHEN I AM HOLDING THE INSTRUMENT IT'S AS THOUGH MY FINGERS RECOGNISE IT, AS THOUGH... THEY KNOW BY THEMSELVES WHERE TO GO...
CUT IT SHORT, KIDDO! CAN WE HEAR OR WHAT?

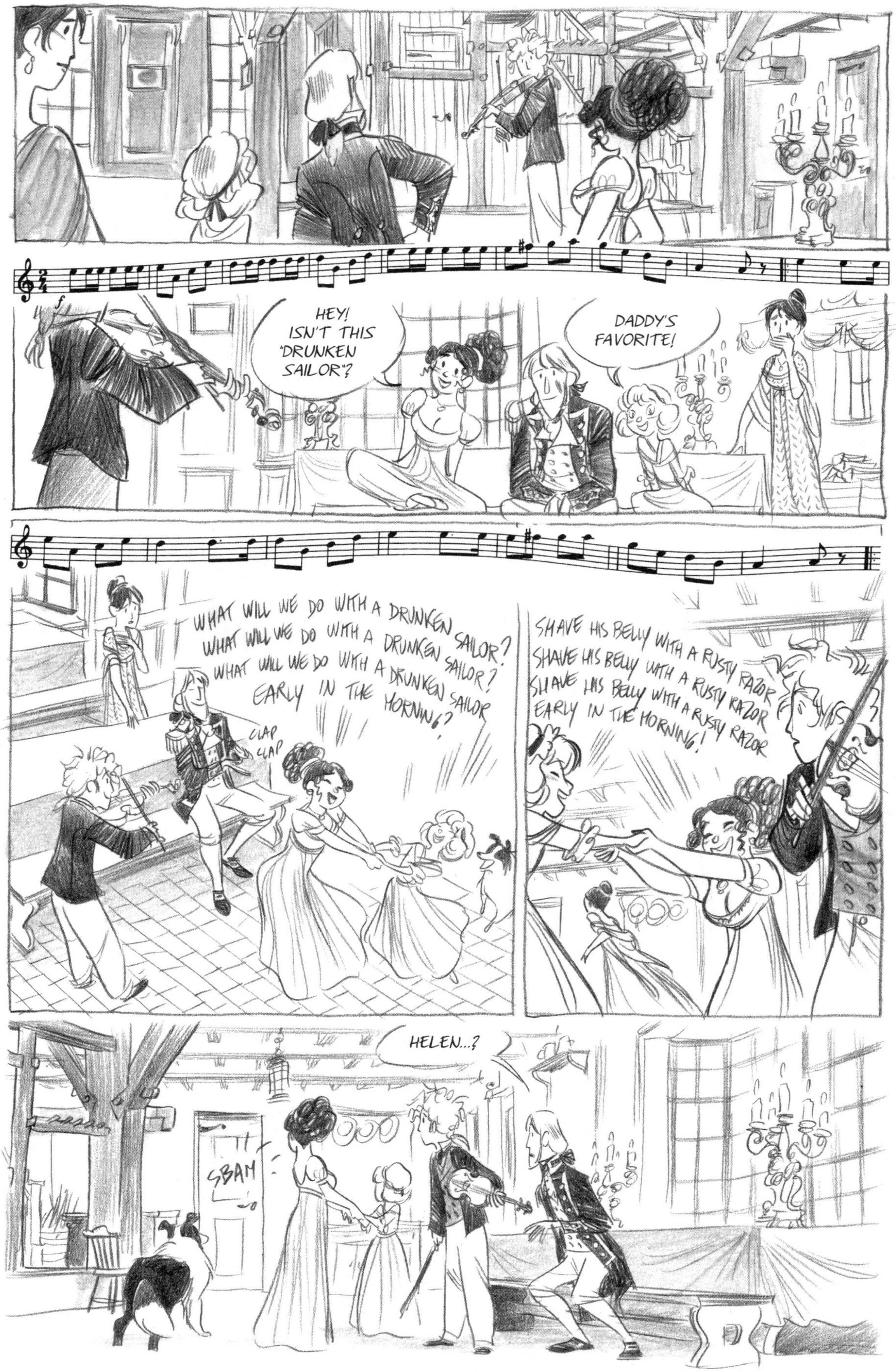
HEY! ISN'T THIS "DRUNKEN SAILOR"?
DADDY'S FAVORITE!
WHAT WILL WE DO WITH A DRUNKEN SAILOR? WHAT WILL WE DO WITH A DRUNKEN SAILOR? WHAT WILL WE DO WITH A DRUNKEN SAILOR? EARLY IN THE MORNING?
CLAP CLAP
SHAVE HIS BELLY WITH A RUSTY RAZOR SHAVE HIS BELLY WITH A RUSTY RAZOR SHAVE HIS BELLY WITH A RUSTY RAZOR EARLY IN THE MORNING!
HELEN...?
SBAM

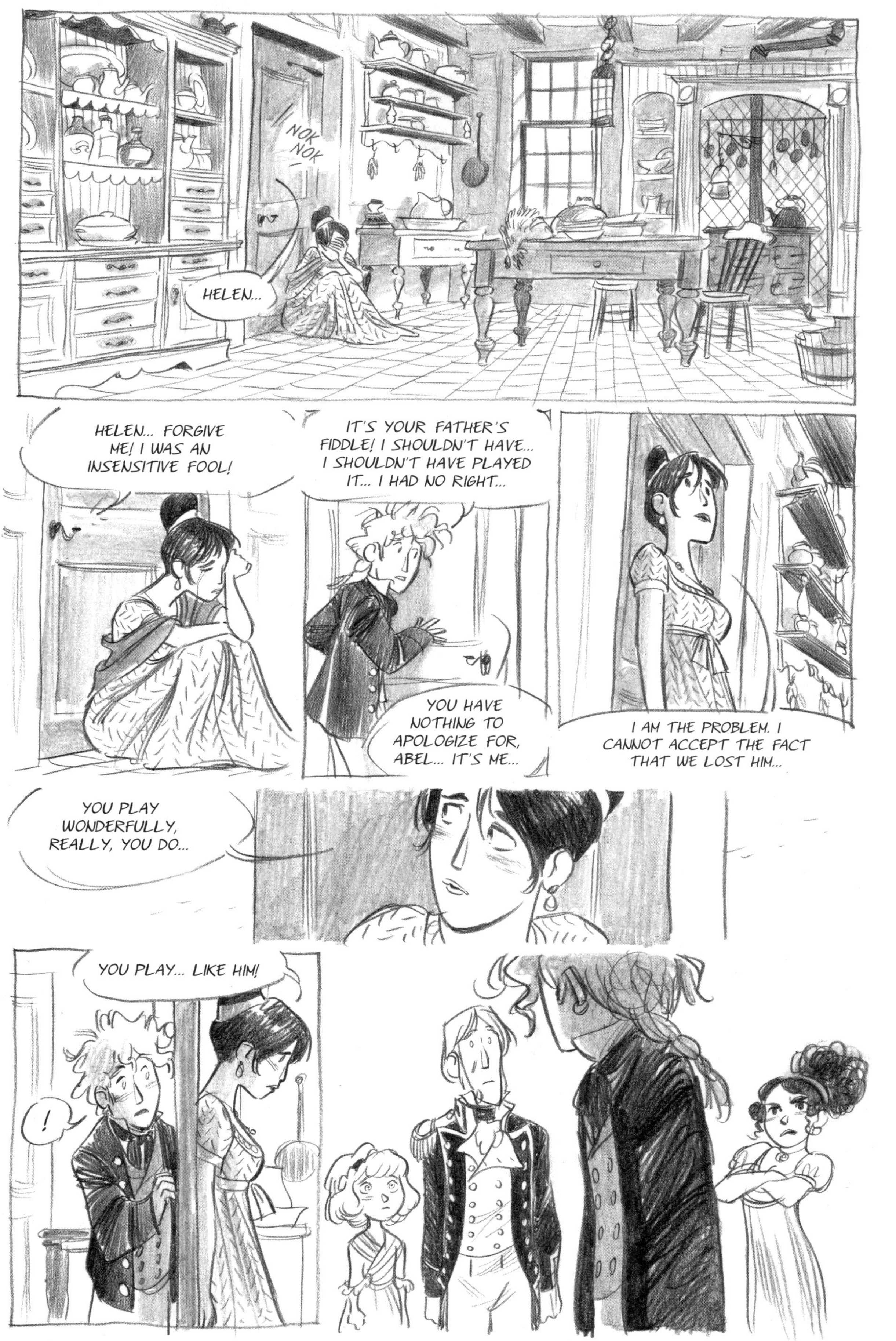
NOK NOK
HELEN...
HELEN... FORGIVE ME! I WAS AN INSENSITIVE FOOL!
IT'S YOUR FATHER'S FIDDLE! I SHOULDN'T HAVE... I SHOULDN'T HAVE PLAYED IT... I HAD NO RIGHT...
YOU HAVE NOTHING TO APOLOGIZE FOR, ABEL... IT'S ME...
I AM THE PROBLEM. I CANNOT ACCEPT THE FACT THAT WE LOST HIM...
YOU PLAY WONDERFULLY, REALLY, YOU DO...
YOU PLAY... LIKE HIM!
!

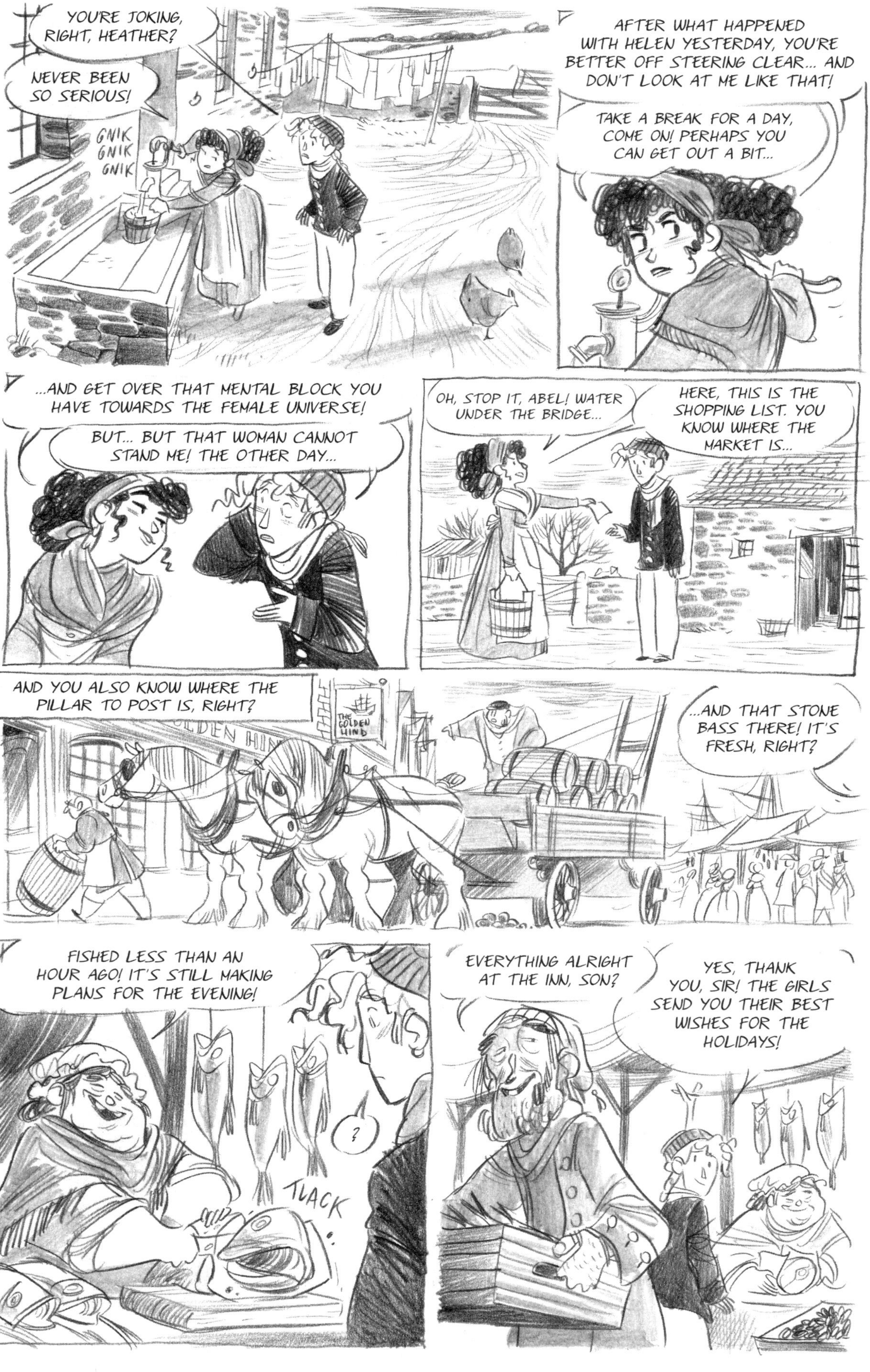
YOU'RE JOKING, RIGHT, HEATHER?
NEVER BEEN SO SERIOUS!
GNIK GNIK GNIK
AFTER WHAT HAPPENED WITH HELEN YESTERDAY, YOU'RE BETTER OFF STEERING CLEAR... AND DON'T LOOK AT ME LIKE THAT!
TAKE A BREAK FOR A DAY, COME ON! PERHAPS YOU CAN GET OUT A BIT...
...AND GET OVER THAT MENTAL BLOCK YOU HAVE TOWARDS THE FEMALE UNIVERSE!
BUT... BUT THAT WOMAN CANNOT STAND ME! THE OTHER DAY...
OH, STOP IT, ABEL! WATER UNDER THE BRIDGE...
HERE, THIS IS THE SHOPPING LIST. YOU KNOW WHERE THE MARKET IS...
AND YOU ALSO KNOW WHERE THE PILLAR TO POST IS, RIGHT?
THE GOLDEN HIND
...AND THAT STONE BASS THERE! IT'S FRESH, RIGHT?
FISHED LESS THAN AN HOUR AGO! IT'S STILL MAKING PLANS FOR THE EVENING!
?
TLACK
EVERYTHING ALRIGHT AT THE INN, SON?
YES, THANK YOU, SIR! THE GIRLS SEND YOU THEIR BEST WISHES FOR THE HOLIDAYS!

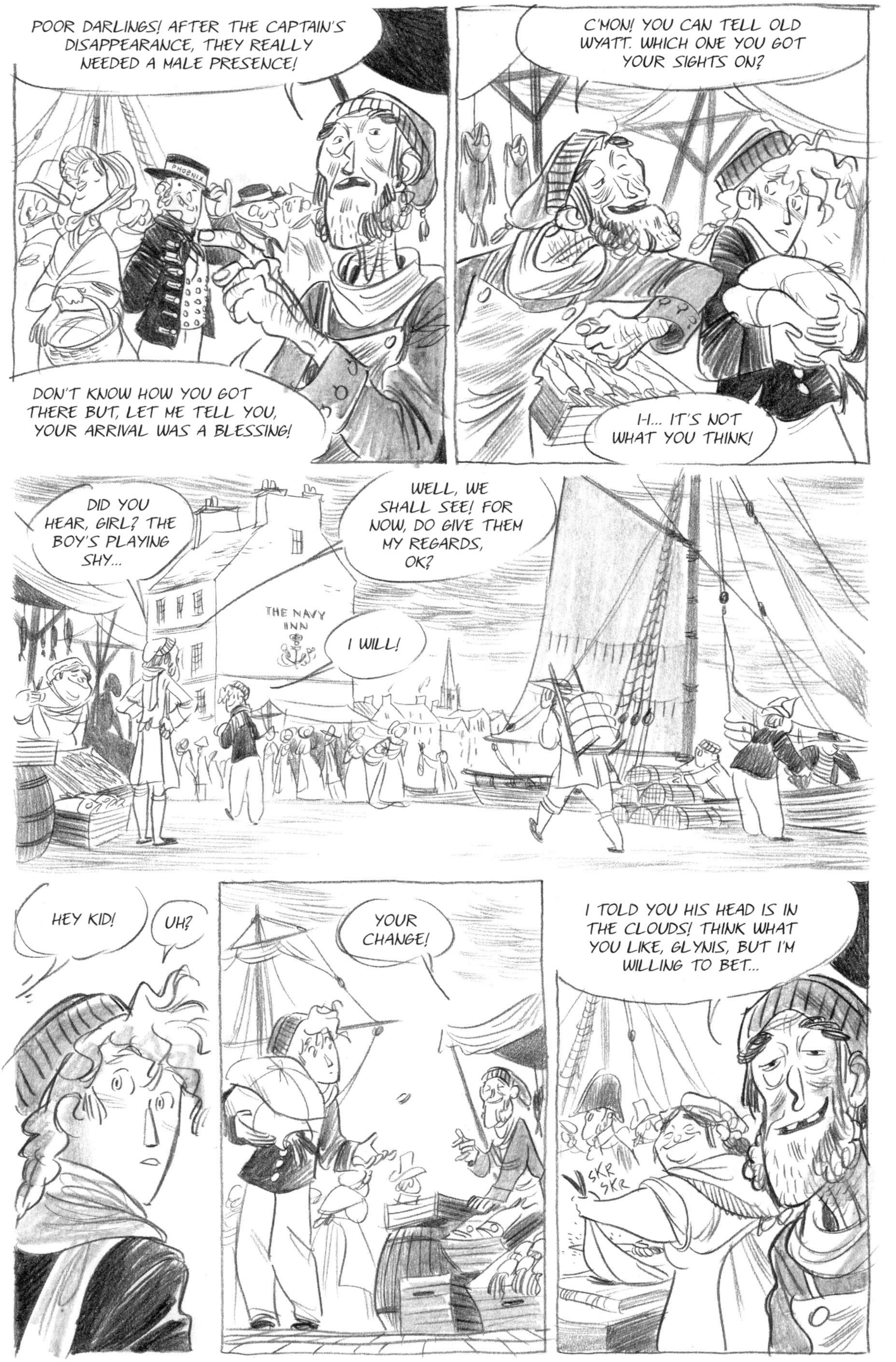
POOR DARLINGS! AFTER THE CAPTAIN'S DISAPPEARANCE, THEY REALLY NEEDED A MALE PRESENCE!
PHOENIX
DON'T KNOW HOW YOU GOT THERE BUT, LET ME TELL YOU, YOUR ARRIVAL WAS A BLESSING!
C'MON! YOU CAN TELL OLD WYATT. WHICH ONE YOU GOT YOUR SIGHTS ON?
I-I... IT'S NOT WHAT YOU THINK!
DID YOU HEAR, GIRL? THE BOY'S PLAYING SHY...
WELL, WE SHALL SEE! FOR NOW, DO GIVE THEM MY REGARDS, OK?
THE NAVY INN
I WILL!
HEY KID!
UH?
YOUR CHANGE!
I TOLD YOU HIS HEAD IS IN THE CLOUDS! THINK WHAT YOU LIKE, GLYNIS, BUT I'M WILLING TO BET...
SKR SKR

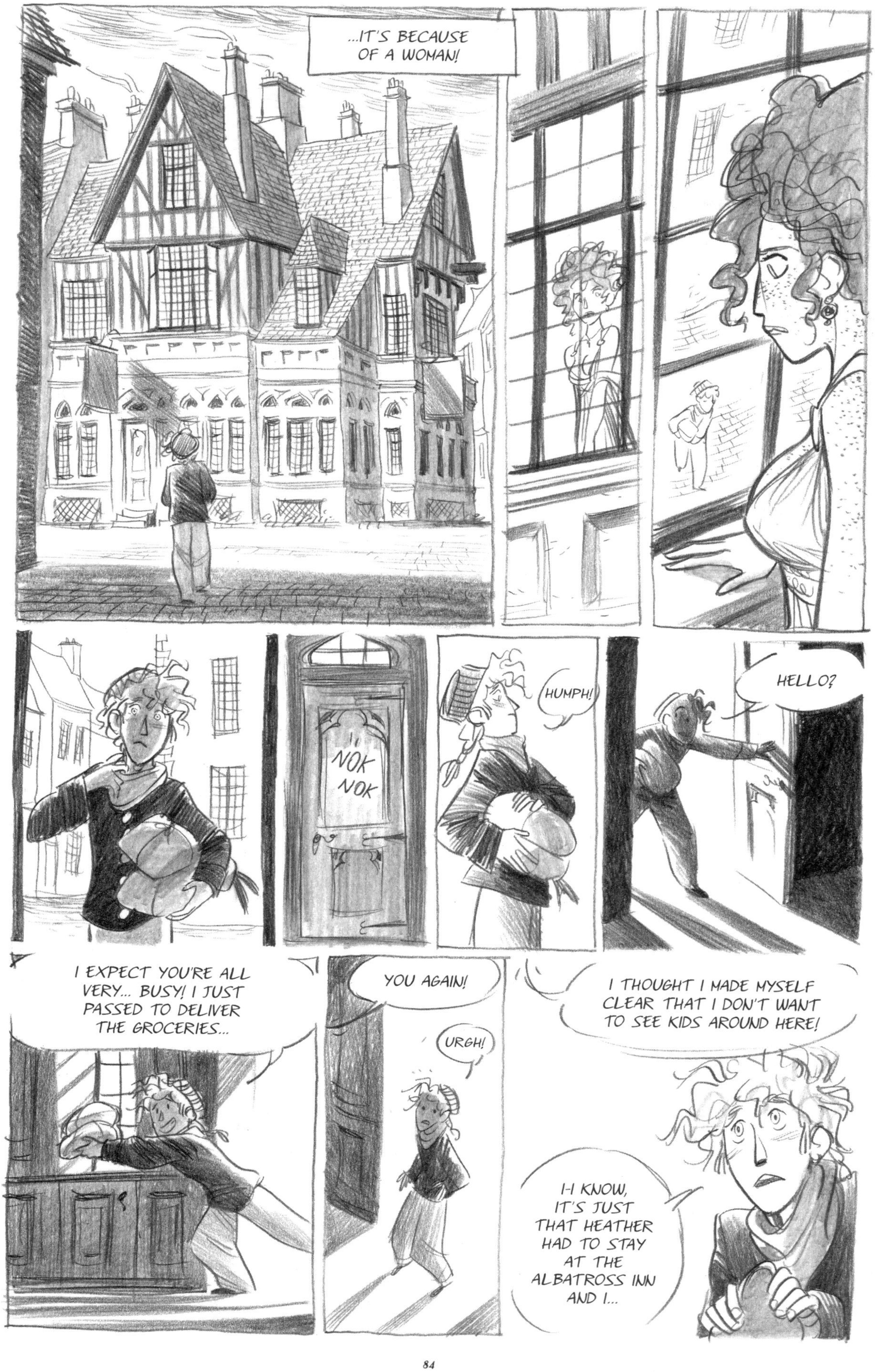

...IT'S BECAUSE OF A WOMAN!
NOK NOK
HUMPH!
HELLO?
I EXPECT YOU'RE ALL VERY... BUSY! I JUST PASSED TO DELIVER THE GROCERIES...
YOU AGAIN!
URGH!
I THOUGHT I MADE MYSELF CLEAR THAT I DON'T WANT TO SEE KIDS AROUND HERE!
I-I KNOW, IT'S JUST THAT HEATHER HAD TO STAY AT THE ALBATROSS INN AND I...

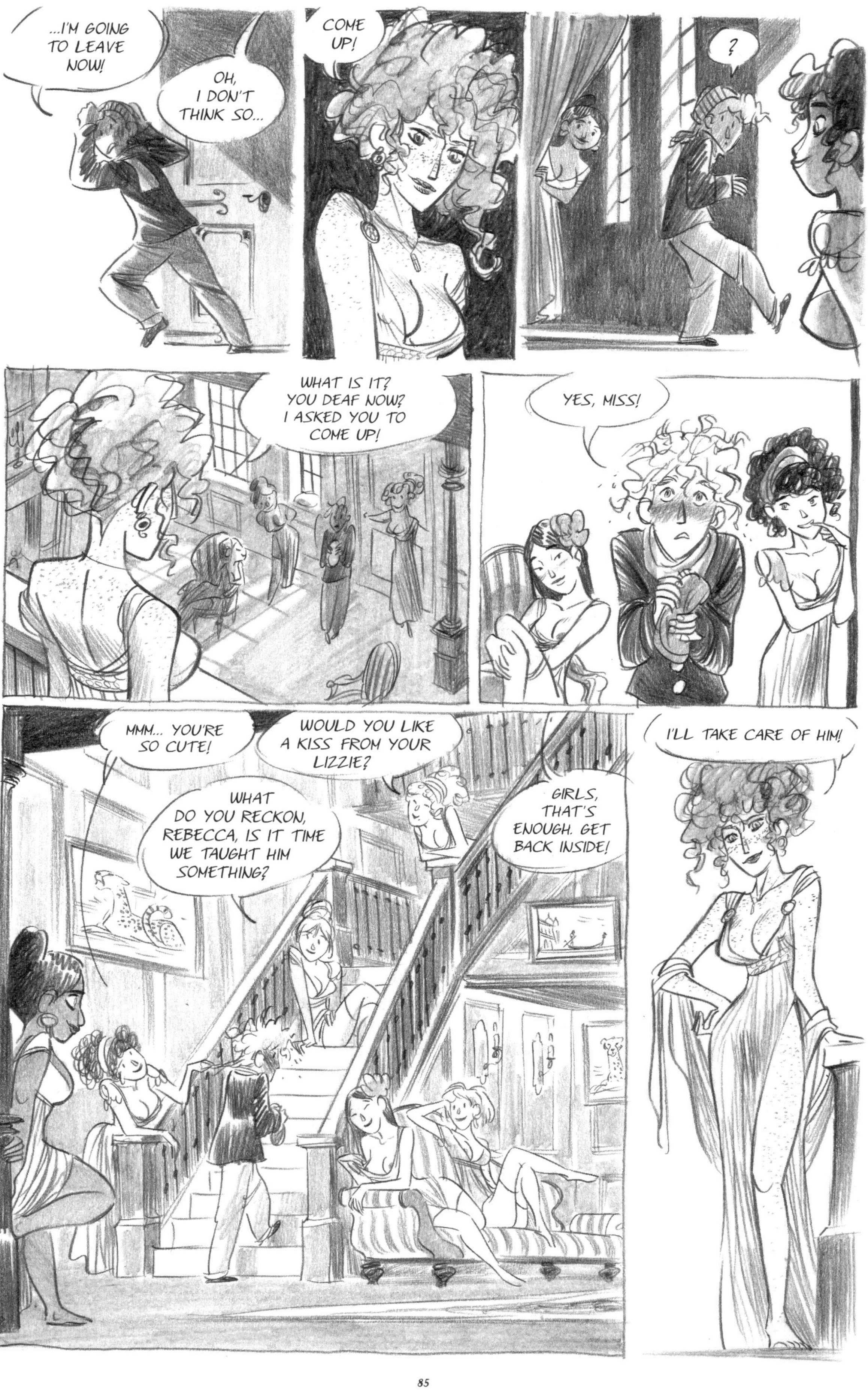

...I'M GOING TO LEAVE NOW!
OH, I DON'T THINK SO...
COME UP!
?
WHAT IS IT? YOU DEAF NOW? I ASKED YOU TO COME UP!
YES, MISS!
MMM... YOU'RE SO CUTE!
WOULD YOU LIKE A KISS FROM YOUR LIZZIE?
WHAT DO YOU RECKON, REBECCA, IS IT TIME WE TAUGHT HIM SOMETHING?
GIRLS, THAT'S ENOUGH. GET BACK INSIDE!
I'LL TAKE CARE OF HIM!

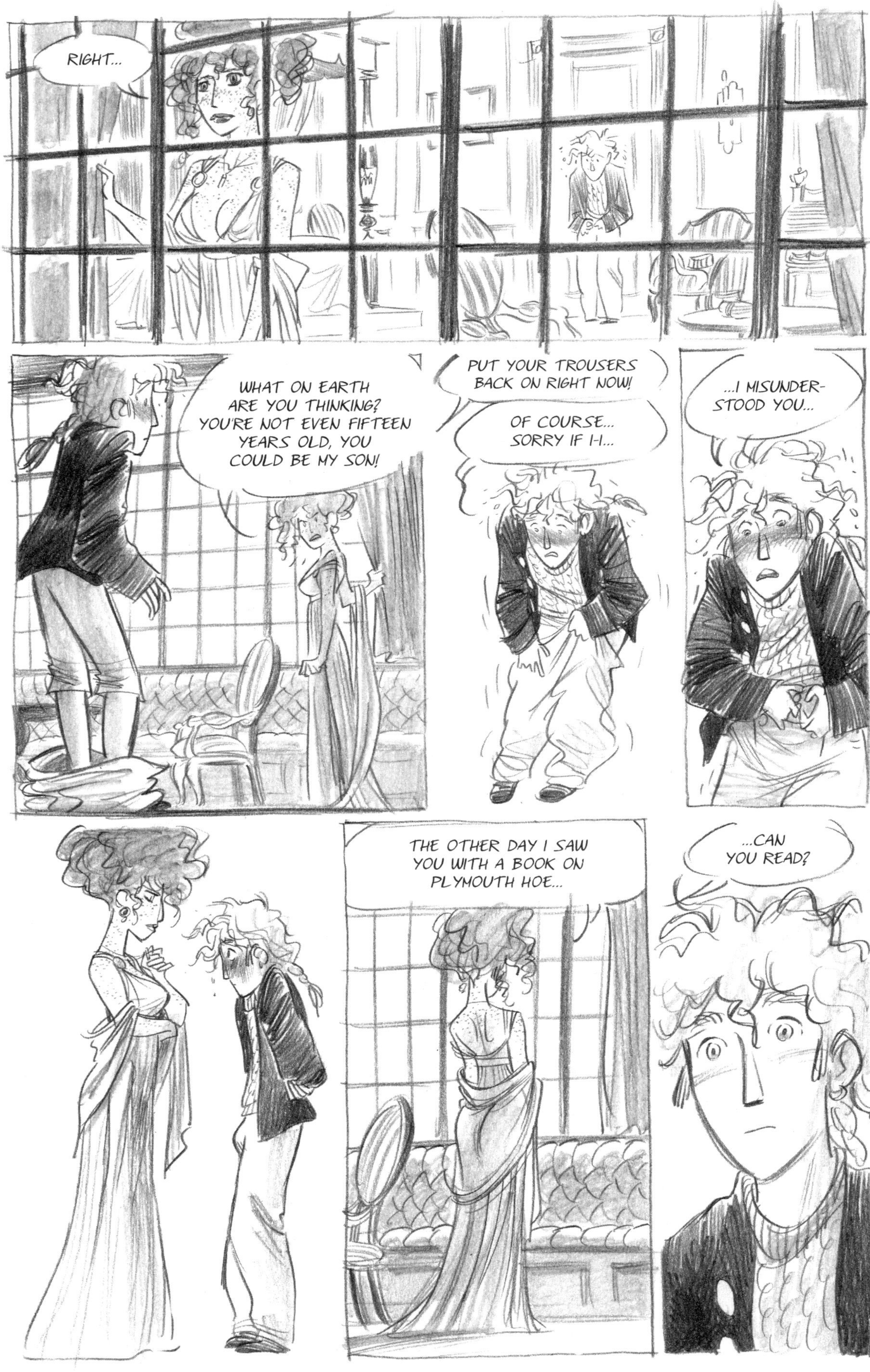
RIGHT...
WHAT ON EARTH ARE YOU THINKING? YOU'RE NOT EVEN FIFTEEN YEARS OLD, YOU COULD BE MY SON!
PUT YOUR TROUSERS BACK ON RIGHT NOW!
OF COURSE... SORRY IF I-I...
...I MISUNDER-STOOD YOU...
THE OTHER DAY I SAW YOU WITH A BOOK ON PLYMOUTH HOE...
...CAN YOU READ?

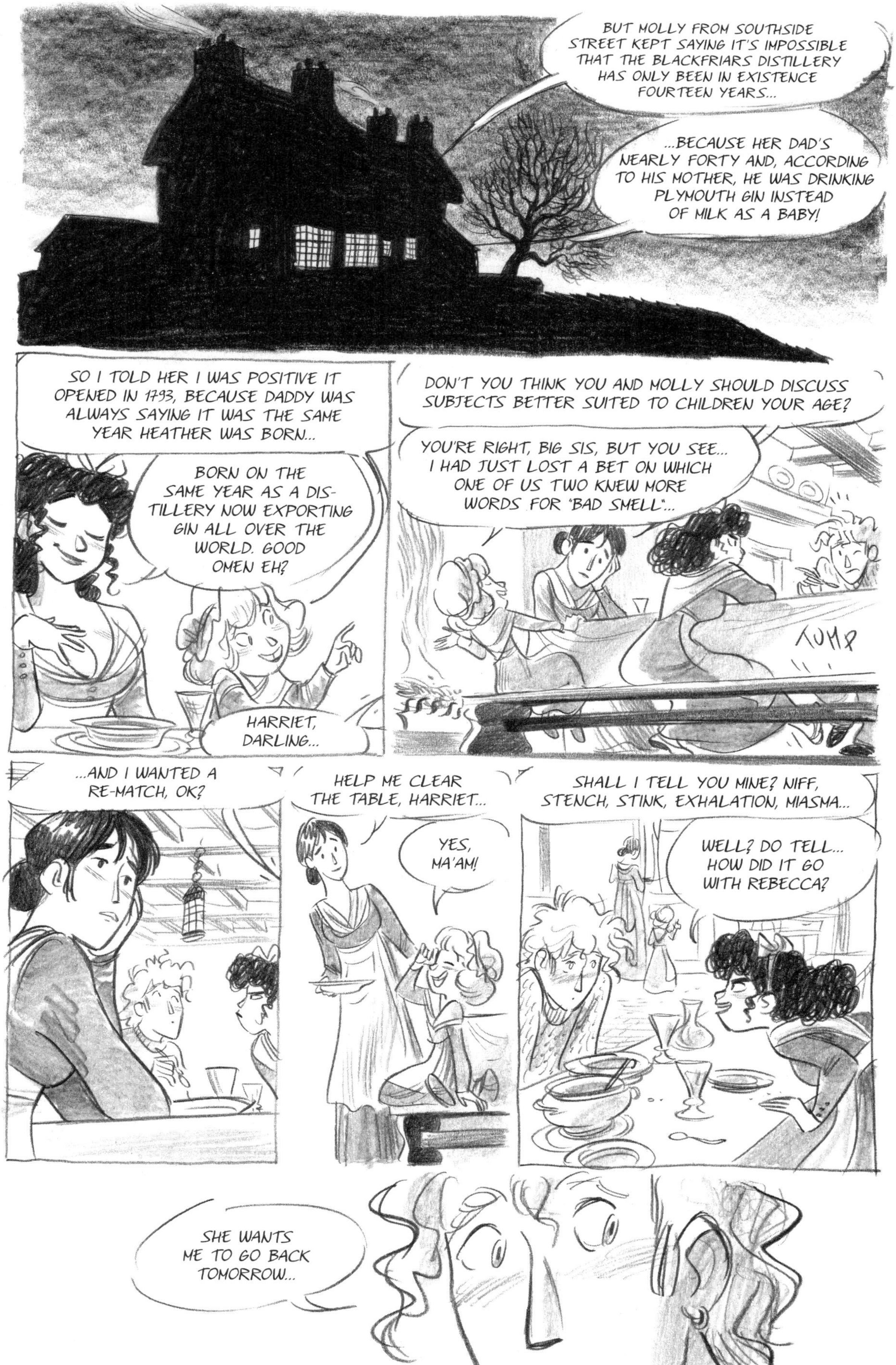
BUT MOLLY FROM SOUTHSIDE STREET KEPT SAYING IT'S IMPOSSIBLE THAT THE BLACKFRIARS DISTILLERY HAS ONLY BEEN IN EXISTENCE FOURTEEN YEARS...
...BECAUSE HER DAD'S NEARLY FORTY AND, ACCORDING TO HIS MOTHER, HE WAS DRINKING PLYMOUTH GIN INSTEAD OF MILK AS A BABY!
SO I TOLD HER I WAS POSITIVE IT OPENED IN 1793, BECAUSE DADDY WAS ALWAYS SAYING IT WAS THE SAME YEAR HEATHER WAS BORN...
BORN ON THE SAME YEAR AS A DISTILLERY NOW EXPORTING GIN ALL OVER THE WORLD. GOOD OMEN EH?
HARRIET, DARLING...
DON'T YOU THINK YOU AND MOLLY SHOULD DISCUSS SUBJECTS BETTER SUITED TO CHILDREN YOUR AGE?
YOU'RE RIGHT, BIG SIS, BUT YOU SEE... I HAD JUST LOST A BET ON WHICH ONE OF US TWO KNEW MORE WORDS FOR "BAD SMELL"...
TUMP
...AND I WANTED A RE-MATCH, OK?
HELP ME CLEAR THE TABLE, HARRIET...
YES, MA'AM!
SHALL I TELL YOU MINE? NIFF, STENCH, STINK, EXHALATION, MIASMA...
WELL? DO TELL... HOW DID IT GO WITH REBECCA?
SHE WANTS ME TO GO BACK TOMORROW...

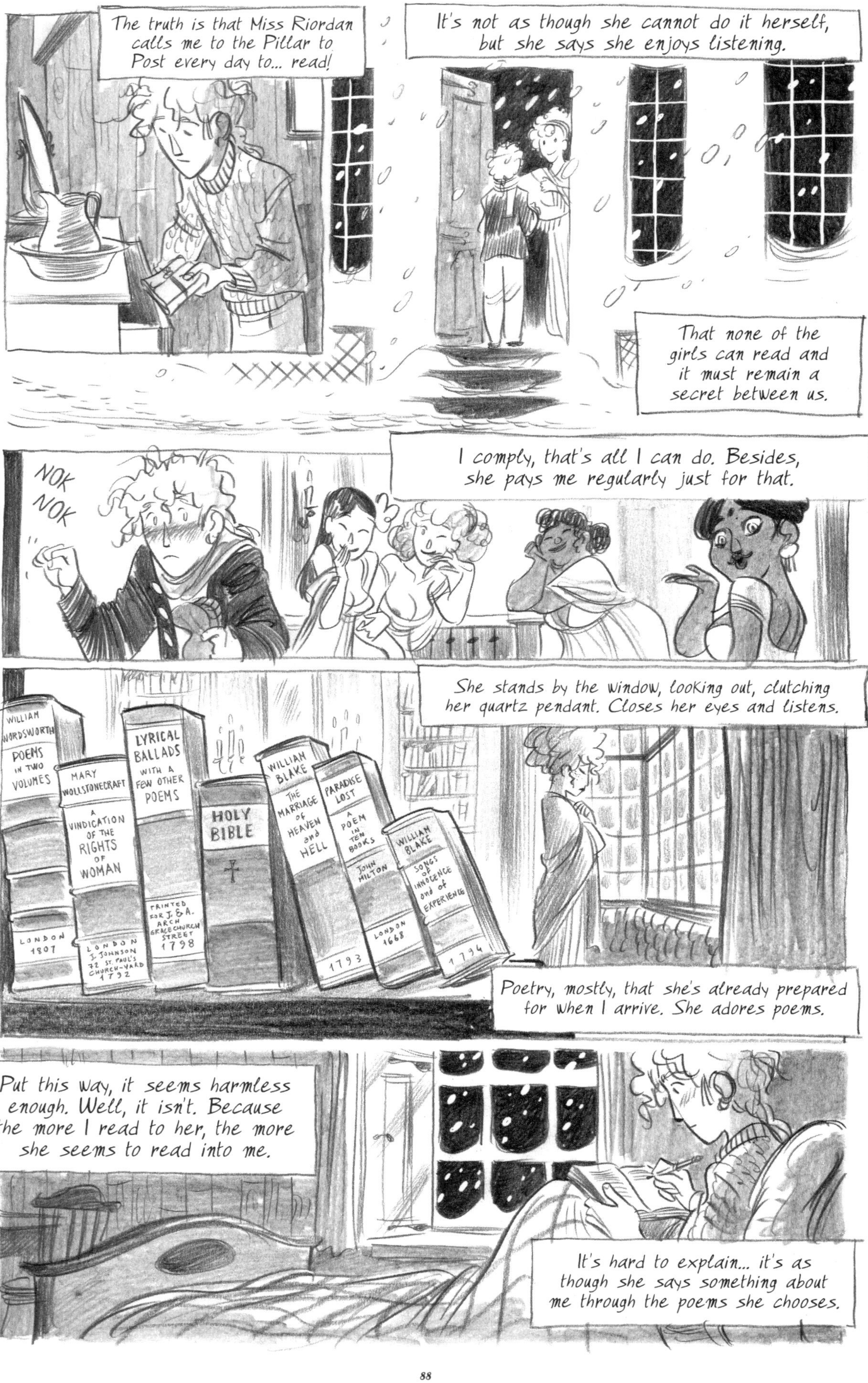
The truth is that Miss Riordan calls me to the Pillar to Post every day to... read!
It's not as though she cannot do it herself, but she says she enjoys listening.
That none of the girls can read and it must remain a secret between us.
I comply, that's all I can do. Besides, she pays me regularly just for that.
NOK NOK
She stands by the window, looking out, clutching her quartz pendant. Closes her eyes and listens.
WILLIAM WORDSWORTH POEMS IN TWO VOLUMES LONDON 1807
MARY WOLLSTONECRAFT A VINDICATION OF THE RIGHTS OF WOMAN LONDON J. JOHNSON 72 ST. PAUL'S CHURCH-YARD 1792
LYRICAL BALLADS WITH A FEW OTHER POEMS PRINTED FOR J. & A. ARCH GRACECHURCH STREET 1798
HOLY BIBLE
WILLIAM BLAKE THE MARRIAGE OF HEAVEN and HELL 1793
PARADISE LOST A POEM IN TEN BOOKS JOHN MILTON LONDON 1668
WILLIAM BLAKE SONGS OF INNOCENCE and of EXPERIENCE 1794
Poetry, mostly, that she's already prepared for when I arrive. She adores poems.
Put this way, it seems harmless enough. Well, it isn't. Because the more I read to her, the more she seems to read into me.
It's hard to explain... it's as though she says something about me through the poems she chooses.

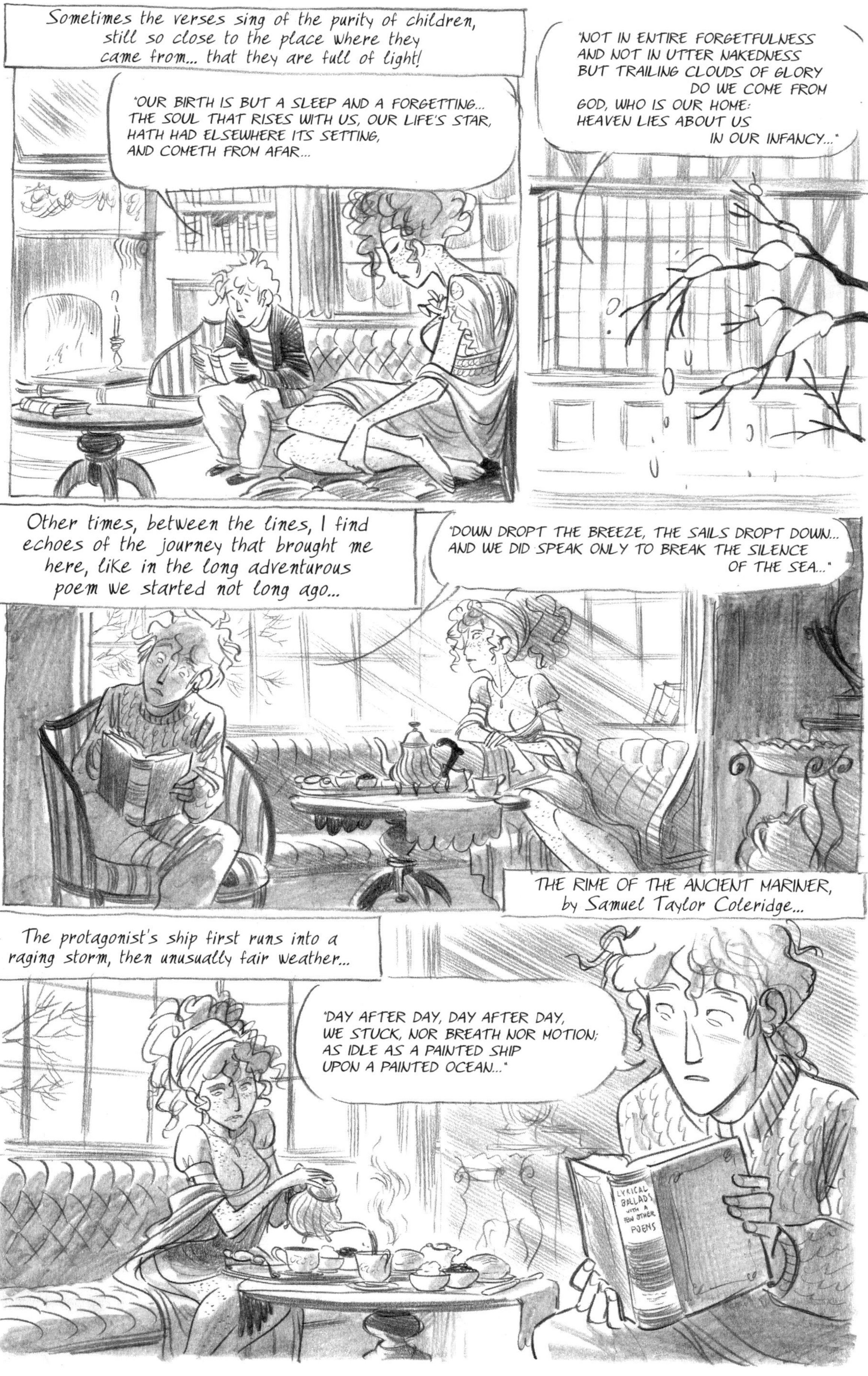
Sometimes the verses sing of the purity of children, still so close to the place where they came from... that they are full of light!
"OUR BIRTH IS BUT A SLEEP AND A FORGETTING... THE SOUL THAT RISES WITH US, OUR LIFE'S STAR, HATH HAD ELSEWHERE ITS SETTING, AND COMETH FROM AFAR...
"NOT IN ENTIRE FORGETFULNESS AND NOT IN UTTER NAKEDNESS BUT TRAILING CLOUDS OF GLORY DO WE COME FROM GOD, WHO IS OUR HOME: HEAVEN LIES ABOUT US IN OUR INFANCY..."
Other times, between the lines, I find echoes of the journey that brought me here, like in the long adventurous poem we started not long ago...
"DOWN DROPT THE BREEZE, THE SAILS DROPT DOWN... AND WE DID SPEAK ONLY TO BREAK THE SILENCE OF THE SEA..."
THE RIME OF THE ANCIENT MARINER, by Samuel Taylor Coleridge...
The protagonist's ship first runs into a raging storm, then unusually fair weather...
"DAY AFTER DAY, DAY AFTER DAY, WE STUCK, NOR BREATH NOR MOTION; AS IDLE AS A PAINTED SHIP UPON A PAINTED OCEAN..."
LYRICAL BALLADS WITH A FEW OTHER POEMS

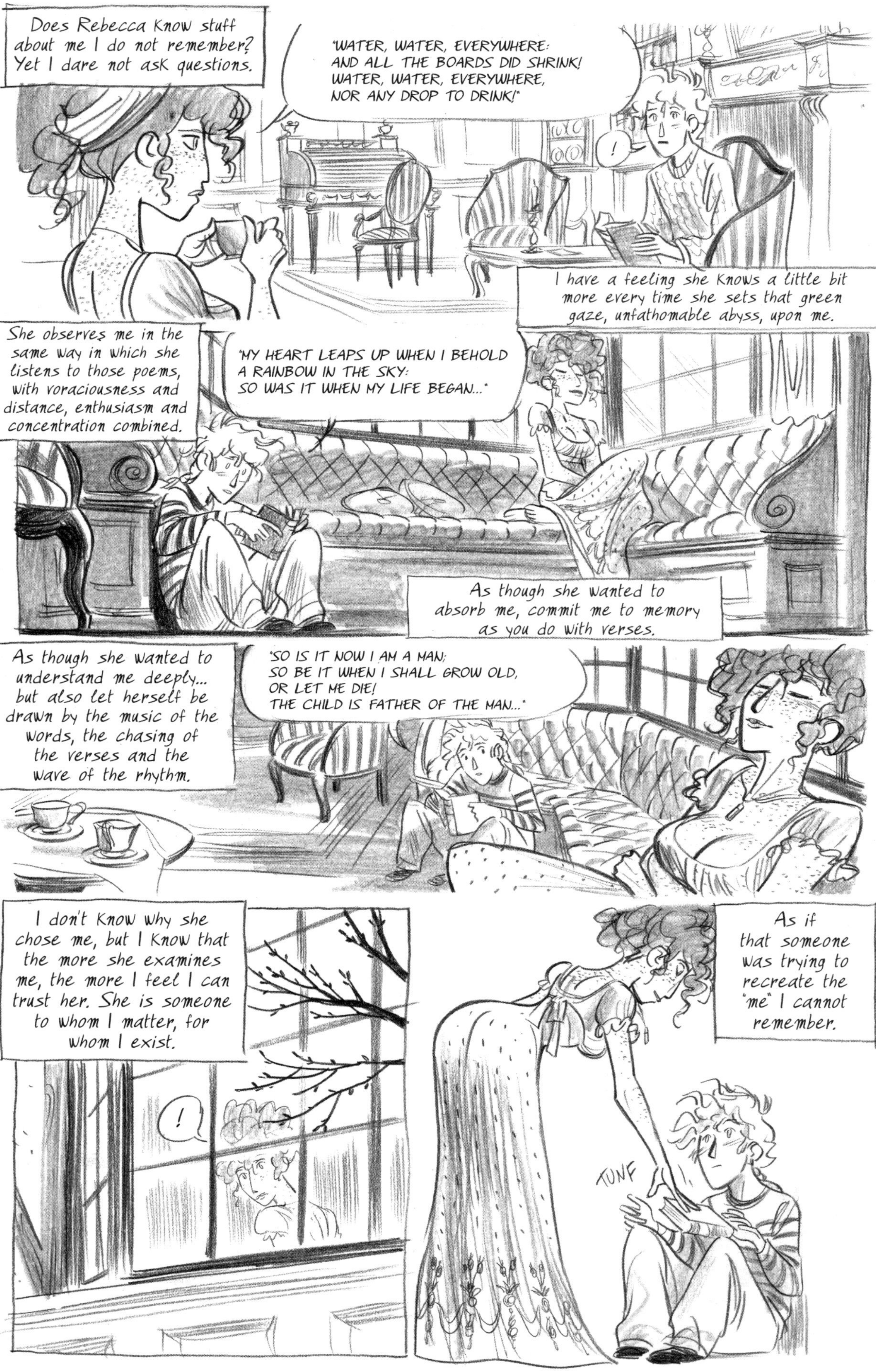
Does Rebecca know stuff about me I do not remember? Yet I dare not ask questions.
"WATER, WATER, EVERYWHERE: AND ALL THE BOARDS DID SHRINK! WATER, WATER, EVERYWHERE, NOR ANY DROP TO DRINK!"
!
I have a feeling she knows a little bit more every time she sets that green gaze, unfathomable abyss, upon me.
She observes me in the same way in which she listens to those poems, with voraciousness and distance, enthusiasm and concentration combined.
"MY HEART LEAPS UP WHEN I BEHOLD A RAINBOW IN THE SKY: SO WAS IT WHEN MY LIFE BEGAN..."
As though she wanted to absorb me, commit me to memory as you do with verses.
As though she wanted to understand me deeply... but also let herself be drawn by the music of the words, the chasing of the verses and the wave of the rhythm.
"SO IS IT NOW I AM A MAN; SO BE IT WHEN I SHALL GROW OLD, OR LET ME DIE! THE CHILD IS FATHER OF THE MAN..."
I don't know why she chose me, but I know that the more she examines me, the more I feel I can trust her. She is someone to whom I matter, for whom I exist.
!
As if that someone was trying to recreate the "me" I cannot remember.
TUNF

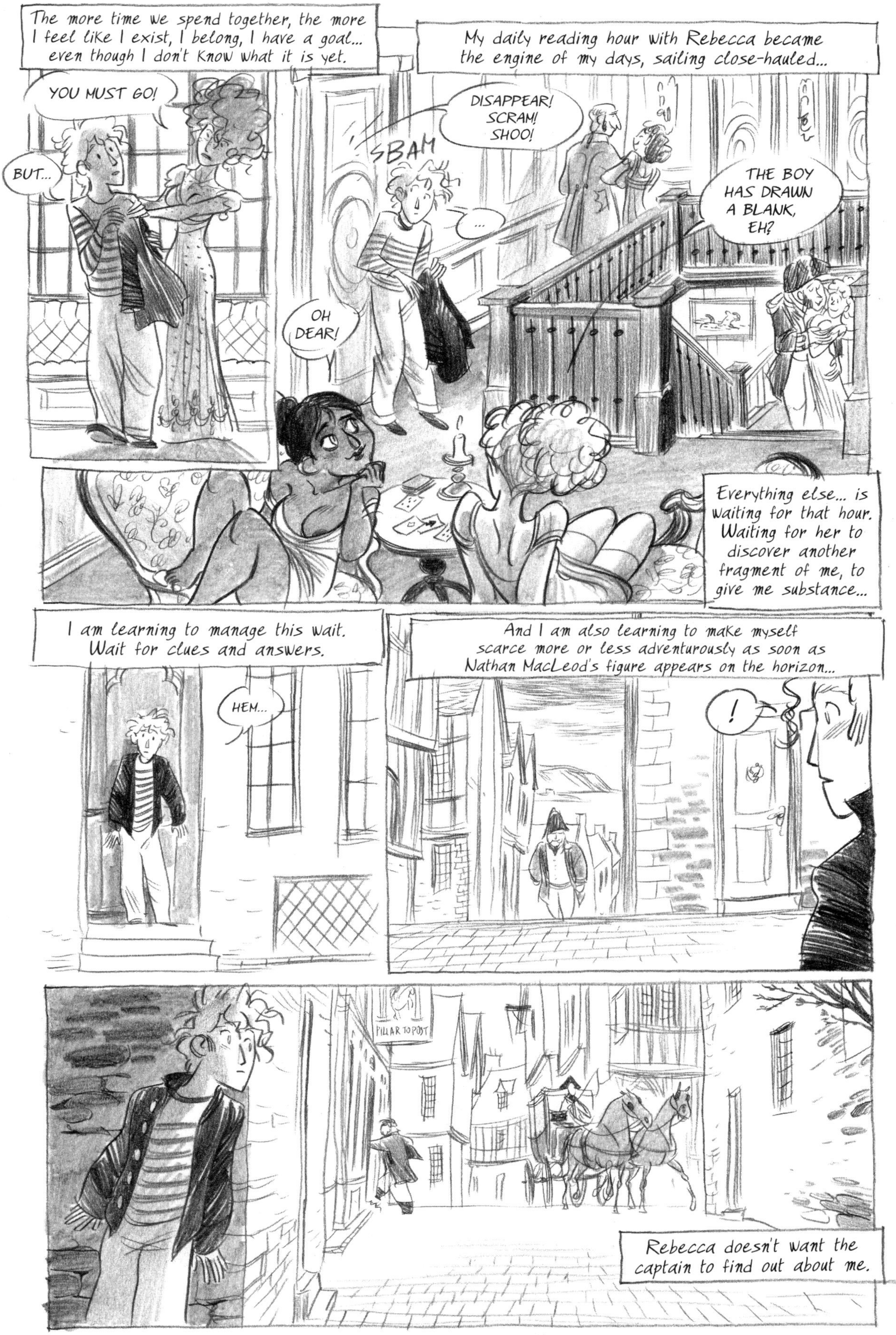

The more time we spend together, the more I feel like I exist, I belong, I have a goal... even though I don't know what it is yet.
YOU MUST GO!
BUT...
My daily reading hour with Rebecca became the engine of my days, sailing close-hauled...
DISAPPEAR! SCRAM! SHOO!
SBAM
...
THE BOY HAS DRAWN A BLANK, EH?
OH DEAR!
Everything else... is waiting for that hour. Waiting for her to discover another fragment of me, to give me substance...
I am learning to manage this wait. Wait for clues and answers.
HEM...
And I am also learning to make myself scarce more or less adventurously as soon as Nathan MacLeod's figure appears on the horizon...
!
PILLAR TO POST
Rebecca doesn't want the captain to find out about me.

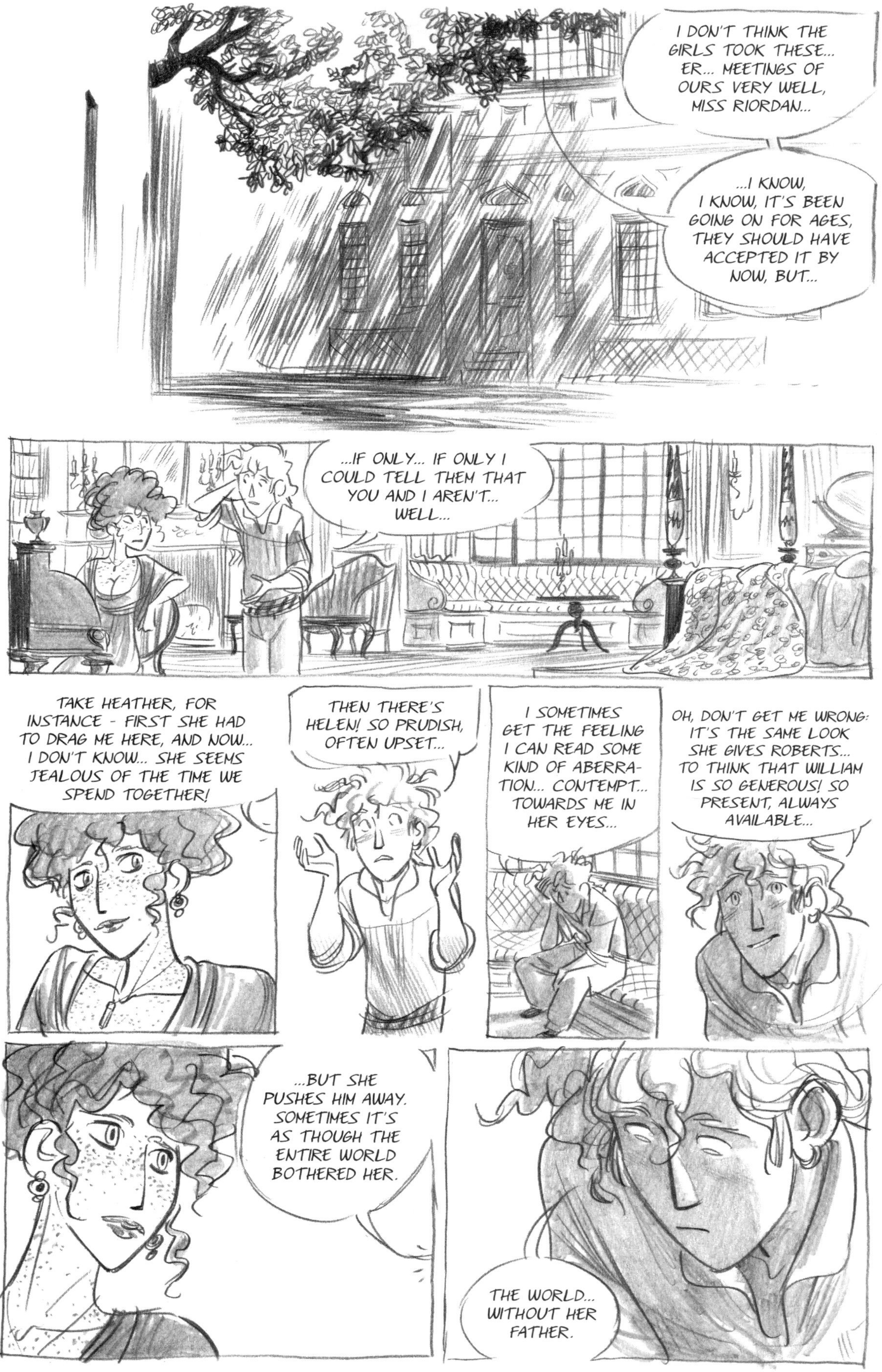
I DON'T THINK THE GIRLS TOOK THESE... ER... MEETINGS OF OURS VERY WELL, MISS RIORDAN...
...I KNOW, I KNOW, IT'S BEEN GOING ON FOR AGES, THEY SHOULD HAVE ACCEPTED IT BY NOW, BUT...
...IF ONLY... IF ONLY I COULD TELL THEM THAT YOU AND I AREN'T... WELL...
TAKE HEATHER, FOR INSTANCE - FIRST SHE HAD TO DRAG ME HERE, AND NOW... I DON'T KNOW... SHE SEEMS JEALOUS OF THE TIME WE SPEND TOGETHER!
THEN THERE'S HELEN! SO PRUDISH, OFTEN UPSET...
I SOMETIMES GET THE FEELING I CAN READ SOME KIND OF ABERRATION... CONTEMPT... TOWARDS ME IN HER EYES...
OH, DON'T GET ME WRONG: IT'S THE SAME LOOK SHE GIVES ROBERTS... TO THINK THAT WILLIAM IS SO GENEROUS! SO PRESENT, ALWAYS AVAILABLE...
...BUT SHE PUSHES HIM AWAY. SOMETIMES IT'S AS THOUGH THE ENTIRE WORLD BOTHERED HER.
THE WORLD... WITHOUT HER FATHER.

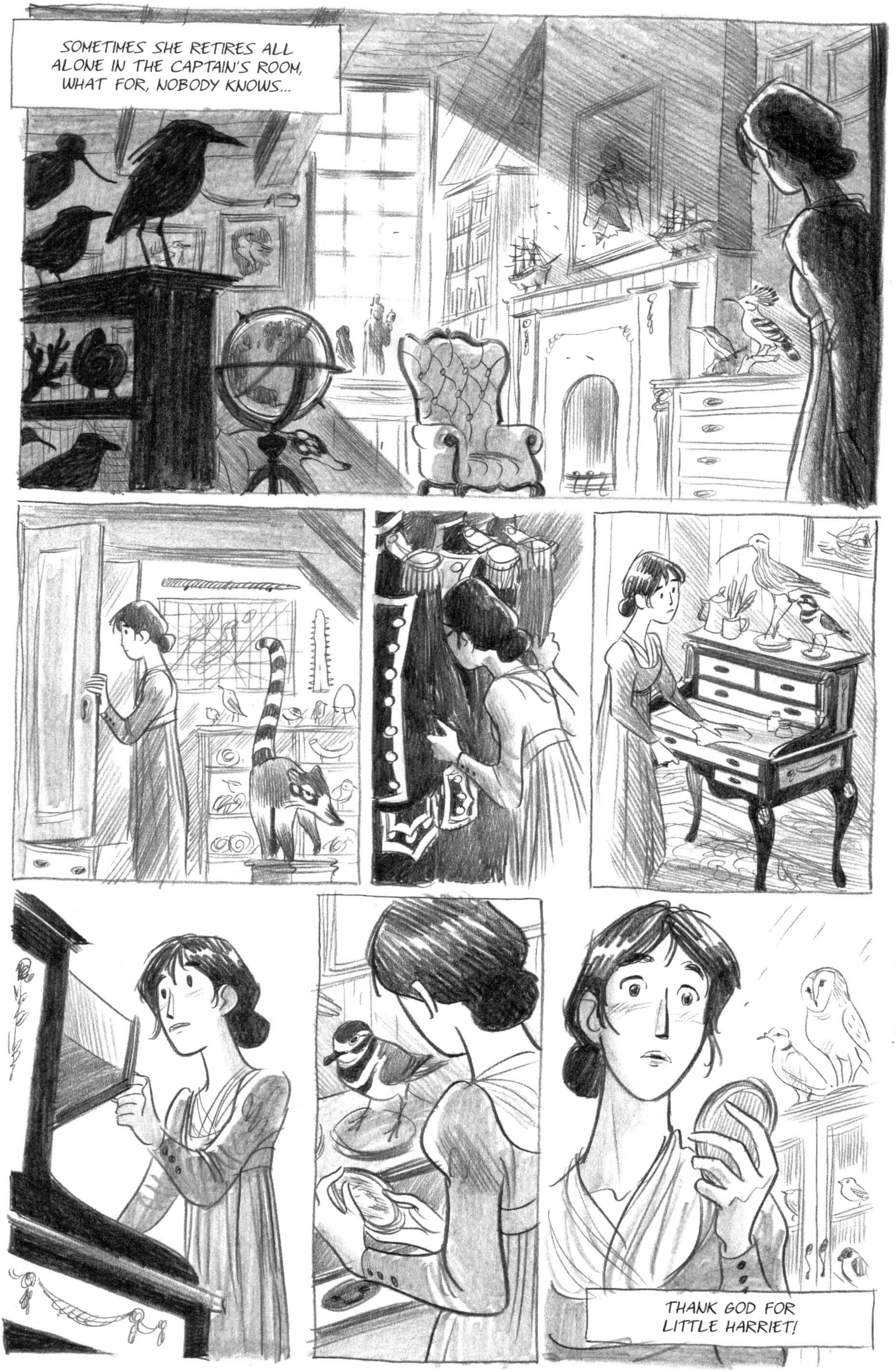
SOMETIMES SHE RETIRES ALL ALONE IN THE CAPTAIN'S ROOM, WHAT FOR, NOBODY KNOWS...
THANK GOD FOR LITTLE HARRIET!

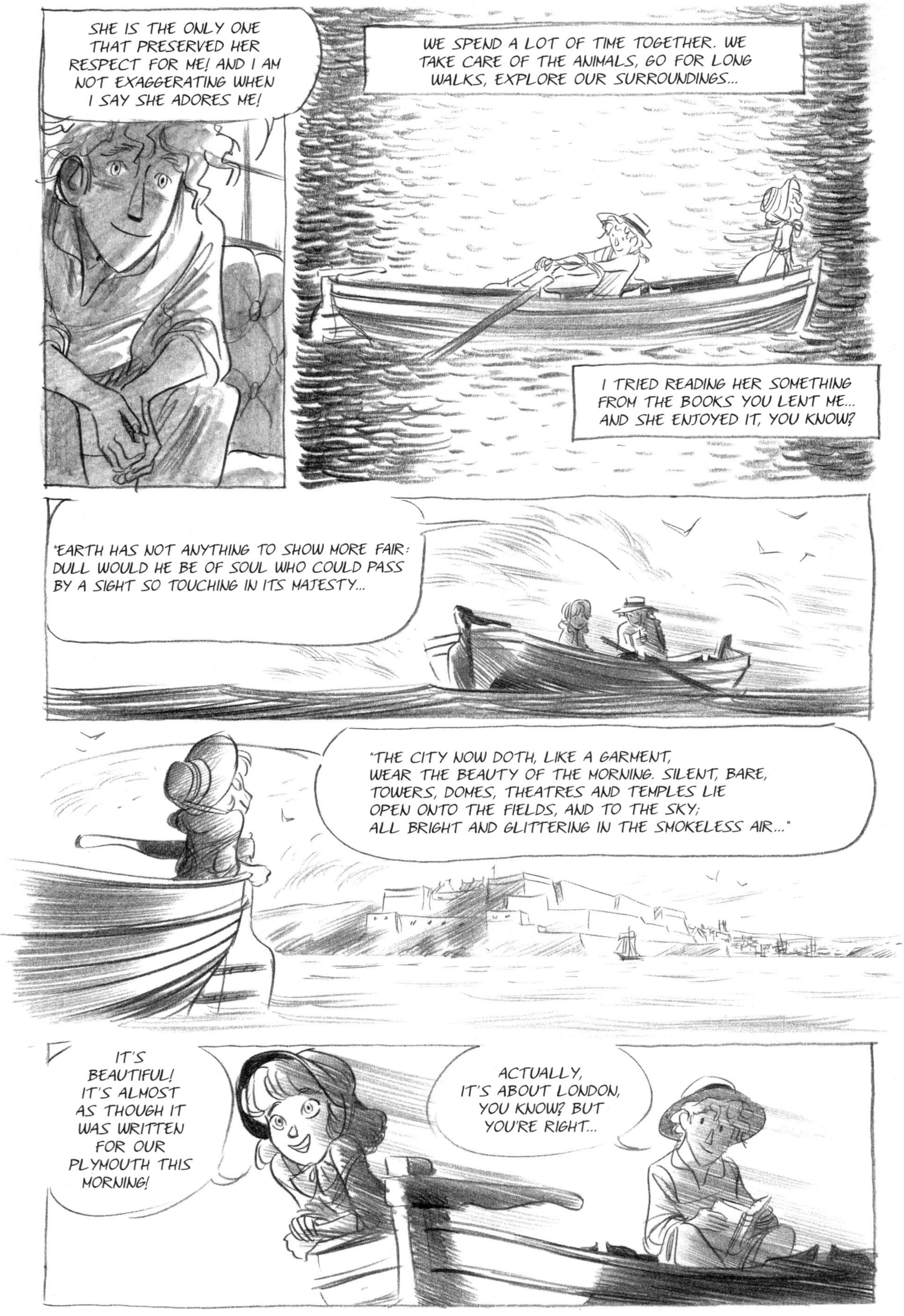
SHE IS THE ONLY ONE THAT PRESERVED HER RESPECT FOR ME! AND I AM NOT EXAGGERATING WHEN I SAY SHE ADORES ME!
WE SPEND A LOT OF TIME TOGETHER. WE TAKE CARE OF THE ANIMALS, GO FOR LONG WALKS, EXPLORE OUR SURROUNDINGS...
I TRIED READING HER SOMETHING FROM THE BOOKS YOU LENT ME... AND SHE ENJOYED IT, YOU KNOW?
"EARTH HAS NOT ANYTHING TO SHOW MORE FAIR: DULL WOULD HE BE OF SOUL WHO COULD PASS BY A SIGHT SO TOUCHING IN ITS MAJESTY...
"THE CITY NOW DOTH, LIKE A GARMENT, WEAR THE BEAUTY OF THE MORNING. SILENT, BARE, TOWERS, DOMES, THEATRES AND TEMPLES LIE OPEN ONTO THE FIELDS, AND TO THE SKY; ALL BRIGHT AND GLITTERING IN THE SMOKELESS AIR..."
IT'S BEAUTIFUL! IT'S ALMOST AS THOUGH IT WAS WRITTEN FOR OUR PLYMOUTH THIS MORNING!
ACTUALLY, IT'S ABOUT LONDON, YOU KNOW? BUT YOU'RE RIGHT...

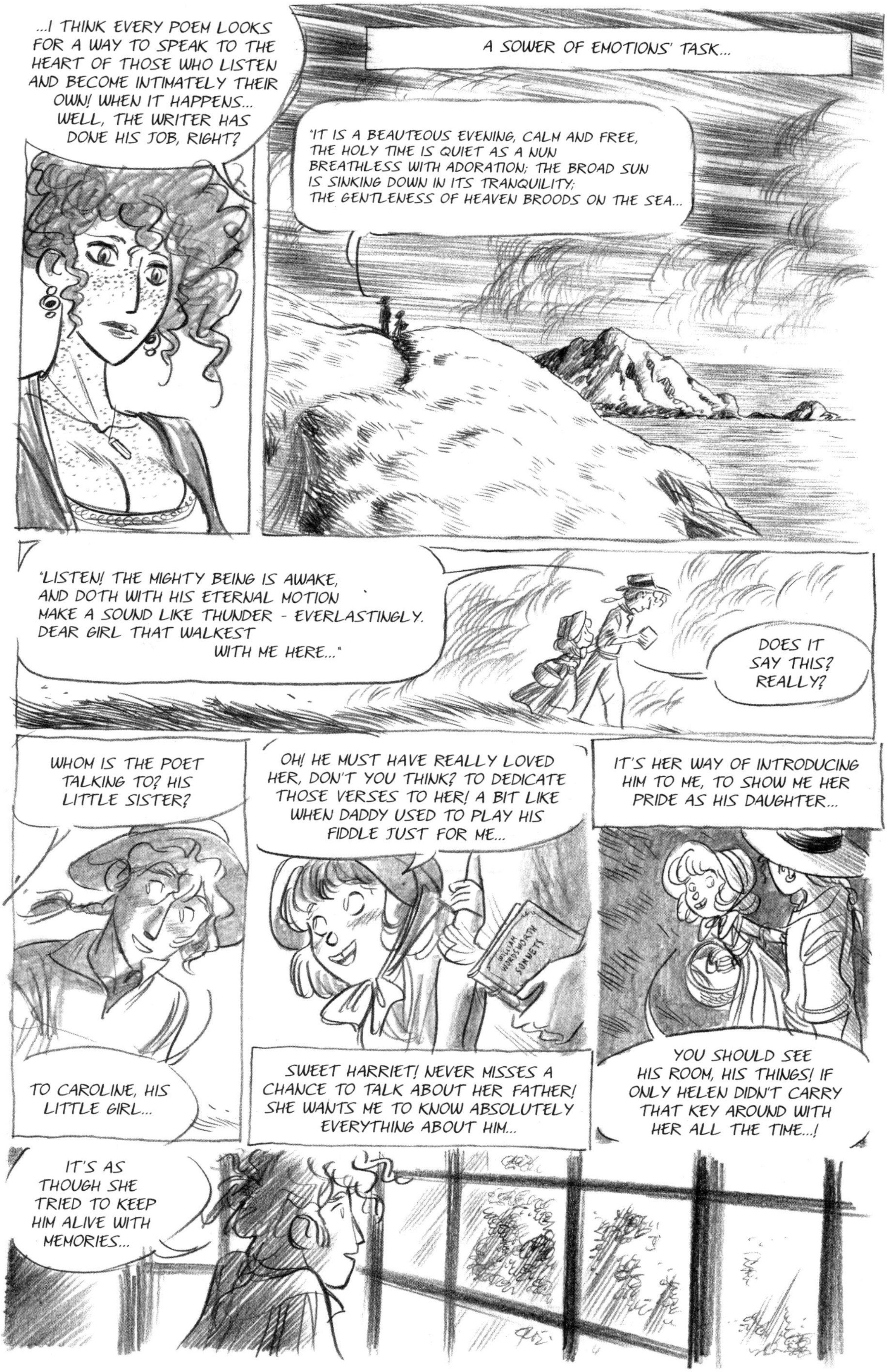
...I THINK EVERY POEM LOOKS FOR A WAY TO SPEAK TO THE HEART OF THOSE WHO LISTEN AND BECOME INTIMATELY THEIR OWN! WHEN IT HAPPENS... WELL, THE WRITER HAS DONE HIS JOB, RIGHT?
A SOWER OF EMOTIONS' TASK...
"IT IS A BEAUTEOUS EVENING, CALM AND FREE, THE HOLY TIME IS QUIET AS A NUN BREATHLESS WITH ADORATION; THE BROAD SUN IS SINKING DOWN IN ITS TRANQUILITY; THE GENTLENESS OF HEAVEN BROODS ON THE SEA...
"LISTEN! THE MIGHTY BEING IS AWAKE, AND DOTH WITH HIS ETERNAL MOTION MAKE A SOUND LIKE THUNDER - EVERLASTINGLY. DEAR GIRL THAT WALKEST WITH ME HERE..."
DOES IT SAY THIS? REALLY?
WHOM IS THE POET TALKING TO? HIS LITTLE SISTER?
TO CAROLINE, HIS LITTLE GIRL...
OH! HE MUST HAVE REALLY LOVED HER, DON'T YOU THINK? TO DEDICATE THOSE VERSES TO HER! A BIT LIKE WHEN DADDY USED TO PLAY HIS FIDDLE JUST FOR ME...
WILLIAM WORDSWORTH SONNETS
SWEET HARRIET! NEVER MISSES A CHANCE TO TALK ABOUT HER FATHER! SHE WANTS ME TO KNOW ABSOLUTELY EVERYTHING ABOUT HIM...
IT'S HER WAY OF INTRODUCING HIM TO ME, TO SHOW ME HER PRIDE AS HIS DAUGHTER...
YOU SHOULD SEE HIS ROOM, HIS THINGS! IF ONLY HELEN DIDN'T CARRY THAT KEY AROUND WITH HER ALL THE TIME...!
IT'S AS THOUGH SHE TRIED TO KEEP HIM ALIVE WITH MEMORIES...

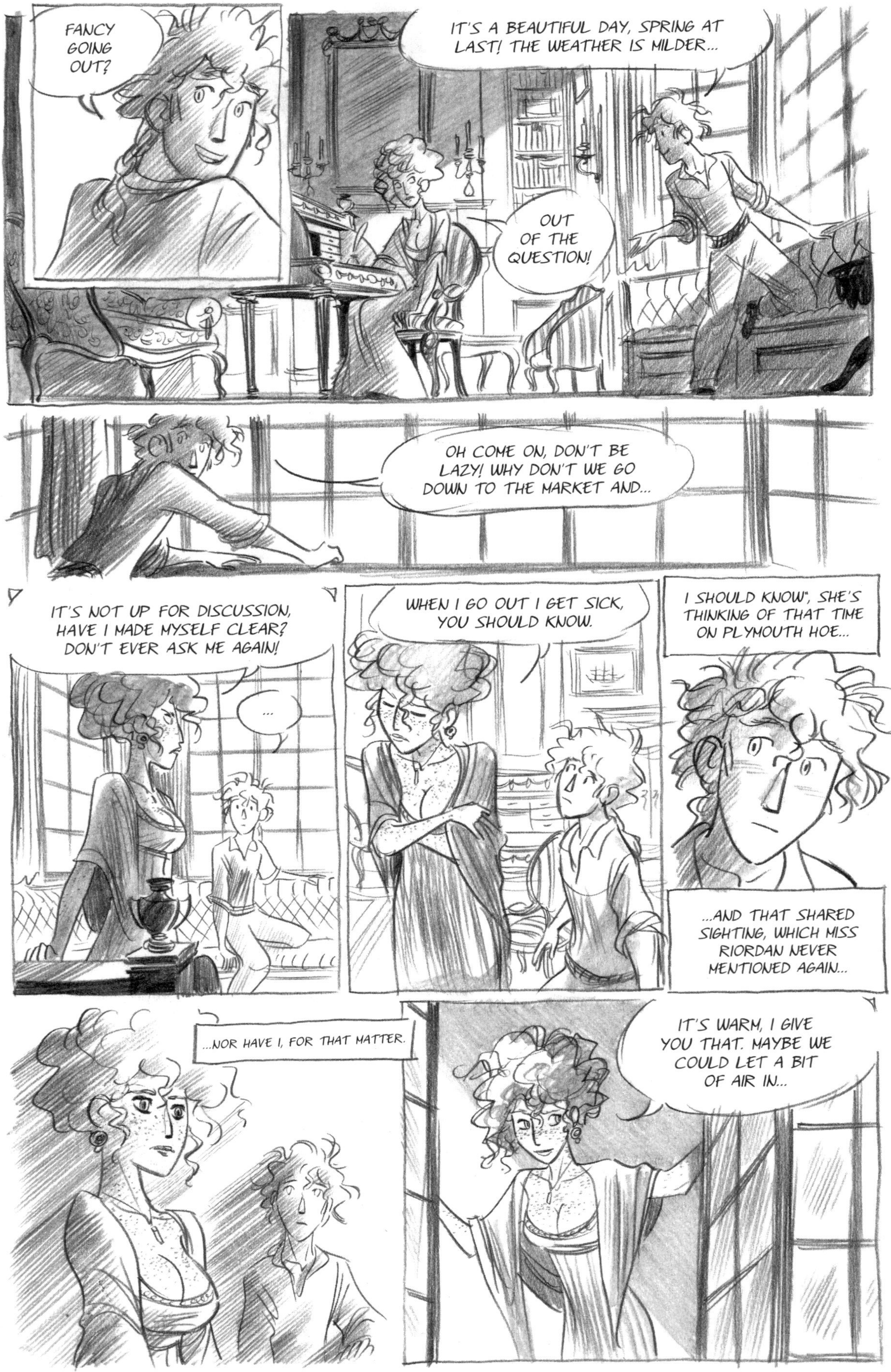
FANCY GOING OUT?
IT'S A BEAUTIFUL DAY, SPRING AT LAST! THE WEATHER IS MILDER...
OUT OF THE QUESTION!
OH COME ON, DON'T BE LAZY! WHY DON'T WE GO DOWN TO THE MARKET AND...
IT'S NOT UP FOR DISCUSSION, HAVE I MADE MYSELF CLEAR? DON'T EVER ASK ME AGAIN!
...
WHEN I GO OUT I GET SICK, YOU SHOULD KNOW.
I SHOULD KNOW", SHE'S THINKING OF THAT TIME ON PLYMOUTH HOE...
...AND THAT SHARED SIGHTING, WHICH MISS RIORDAN NEVER MENTIONED AGAIN...
...NOR HAVE I, FOR THAT MATTER.
IT'S WARM, I GIVE YOU THAT. MAYBE WE COULD LET A BIT OF AIR IN...

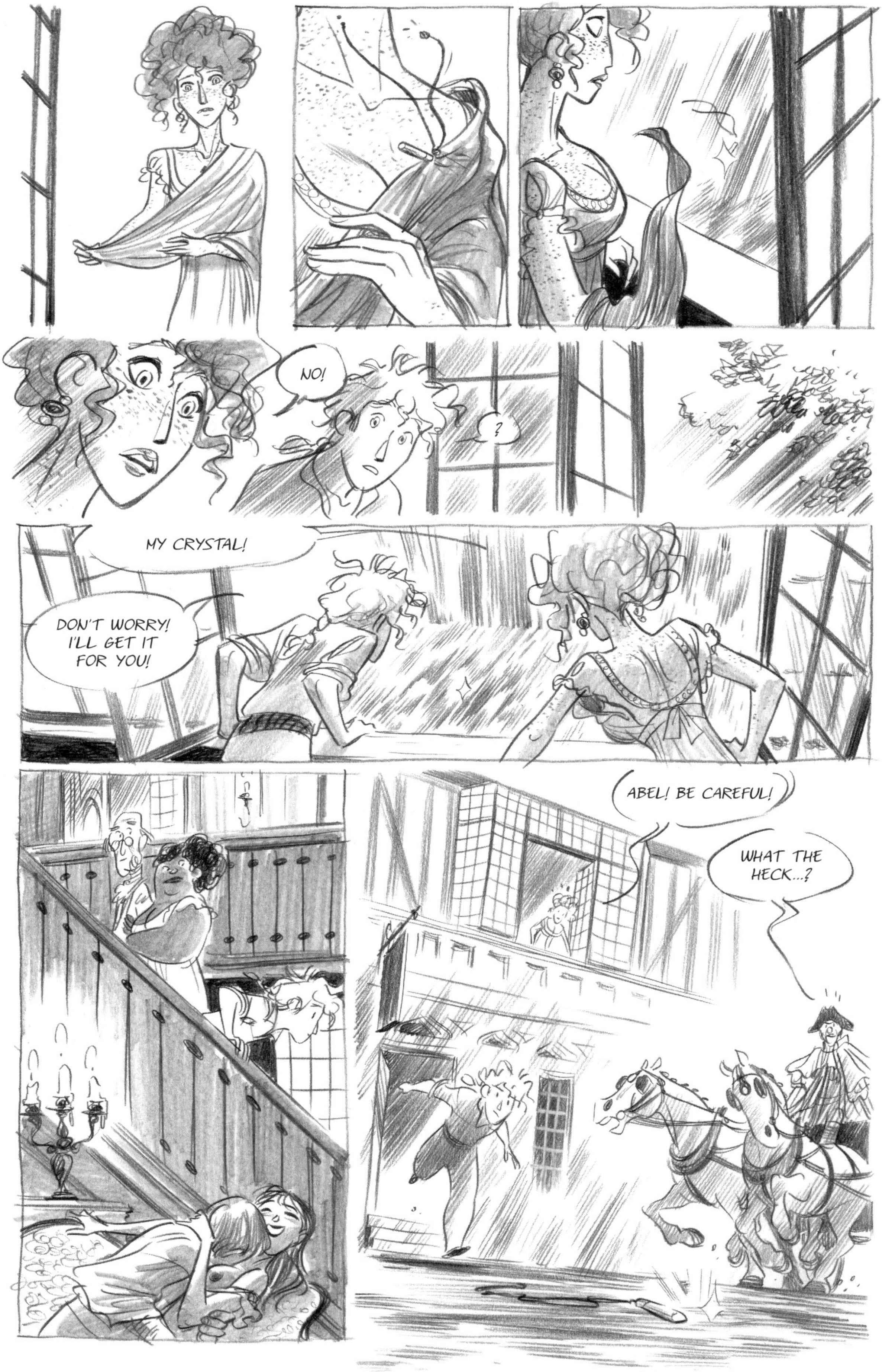
NO!
?
MY CRYSTAL!
DON'T WORRY! I'LL GET IT FOR YOU!
ABEL! BE CAREFUL!
WHAT THE HECK...?

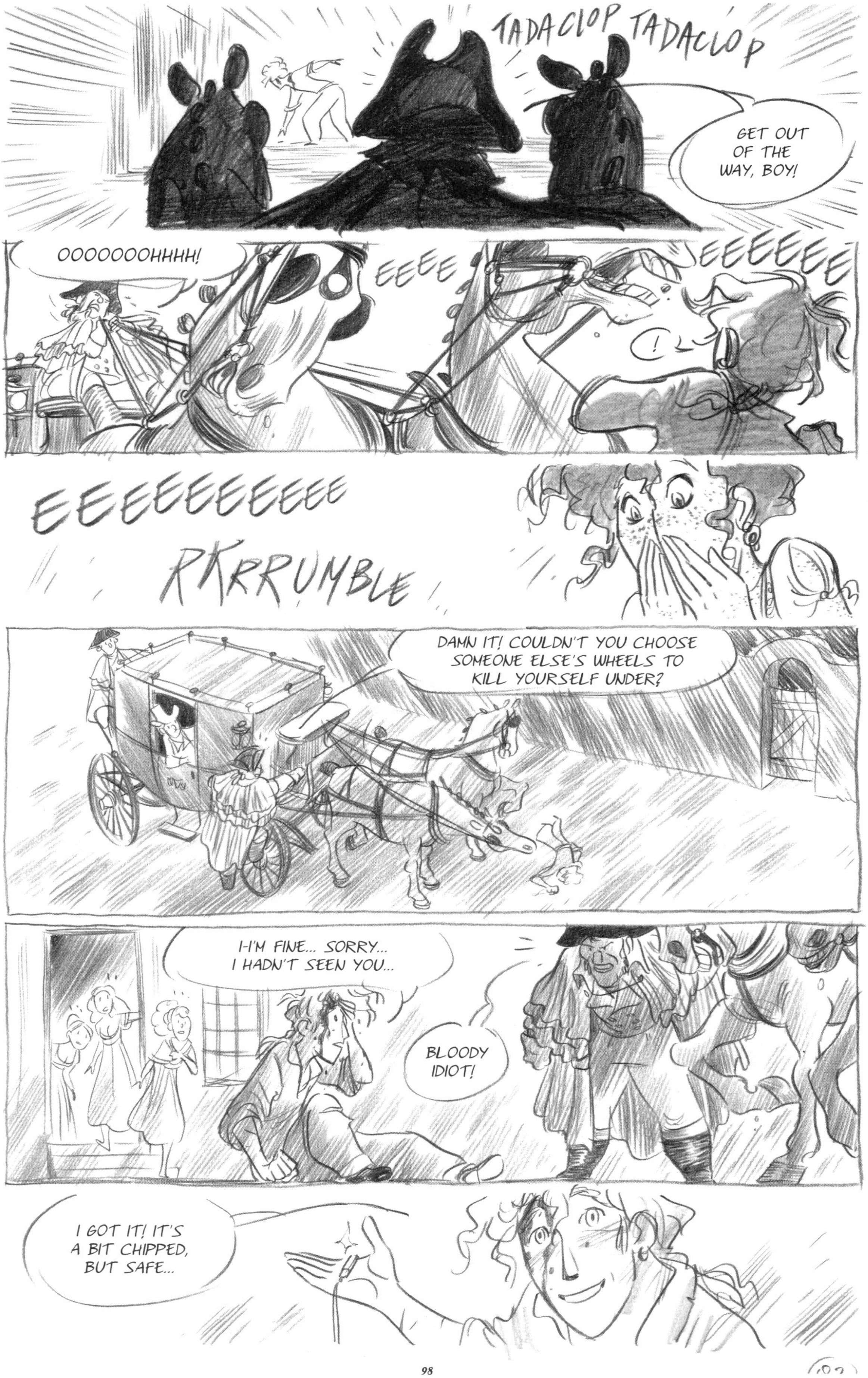
TADACLOP TADACLOP
GET OUT OF THE WAY, BOY!
OOOOOOOHHHH!
EEEE
EEEEEEE
EEEEEEEEEE
RKRRUMBLE
DAMN IT! COULDN'T YOU CHOOSE SOMEONE ELSE'S WHEELS TO KILL YOURSELF UNDER?
I-I'M FINE... SORRY... I HADN'T SEEN YOU...
BLOODY IDIOT!
I GOT IT! IT'S A BIT CHIPPED, BUT SAFE...

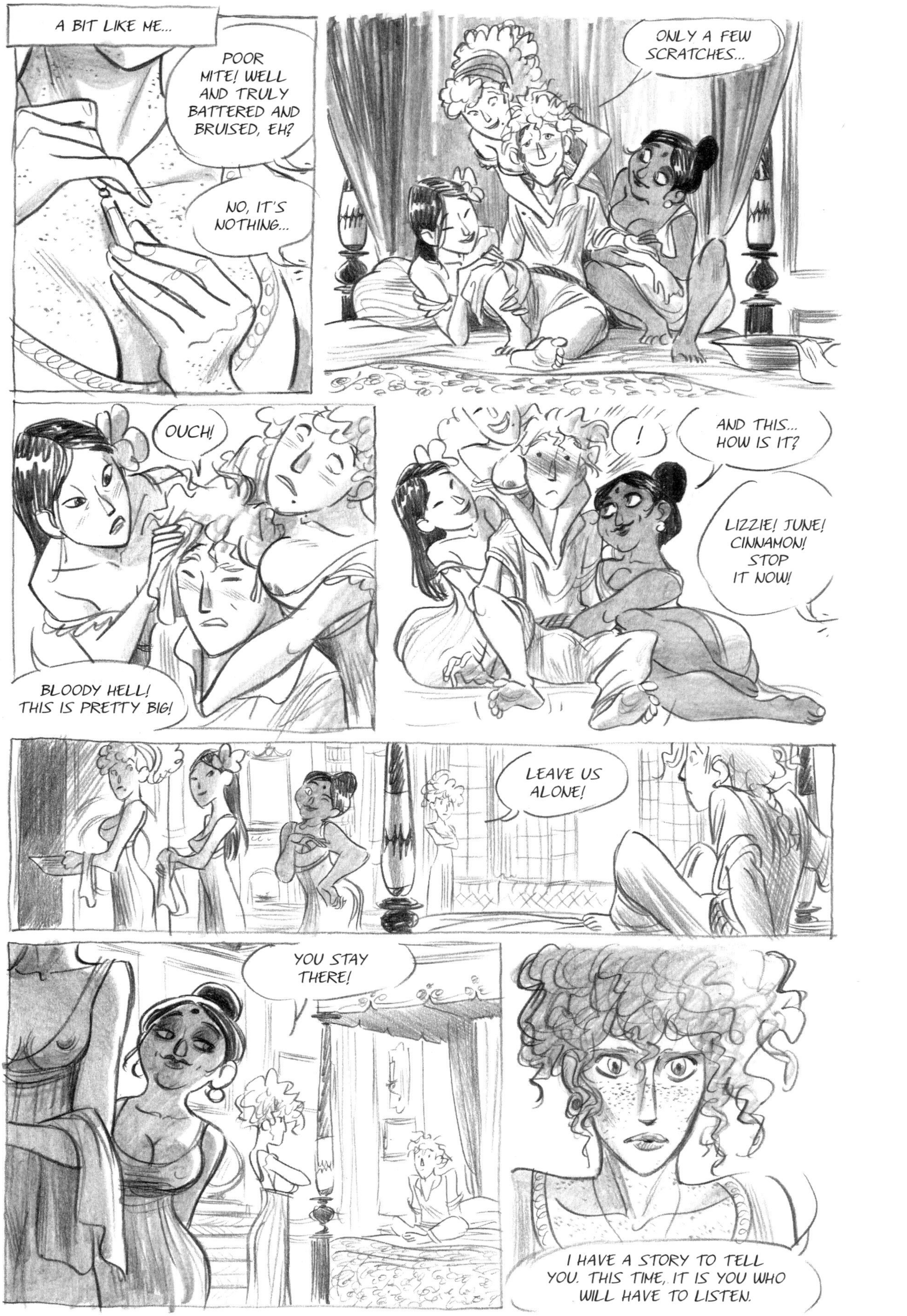

A BIT LIKE ME...
POOR MITE! WELL AND TRULY BATTERED AND BRUISED, EH?
NO, IT'S NOTHING...
ONLY A FEW SCRATCHES...
OUCH!
BLOODY HELL! THIS IS PRETTY BIG!
!
AND THIS... HOW IS IT?
LIZZIE! JUNE! CINNAMON! STOP IT NOW!
LEAVE US ALONE!
YOU STAY THERE!
I HAVE A STORY TO TELL YOU. THIS TIME, IT IS YOU WHO WILL HAVE TO LISTEN.

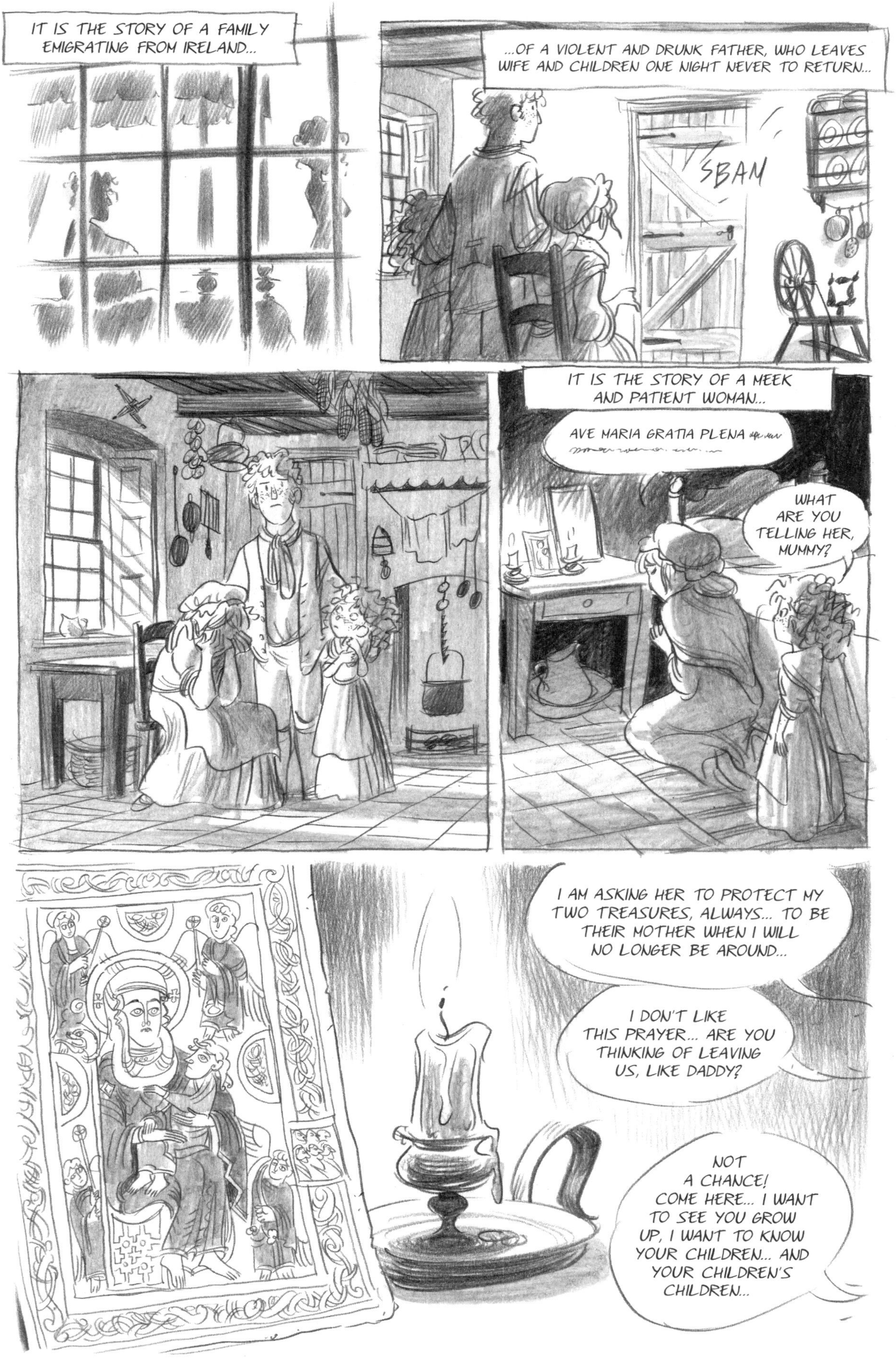

IT IS THE STORY OF A FAMILY EMIGRATING FROM IRELAND...
...OF A VIOLENT AND DRUNK FATHER, WHO LEAVES WIFE AND CHILDREN ONE NIGHT NEVER TO RETURN...
SBAM
IT IS THE STORY OF A MEEK AND PATIENT WOMAN...
AVE MARIA GRATIA PLENA
WHAT ARE YOU TELLING HER, MUMMY?
I AM ASKING HER TO PROTECT MY TWO TREASURES, ALWAYS... TO BE THEIR MOTHER WHEN I WILL NO LONGER BE AROUND...
I DON'T LIKE THIS PRAYER... ARE YOU THINKING OF LEAVING US, LIKE DADDY?
NOT A CHANCE! COME HERE... I WANT TO SEE YOU GROW UP, I WANT TO KNOW YOUR CHILDREN... AND YOUR CHILDREN'S CHILDREN...

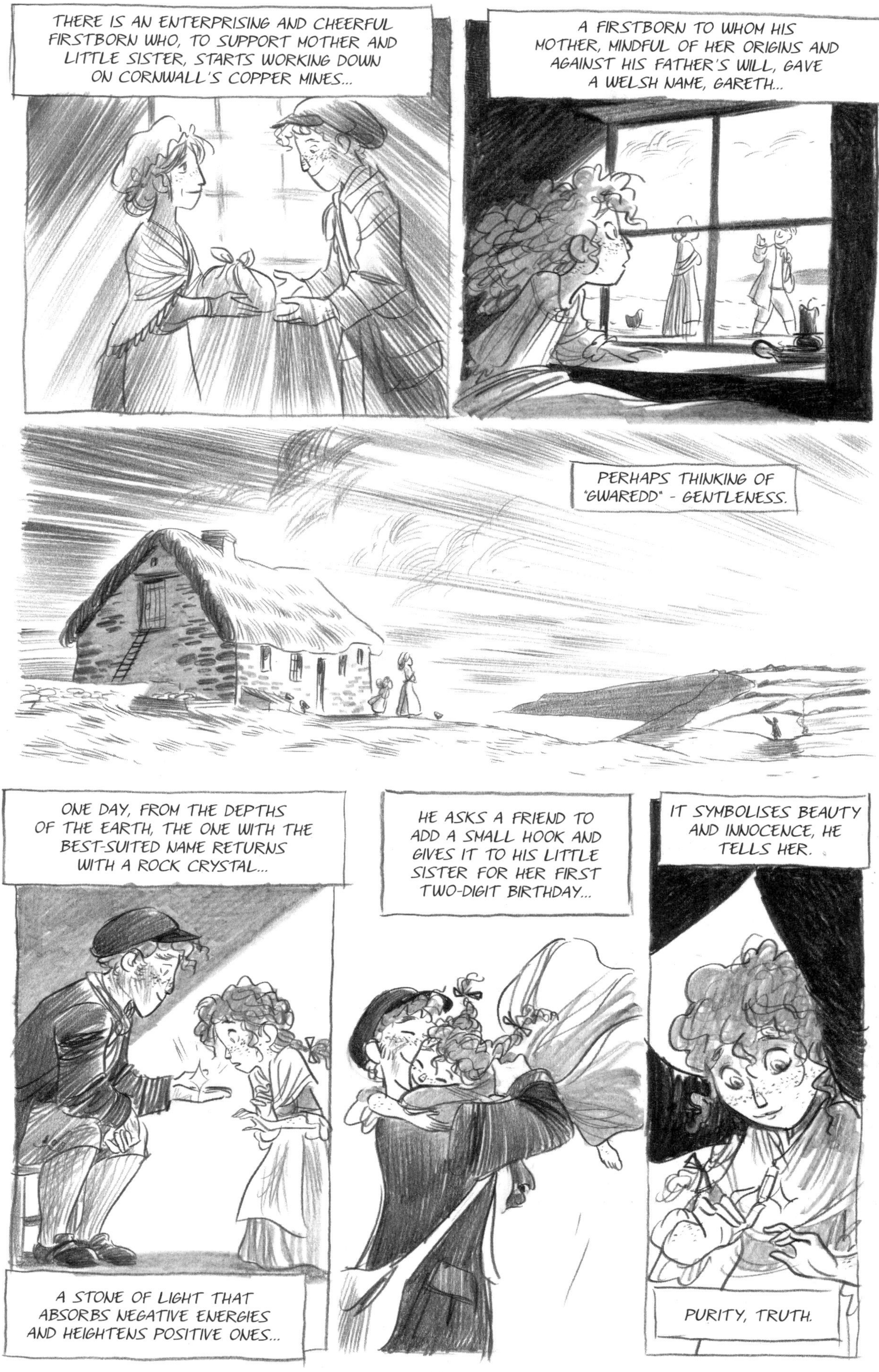
THERE IS AN ENTERPRISING AND CHEERFUL FIRSTBORN WHO, TO SUPPORT MOTHER AND LITTLE SISTER, STARTS WORKING DOWN ON CORNWALL'S COPPER MINES...
A FIRSTBORN TO WHOM HIS MOTHER, MINDFUL OF HER ORIGINS AND AGAINST HIS FATHER'S WILL, GAVE A WELSH NAME, GARETH...
PERHAPS THINKING OF "GWAREDD" - GENTLENESS.
ONE DAY, FROM THE DEPTHS OF THE EARTH, THE ONE WITH THE BEST-SUITED NAME RETURNS WITH A ROCK CRYSTAL...
A STONE OF LIGHT THAT ABSORBS NEGATIVE ENERGIES AND HEIGHTENS POSITIVE ONES...
HE ASKS A FRIEND TO ADD A SMALL HOOK AND GIVES IT TO HIS LITTLE SISTER FOR HER FIRST TWO-DIGIT BIRTHDAY...
IT SYMBOLISES BEAUTY AND INNOCENCE, HE TELLS HER.
PURITY, TRUTH.

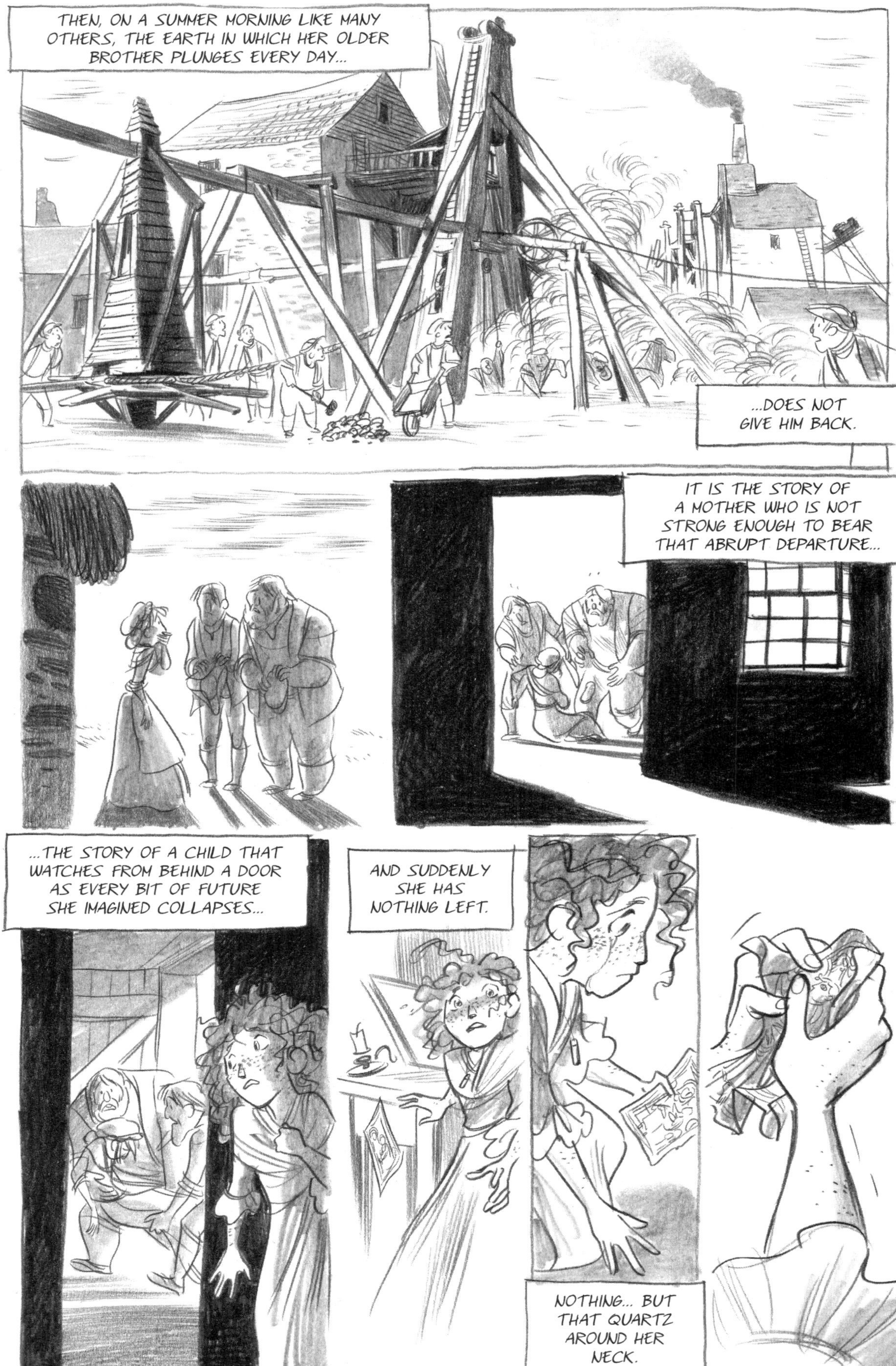
THEN, ON A SUMMER MORNING LIKE MANY OTHERS, THE EARTH IN WHICH HER OLDER BROTHER PLUNGES EVERY DAY...
...DOES NOT GIVE HIM BACK.
IT IS THE STORY OF A MOTHER WHO IS NOT STRONG ENOUGH TO BEAR THAT ABRUPT DEPARTURE...
...THE STORY OF A CHILD THAT WATCHES FROM BEHIND A DOOR AS EVERY BIT OF FUTURE SHE IMAGINED COLLAPSES...
AND SUDDENLY SHE HAS NOTHING LEFT.
NOTHING... BUT THAT QUARTZ AROUND HER NECK.

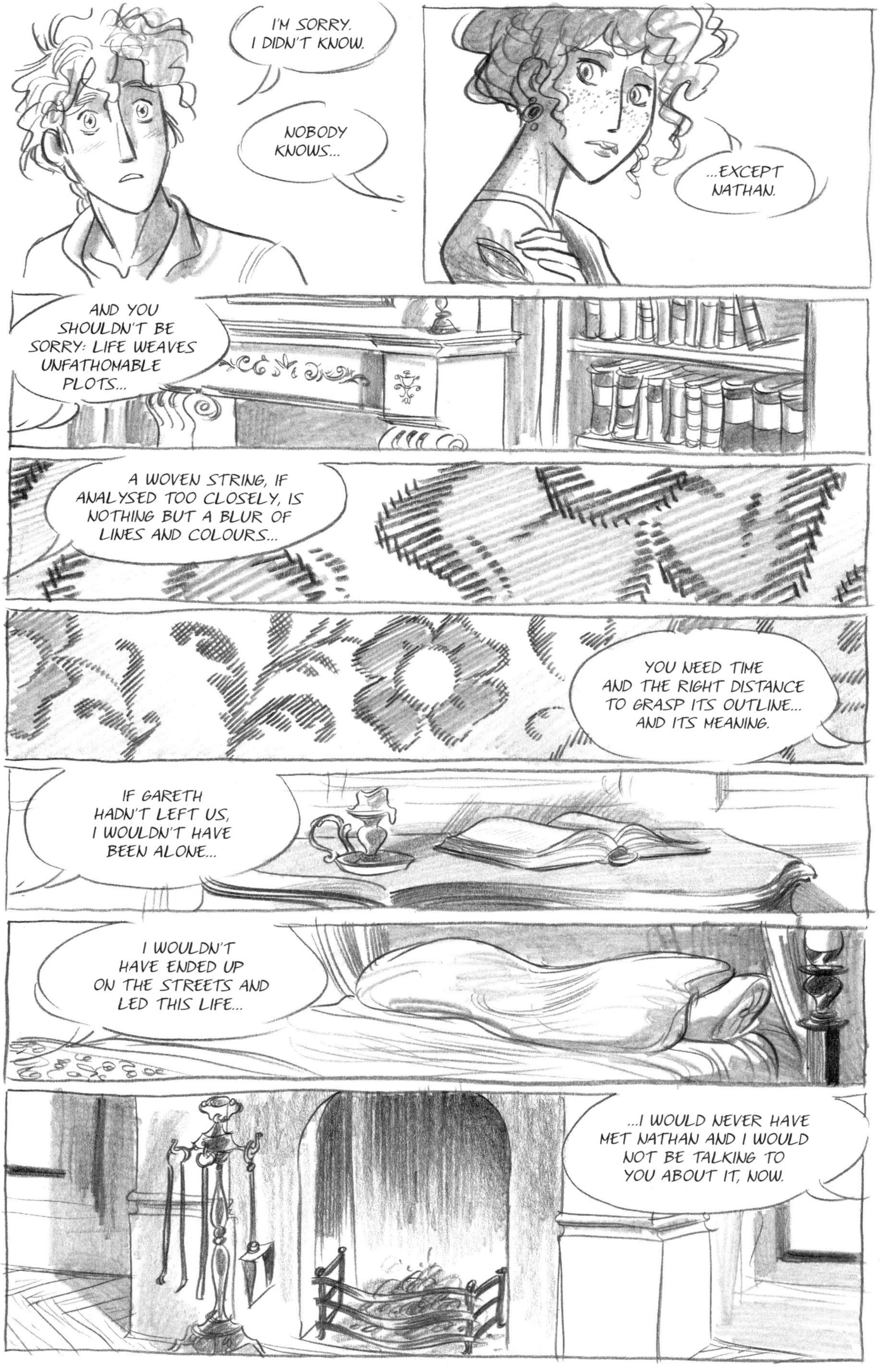
I'M SORRY. I DIDN'T KNOW.
NOBODY KNOWS...
...EXCEPT NATHAN.
AND YOU SHOULDN'T BE SORRY: LIFE WEAVES UNFATHOMABLE PLOTS...
A WOVEN STRING, IF ANALYSED TOO CLOSELY, IS NOTHING BUT A BLUR OF LINES AND COLOURS...
YOU NEED TIME AND THE RIGHT DISTANCE TO GRASP ITS OUTLINE... AND ITS MEANING.
IF GARETH HADN'T LEFT US, I WOULDN'T HAVE BEEN ALONE...
I WOULDN'T HAVE ENDED UP ON THE STREETS AND LED THIS LIFE...
...I WOULD NEVER HAVE MET NATHAN AND I WOULD NOT BE TALKING TO YOU ABOUT IT, NOW.

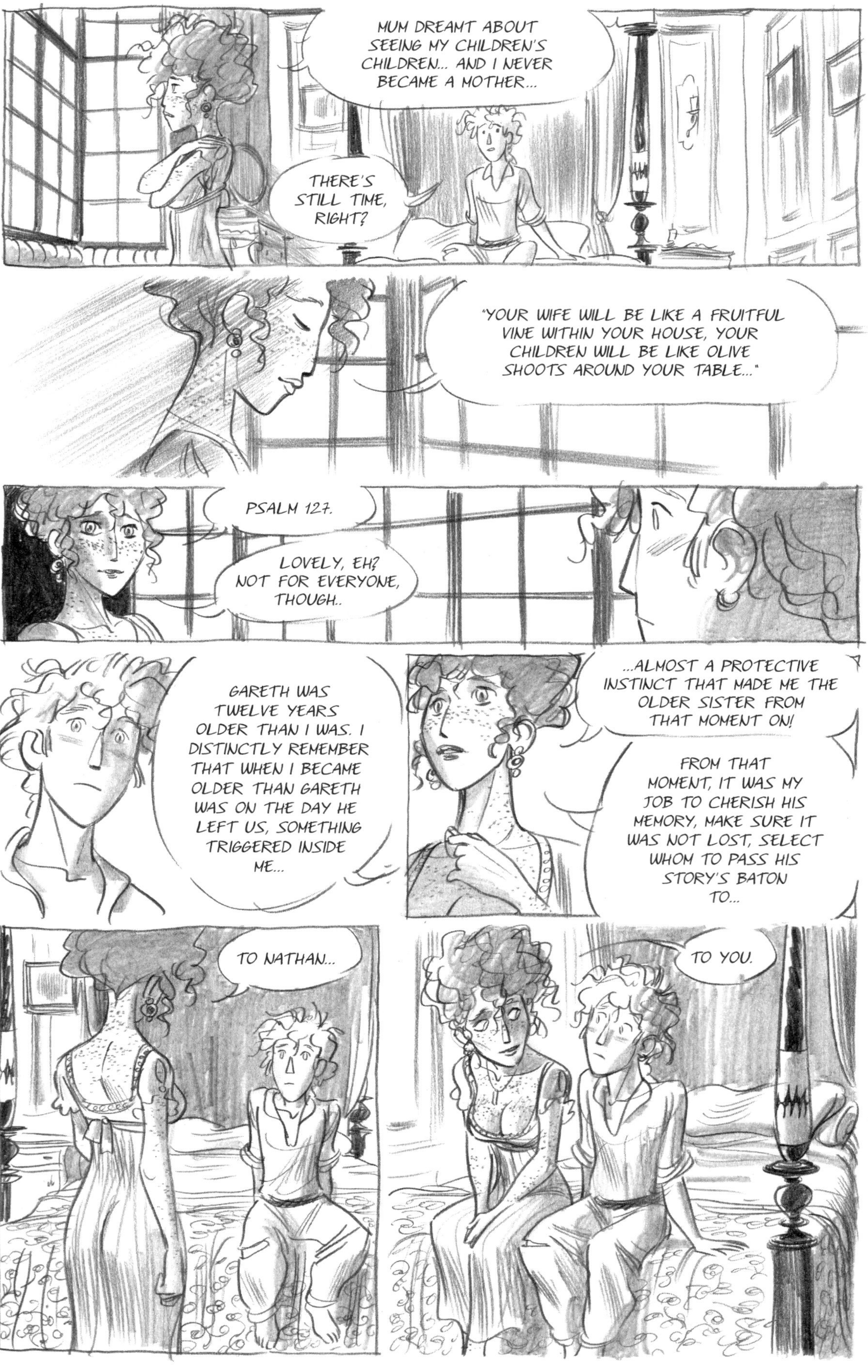
MUM DREAMT ABOUT SEEING MY CHILDREN'S CHILDREN... AND I NEVER BECAME A MOTHER...
THERE'S STILL TIME, RIGHT?
"YOUR WIFE WILL BE LIKE A FRUITFUL VINE WITHIN YOUR HOUSE, YOUR CHILDREN WILL BE LIKE OLIVE SHOOTS AROUND YOUR TABLE..."
PSALM 127.
LOVELY, EH? NOT FOR EVERYONE, THOUGH..
GARETH WAS TWELVE YEARS OLDER THAN I WAS. I DISTINCTLY REMEMBER THAT WHEN I BECAME OLDER THAN GARETH WAS ON THE DAY HE LEFT US, SOMETHING TRIGGERED INSIDE ME...
...ALMOST A PROTECTIVE INSTINCT THAT MADE ME THE OLDER SISTER FROM THAT MOMENT ON!
FROM THAT MOMENT, IT WAS MY JOB TO CHERISH HIS MEMORY, MAKE SURE IT WAS NOT LOST, SELECT WHOM TO PASS HIS STORY'S BATON TO...
TO NATHAN...
TO YOU.

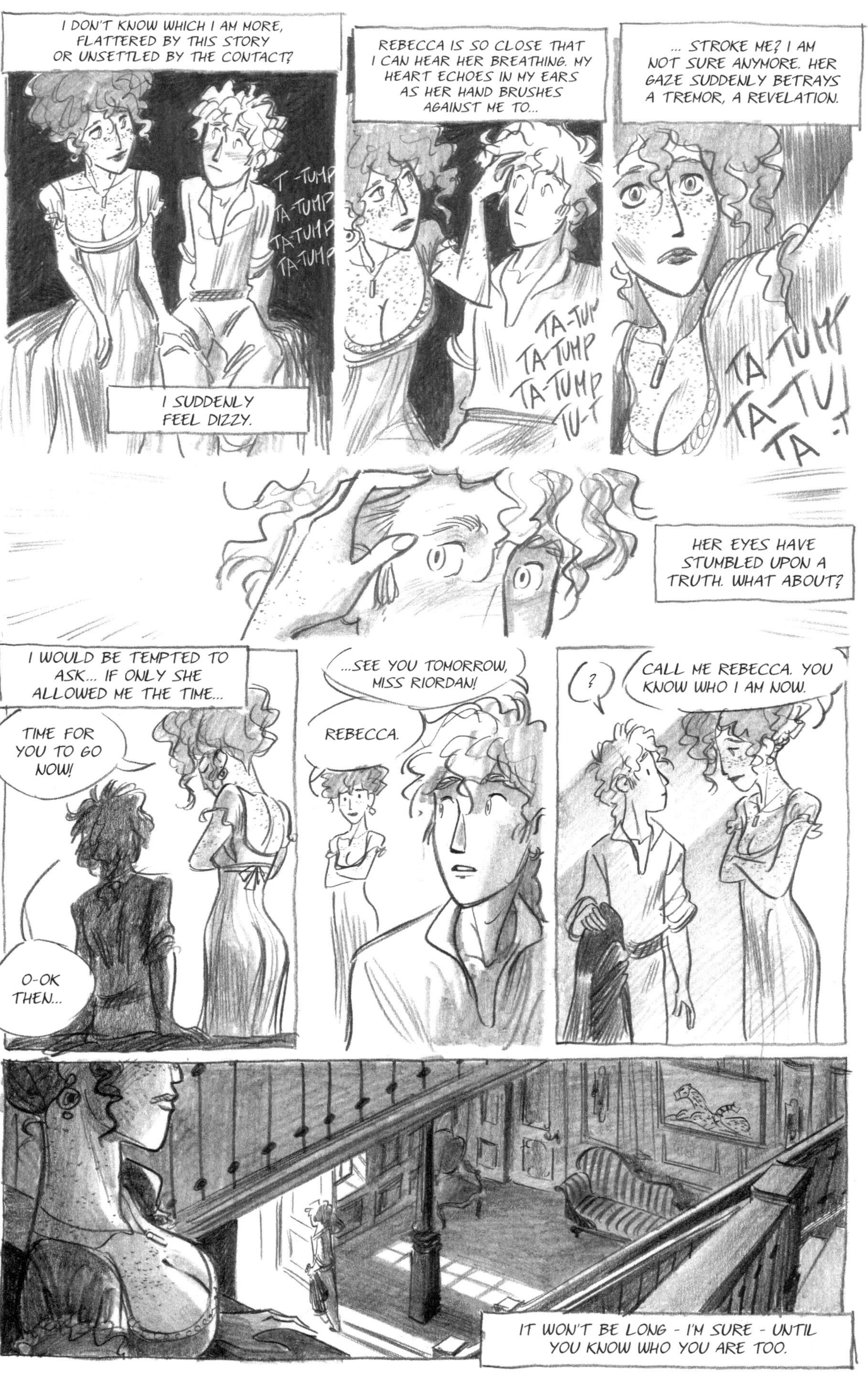
I DON'T KNOW WHICH I AM MORE, FLATTERED BY THIS STORY OR UNSETTLED BY THE CONTACT?
T-TUMP TA-TUMP TA-TUMP TA-TUMP
I SUDDENLY FEEL DIZZY.
REBECCA IS SO CLOSE THAT I CAN HEAR HER BREATHING. MY HEART ECHOES IN MY EARS AS HER HAND BRUSHES AGAINST ME TO...
TA-TUMP TA-TUMP TA-TUMP TU-T
... STROKE ME? I AM NOT SURE ANYMORE. HER GAZE SUDDENLY BETRAYS A TREMOR, A REVELATION.
HER EYES HAVE STUMBLED UPON A TRUTH. WHAT ABOUT?
I WOULD BE TEMPTED TO ASK... IF ONLY SHE ALLOWED ME THE TIME...
TIME FOR YOU TO GO NOW!
O-OK THEN...
...SEE YOU TOMORROW, MISS RIORDAN!
REBECCA.
?
CALL ME REBECCA. YOU KNOW WHO I AM NOW.
IT WON'T BE LONG - I'M SURE - UNTIL YOU KNOW WHO YOU ARE TOO.

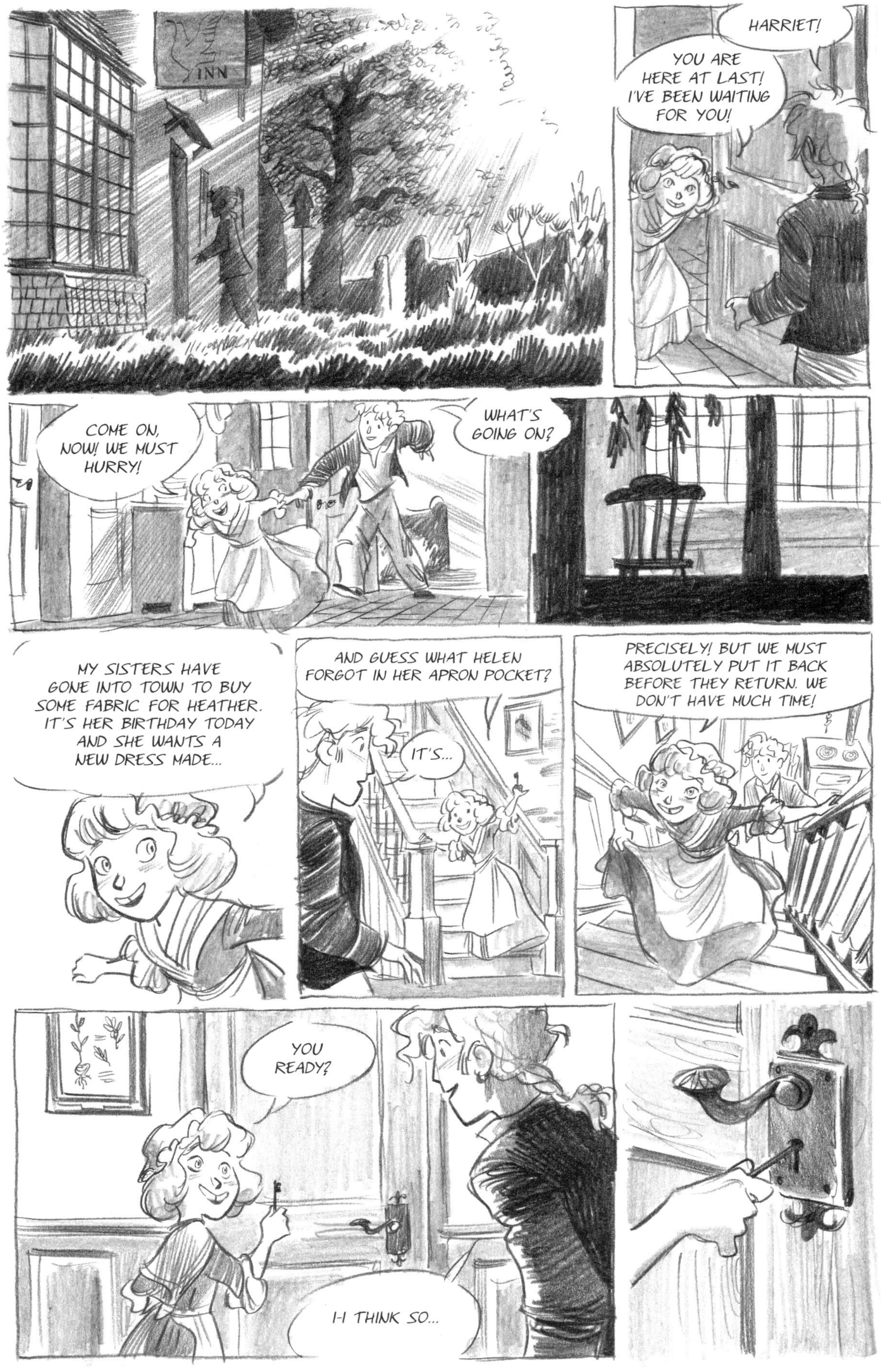
INN
HARRIET!
YOU ARE HERE AT LAST! I'VE BEEN WAITING FOR YOU!
COME ON, NOW! WE MUST HURRY!
WHAT'S GOING ON?
MY SISTERS HAVE GONE INTO TOWN TO BUY SOME FABRIC FOR HEATHER. IT'S HER BIRTHDAY TODAY AND SHE WANTS A NEW DRESS MADE...
AND GUESS WHAT HELEN FORGOT IN HER APRON POCKET?
IT'S...
PRECISELY! BUT WE MUST ABSOLUTELY PUT IT BACK BEFORE THEY RETURN. WE DON'T HAVE MUCH TIME!
YOU READY?
I-I THINK SO...

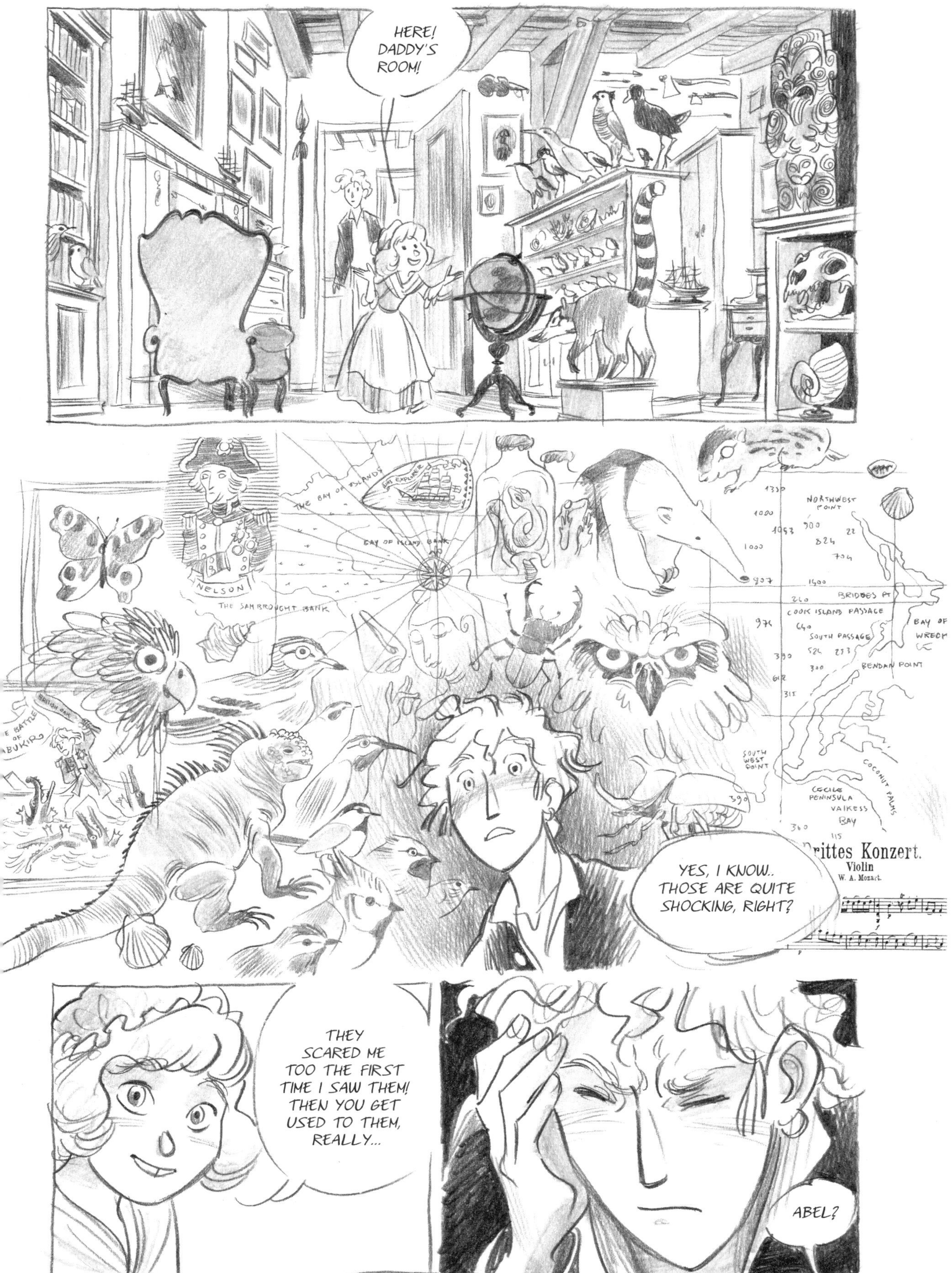
HERE! DADDY'S ROOM!
NELSON
THE BAY OF ISLANDS
BAY OF ISLAND BANK
THE SAMBROUGHT BANK
NORTHWEST POINT
BRIDGES PT
COOK ISLAND PASSAGE
SOUTH PASSAGE
BENDAN POINT
SOUTH WEST POINT
CECILE PENINSULA
VAIKESS BAY
COCONUT PALMS
rittes Konzert.
Violin
W. A. Mozart.
YES, I KNOW.. THOSE ARE QUITE SHOCKING, RIGHT?
THEY SCARED ME TOO THE FIRST TIME I SAW THEM! THEN YOU GET USED TO THEM, REALLY...
ABEL?

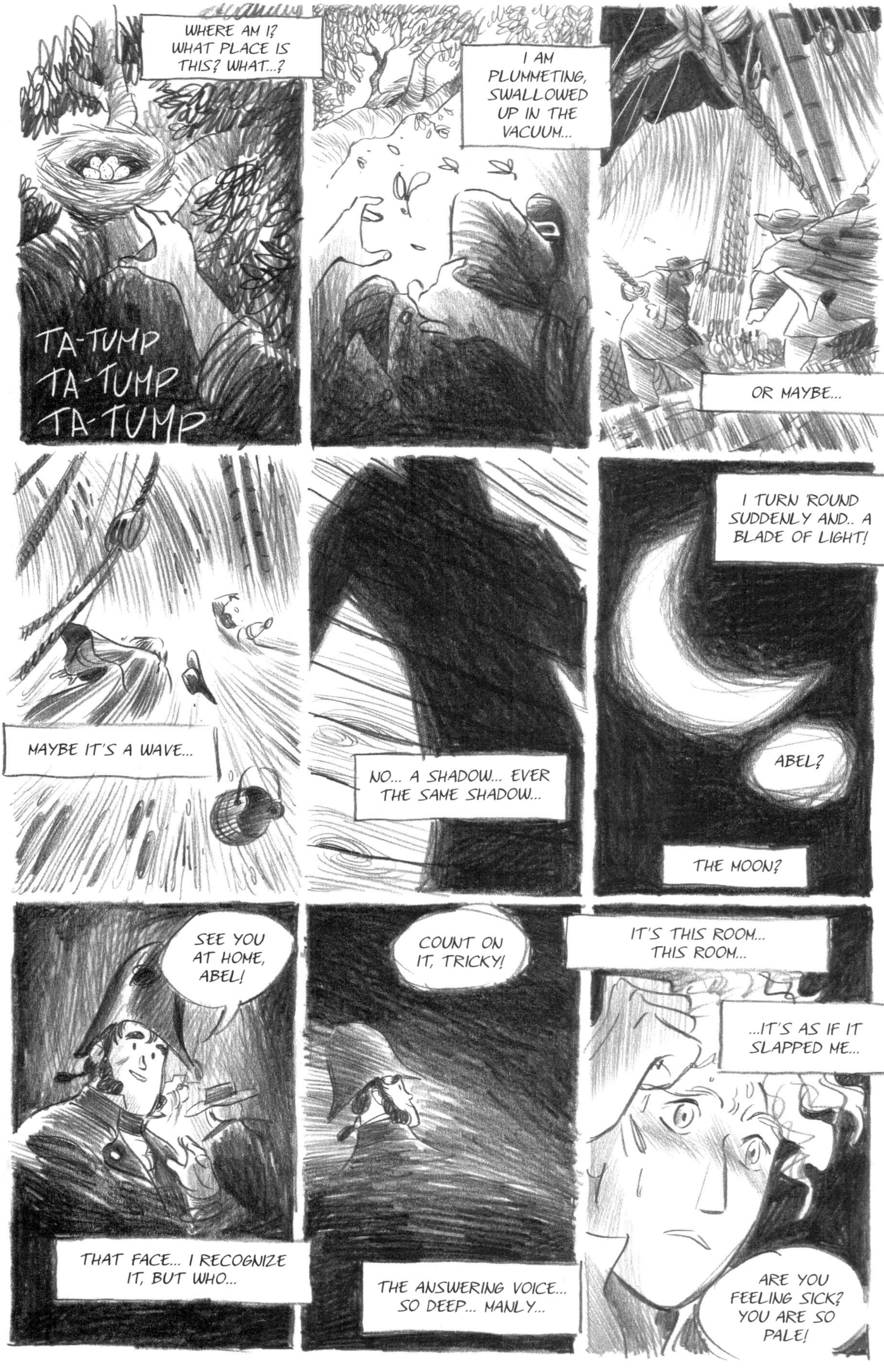

WHERE AM I? WHAT PLACE IS THIS? WHAT...?
TA-TUMP TA-TUMP TA-TUMP
I AM PLUMMETING, SWALLOWED UP IN THE VACUUM...
OR MAYBE...
MAYBE IT'S A WAVE...
NO... A SHADOW... EVER THE SAME SHADOW...
I TURN ROUND SUDDENLY AND.. A BLADE OF LIGHT!
ABEL?
THE MOON?
SEE YOU AT HOME, ABEL!
THAT FACE... I RECOGNIZE IT, BUT WHO...
COUNT ON IT, TRICKY!
THE ANSWERING VOICE... SO DEEP... MANLY...
IT'S THIS ROOM... THIS ROOM...
...IT'S AS IF IT SLAPPED ME...
ARE YOU FEELING SICK? YOU ARE SO PALE!

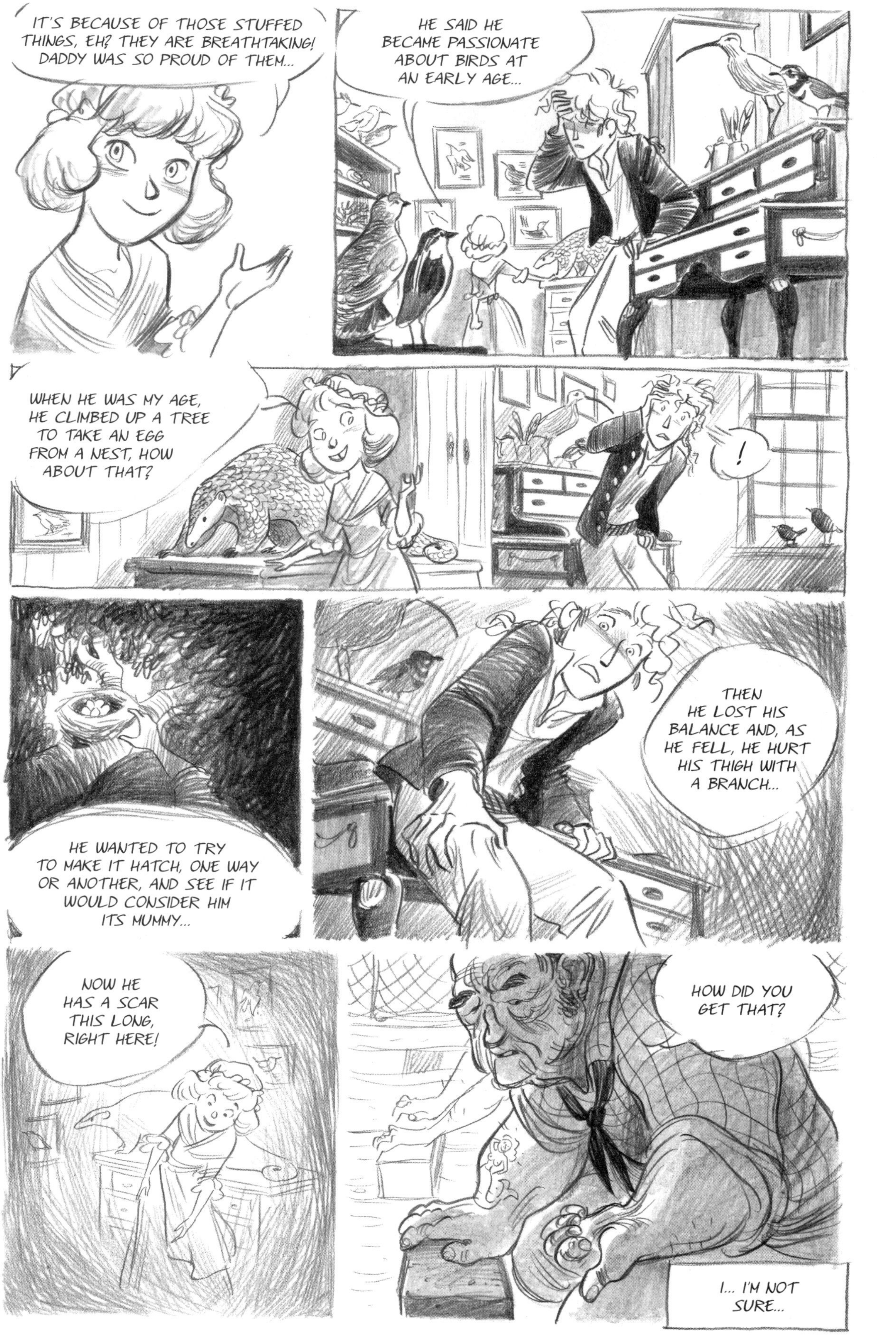
IT'S BECAUSE OF THOSE STUFFED THINGS, EH? THEY ARE BREATHTAKING! DADDY WAS SO PROUD OF THEM...
HE SAID HE BECAME PASSIONATE ABOUT BIRDS AT AN EARLY AGE...
WHEN HE WAS MY AGE, HE CLIMBED UP A TREE TO TAKE AN EGG FROM A NEST, HOW ABOUT THAT?
!
HE WANTED TO TRY TO MAKE IT HATCH, ONE WAY OR ANOTHER, AND SEE IF IT WOULD CONSIDER HIM ITS MUMMY...
THEN HE LOST HIS BALANCE AND, AS HE FELL, HE HURT HIS THIGH WITH A BRANCH...
NOW HE HAS A SCAR THIS LONG, RIGHT HERE!
HOW DID YOU GET THAT?
I... I'M NOT SURE...

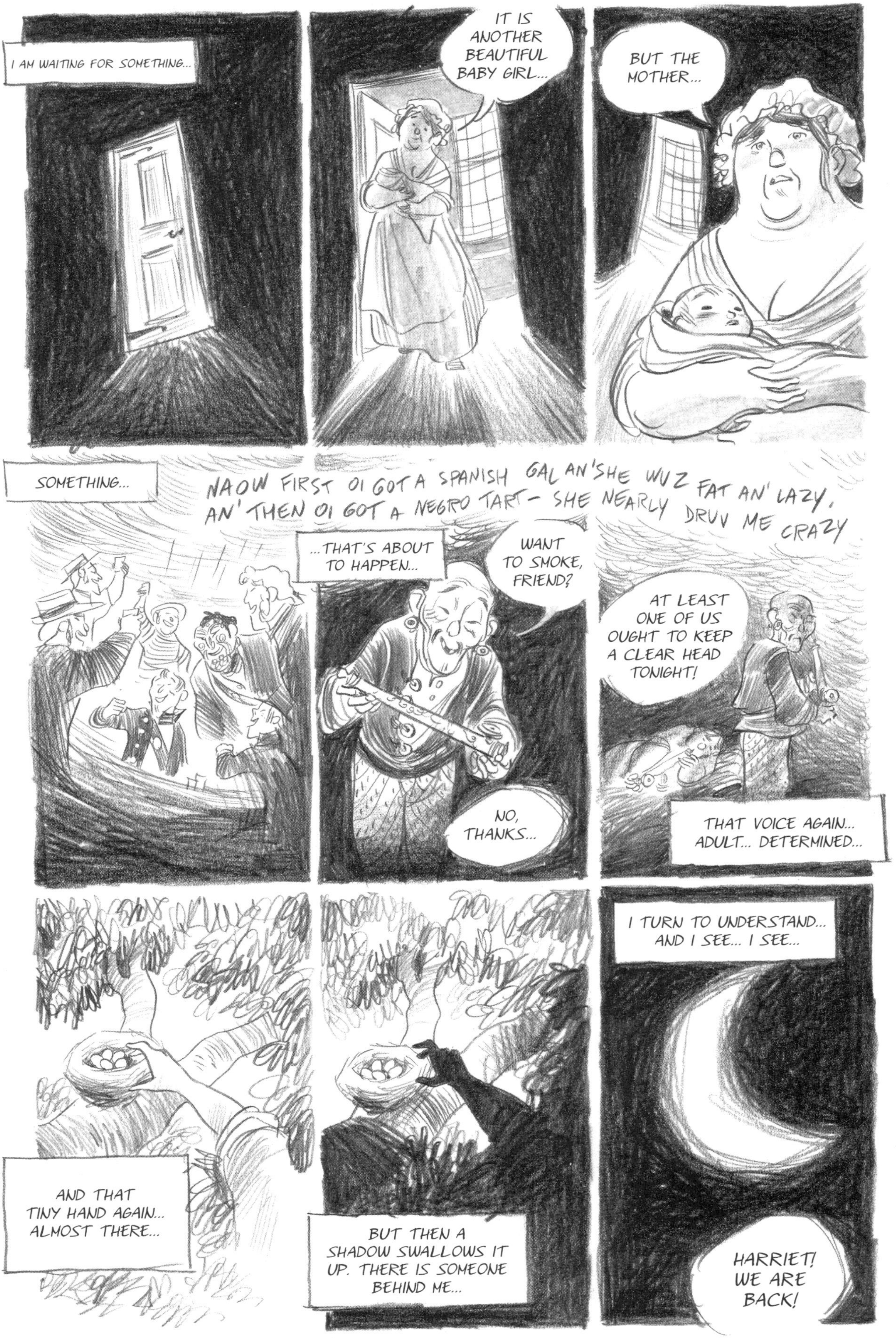
I AM WAITING FOR SOMETHING...
IT IS ANOTHER BEAUTIFUL BABY GIRL...
BUT THE MOTHER...
SOMETHING...
NAOW FIRST OI GOT A SPANISH GAL AN'SHE WUZ FAT AN' LAZY, AN' THEN OI GOT A NEGRO TART – SHE NEARLY DRUV ME CRAZY
...THAT'S ABOUT TO HAPPEN...
WANT TO SMOKE, FRIEND?
NO, THANKS...
AT LEAST ONE OF US OUGHT TO KEEP A CLEAR HEAD TONIGHT!
THAT VOICE AGAIN... ADULT... DETERMINED...
AND THAT TINY HAND AGAIN... ALMOST THERE...
BUT THEN A SHADOW SWALLOWS IT UP. THERE IS SOMEONE BEHIND ME...
I TURN TO UNDERSTAND... AND I SEE... I SEE...
HARRIET! WE ARE BACK!

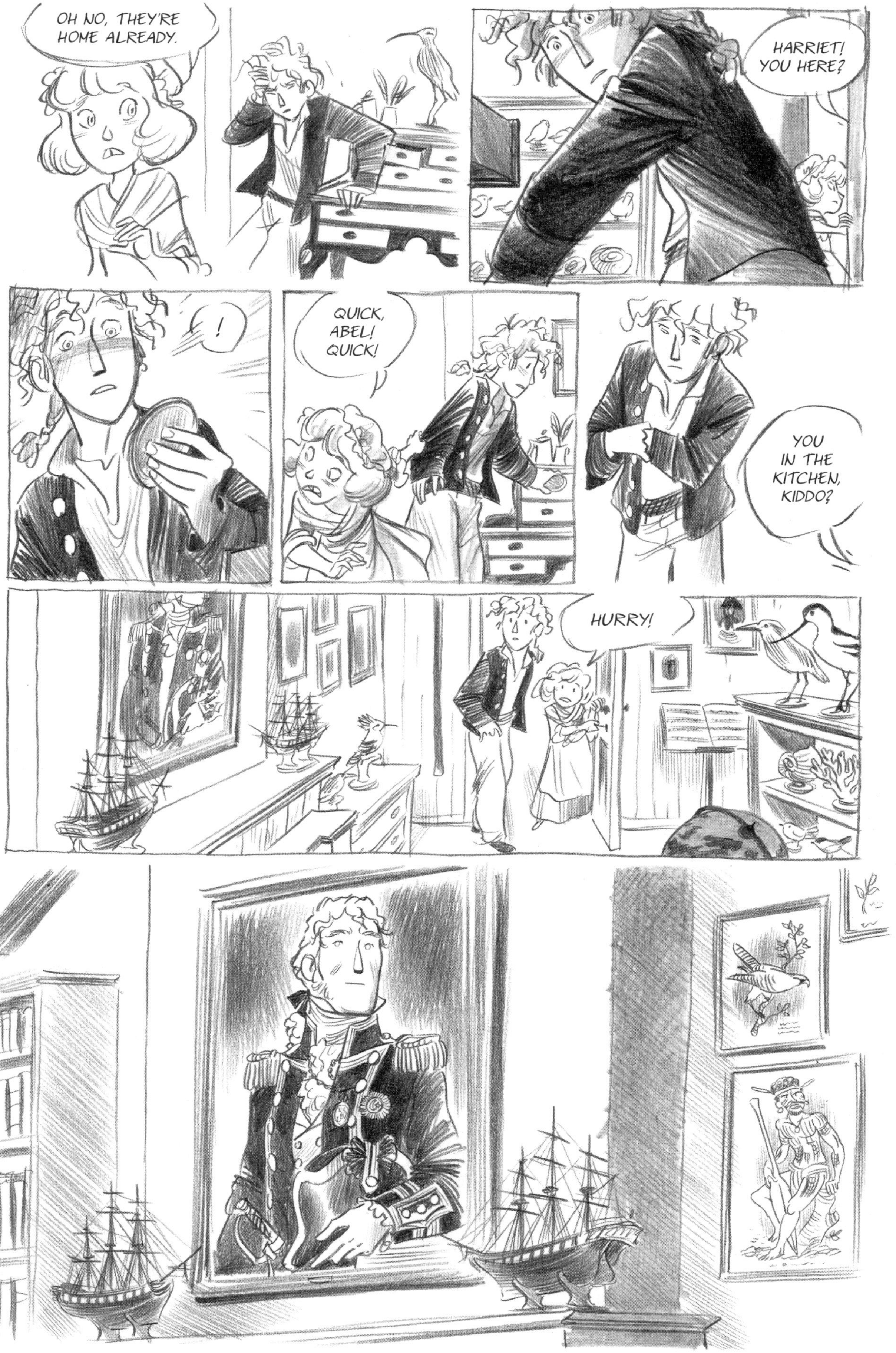
OH NO, THEY'RE HOME ALREADY.
HARRIET! YOU HERE?
!
QUICK, ABEL! QUICK!
YOU IN THE KITCHEN, KIDDO?
HURRY!

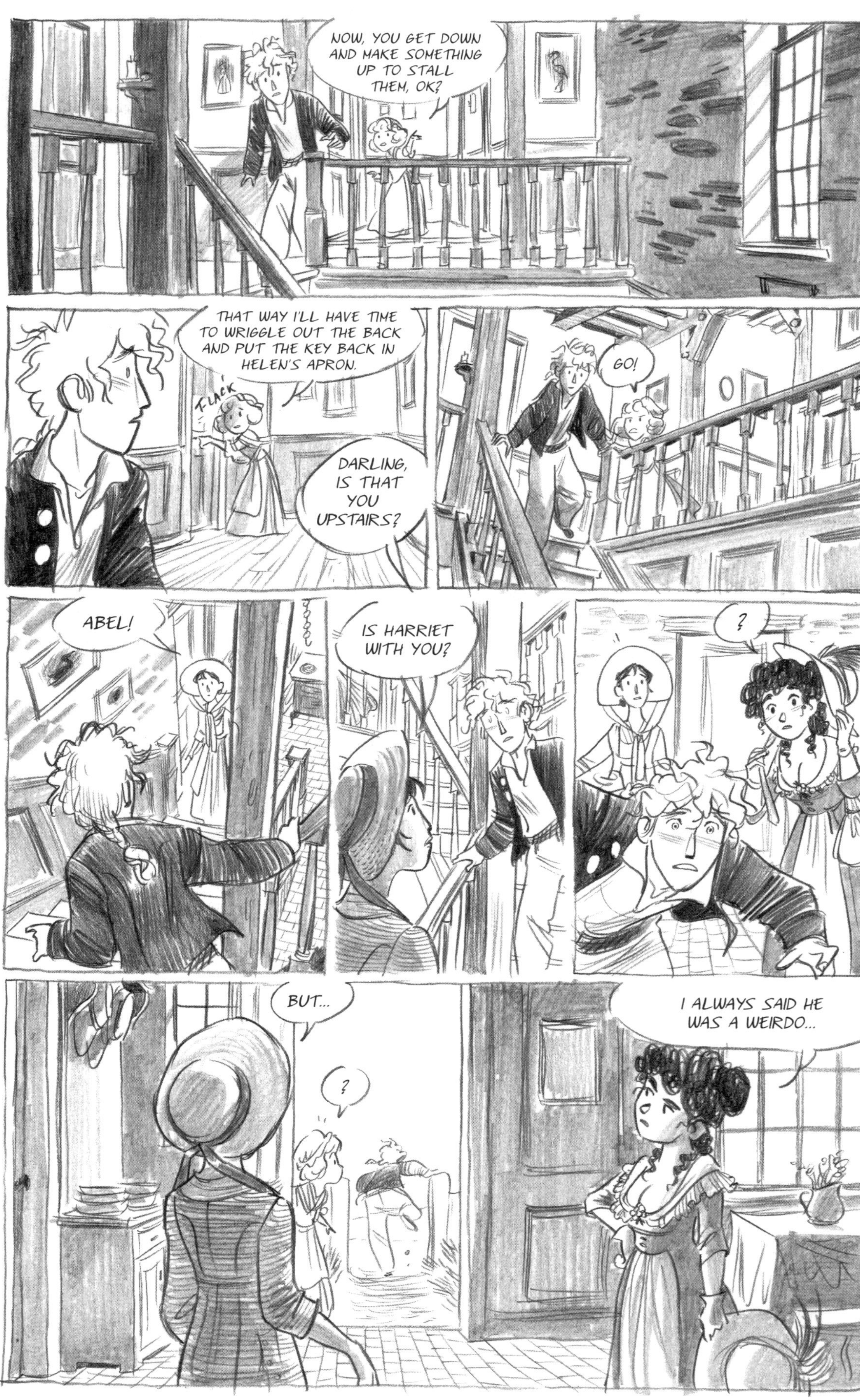
NOW, YOU GET DOWN AND MAKE SOMETHING UP TO STALL THEM, OK?
THAT WAY I'LL HAVE TIME TO WRIGGLE OUT THE BACK AND PUT THE KEY BACK IN HELEN'S APRON.
FLACK
DARLING, IS THAT YOU UPSTAIRS?
GO!
ABEL!
IS HARRIET WITH YOU?
?
BUT...
?
I ALWAYS SAID HE WAS A WEIRDO...

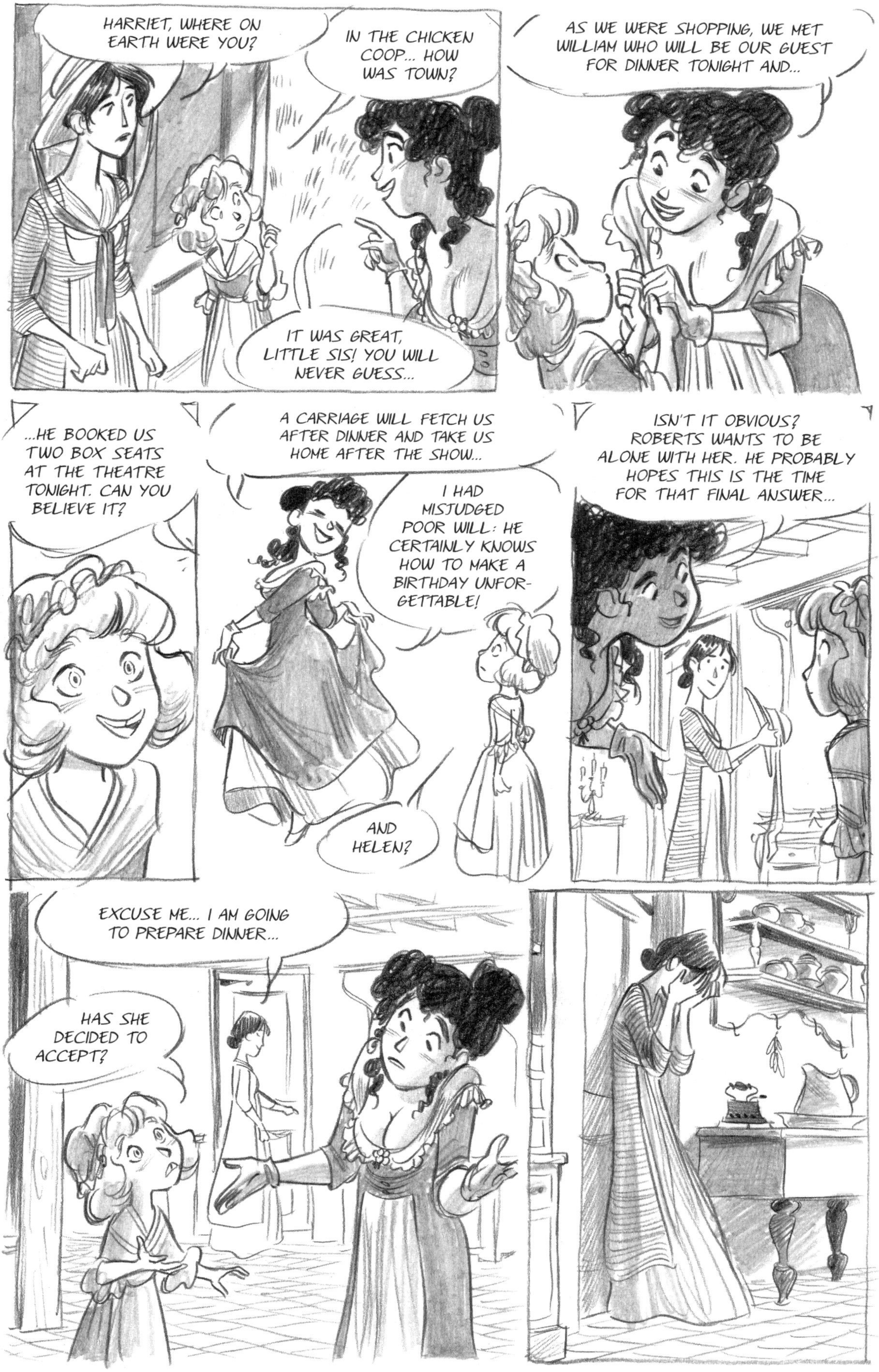
HARRIET, WHERE ON EARTH WERE YOU?
IN THE CHICKEN COOP... HOW WAS TOWN?
IT WAS GREAT, LITTLE SIS! YOU WILL NEVER GUESS...
AS WE WERE SHOPPING, WE MET WILLIAM WHO WILL BE OUR GUEST FOR DINNER TONIGHT AND...
...HE BOOKED US TWO BOX SEATS AT THE THEATRE TONIGHT. CAN YOU BELIEVE IT?
A CARRIAGE WILL FETCH US AFTER DINNER AND TAKE US HOME AFTER THE SHOW...
I HAD MISJUDGED POOR WILL: HE CERTAINLY KNOWS HOW TO MAKE A BIRTHDAY UNFOR-GETTABLE!
AND HELEN?
ISN'T IT OBVIOUS? ROBERTS WANTS TO BE ALONE WITH HER. HE PROBABLY HOPES THIS IS THE TIME FOR THAT FINAL ANSWER...
EXCUSE ME... I AM GOING TO PREPARE DINNER...
HAS SHE DECIDED TO ACCEPT?

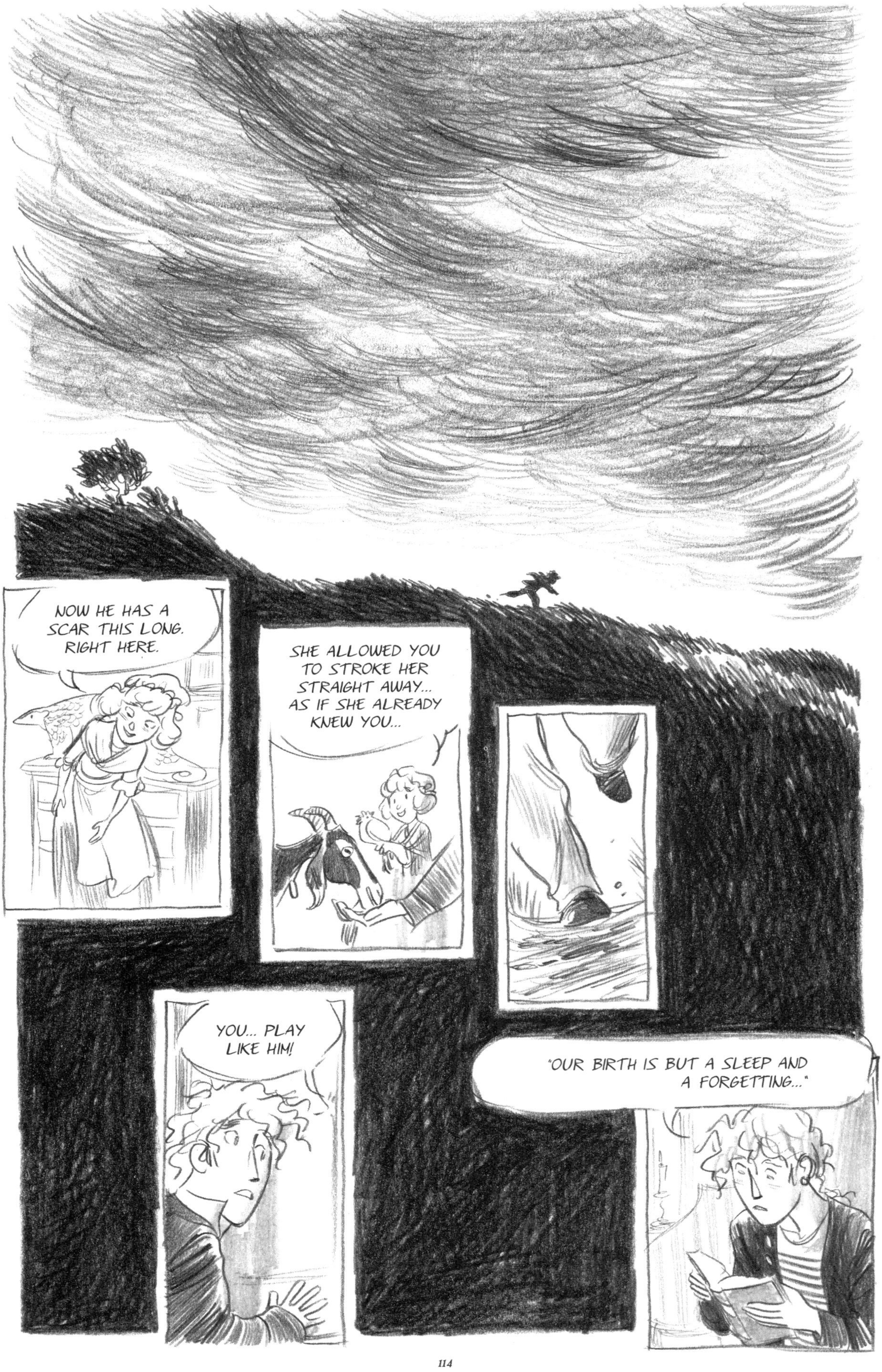
NOW HE HAS A SCAR THIS LONG. RIGHT HERE.
SHE ALLOWED YOU TO STROKE HER STRAIGHT AWAY... AS IF SHE ALREADY KNEW YOU...
YOU... PLAY LIKE HIM!
"OUR BIRTH IS BUT A SLEEP AND A FORGETTING..."

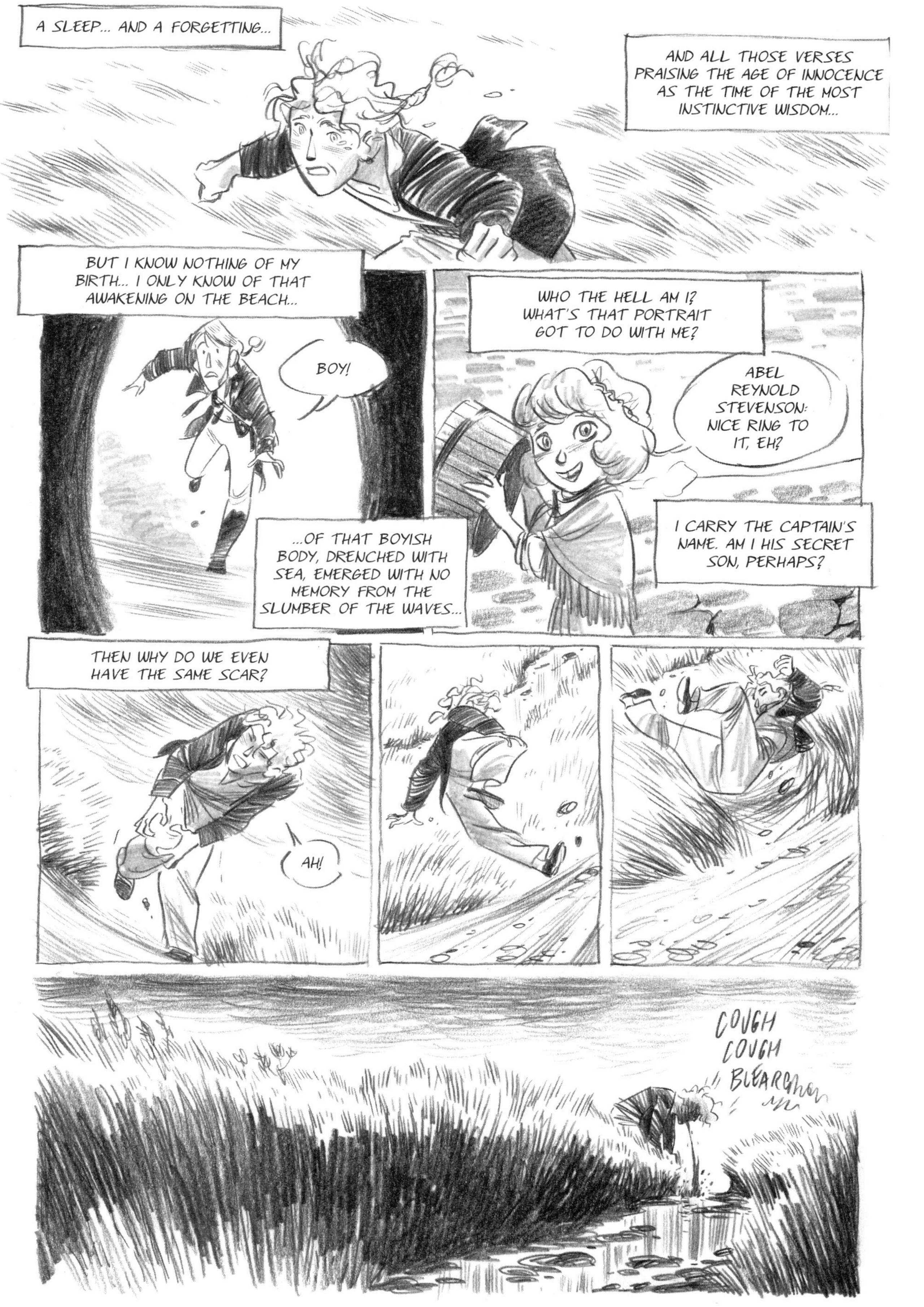
A SLEEP... AND A FORGETTING...
AND ALL THOSE VERSES PRAISING THE AGE OF INNOCENCE AS THE TIME OF THE MOST INSTINCTIVE WISDOM...
BUT I KNOW NOTHING OF MY BIRTH... I ONLY KNOW OF THAT AWAKENING ON THE BEACH...
BOY!
...OF THAT BOYISH BODY, DRENCHED WITH SEA, EMERGED WITH NO MEMORY FROM THE SLUMBER OF THE WAVES...
WHO THE HELL AM I? WHAT'S THAT PORTRAIT GOT TO DO WITH ME?
ABEL REYNOLD STEVENSON: NICE RING TO IT, EH?
I CARRY THE CAPTAIN'S NAME. AM I HIS SECRET SON, PERHAPS?
THEN WHY DO WE EVEN HAVE THE SAME SCAR?
AH!
COUGH
COUGH
BLEARGHH

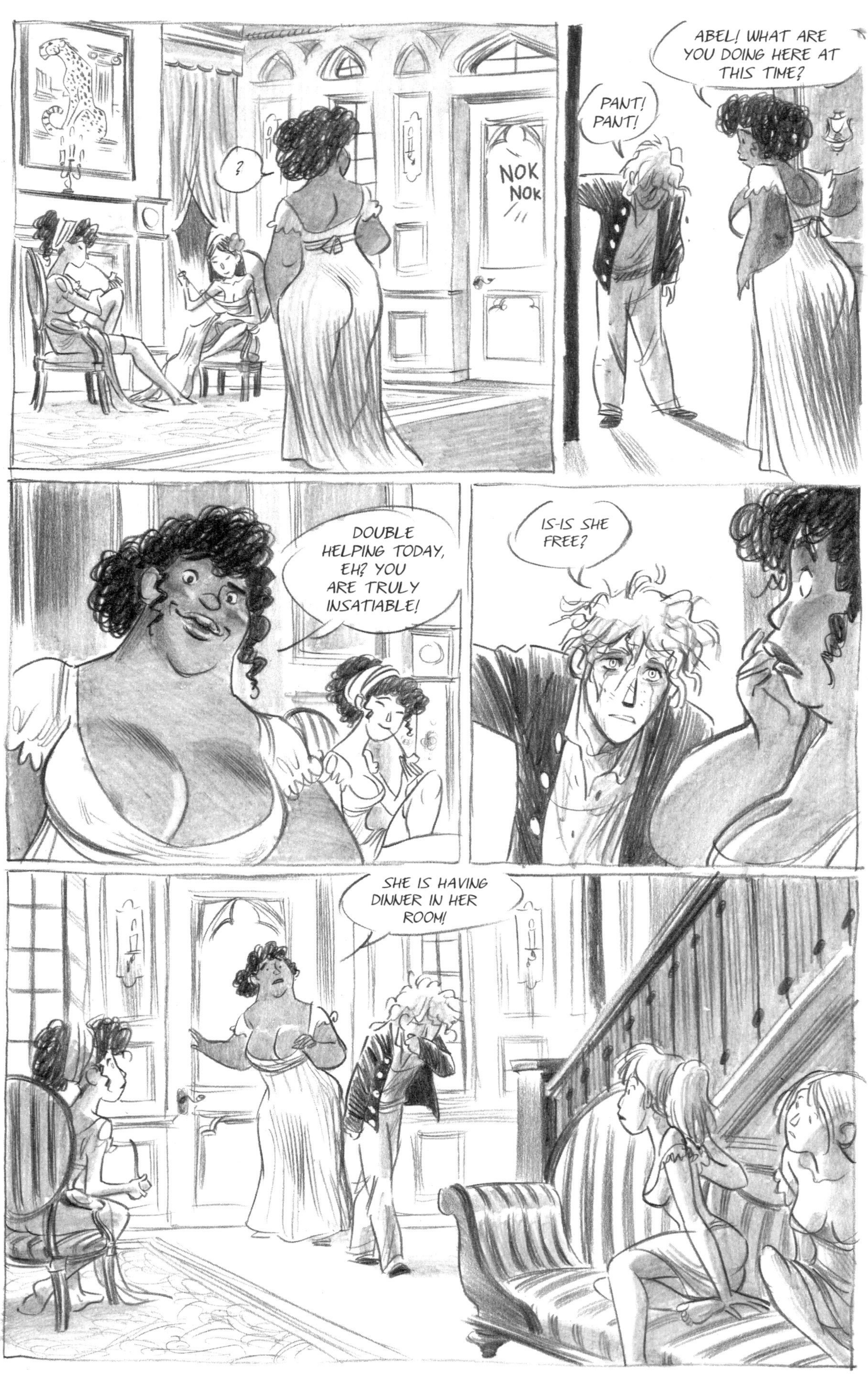

?
NOK NOK
PANT! PANT!
ABEL! WHAT ARE YOU DOING HERE AT THIS TIME?
DOUBLE HELPING TODAY, EH? YOU ARE TRULY INSATIABLE!
IS-IS SHE FREE?
SHE IS HAVING DINNER IN HER ROOM!

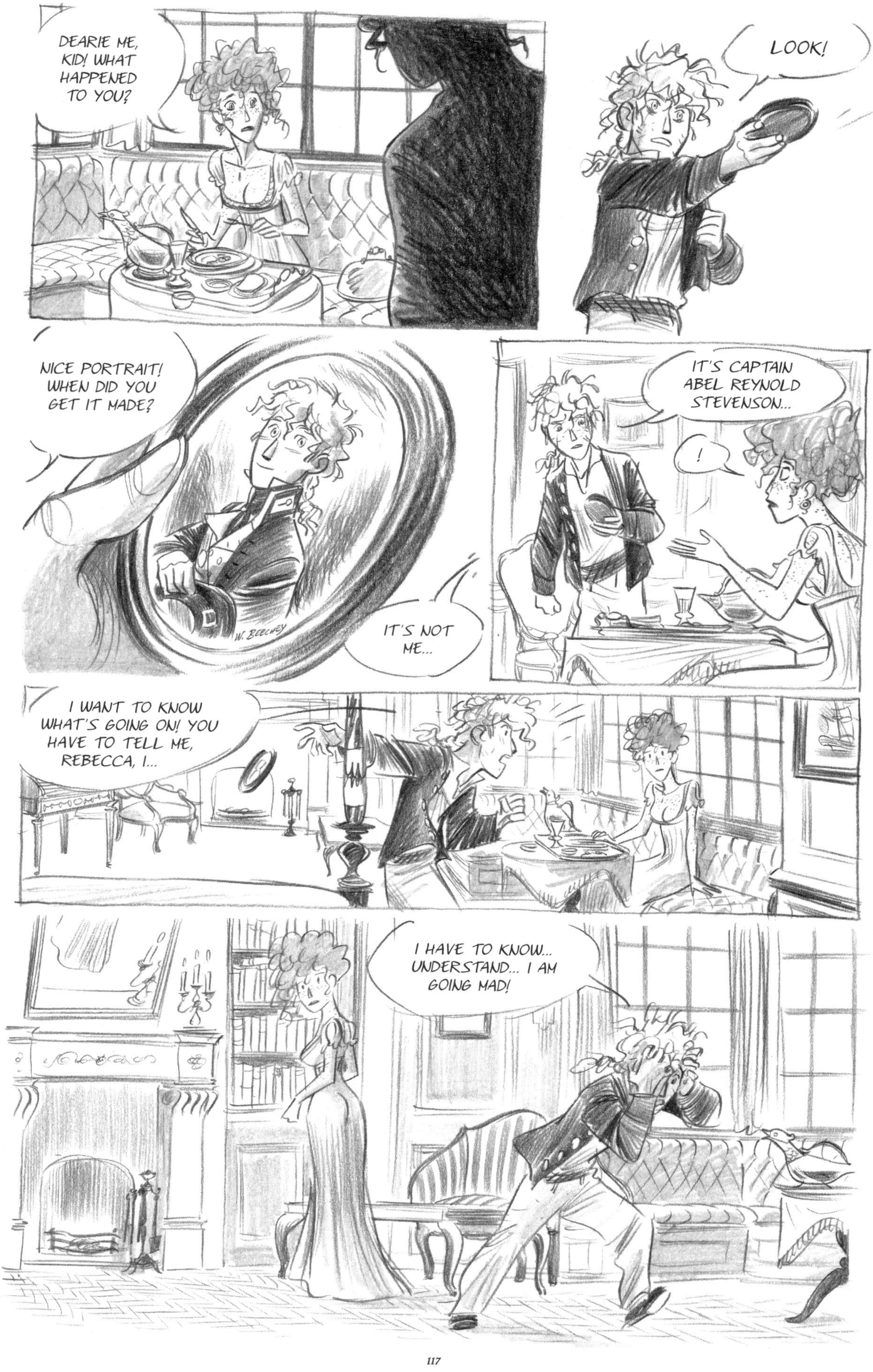
DEARIE ME, KID! WHAT HAPPENED TO YOU?
LOOK!
NICE PORTRAIT! WHEN DID YOU GET IT MADE?
W. BEECHEY
IT'S NOT ME...
IT'S CAPTAIN ABEL REYNOLD STEVENSON...
!
I WANT TO KNOW WHAT'S GOING ON! YOU HAVE TO TELL ME, REBECCA, I...
I HAVE TO KNOW... UNDERSTAND... I AM GOING MAD!

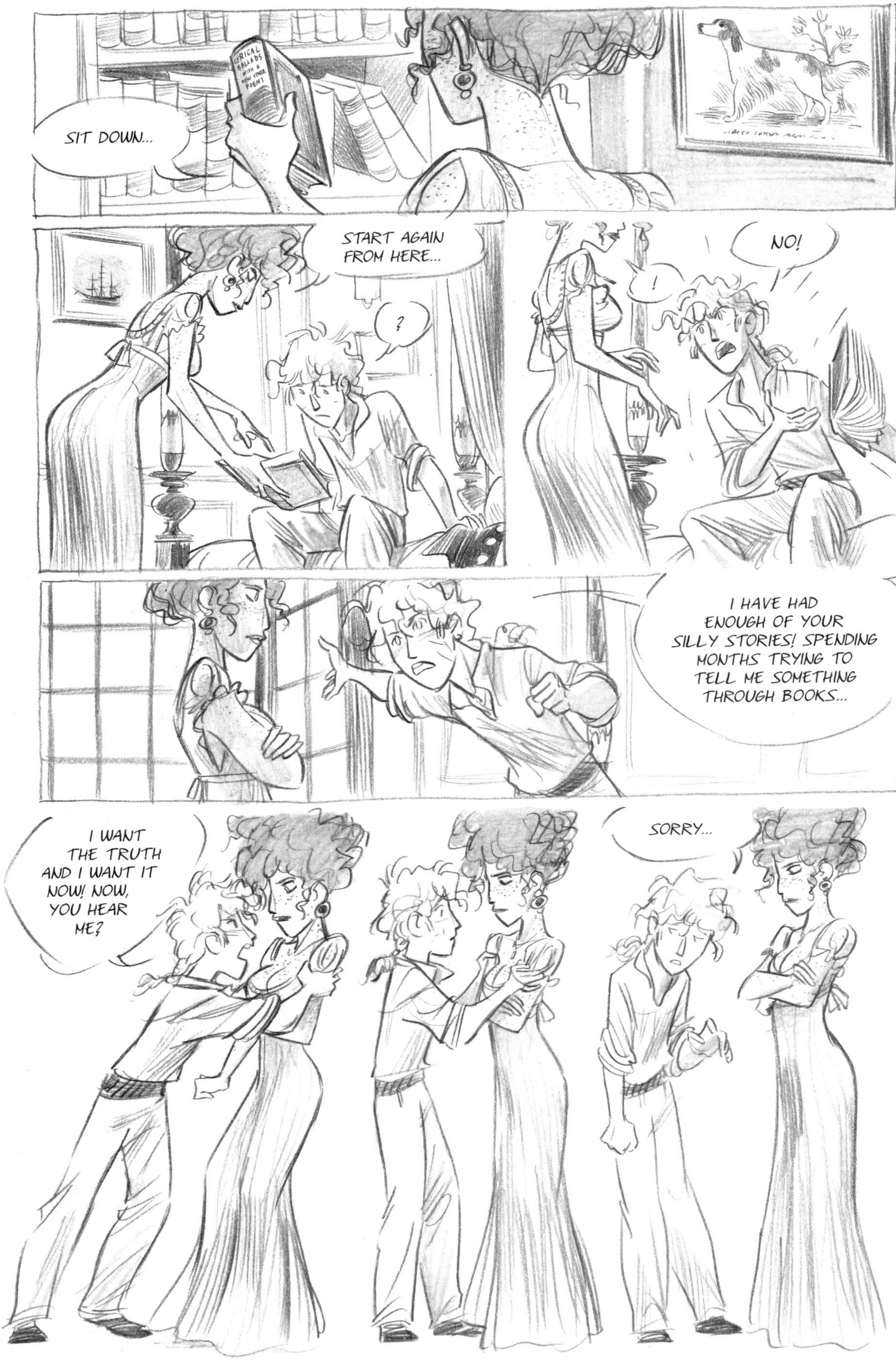
SIT DOWN...
LYRICAL BALLADS WITH A FEW OTHER POEMS
START AGAIN FROM HERE...
?
!
NO!
I HAVE HAD ENOUGH OF YOUR SILLY STORIES! SPENDING MONTHS TRYING TO TELL ME SOMETHING THROUGH BOOKS...
I WANT THE TRUTH AND I WANT IT NOW! NOW, YOU HEAR ME?
SORRY...

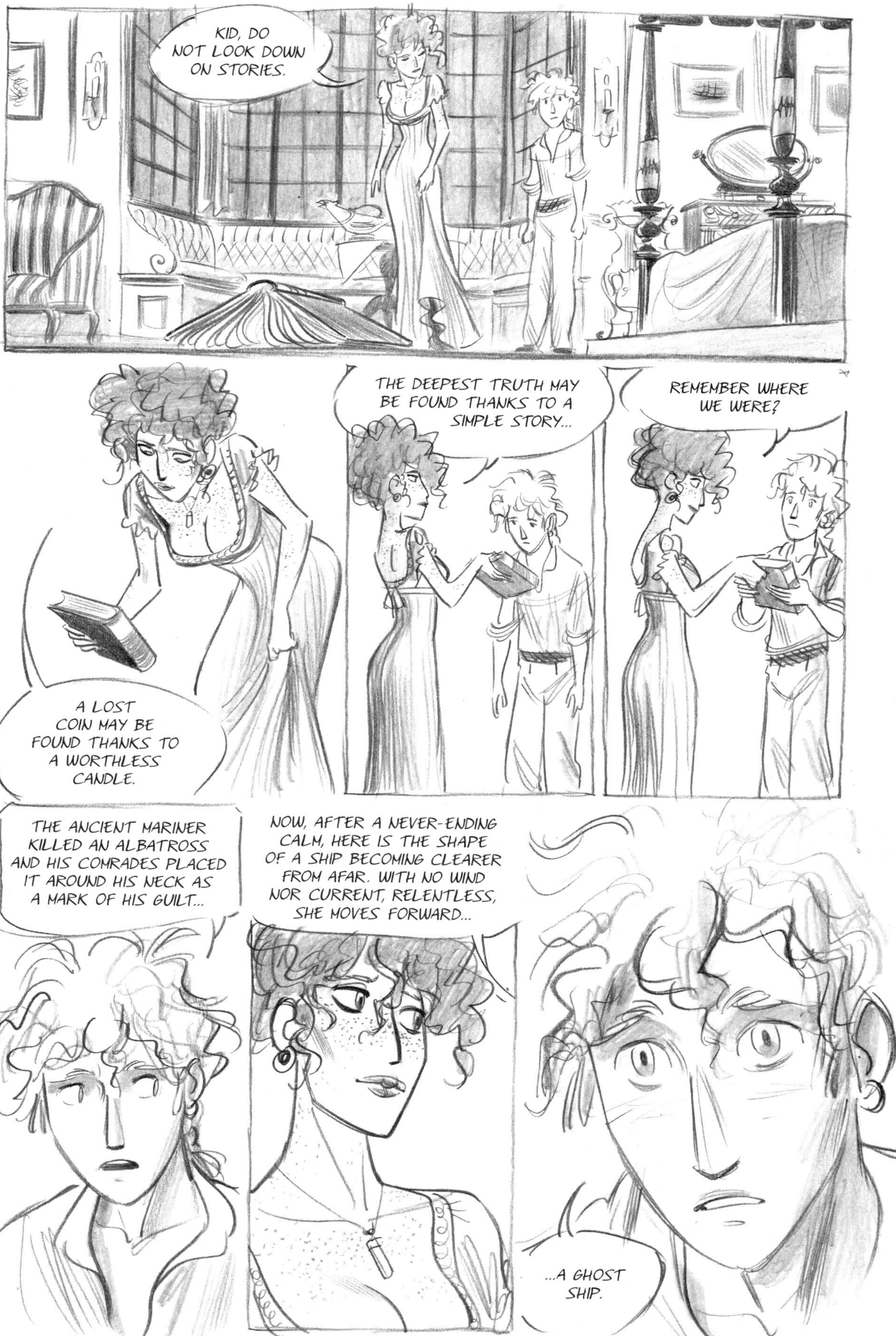
KID, DO NOT LOOK DOWN ON STORIES.
A LOST COIN MAY BE FOUND THANKS TO A WORTHLESS CANDLE.
THE DEEPEST TRUTH MAY BE FOUND THANKS TO A SIMPLE STORY...
REMEMBER WHERE WE WERE?
THE ANCIENT MARINER KILLED AN ALBATROSS AND HIS COMRADES PLACED IT AROUND HIS NECK AS A MARK OF HIS GUILT...
NOW, AFTER A NEVER-ENDING CALM, HERE IS THE SHAPE OF A SHIP BECOMING CLEARER FROM AFAR. WITH NO WIND NOR CURRENT, RELENTLESS, SHE MOVES FORWARD...
...A GHOST SHIP.

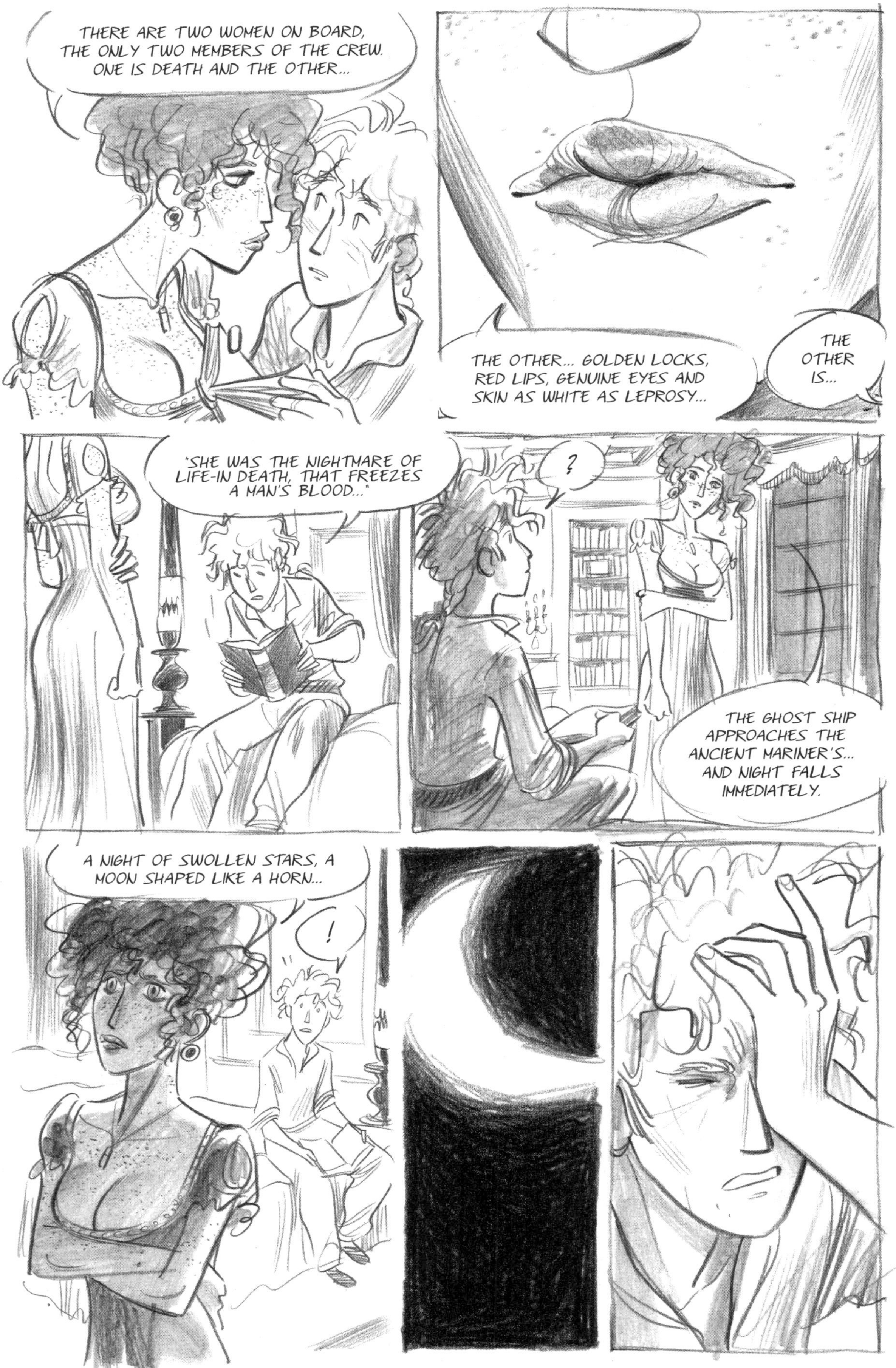
THERE ARE TWO WOMEN ON BOARD, THE ONLY TWO MEMBERS OF THE CREW. ONE IS DEATH AND THE OTHER...
THE OTHER... GOLDEN LOCKS, RED LIPS, GENUINE EYES AND SKIN AS WHITE AS LEPROSY...
THE OTHER IS...
"SHE WAS THE NIGHTMARE OF LIFE-IN DEATH, THAT FREEZES A MAN'S BLOOD..."
?
THE GHOST SHIP APPROACHES THE ANCIENT MARINER'S... AND NIGHT FALLS IMMEDIATELY.
A NIGHT OF SWOLLEN STARS, A MOON SHAPED LIKE A HORN...
!

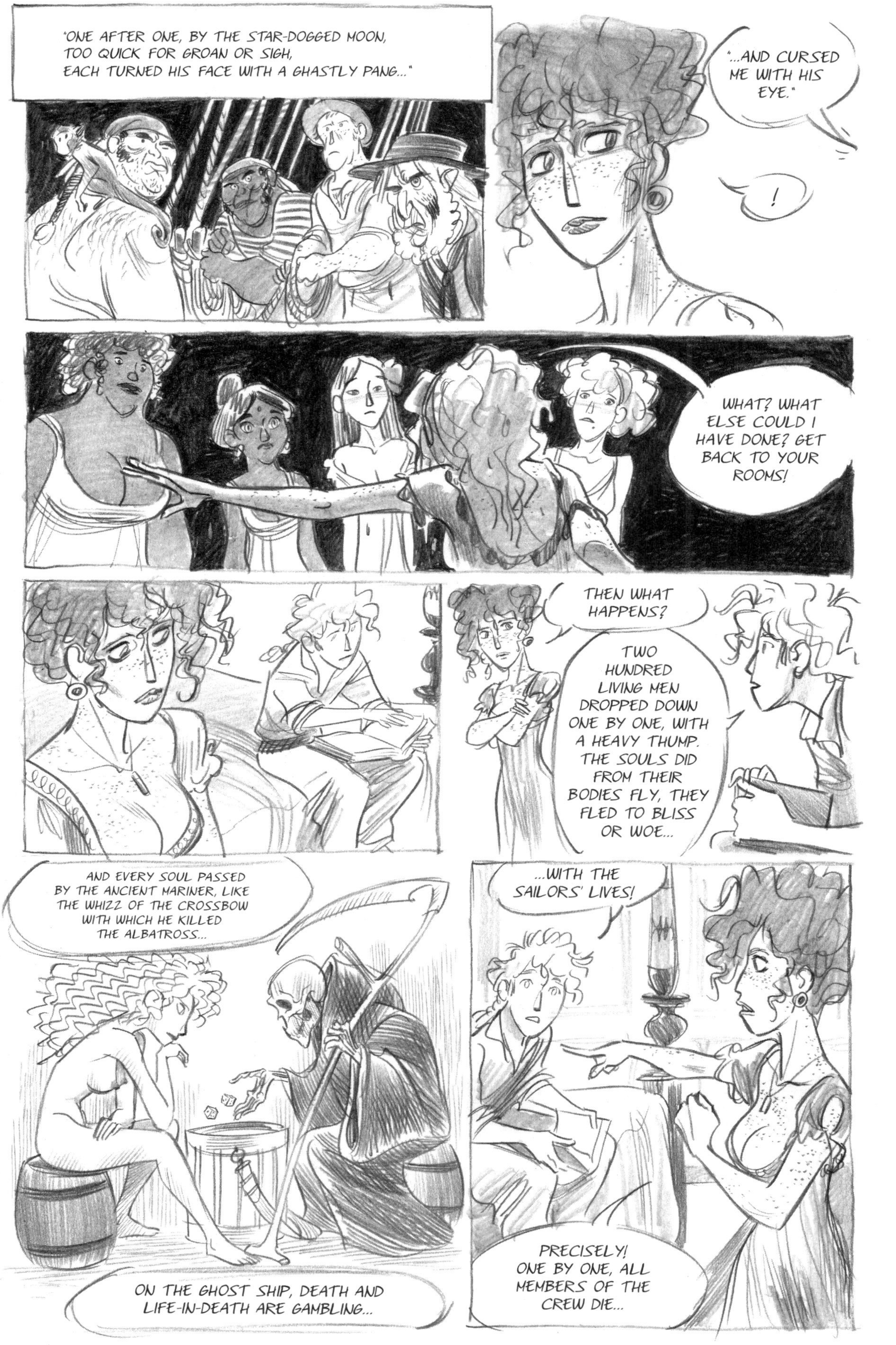
"ONE AFTER ONE, BY THE STAR-DOGGED MOON, TOO QUICK FOR GROAN OR SIGH, EACH TURNED HIS FACE WITH A GHASTLY PANG..."
"...AND CURSED ME WITH HIS EYE."
!
WHAT? WHAT ELSE COULD I HAVE DONE? GET BACK TO YOUR ROOMS!
THEN WHAT HAPPENS?
TWO HUNDRED LIVING MEN DROPPED DOWN ONE BY ONE, WITH A HEAVY THUMP. THE SOULS DID FROM THEIR BODIES FLY, THEY FLED TO BLISS OR WOE...
AND EVERY SOUL PASSED BY THE ANCIENT MARINER, LIKE THE WHIZZ OF THE CROSSBOW WITH WHICH HE KILLED THE ALBATROSS...
ON THE GHOST SHIP, DEATH AND LIFE-IN-DEATH ARE GAMBLING...
...WITH THE SAILORS' LIVES!
PRECISELY! ONE BY ONE, ALL MEMBERS OF THE CREW DIE...

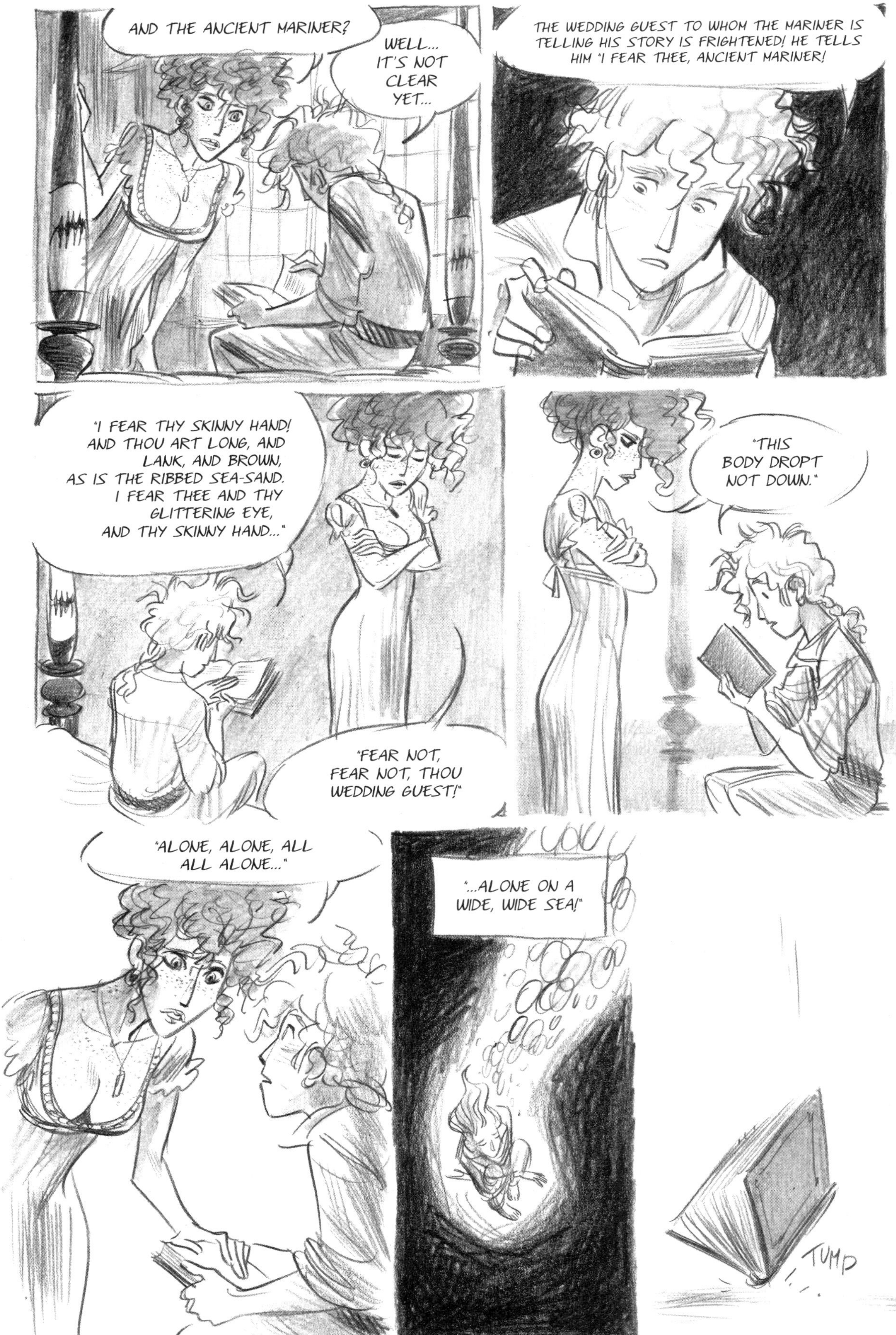
AND THE ANCIENT MARINER?
WELL... IT'S NOT CLEAR YET...
THE WEDDING GUEST TO WHOM THE MARINER IS TELLING HIS STORY IS FRIGHTENED! HE TELLS HIM "I FEAR THEE, ANCIENT MARINER!
"I FEAR THY SKINNY HAND! AND THOU ART LONG, AND LANK, AND BROWN, AS IS THE RIBBED SEA-SAND. I FEAR THEE AND THY GLITTERING EYE, AND THY SKINNY HAND..."
"FEAR NOT, FEAR NOT, THOU WEDDING GUEST!"
"THIS BODY DROPT NOT DOWN."
"ALONE, ALONE, ALL ALL ALONE..."
"...ALONE ON A WIDE, WIDE SEA!"
TUMP

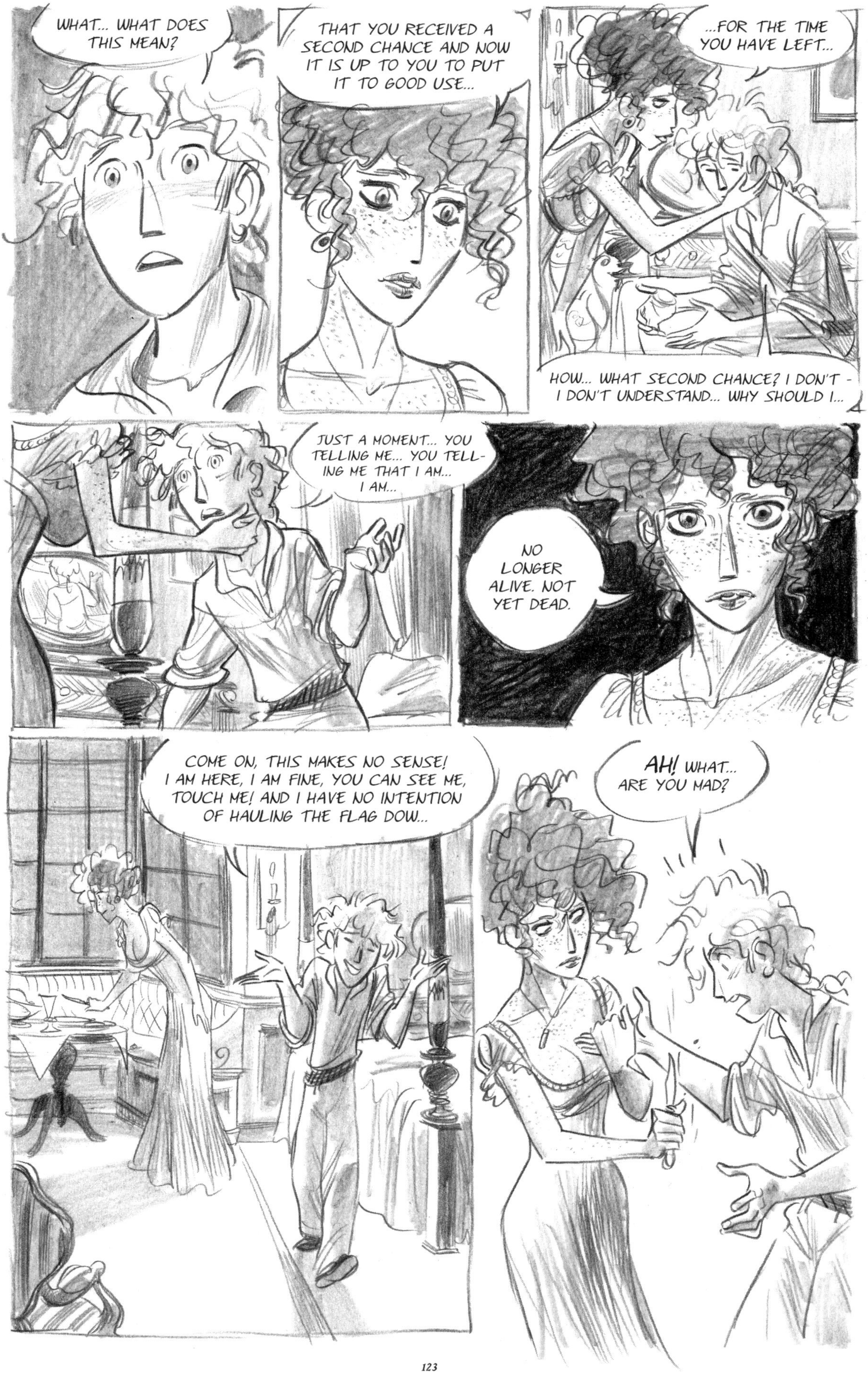
WHAT... WHAT DOES THIS MEAN?
THAT YOU RECEIVED A SECOND CHANCE AND NOW IT IS UP TO YOU TO PUT IT TO GOOD USE...
...FOR THE TIME YOU HAVE LEFT...
HOW... WHAT SECOND CHANCE? I DON'T - I DON'T UNDERSTAND... WHY SHOULD I...
JUST A MOMENT... YOU TELLING ME... YOU TELLING ME THAT I AM... I AM...
NO LONGER ALIVE. NOT YET DEAD.
COME ON, THIS MAKES NO SENSE! I AM HERE, I AM FINE, YOU CAN SEE ME, TOUCH ME! AND I HAVE NO INTENTION OF HAULING THE FLAG DOW...
AH! WHAT... ARE YOU MAD?

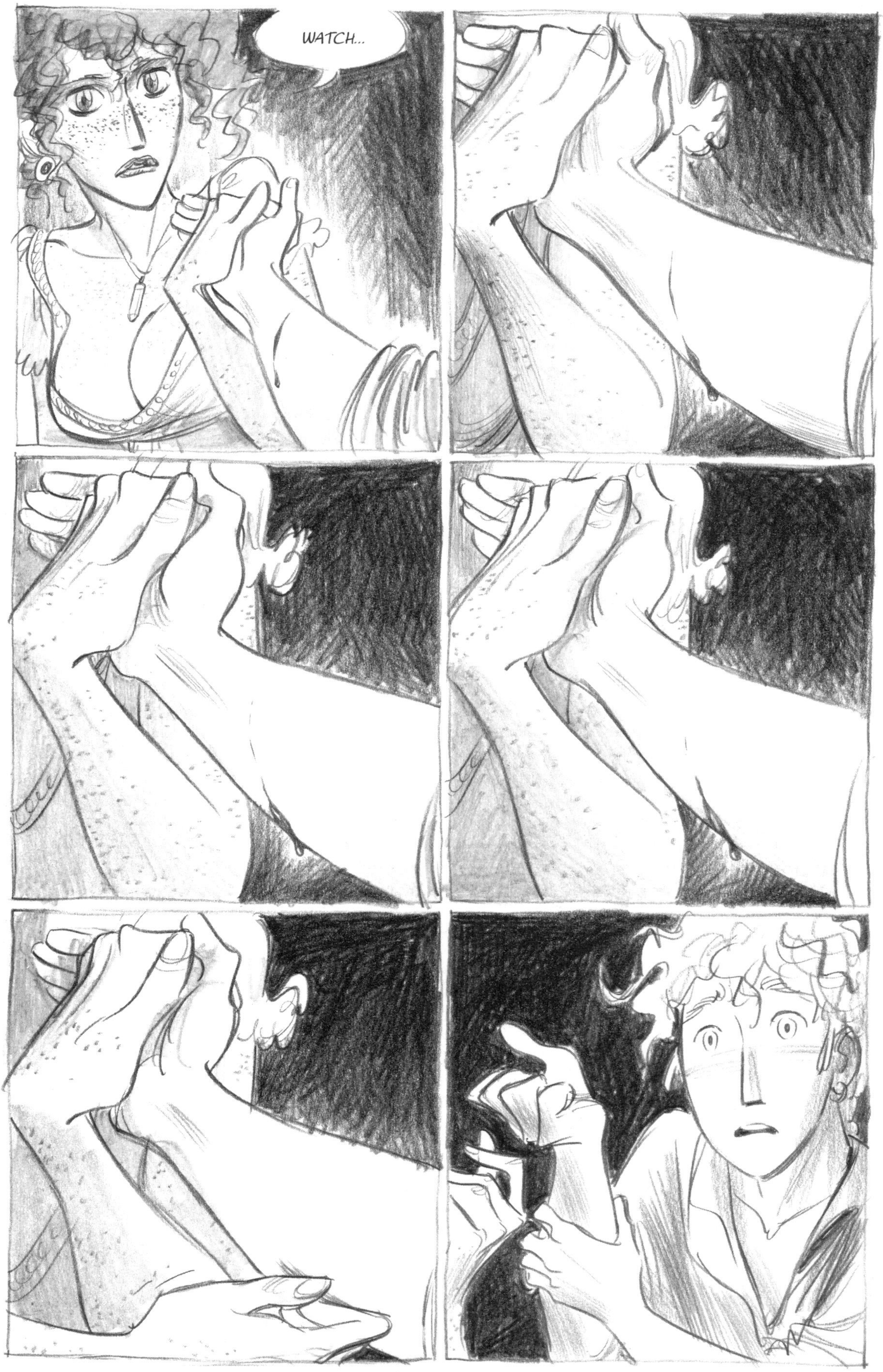
WATCH...

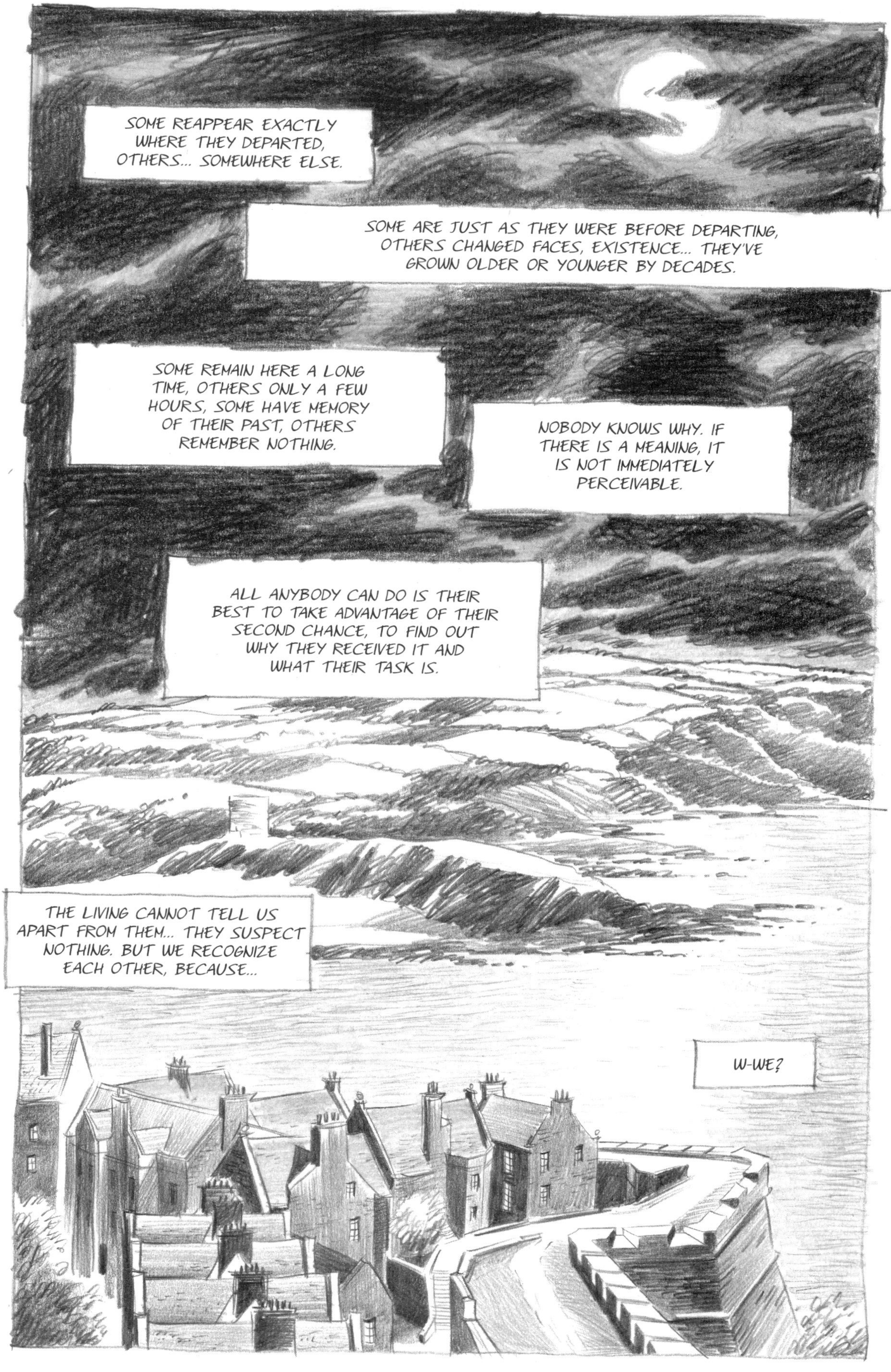
SOME REAPPEAR EXACTLY WHERE THEY DEPARTED, OTHERS... SOMEWHERE ELSE.
SOME ARE JUST AS THEY WERE BEFORE DEPARTING, OTHERS CHANGED FACES, EXISTENCE... THEY'VE GROWN OLDER OR YOUNGER BY DECADES.
SOME REMAIN HERE A LONG TIME, OTHERS ONLY A FEW HOURS, SOME HAVE MEMORY OF THEIR PAST, OTHERS REMEMBER NOTHING.
NOBODY KNOWS WHY. IF THERE IS A MEANING, IT IS NOT IMMEDIATELY PERCEIVABLE.
ALL ANYBODY CAN DO IS THEIR BEST TO TAKE ADVANTAGE OF THEIR SECOND CHANCE, TO FIND OUT WHY THEY RECEIVED IT AND WHAT THEIR TASK IS.
THE LIVING CANNOT TELL US APART FROM THEM... THEY SUSPECT NOTHING. BUT WE RECOGNIZE EACH OTHER, BECAUSE...
W-WE?

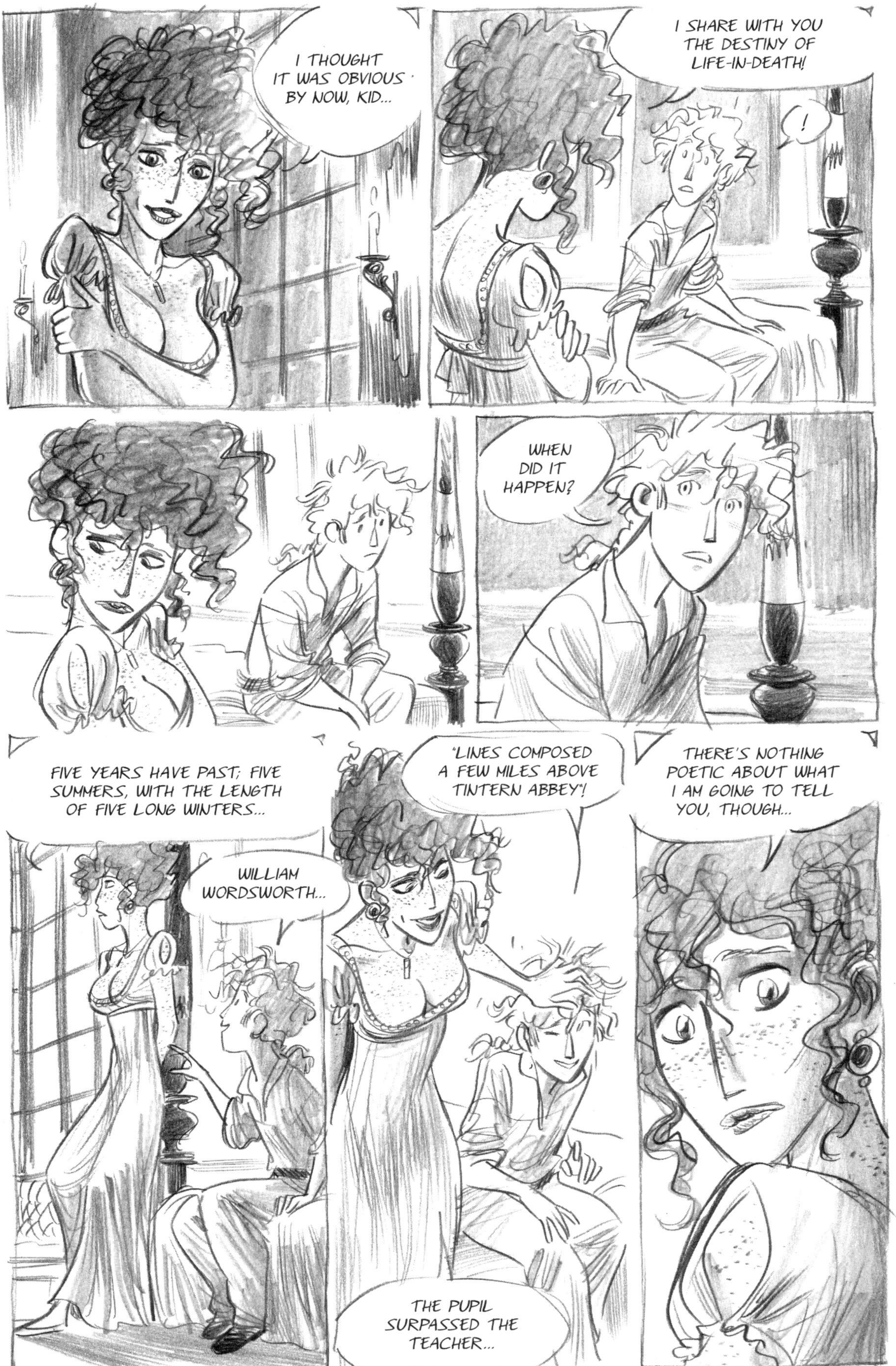
I THOUGHT IT WAS OBVIOUS BY NOW, KID...
I SHARE WITH YOU THE DESTINY OF LIFE-IN-DEATH!
!
WHEN DID IT HAPPEN?
FIVE YEARS HAVE PAST; FIVE SUMMERS, WITH THE LENGTH OF FIVE LONG WINTERS...
WILLIAM WORDSWORTH...
"LINES COMPOSED A FEW MILES ABOVE TINTERN ABBEY"!
THE PUPIL SURPASSED THE TEACHER...
THERE'S NOTHING POETIC ABOUT WHAT I AM GOING TO TELL YOU, THOUGH...

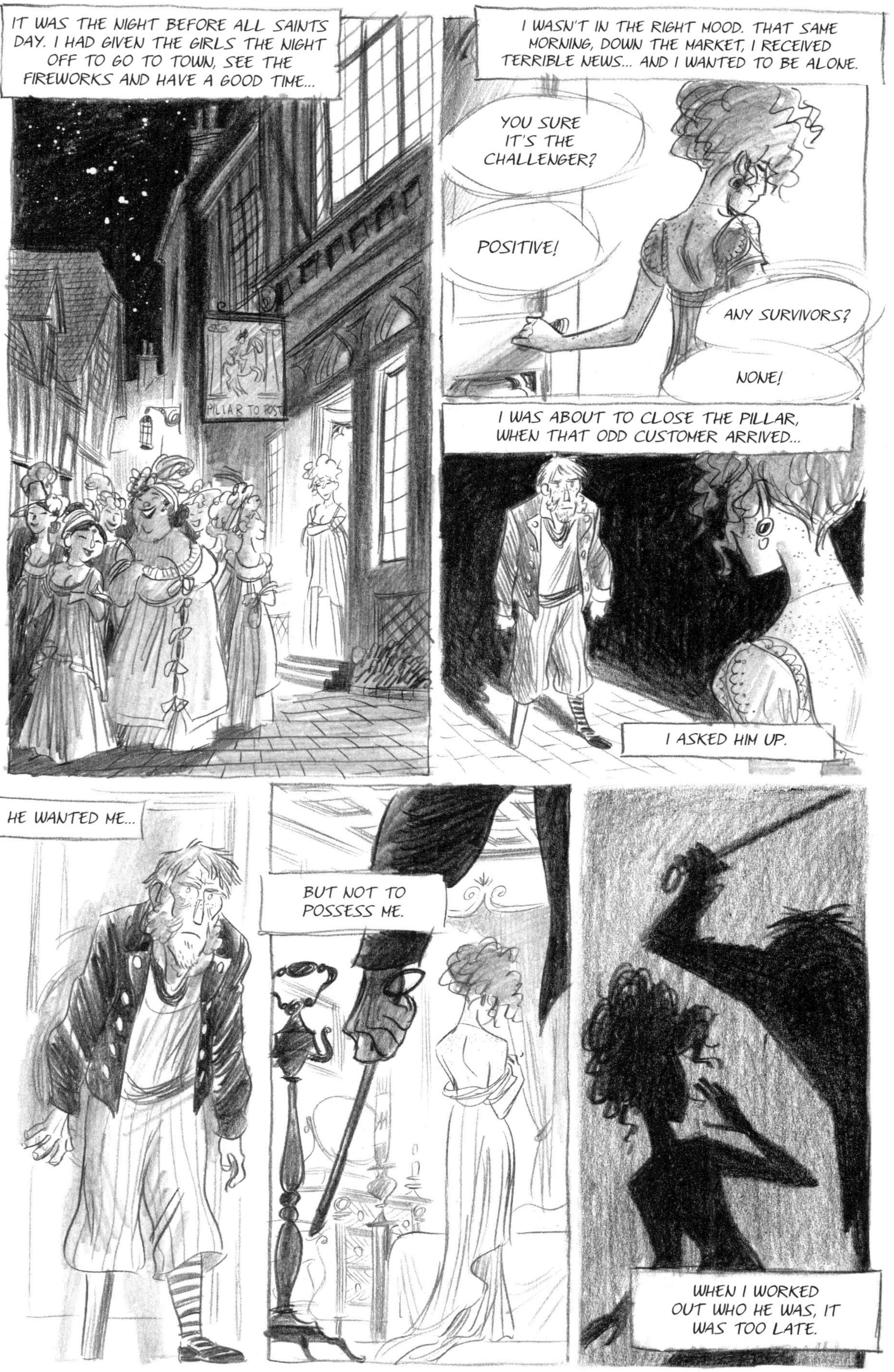
IT WAS THE NIGHT BEFORE ALL SAINTS DAY. I HAD GIVEN THE GIRLS THE NIGHT OFF TO GO TO TOWN, SEE THE FIREWORKS AND HAVE A GOOD TIME...
PILLAR TO POST
I WASN'T IN THE RIGHT MOOD. THAT SAME MORNING, DOWN THE MARKET, I RECEIVED TERRIBLE NEWS... AND I WANTED TO BE ALONE.
YOU SURE IT'S THE CHALLENGER?
POSITIVE!
ANY SURVIVORS?
NONE!
I WAS ABOUT TO CLOSE THE PILLAR, WHEN THAT ODD CUSTOMER ARRIVED...
I ASKED HIM UP.
HE WANTED ME...
BUT NOT TO POSSESS ME.
WHEN I WORKED OUT WHO HE WAS, IT WAS TOO LATE.

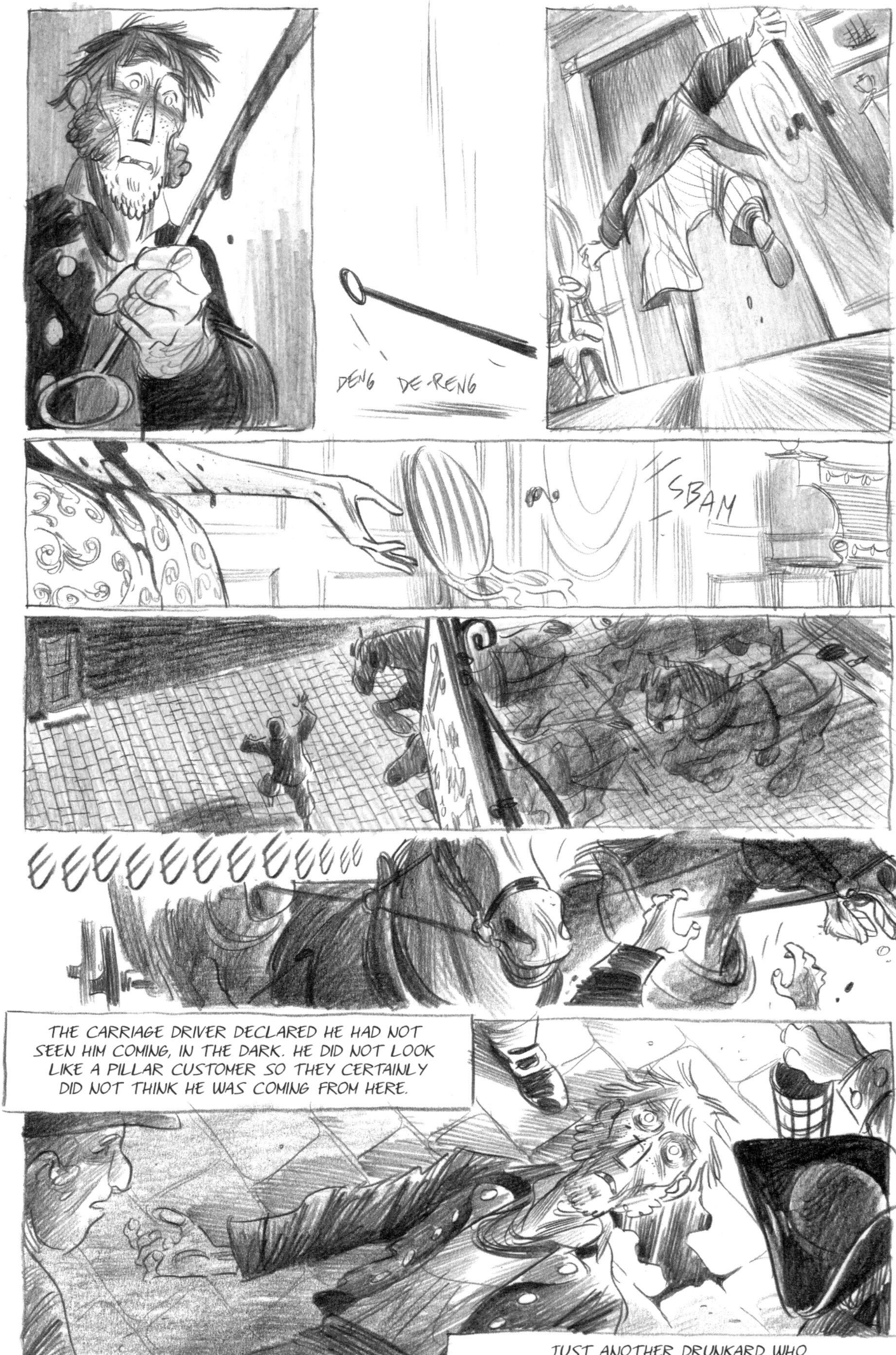
DENG DE-RENG
SBAM
EEEEEEEEEEEEEEEEE
THE CARRIAGE DRIVER DECLARED HE HAD NOT SEEN HIM COMING, IN THE DARK. HE DID NOT LOOK LIKE A PILLAR CUSTOMER SO THEY CERTAINLY DID NOT THINK HE WAS COMING FROM HERE.
JUST ANOTHER DRUNKARD WHO DID NOT LOOK BEFORE CROSSING.

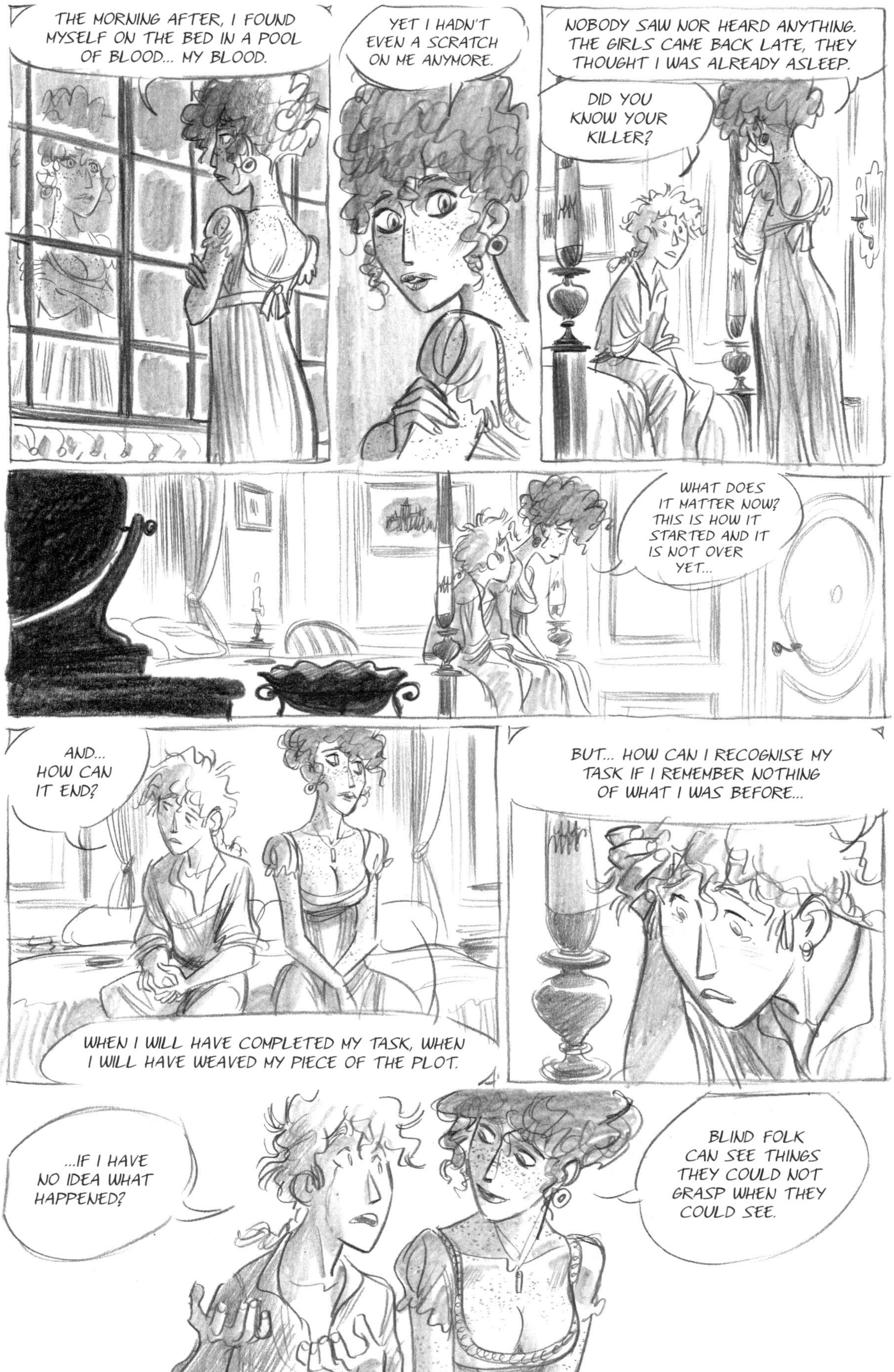
THE MORNING AFTER, I FOUND MYSELF ON THE BED IN A POOL OF BLOOD... MY BLOOD.
YET I HADN'T EVEN A SCRATCH ON ME ANYMORE.
NOBODY SAW NOR HEARD ANYTHING. THE GIRLS CAME BACK LATE, THEY THOUGHT I WAS ALREADY ASLEEP.
DID YOU KNOW YOUR KILLER?
WHAT DOES IT MATTER NOW? THIS IS HOW IT STARTED AND IT IS NOT OVER YET...
AND... HOW CAN IT END?
WHEN I WILL HAVE COMPLETED MY TASK, WHEN I WILL HAVE WEAVED MY PIECE OF THE PLOT.
BUT... HOW CAN I RECOGNISE MY TASK IF I REMEMBER NOTHING OF WHAT I WAS BEFORE...
...IF I HAVE NO IDEA WHAT HAPPENED?
BLIND FOLK CAN SEE THINGS THEY COULD NOT GRASP WHEN THEY COULD SEE.

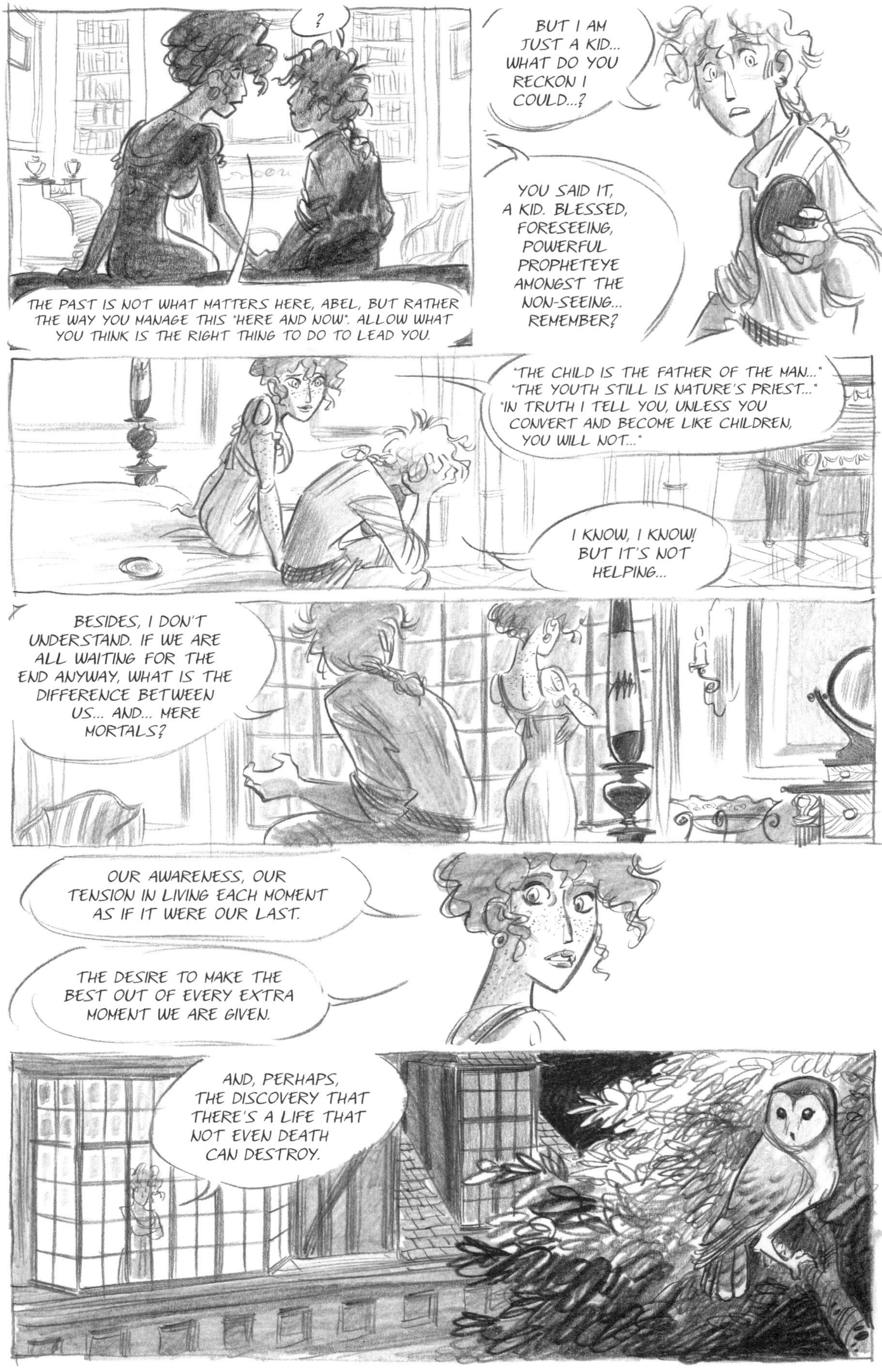
?
THE PAST IS NOT WHAT MATTERS HERE, ABEL, BUT RATHER THE WAY YOU MANAGE THIS "HERE AND NOW". ALLOW WHAT YOU THINK IS THE RIGHT THING TO DO TO LEAD YOU.
BUT I AM JUST A KID... WHAT DO YOU RECKON I COULD...?
YOU SAID IT, A KID. BLESSED, FORESEEING, POWERFUL PROPHETEYE AMONGST THE NON-SEEING... REMEMBER?
"THE CHILD IS THE FATHER OF THE MAN..." "THE YOUTH STILL IS NATURE'S PRIEST..." "IN TRUTH I TELL YOU, UNLESS YOU CONVERT AND BECOME LIKE CHILDREN, YOU WILL NOT..."
I KNOW, I KNOW! BUT IT'S NOT HELPING...
BESIDES, I DON'T UNDERSTAND. IF WE ARE ALL WAITING FOR THE END ANYWAY, WHAT IS THE DIFFERENCE BETWEEN US... AND... MERE MORTALS?
OUR AWARENESS, OUR TENSION IN LIVING EACH MOMENT AS IF IT WERE OUR LAST.
THE DESIRE TO MAKE THE BEST OUT OF EVERY EXTRA MOMENT WE ARE GIVEN.
AND, PERHAPS, THE DISCOVERY THAT THERE'S A LIFE THAT NOT EVEN DEATH CAN DESTROY.

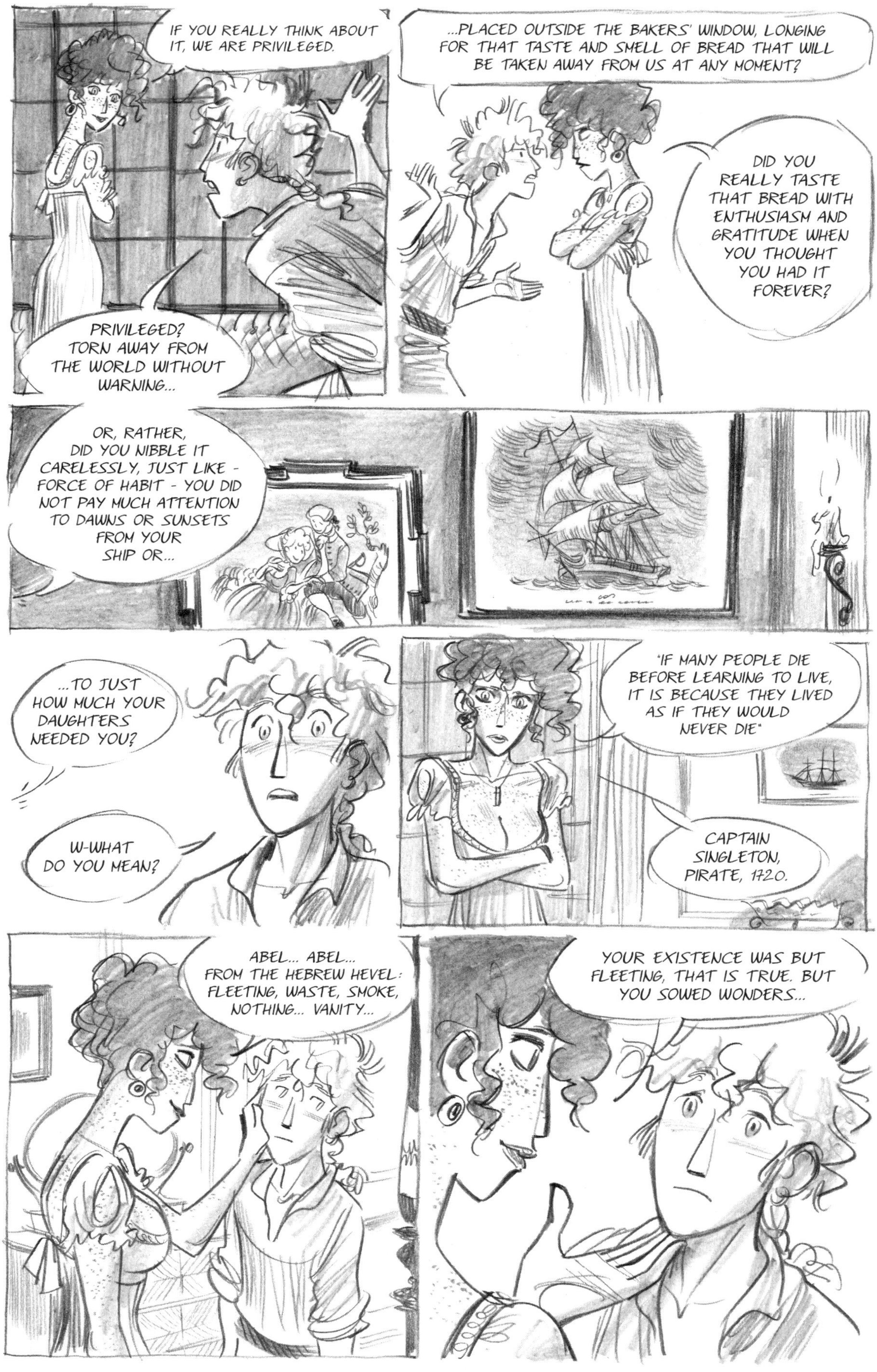
IF YOU REALLY THINK ABOUT IT, WE ARE PRIVILEGED.
PRIVILEGED? TORN AWAY FROM THE WORLD WITHOUT WARNING...
...PLACED OUTSIDE THE BAKERS' WINDOW, LONGING FOR THAT TASTE AND SMELL OF BREAD THAT WILL BE TAKEN AWAY FROM US AT ANY MOMENT?
DID YOU REALLY TASTE THAT BREAD WITH ENTHUSIASM AND GRATITUDE WHEN YOU THOUGHT YOU HAD IT FOREVER?
OR, RATHER, DID YOU NIBBLE IT CARELESSLY, JUST LIKE - FORCE OF HABIT - YOU DID NOT PAY MUCH ATTENTION TO DAWNS OR SUNSETS FROM YOUR SHIP OR...
...TO JUST HOW MUCH YOUR DAUGHTERS NEEDED YOU?
W-WHAT DO YOU MEAN?
"IF MANY PEOPLE DIE BEFORE LEARNING TO LIVE, IT IS BECAUSE THEY LIVED AS IF THEY WOULD NEVER DIE"
CAPTAIN SINGLETON, PIRATE, 1720.
ABEL... ABEL... FROM THE HEBREW HEVEL: FLEETING, WASTE, SMOKE, NOTHING... VANITY...
YOUR EXISTENCE WAS BUT FLEETING, THAT IS TRUE. BUT YOU SOWED WONDERS...

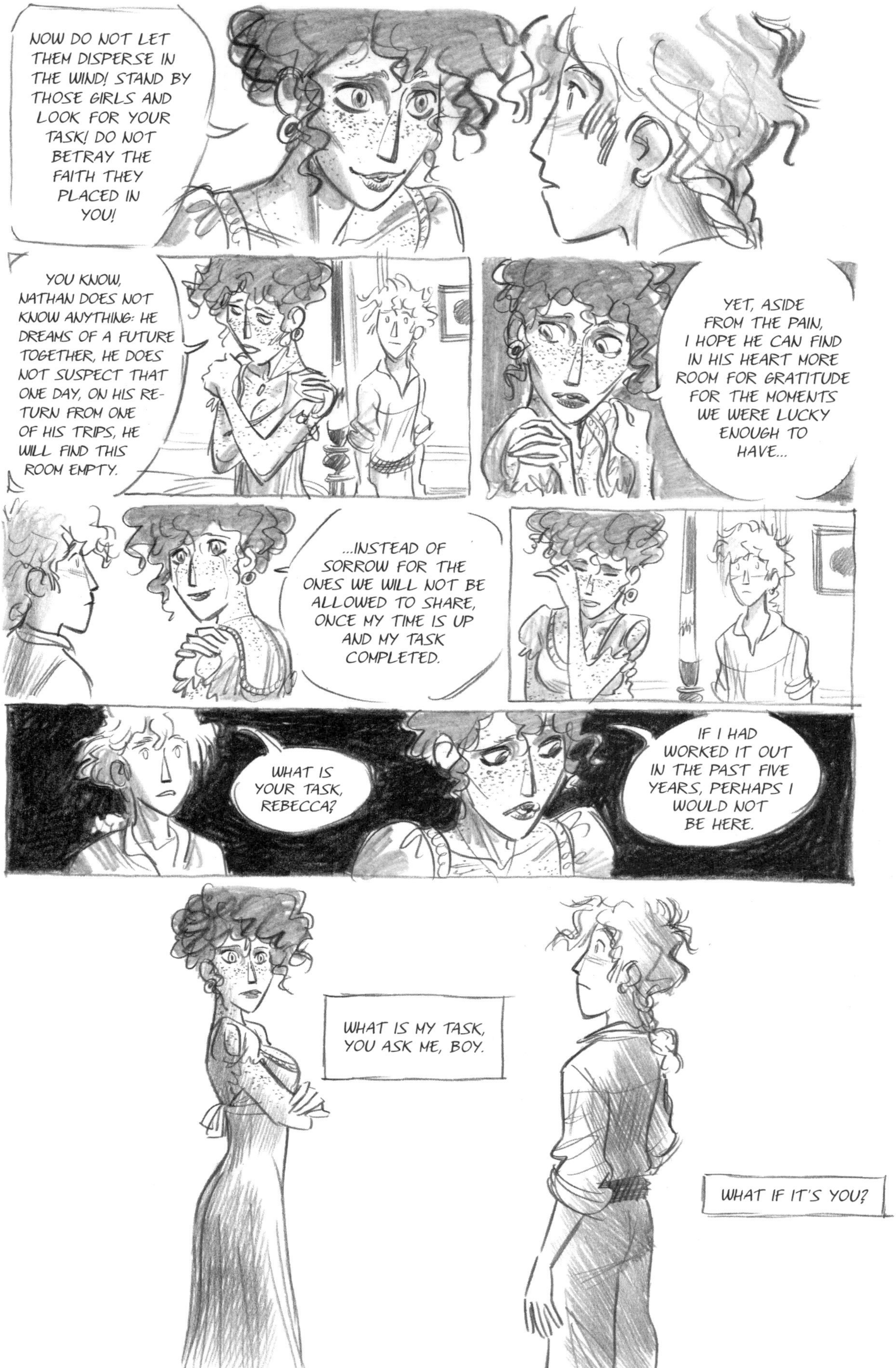
NOW DO NOT LET THEM DISPERSE IN THE WIND! STAND BY THOSE GIRLS AND LOOK FOR YOUR TASK! DO NOT BETRAY THE FAITH THEY PLACED IN YOU!
YOU KNOW, NATHAN DOES NOT KNOW ANYTHING: HE DREAMS OF A FUTURE TOGETHER, HE DOES NOT SUSPECT THAT ONE DAY, ON HIS RETURN FROM ONE OF HIS TRIPS, HE WILL FIND THIS ROOM EMPTY.
YET, ASIDE FROM THE PAIN, I HOPE HE CAN FIND IN HIS HEART MORE ROOM FOR GRATITUDE FOR THE MOMENTS WE WERE LUCKY ENOUGH TO HAVE...
...INSTEAD OF SORROW FOR THE ONES WE WILL NOT BE ALLOWED TO SHARE, ONCE MY TIME IS UP AND MY TASK COMPLETED.
WHAT IS YOUR TASK, REBECCA?
IF I HAD WORKED IT OUT IN THE PAST FIVE YEARS, PERHAPS I WOULD NOT BE HERE.
WHAT IS MY TASK, YOU ASK ME, BOY.
WHAT IF IT'S YOU?

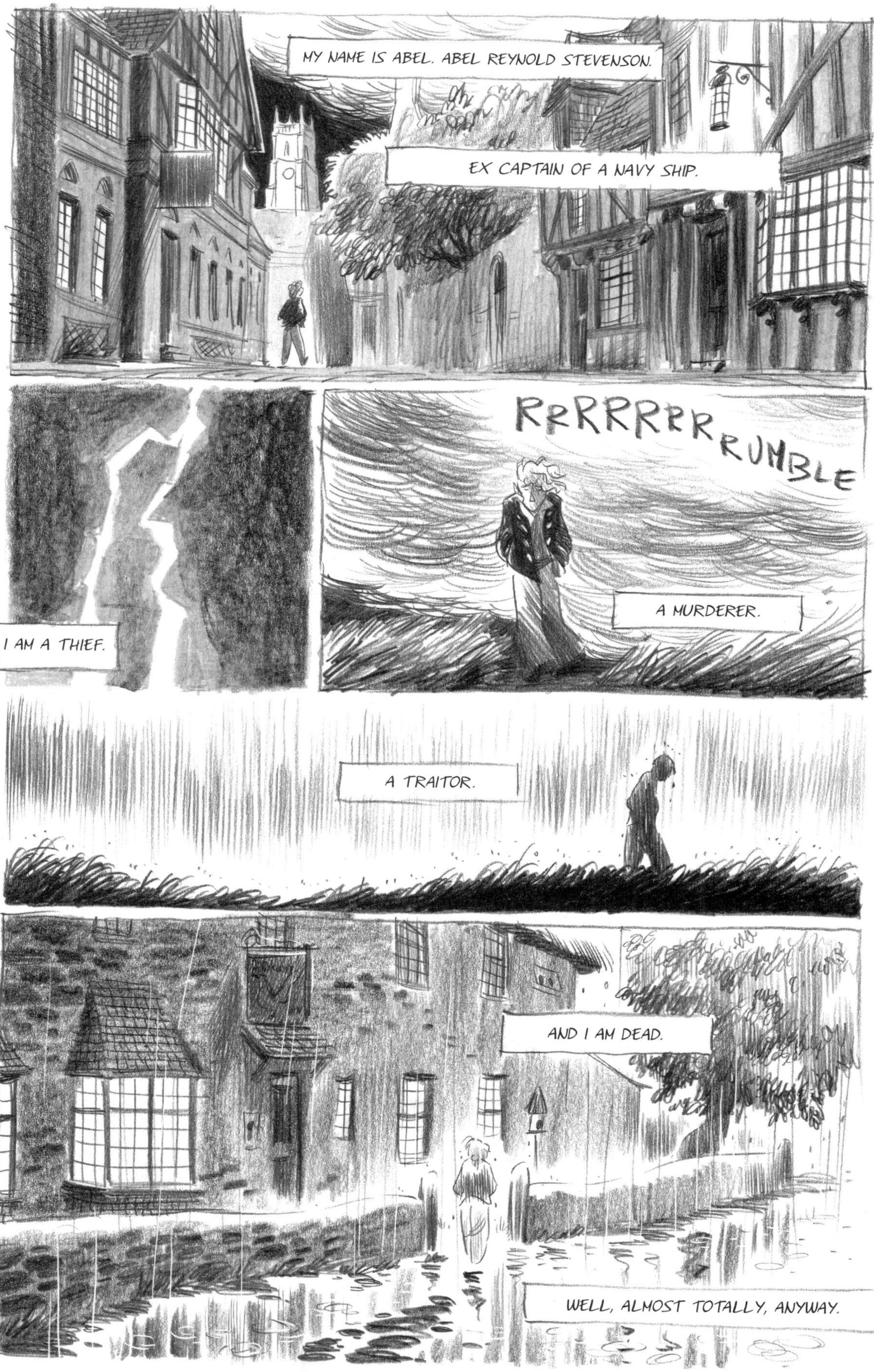
MY NAME IS ABEL. ABEL REYNOLD STEVENSON.
EX CAPTAIN OF A NAVY SHIP.
I AM A THIEF.
RRRRRRRRRUMBLE
A MURDERER.
A TRAITOR.
AND I AM DEAD.
WELL, ALMOST TOTALLY, ANYWAY.

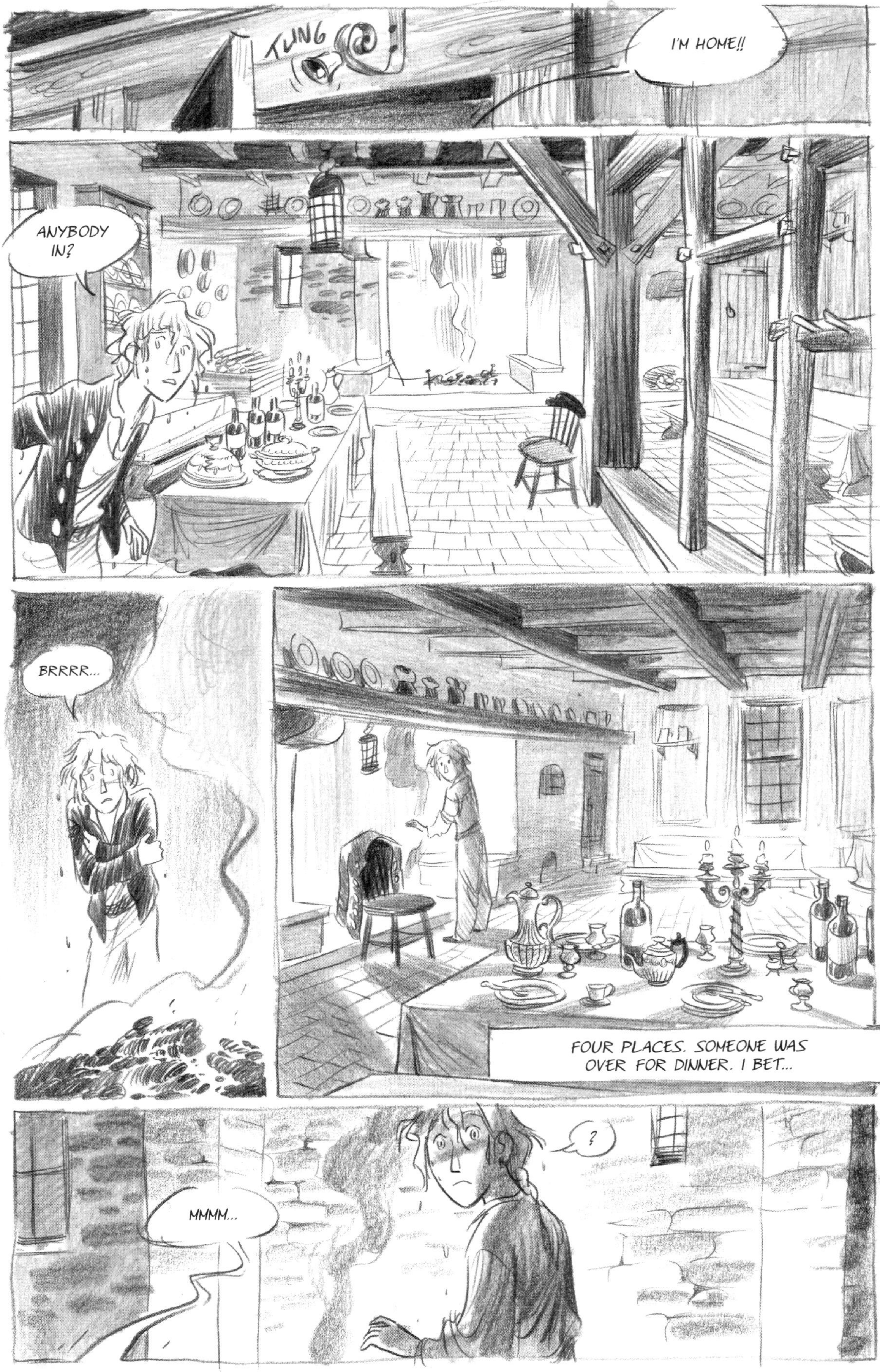
TUNG
I'M HOME!!
ANYBODY IN?
BRRRR...
FOUR PLACES. SOMEONE WAS OVER FOR DINNER. I BET...
MMMM...
?

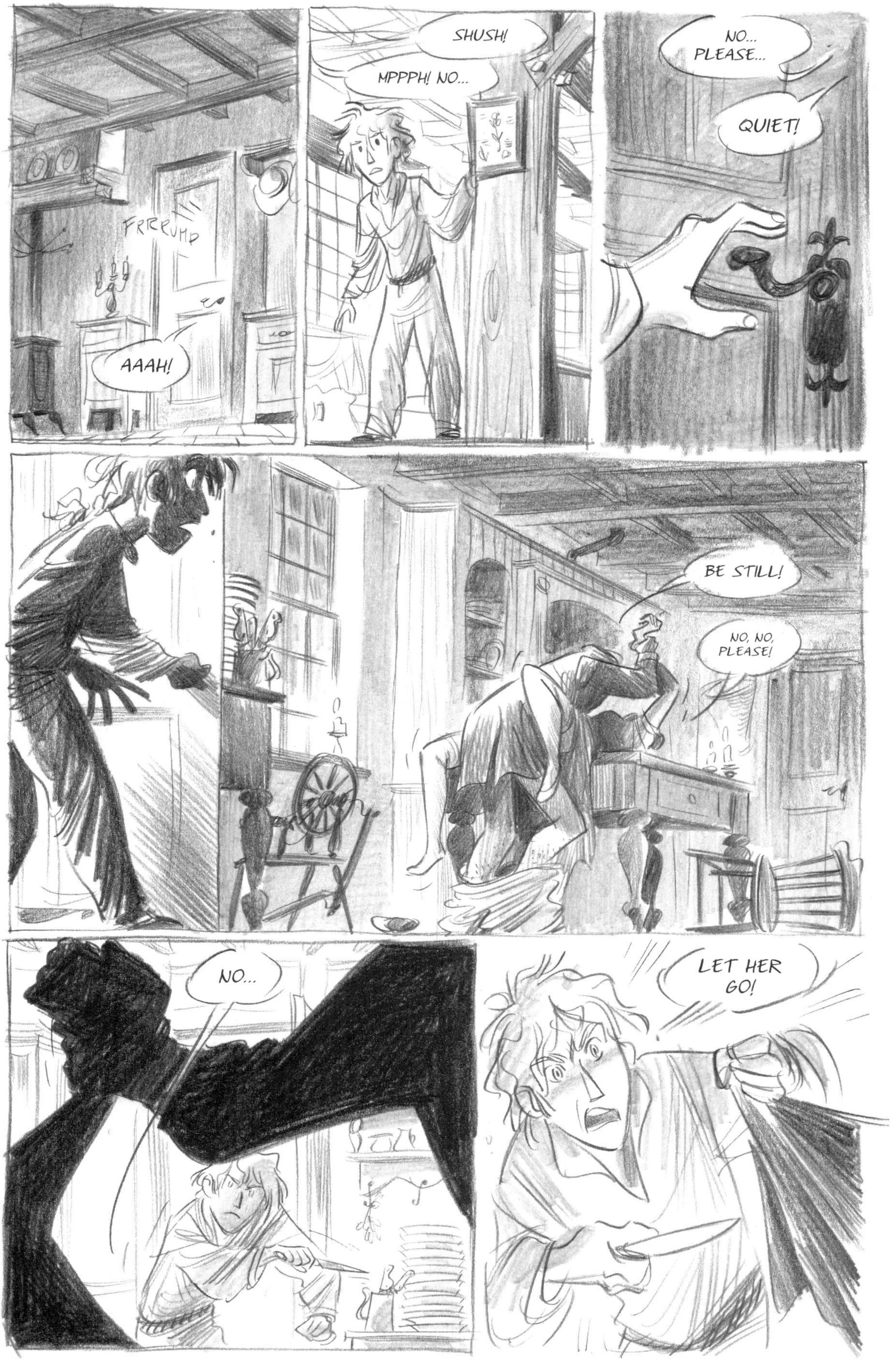
FRRRUMP
AAAH!
SHUSH!
MPPPH! NO...
NO... PLEASE...
QUIET!
BE STILL!
NO, NO, PLEASE!
NO...
LET HER GO!

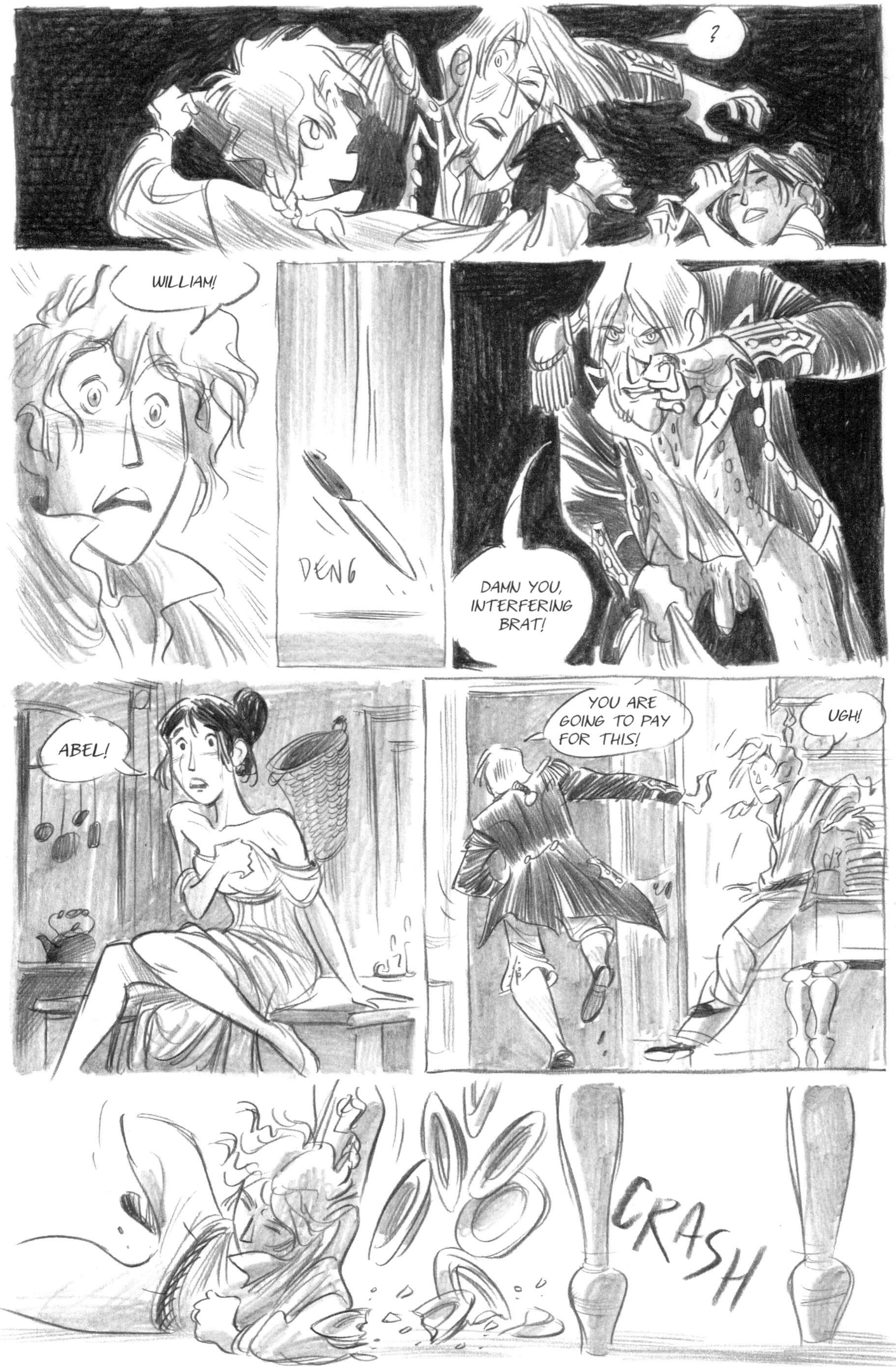
?
WILLIAM!
DENG
DAMN YOU, INTERFERING BRAT!
ABEL!
YOU ARE GOING TO PAY FOR THIS!
UGH!
CRASH

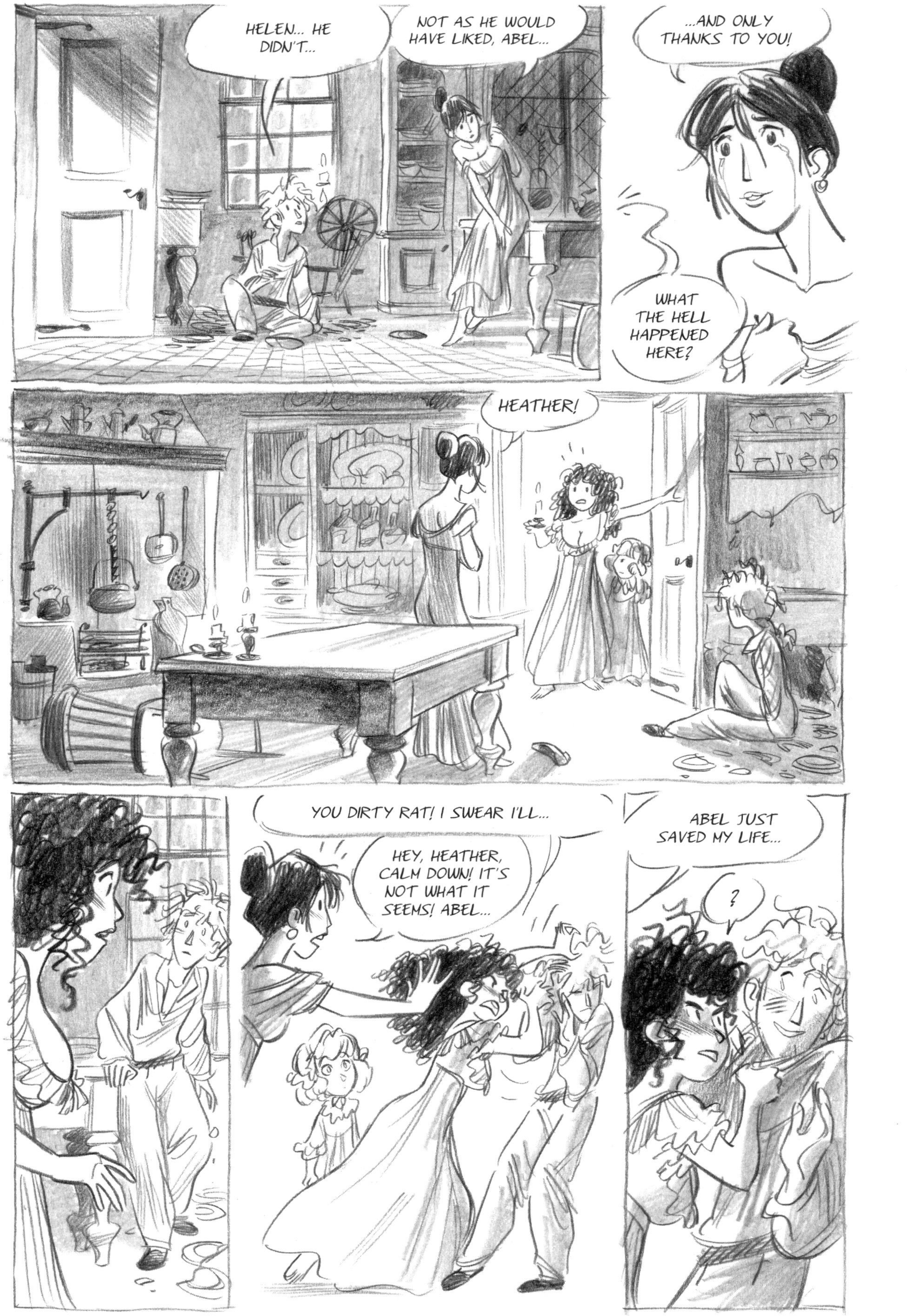
HELEN... HE DIDN'T...
NOT AS HE WOULD HAVE LIKED, ABEL...
...AND ONLY THANKS TO YOU!
WHAT THE HELL HAPPENED HERE?
HEATHER!
YOU DIRTY RAT! I SWEAR I'LL...
HEY, HEATHER, CALM DOWN! IT'S NOT WHAT IT SEEMS! ABEL...
ABEL JUST SAVED MY LIFE...
?

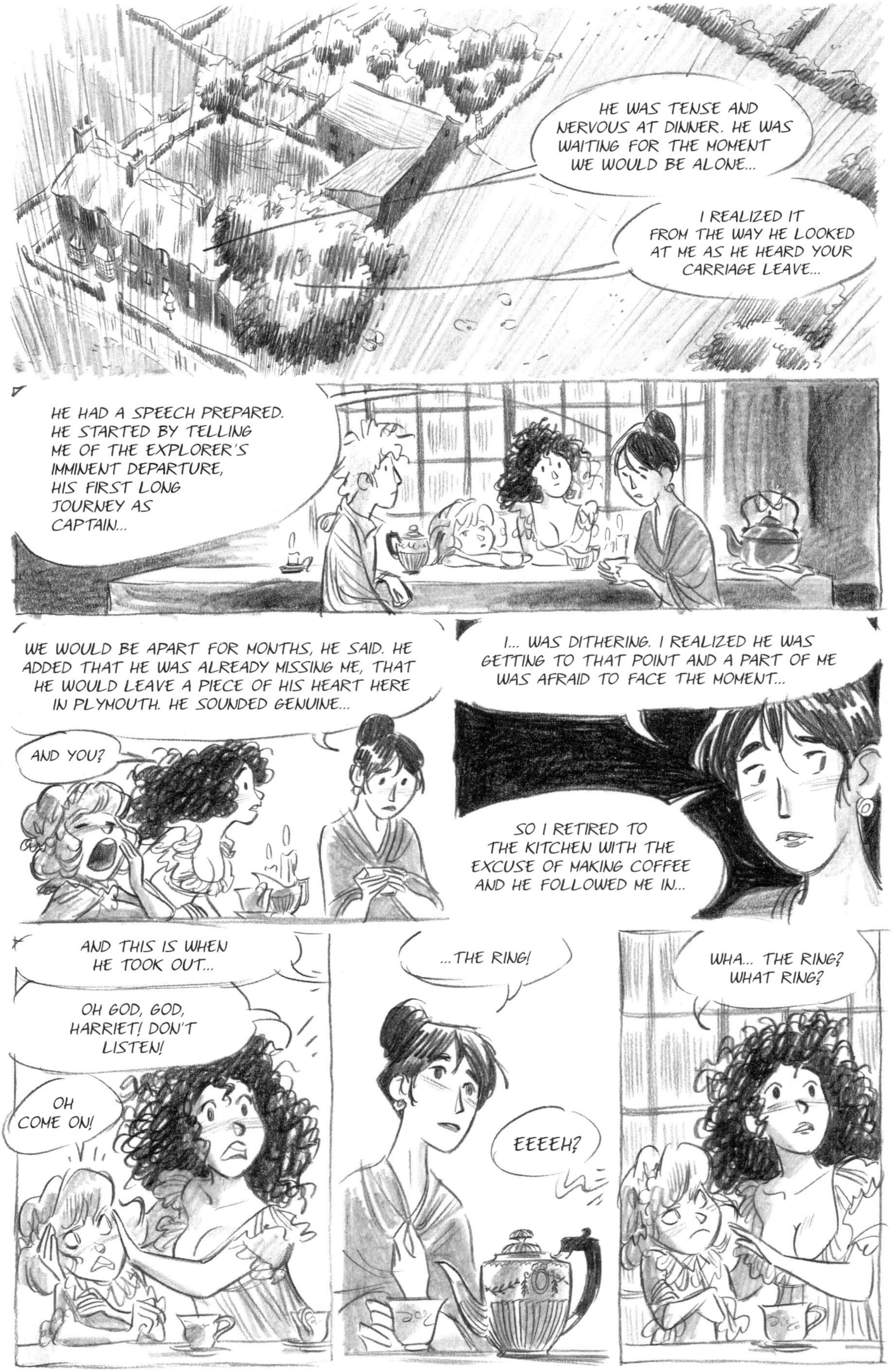
HE WAS TENSE AND NERVOUS AT DINNER. HE WAS WAITING FOR THE MOMENT WE WOULD BE ALONE...
I REALIZED IT FROM THE WAY HE LOOKED AT ME AS HE HEARD YOUR CARRIAGE LEAVE...
HE HAD A SPEECH PREPARED. HE STARTED BY TELLING ME OF THE EXPLORER'S IMMINENT DEPARTURE, HIS FIRST LONG JOURNEY AS CAPTAIN...
WE WOULD BE APART FOR MONTHS, HE SAID. HE ADDED THAT HE WAS ALREADY MISSING ME, THAT HE WOULD LEAVE A PIECE OF HIS HEART HERE IN PLYMOUTH. HE SOUNDED GENUINE...
AND YOU?
I... WAS DITHERING. I REALIZED HE WAS GETTING TO THAT POINT AND A PART OF ME WAS AFRAID TO FACE THE MOMENT...
SO I RETIRED TO THE KITCHEN WITH THE EXCUSE OF MAKING COFFEE AND HE FOLLOWED ME IN...
AND THIS IS WHEN HE TOOK OUT...
OH GOD, GOD, HARRIET! DON'T LISTEN!
OH COME ON!
...THE RING!
EEEEH?
WHA... THE RING? WHAT RING?

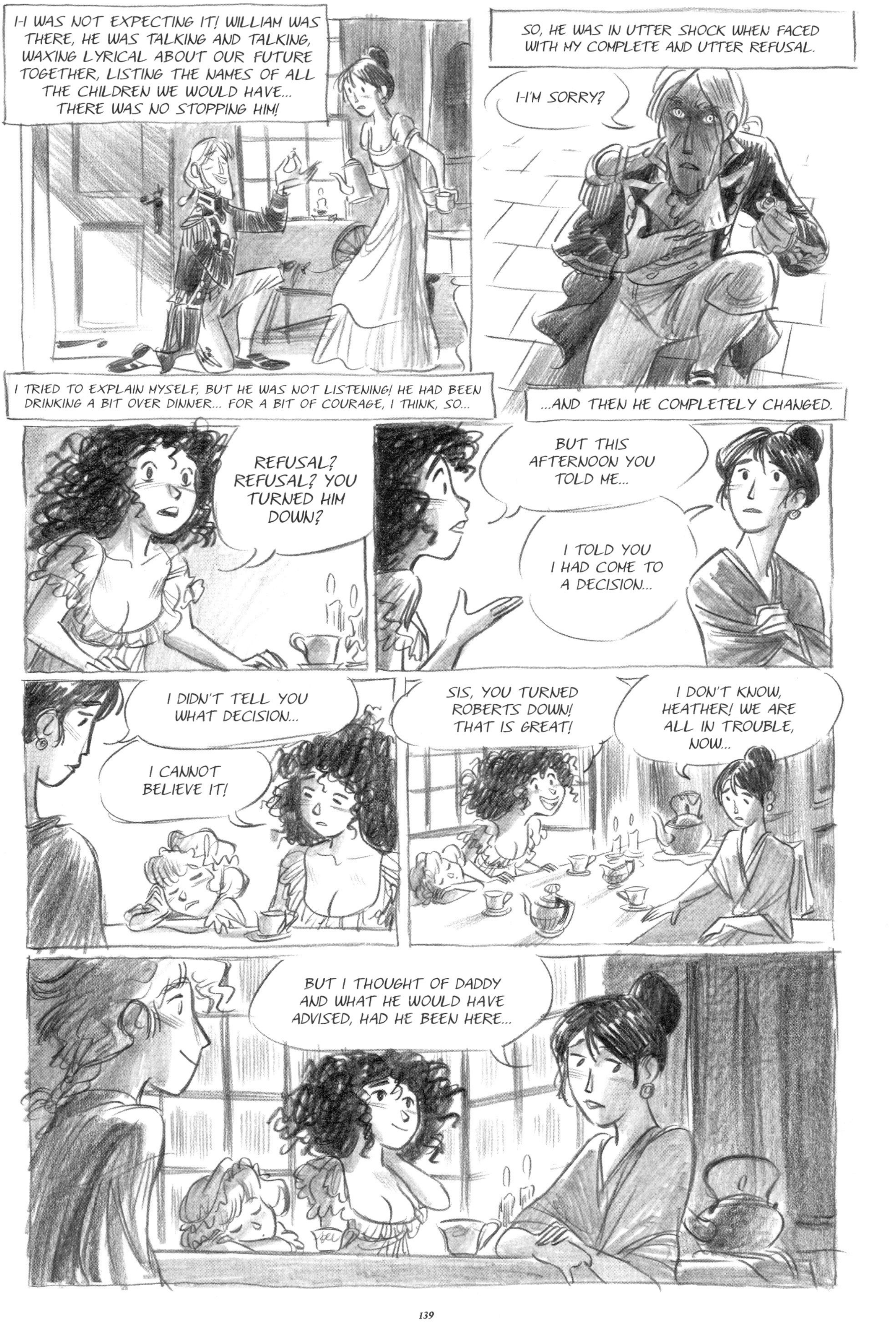
I-I WAS NOT EXPECTING IT! WILLIAM WAS THERE, HE WAS TALKING AND TALKING, WAXING LYRICAL ABOUT OUR FUTURE TOGETHER, LISTING THE NAMES OF ALL THE CHILDREN WE WOULD HAVE... THERE WAS NO STOPPING HIM!
I TRIED TO EXPLAIN MYSELF, BUT HE WAS NOT LISTENING! HE HAD BEEN DRINKING A BIT OVER DINNER... FOR A BIT OF COURAGE, I THINK, SO...
SO, HE WAS IN UTTER SHOCK WHEN FACED WITH MY COMPLETE AND UTTER REFUSAL.
I-I'M SORRY?
...AND THEN HE COMPLETELY CHANGED.
REFUSAL? REFUSAL? YOU TURNED HIM DOWN?
BUT THIS AFTERNOON YOU TOLD ME...
I TOLD YOU I HAD COME TO A DECISION...
I DIDN'T TELL YOU WHAT DECISION...
I CANNOT BELIEVE IT!
SIS, YOU TURNED ROBERTS DOWN! THAT IS GREAT!
I DON'T KNOW, HEATHER! WE ARE ALL IN TROUBLE, NOW...
BUT I THOUGHT OF DADDY AND WHAT HE WOULD HAVE ADVISED, HAD HE BEEN HERE...

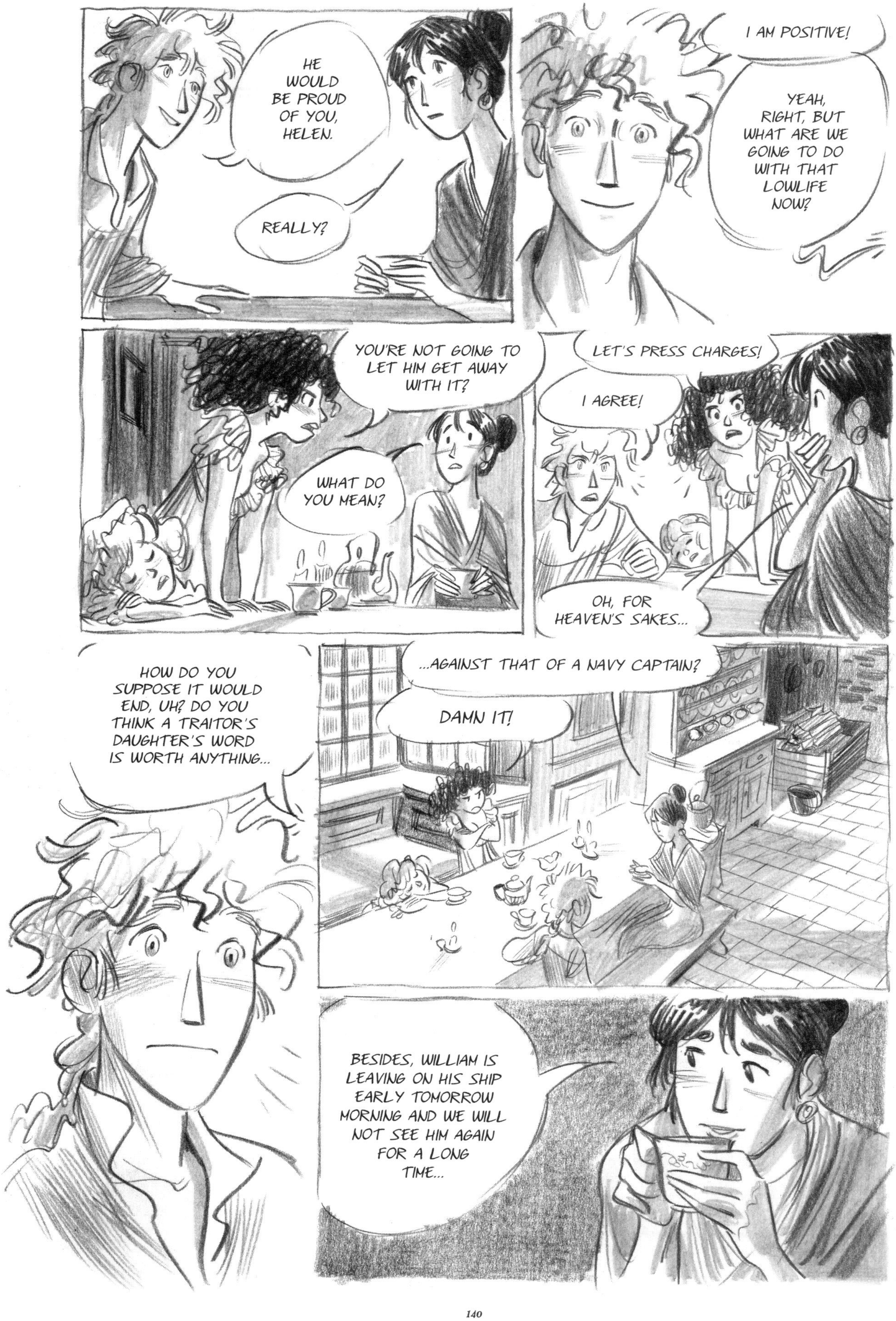

HE WOULD BE PROUD OF YOU, HELEN.
REALLY?
I AM POSITIVE!
YEAH, RIGHT, BUT WHAT ARE WE GOING TO DO WITH THAT LOWLIFE NOW?
YOU'RE NOT GOING TO LET HIM GET AWAY WITH IT?
WHAT DO YOU MEAN?
LET'S PRESS CHARGES!
I AGREE!
OH, FOR HEAVEN'S SAKES...
HOW DO YOU SUPPOSE IT WOULD END, UH? DO YOU THINK A TRAITOR'S DAUGHTER'S WORD IS WORTH ANYTHING...
...AGAINST THAT OF A NAVY CAPTAIN?
DAMN IT!
BESIDES, WILLIAM IS LEAVING ON HIS SHIP EARLY TOMORROW MORNING AND WE WILL NOT SEE HIM AGAIN FOR A LONG TIME...

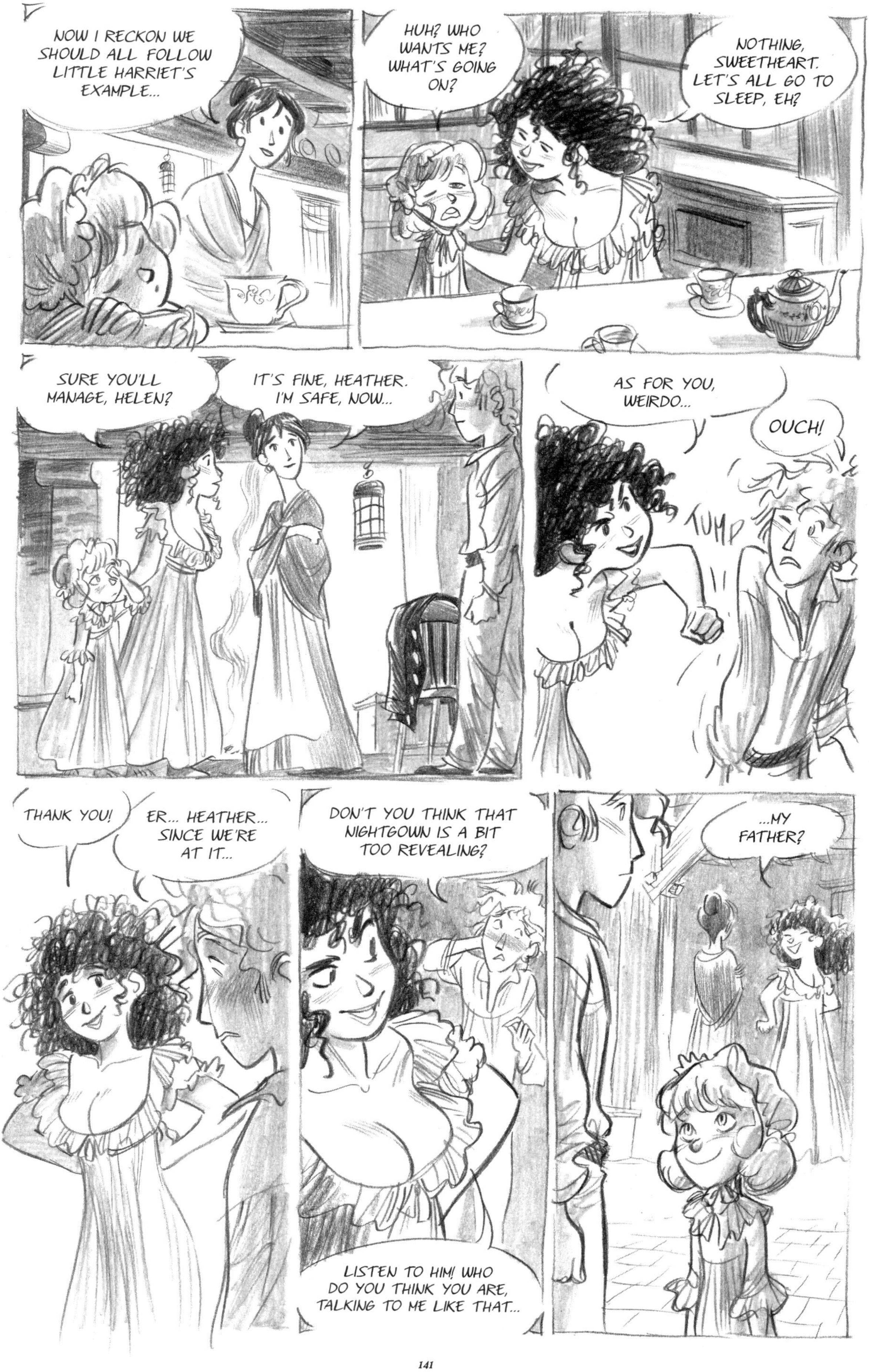
NOW I RECKON WE SHOULD ALL FOLLOW LITTLE HARRIET'S EXAMPLE...
HUH? WHO WANTS ME? WHAT'S GOING ON?
NOTHING, SWEETHEART. LET'S ALL GO TO SLEEP, EH?
SURE YOU'LL MANAGE, HELEN?
IT'S FINE, HEATHER. I'M SAFE, NOW...
AS FOR YOU, WEIRDO...
OUCH!
TUMP
THANK YOU!
ER... HEATHER... SINCE WE'RE AT IT...
DON'T YOU THINK THAT NIGHTGOWN IS A BIT TOO REVEALING?
LISTEN TO HIM! WHO DO YOU THINK YOU ARE, TALKING TO ME LIKE THAT...
...MY FATHER?

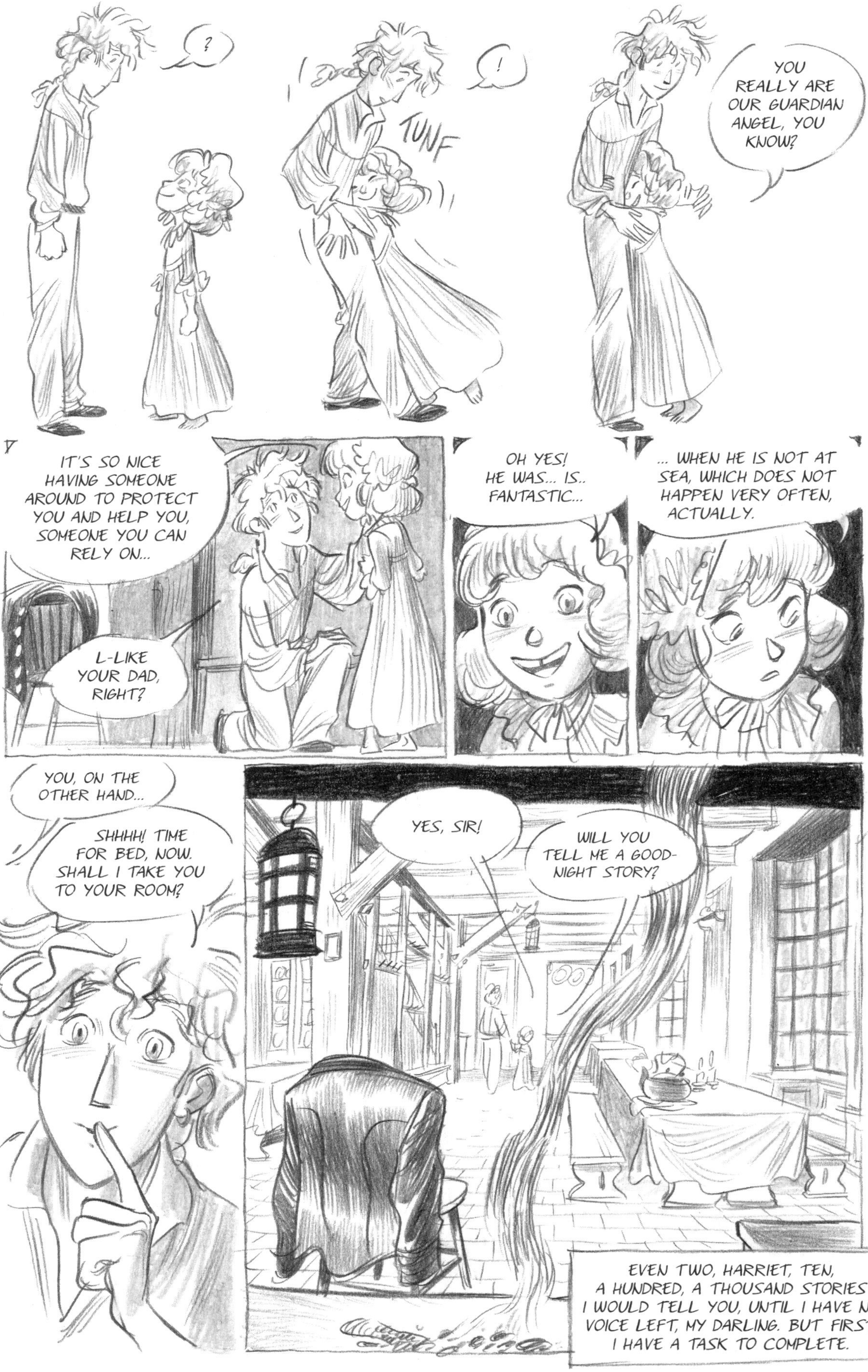
?
!
TUNF
YOU REALLY ARE OUR GUARDIAN ANGEL, YOU KNOW?
IT'S SO NICE HAVING SOMEONE AROUND TO PROTECT YOU AND HELP YOU, SOMEONE YOU CAN RELY ON...
L-LIKE YOUR DAD, RIGHT?
OH YES! HE WAS... IS.. FANTASTIC...
... WHEN HE IS NOT AT SEA, WHICH DOES NOT HAPPEN VERY OFTEN, ACTUALLY.
YOU, ON THE OTHER HAND...
SHHHH! TIME FOR BED, NOW. SHALL I TAKE YOU TO YOUR ROOM?
YES, SIR!
WILL YOU TELL ME A GOOD-NIGHT STORY?
EVEN TWO, HARRIET, TEN, A HUNDRED, A THOUSAND STORIES I WOULD TELL YOU, UNTIL I HAVE NO VOICE LEFT, MY DARLING. BUT FIRST, I HAVE A TASK TO COMPLETE.

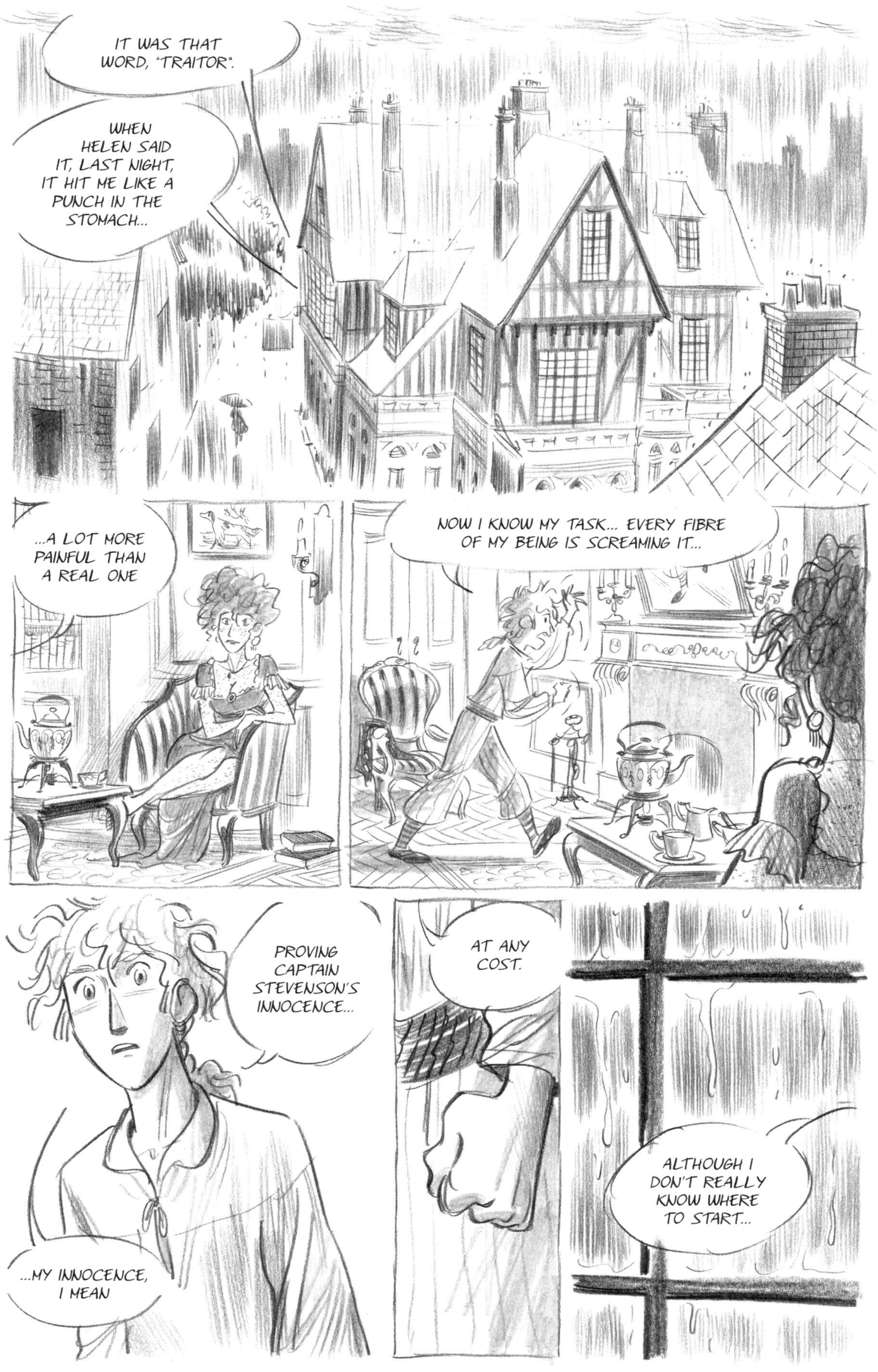

IT WAS THAT WORD, "TRAITOR".
WHEN HELEN SAID IT, LAST NIGHT, IT HIT ME LIKE A PUNCH IN THE STOMACH...
...A LOT MORE PAINFUL THAN A REAL ONE
NOW I KNOW MY TASK... EVERY FIBRE OF MY BEING IS SCREAMING IT...
PROVING CAPTAIN STEVENSON'S INNOCENCE...
...MY INNOCENCE, I MEAN
AT ANY COST.
ALTHOUGH I DON'T REALLY KNOW WHERE TO START...

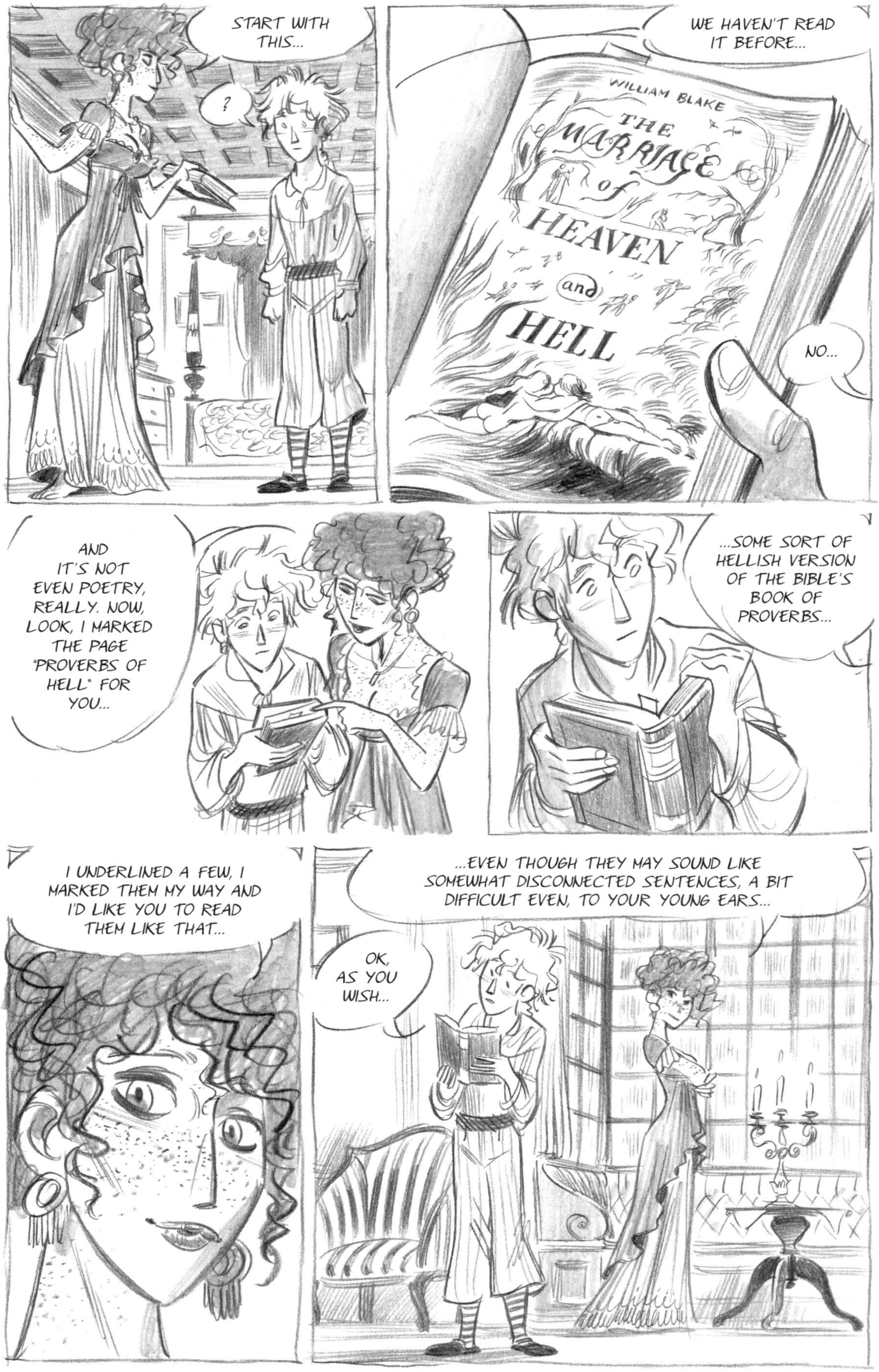
START WITH THIS...
?
WE HAVEN'T READ IT BEFORE...
WILLIAM BLAKE
THE MARRIAGE of HEAVEN and HELL
NO...
AND IT'S NOT EVEN POETRY, REALLY. NOW, LOOK, I MARKED THE PAGE "PROVERBS OF HELL" FOR YOU...
...SOME SORT OF HELLISH VERSION OF THE BIBLE'S BOOK OF PROVERBS...
I UNDERLINED A FEW, I MARKED THEM MY WAY AND I'D LIKE YOU TO READ THEM LIKE THAT...
...EVEN THOUGH THEY MAY SOUND LIKE SOMEWHAT DISCONNECTED SENTENCES, A BIT DIFFICULT EVEN, TO YOUR YOUNG EARS...
OK, AS YOU WISH...

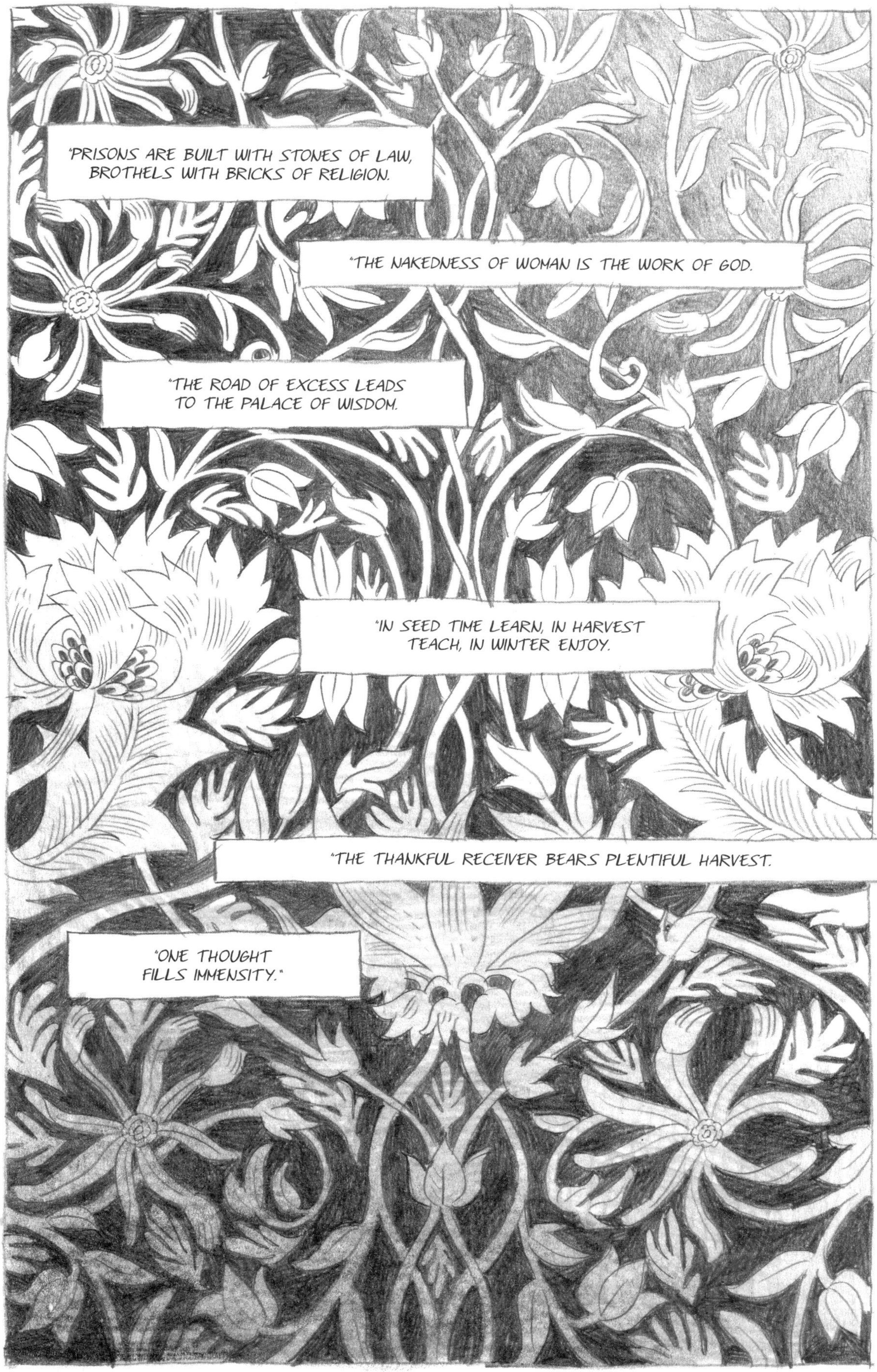
"PRISONS ARE BUILT WITH STONES OF LAW, BROTHELS WITH BRICKS OF RELIGION.
"THE NAKEDNESS OF WOMAN IS THE WORK OF GOD.
"THE ROAD OF EXCESS LEADS TO THE PALACE OF WISDOM.
"IN SEED TIME LEARN, IN HARVEST TEACH, IN WINTER ENJOY.
"THE THANKFUL RECEIVER BEARS PLENTIFUL HARVEST.
"ONE THOUGHT FILLS IMMENSITY."

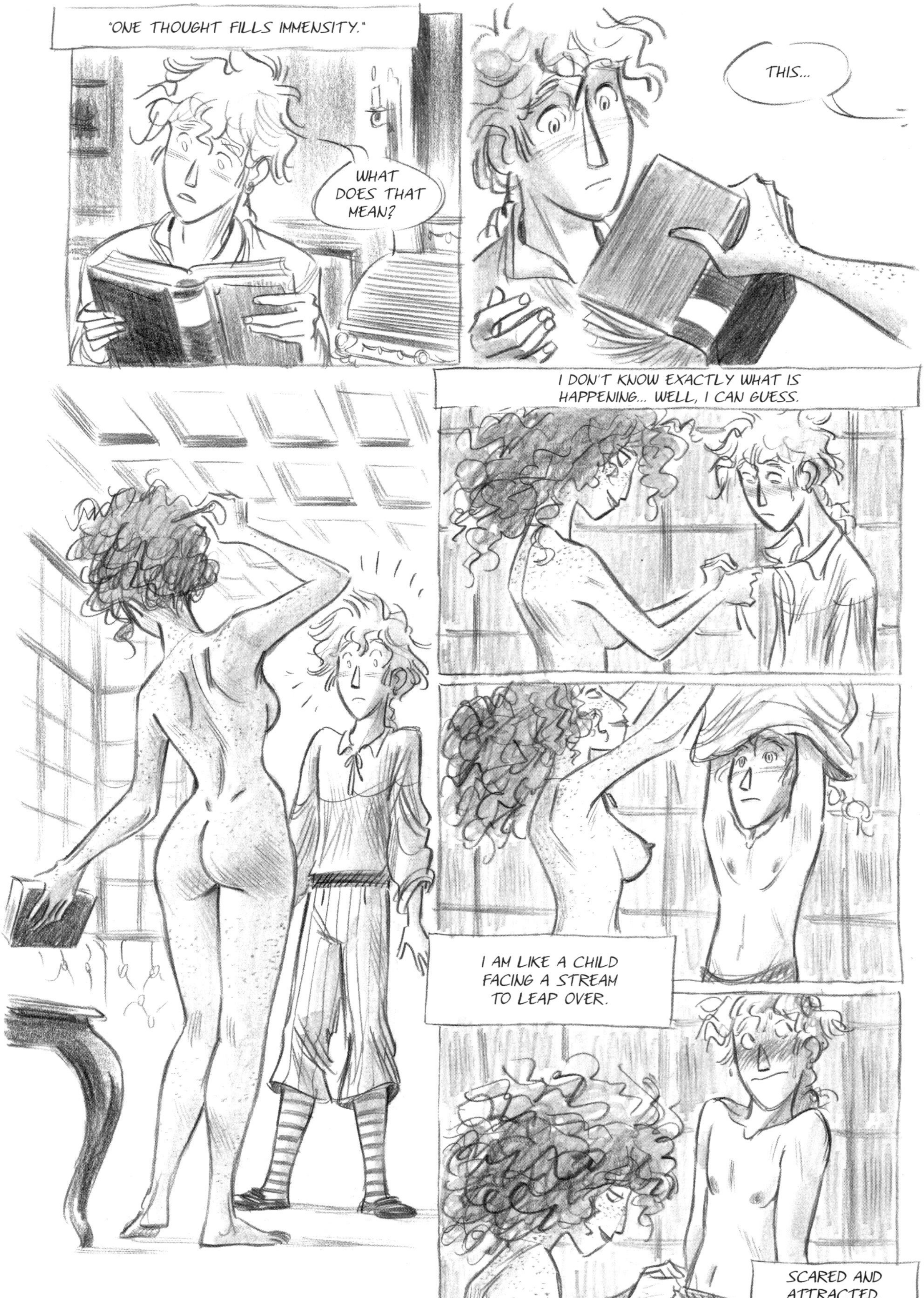
"ONE THOUGHT FILLS IMMENSITY."
WHAT DOES THAT MEAN?
THIS...
I DON'T KNOW EXACTLY WHAT IS HAPPENING... WELL, I CAN GUESS.
I AM LIKE A CHILD FACING A STREAM TO LEAP OVER.
SCARED AND ATTRACTED.

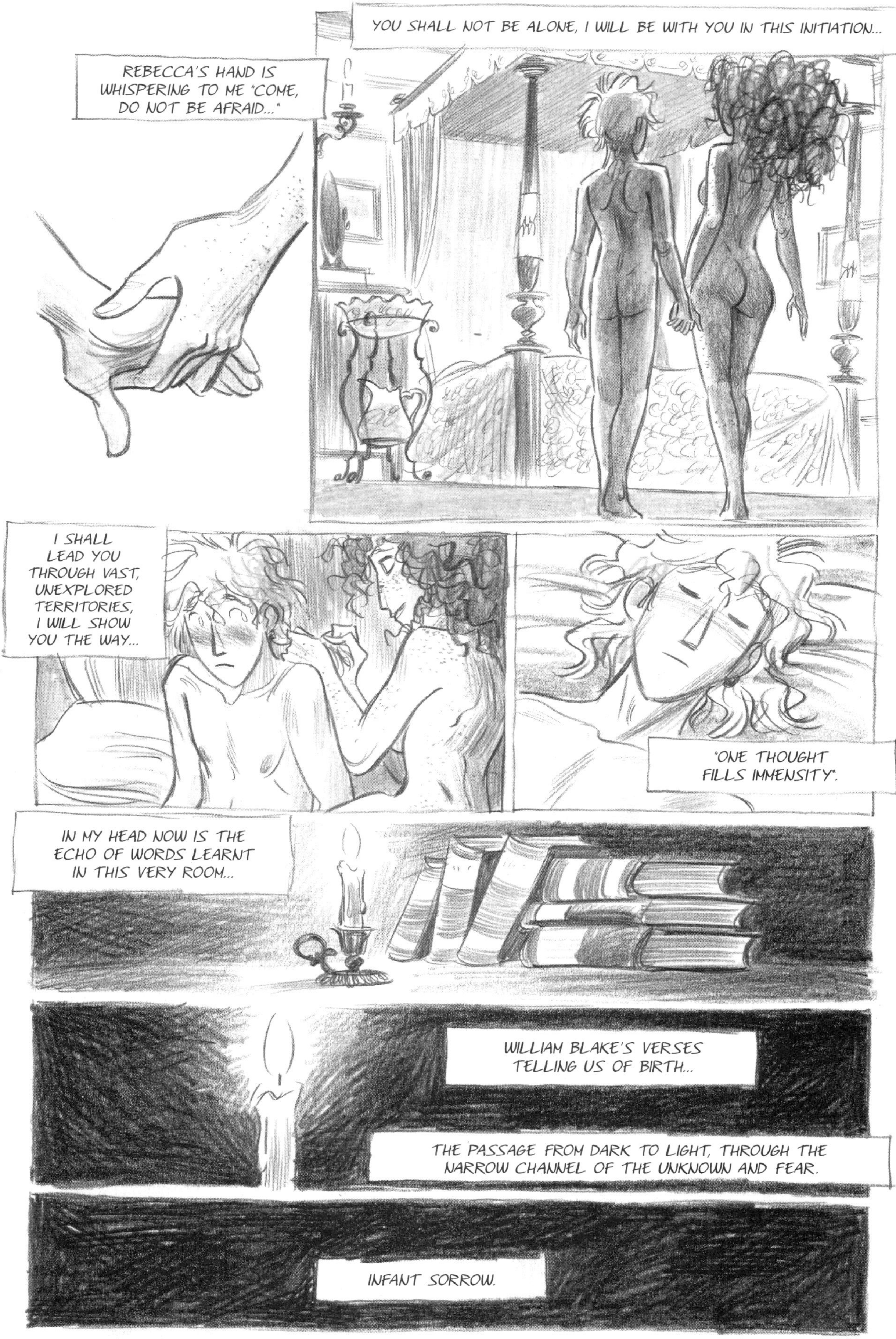
YOU SHALL NOT BE ALONE, I WILL BE WITH YOU IN THIS INITIATION...
REBECCA'S HAND IS WHISPERING TO ME "COME, DO NOT BE AFRAID..."
I SHALL LEAD YOU THROUGH VAST, UNEXPLORED TERRITORIES, I WILL SHOW YOU THE WAY...
"ONE THOUGHT FILLS IMMENSITY".
IN MY HEAD NOW IS THE ECHO OF WORDS LEARNT IN THIS VERY ROOM...
WILLIAM BLAKE'S VERSES TELLING US OF BIRTH...
THE PASSAGE FROM DARK TO LIGHT, THROUGH THE NARROW CHANNEL OF THE UNKNOWN AND FEAR.
INFANT SORROW.

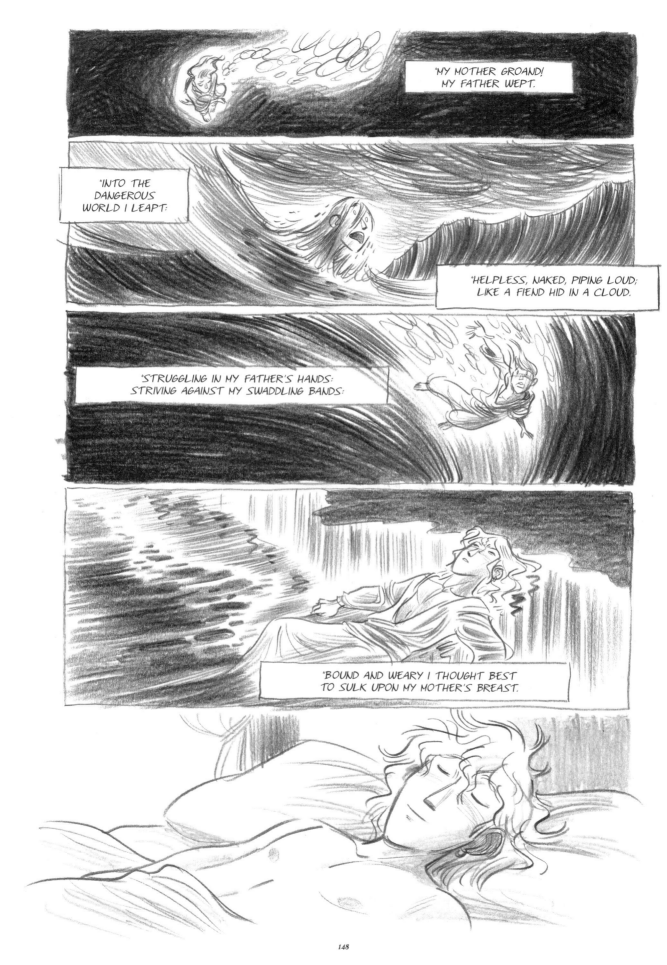

"MY MOTHER GROAN!
MY FATHER WEPT.

"INTO THE
DANGEROUS
WORLD I LEAPT:

"HELPLESS, NAKED, PIPING LOUD;
LIKE A FIEND HID IN A CLOUD.

"STRUGGLING IN MY FATHER'S HANDS:
STRIVING AGAINST MY SWADDLING BANDS:

"BOUND AND WEARY I THOUGHT BEST
TO SULK UPON MY MOTHER'S BREAST.

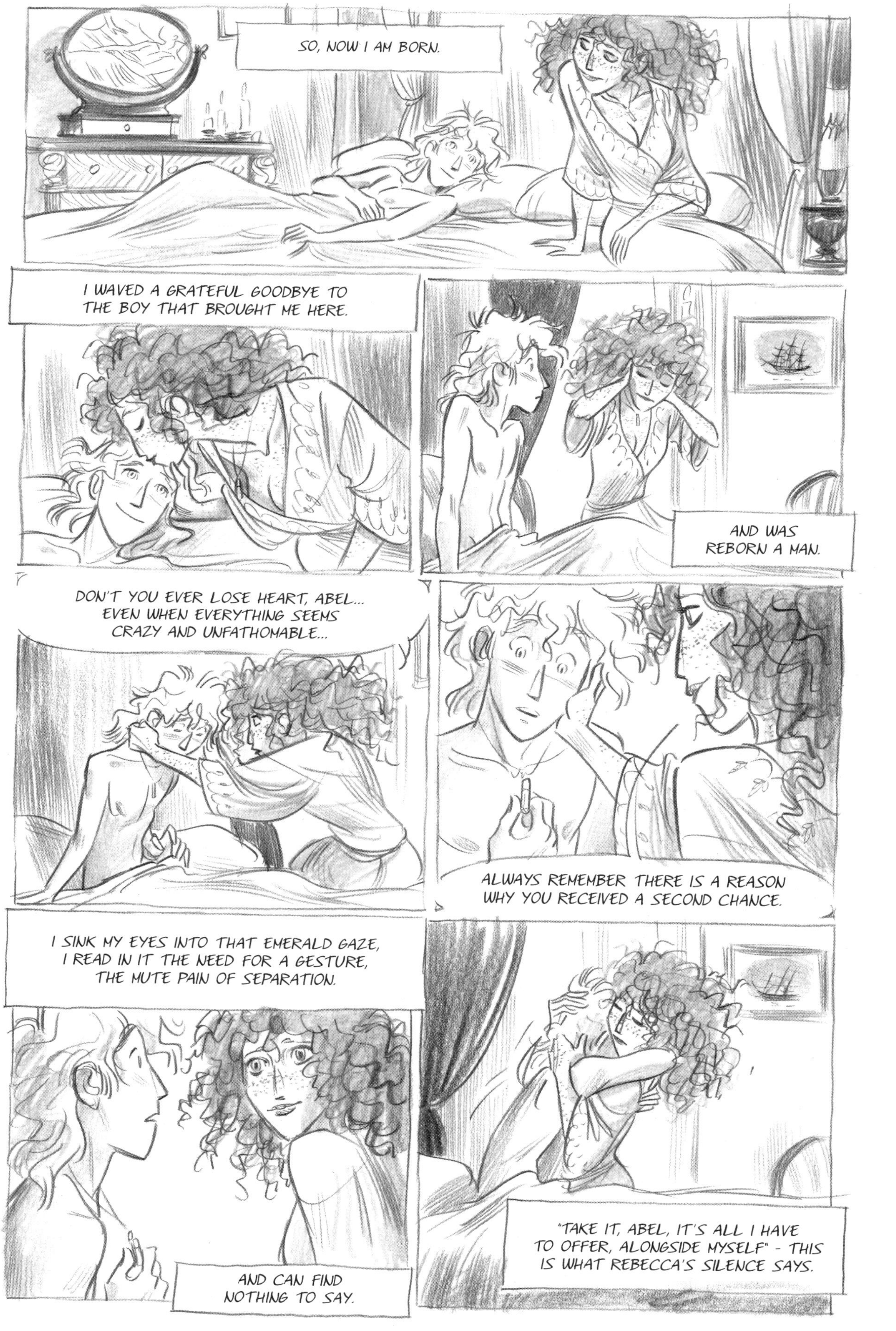
SO, NOW I AM BORN.
I WAVED A GRATEFUL GOODBYE TO THE BOY THAT BROUGHT ME HERE.
AND WAS REBORN A MAN.
DON'T YOU EVER LOSE HEART, ABEL... EVEN WHEN EVERYTHING SEEMS CRAZY AND UNFATHOMABLE...
ALWAYS REMEMBER THERE IS A REASON WHY YOU RECEIVED A SECOND CHANCE.
I SINK MY EYES INTO THAT EMERALD GAZE, I READ IN IT THE NEED FOR A GESTURE, THE MUTE PAIN OF SEPARATION.
AND CAN FIND NOTHING TO SAY.
"TAKE IT, ABEL, IT'S ALL I HAVE TO OFFER, ALONGSIDE MYSELF" - THIS IS WHAT REBECCA'S SILENCE SAYS.

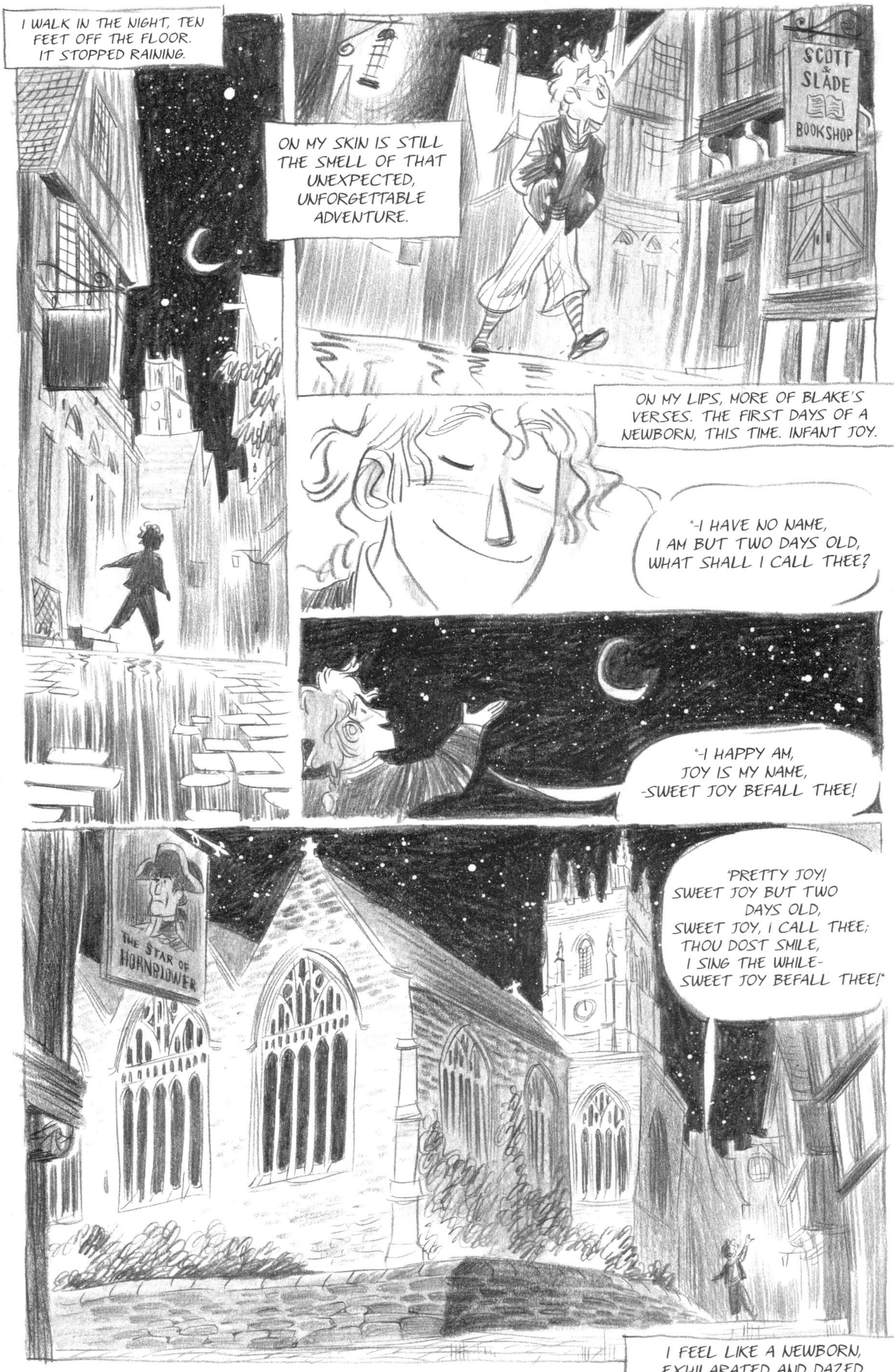
I WALK IN THE NIGHT, TEN FEET OFF THE FLOOR. IT STOPPED RAINING.
ON MY SKIN IS STILL THE SMELL OF THAT UNEXPECTED, UNFORGETTABLE ADVENTURE.
SCOTT & SLADE BOOKSHOP
ON MY LIPS, MORE OF BLAKE'S VERSES. THE FIRST DAYS OF A NEWBORN, THIS TIME. INFANT JOY.
"-I HAVE NO NAME, I AM BUT TWO DAYS OLD, WHAT SHALL I CALL THEE?
"-I HAPPY AM, JOY IS MY NAME, -SWEET JOY BEFALL THEE!
THE STAR OF HORNBLOWER
"PRETTY JOY! SWEET JOY BUT TWO DAYS OLD, SWEET JOY, I CALL THEE; THOU DOST SMILE, I SING THE WHILE- SWEET JOY BEFALL THEE!"
I FEEL LIKE A NEWBORN, EXHILARATED AND DAZED.

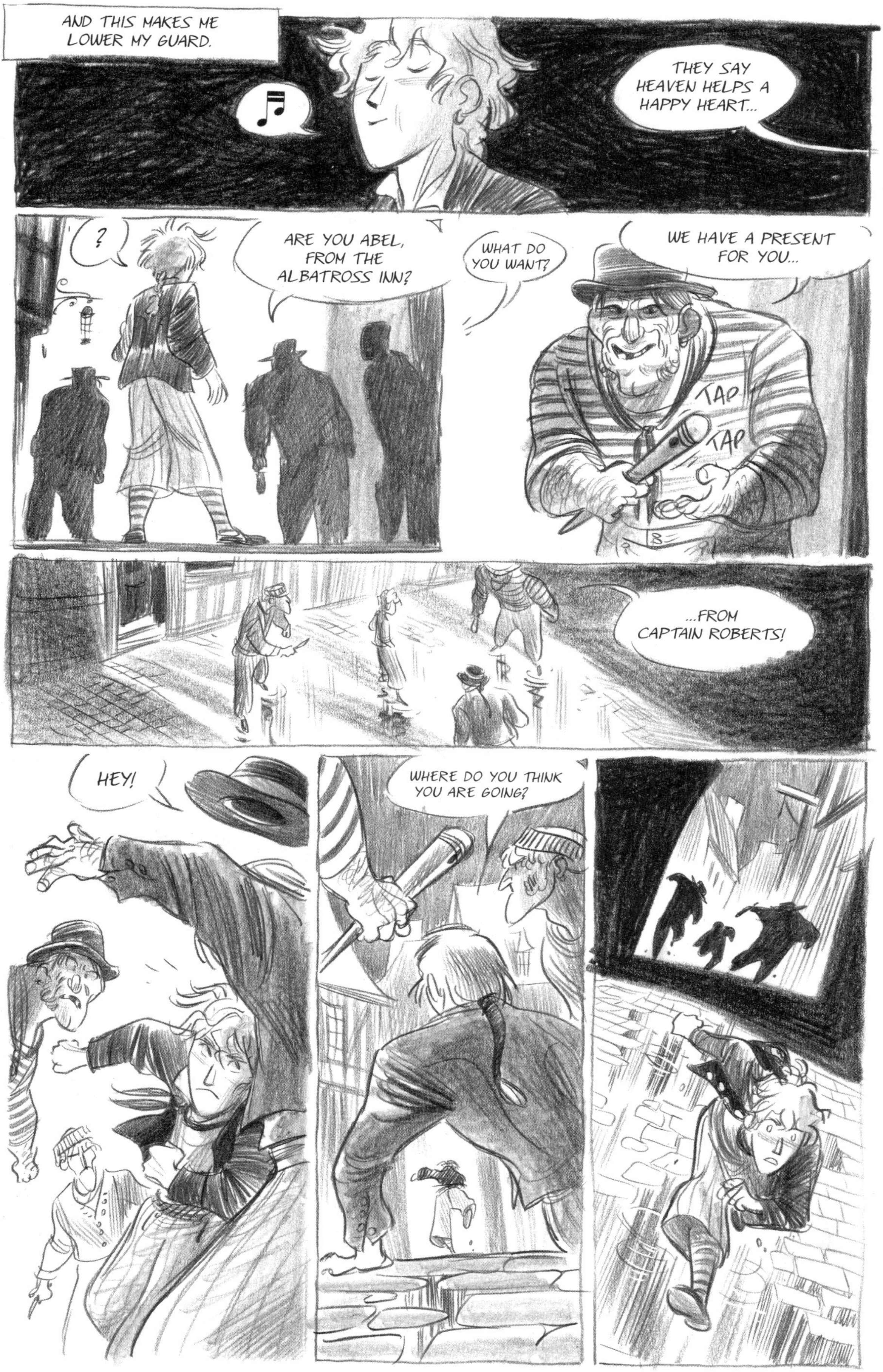
AND THIS MAKES ME LOWER MY GUARD.
THEY SAY HEAVEN HELPS A HAPPY HEART...
?
ARE YOU ABEL, FROM THE ALBATROSS INN?
WHAT DO YOU WANT?
WE HAVE A PRESENT FOR YOU...
TAP
TAP
...FROM CAPTAIN ROBERTS!
HEY!
WHERE DO YOU THINK YOU ARE GOING?

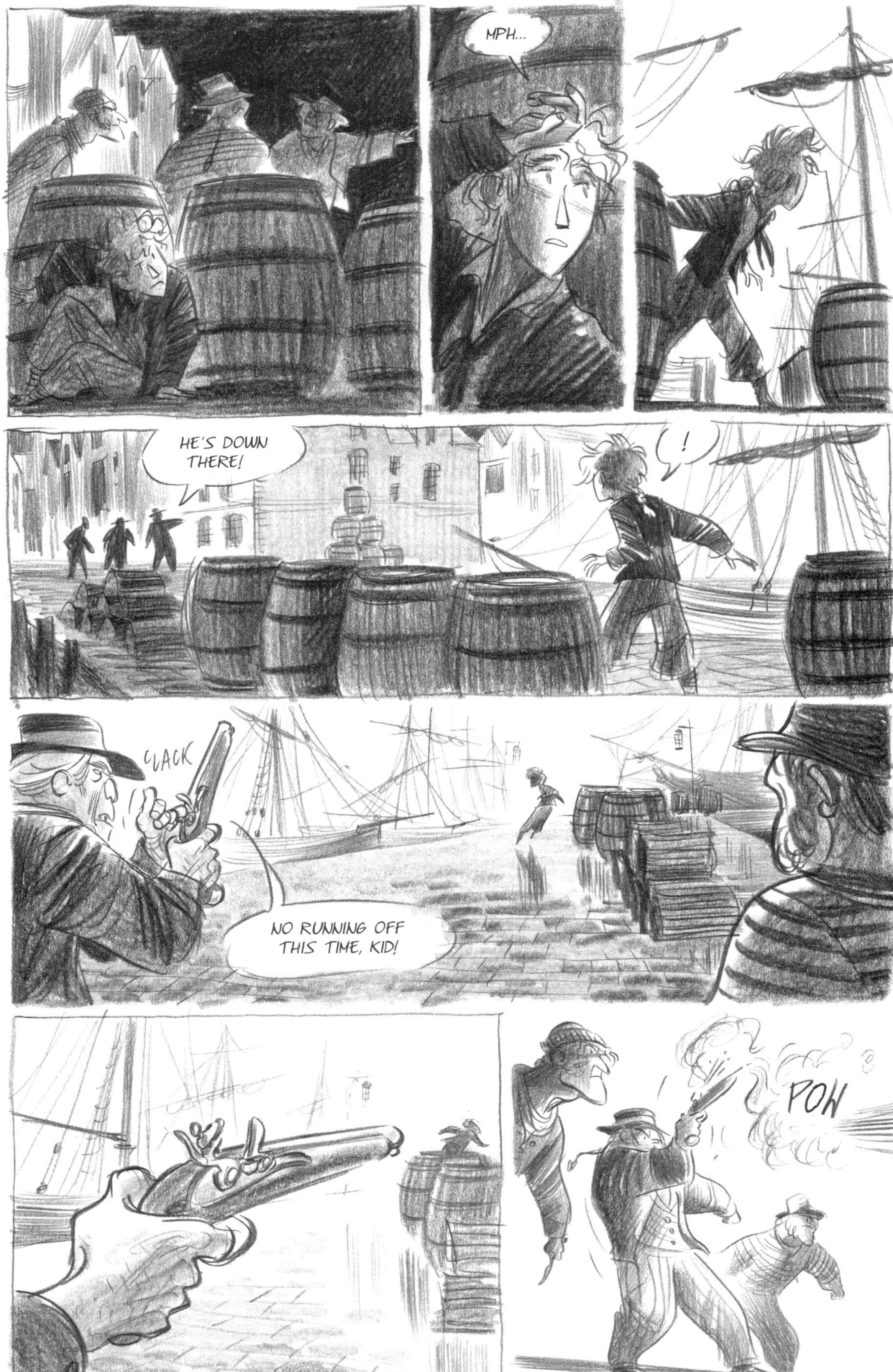
MPH...
HE'S DOWN THERE!
!
CLACK
NO RUNNING OFF THIS TIME, KID!
POW

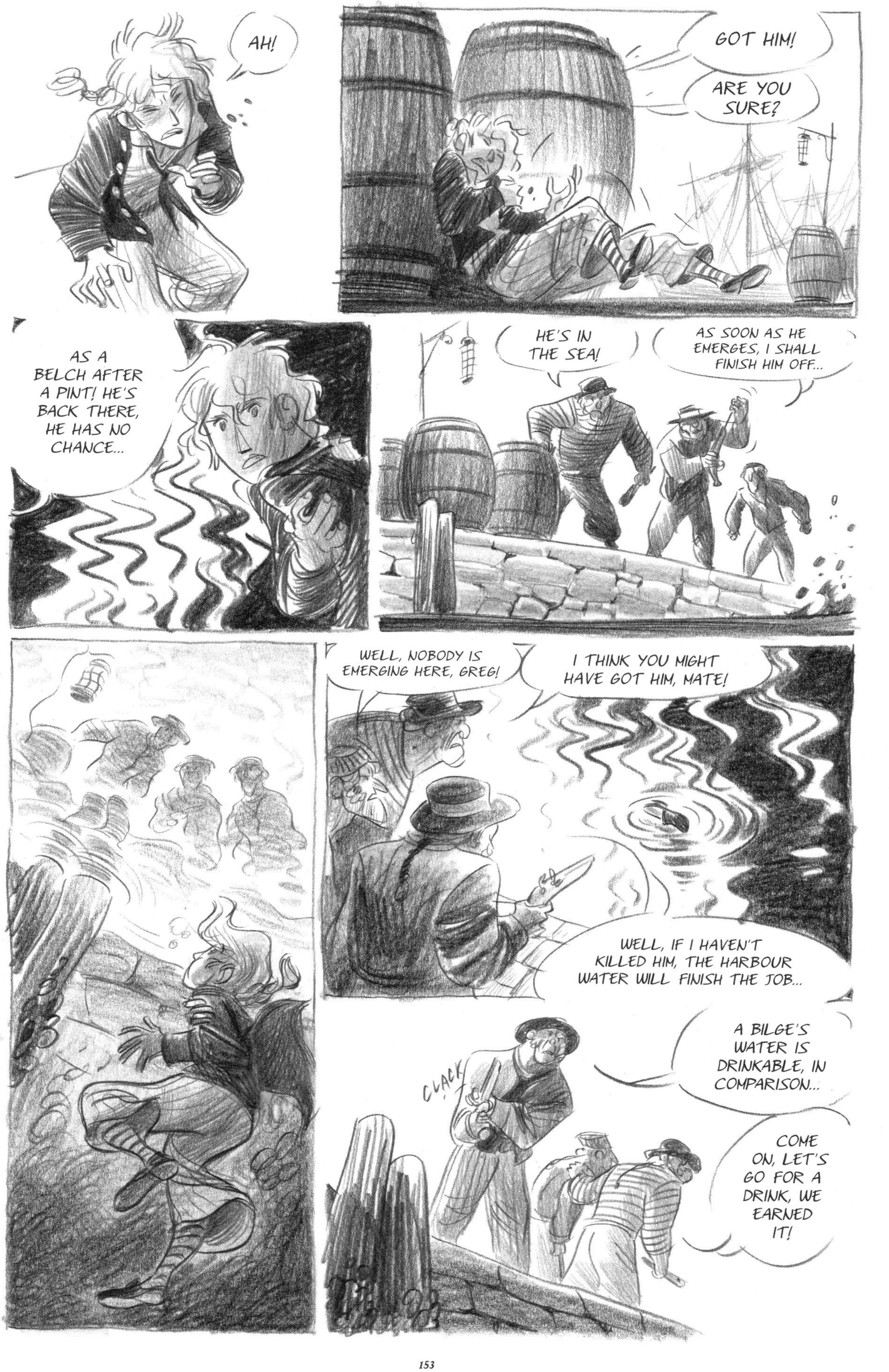
AH!
GOT HIM!
ARE YOU SURE?
AS A BELCH AFTER A PINT! HE'S BACK THERE, HE HAS NO CHANCE...
HE'S IN THE SEA!
AS SOON AS HE EMERGES, I SHALL FINISH HIM OFF...
WELL, NOBODY IS EMERGING HERE, GREG!
I THINK YOU MIGHT HAVE GOT HIM, MATE!
WELL, IF I HAVEN'T KILLED HIM, THE HARBOUR WATER WILL FINISH THE JOB...
CLACK
A BILGE'S WATER IS DRINKABLE, IN COMPARISON...
COME ON, LET'S GO FOR A DRINK, WE EARNED IT!

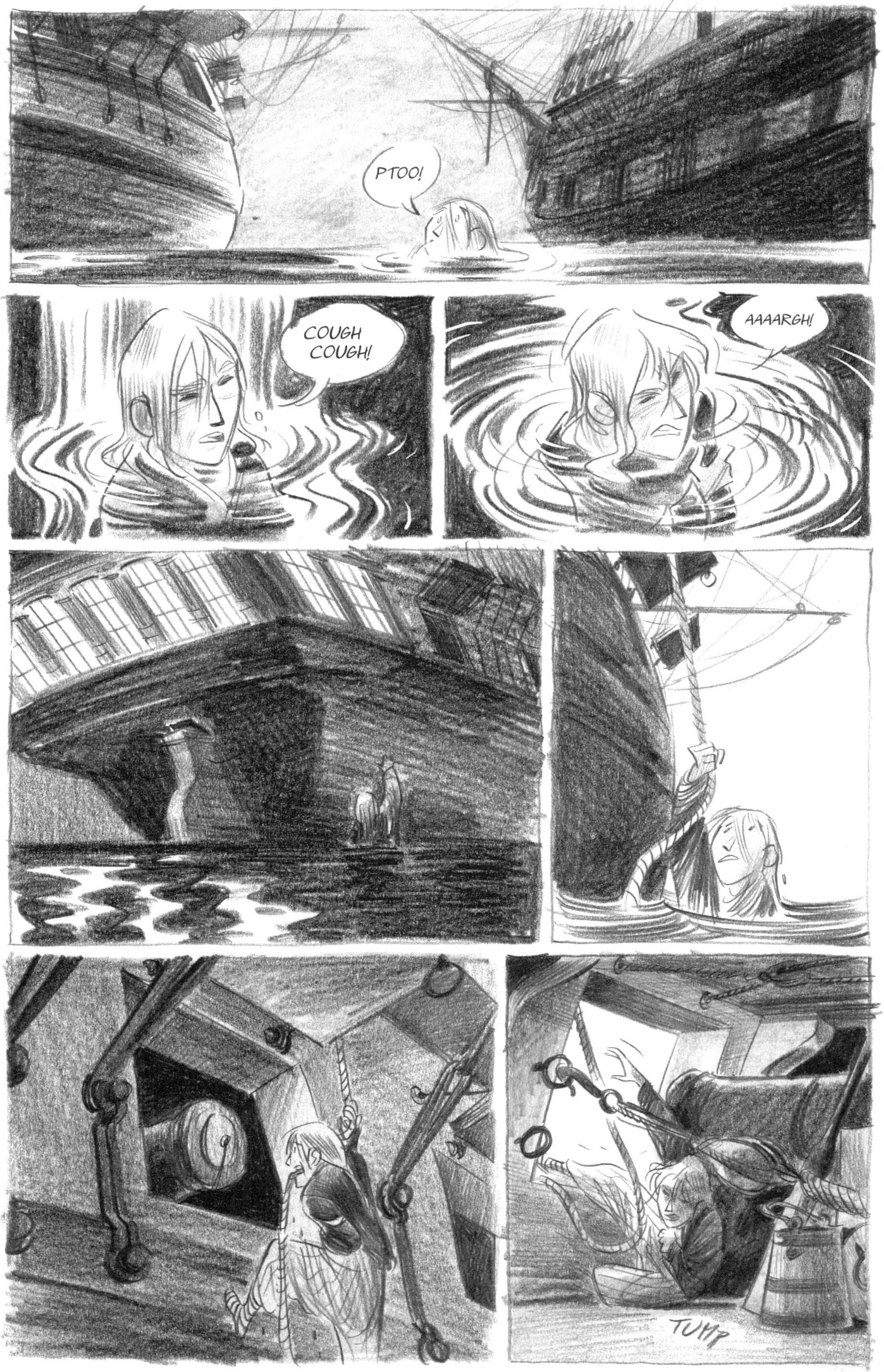
PTOO!
COUGH COUGH!
AAAARGH!
TUMP

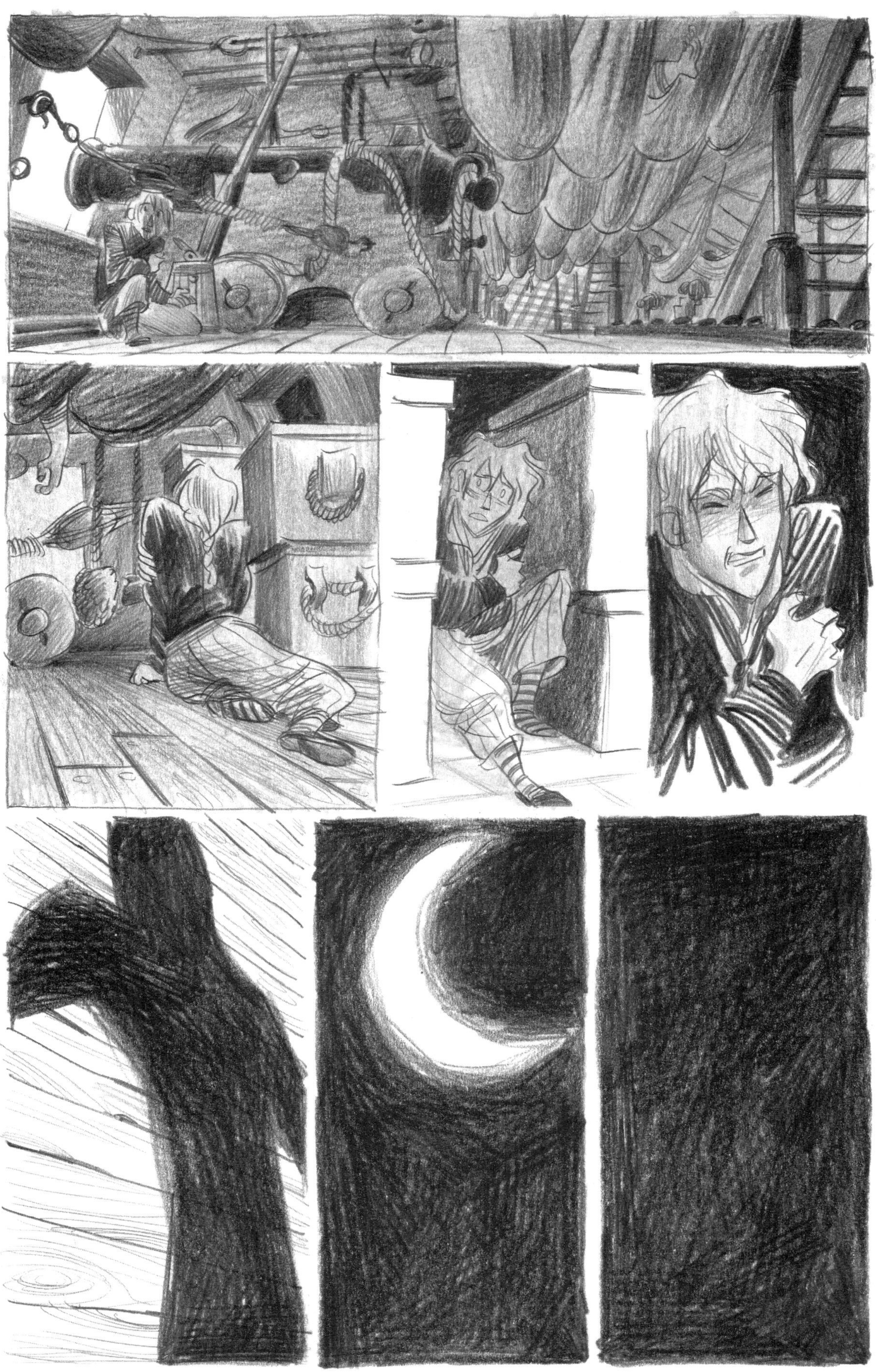

ACT III
EICS LAST CHANCE

THE unfathomable sea, and time, and tears,
The deeds of heroes and the crimes of kings
Dispart us; and the river of events
Has, for an age of years, to east and west
More widely borne our cradles. Thou to me
Art foreign, as when seamen at the dawn
Descry a land far off and know not which.
So I approach uncertain; so I cruise
Round thy mysterious islet, and behold
Surf and great mountains and loud river-bars,
And from the shore hear inland voices call.

Strange is the seaman's heart; he hopes, he fears;
Draws closer and sweeps wider from that coast;
Last, his rent sail refits, and to the deep
His shattered prow uncomforted puts back.
Yet as he goes he ponders at the helm
Of that bright island; where he feared to touch,
His spirit readventures; and for years,
Where by his wife he slumbers safe at home,
Thoughts of that land revisit him; he sees
The eternal mountains beckon, and awakes
Yearning for that far home that might have been.

Robert Louis Stevenson

TO N.V. DE G.S.
(Underwoods)

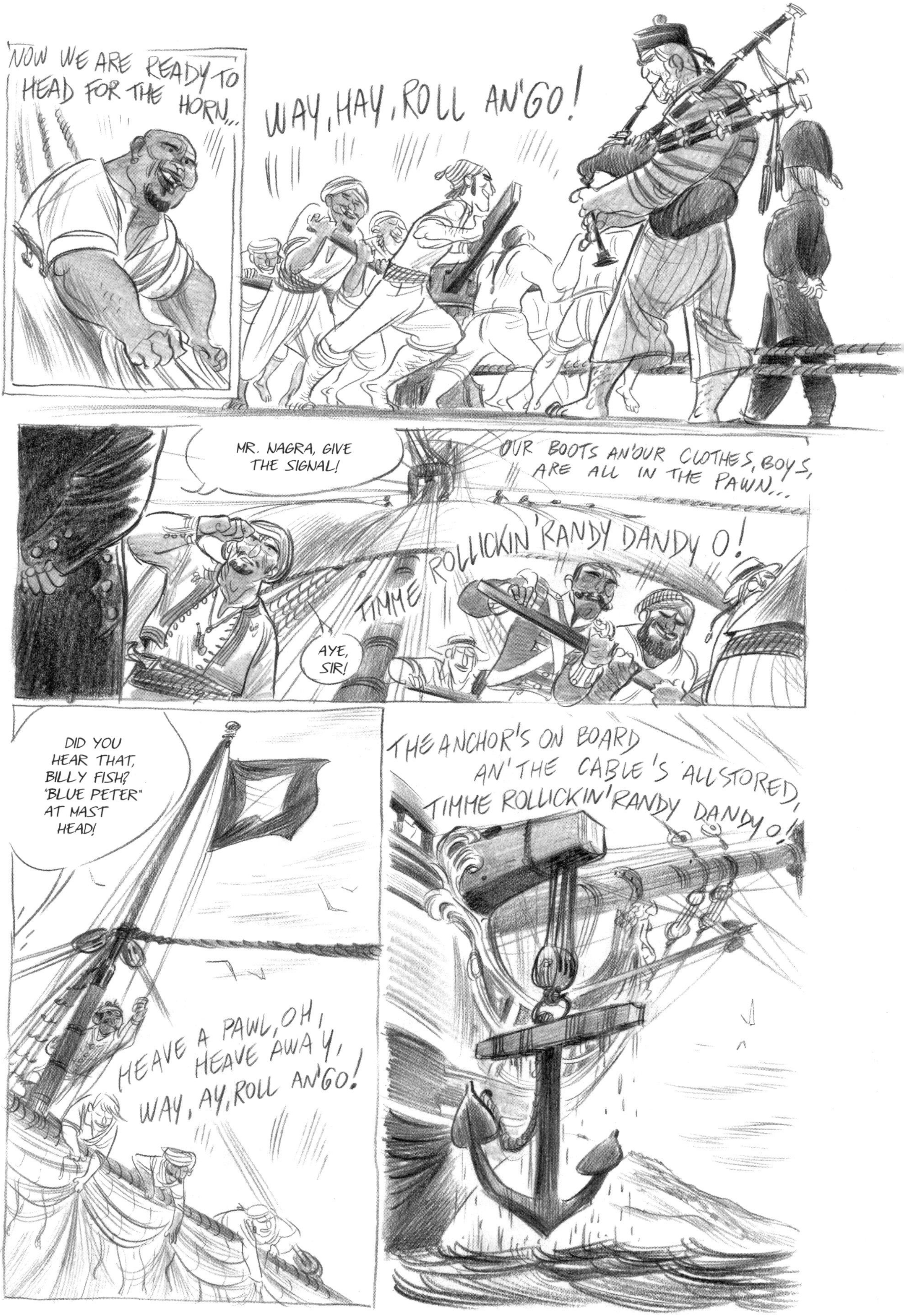

NOW WE ARE READY TO HEAD FOR THE HORN...
WAY, HAY, ROLL AN'GO!
MR. NAGRA, GIVE THE SIGNAL!
OUR BOOTS AN'OUR CLOTHES, BOYS, ARE ALL IN THE PAWN...
TIMME ROLLICKIN' RANDY DANDY O!
AYE, SIR!
DID YOU HEAR THAT, BILLY FISH? "BLUE PETER" AT MAST HEAD!
HEAVE A PAWL, OH, HEAVE AWAY, WAY, AY, ROLL AN'GO!
THE ANCHOR'S ON BOARD AN' THE CABLE'S ALL STORED, TIMME ROLLICKIN' RANDY DANDY O!

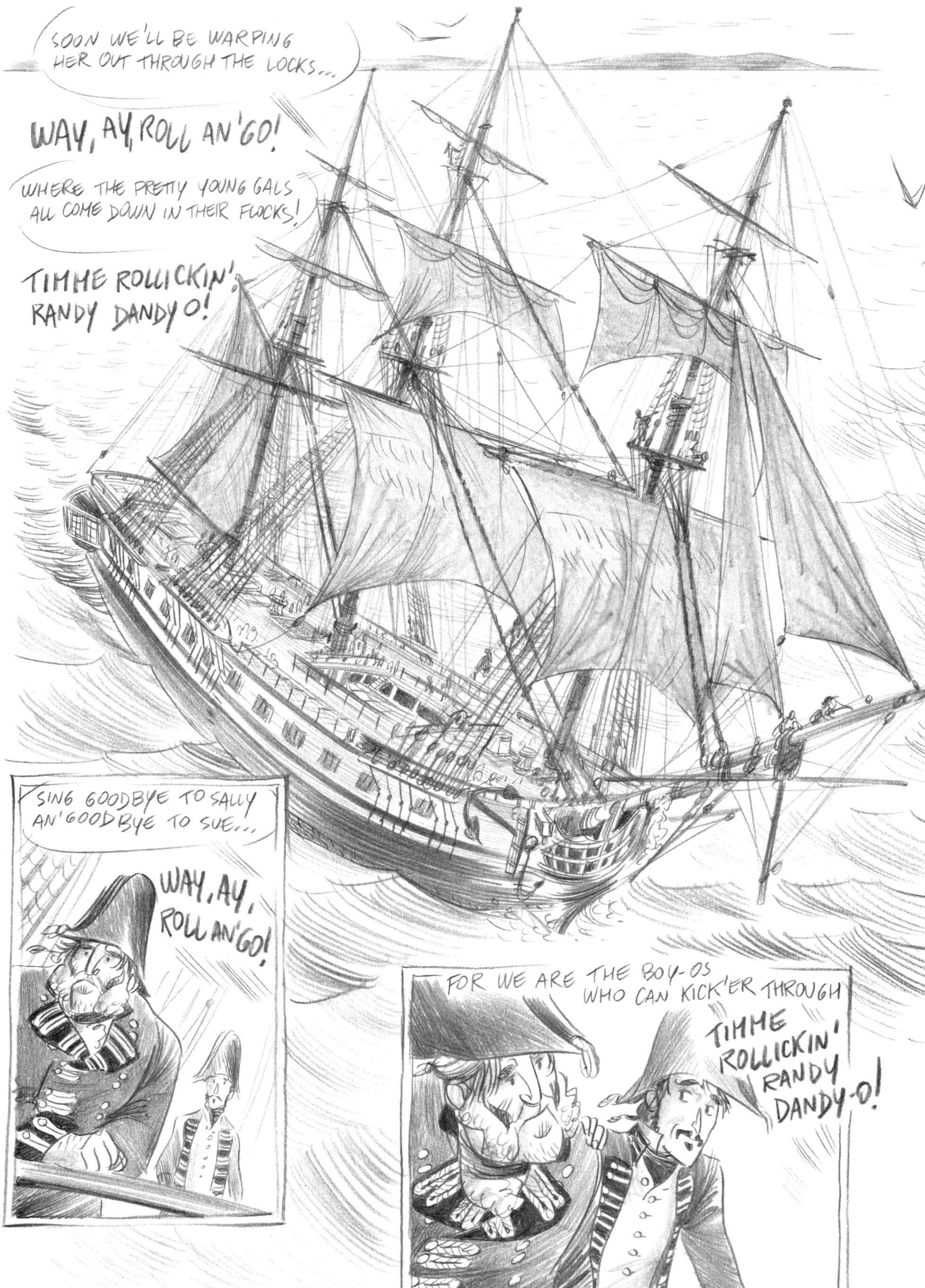
SOON WE'LL BE WARPING HER OUT THROUGH THE LOCKS...
WAY, AY, ROLL AN' GO!
WHERE THE PRETTY YOUNG GALS ALL COME DOWN IN THEIR FLOCKS!
TIMME ROLLICKIN' RANDY DANDY O!
SING GOODBYE TO SALLY AN' GOODBYE TO SUE...
WAY, AY, ROLL AN' GO!
FOR WE ARE THE BOY-OS WHO CAN KICK 'ER THROUGH
TIMME ROLLICKIN' RANDY DANDY-O!

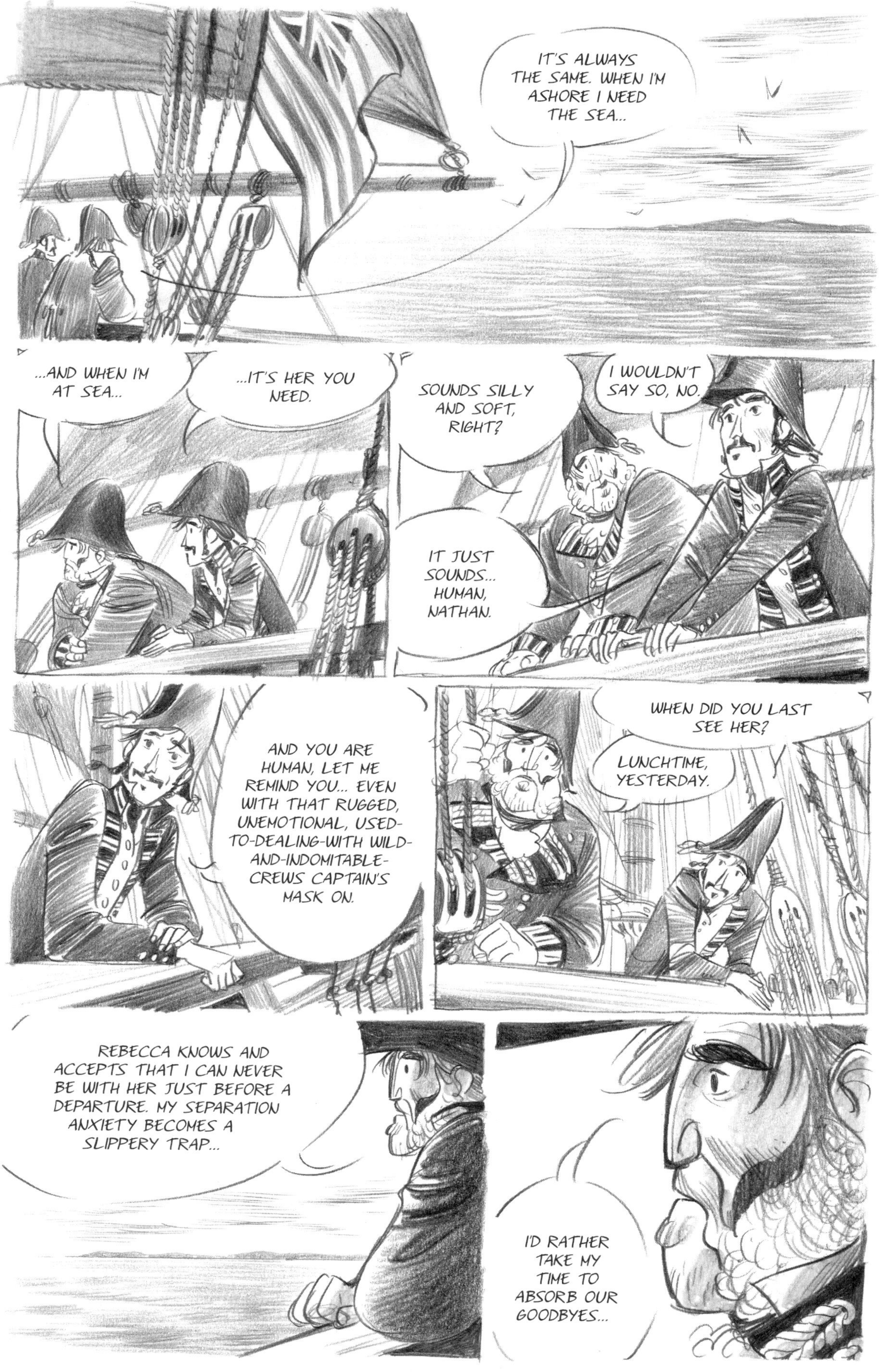
IT'S ALWAYS THE SAME. WHEN I'M ASHORE I NEED THE SEA...
...AND WHEN I'M AT SEA...
...IT'S HER YOU NEED.
SOUNDS SILLY AND SOFT, RIGHT?
I WOULDN'T SAY SO, NO.
IT JUST SOUNDS... HUMAN, NATHAN.
AND YOU ARE HUMAN, LET ME REMIND YOU... EVEN WITH THAT RUGGED, UNEMOTIONAL, USED-TO-DEALING-WITH WILD-AND-INDOMITABLE-CREWS CAPTAIN'S MASK ON.
WHEN DID YOU LAST SEE HER?
LUNCHTIME, YESTERDAY.
REBECCA KNOWS AND ACCEPTS THAT I CAN NEVER BE WITH HER JUST BEFORE A DEPARTURE. MY SEPARATION ANXIETY BECOMES A SLIPPERY TRAP...
I'D RATHER TAKE MY TIME TO ABSORB OUR GOODBYES...

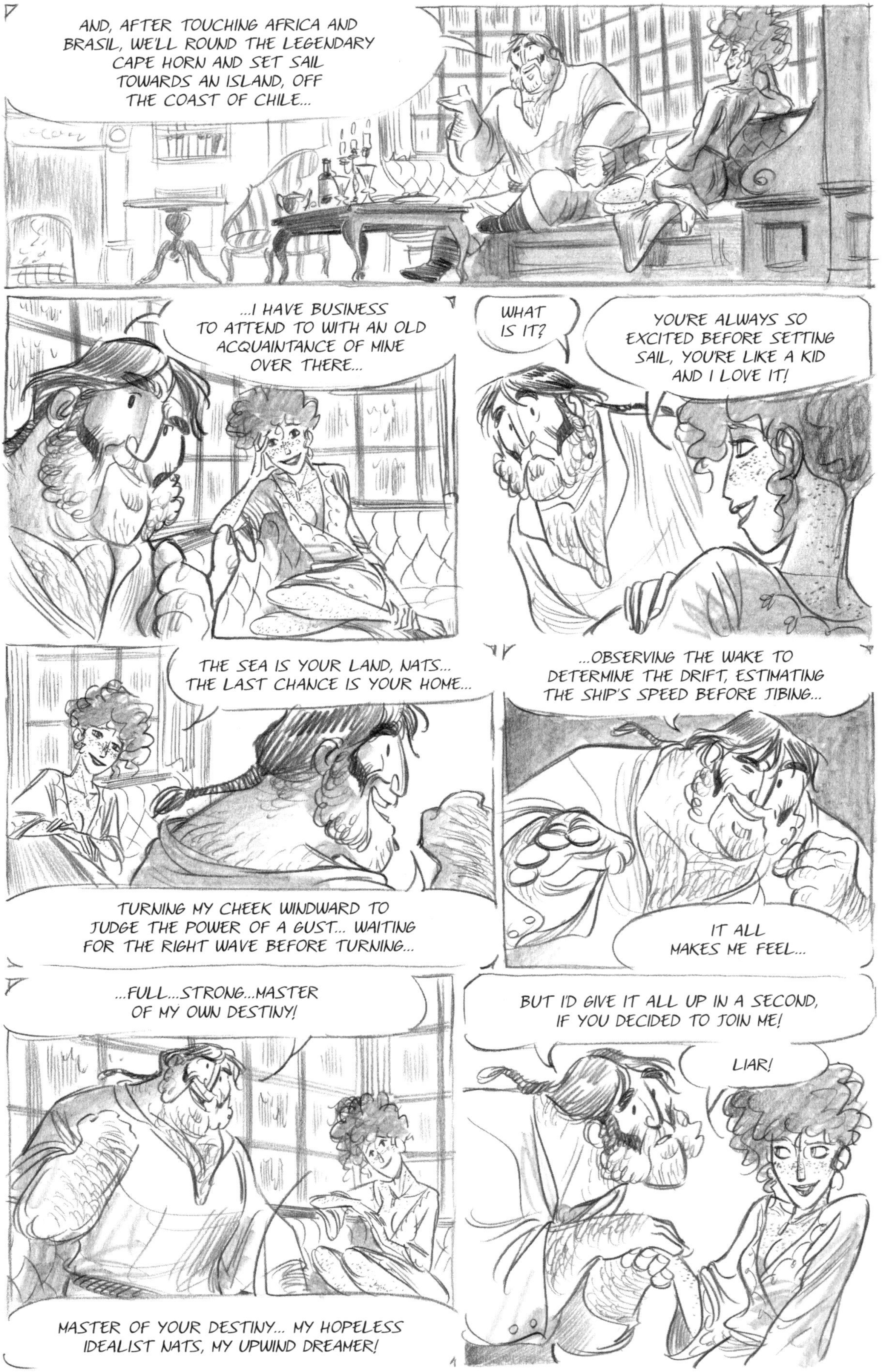
AND, AFTER TOUCHING AFRICA AND BRASIL, WE'LL ROUND THE LEGENDARY CAPE HORN AND SET SAIL TOWARDS AN ISLAND, OFF THE COAST OF CHILE...
...I HAVE BUSINESS TO ATTEND TO WITH AN OLD ACQUAINTANCE OF MINE OVER THERE...
WHAT IS IT?
YOU'RE ALWAYS SO EXCITED BEFORE SETTING SAIL, YOU'RE LIKE A KID AND I LOVE IT!
THE SEA IS YOUR LAND, NATS... THE LAST CHANCE IS YOUR HOME...
TURNING MY CHEEK WINDWARD TO JUDGE THE POWER OF A GUST... WAITING FOR THE RIGHT WAVE BEFORE TURNING...
...OBSERVING THE WAKE TO DETERMINE THE DRIFT, ESTIMATING THE SHIP'S SPEED BEFORE JIBING...
IT ALL MAKES ME FEEL...
...FULL...STRONG...MASTER OF MY OWN DESTINY!
MASTER OF YOUR DESTINY... MY HOPELESS IDEALIST NATS, MY UPWIND DREAMER!
BUT I'D GIVE IT ALL UP IN A SECOND, IF YOU DECIDED TO JOIN ME!
LIAR!

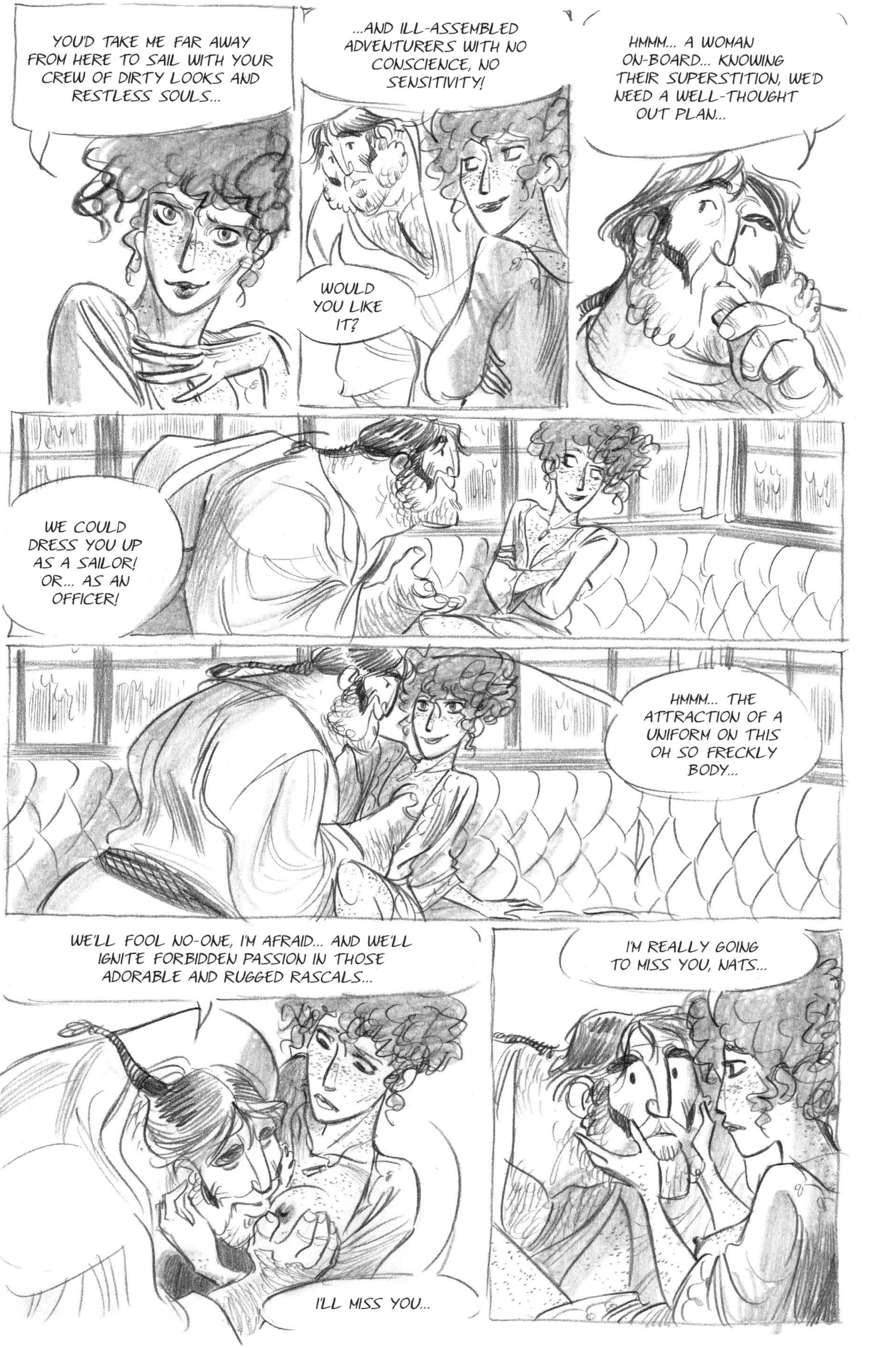
YOU'D TAKE ME FAR AWAY FROM HERE TO SAIL WITH YOUR CREW OF DIRTY LOOKS AND RESTLESS SOULS...
...AND ILL-ASSEMBLED ADVENTURERS WITH NO CONSCIENCE, NO SENSITIVITY!
WOULD YOU LIKE IT?
HMMM... A WOMAN ON-BOARD... KNOWING THEIR SUPERSTITION, WE'D NEED A WELL-THOUGHT OUT PLAN...
WE COULD DRESS YOU UP AS A SAILOR! OR... AS AN OFFICER!
HMMM... THE ATTRACTION OF A UNIFORM ON THIS OH SO FRECKLY BODY...
WE'LL FOOL NO-ONE, I'M AFRAID... AND WE'LL IGNITE FORBIDDEN PASSION IN THOSE ADORABLE AND RUGGED RASCALS...
I'LL MISS YOU...
I'M REALLY GOING TO MISS YOU, NATS...

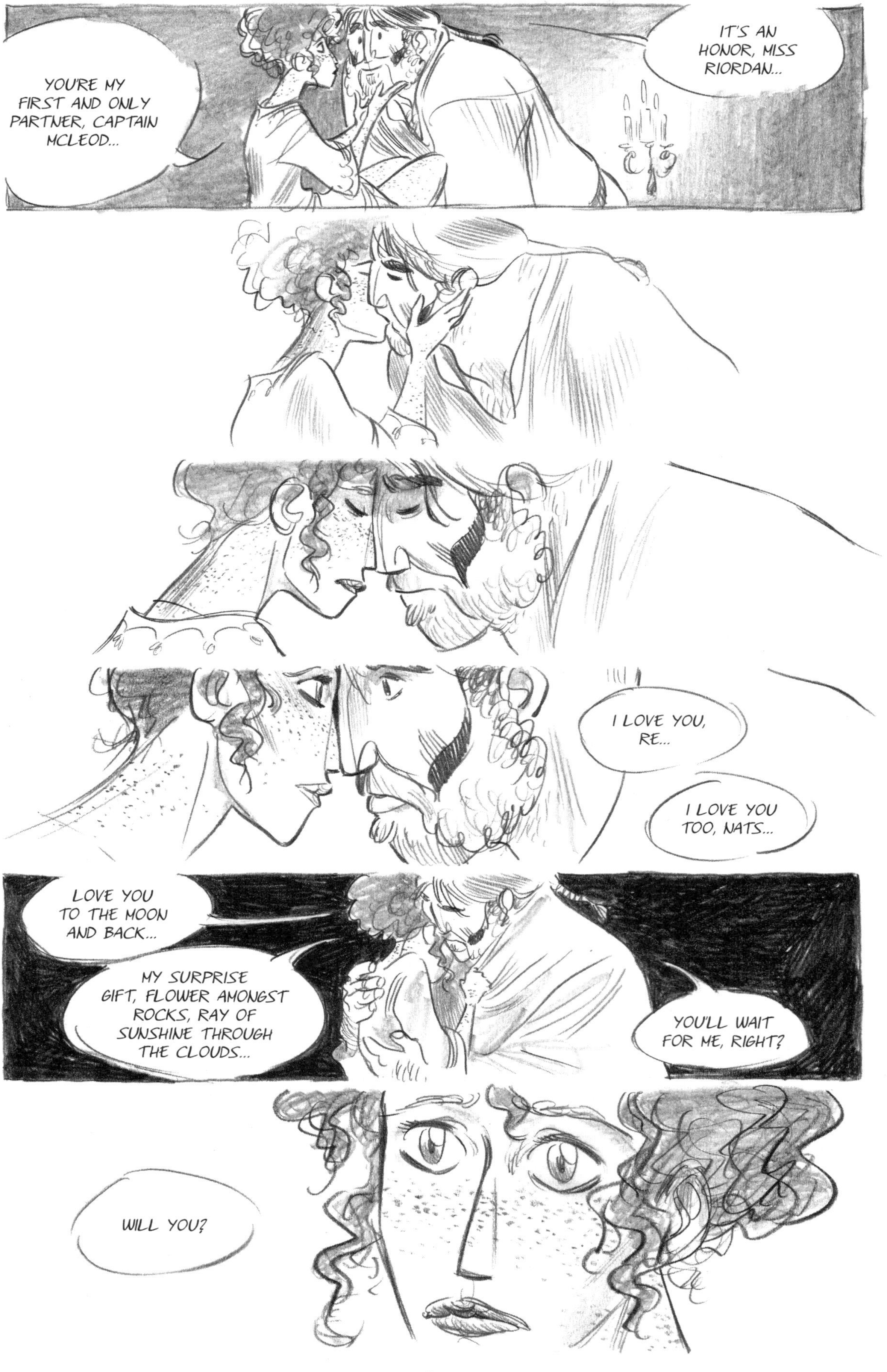
YOU'RE MY FIRST AND ONLY PARTNER, CAPTAIN MCLEOD...
IT'S AN HONOR, MISS RIORDAN...
I LOVE YOU, RE...
I LOVE YOU TOO, NATS...
LOVE YOU TO THE MOON AND BACK...
MY SURPRISE GIFT, FLOWER AMONGST ROCKS, RAY OF SUNSHINE THROUGH THE CLOUDS...
YOU'LL WAIT FOR ME, RIGHT?
WILL YOU?

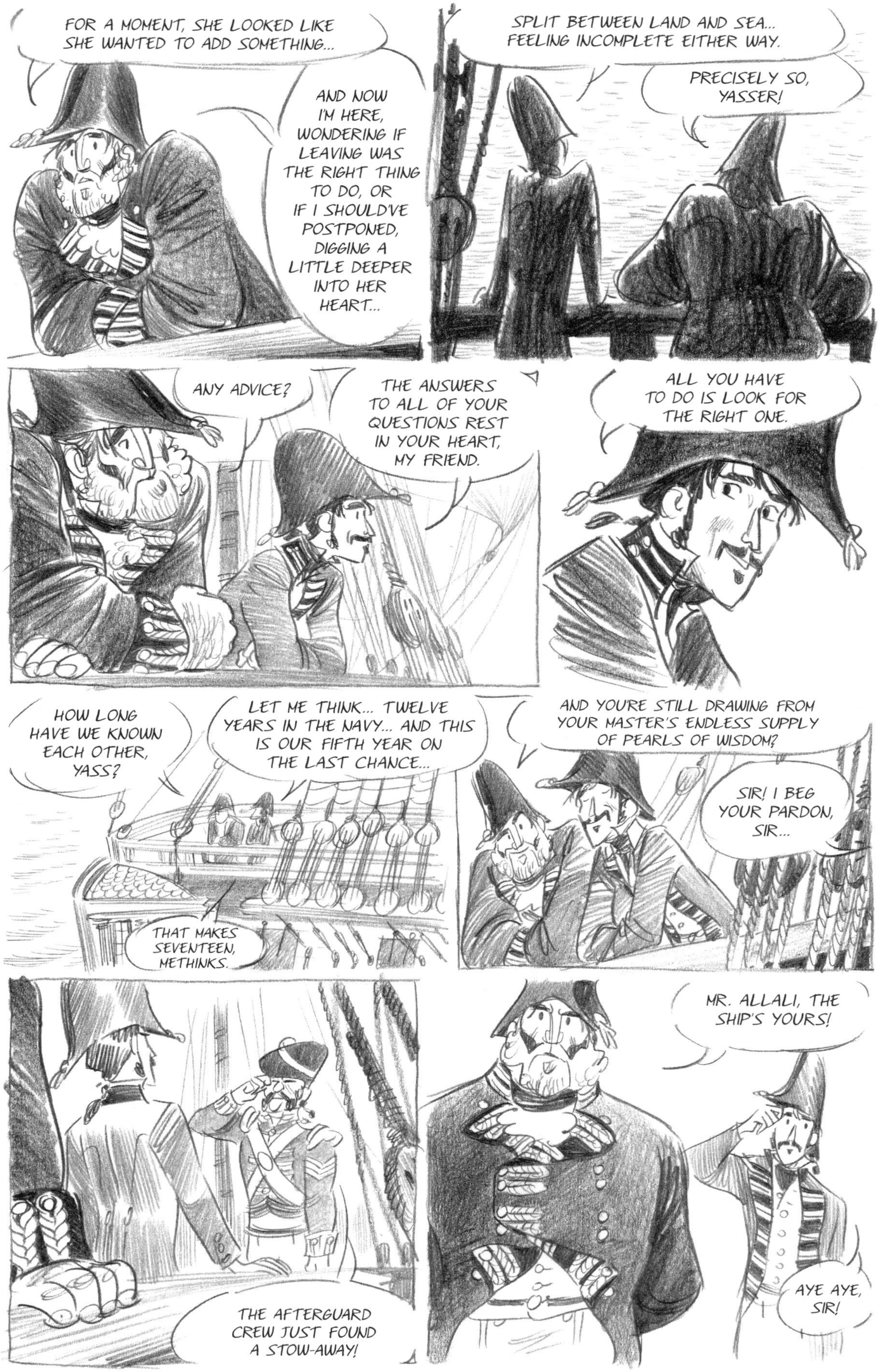
FOR A MOMENT, SHE LOOKED LIKE SHE WANTED TO ADD SOMETHING...
AND NOW I'M HERE, WONDERING IF LEAVING WAS THE RIGHT THING TO DO, OR IF I SHOULD'VE POSTPONED, DIGGING A LITTLE DEEPER INTO HER HEART...
SPLIT BETWEEN LAND AND SEA... FEELING INCOMPLETE EITHER WAY.
PRECISELY SO, YASSER!
ANY ADVICE?
THE ANSWERS TO ALL OF YOUR QUESTIONS REST IN YOUR HEART, MY FRIEND.
ALL YOU HAVE TO DO IS LOOK FOR THE RIGHT ONE.
HOW LONG HAVE WE KNOWN EACH OTHER, YASS?
LET ME THINK... TWELVE YEARS IN THE NAVY... AND THIS IS OUR FIFTH YEAR ON THE LAST CHANCE...
THAT MAKES SEVENTEEN, METHINKS.
AND YOU'RE STILL DRAWING FROM YOUR MASTER'S ENDLESS SUPPLY OF PEARLS OF WISDOM?
SIR! I BEG YOUR PARDON, SIR...
THE AFTERGUARD CREW JUST FOUND A STOW-AWAY!
MR. ALLALI, THE SHIP'S YOURS!
AYE AYE, SIR!

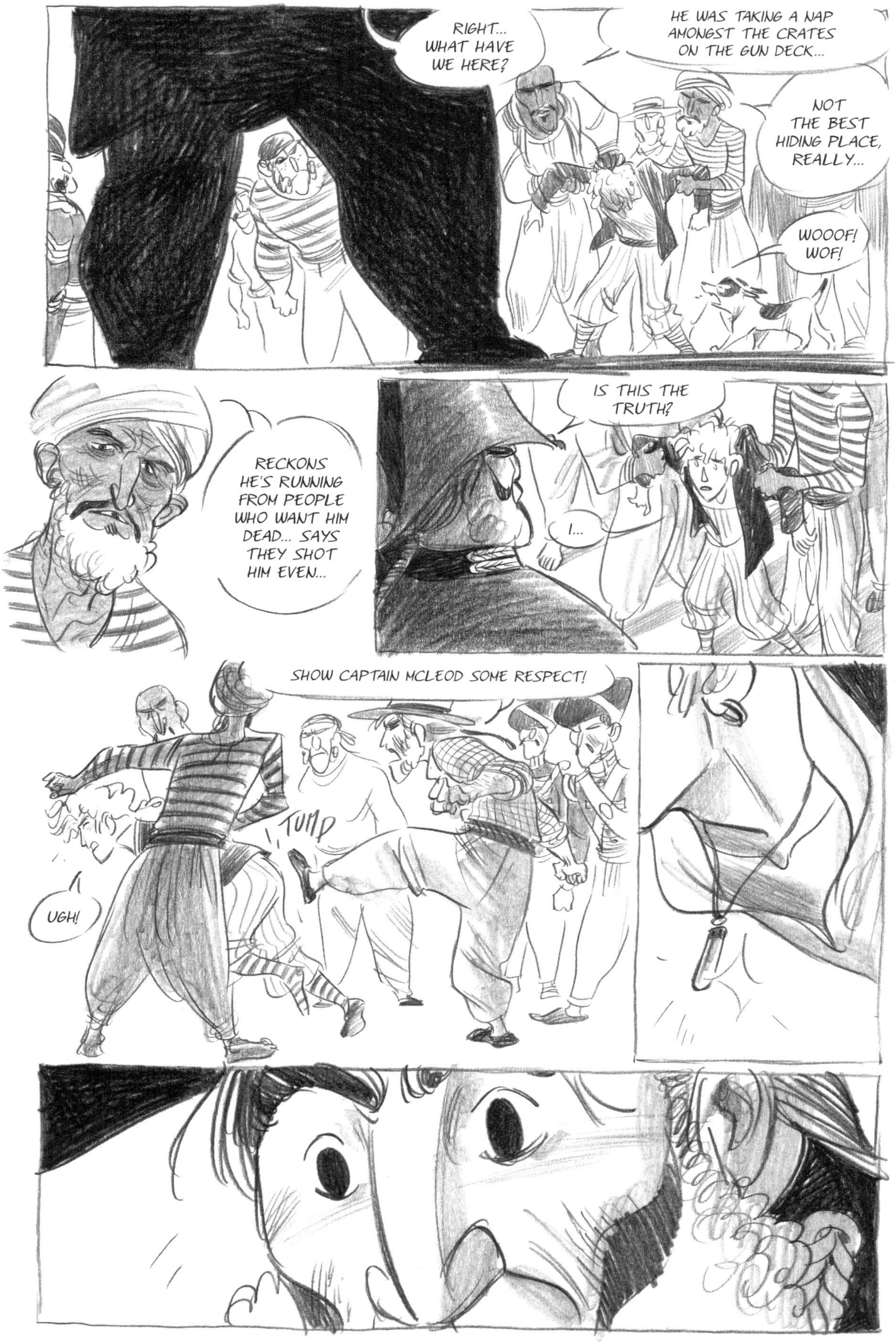
RIGHT... WHAT HAVE WE HERE?
HE WAS TAKING A NAP AMONGST THE CRATES ON THE GUN DECK...
NOT THE BEST HIDING PLACE, REALLY...
WOOOF! WOF!
RECKONS HE'S RUNNING FROM PEOPLE WHO WANT HIM DEAD... SAYS THEY SHOT HIM EVEN...
IS THIS THE TRUTH?
I...
SHOW CAPTAIN MCLEOD SOME RESPECT!
TUMP
UGH!

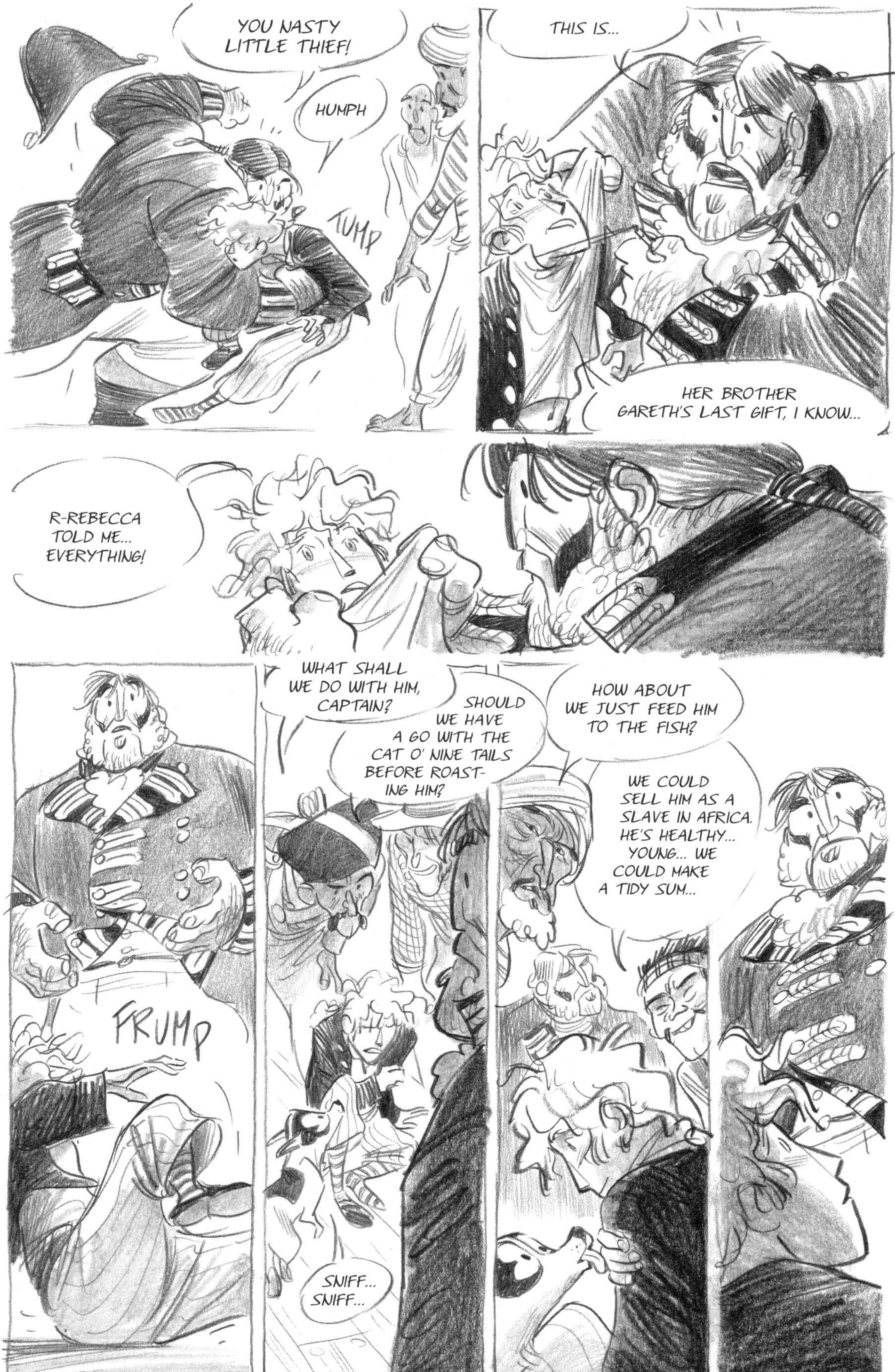
YOU NASTY LITTLE THIEF!
HUMPH
TUMP
THIS IS...
HER BROTHER GARETH'S LAST GIFT, I KNOW...
R-REBECCA TOLD ME... EVERYTHING!
FRUMP
WHAT SHALL WE DO WITH HIM, CAPTAIN?
SHOULD WE HAVE A GO WITH THE CAT O' NINE TAILS BEFORE ROAST-ING HIM?
HOW ABOUT WE JUST FEED HIM TO THE FISH?
WE COULD SELL HIM AS A SLAVE IN AFRICA. HE'S HEALTHY... YOUNG... WE COULD MAKE A TIDY SUM...
SNIFF... SNIFF...

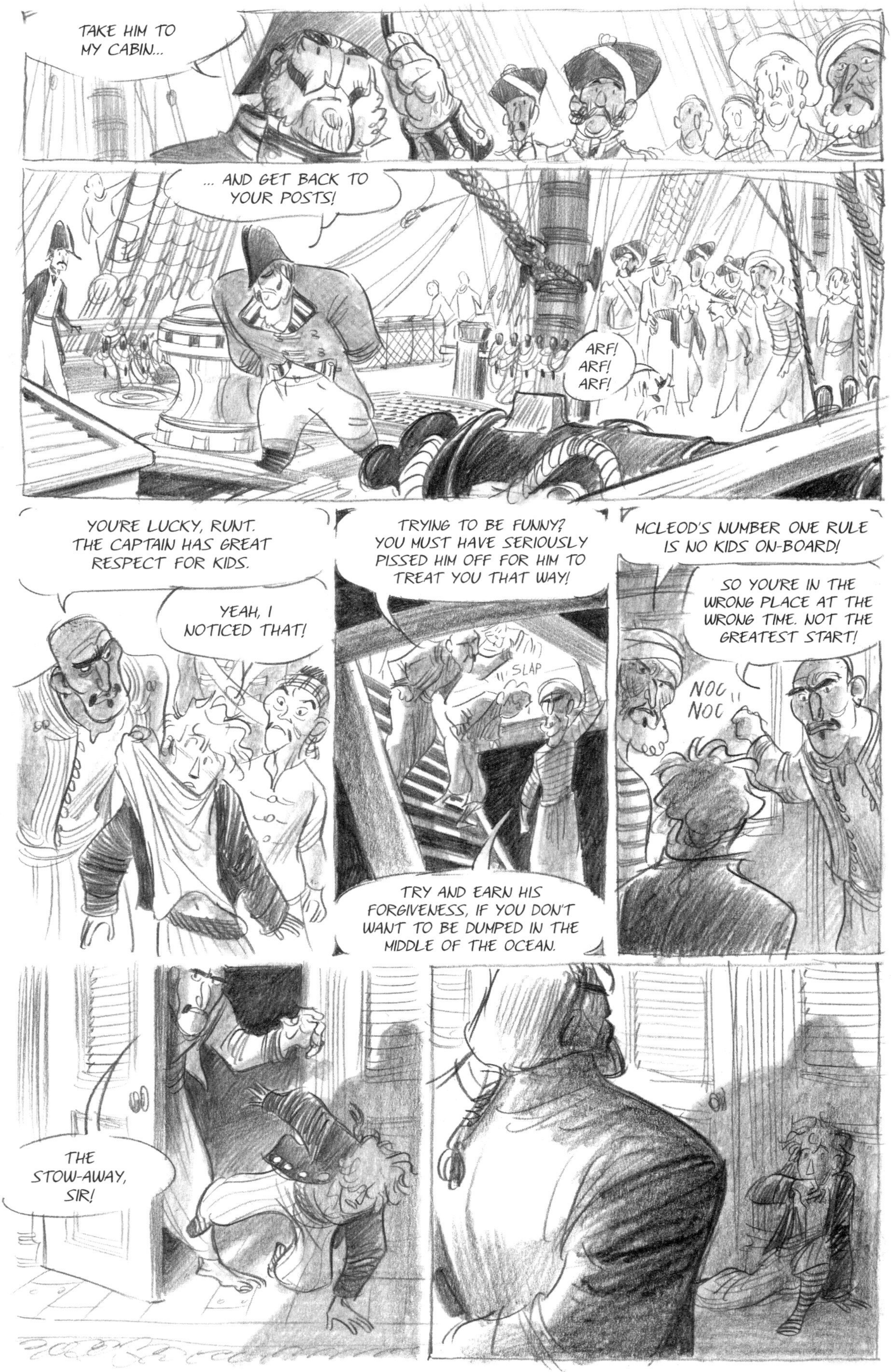
TAKE HIM TO MY CABIN...
... AND GET BACK TO YOUR POSTS!
ARF! ARF! ARF!
YOU'RE LUCKY, RUNT. THE CAPTAIN HAS GREAT RESPECT FOR KIDS.
YEAH, I NOTICED THAT!
TRYING TO BE FUNNY? YOU MUST HAVE SERIOUSLY PISSED HIM OFF FOR HIM TO TREAT YOU THAT WAY!
SLAP
TRY AND EARN HIS FORGIVENESS, IF YOU DON'T WANT TO BE DUMPED IN THE MIDDLE OF THE OCEAN.
MCLEOD'S NUMBER ONE RULE IS NO KIDS ON-BOARD!
SO YOU'RE IN THE WRONG PLACE AT THE WRONG TIME. NOT THE GREATEST START!
NOC NOC
THE STOW-AWAY, SIR!

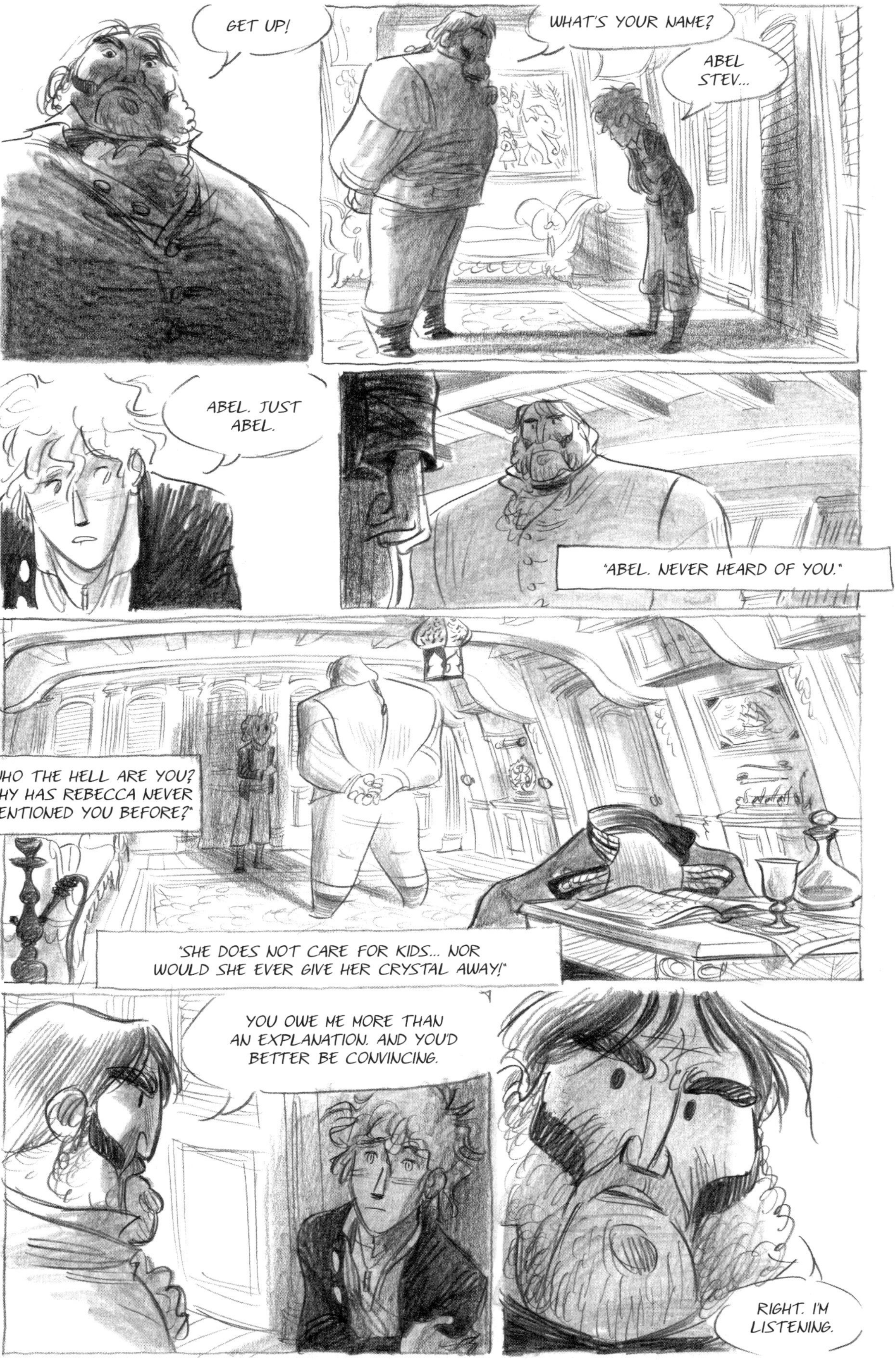
GET UP!
WHAT'S YOUR NAME?
ABEL STEV...
ABEL. JUST ABEL.
"ABEL. NEVER HEARD OF YOU."
"WHO THE HELL ARE YOU? WHY HAS REBECCA NEVER MENTIONED YOU BEFORE?"
"SHE DOES NOT CARE FOR KIDS... NOR WOULD SHE EVER GIVE HER CRYSTAL AWAY!"
YOU OWE ME MORE THAN AN EXPLANATION. AND YOU'D BETTER BE CONVINCING.
RIGHT. I'M LISTENING.

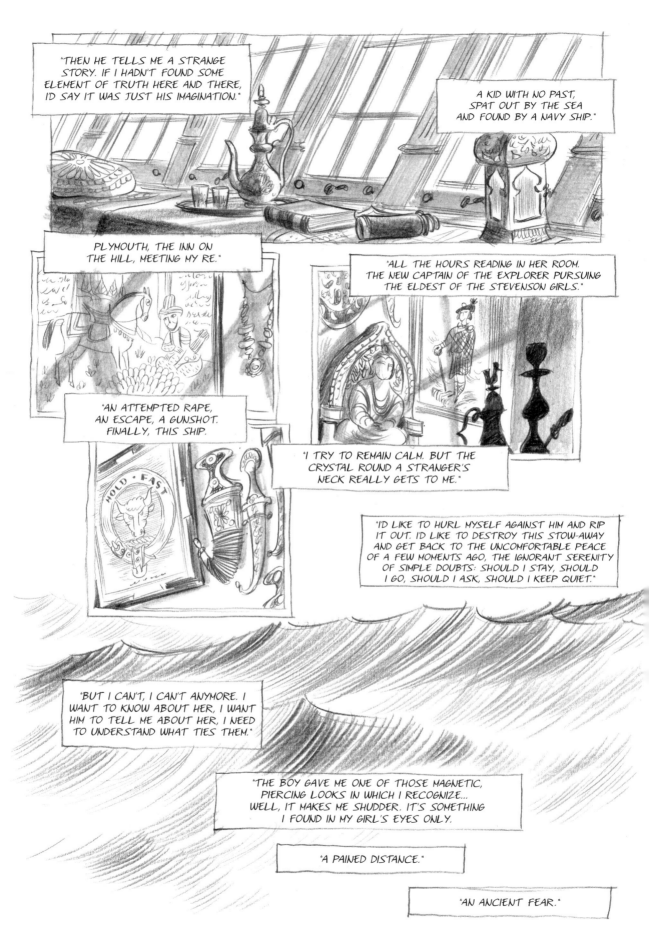

"THEN HE TELLS ME A STRANGE STORY. IF I HADN'T FOUND SOME ELEMENT OF TRUTH HERE AND THERE, I'D SAY IT WAS JUST HIS IMAGINATION."

A KID WITH NO PAST, SPAT OUT BY THE SEA AND FOUND BY A NAVY SHIP."

PLYMOUTH, THE INN ON THE HILL, MEETING MY RE."

"ALL THE HOURS READING IN HER ROOM. THE NEW CAPTAIN OF THE EXPLORER PURSUING THE ELDEST OF THE STEVENSON GIRLS."

"AN ATTEMPTED RAPE, AN ESCAPE, A GUNSHOT. FINALLY, THIS SHIP.

"I TRY TO REMAIN CALM. BUT THE CRYSTAL ROUND A STRANGER'S NECK REALLY GETS TO ME."

"I'D LIKE TO HURL MYSELF AGAINST HIM AND RIP IT OUT. I'D LIKE TO DESTROY THIS STOW-AWAY AND GET BACK TO THE UNCOMFORTABLE PEACE OF A FEW MOMENTS AGO, THE IGNORANT SERENITY OF SIMPLE DOUBTS: SHOULD I STAY, SHOULD I GO, SHOULD I ASK, SHOULD I KEEP QUIET."

"BUT I CAN'T, I CAN'T ANYMORE. I WANT TO KNOW ABOUT HER, I WANT HIM TO TELL ME ABOUT HER, I NEED TO UNDERSTAND WHAT TIES THEM."

"THE BOY GAVE ME ONE OF THOSE MAGNETIC, PIERCING LOOKS IN WHICH I RECOGNIZE... WELL, IT MAKES ME SHUDDER. IT'S SOMETHING I FOUND IN MY GIRL'S EYES ONLY.

"A PAINED DISTANCE."

"AN ANCIENT FEAR."

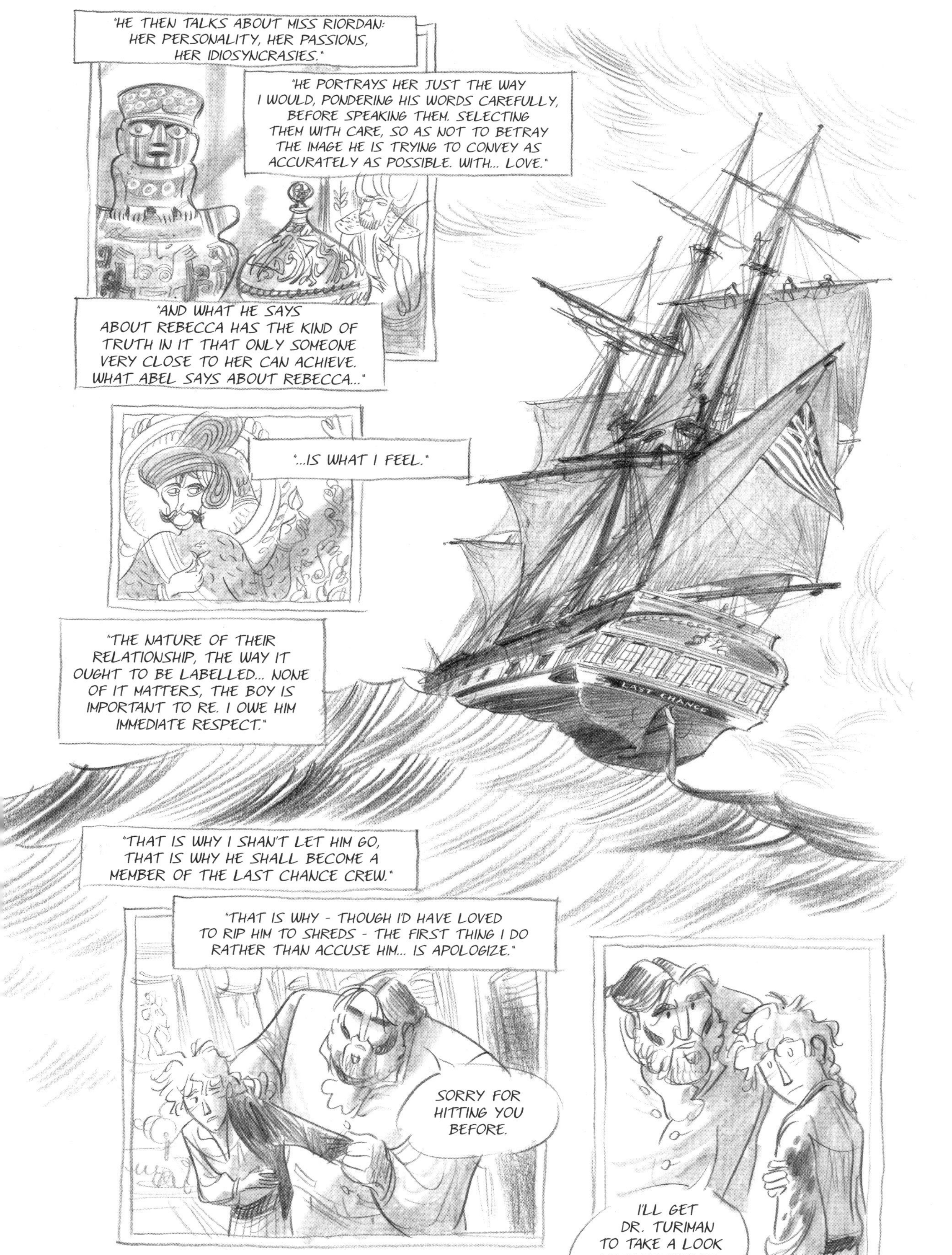
"HE THEN TALKS ABOUT MISS RIORDAN: HER PERSONALITY, HER PASSIONS, HER IDIOSYNCRASIES."
"HE PORTRAYS HER JUST THE WAY I WOULD, PONDERING HIS WORDS CAREFULLY, BEFORE SPEAKING THEM. SELECTING THEM WITH CARE, SO AS NOT TO BETRAY THE IMAGE HE IS TRYING TO CONVEY AS ACCURATELY AS POSSIBLE. WITH... LOVE."
"AND WHAT HE SAYS ABOUT REBECCA HAS THE KIND OF TRUTH IN IT THAT ONLY SOMEONE VERY CLOSE TO HER CAN ACHIEVE. WHAT ABEL SAYS ABOUT REBECCA..."
"...IS WHAT I FEEL."
"THE NATURE OF THEIR RELATIONSHIP, THE WAY IT OUGHT TO BE LABELLED... NONE OF IT MATTERS, THE BOY IS IMPORTANT TO RE. I OWE HIM IMMEDIATE RESPECT."
LAST CHANCE
"THAT IS WHY I SHAN'T LET HIM GO, THAT IS WHY HE SHALL BECOME A MEMBER OF THE LAST CHANCE CREW."
"THAT IS WHY - THOUGH I'D HAVE LOVED TO RIP HIM TO SHREDS - THE FIRST THING I DO RATHER THAN ACCUSE HIM... IS APOLOGIZE."
SORRY FOR HITTING YOU BEFORE.
I'LL GET DR. TURIMAN TO TAKE A LOOK AT THAT WOUND NOW...

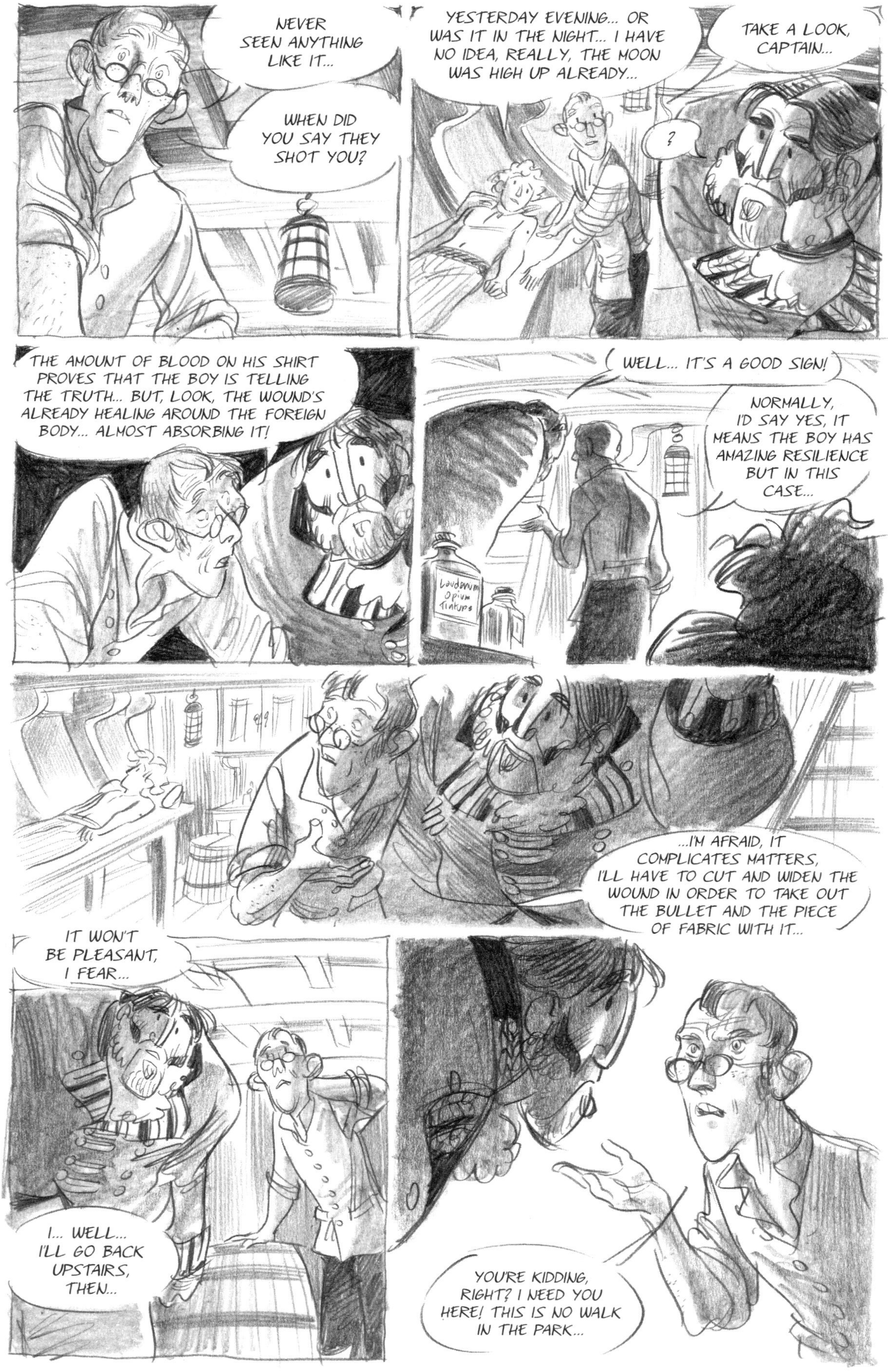
NEVER SEEN ANYTHING LIKE IT...
WHEN DID YOU SAY THEY SHOT YOU?
YESTERDAY EVENING... OR WAS IT IN THE NIGHT... I HAVE NO IDEA, REALLY, THE MOON WAS HIGH UP ALREADY...
TAKE A LOOK, CAPTAIN...
?
THE AMOUNT OF BLOOD ON HIS SHIRT PROVES THAT THE BOY IS TELLING THE TRUTH... BUT, LOOK, THE WOUND'S ALREADY HEALING AROUND THE FOREIGN BODY... ALMOST ABSORBING IT!
WELL... IT'S A GOOD SIGN!
NORMALLY, I'D SAY YES, IT MEANS THE BOY HAS AMAZING RESILIENCE BUT IN THIS CASE...
...I'M AFRAID, IT COMPLICATES MATTERS, I'LL HAVE TO CUT AND WIDEN THE WOUND IN ORDER TO TAKE OUT THE BULLET AND THE PIECE OF FABRIC WITH IT...
IT WON'T BE PLEASANT, I FEAR...
I... WELL... I'LL GO BACK UPSTAIRS, THEN...
YOU'RE KIDDING, RIGHT? I NEED YOU HERE! THIS IS NO WALK IN THE PARK...

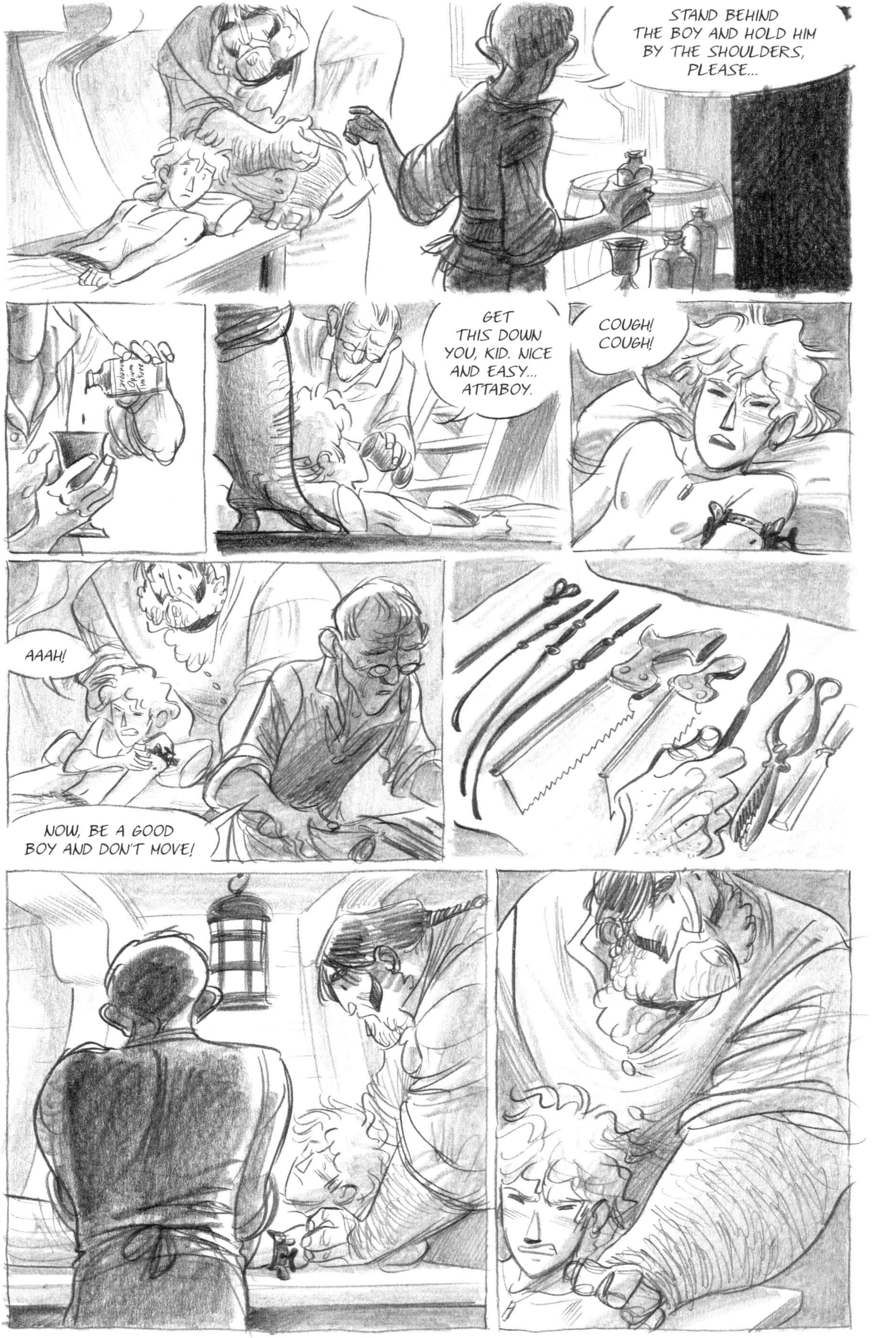
STAND BEHIND THE BOY AND HOLD HIM BY THE SHOULDERS, PLEASE...
GET THIS DOWN YOU, KID. NICE AND EASY... ATTABOY.
COUGH! COUGH!
AAAH!
NOW, BE A GOOD BOY AND DON'T MOVE!

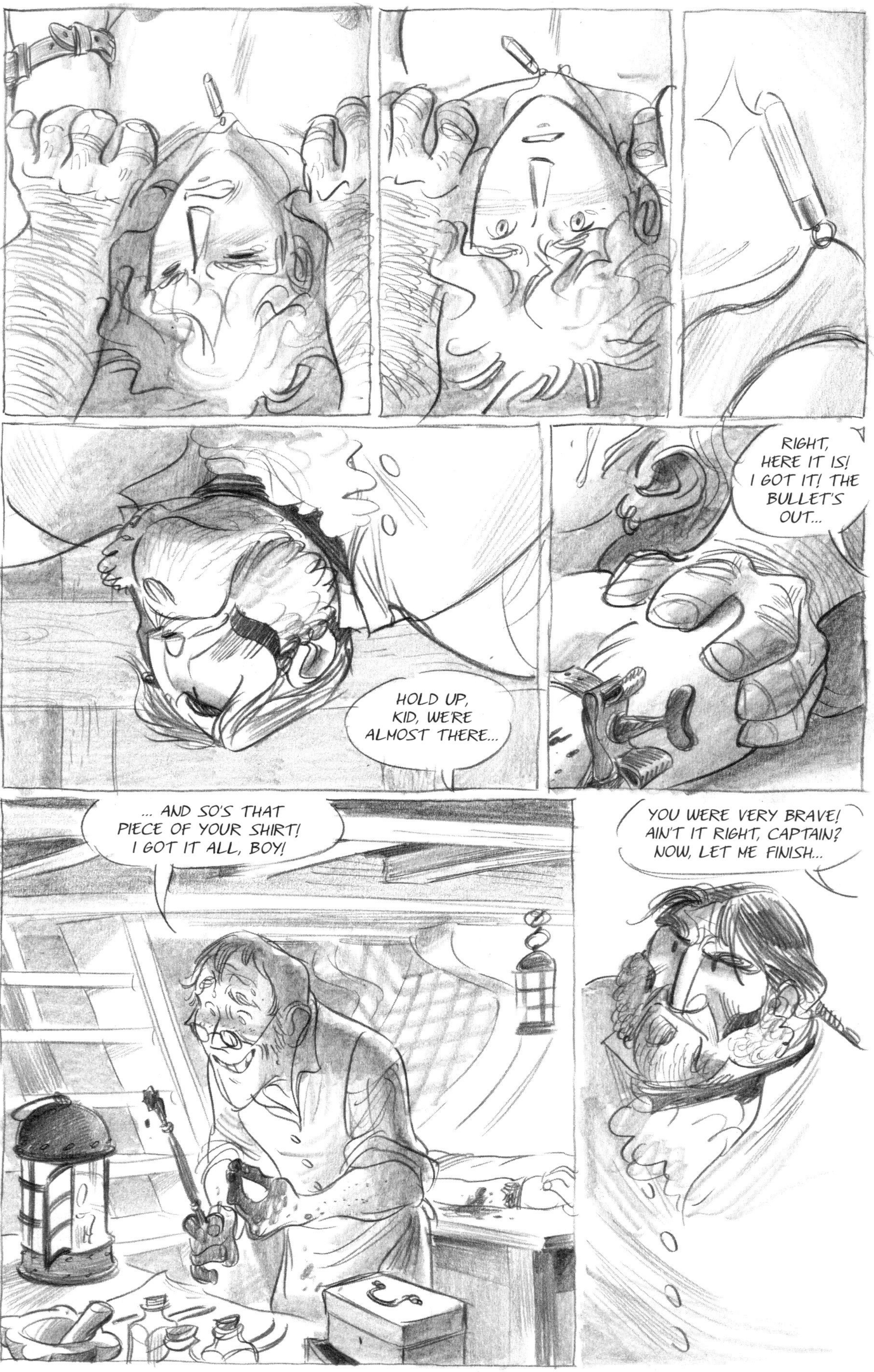
HOLD UP, KID, WE'RE ALMOST THERE...
RIGHT, HERE IT IS! I GOT IT! THE BULLET'S OUT...
... AND SO'S THAT PIECE OF YOUR SHIRT! I GOT IT ALL, BOY!
YOU WERE VERY BRAVE! AIN'T IT RIGHT, CAPTAIN? NOW, LET ME FINISH...

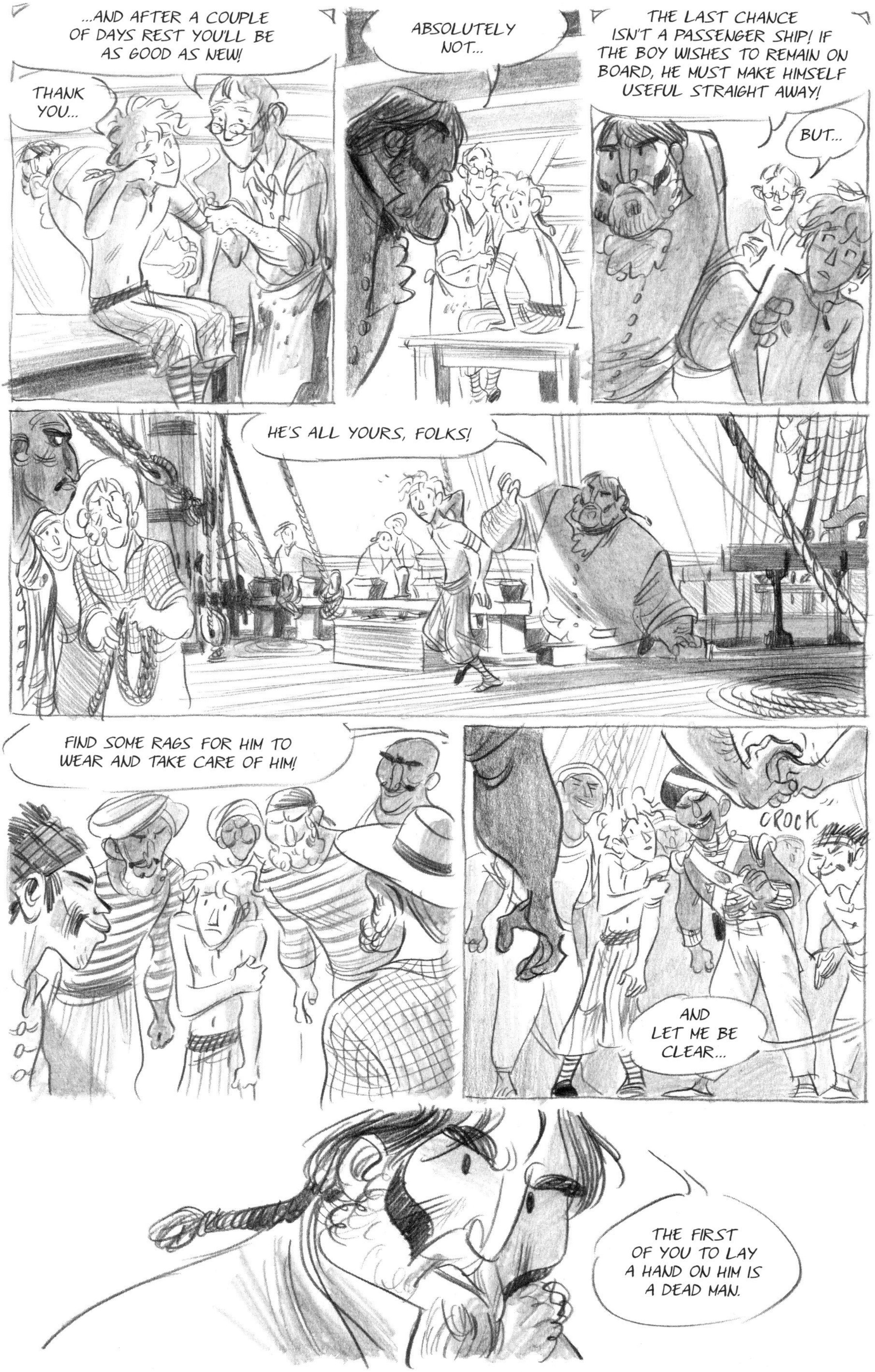
...AND AFTER A COUPLE OF DAYS REST YOU'LL BE AS GOOD AS NEW!
THANK YOU...
ABSOLUTELY NOT...
THE LAST CHANCE ISN'T A PASSENGER SHIP! IF THE BOY WISHES TO REMAIN ON BOARD, HE MUST MAKE HIMSELF USEFUL STRAIGHT AWAY!
BUT...
HE'S ALL YOURS, FOLKS!
FIND SOME RAGS FOR HIM TO WEAR AND TAKE CARE OF HIM!
CROCK
AND LET ME BE CLEAR...
THE FIRST OF YOU TO LAY A HAND ON HIM IS A DEAD MAN.

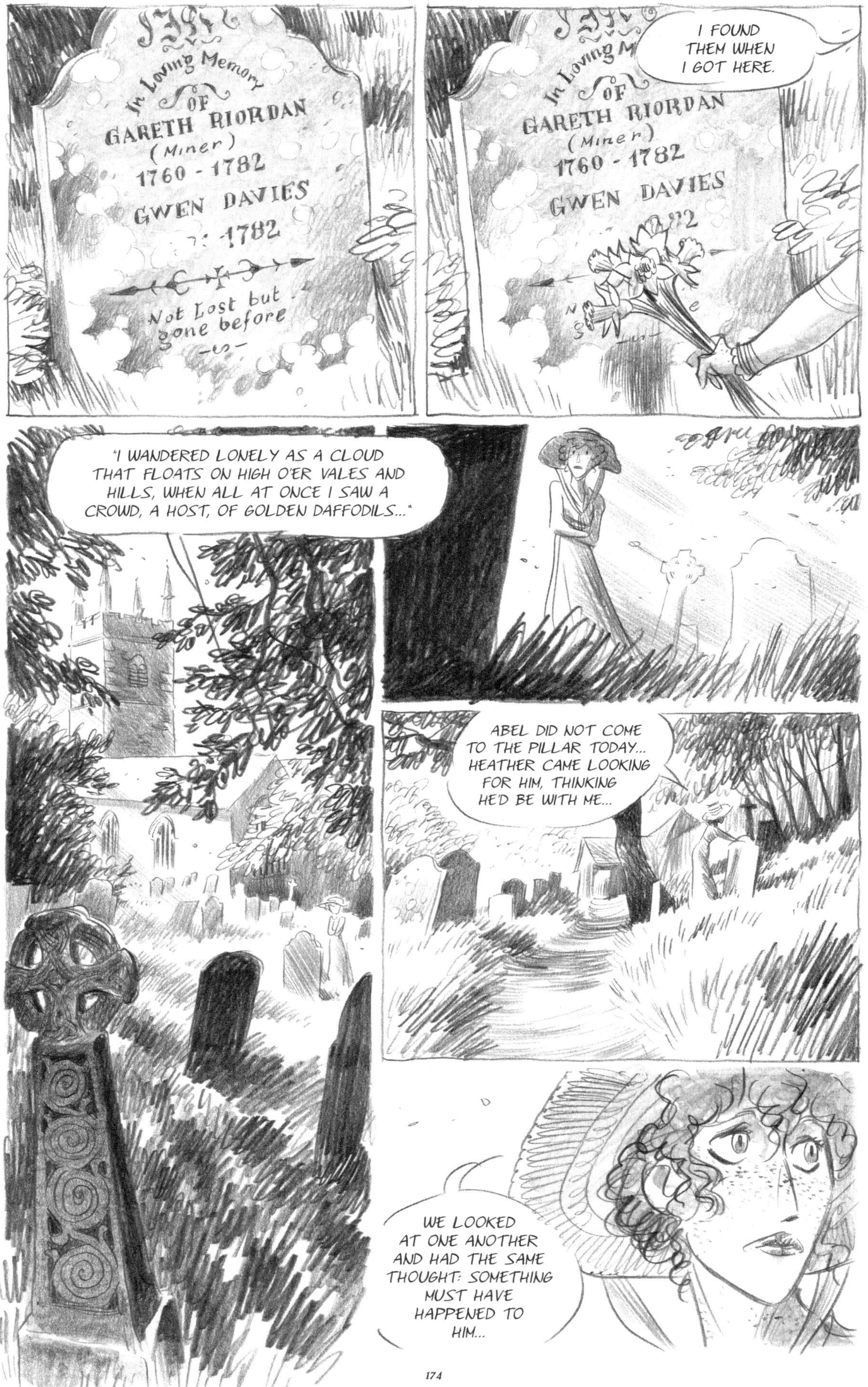
In Loving Memory
OF
GARETH RIORDAN
(Miner)
1760 - 1782
GWEN DAVIES
1782
Not Lost but gone before
I FOUND THEM WHEN I GOT HERE.
"I WANDERED LONELY AS A CLOUD THAT FLOATS ON HIGH O'ER VALES AND HILLS, WHEN ALL AT ONCE I SAW A CROWD, A HOST, OF GOLDEN DAFFODILS..."
ABEL DID NOT COME TO THE PILLAR TODAY... HEATHER CAME LOOKING FOR HIM, THINKING HE'D BE WITH ME...
WE LOOKED AT ONE ANOTHER AND HAD THE SAME THOUGHT: SOMETHING MUST HAVE HAPPENED TO HIM...

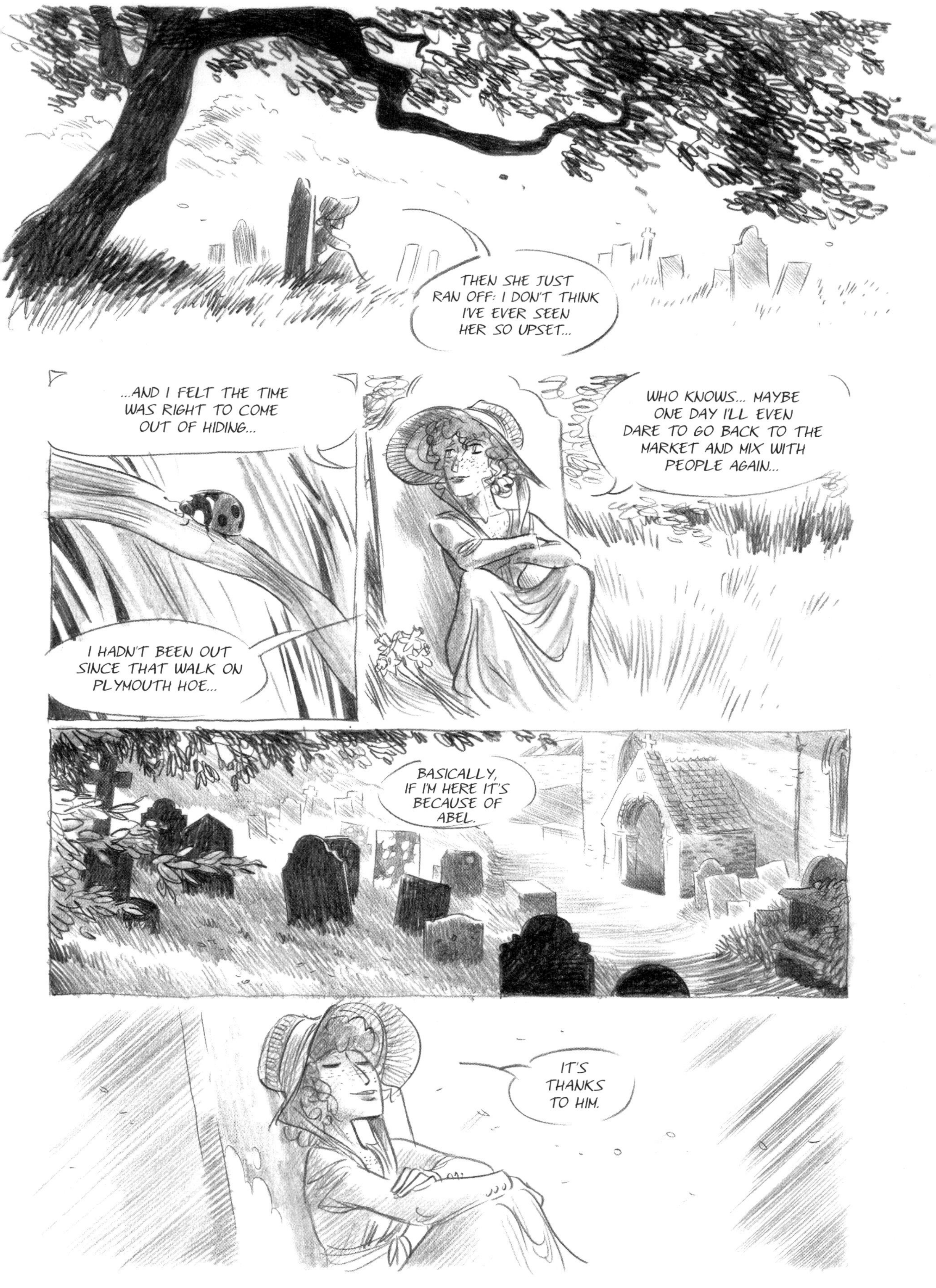
THEN SHE JUST RAN OFF: I DON'T THINK I'VE EVER SEEN HER SO UPSET...
...AND I FELT THE TIME WAS RIGHT TO COME OUT OF HIDING...
I HADN'T BEEN OUT SINCE THAT WALK ON PLYMOUTH HOE...
WHO KNOWS... MAYBE ONE DAY I'LL EVEN DARE TO GO BACK TO THE MARKET AND MIX WITH PEOPLE AGAIN...
BASICALLY, IF I'M HERE IT'S BECAUSE OF ABEL.
IT'S THANKS TO HIM.

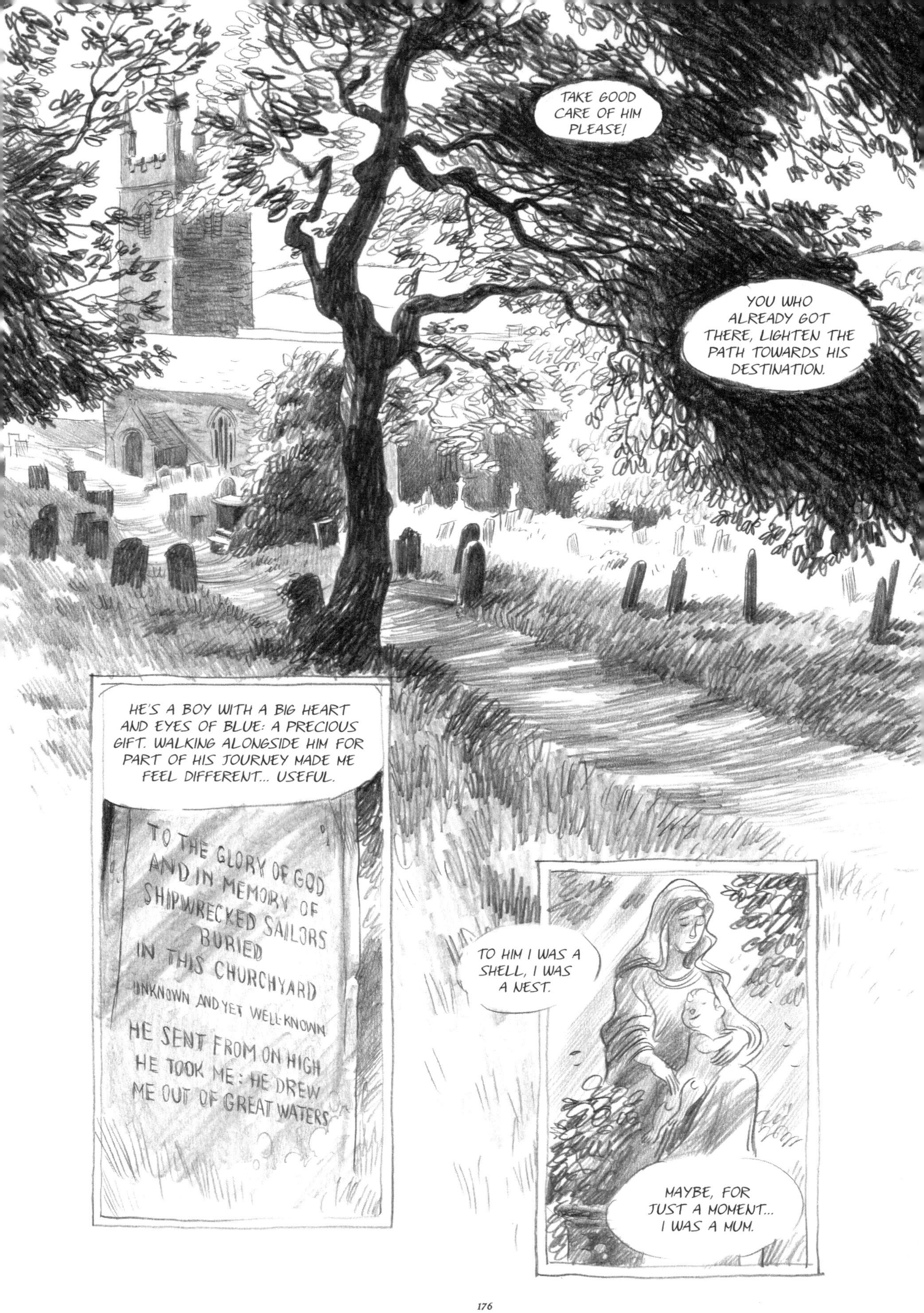
TAKE GOOD CARE OF HIM PLEASE!
YOU WHO ALREADY GOT THERE, LIGHTEN THE PATH TOWARDS HIS DESTINATION.
HE'S A BOY WITH A BIG HEART AND EYES OF BLUE: A PRECIOUS GIFT. WALKING ALONGSIDE HIM FOR PART OF HIS JOURNEY MADE ME FEEL DIFFERENT... USEFUL.
TO THE GLORY OF GOD AND IN MEMORY OF SHIPWRECKED SAILORS BURIED IN THIS CHURCHYARD
UNKNOWN AND YET WELL-KNOWN
HE SENT FROM ON HIGH HE TOOK ME: HE DREW ME OUT OF GREAT WATERS
TO HIM I WAS A SHELL, I WAS A NEST.
MAYBE, FOR JUST A MOMENT... I WAS A MUM.

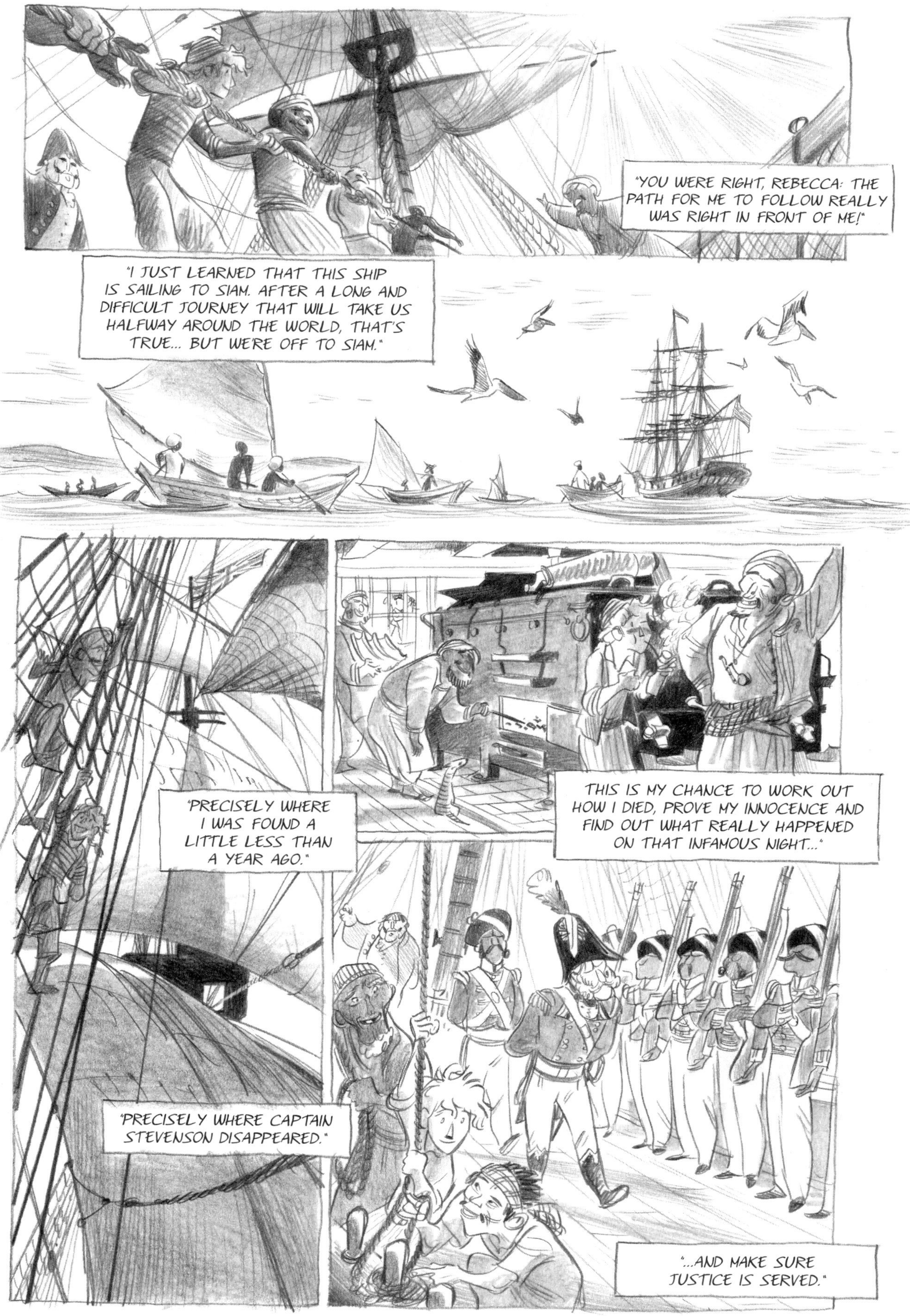
"YOU WERE RIGHT, REBECCA: THE PATH FOR ME TO FOLLOW REALLY WAS RIGHT IN FRONT OF ME!"
"I JUST LEARNED THAT THIS SHIP IS SAILING TO SIAM. AFTER A LONG AND DIFFICULT JOURNEY THAT WILL TAKE US HALFWAY AROUND THE WORLD, THAT'S TRUE... BUT WE'RE OFF TO SIAM."
"PRECISELY WHERE I WAS FOUND A LITTLE LESS THAN A YEAR AGO."
"PRECISELY WHERE CAPTAIN STEVENSON DISAPPEARED."
THIS IS MY CHANCE TO WORK OUT HOW I DIED, PROVE MY INNOCENCE AND FIND OUT WHAT REALLY HAPPENED ON THAT INFAMOUS NIGHT..."
"...AND MAKE SURE JUSTICE IS SERVED."

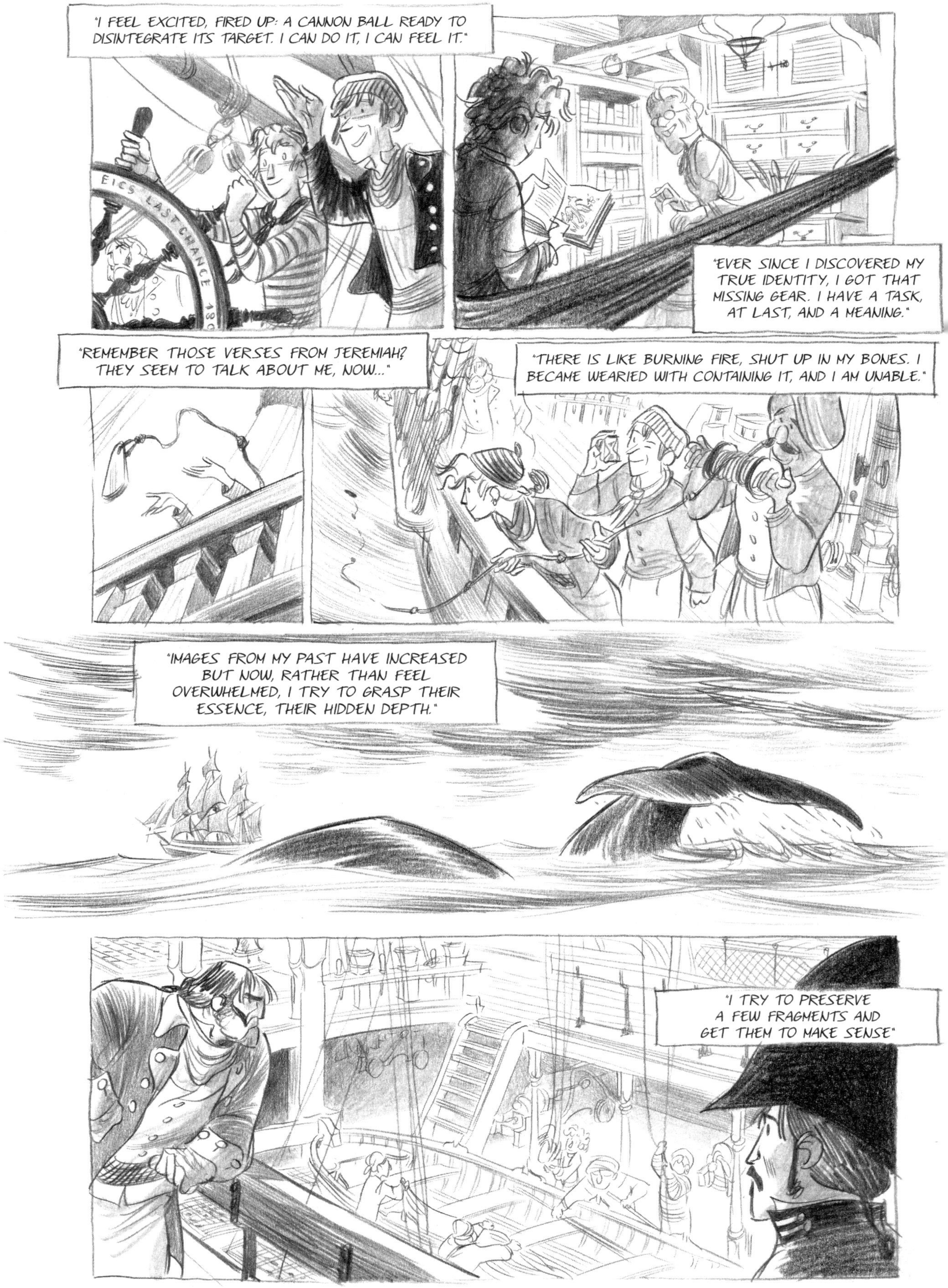
"I FEEL EXCITED, FIRED UP: A CANNON BALL READY TO DISINTEGRATE ITS TARGET. I CAN DO IT, I CAN FEEL IT."
EICS LAST CHANCE
"EVER SINCE I DISCOVERED MY TRUE IDENTITY, I GOT THAT MISSING GEAR. I HAVE A TASK, AT LAST, AND A MEANING."
"REMEMBER THOSE VERSES FROM JEREMIAH? THEY SEEM TO TALK ABOUT ME, NOW..."
"THERE IS LIKE BURNING FIRE, SHUT UP IN MY BONES. I BECAME WEARIED WITH CONTAINING IT, AND I AM UNABLE."
"IMAGES FROM MY PAST HAVE INCREASED BUT NOW, RATHER THAN FEEL OVERWHELMED, I TRY TO GRASP THEIR ESSENCE, THEIR HIDDEN DEPTH."
"I TRY TO PRESERVE A FEW FRAGMENTS AND GET THEM TO MAKE SENSE"

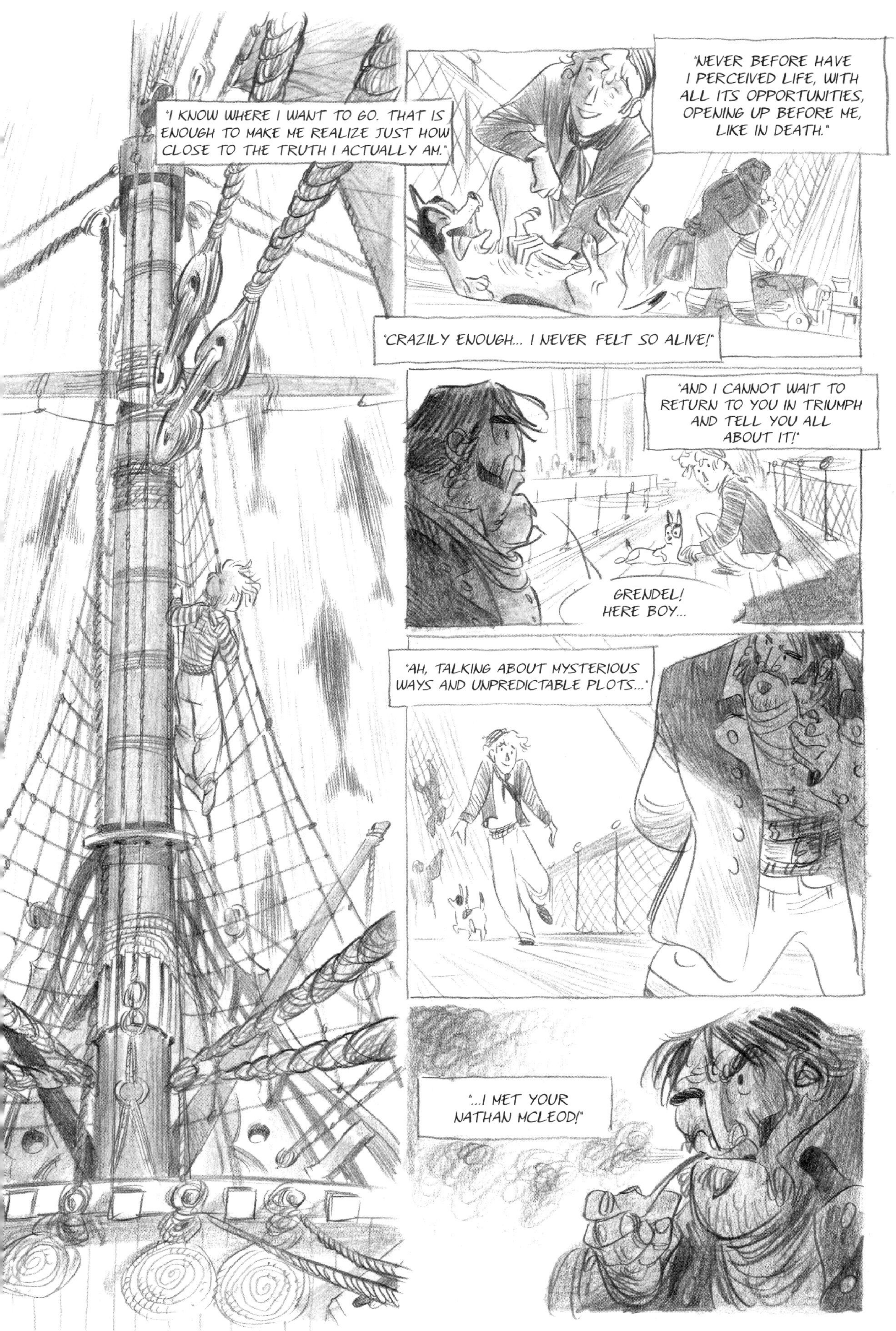
"I KNOW WHERE I WANT TO GO. THAT IS ENOUGH TO MAKE ME REALIZE JUST HOW CLOSE TO THE TRUTH I ACTUALLY AM."
"NEVER BEFORE HAVE I PERCEIVED LIFE, WITH ALL ITS OPPORTUNITIES, OPENING UP BEFORE ME, LIKE IN DEATH."
"CRAZILY ENOUGH... I NEVER FELT SO ALIVE!"
"AND I CANNOT WAIT TO RETURN TO YOU IN TRIUMPH AND TELL YOU ALL ABOUT IT!"
GRENDEL! HERE BOY...
"AH, TALKING ABOUT MYSTERIOUS WAYS AND UNPREDICTABLE PLOTS..."
"...I MET YOUR NATHAN MCLEOD!"

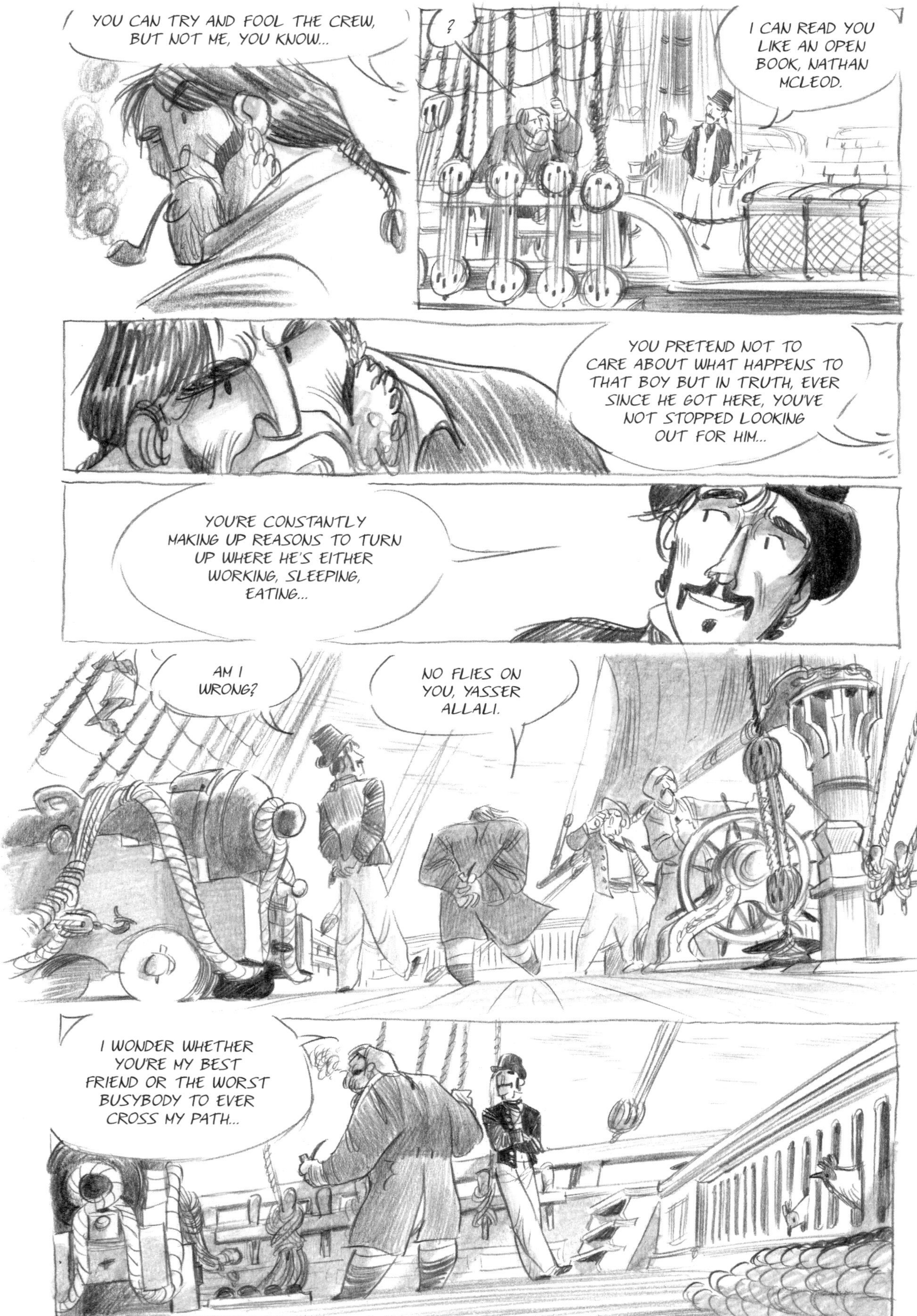
YOU CAN TRY AND FOOL THE CREW, BUT NOT ME, YOU KNOW...
?
I CAN READ YOU LIKE AN OPEN BOOK, NATHAN MCLEOD.
YOU PRETEND NOT TO CARE ABOUT WHAT HAPPENS TO THAT BOY BUT IN TRUTH, EVER SINCE HE GOT HERE, YOU'VE NOT STOPPED LOOKING OUT FOR HIM...
YOU'RE CONSTANTLY MAKING UP REASONS TO TURN UP WHERE HE'S EITHER WORKING, SLEEPING, EATING...
AM I WRONG?
NO FLIES ON YOU, YASSER ALLALI.
I WONDER WHETHER YOU'RE MY BEST FRIEND OR THE WORST BUSYBODY TO EVER CROSS MY PATH...

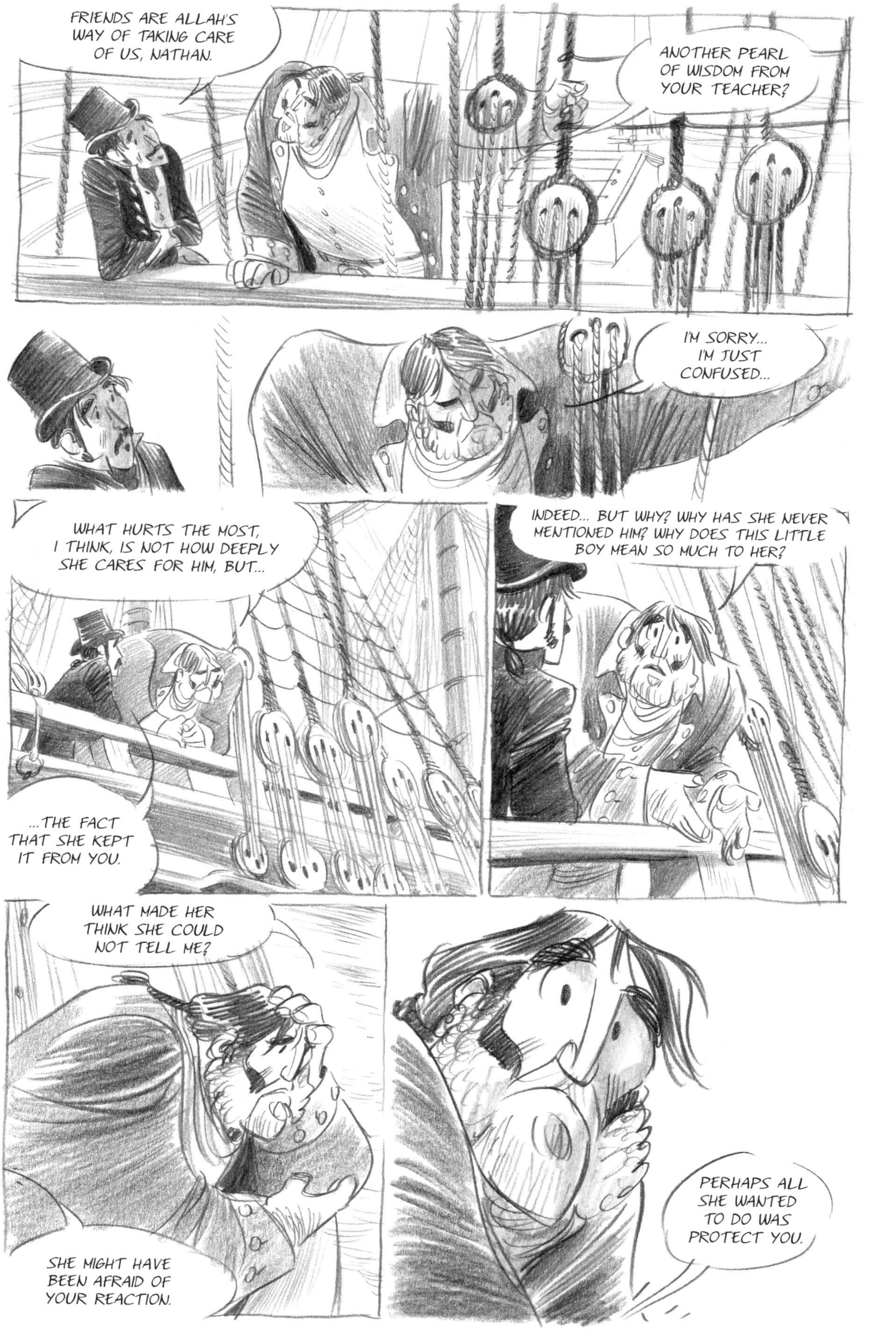
FRIENDS ARE ALLAH'S WAY OF TAKING CARE OF US, NATHAN.
ANOTHER PEARL OF WISDOM FROM YOUR TEACHER?
I'M SORRY... I'M JUST CONFUSED...
WHAT HURTS THE MOST, I THINK, IS NOT HOW DEEPLY SHE CARES FOR HIM, BUT...
...THE FACT THAT SHE KEPT IT FROM YOU.
INDEED... BUT WHY? WHY HAS SHE NEVER MENTIONED HIM? WHY DOES THIS LITTLE BOY MEAN SO MUCH TO HER?
WHAT MADE HER THINK SHE COULD NOT TELL ME?
SHE MIGHT HAVE BEEN AFRAID OF YOUR REACTION.
PERHAPS ALL SHE WANTED TO DO WAS PROTECT YOU.

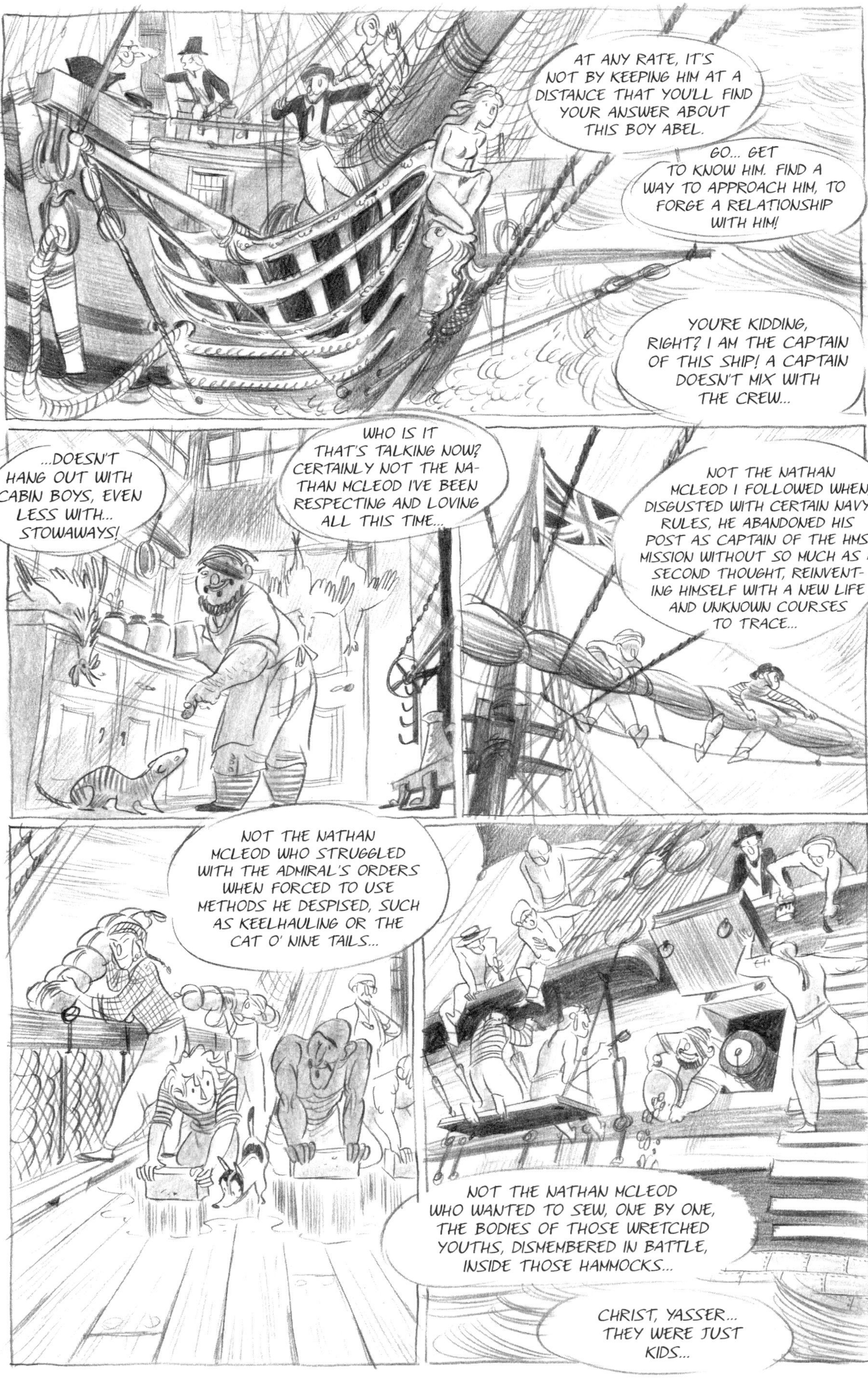
AT ANY RATE, IT'S NOT BY KEEPING HIM AT A DISTANCE THAT YOU'LL FIND YOUR ANSWER ABOUT THIS BOY ABEL.
GO... GET TO KNOW HIM. FIND A WAY TO APPROACH HIM, TO FORGE A RELATIONSHIP WITH HIM!
YOU'RE KIDDING, RIGHT? I AM THE CAPTAIN OF THIS SHIP! A CAPTAIN DOESN'T MIX WITH THE CREW...
...DOESN'T HANG OUT WITH CABIN BOYS, EVEN LESS WITH... STOWAWAYS!
WHO IS IT THAT'S TALKING NOW? CERTAINLY NOT THE NATHAN MCLEOD I'VE BEEN RESPECTING AND LOVING ALL THIS TIME...
NOT THE NATHAN MCLEOD I FOLLOWED WHEN, DISGUSTED WITH CERTAIN NAVY RULES, HE ABANDONED HIS POST AS CAPTAIN OF THE HMS MISSION WITHOUT SO MUCH AS A SECOND THOUGHT, REINVENTING HIMSELF WITH A NEW LIFE AND UNKNOWN COURSES TO TRACE...
NOT THE NATHAN MCLEOD WHO STRUGGLED WITH THE ADMIRAL'S ORDERS WHEN FORCED TO USE METHODS HE DESPISED, SUCH AS KEELHAULING OR THE CAT O' NINE TAILS...
NOT THE NATHAN MCLEOD WHO WANTED TO SEW, ONE BY ONE, THE BODIES OF THOSE WRETCHED YOUTHS, DISMEMBERED IN BATTLE, INSIDE THOSE HAMMOCKS...
CHRIST, YASSER... THEY WERE JUST KIDS...

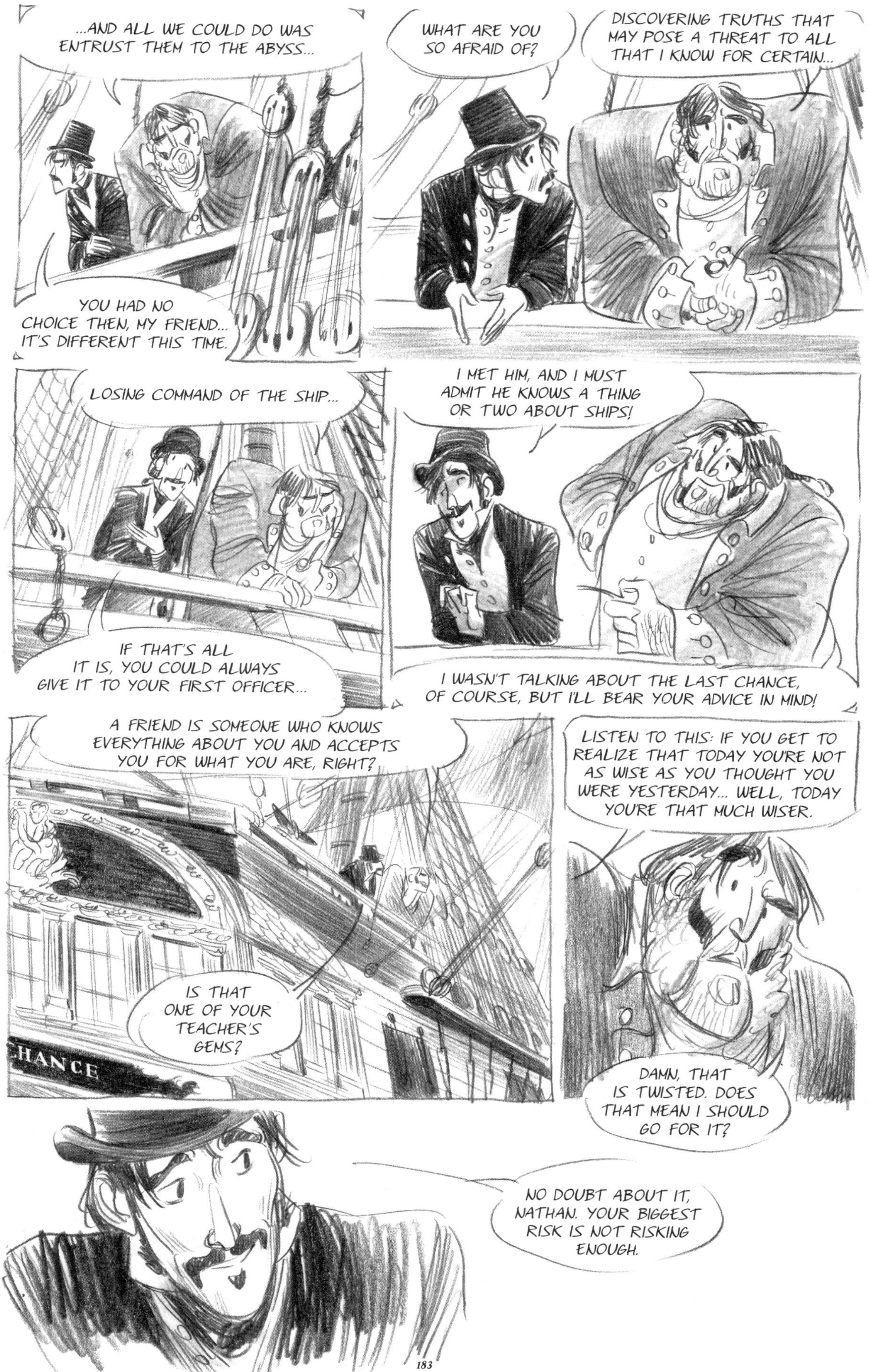
...AND ALL WE COULD DO WAS ENTRUST THEM TO THE ABYSS...
YOU HAD NO CHOICE THEN, MY FRIEND... IT'S DIFFERENT THIS TIME.
WHAT ARE YOU SO AFRAID OF?
DISCOVERING TRUTHS THAT MAY POSE A THREAT TO ALL THAT I KNOW FOR CERTAIN...
LOSING COMMAND OF THE SHIP...
IF THAT'S ALL IT IS, YOU COULD ALWAYS GIVE IT TO YOUR FIRST OFFICER...
I MET HIM, AND I MUST ADMIT HE KNOWS A THING OR TWO ABOUT SHIPS!
I WASN'T TALKING ABOUT THE LAST CHANCE, OF COURSE, BUT I'LL BEAR YOUR ADVICE IN MIND!
A FRIEND IS SOMEONE WHO KNOWS EVERYTHING ABOUT YOU AND ACCEPTS YOU FOR WHAT YOU ARE, RIGHT?
IS THAT ONE OF YOUR TEACHER'S GEMS?
CHANCE
LISTEN TO THIS: IF YOU GET TO REALIZE THAT TODAY YOU'RE NOT AS WISE AS YOU THOUGHT YOU WERE YESTERDAY... WELL, TODAY YOU'RE THAT MUCH WISER.
DAMN, THAT IS TWISTED. DOES THAT MEAN I SHOULD GO FOR IT?
NO DOUBT ABOUT IT, NATHAN. YOUR BIGGEST RISK IS NOT RISKING ENOUGH.

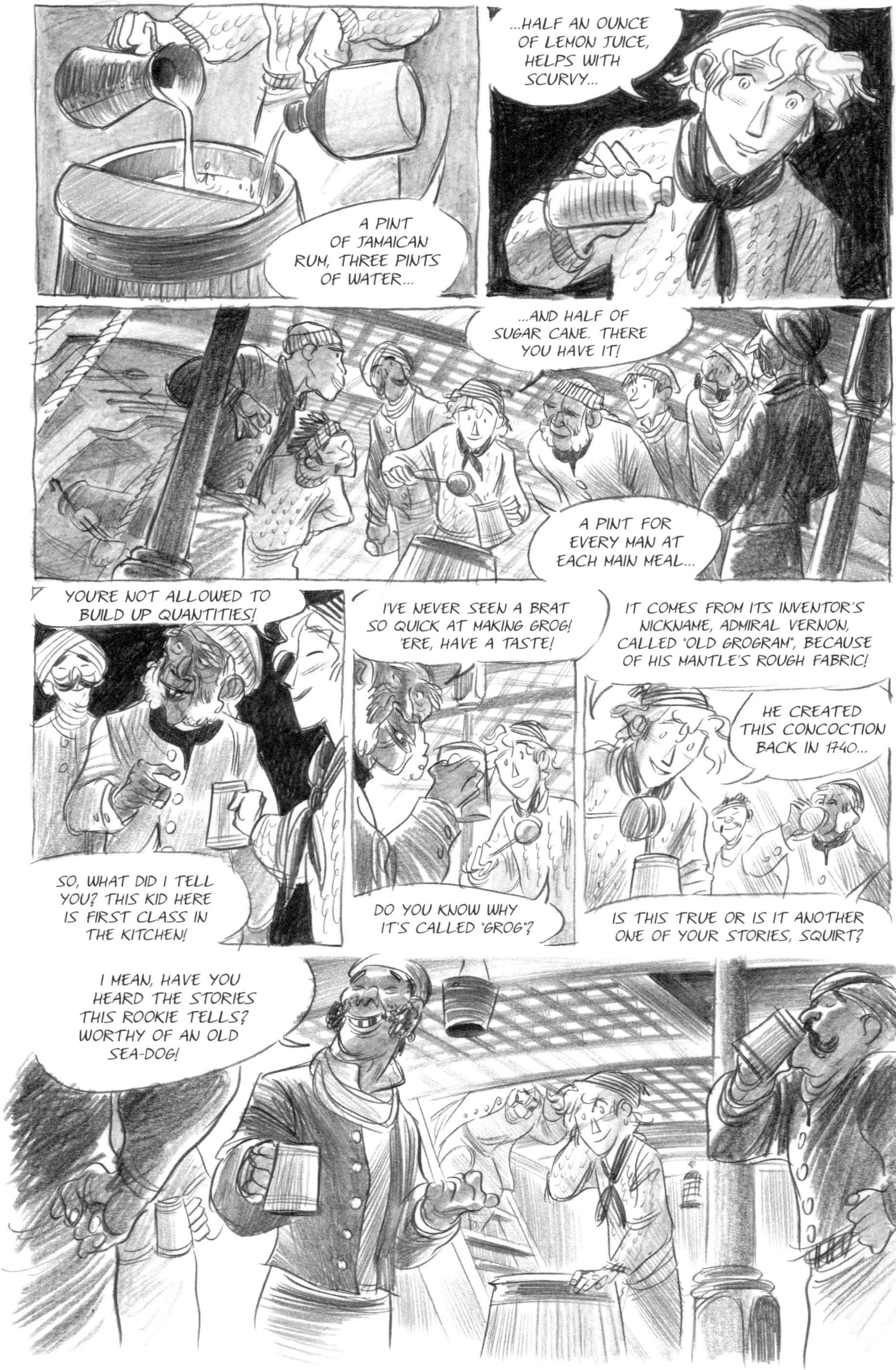
A PINT OF JAMAICAN RUM, THREE PINTS OF WATER...
...HALF AN OUNCE OF LEMON JUICE, HELPS WITH SCURVY...
...AND HALF OF SUGAR CANE. THERE YOU HAVE IT!
A PINT FOR EVERY MAN AT EACH MAIN MEAL...
YOU'RE NOT ALLOWED TO BUILD UP QUANTITIES!
SO, WHAT DID I TELL YOU? THIS KID HERE IS FIRST CLASS IN THE KITCHEN!
I'VE NEVER SEEN A BRAT SO QUICK AT MAKING GROG! 'ERE, HAVE A TASTE!
DO YOU KNOW WHY IT'S CALLED "GROG"?
IT COMES FROM ITS INVENTOR'S NICKNAME, ADMIRAL VERNON, CALLED "OLD GROGRAM", BECAUSE OF HIS MANTLE'S ROUGH FABRIC!
HE CREATED THIS CONCOCTION BACK IN 1740...
IS THIS TRUE OR IS IT ANOTHER ONE OF YOUR STORIES, SQUIRT?
I MEAN, HAVE YOU HEARD THE STORIES THIS ROOKIE TELLS? WORTHY OF AN OLD SEA-DOG!

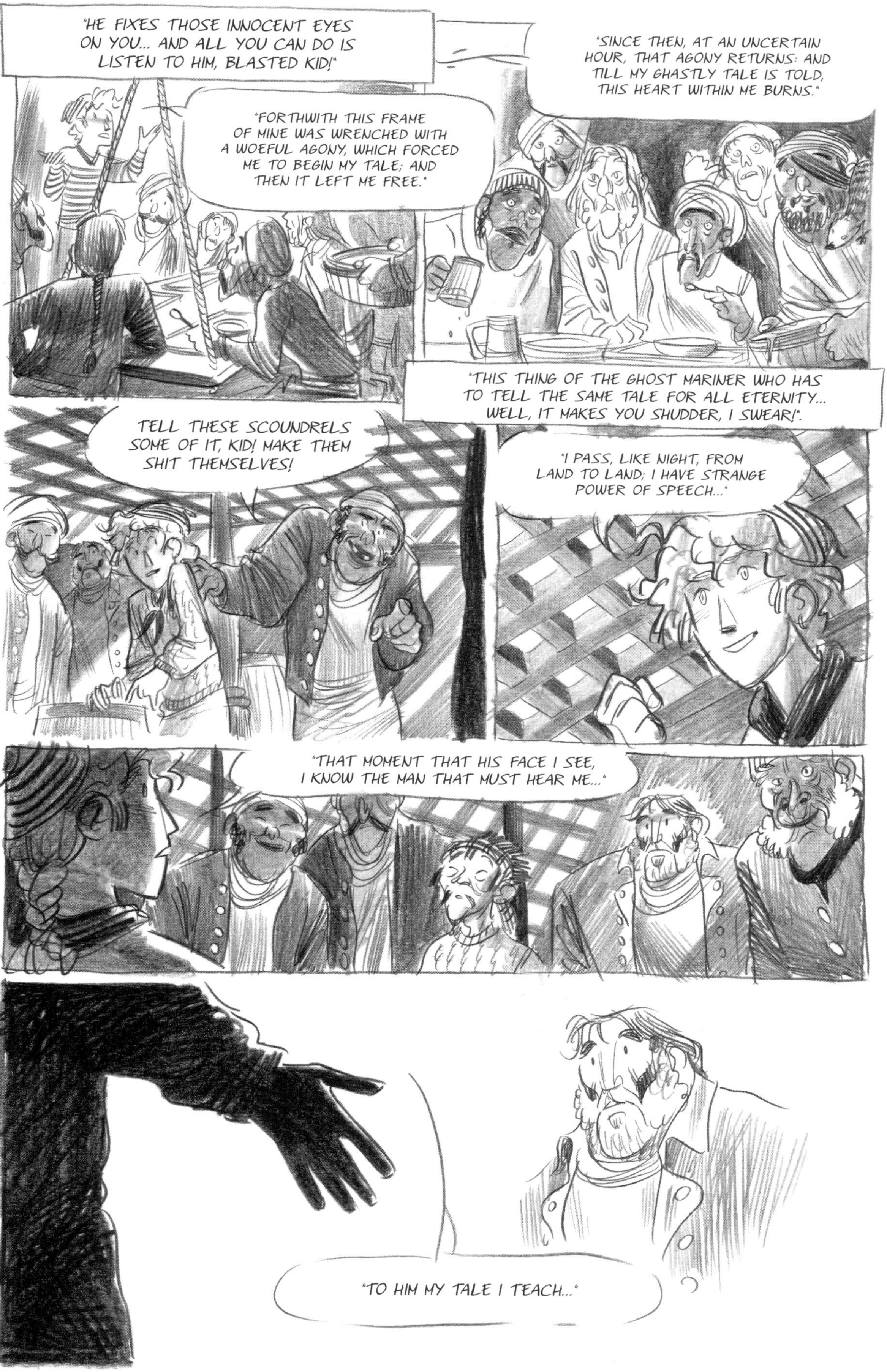
"HE FIXES THOSE INNOCENT EYES ON YOU... AND ALL YOU CAN DO IS LISTEN TO HIM, BLASTED KID!"
"FORTHWITH THIS FRAME OF MINE WAS WRENCHED WITH A WOEFUL AGONY, WHICH FORCED ME TO BEGIN MY TALE; AND THEN IT LEFT ME FREE."
"SINCE THEN, AT AN UNCERTAIN HOUR, THAT AGONY RETURNS: AND TILL MY GHASTLY TALE IS TOLD, THIS HEART WITHIN ME BURNS."
"THIS THING OF THE GHOST MARINER WHO HAS TO TELL THE SAME TALE FOR ALL ETERNITY... WELL, IT MAKES YOU SHUDDER, I SWEAR!".
TELL THESE SCOUNDRELS SOME OF IT, KID! MAKE THEM SHIT THEMSELVES!
"I PASS, LIKE NIGHT, FROM LAND TO LAND; I HAVE STRANGE POWER OF SPEECH..."
"THAT MOMENT THAT HIS FACE I SEE, I KNOW THE MAN THAT MUST HEAR ME..."
"TO HIM MY TALE I TEACH..."

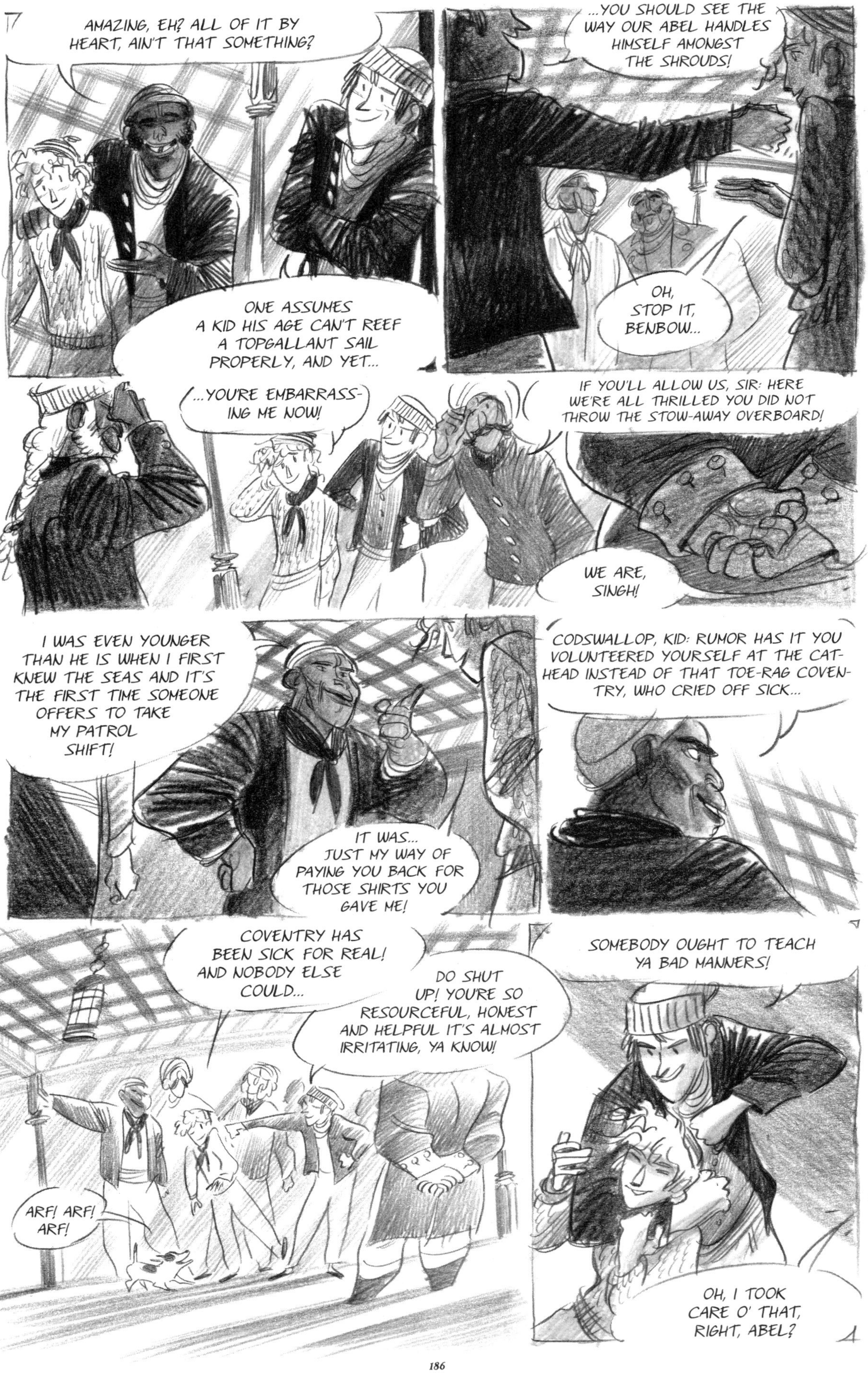
AMAZING, EH? ALL OF IT BY HEART, AIN'T THAT SOMETHING?
ONE ASSUMES A KID HIS AGE CAN'T REEF A TOPGALLANT SAIL PROPERLY, AND YET...
...YOU SHOULD SEE THE WAY OUR ABEL HANDLES HIMSELF AMONGST THE SHROUDS!
OH, STOP IT, BENBOW...
...YOU'RE EMBARRASSING ME NOW!
IF YOU'LL ALLOW US, SIR: HERE WE'RE ALL THRILLED YOU DID NOT THROW THE STOW-AWAY OVERBOARD!
WE ARE, SINGH!
I WAS EVEN YOUNGER THAN HE IS WHEN I FIRST KNEW THE SEAS AND IT'S THE FIRST TIME SOMEONE OFFERS TO TAKE MY PATROL SHIFT!
IT WAS... JUST MY WAY OF PAYING YOU BACK FOR THOSE SHIRTS YOU GAVE ME!
CODSWALLOP, KID: RUMOR HAS IT YOU VOLUNTEERED YOURSELF AT THE CAT-HEAD INSTEAD OF THAT TOE-RAG COVENTRY, WHO CRIED OFF SICK...
COVENTRY HAS BEEN SICK FOR REAL! AND NOBODY ELSE COULD...
DO SHUT UP! YOU'RE SO RESOURCEFUL, HONEST AND HELPFUL IT'S ALMOST IRRITATING, YA KNOW!
ARF! ARF! ARF!
SOMEBODY OUGHT TO TEACH YA BAD MANNERS!
OH, I TOOK CARE O' THAT, RIGHT, ABEL?

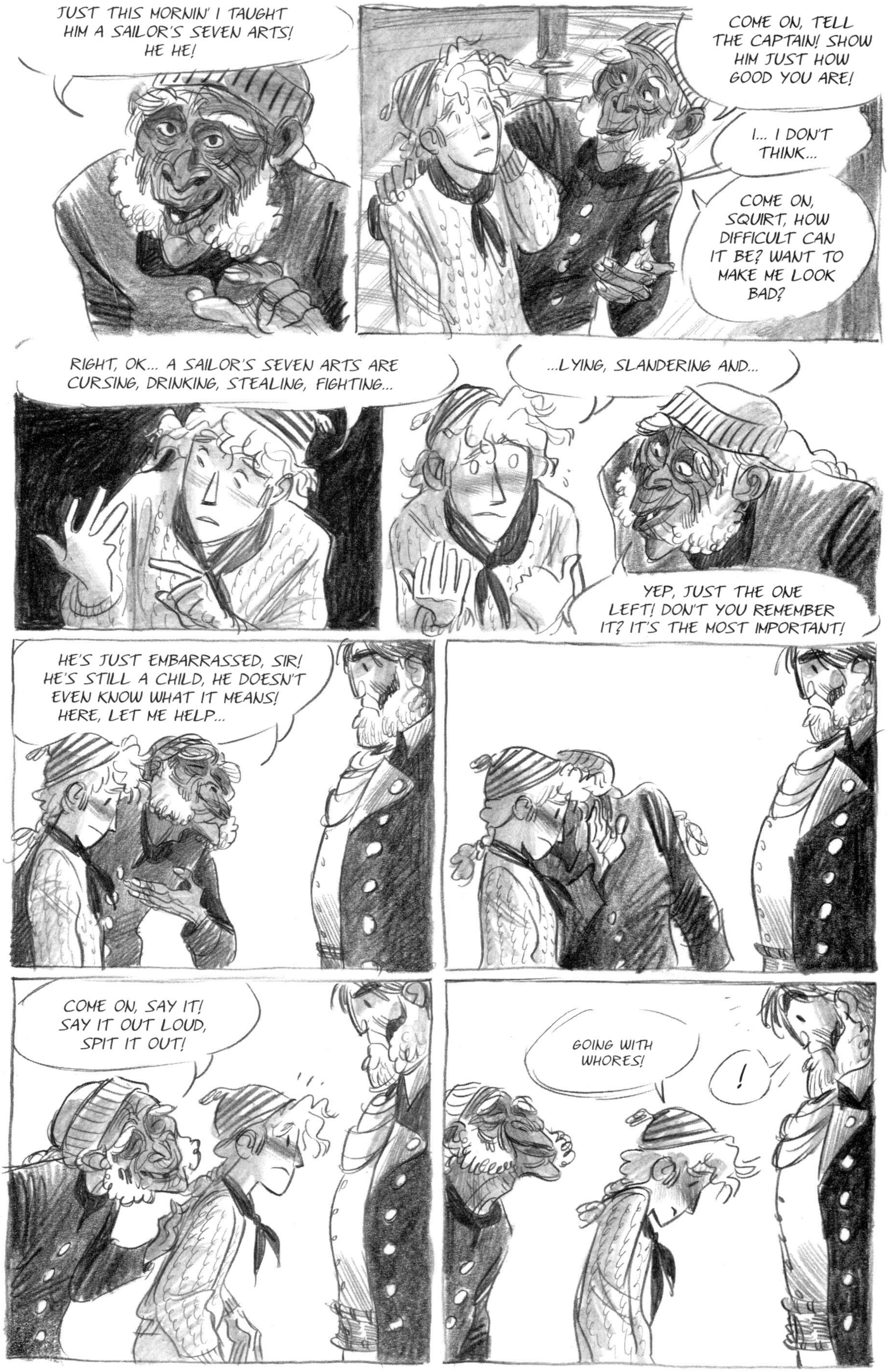
JUST THIS MORNIN' I TAUGHT HIM A SAILOR'S SEVEN ARTS! HE HE!
COME ON, TELL THE CAPTAIN! SHOW HIM JUST HOW GOOD YOU ARE!
I... I DON'T THINK...
COME ON, SQUIRT, HOW DIFFICULT CAN IT BE? WANT TO MAKE ME LOOK BAD?
RIGHT, OK... A SAILOR'S SEVEN ARTS ARE CURSING, DRINKING, STEALING, FIGHTING...
...LYING, SLANDERING AND...
YEP, JUST THE ONE LEFT! DON'T YOU REMEMBER IT? IT'S THE MOST IMPORTANT!
HE'S JUST EMBARRASSED, SIR! HE'S STILL A CHILD, HE DOESN'T EVEN KNOW WHAT IT MEANS! HERE, LET ME HELP...
COME ON, SAY IT! SAY IT OUT LOUD, SPIT IT OUT!
GOING WITH WHORES!
!

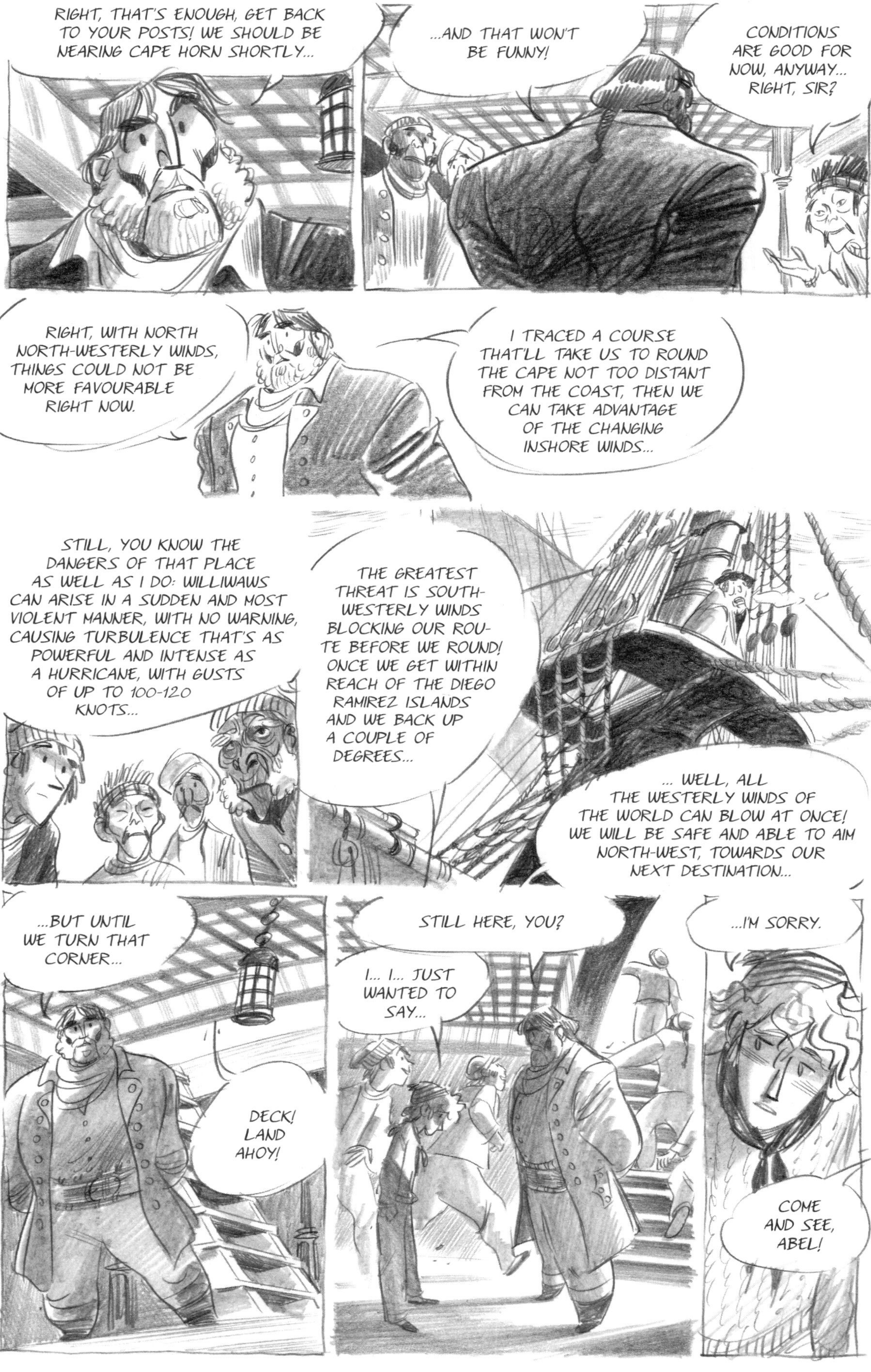
RIGHT, THAT'S ENOUGH, GET BACK TO YOUR POSTS! WE SHOULD BE NEARING CAPE HORN SHORTLY...
...AND THAT WON'T BE FUNNY!
CONDITIONS ARE GOOD FOR NOW, ANYWAY... RIGHT, SIR?
RIGHT, WITH NORTH NORTH-WESTERLY WINDS, THINGS COULD NOT BE MORE FAVOURABLE RIGHT NOW.
I TRACED A COURSE THAT'LL TAKE US TO ROUND THE CAPE NOT TOO DISTANT FROM THE COAST, THEN WE CAN TAKE ADVANTAGE OF THE CHANGING INSHORE WINDS...
STILL, YOU KNOW THE DANGERS OF THAT PLACE AS WELL AS I DO: WILLIWAWS CAN ARISE IN A SUDDEN AND MOST VIOLENT MANNER, WITH NO WARNING, CAUSING TURBULENCE THAT'S AS POWERFUL AND INTENSE AS A HURRICANE, WITH GUSTS OF UP TO 100-120 KNOTS...
THE GREATEST THREAT IS SOUTH-WESTERLY WINDS BLOCKING OUR ROUTE BEFORE WE ROUND! ONCE WE GET WITHIN REACH OF THE DIEGO RAMIREZ ISLANDS AND WE BACK UP A COUPLE OF DEGREES...
... WELL, ALL THE WESTERLY WINDS OF THE WORLD CAN BLOW AT ONCE! WE WILL BE SAFE AND ABLE TO AIM NORTH-WEST, TOWARDS OUR NEXT DESTINATION...
...BUT UNTIL WE TURN THAT CORNER...
DECK! LAND AHOY!
STILL HERE, YOU?
I... I... JUST WANTED TO SAY...
...I'M SORRY.
COME AND SEE, ABEL!

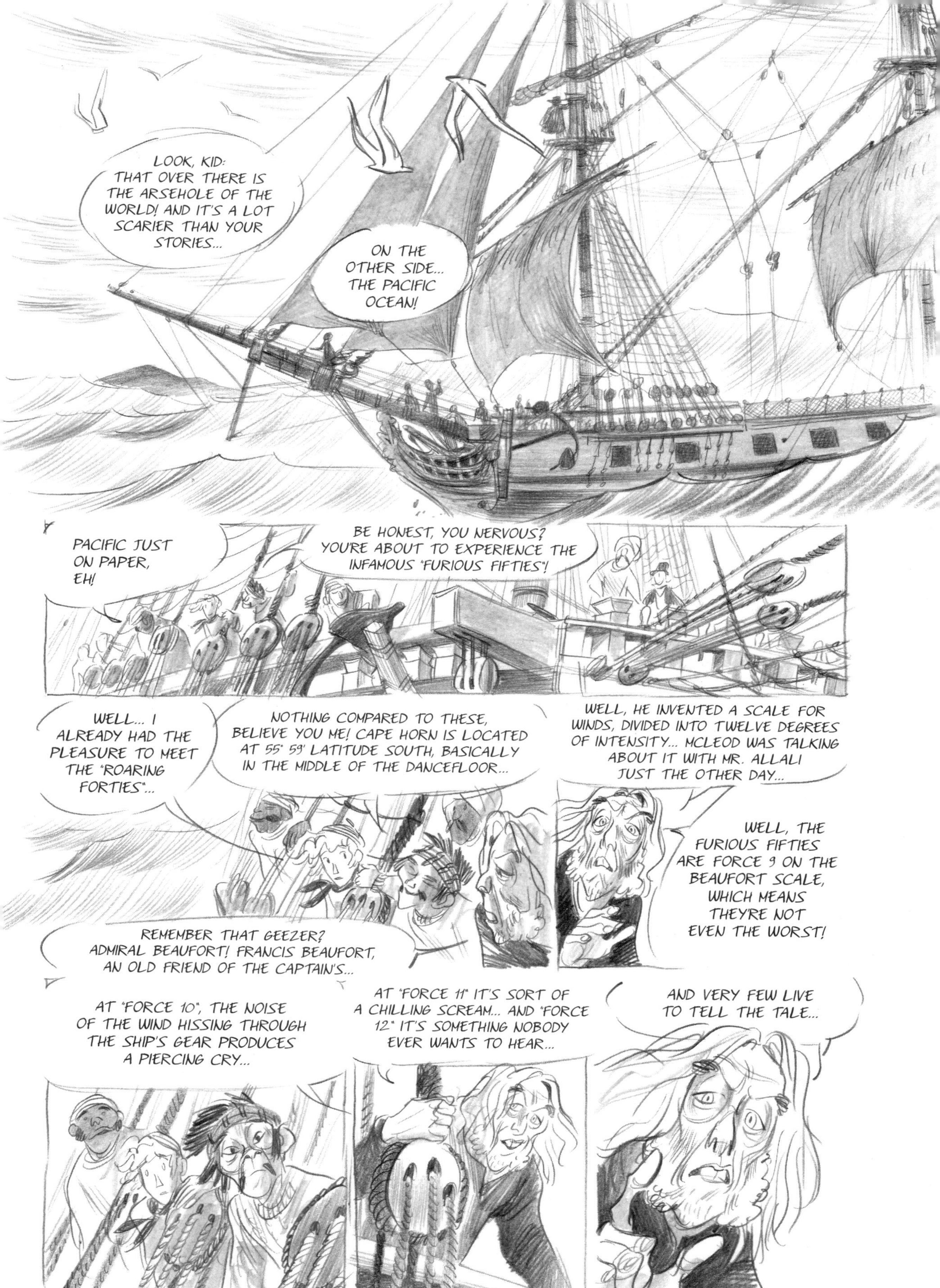

LOOK, KID: THAT OVER THERE IS THE ARSEHOLE OF THE WORLD! AND IT'S A LOT SCARIER THAN YOUR STORIES...
ON THE OTHER SIDE... THE PACIFIC OCEAN!
PACIFIC JUST ON PAPER, EH!
BE HONEST, YOU NERVOUS? YOU'RE ABOUT TO EXPERIENCE THE INFAMOUS "FURIOUS FIFTIES"!
WELL... I ALREADY HAD THE PLEASURE TO MEET THE "ROARING FORTIES"...
NOTHING COMPARED TO THESE, BELIEVE YOU ME! CAPE HORN IS LOCATED AT 55° 59' LATITUDE SOUTH, BASICALLY IN THE MIDDLE OF THE DANCEFLOOR...
REMEMBER THAT GEEZER? ADMIRAL BEAUFORT! FRANCIS BEAUFORT, AN OLD FRIEND OF THE CAPTAIN'S...
WELL, HE INVENTED A SCALE FOR WINDS, DIVIDED INTO TWELVE DEGREES OF INTENSITY... MCLEOD WAS TALKING ABOUT IT WITH MR. ALLALI JUST THE OTHER DAY...
WELL, THE FURIOUS FIFTIES ARE FORCE 9 ON THE BEAUFORT SCALE, WHICH MEANS THEY'RE NOT EVEN THE WORST!
AT "FORCE 10", THE NOISE OF THE WIND HISSING THROUGH THE SHIP'S GEAR PRODUCES A PIERCING CRY...
AT "FORCE 11" IT'S SORT OF A CHILLING SCREAM... AND "FORCE 12" IT'S SOMETHING NOBODY EVER WANTS TO HEAR...
AND VERY FEW LIVE TO TELL THE TALE...

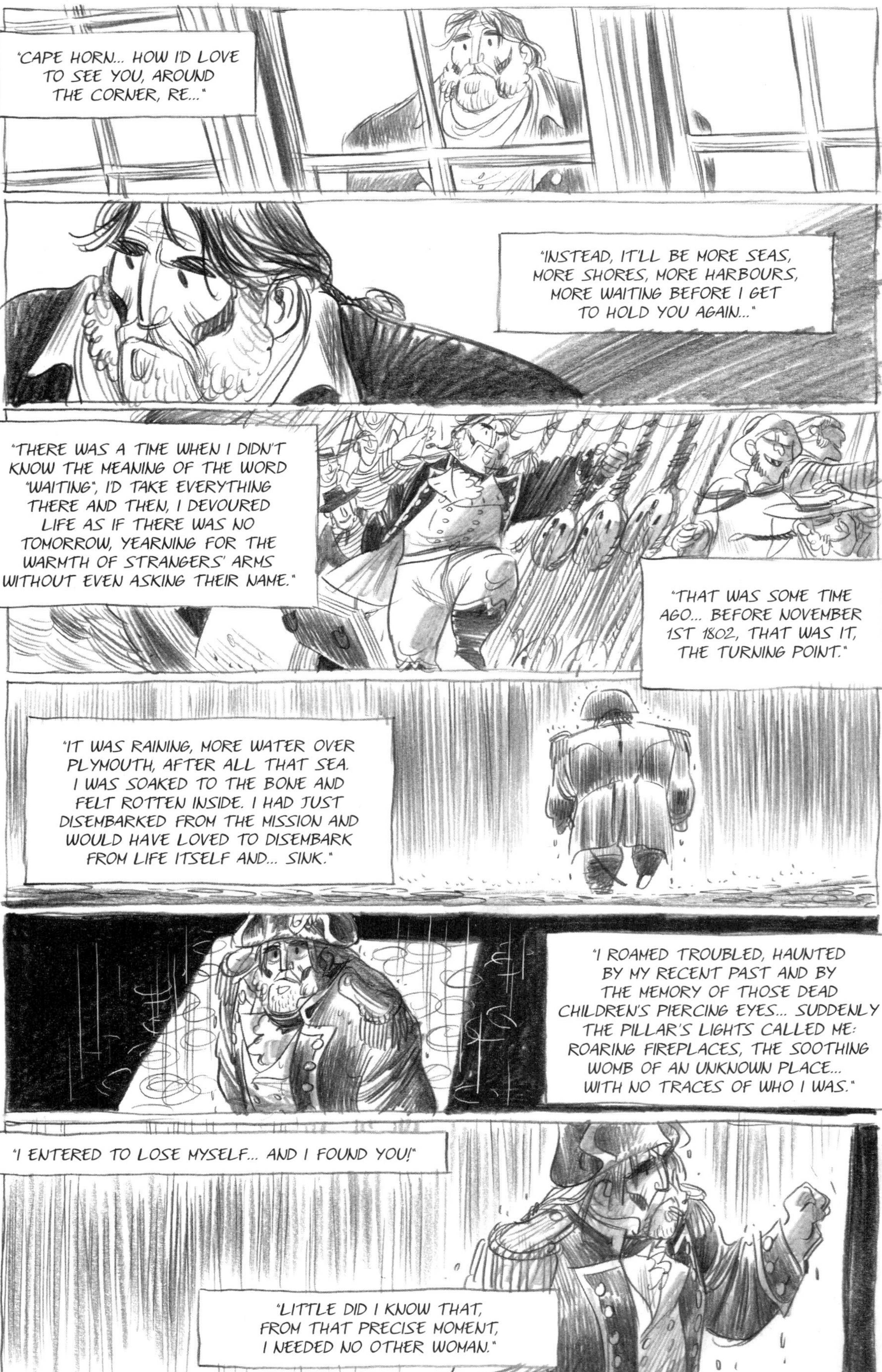
"CAPE HORN... HOW I'D LOVE TO SEE YOU, AROUND THE CORNER, RE..."
"INSTEAD, IT'LL BE MORE SEAS, MORE SHORES, MORE HARBOURS, MORE WAITING BEFORE I GET TO HOLD YOU AGAIN..."
"THERE WAS A TIME WHEN I DIDN'T KNOW THE MEANING OF THE WORD "WAITING", I'D TAKE EVERYTHING THERE AND THEN, I DEVOURED LIFE AS IF THERE WAS NO TOMORROW, YEARNING FOR THE WARMTH OF STRANGERS' ARMS WITHOUT EVEN ASKING THEIR NAME."
"THAT WAS SOME TIME AGO... BEFORE NOVEMBER 1ST 1802, THAT WAS IT, THE TURNING POINT."
"IT WAS RAINING, MORE WATER OVER PLYMOUTH, AFTER ALL THAT SEA. I WAS SOAKED TO THE BONE AND FELT ROTTEN INSIDE. I HAD JUST DISEMBARKED FROM THE MISSION AND WOULD HAVE LOVED TO DISEMBARK FROM LIFE ITSELF AND... SINK."
"I ROAMED TROUBLED, HAUNTED BY MY RECENT PAST AND BY THE MEMORY OF THOSE DEAD CHILDREN'S PIERCING EYES... SUDDENLY THE PILLAR'S LIGHTS CALLED ME: ROARING FIREPLACES, THE SOOTHING WOMB OF AN UNKNOWN PLACE... WITH NO TRACES OF WHO I WAS."
"I ENTERED TO LOSE MYSELF... AND I FOUND YOU!"
"LITTLE DID I KNOW THAT, FROM THAT PRECISE MOMENT, I NEEDED NO OTHER WOMAN."

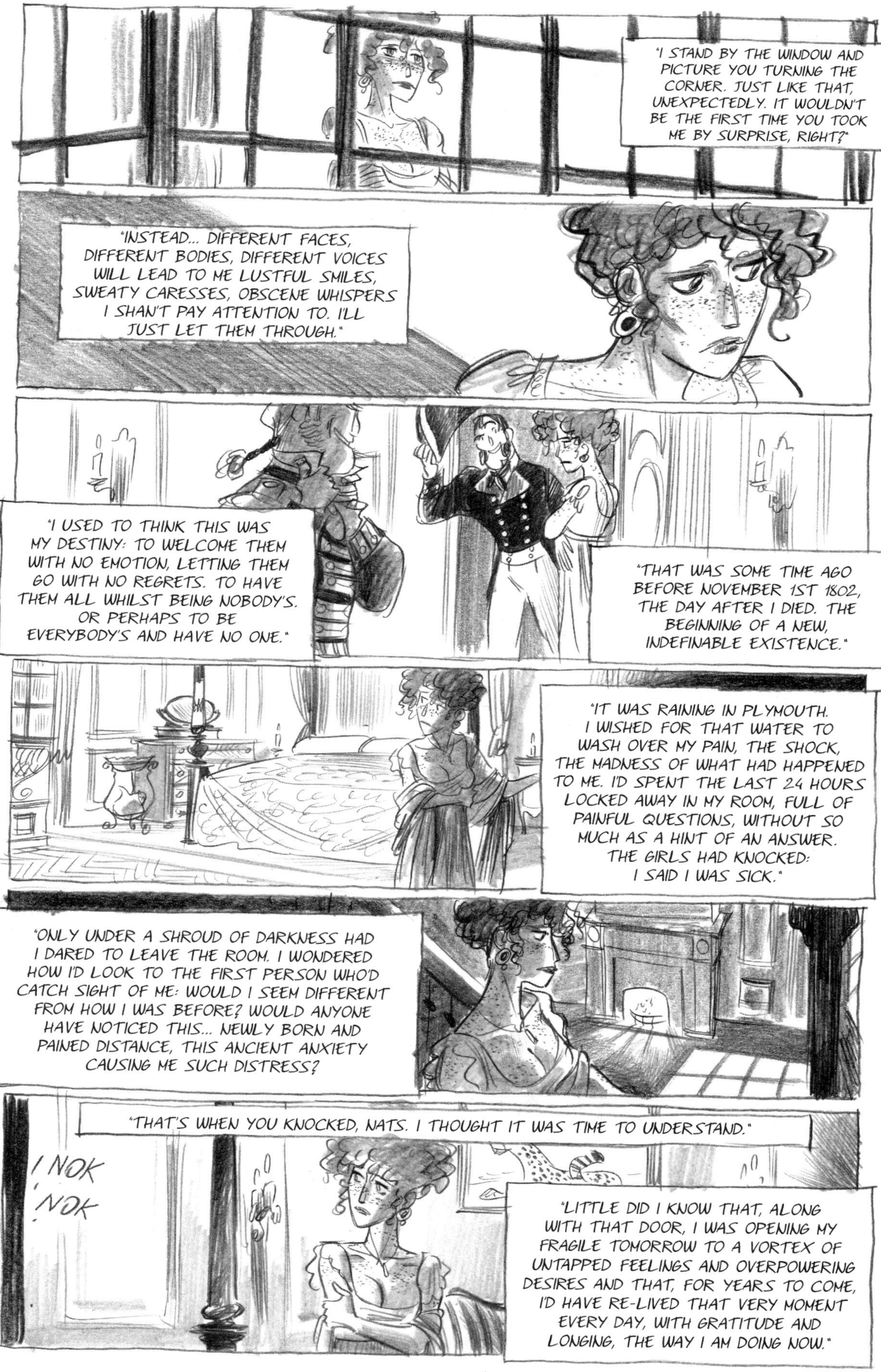

"I STAND BY THE WINDOW AND PICTURE YOU TURNING THE CORNER. JUST LIKE THAT, UNEXPECTEDLY. IT WOULDN'T BE THE FIRST TIME YOU TOOK ME BY SURPRISE, RIGHT?"
"INSTEAD... DIFFERENT FACES, DIFFERENT BODIES, DIFFERENT VOICES WILL LEAD TO ME LUSTFUL SMILES, SWEATY CARESSES, OBSCENE WHISPERS I SHAN'T PAY ATTENTION TO. I'LL JUST LET THEM THROUGH."
"I USED TO THINK THIS WAS MY DESTINY: TO WELCOME THEM WITH NO EMOTION, LETTING THEM GO WITH NO REGRETS. TO HAVE THEM ALL WHILST BEING NOBODY'S. OR PERHAPS TO BE EVERYBODY'S AND HAVE NO ONE."
"THAT WAS SOME TIME AGO BEFORE NOVEMBER 1ST 1802, THE DAY AFTER I DIED. THE BEGINNING OF A NEW, INDEFINABLE EXISTENCE."
"IT WAS RAINING IN PLYMOUTH. I WISHED FOR THAT WATER TO WASH OVER MY PAIN, THE SHOCK, THE MADNESS OF WHAT HAD HAPPENED TO ME. I'D SPENT THE LAST 24 HOURS LOCKED AWAY IN MY ROOM, FULL OF PAINFUL QUESTIONS, WITHOUT SO MUCH AS A HINT OF AN ANSWER. THE GIRLS HAD KNOCKED: I SAID I WAS SICK."
"ONLY UNDER A SHROUD OF DARKNESS HAD I DARED TO LEAVE THE ROOM. I WONDERED HOW I'D LOOK TO THE FIRST PERSON WHO'D CATCH SIGHT OF ME: WOULD I SEEM DIFFERENT FROM HOW I WAS BEFORE? WOULD ANYONE HAVE NOTICED THIS... NEWLY BORN AND PAINED DISTANCE, THIS ANCIENT ANXIETY CAUSING ME SUCH DISTRESS?
"THAT'S WHEN YOU KNOCKED, NATS. I THOUGHT IT WAS TIME TO UNDERSTAND."
!NOK
!NOK
"LITTLE DID I KNOW THAT, ALONG WITH THAT DOOR, I WAS OPENING MY FRAGILE TOMORROW TO A VORTEX OF UNTAPPED FEELINGS AND OVERPOWERING DESIRES AND THAT, FOR YEARS TO COME, I'D HAVE RE-LIVED THAT VERY MOMENT EVERY DAY, WITH GRATITUDE AND LONGING, THE WAY I AM DOING NOW."

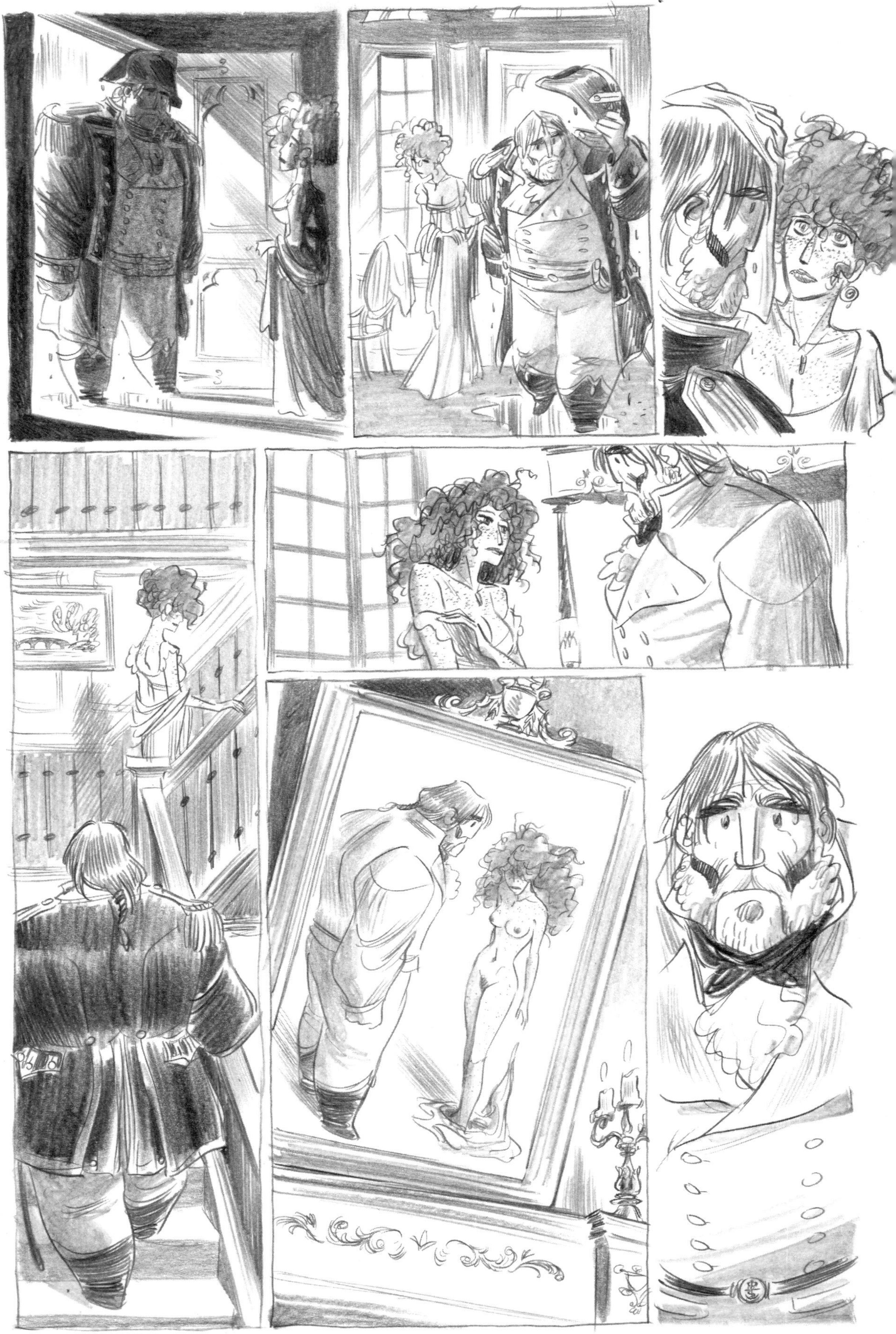

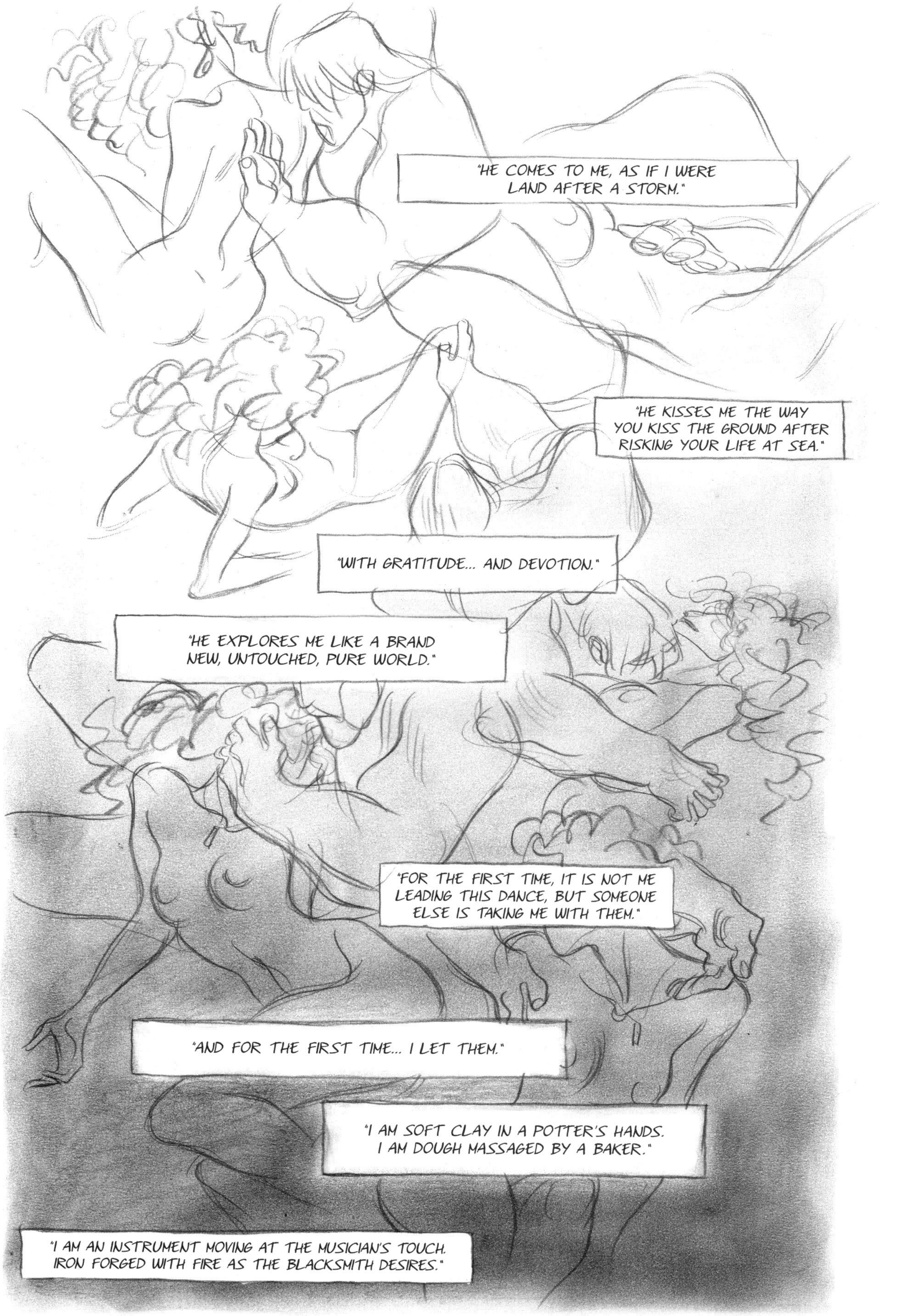
"HE COMES TO ME, AS IF I WERE LAND AFTER A STORM."
"HE KISSES ME THE WAY YOU KISS THE GROUND AFTER RISKING YOUR LIFE AT SEA."
"WITH GRATITUDE... AND DEVOTION."
"HE EXPLORES ME LIKE A BRAND NEW, UNTOUCHED, PURE WORLD."
"FOR THE FIRST TIME, IT IS NOT ME LEADING THIS DANCE, BUT SOMEONE ELSE IS TAKING ME WITH THEM."
"AND FOR THE FIRST TIME... I LET THEM."
"I AM SOFT CLAY IN A POTTER'S HANDS. I AM DOUGH MASSAGED BY A BAKER."
"I AM AN INSTRUMENT MOVING AT THE MUSICIAN'S TOUCH. IRON FORGED WITH FIRE AS THE BLACKSMITH DESIRES."

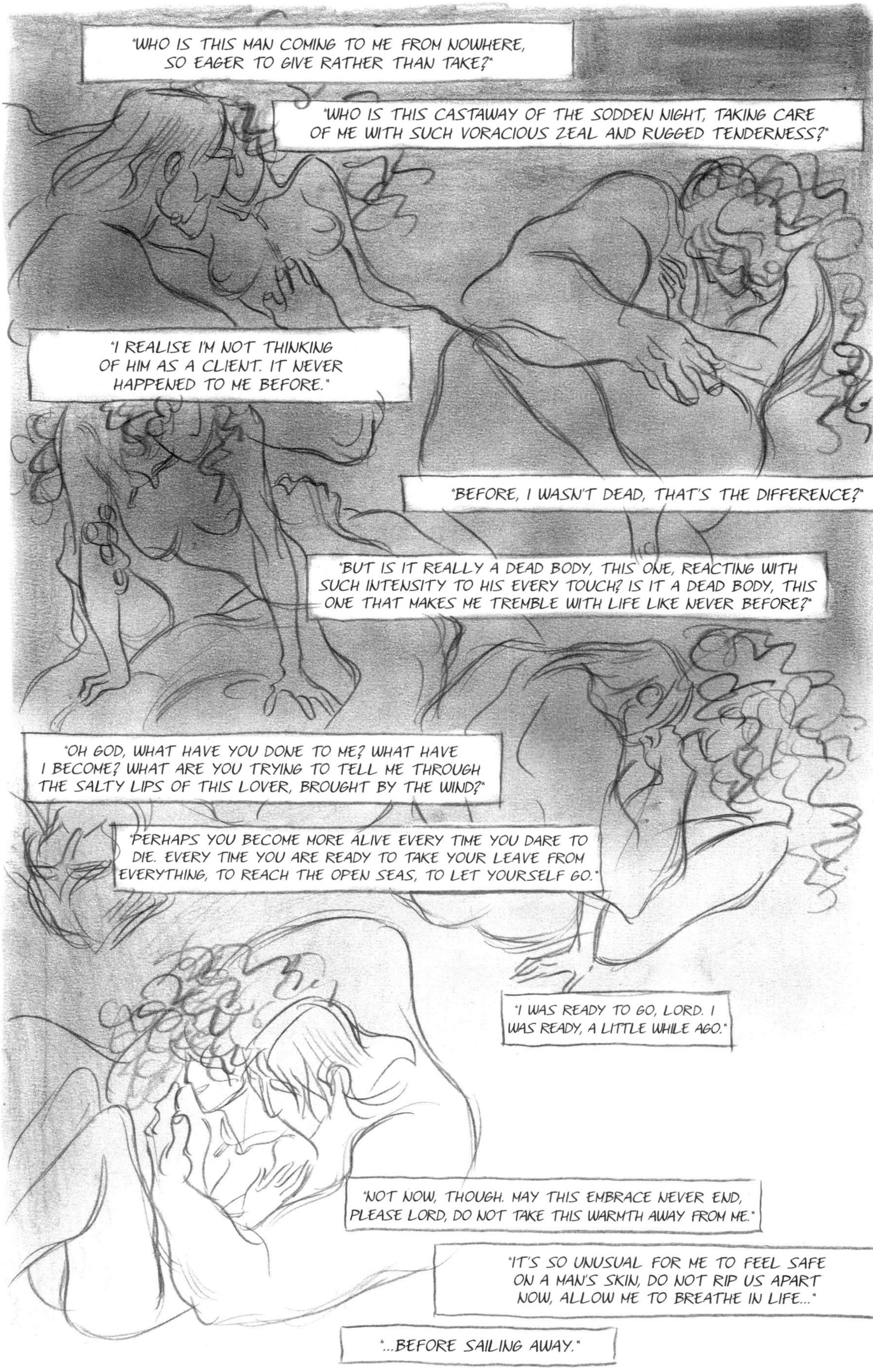
"WHO IS THIS MAN COMING TO ME FROM NOWHERE, SO EAGER TO GIVE RATHER THAN TAKE?"
"WHO IS THIS CASTAWAY OF THE SODDEN NIGHT, TAKING CARE OF ME WITH SUCH VORACIOUS ZEAL AND RUGGED TENDERNESS?"
"I REALISE I'M NOT THINKING OF HIM AS A CLIENT. IT NEVER HAPPENED TO ME BEFORE."
"BEFORE, I WASN'T DEAD, THAT'S THE DIFFERENCE?"
"BUT IS IT REALLY A DEAD BODY, THIS ONE, REACTING WITH SUCH INTENSITY TO HIS EVERY TOUCH? IS IT A DEAD BODY, THIS ONE THAT MAKES ME TREMBLE WITH LIFE LIKE NEVER BEFORE?"
"OH GOD, WHAT HAVE YOU DONE TO ME? WHAT HAVE I BECOME? WHAT ARE YOU TRYING TO TELL ME THROUGH THE SALTY LIPS OF THIS LOVER, BROUGHT BY THE WIND?"
"PERHAPS YOU BECOME MORE ALIVE EVERY TIME YOU DARE TO DIE. EVERY TIME YOU ARE READY TO TAKE YOUR LEAVE FROM EVERYTHING, TO REACH THE OPEN SEAS, TO LET YOURSELF GO."
"I WAS READY TO GO, LORD. I WAS READY, A LITTLE WHILE AGO."
"NOT NOW, THOUGH. MAY THIS EMBRACE NEVER END, PLEASE LORD, DO NOT TAKE THIS WARMTH AWAY FROM ME."
"IT'S SO UNUSUAL FOR ME TO FEEL SAFE ON A MAN'S SKIN, DO NOT RIP US APART NOW, ALLOW ME TO BREATHE IN LIFE..."
"...BEFORE SAILING AWAY."

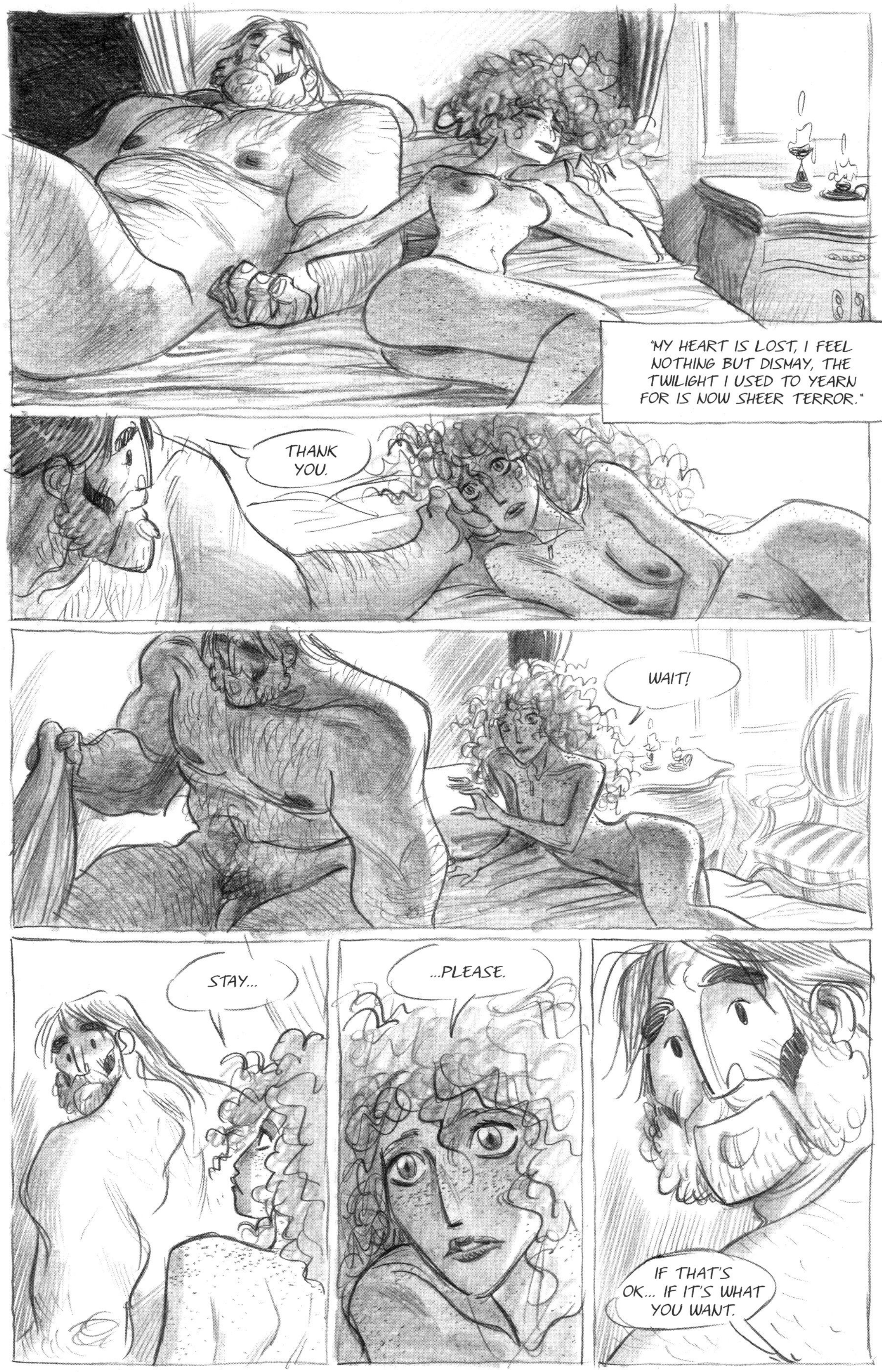
"MY HEART IS LOST, I FEEL NOTHING BUT DISMAY, THE TWILIGHT I USED TO YEARN FOR IS NOW SHEER TERROR."
THANK YOU.
WAIT!
STAY...
...PLEASE.
IF THAT'S OK... IF IT'S WHAT YOU WANT.

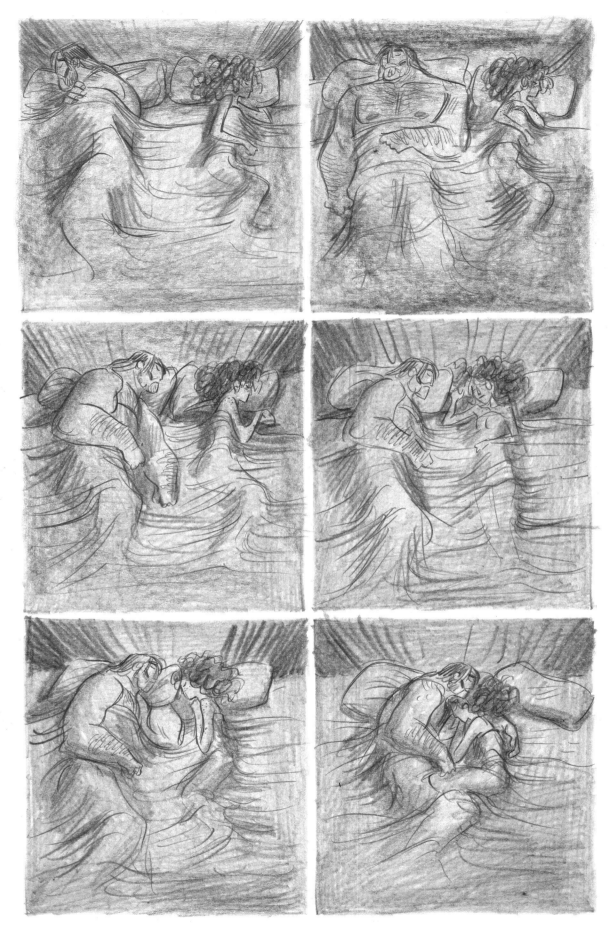

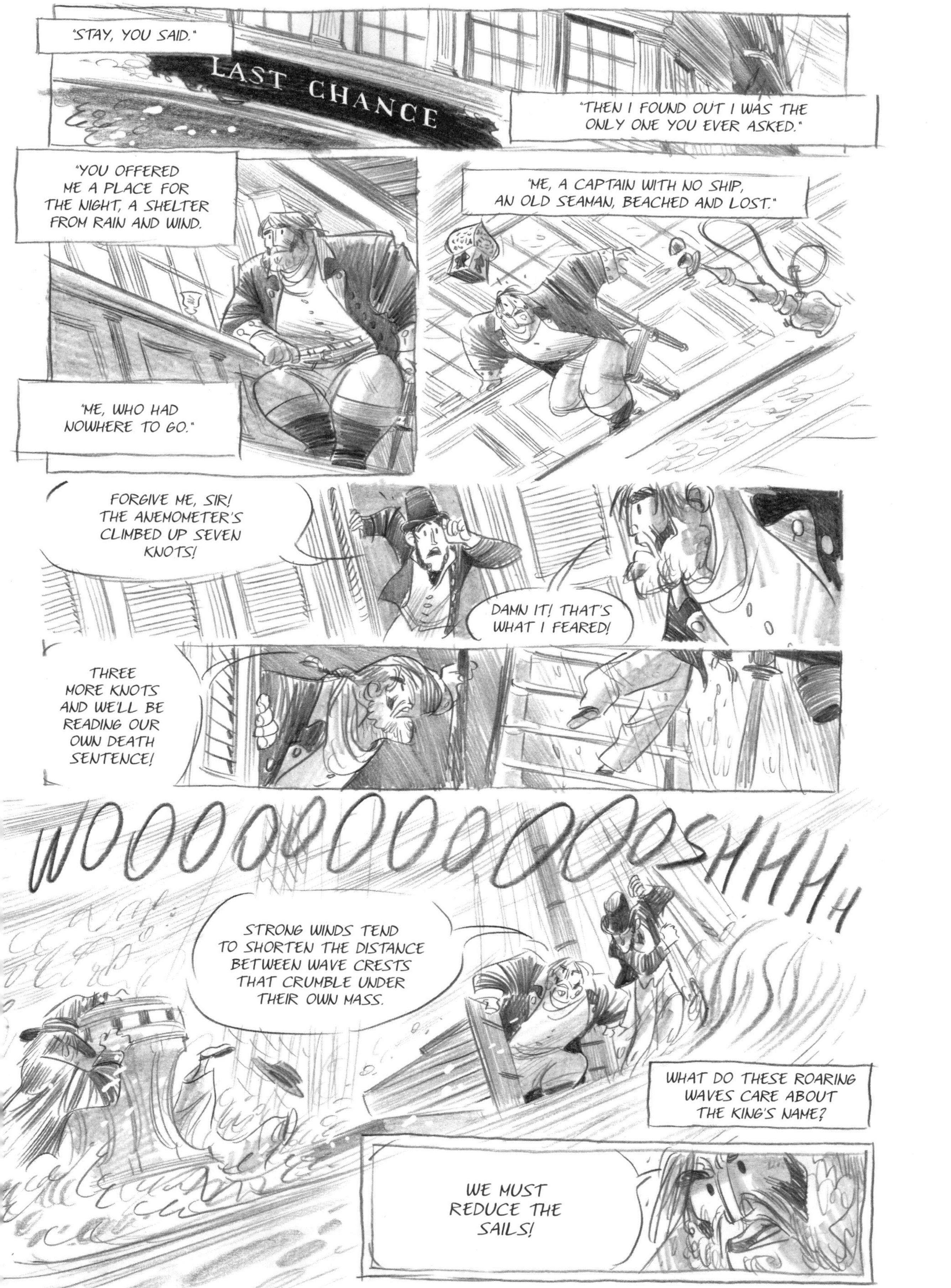
"STAY, YOU SAID."
LAST CHANCE
"THEN I FOUND OUT I WAS THE ONLY ONE YOU EVER ASKED."
"YOU OFFERED ME A PLACE FOR THE NIGHT, A SHELTER FROM RAIN AND WIND.
"ME, WHO HAD NOWHERE TO GO."
"ME, A CAPTAIN WITH NO SHIP, AN OLD SEAMAN, BEACHED AND LOST."
FORGIVE ME, SIR! THE ANEMOMETER'S CLIMBED UP SEVEN KNOTS!
DAMN IT! THAT'S WHAT I FEARED!
THREE MORE KNOTS AND WE'LL BE READING OUR OWN DEATH SENTENCE!
WOOOOOOOOOOOSHHHH
STRONG WINDS TEND TO SHORTEN THE DISTANCE BETWEEN WAVE CRESTS THAT CRUMBLE UNDER THEIR OWN MASS.
WHAT DO THESE ROARING WAVES CARE ABOUT THE KING'S NAME?
WE MUST REDUCE THE SAILS!

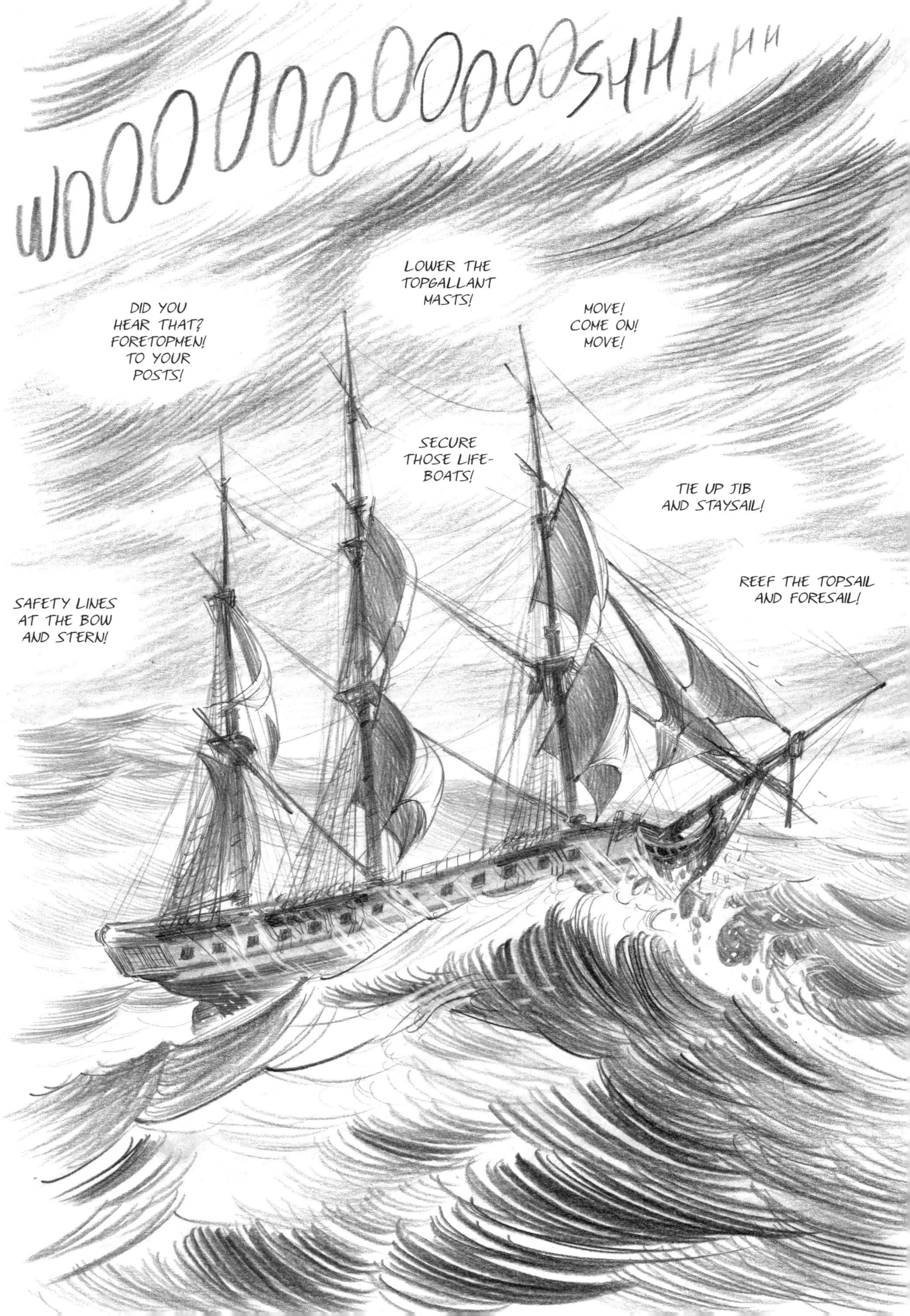
WOOOOOOOOOOOOSHHHHHH
LOWER THE TOPGALLANT MASTS!
DID YOU HEAR THAT? FORETOPMEN! TO YOUR POSTS!
MOVE! COME ON! MOVE!
SECURE THOSE LIFE-BOATS!
TIE UP JIB AND STAYSAIL!
REEF THE TOPSAIL AND FORESAIL!
SAFETY LINES AT THE BOW AND STERN!

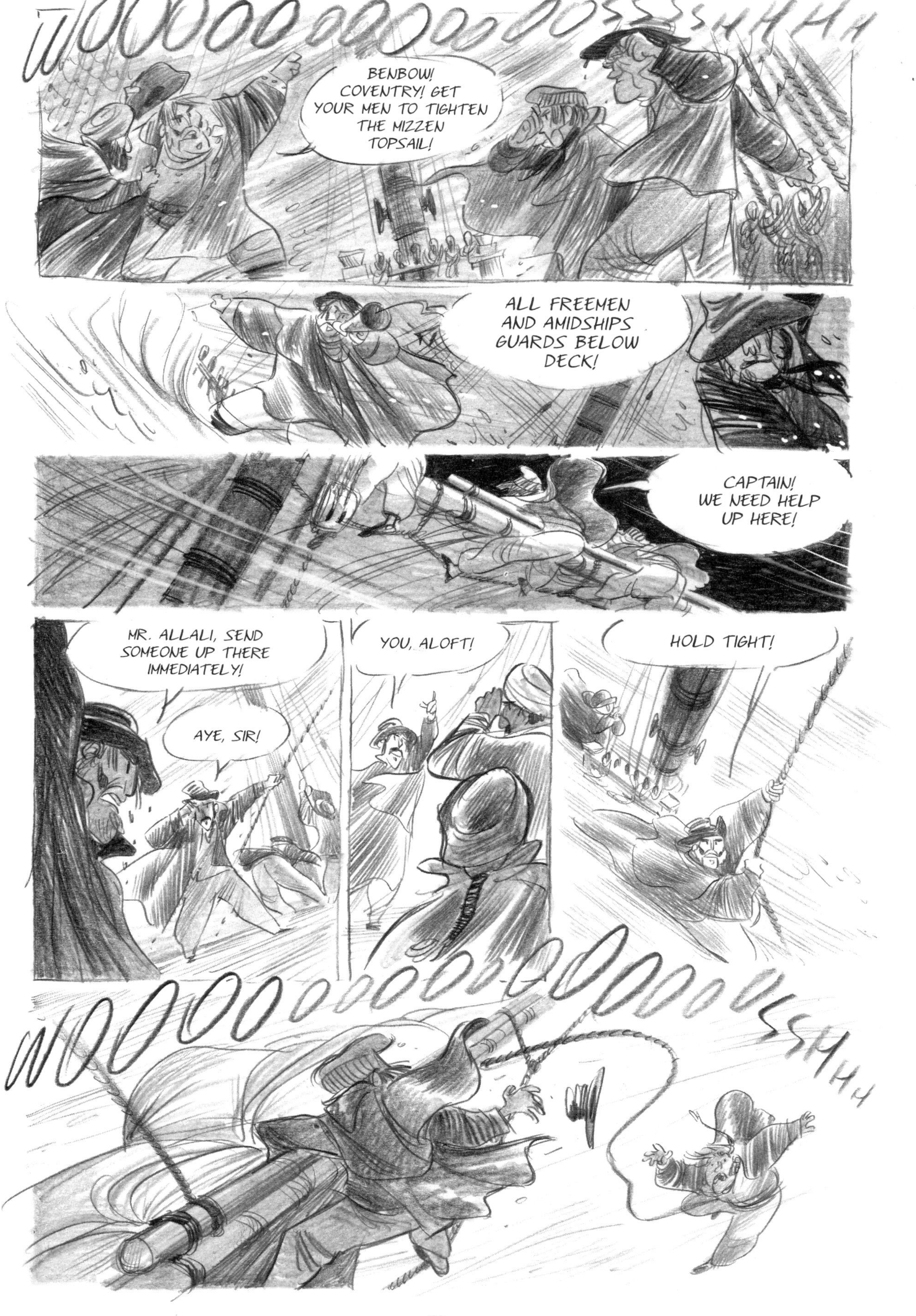
WOOOOOOOOOOOOOOOOOOSSSSHHHHH
BENBOW! COVENTRY! GET YOUR MEN TO TIGHTEN THE MIZZEN TOPSAIL!
ALL FREEMEN AND AMIDSHIPS GUARDS BELOW DECK!
CAPTAIN! WE NEED HELP UP HERE!
MR. ALLALI, SEND SOMEONE UP THERE IMMEDIATELY!
AYE, SIR!
YOU, ALOFT!
HOLD TIGHT!
WOOOOOOOOOOOOOOOOOOOOSSHHH

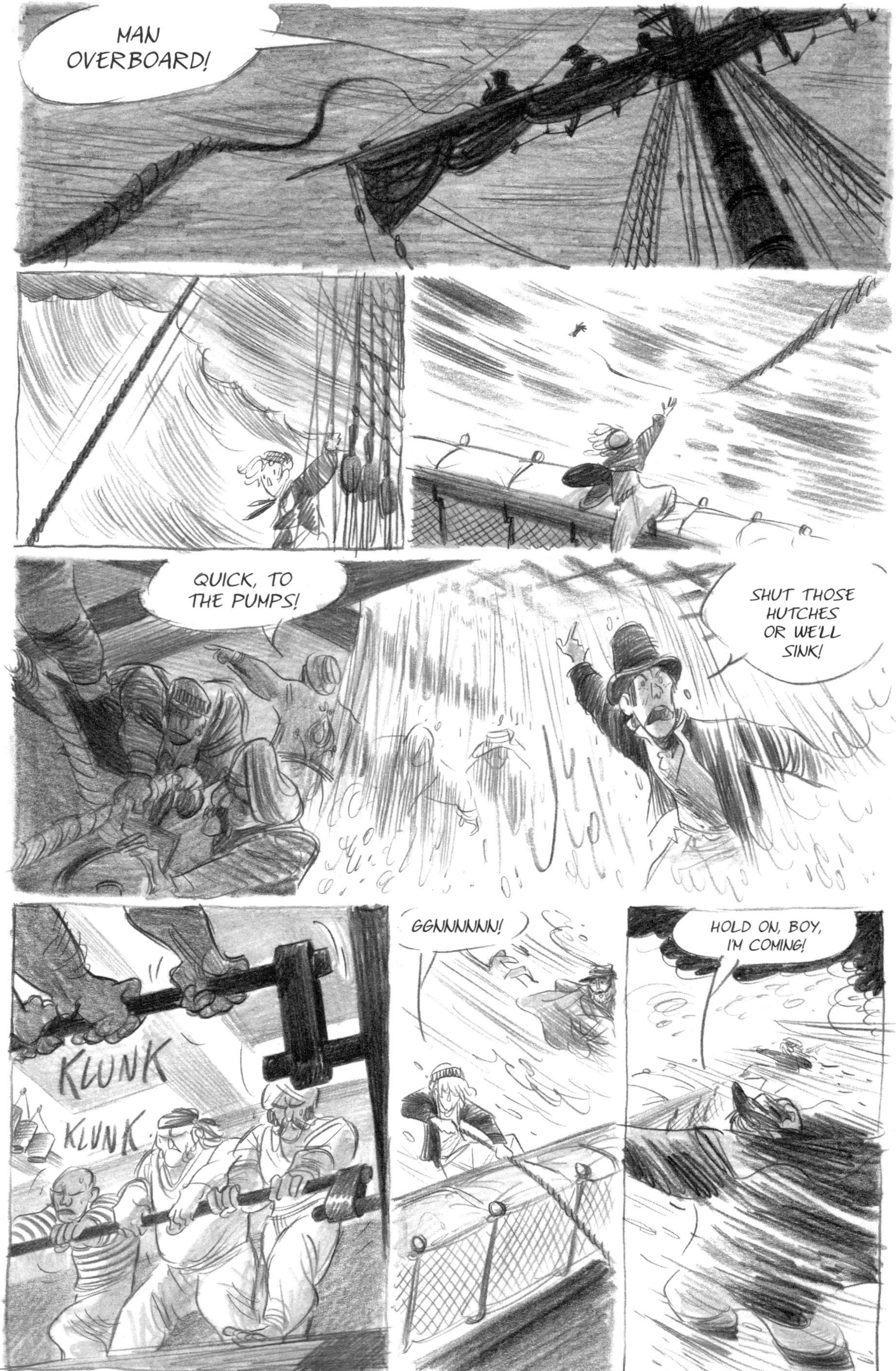
MAN OVERBOARD!
QUICK, TO THE PUMPS!
SHUT THOSE HUTCHES OR WE'LL SINK!
KLUNK
KLUNK
GGNNNNNN!
HOLD ON, BOY, I'M COMING!

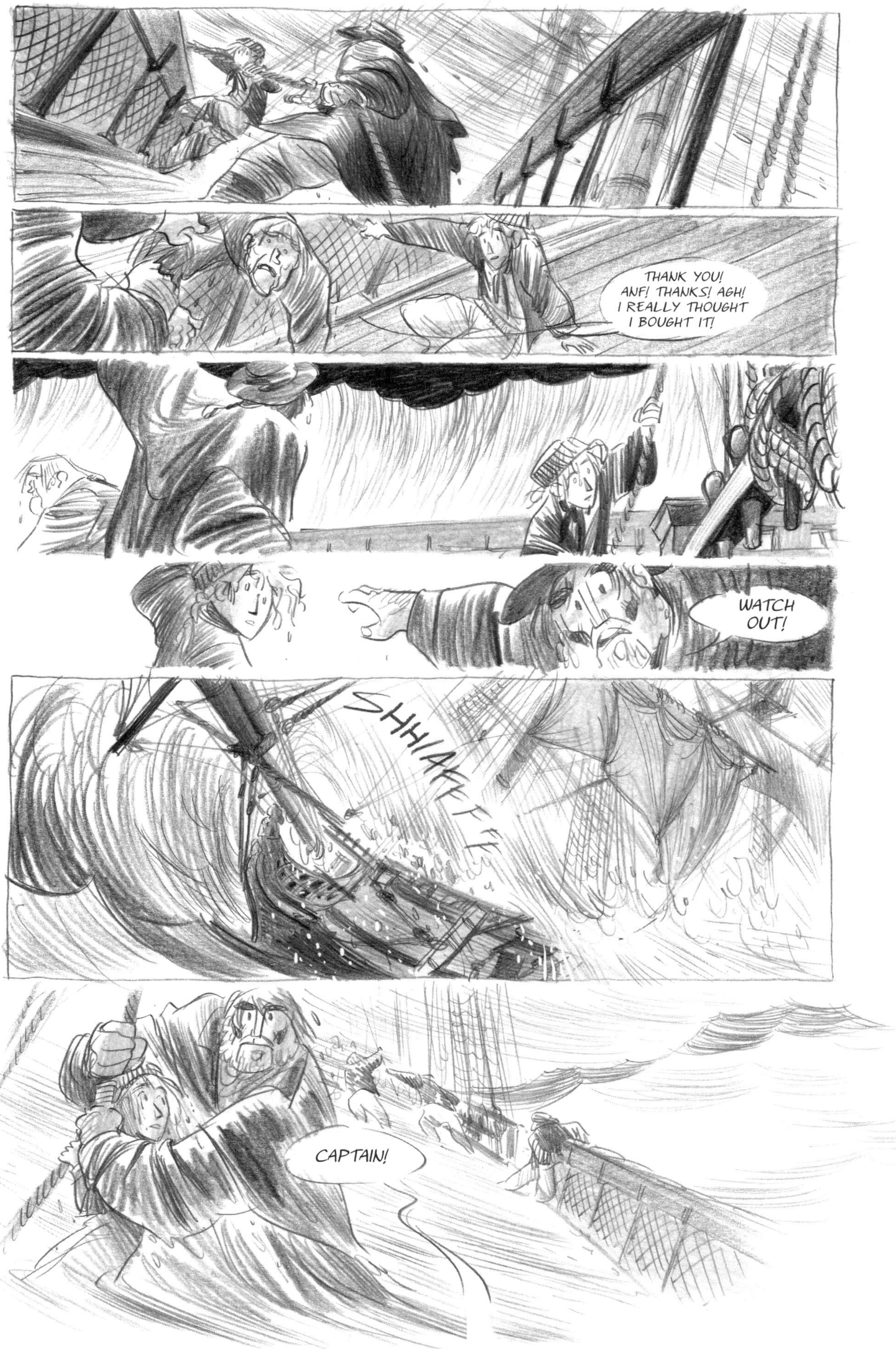
THANK YOU! ANF! THANKS! AGH! I REALLY THOUGHT I BOUGHT IT!
WATCH OUT!
SHHIAKKFFF
CAPTAIN!

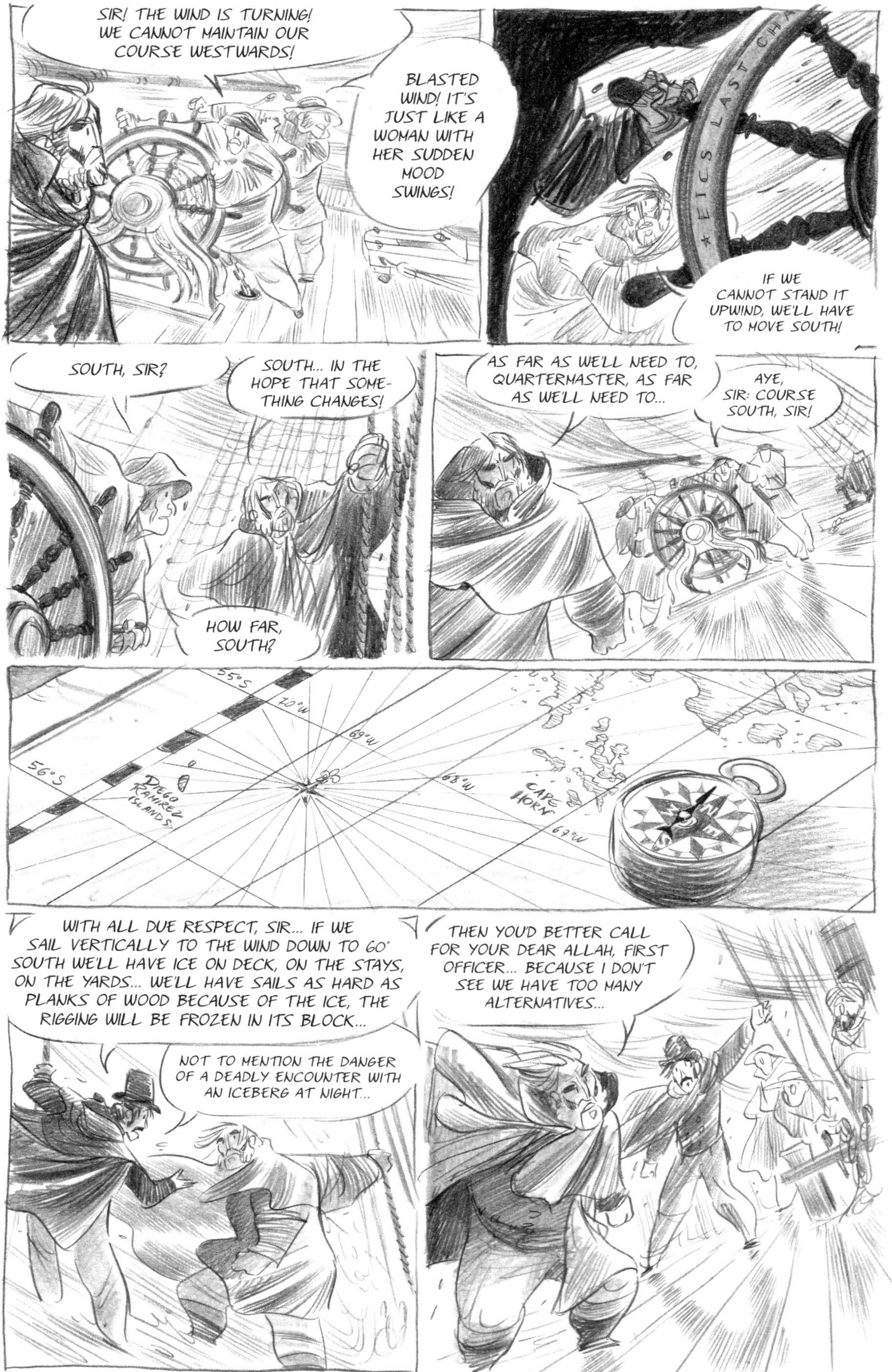
SIR! THE WIND IS TURNING! WE CANNOT MAINTAIN OUR COURSE WESTWARDS!
BLASTED WIND! IT'S JUST LIKE A WOMAN WITH HER SUDDEN MOOD SWINGS!
IF WE CANNOT STAND IT UPWIND, WE'LL HAVE TO MOVE SOUTH!
SOUTH, SIR?
SOUTH... IN THE HOPE THAT SOMETHING CHANGES!
HOW FAR, SOUTH?
AS FAR AS WE'LL NEED TO, QUARTERMASTER, AS FAR AS WE'LL NEED TO...
AYE, SIR: COURSE SOUTH, SIR!
55°S
70°W
69°W
56°S
DIEGO RAMIREZ ISLANDS
68°W
CAPE HORN
67°W
WITH ALL DUE RESPECT, SIR... IF WE SAIL VERTICALLY TO THE WIND DOWN TO 60° SOUTH WE'LL HAVE ICE ON DECK, ON THE STAYS, ON THE YARDS... WE'LL HAVE SAILS AS HARD AS PLANKS OF WOOD BECAUSE OF THE ICE, THE RIGGING WILL BE FROZEN IN ITS BLOCK...
NOT TO MENTION THE DANGER OF A DEADLY ENCOUNTER WITH AN ICEBERG AT NIGHT...
THEN YOU'D BETTER CALL FOR YOUR DEAR ALLAH, FIRST OFFICER... BECAUSE I DON'T SEE WE HAVE TOO MANY ALTERNATIVES...

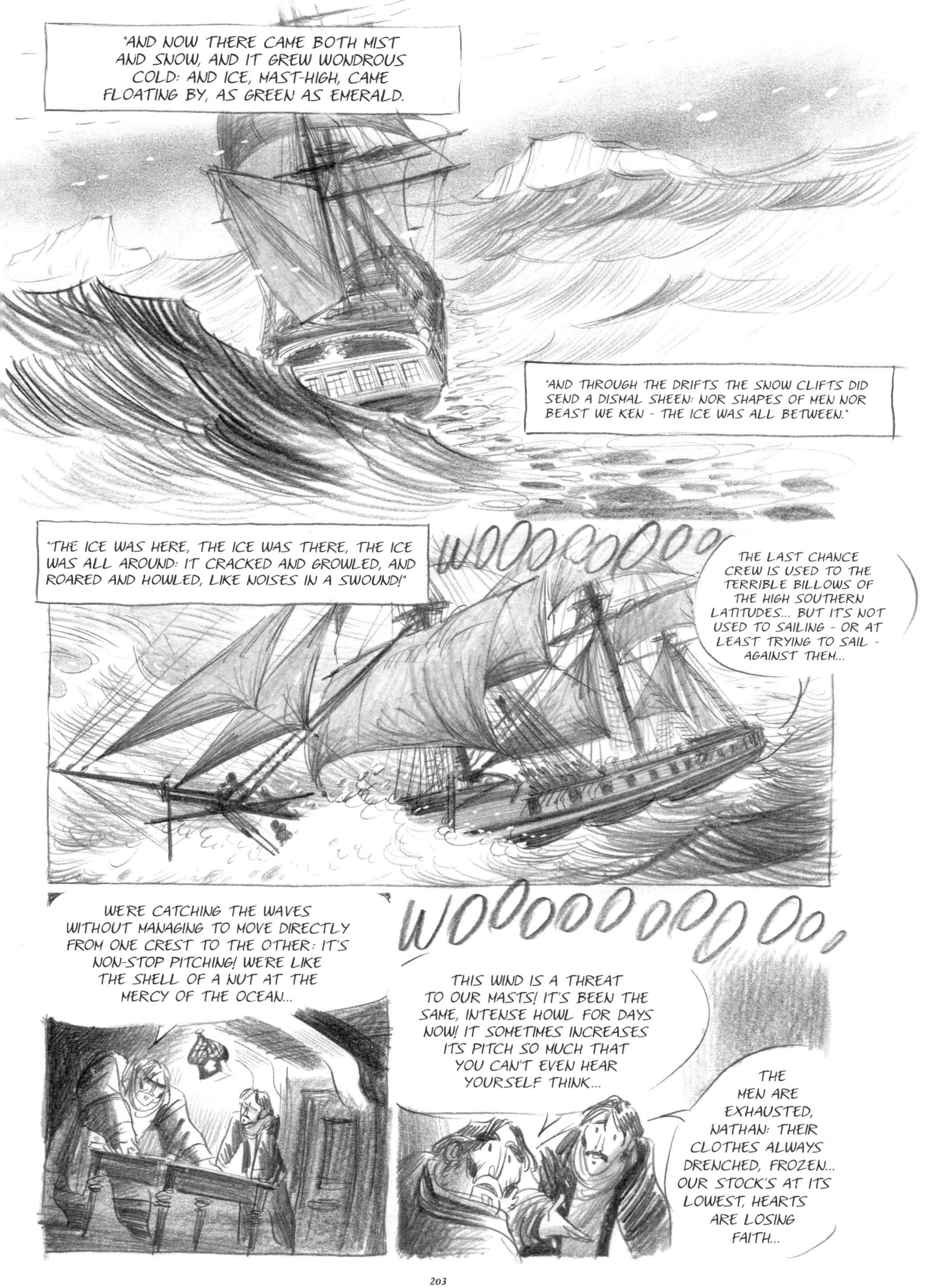
"AND NOW THERE CAME BOTH MIST AND SNOW, AND IT GREW WONDROUS COLD: AND ICE, MAST-HIGH, CAME FLOATING BY, AS GREEN AS EMERALD.
"AND THROUGH THE DRIFTS THE SNOW CLIFTS DID SEND A DISMAL SHEEN: NOR SHAPES OF MEN NOR BEAST WE KEN - THE ICE WAS ALL BETWEEN."
"THE ICE WAS HERE, THE ICE WAS THERE, THE ICE WAS ALL AROUND: IT CRACKED AND GROWLED, AND ROARED AND HOWLED, LIKE NOISES IN A SWOUND!"
WOOOOOOOOO
THE LAST CHANCE CREW IS USED TO THE TERRIBLE BILLOWS OF THE HIGH SOUTHERN LATITUDES... BUT IT'S NOT USED TO SAILING - OR AT LEAST TRYING TO SAIL - AGAINST THEM...
WE'RE CATCHING THE WAVES WITHOUT MANAGING TO MOVE DIRECTLY FROM ONE CREST TO THE OTHER: IT'S NON-STOP PITCHING! WE'RE LIKE THE SHELL OF A NUT AT THE MERCY OF THE OCEAN...
WOOOOOOOOOOOO
THIS WIND IS A THREAT TO OUR MASTS! IT'S BEEN THE SAME, INTENSE HOWL FOR DAYS NOW! IT SOMETIMES INCREASES ITS PITCH SO MUCH THAT YOU CAN'T EVEN HEAR YOURSELF THINK...
THE MEN ARE EXHAUSTED, NATHAN: THEIR CLOTHES ALWAYS DRENCHED, FROZEN... OUR STOCK'S AT ITS LOWEST, HEARTS ARE LOSING FAITH...

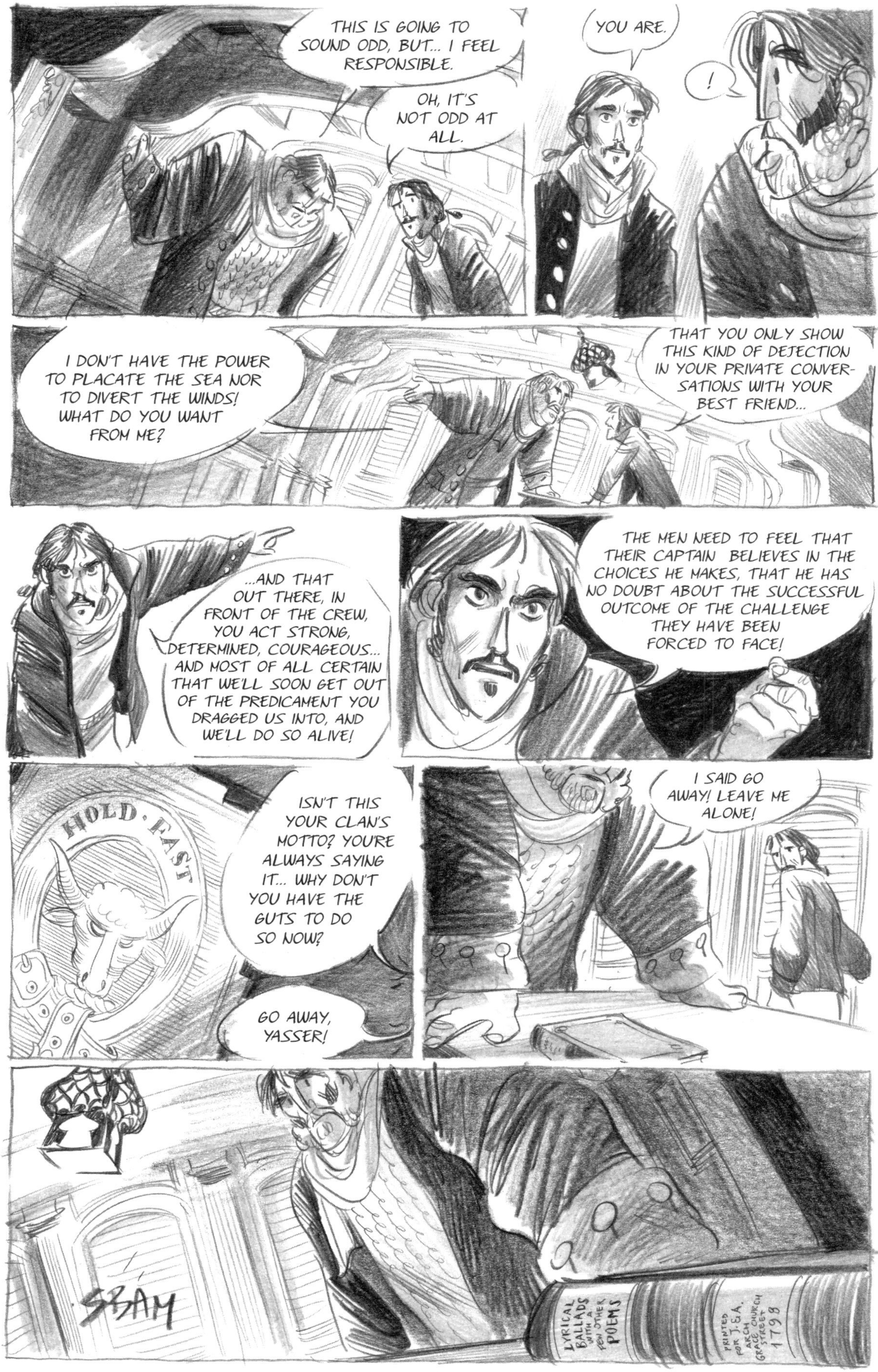
THIS IS GOING TO SOUND ODD, BUT... I FEEL RESPONSIBLE.
OH, IT'S NOT ODD AT ALL.
YOU ARE.
!
I DON'T HAVE THE POWER TO PLACATE THE SEA NOR TO DIVERT THE WINDS! WHAT DO YOU WANT FROM ME?
THAT YOU ONLY SHOW THIS KIND OF DEJECTION IN YOUR PRIVATE CONVER-SATIONS WITH YOUR BEST FRIEND...
...AND THAT OUT THERE, IN FRONT OF THE CREW, YOU ACT STRONG, DETERMINED, COURAGEOUS... AND MOST OF ALL CERTAIN THAT WE'LL SOON GET OUT OF THE PREDICAMENT YOU DRAGGED US INTO, AND WE'LL DO SO ALIVE!
THE MEN NEED TO FEEL THAT THEIR CAPTAIN BELIEVES IN THE CHOICES HE MAKES, THAT HE HAS NO DOUBT ABOUT THE SUCCESSFUL OUTCOME OF THE CHALLENGE THEY HAVE BEEN FORCED TO FACE!
HOLD · FAST
ISN'T THIS YOUR CLAN'S MOTTO? YOU'RE ALWAYS SAYING IT... WHY DON'T YOU HAVE THE GUTS TO DO SO NOW?
GO AWAY, YASSER!
I SAID GO AWAY! LEAVE ME ALONE!
SBAM
LYRICAL BALLADS WITH A FEW OTHER POEMS
PRINTED FOR J.&A. ARCH GRACECHURCH STREET 1798

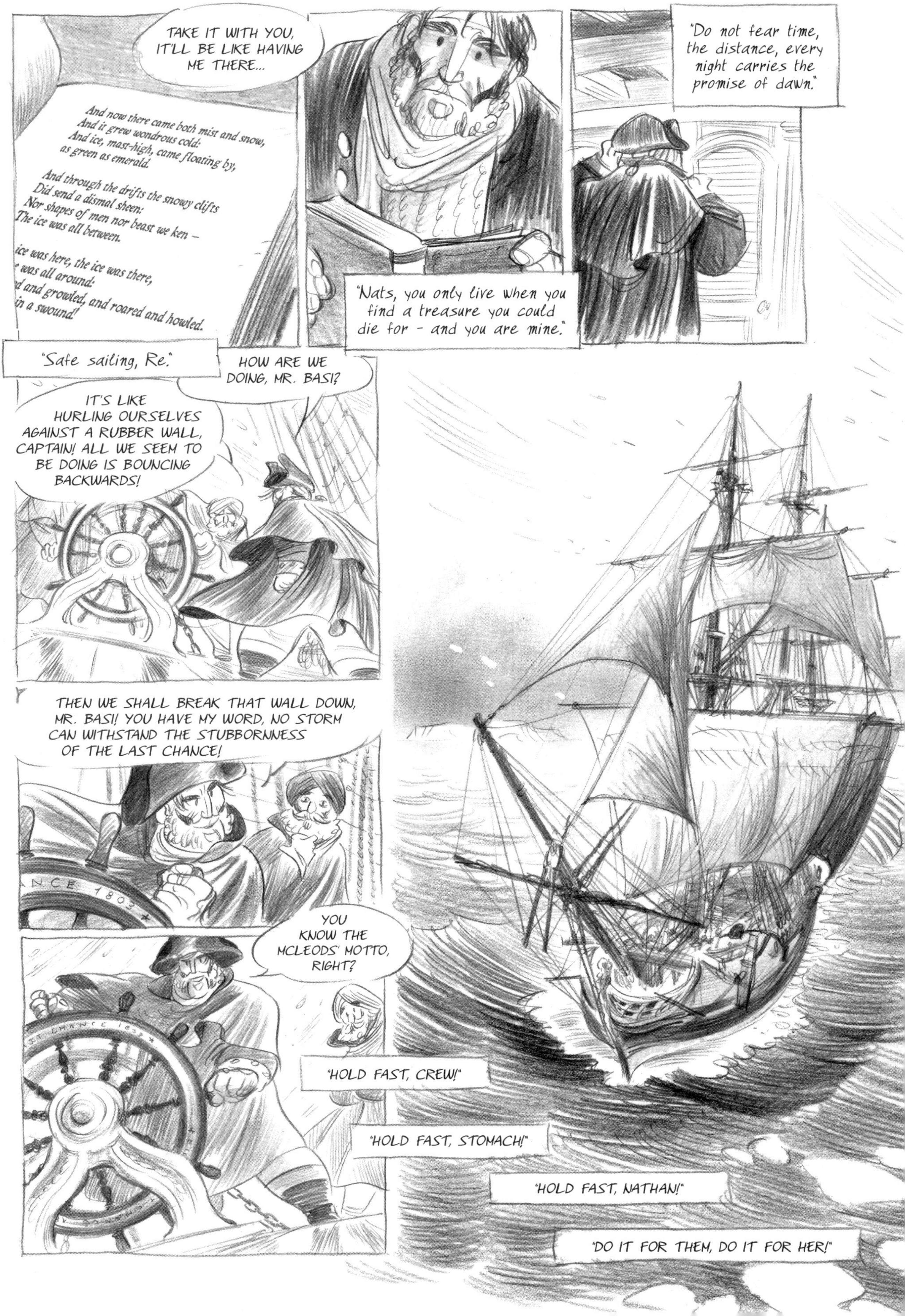

TAKE IT WITH YOU, IT'LL BE LIKE HAVING ME THERE...
And now there came both mist and snow,
And it grew wondrous cold:
And ice, mast-high, came floating by,
as green as emerald.
And through the drifts the snowy clifts
Did send a dismal sheen:
Nor shapes of men nor beast we ken –
The ice was all between.
ice was here, the ice was there,
was all around:
d and growled, and roared and howled.
in a swound!"
"Nats, you only live when you find a treasure you could die for - and you are mine."
"Do not fear time, the distance, every night carries the promise of dawn."
"Safe sailing, Re."
HOW ARE WE DOING, MR. BASI?
IT'S LIKE HURLING OURSELVES AGAINST A RUBBER WALL, CAPTAIN! ALL WE SEEM TO BE DOING IS BOUNCING BACKWARDS!
THEN WE SHALL BREAK THAT WALL DOWN, MR. BASI! YOU HAVE MY WORD, NO STORM CAN WITHSTAND THE STUBBORNNESS OF THE LAST CHANCE!
NCE 1803
YOU KNOW THE MCLEODS' MOTTO, RIGHT?
"HOLD FAST, CREW!"
"HOLD FAST, STOMACH!"
"HOLD FAST, NATHAN!"
"DO IT FOR THEM, DO IT FOR HER!"

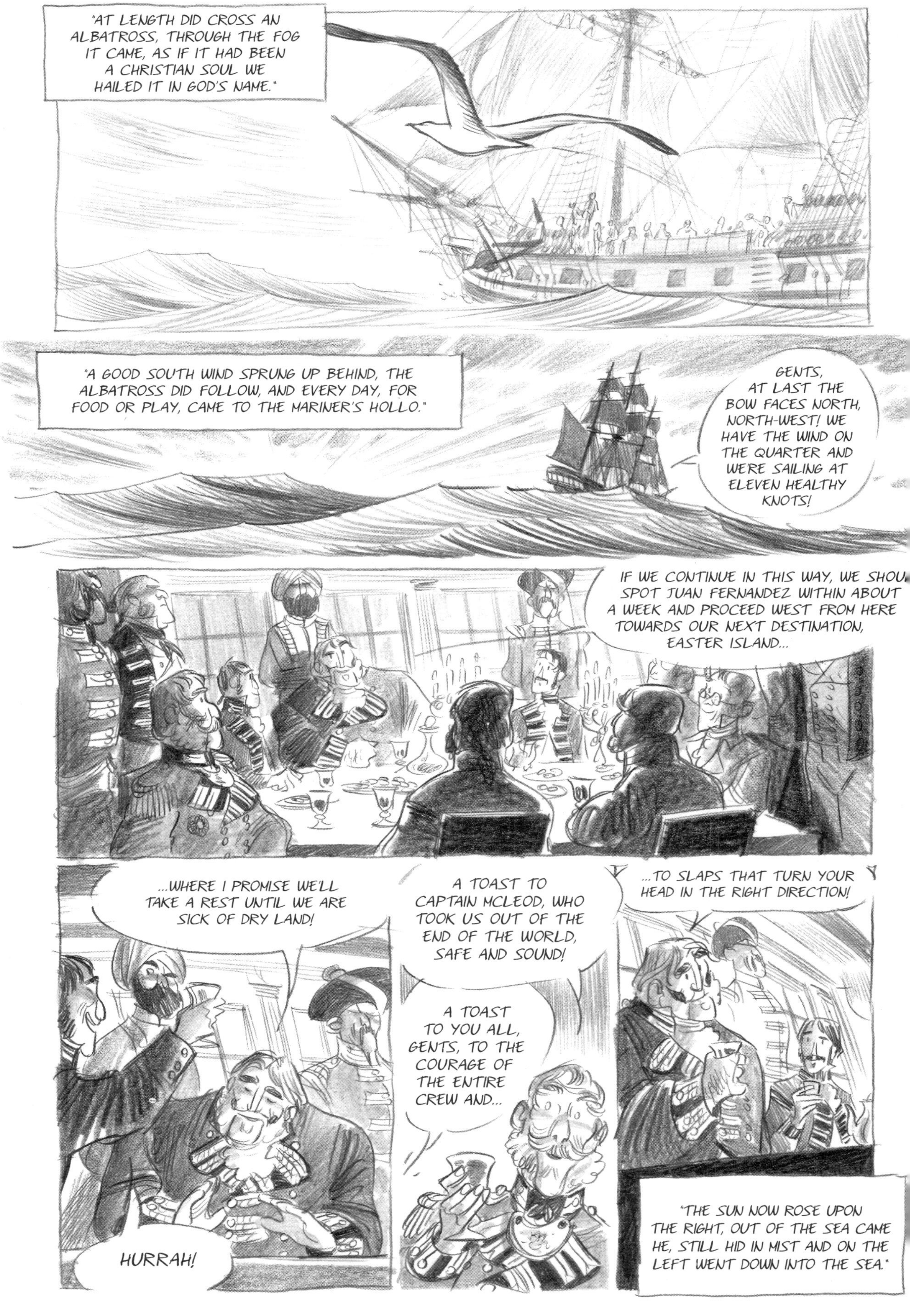
"AT LENGTH DID CROSS AN ALBATROSS, THROUGH THE FOG IT CAME, AS IF IT HAD BEEN A CHRISTIAN SOUL WE HAILED IT IN GOD'S NAME."
"A GOOD SOUTH WIND SPRUNG UP BEHIND, THE ALBATROSS DID FOLLOW, AND EVERY DAY, FOR FOOD OR PLAY, CAME TO THE MARINER'S HOLLO."
GENTS, AT LAST THE BOW FACES NORTH, NORTH-WEST! WE HAVE THE WIND ON THE QUARTER AND WE'RE SAILING AT ELEVEN HEALTHY KNOTS!
IF WE CONTINUE IN THIS WAY, WE SHOU SPOT JUAN FERNANDEZ WITHIN ABOUT A WEEK AND PROCEED WEST FROM HERE TOWARDS OUR NEXT DESTINATION, EASTER ISLAND...
...WHERE I PROMISE WE'LL TAKE A REST UNTIL WE ARE SICK OF DRY LAND!
HURRAH!
A TOAST TO CAPTAIN MCLEOD, WHO TOOK US OUT OF THE END OF THE WORLD, SAFE AND SOUND!
A TOAST TO YOU ALL, GENTS, TO THE COURAGE OF THE ENTIRE CREW AND...
...TO SLAPS THAT TURN YOUR HEAD IN THE RIGHT DIRECTION!
"THE SUN NOW ROSE UPON THE RIGHT, OUT OF THE SEA CAME HE, STILL HID IN MIST AND ON THE LEFT WENT DOWN INTO THE SEA."

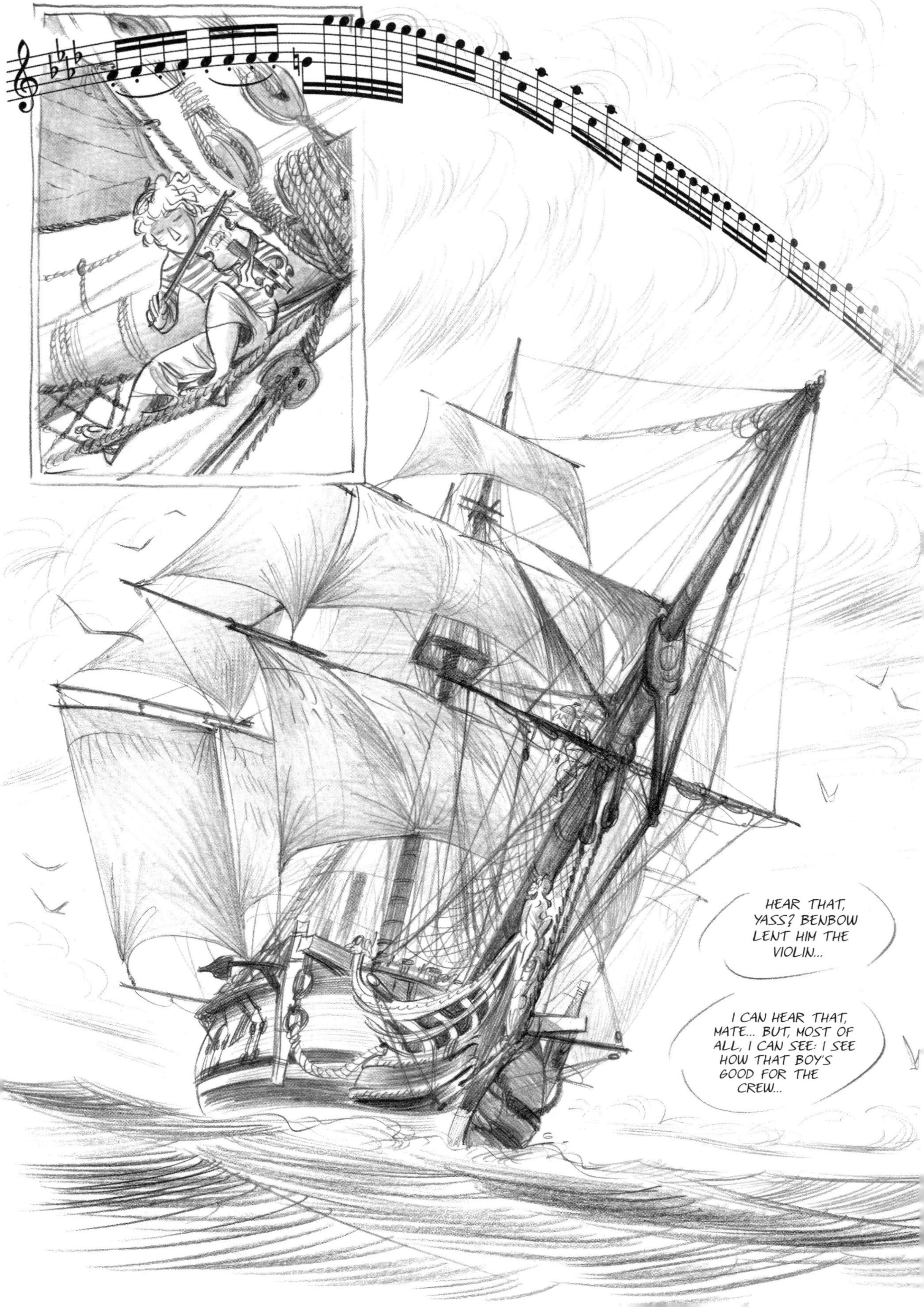
HEAR THAT, YASS? BENBOW LENT HIM THE VIOLIN...
I CAN HEAR THAT, MATE... BUT, MOST OF ALL, I CAN SEE: I SEE HOW THAT BOY'S GOOD FOR THE CREW...

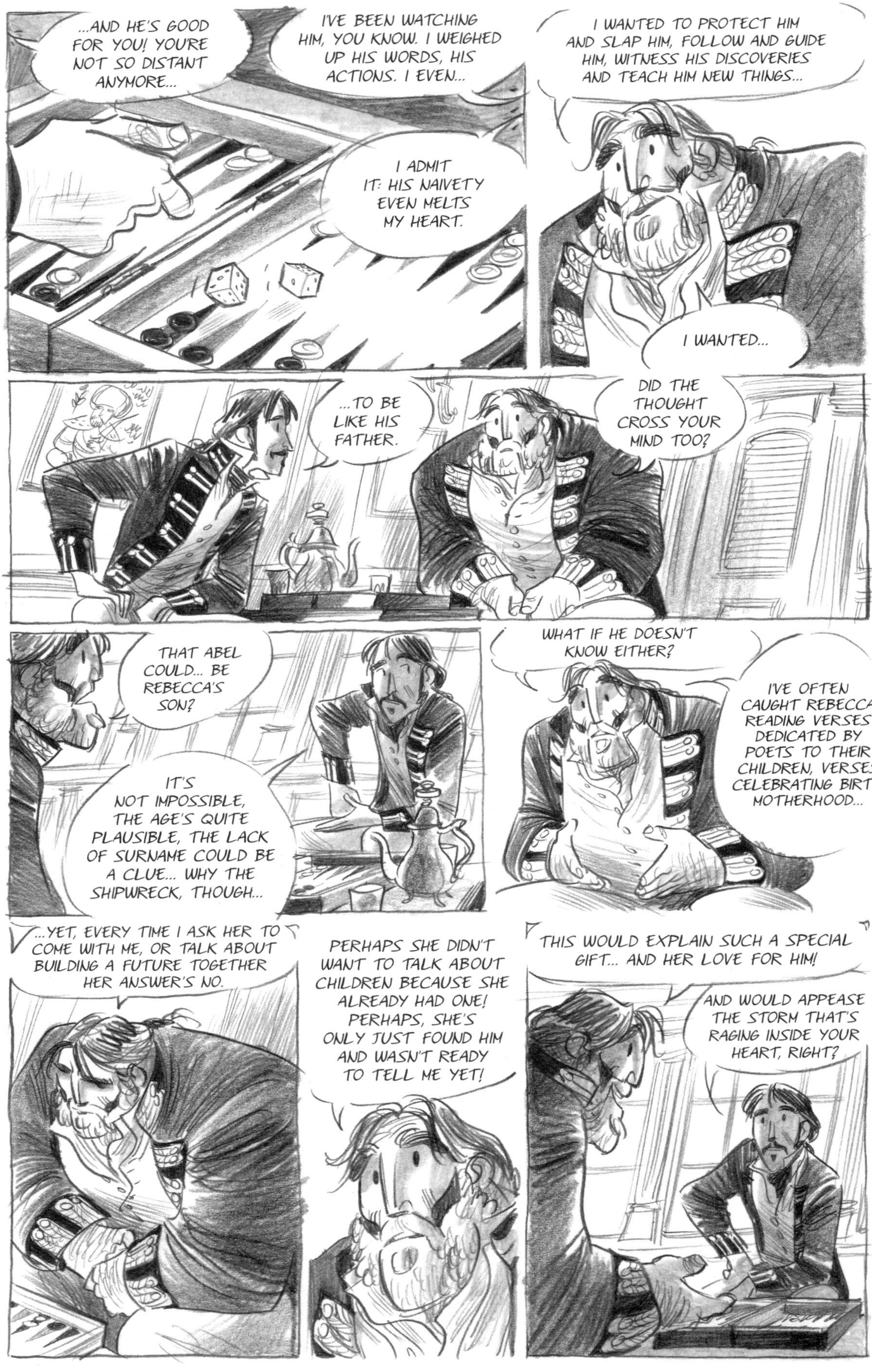
...AND HE'S GOOD FOR YOU! YOU'RE NOT SO DISTANT ANYMORE...
I'VE BEEN WATCHING HIM, YOU KNOW. I WEIGHED UP HIS WORDS, HIS ACTIONS. I EVEN...
I ADMIT IT: HIS NAIVETY EVEN MELTS MY HEART.
I WANTED TO PROTECT HIM AND SLAP HIM, FOLLOW AND GUIDE HIM, WITNESS HIS DISCOVERIES AND TEACH HIM NEW THINGS...
I WANTED...
...TO BE LIKE HIS FATHER.
DID THE THOUGHT CROSS YOUR MIND TOO?
THAT ABEL COULD... BE REBECCA'S SON?
IT'S NOT IMPOSSIBLE, THE AGE'S QUITE PLAUSIBLE, THE LACK OF SURNAME COULD BE A CLUE... WHY THE SHIPWRECK, THOUGH...
WHAT IF HE DOESN'T KNOW EITHER?
I'VE OFTEN CAUGHT REBECCA READING VERSES DEDICATED BY POETS TO THEIR CHILDREN, VERSES CELEBRATING BIRTH, MOTHERHOOD...
...YET, EVERY TIME I ASK HER TO COME WITH ME, OR TALK ABOUT BUILDING A FUTURE TOGETHER HER ANSWER'S NO.
PERHAPS SHE DIDN'T WANT TO TALK ABOUT CHILDREN BECAUSE SHE ALREADY HAD ONE! PERHAPS, SHE'S ONLY JUST FOUND HIM AND WASN'T READY TO TELL ME YET!
THIS WOULD EXPLAIN SUCH A SPECIAL GIFT... AND HER LOVE FOR HIM!
AND WOULD APPEASE THE STORM THAT'S RAGING INSIDE YOUR HEART, RIGHT?

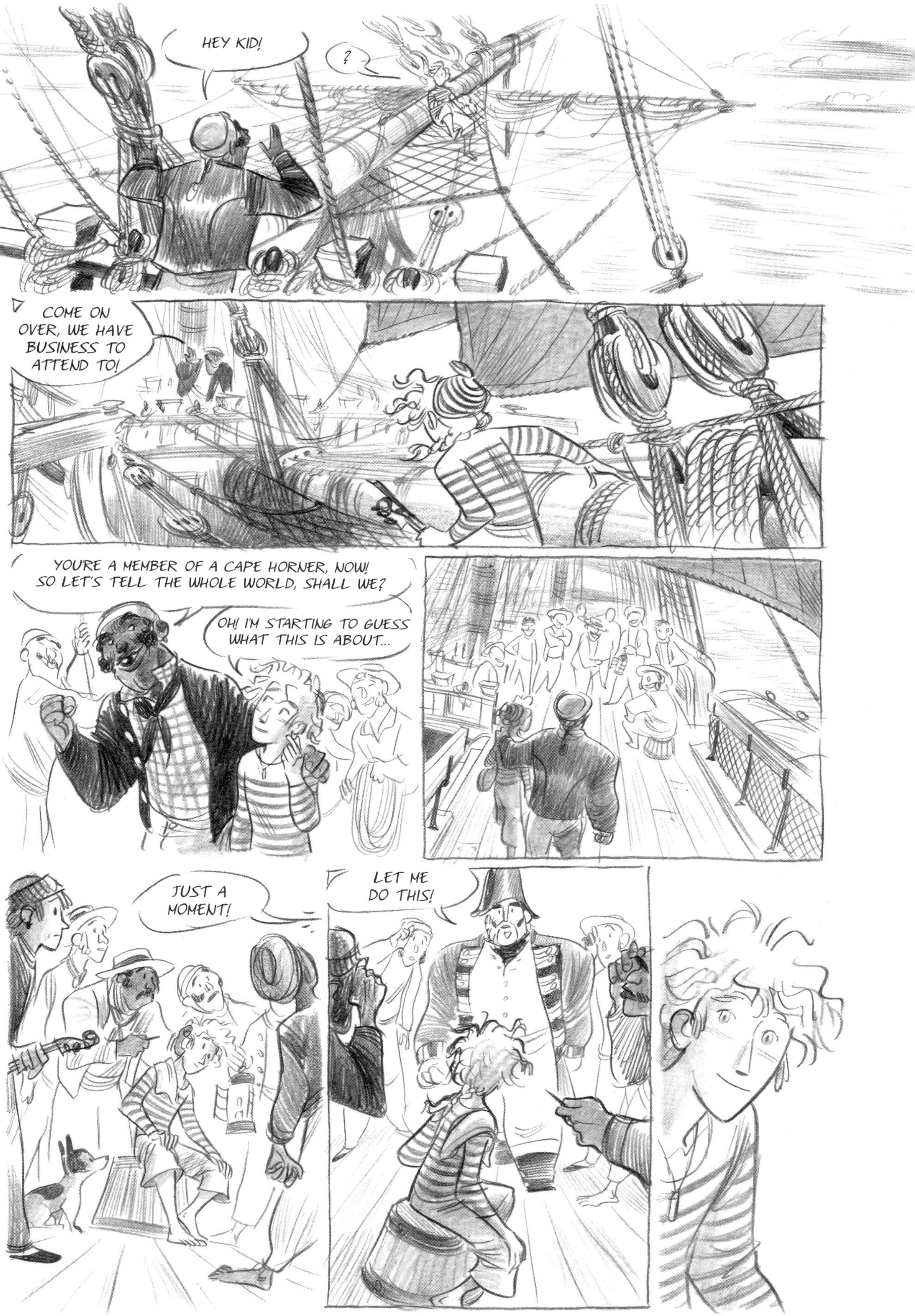
HEY KID!
?
COME ON OVER, WE HAVE BUSINESS TO ATTEND TO!
YOU'RE A MEMBER OF A CAPE HORNER, NOW! SO LET'S TELL THE WHOLE WORLD, SHALL WE?
OH! I'M STARTING TO GUESS WHAT THIS IS ABOUT...
JUST A MOMENT!
LET ME DO THIS!

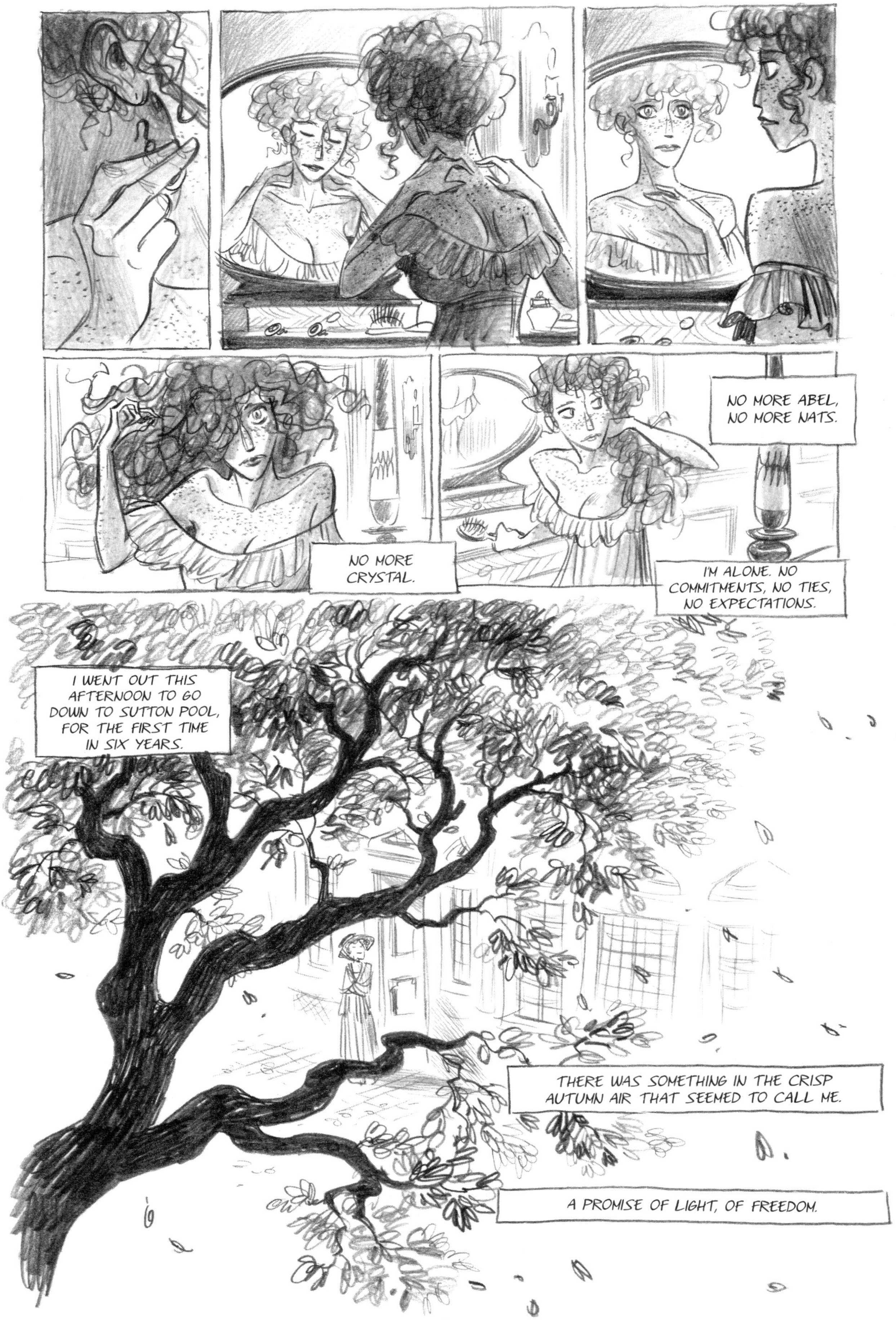

NO MORE CRYSTAL.
NO MORE ABEL, NO MORE NATS.
I'M ALONE. NO COMMITMENTS, NO TIES, NO EXPECTATIONS.
I WENT OUT THIS AFTERNOON TO GO DOWN TO SUTTON POOL, FOR THE FIRST TIME IN SIX YEARS.
THERE WAS SOMETHING IN THE CRISP AUTUMN AIR THAT SEEMED TO CALL ME.
A PROMISE OF LIGHT, OF FREEDOM.

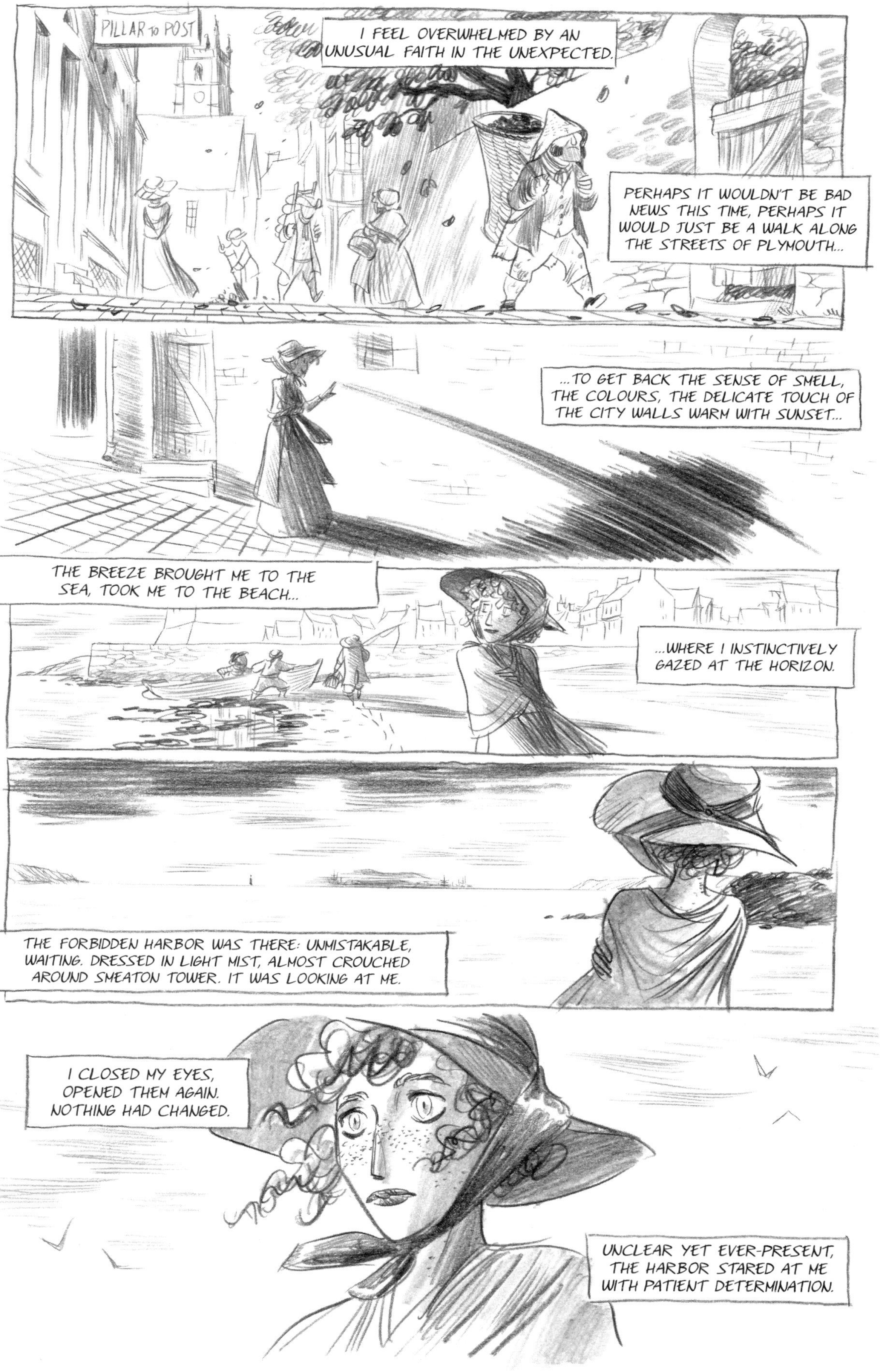
PILLAR TO POST
I FEEL OVERWHELMED BY AN UNUSUAL FAITH IN THE UNEXPECTED.
PERHAPS IT WOULDN'T BE BAD NEWS THIS TIME, PERHAPS IT WOULD JUST BE A WALK ALONG THE STREETS OF PLYMOUTH...
...TO GET BACK THE SENSE OF SMELL, THE COLOURS, THE DELICATE TOUCH OF THE CITY WALLS WARM WITH SUNSET...
THE BREEZE BROUGHT ME TO THE SEA, TOOK ME TO THE BEACH...
...WHERE I INSTINCTIVELY GAZED AT THE HORIZON.
THE FORBIDDEN HARBOR WAS THERE: UNMISTAKABLE, WAITING. DRESSED IN LIGHT MIST, ALMOST CROUCHED AROUND SMEATON TOWER. IT WAS LOOKING AT ME.
I CLOSED MY EYES, OPENED THEM AGAIN. NOTHING HAD CHANGED.
UNCLEAR YET EVER-PRESENT, THE HARBOR STARED AT ME WITH PATIENT DETERMINATION.

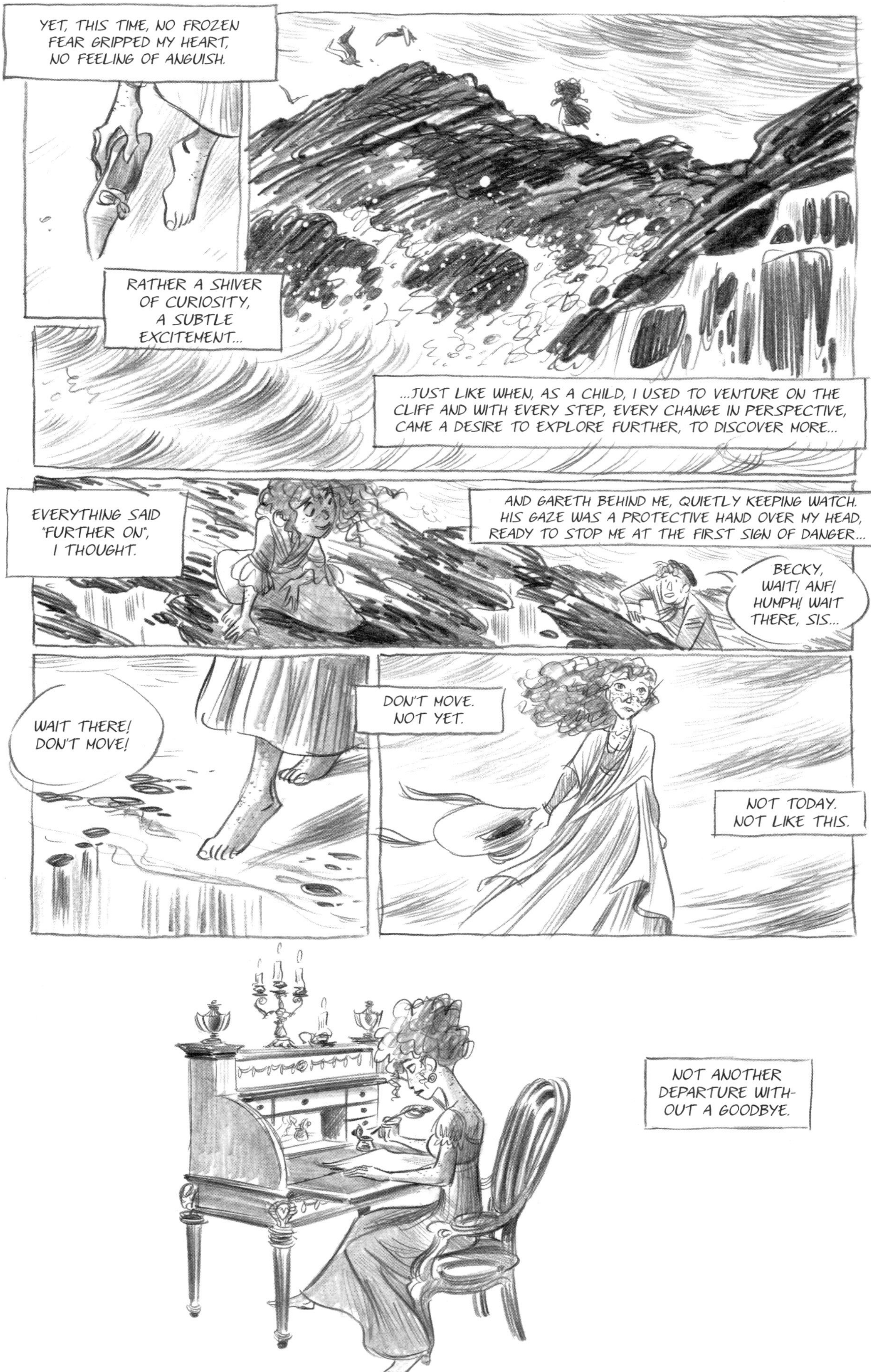
YET, THIS TIME, NO FROZEN FEAR GRIPPED MY HEART, NO FEELING OF ANGUISH.
RATHER A SHIVER OF CURIOSITY, A SUBTLE EXCITEMENT...
...JUST LIKE WHEN, AS A CHILD, I USED TO VENTURE ON THE CLIFF AND WITH EVERY STEP, EVERY CHANGE IN PERSPECTIVE, CAME A DESIRE TO EXPLORE FURTHER, TO DISCOVER MORE...
EVERYTHING SAID "FURTHER ON", I THOUGHT.
AND GARETH BEHIND ME, QUIETLY KEEPING WATCH. HIS GAZE WAS A PROTECTIVE HAND OVER MY HEAD, READY TO STOP ME AT THE FIRST SIGN OF DANGER...
BECKY, WAIT! ANF! HUMPH! WAIT THERE, SIS...
WAIT THERE! DON'T MOVE!
DON'T MOVE. NOT YET.
NOT TODAY. NOT LIKE THIS.
NOT ANOTHER DEPARTURE WITH-OUT A GOODBYE.

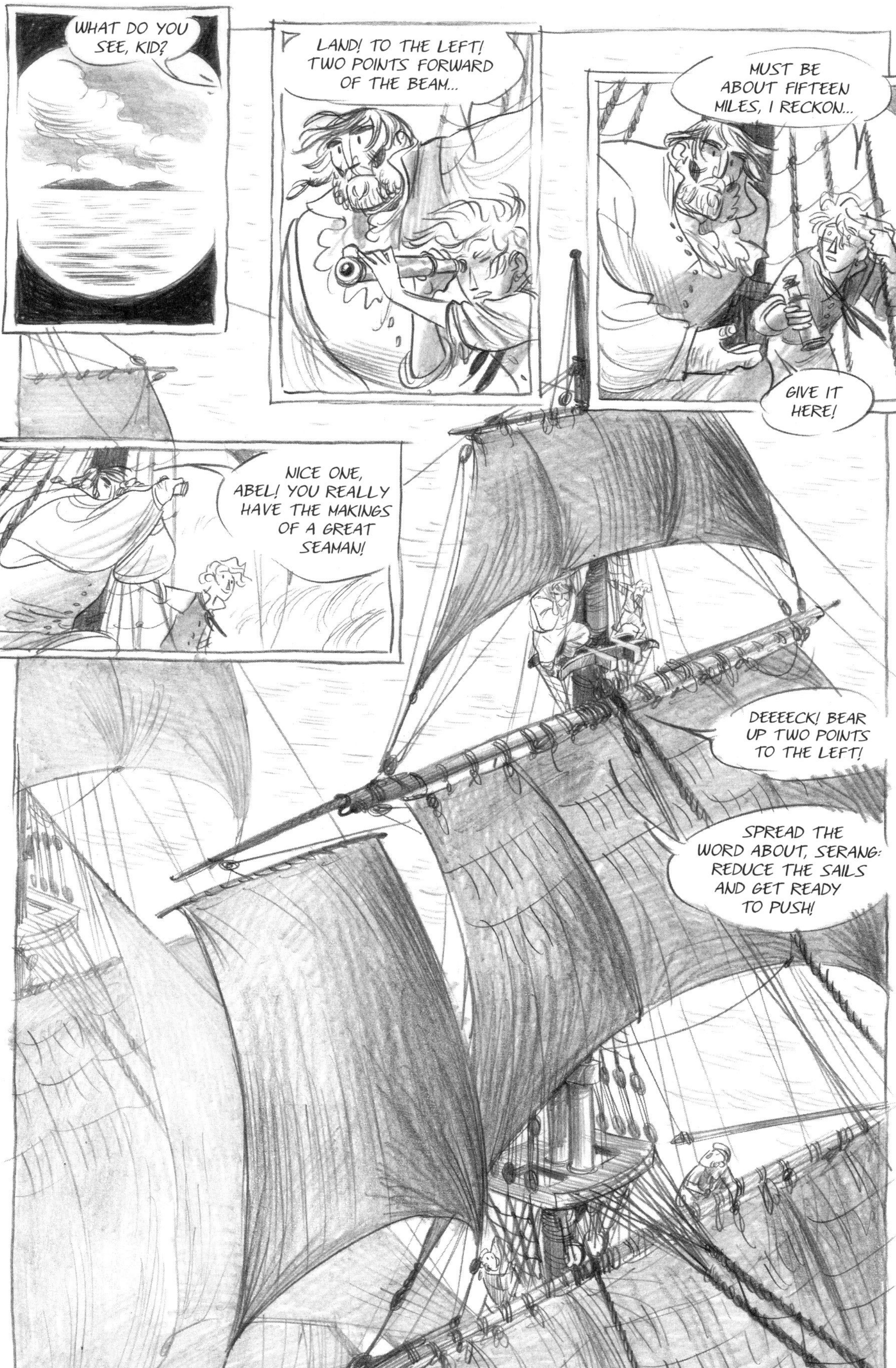
WHAT DO YOU SEE, KID?
LAND! TO THE LEFT! TWO POINTS FORWARD OF THE BEAM...
MUST BE ABOUT FIFTEEN MILES, I RECKON...
GIVE IT HERE!
NICE ONE, ABEL! YOU REALLY HAVE THE MAKINGS OF A GREAT SEAMAN!
DEEEECK! BEAR UP TWO POINTS TO THE LEFT!
SPREAD THE WORD ABOUT, SERANG: REDUCE THE SAILS AND GET READY TO PUSH!

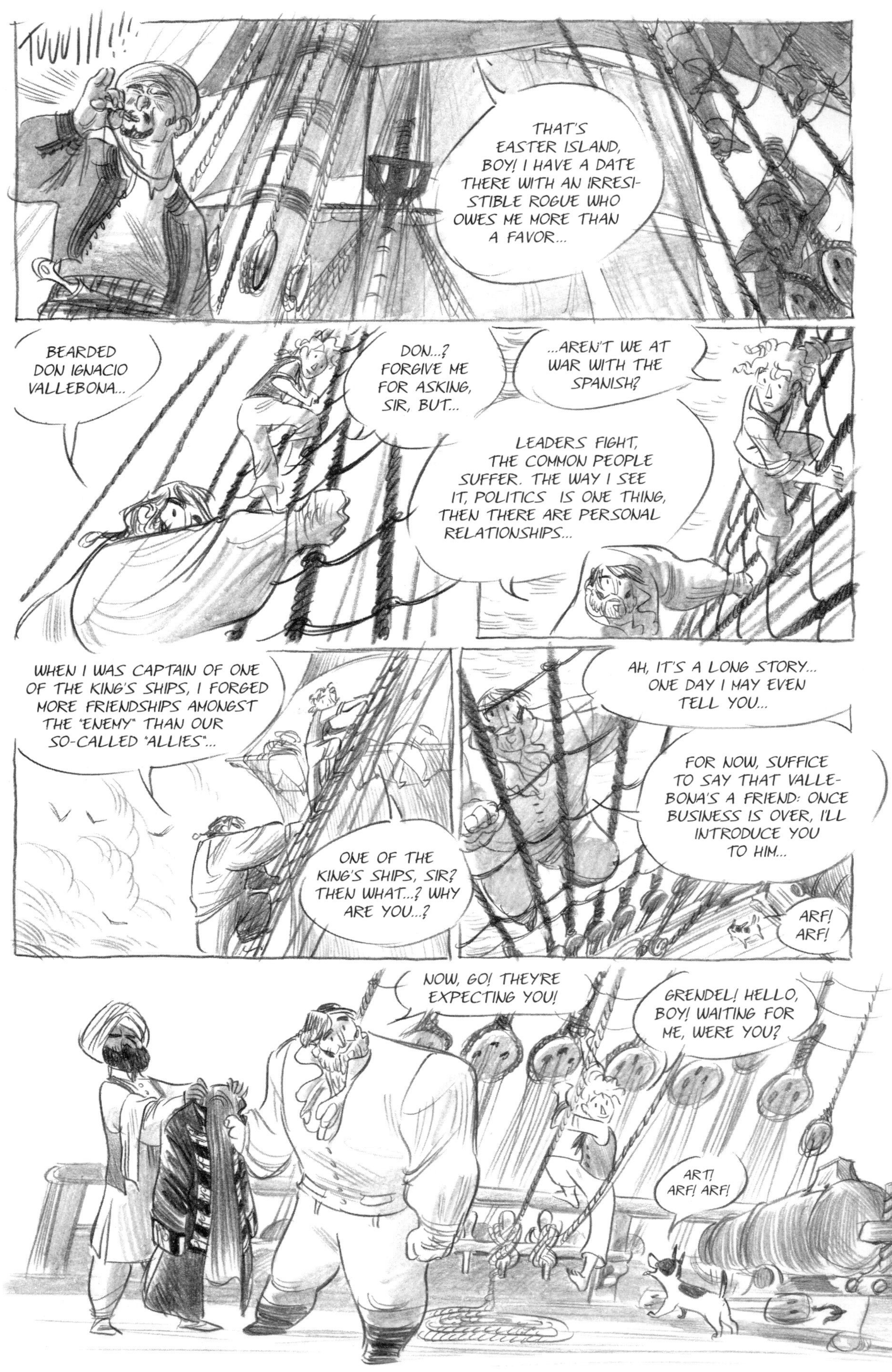
TUUUIII!!!
THAT'S EASTER ISLAND, BOY! I HAVE A DATE THERE WITH AN IRRESISTIBLE ROGUE WHO OWES ME MORE THAN A FAVOR...
BEARDED DON IGNACIO VALLEBONA...
DON...? FORGIVE ME FOR ASKING, SIR, BUT...
...AREN'T WE AT WAR WITH THE SPANISH?
LEADERS FIGHT, THE COMMON PEOPLE SUFFER. THE WAY I SEE IT, POLITICS IS ONE THING, THEN THERE ARE PERSONAL RELATIONSHIPS...
WHEN I WAS CAPTAIN OF ONE OF THE KING'S SHIPS, I FORGED MORE FRIENDSHIPS AMONGST THE "ENEMY" THAN OUR SO-CALLED "ALLIES"...
ONE OF THE KING'S SHIPS, SIR? THEN WHAT...? WHY ARE YOU...?
AH, IT'S A LONG STORY... ONE DAY I MAY EVEN TELL YOU...
FOR NOW, SUFFICE TO SAY THAT VALLEBONA'S A FRIEND: ONCE BUSINESS IS OVER, I'LL INTRODUCE YOU TO HIM...
ARF! ARF!
NOW, GO! THEY'RE EXPECTING YOU!
GRENDEL! HELLO, BOY! WAITING FOR ME, WERE YOU?
ART! ARF! ARF!

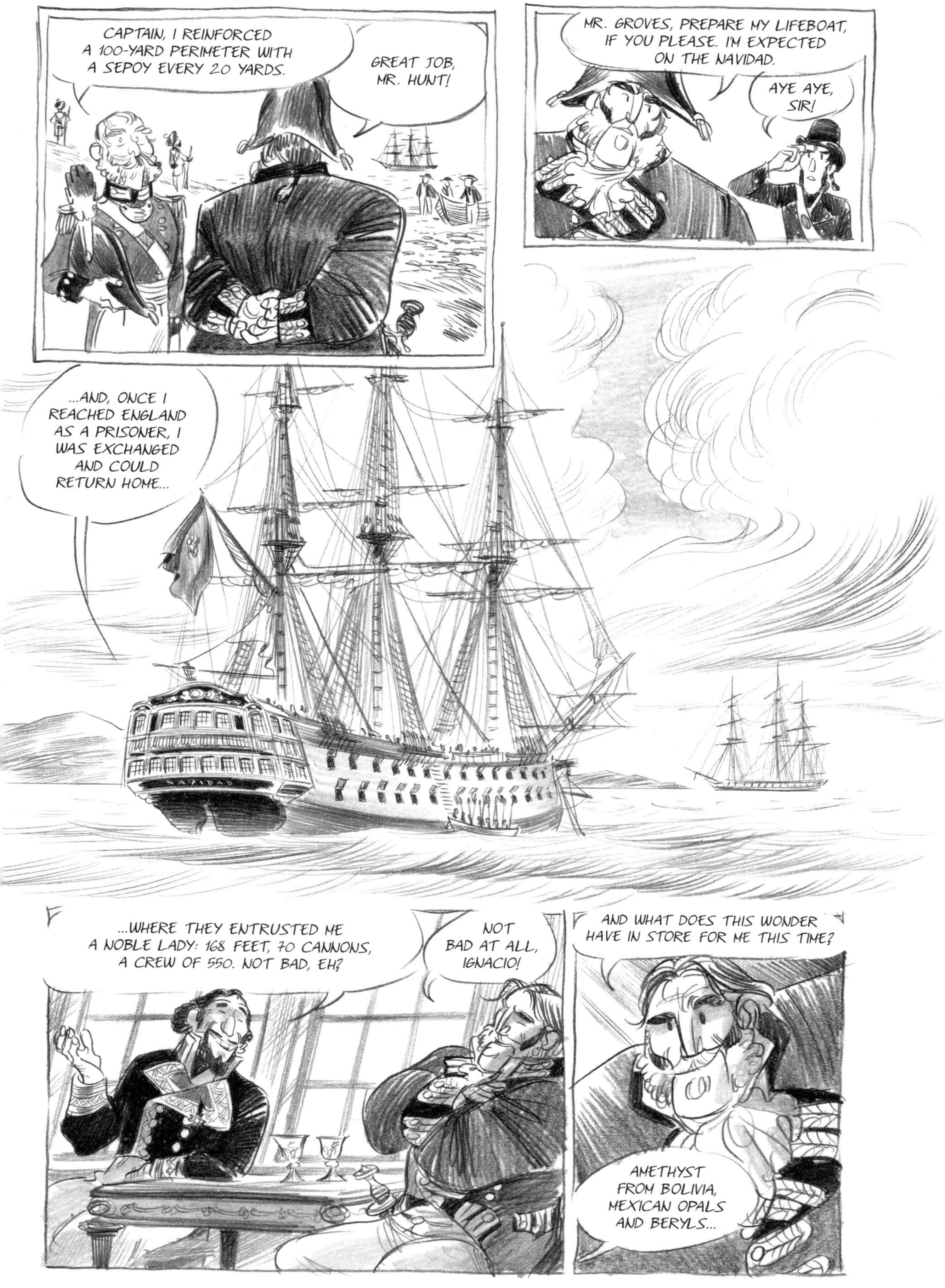
CAPTAIN, I REINFORCED A 100-YARD PERIMETER WITH A SEPOY EVERY 20 YARDS.
GREAT JOB, MR. HUNT!
MR. GROVES, PREPARE MY LIFEBOAT, IF YOU PLEASE. I'M EXPECTED ON THE NAVIDAD.
AYE AYE, SIR!
...AND, ONCE I REACHED ENGLAND AS A PRISONER, I WAS EXCHANGED AND COULD RETURN HOME...
NAVIDAD
...WHERE THEY ENTRUSTED ME A NOBLE LADY: 168 FEET, 70 CANNONS, A CREW OF 550. NOT BAD, EH?
NOT BAD AT ALL, IGNACIO!
AND WHAT DOES THIS WONDER HAVE IN STORE FOR ME THIS TIME?
AMETHYST FROM BOLIVIA, MEXICAN OPALS AND BERYLS...

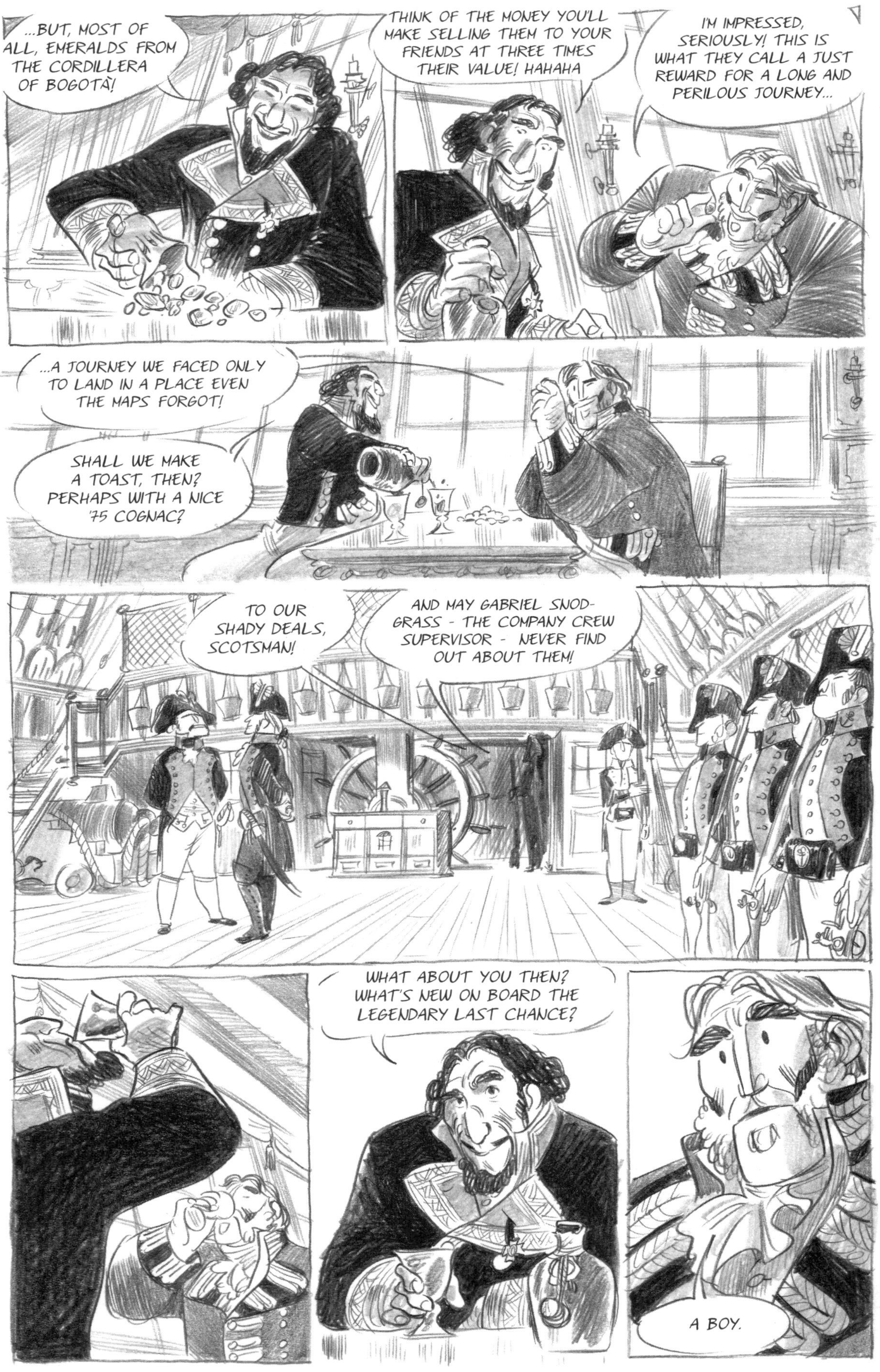
...BUT, MOST OF ALL, EMERALDS FROM THE CORDILLERA OF BOGOTÀ!
THINK OF THE MONEY YOU'LL MAKE SELLING THEM TO YOUR FRIENDS AT THREE TIMES THEIR VALUE! HAHAHA
I'M IMPRESSED, SERIOUSLY! THIS IS WHAT THEY CALL A JUST REWARD FOR A LONG AND PERILOUS JOURNEY...
...A JOURNEY WE FACED ONLY TO LAND IN A PLACE EVEN THE MAPS FORGOT!
SHALL WE MAKE A TOAST, THEN? PERHAPS WITH A NICE '75 COGNAC?
TO OUR SHADY DEALS, SCOTSMAN!
AND MAY GABRIEL SNOD-GRASS - THE COMPANY CREW SUPERVISOR - NEVER FIND OUT ABOUT THEM!
WHAT ABOUT YOU THEN? WHAT'S NEW ON BOARD THE LEGENDARY LAST CHANCE?
A BOY.

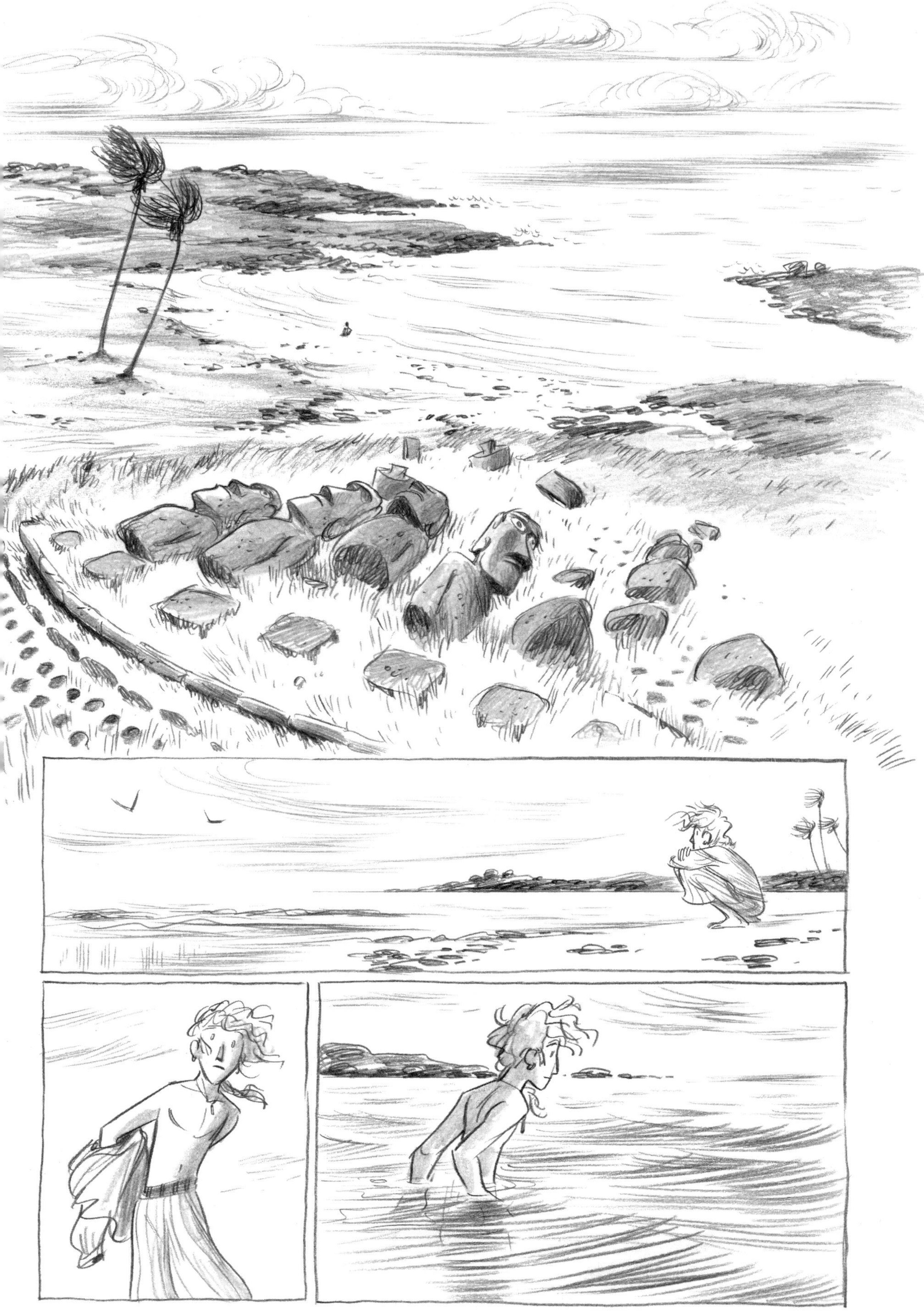

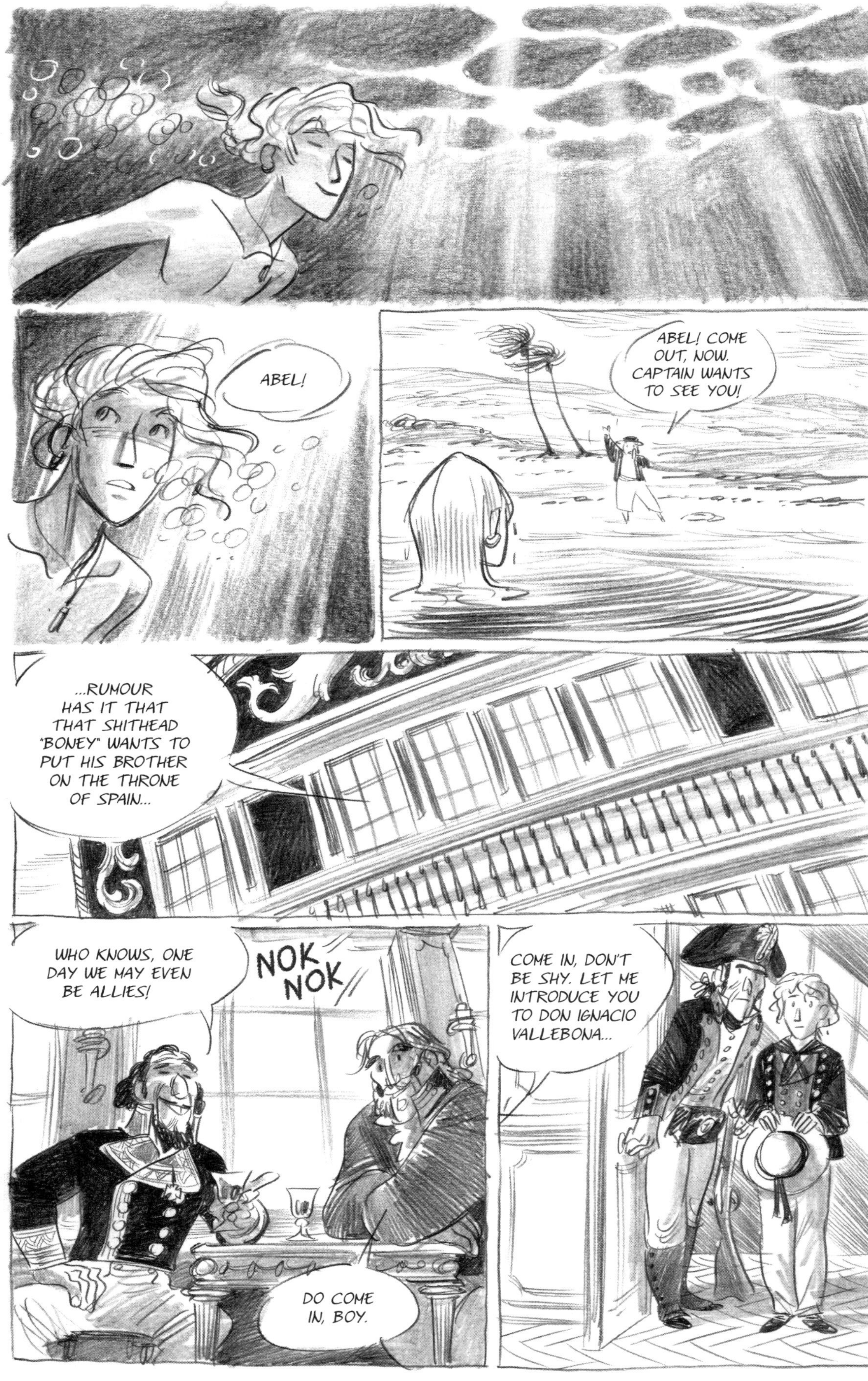
ABEL!
ABEL! COME OUT, NOW. CAPTAIN WANTS TO SEE YOU!
...RUMOUR HAS IT THAT THAT SHITHEAD "BONEY" WANTS TO PUT HIS BROTHER ON THE THRONE OF SPAIN...
WHO KNOWS, ONE DAY WE MAY EVEN BE ALLIES!
NOK NOK
DO COME IN, BOY.
COME IN, DON'T BE SHY. LET ME INTRODUCE YOU TO DON IGNACIO VALLEBONA...

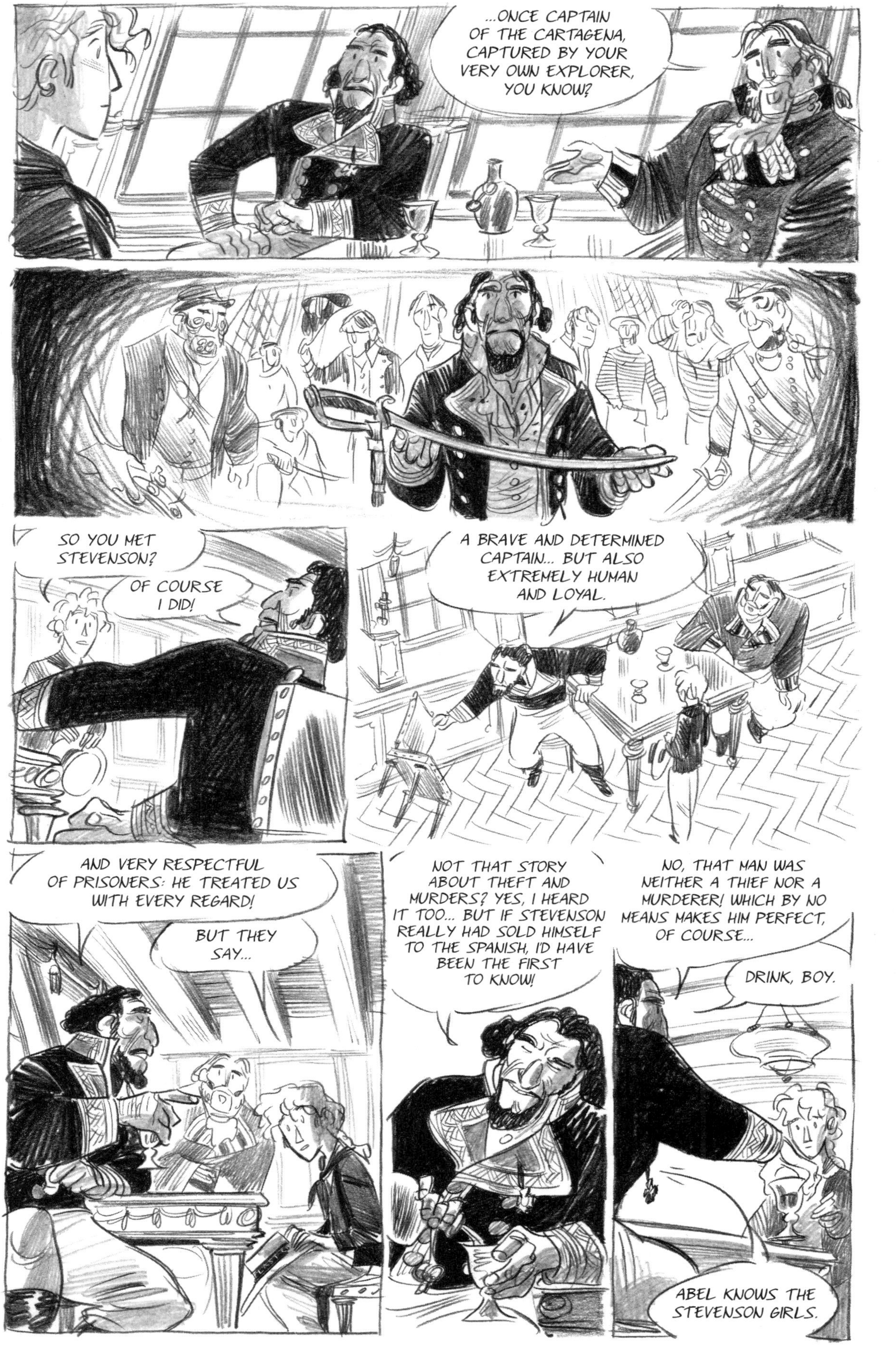
...ONCE CAPTAIN OF THE CARTAGENA, CAPTURED BY YOUR VERY OWN EXPLORER, YOU KNOW?
SO YOU MET STEVENSON?
OF COURSE I DID!
A BRAVE AND DETERMINED CAPTAIN... BUT ALSO EXTREMELY HUMAN AND LOYAL.
AND VERY RESPECTFUL OF PRISONERS: HE TREATED US WITH EVERY REGARD!
BUT THEY SAY...
NOT THAT STORY ABOUT THEFT AND MURDERS? YES, I HEARD IT TOO... BUT IF STEVENSON REALLY HAD SOLD HIMSELF TO THE SPANISH, I'D HAVE BEEN THE FIRST TO KNOW!
NO, THAT MAN WAS NEITHER A THIEF NOR A MURDERER! WHICH BY NO MEANS MAKES HIM PERFECT, OF COURSE...
DRINK, BOY.
ABEL KNOWS THE STEVENSON GIRLS.

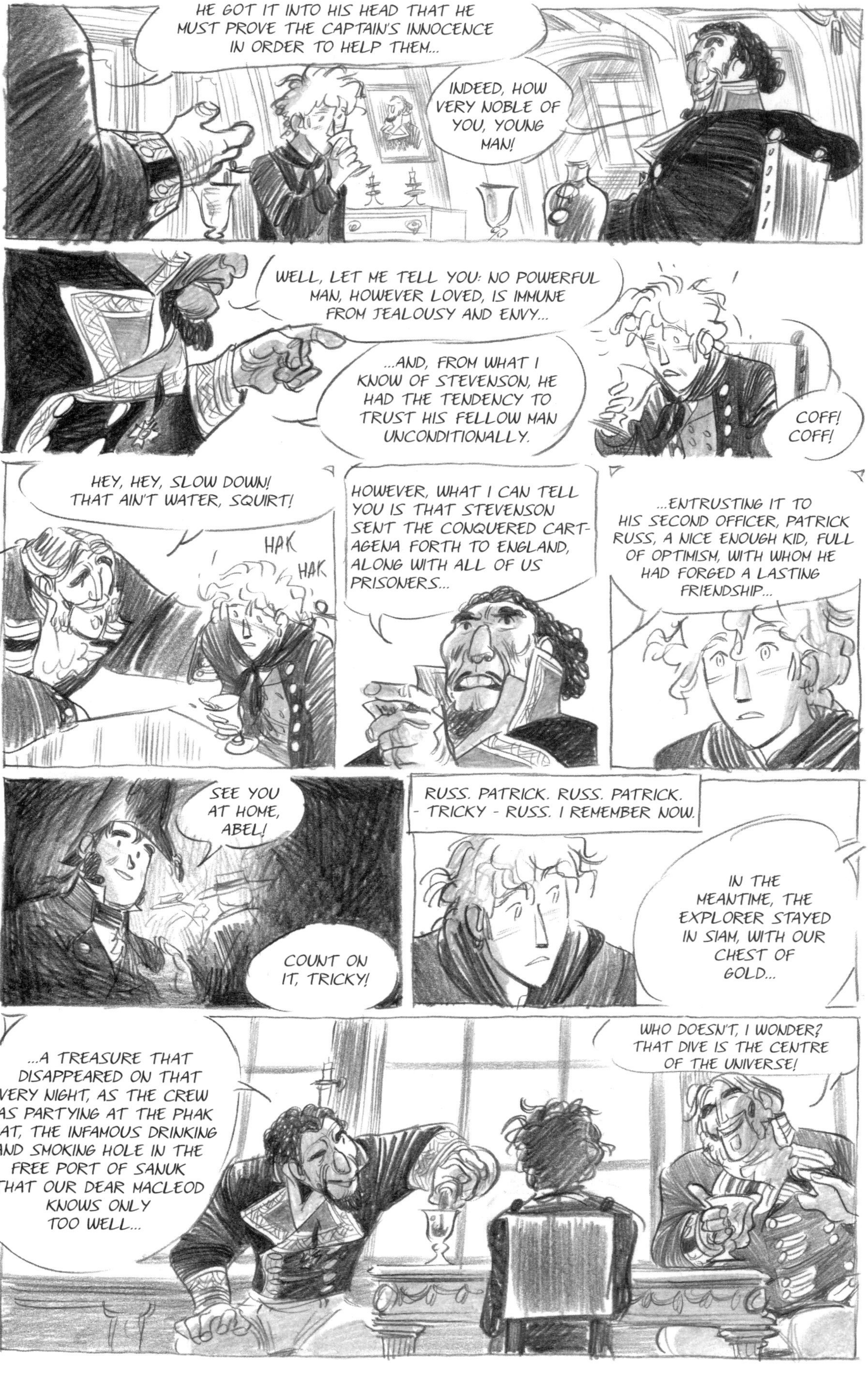
HE GOT IT INTO HIS HEAD THAT HE MUST PROVE THE CAPTAIN'S INNOCENCE IN ORDER TO HELP THEM...
INDEED, HOW VERY NOBLE OF YOU, YOUNG MAN!
WELL, LET ME TELL YOU: NO POWERFUL MAN, HOWEVER LOVED, IS IMMUNE FROM JEALOUSY AND ENVY...
...AND, FROM WHAT I KNOW OF STEVENSON, HE HAD THE TENDENCY TO TRUST HIS FELLOW MAN UNCONDITIONALLY.
COFF! COFF!
HEY, HEY, SLOW DOWN! THAT AIN'T WATER, SQUIRT!
HAK HAK
HOWEVER, WHAT I CAN TELL YOU IS THAT STEVENSON SENT THE CONQUERED CART-AGENA FORTH TO ENGLAND, ALONG WITH ALL OF US PRISONERS...
...ENTRUSTING IT TO HIS SECOND OFFICER, PATRICK RUSS, A NICE ENOUGH KID, FULL OF OPTIMISM, WITH WHOM HE HAD FORGED A LASTING FRIENDSHIP...
SEE YOU AT HOME, ABEL!
COUNT ON IT, TRICKY!
RUSS. PATRICK. RUSS. PATRICK. - TRICKY - RUSS. I REMEMBER NOW.
IN THE MEANTIME, THE EXPLORER STAYED IN SIAM, WITH OUR CHEST OF GOLD...
...A TREASURE THAT DISAPPEARED ON THAT VERY NIGHT, AS THE CREW WAS PARTYING AT THE PHAK PHAT, THE INFAMOUS DRINKING AND SMOKING HOLE IN THE FREE PORT OF SANUK THAT OUR DEAR MACLEOD KNOWS ONLY TOO WELL...
WHO DOESN'T, I WONDER? THAT DIVE IS THE CENTRE OF THE UNIVERSE!

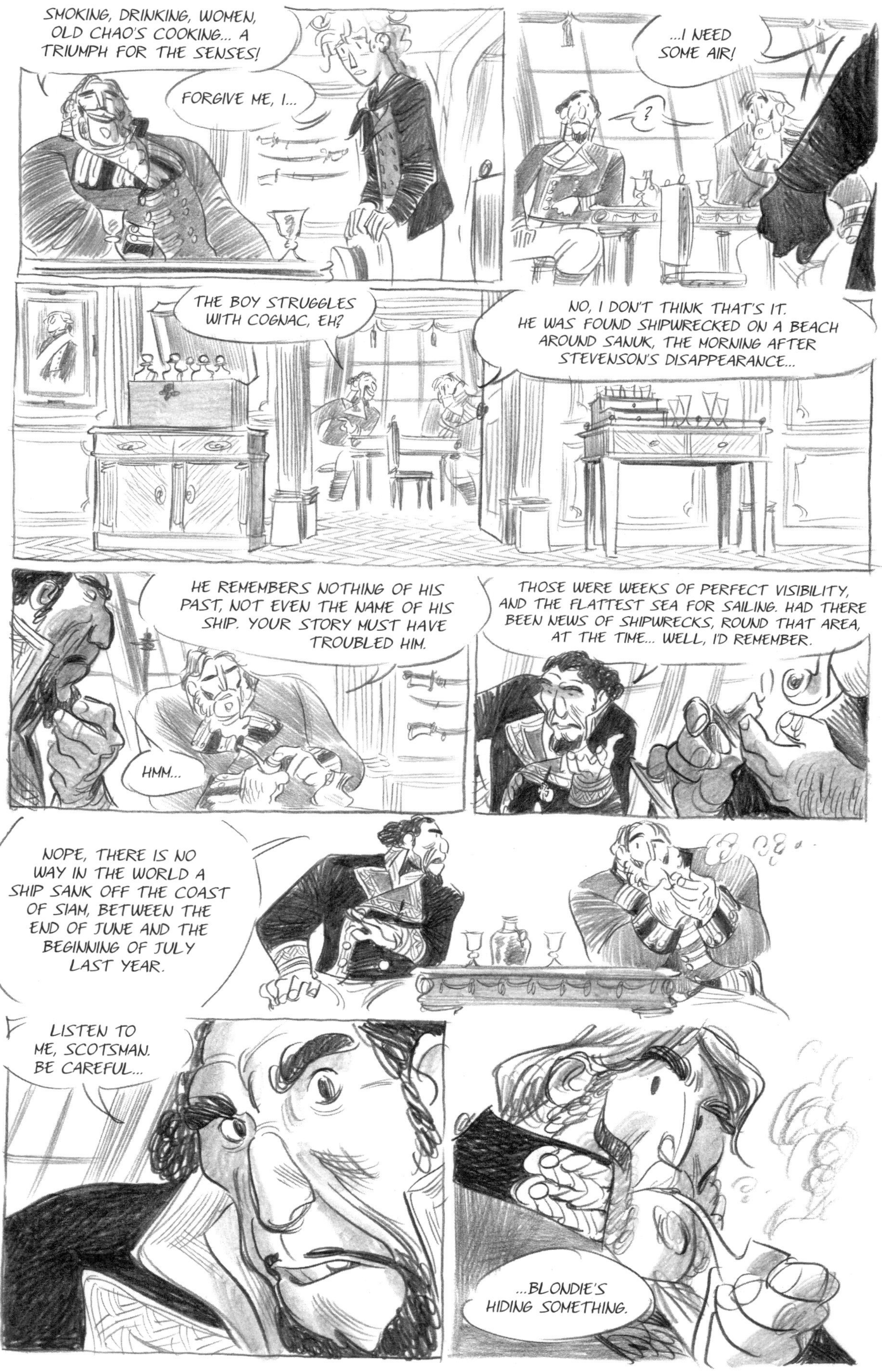
SMOKING, DRINKING, WOMEN, OLD CHAO'S COOKING... A TRIUMPH FOR THE SENSES!
FORGIVE ME, I...
...I NEED SOME AIR!
?
THE BOY STRUGGLES WITH COGNAC, EH?
NO, I DON'T THINK THAT'S IT. HE WAS FOUND SHIPWRECKED ON A BEACH AROUND SANUK, THE MORNING AFTER STEVENSON'S DISAPPEARANCE...
HE REMEMBERS NOTHING OF HIS PAST, NOT EVEN THE NAME OF HIS SHIP. YOUR STORY MUST HAVE TROUBLED HIM.
HMM...
THOSE WERE WEEKS OF PERFECT VISIBILITY, AND THE FLATTEST SEA FOR SAILING. HAD THERE BEEN NEWS OF SHIPWRECKS, ROUND THAT AREA, AT THE TIME... WELL, I'D REMEMBER.
NOPE, THERE IS NO WAY IN THE WORLD A SHIP SANK OFF THE COAST OF SIAM, BETWEEN THE END OF JUNE AND THE BEGINNING OF JULY LAST YEAR.
LISTEN TO ME, SCOTSMAN. BE CAREFUL...
...BLONDIE'S HIDING SOMETHING.

ACT IV
THE ALBATROSS INN

Io vengo da mari lontani —
io sono una nave sferzata
dai flutti
dai venti —
corrosa dal sole —
macerata
dagli uragani —

io vengo da mari lontani
e carica d'innumeri cose
disfatte
di frutti strani
corrotti
di sete vermiglie
spaccate —
stremate
le braccia lucenti dei mozzi
e sradicate le antenne
spente le vele
ammollite le corde
fracidi
gli assi dei ponti —

io sono una nave
una nave che porta
in sé l'orma di tutti i tramonti
solcati sofferti —
io sono una nave che cerca
per tutte le rive
un approdo.
Risogna la nave ferita
il primissimo porto —
che vale
se sopra la scia
del suo viaggio
ricade
l'ondata sfinita?

Oh, il cuore ben sa
la sua scia
ritrovare
dentro tutte le onde!
Oh, il cuore ben sa
ritornare
al suo lido!

O tu, lido eterno —
tu, nido
ultimo della mia anima migrante —
o tu, terra —
tu, patria —
tu, radice profonda
del mio cammino sulle acque —
o tu, quiete
della mia errabonda
pena —
oh, accoglimi tu
fra i tuoi moli —
tu, porto —
e in te sia il cadere
d'ogni carico morto —
nel tuo grembo il calare
lento dell'ancora —
nel tuo cuore il sognare
di una sera velata —
quando per troppa vecchiezza
per troppa stanchezza
naufragherà
nelle tue mute
acque
la greve nave
sfasciata —

Antonia Pozzi - *Il porto*

I come from faraway seas—
I'm a ship that's been lashed by the rains
By wind
By waves
By sunlight decayed—
Consumed
By fierce hurricanes.

I come from faraway seas
And laden with countless things:
Strange, tainted
Fruit,
Scarlet silks
Torn—
Worn,
The once-shining jibs,
The uprooted lateen yards,
The listless sails,
The lines now soft,
The waterlogged
Planks of the bridge—

I'm a ship,
A ship that carries within itself
The traces of all the sunsets
Ploughed through and experienced—
I'm a ship that's searching
'Cross every shore
For a berth.
The wounded ship
Dreams once more
Of its very first harbor;
What is it worth
If across the slipstream
Of its journey,
The exhausted wave
Should fall down once again?

Oh, the heart knows well
Its slipstream,
Recovering
Within all the waves!
Oh, the heart knows well
Returning
To its shore!

O, you, eternal shore—
You, nest,
Last of my migrant soul—
O, you, ground—
You, my homeland—
You, deep root
Of my path across the water—
O, you, the stillness
Of my wandering
Pain—
Oh, welcome me
Amongst your jetties—
You, harbor—
And in you, may
Every dead burden fall—
In your bosom, the anchor
Slowly drop—
In your heart, a veiled evening
Dream—
When through too great old age
Through too much fatigue
Shall founder
In your silent
Waters
The sorrowful, shattered
Ship—

Antonia Pozzi—*The Harbor*

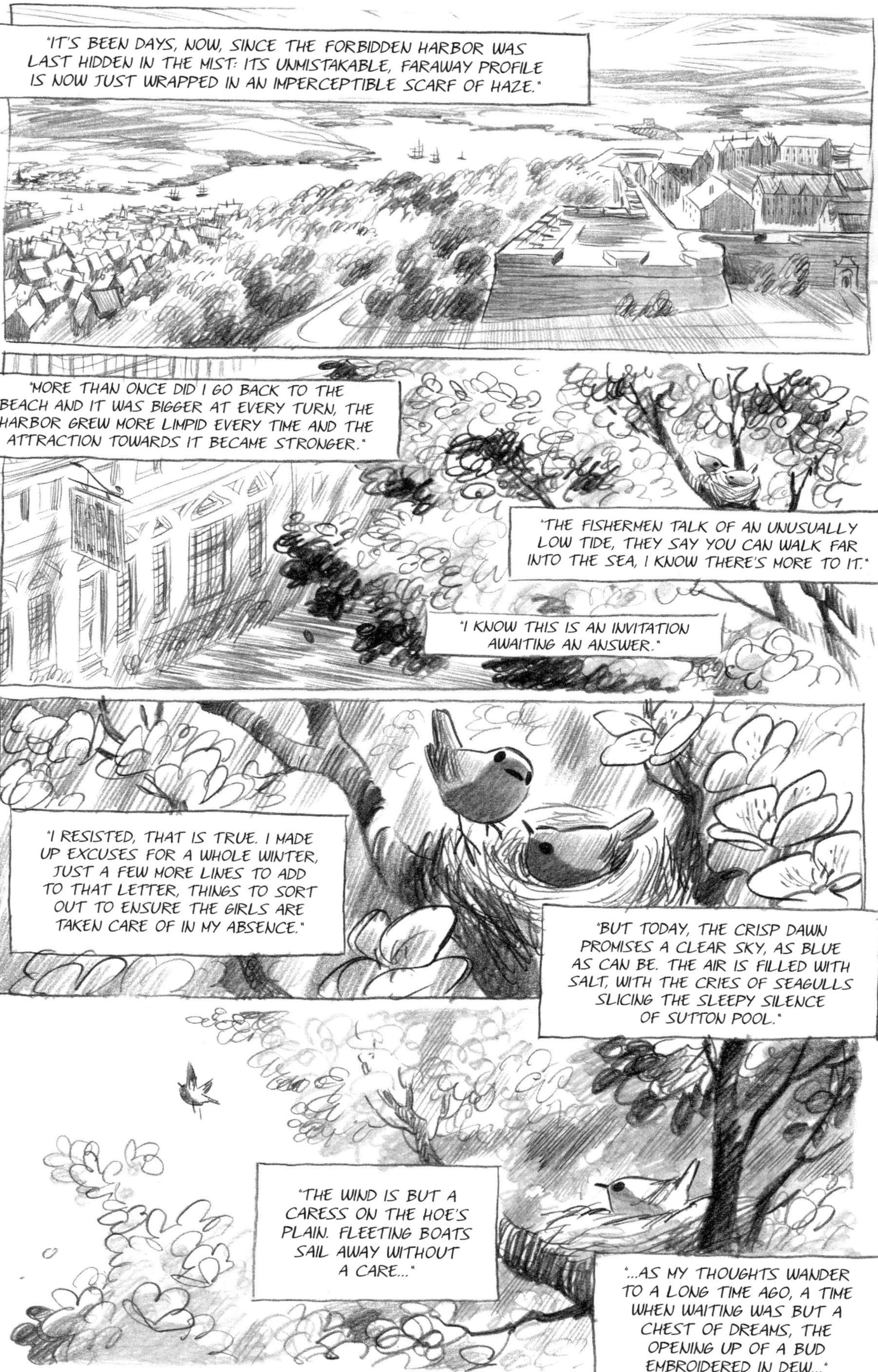
"IT'S BEEN DAYS, NOW, SINCE THE FORBIDDEN HARBOR WAS LAST HIDDEN IN THE MIST: ITS UNMISTAKABLE, FARAWAY PROFILE IS NOW JUST WRAPPED IN AN IMPERCEPTIBLE SCARF OF HAZE."
"MORE THAN ONCE DID I GO BACK TO THE BEACH AND IT WAS BIGGER AT EVERY TURN, THE HARBOR GREW MORE LIMPID EVERY TIME AND THE ATTRACTION TOWARDS IT BECAME STRONGER."
"THE FISHERMEN TALK OF AN UNUSUALLY LOW TIDE, THEY SAY YOU CAN WALK FAR INTO THE SEA, I KNOW THERE'S MORE TO IT."
"I KNOW THIS IS AN INVITATION AWAITING AN ANSWER."
"I RESISTED, THAT IS TRUE. I MADE UP EXCUSES FOR A WHOLE WINTER, JUST A FEW MORE LINES TO ADD TO THAT LETTER, THINGS TO SORT OUT TO ENSURE THE GIRLS ARE TAKEN CARE OF IN MY ABSENCE."
"BUT TODAY, THE CRISP DAWN PROMISES A CLEAR SKY, AS BLUE AS CAN BE. THE AIR IS FILLED WITH SALT, WITH THE CRIES OF SEAGULLS SLICING THE SLEEPY SILENCE OF SUTTON POOL."
"THE WIND IS BUT A CARESS ON THE HOE'S PLAIN. FLEETING BOATS SAIL AWAY WITHOUT A CARE..."
"...AS MY THOUGHTS WANDER TO A LONG TIME AGO, A TIME WHEN WAITING WAS BUT A CHEST OF DREAMS, THE OPENING UP OF A BUD EMBROIDERED IN DEW..."

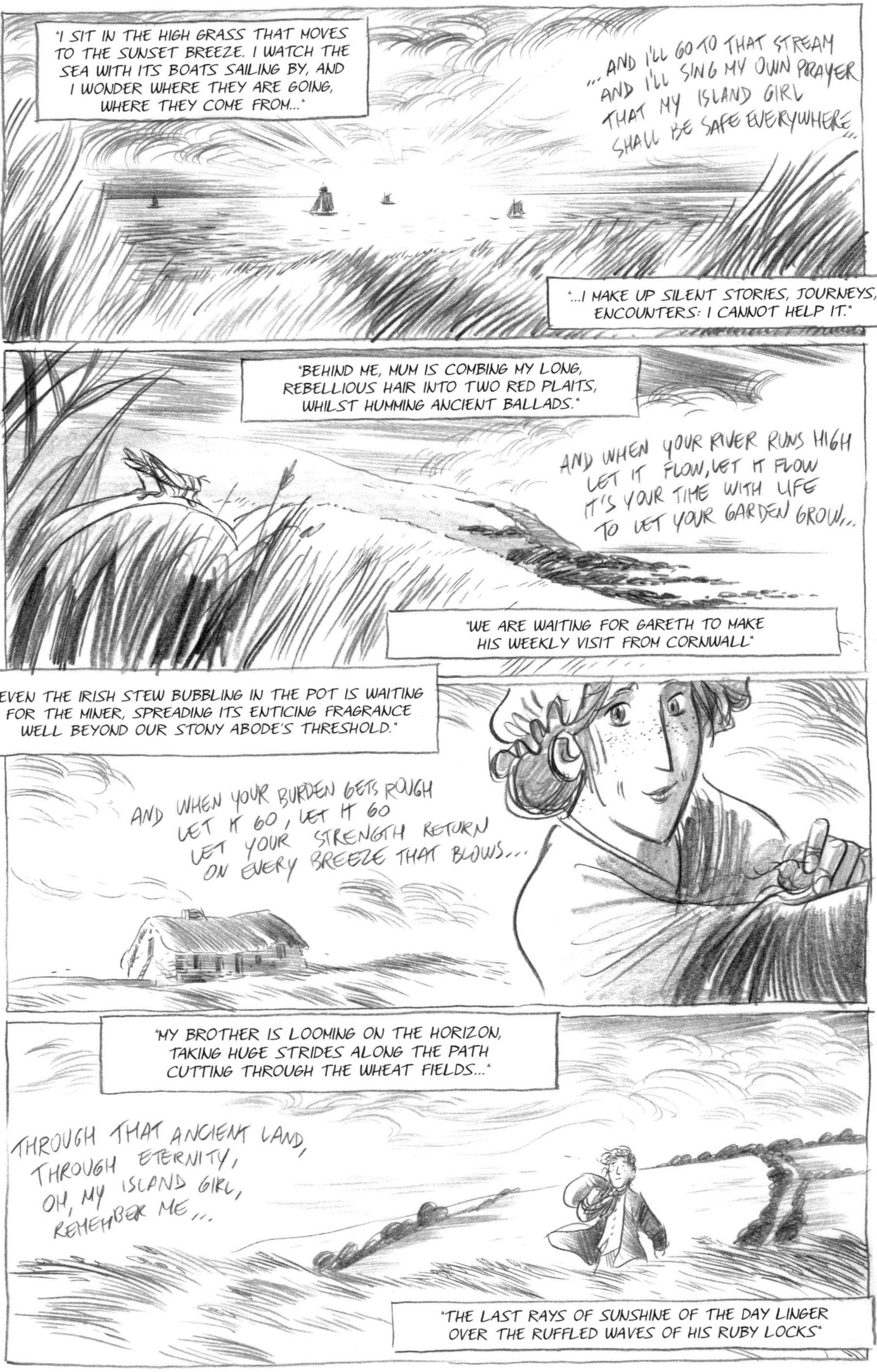
"I SIT IN THE HIGH GRASS THAT MOVES TO THE SUNSET BREEZE. I WATCH THE SEA WITH ITS BOATS SAILING BY, AND I WONDER WHERE THEY ARE GOING, WHERE THEY COME FROM..."
...AND I'LL GO TO THAT STREAM AND I'LL SING MY OWN PRAYER THAT MY ISLAND GIRL SHALL BE SAFE EVERYWHERE
"...I MAKE UP SILENT STORIES, JOURNEYS, ENCOUNTERS: I CANNOT HELP IT."
"BEHIND ME, MUM IS COMBING MY LONG, REBELLIOUS HAIR INTO TWO RED PLAITS, WHILST HUMMING ANCIENT BALLADS."
AND WHEN YOUR RIVER RUNS HIGH LET IT FLOW, LET IT FLOW IT'S YOUR TIME WITH LIFE TO LET YOUR GARDEN GROW...
"WE ARE WAITING FOR GARETH TO MAKE HIS WEEKLY VISIT FROM CORNWALL"
"EVEN THE IRISH STEW BUBBLING IN THE POT IS WAITING FOR THE MINER, SPREADING ITS ENTICING FRAGRANCE WELL BEYOND OUR STONY ABODE'S THRESHOLD."
AND WHEN YOUR BURDEN GETS ROUGH LET IT GO, LET IT GO LET YOUR STRENGTH RETURN ON EVERY BREEZE THAT BLOWS...
"MY BROTHER IS LOOMING ON THE HORIZON, TAKING HUGE STRIDES ALONG THE PATH CUTTING THROUGH THE WHEAT FIELDS..."
THROUGH THAT ANCIENT LAND, THROUGH ETERNITY, OH, MY ISLAND GIRL, REMEMBER ME...
"THE LAST RAYS OF SUNSHINE OF THE DAY LINGER OVER THE RUFFLED WAVES OF HIS RUBY LOCKS"

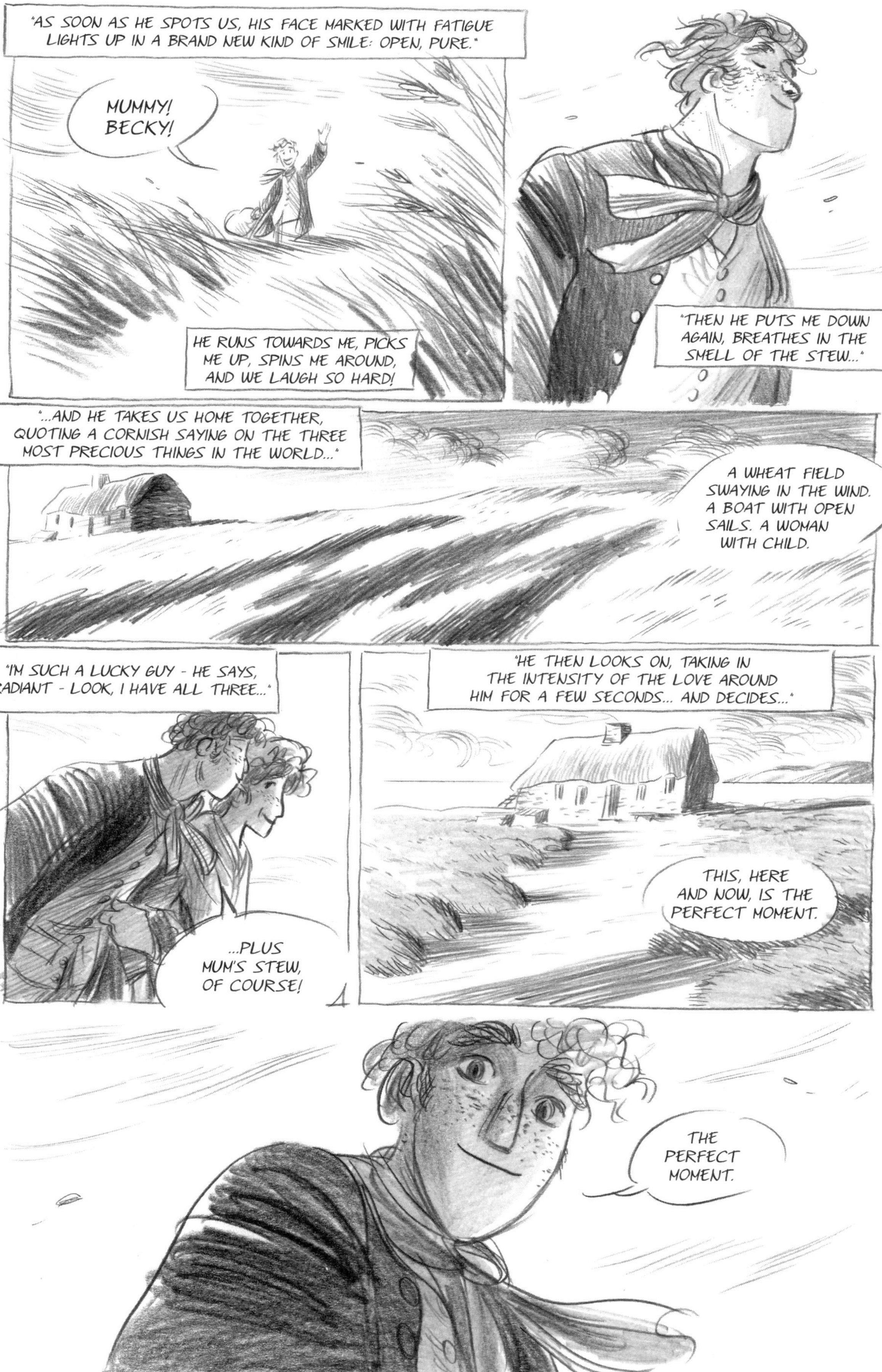
"AS SOON AS HE SPOTS US, HIS FACE MARKED WITH FATIGUE LIGHTS UP IN A BRAND NEW KIND OF SMILE: OPEN, PURE."
MUMMY! BECKY!
HE RUNS TOWARDS ME, PICKS ME UP, SPINS ME AROUND, AND WE LAUGH SO HARD!
"THEN HE PUTS ME DOWN AGAIN, BREATHES IN THE SMELL OF THE STEW..."
"...AND HE TAKES US HOME TOGETHER, QUOTING A CORNISH SAYING ON THE THREE MOST PRECIOUS THINGS IN THE WORLD..."
A WHEAT FIELD SWAYING IN THE WIND. A BOAT WITH OPEN SAILS. A WOMAN WITH CHILD.
"I'M SUCH A LUCKY GUY - HE SAYS, RADIANT - LOOK, I HAVE ALL THREE..."
...PLUS MUM'S STEW, OF COURSE!
"HE THEN LOOKS ON, TAKING IN THE INTENSITY OF THE LOVE AROUND HIM FOR A FEW SECONDS... AND DECIDES..."
THIS, HERE AND NOW, IS THE PERFECT MOMENT.
THE PERFECT MOMENT.

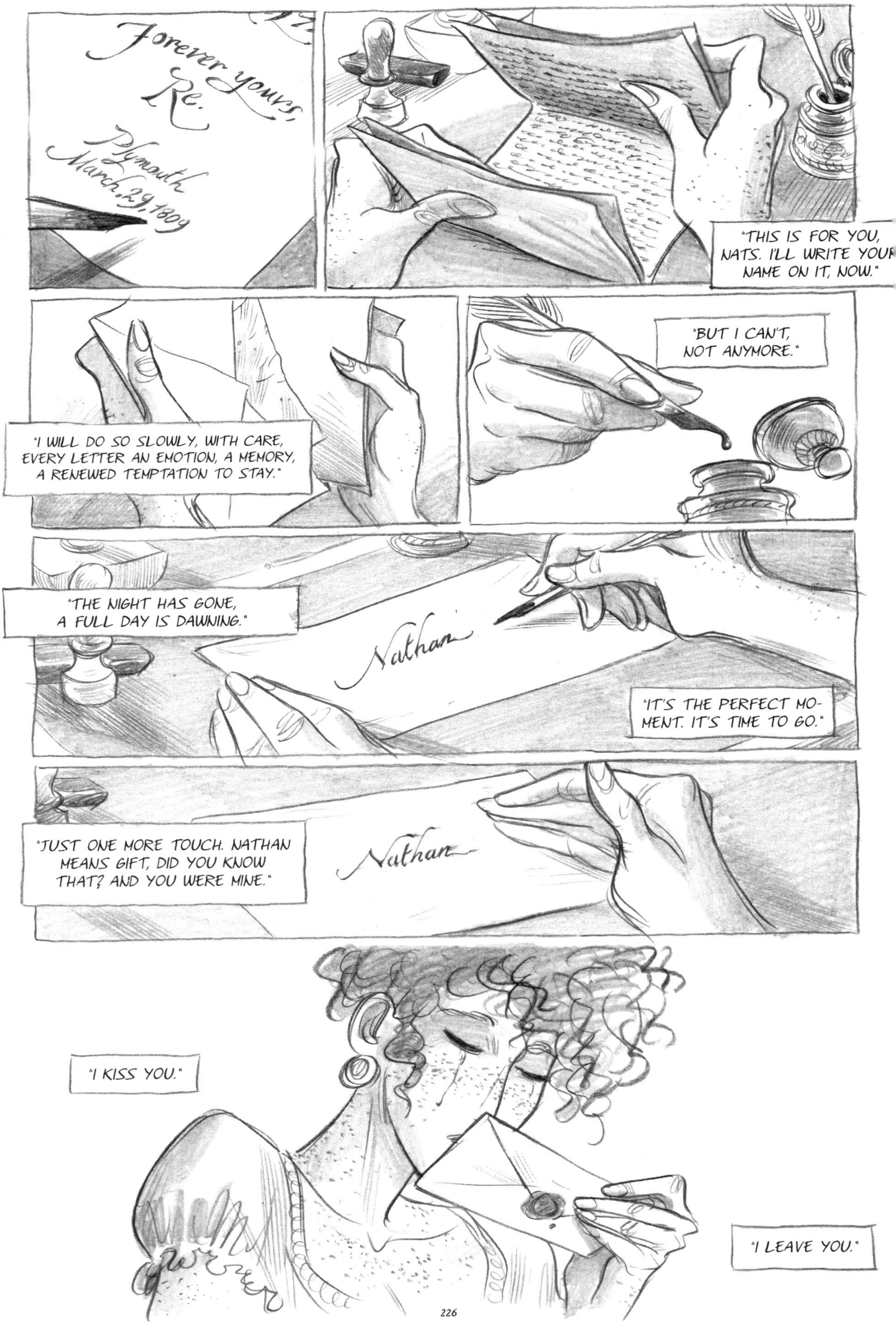
Forever yours,
Re.
Plymouth
March.29.1809
"THIS IS FOR YOU, NATS. I'LL WRITE YOUR NAME ON IT, NOW."
"I WILL DO SO SLOWLY, WITH CARE, EVERY LETTER AN EMOTION, A MEMORY, A RENEWED TEMPTATION TO STAY."
"BUT I CAN'T, NOT ANYMORE."
"THE NIGHT HAS GONE, A FULL DAY IS DAWNING."
Nathan
"IT'S THE PERFECT MOMENT. IT'S TIME TO GO."
"JUST ONE MORE TOUCH. NATHAN MEANS GIFT, DID YOU KNOW THAT? AND YOU WERE MINE."
Nathan
"I KISS YOU."
"I LEAVE YOU."

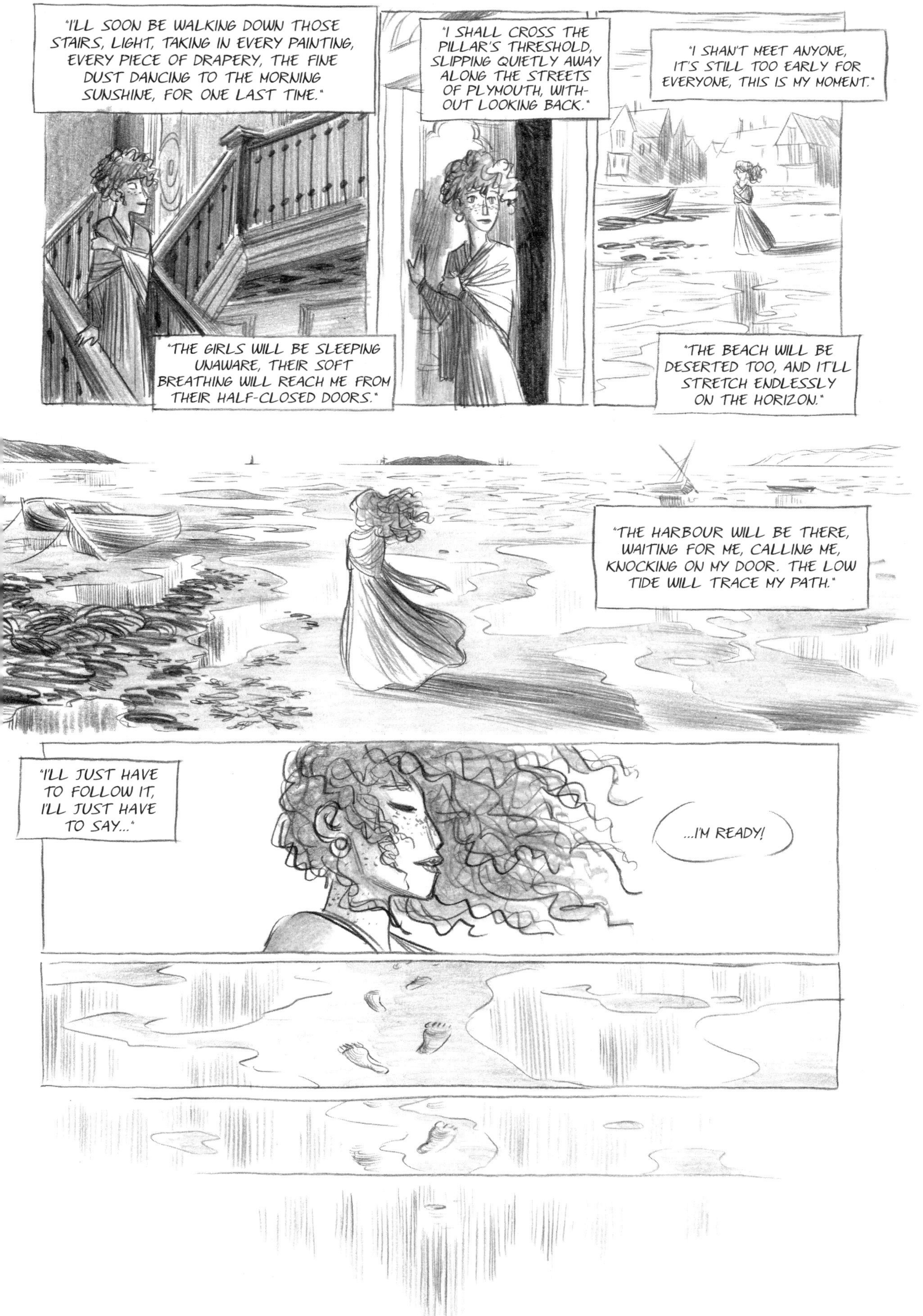
"I'LL SOON BE WALKING DOWN THOSE STAIRS, LIGHT, TAKING IN EVERY PAINTING, EVERY PIECE OF DRAPERY, THE FINE DUST DANCING TO THE MORNING SUNSHINE, FOR ONE LAST TIME."
"THE GIRLS WILL BE SLEEPING UNAWARE, THEIR SOFT BREATHING WILL REACH ME FROM THEIR HALF-CLOSED DOORS."
"I SHALL CROSS THE PILLAR'S THRESHOLD, SLIPPING QUIETLY AWAY ALONG THE STREETS OF PLYMOUTH, WITHOUT LOOKING BACK."
"I SHAN'T MEET ANYONE, IT'S STILL TOO EARLY FOR EVERYONE, THIS IS MY MOMENT."
"THE BEACH WILL BE DESERTED TOO, AND IT'LL STRETCH ENDLESSLY ON THE HORIZON."
"THE HARBOUR WILL BE THERE, WAITING FOR ME, CALLING ME, KNOCKING ON MY DOOR. THE LOW TIDE WILL TRACE MY PATH."
"I'LL JUST HAVE TO FOLLOW IT, I'LL JUST HAVE TO SAY..."
...I'M READY!

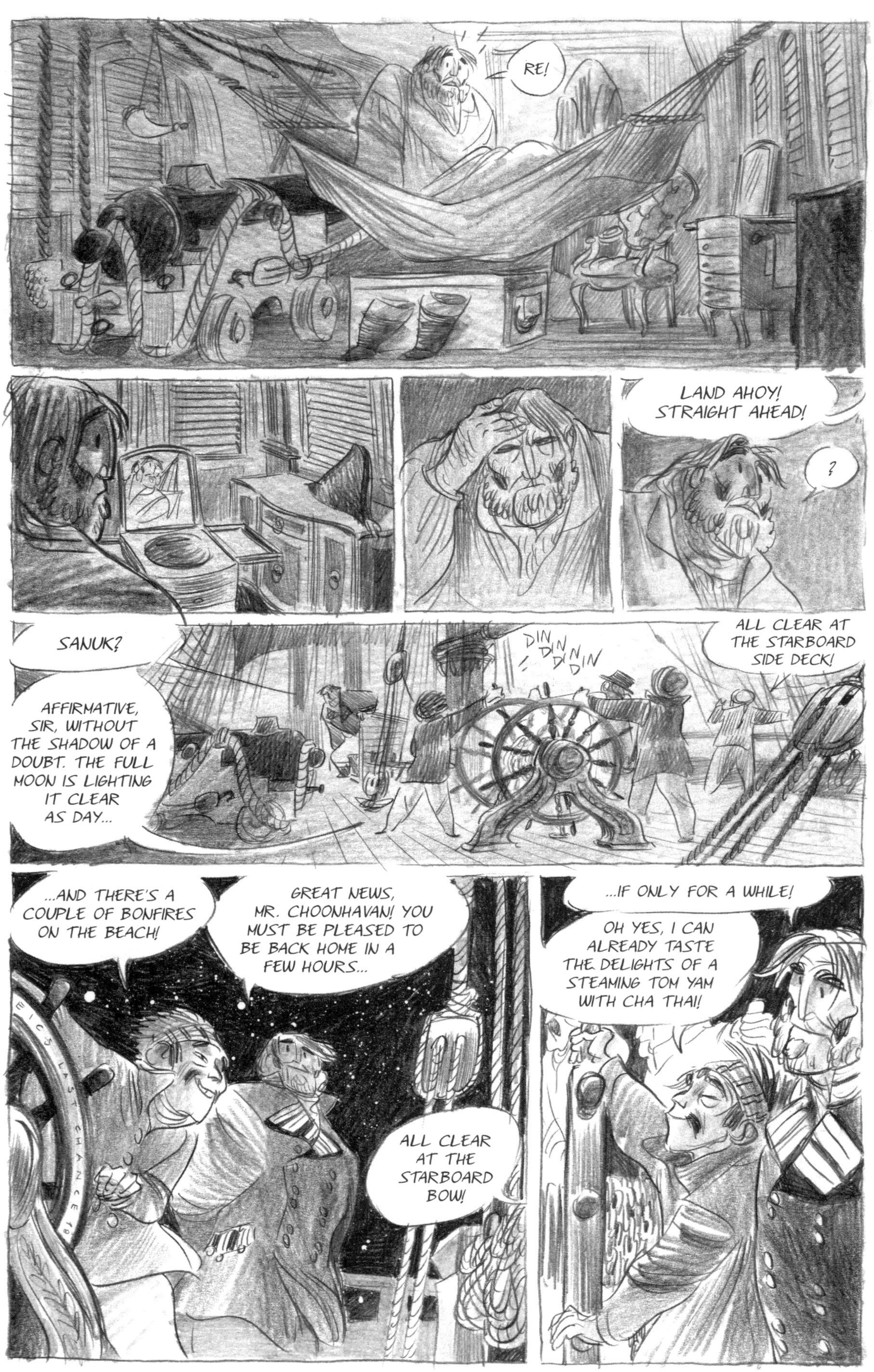
RE!
LAND AHOY! STRAIGHT AHEAD!
?
SANUK?
AFFIRMATIVE, SIR, WITHOUT THE SHADOW OF A DOUBT. THE FULL MOON IS LIGHTING IT CLEAR AS DAY...
DIN DIN DIN DIN
ALL CLEAR AT THE STARBOARD SIDE DECK!
...AND THERE'S A COUPLE OF BONFIRES ON THE BEACH!
GREAT NEWS, MR. CHOONHAVAN! YOU MUST BE PLEASED TO BE BACK HOME IN A FEW HOURS...
ALL CLEAR AT THE STARBOARD BOW!
...IF ONLY FOR A WHILE!
OH YES, I CAN ALREADY TASTE THE DELIGHTS OF A STEAMING TOM YAM WITH CHA THAI!

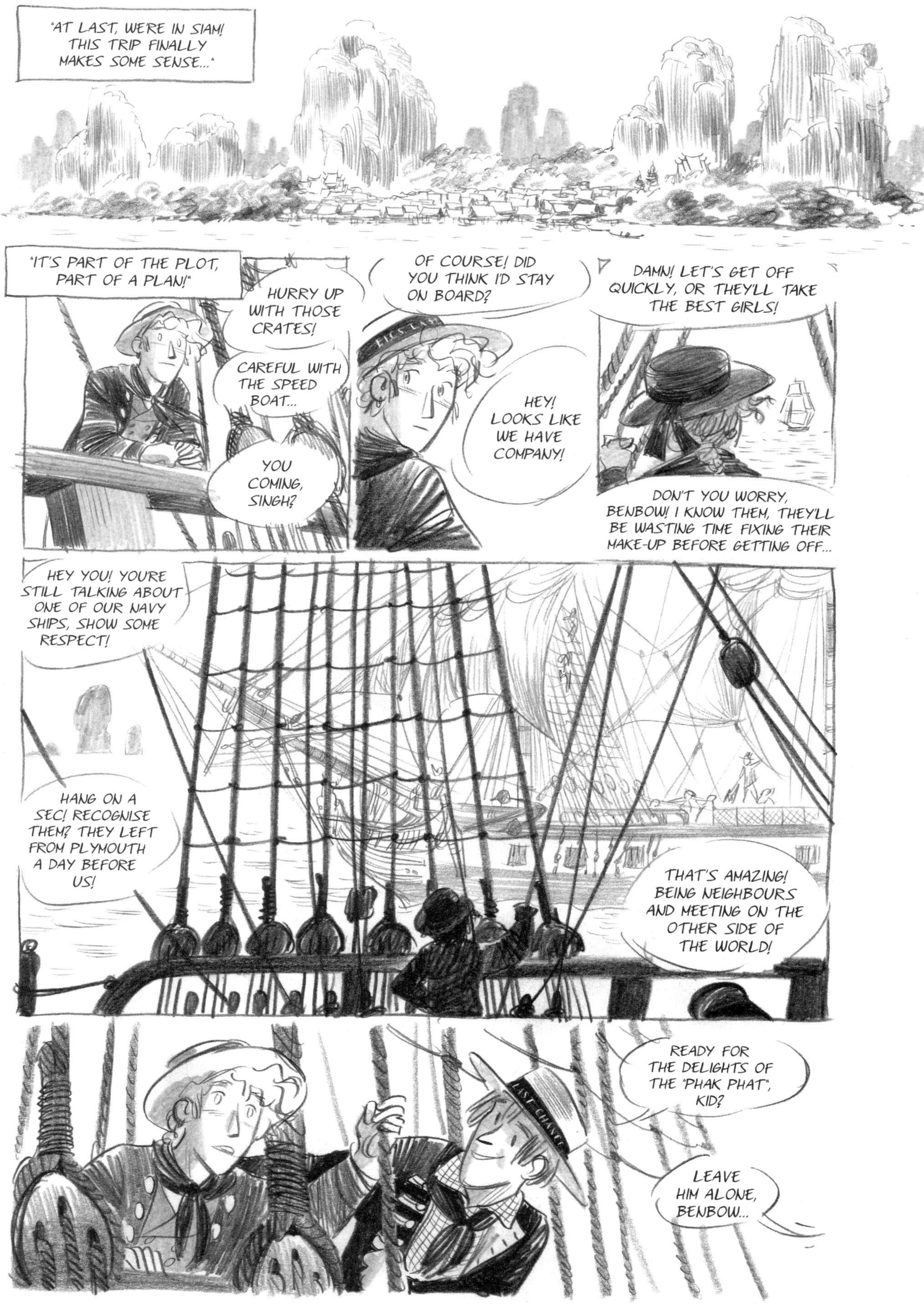
"AT LAST, WE'RE IN SIAM! THIS TRIP FINALLY MAKES SOME SENSE..."
"IT'S PART OF THE PLOT, PART OF A PLAN!"
HURRY UP WITH THOSE CRATES!
CAREFUL WITH THE SPEED BOAT...
YOU COMING, SINGH?
OF COURSE! DID YOU THINK I'D STAY ON BOARD?
HEY! LOOKS LIKE WE HAVE COMPANY!
DAMN! LET'S GET OFF QUICKLY, OR THEY'LL TAKE THE BEST GIRLS!
DON'T YOU WORRY, BENBOW! I KNOW THEM, THEY'LL BE WASTING TIME FIXING THEIR MAKE-UP BEFORE GETTING OFF...
HEY YOU! YOU'RE STILL TALKING ABOUT ONE OF OUR NAVY SHIPS, SHOW SOME RESPECT!
HANG ON A SEC! RECOGNISE THEM? THEY LEFT FROM PLYMOUTH A DAY BEFORE US!
THAT'S AMAZING! BEING NEIGHBOURS AND MEETING ON THE OTHER SIDE OF THE WORLD!
READY FOR THE DELIGHTS OF THE "PHAK PHAT", KID?
LEAVE HIM ALONE, BENBOW...

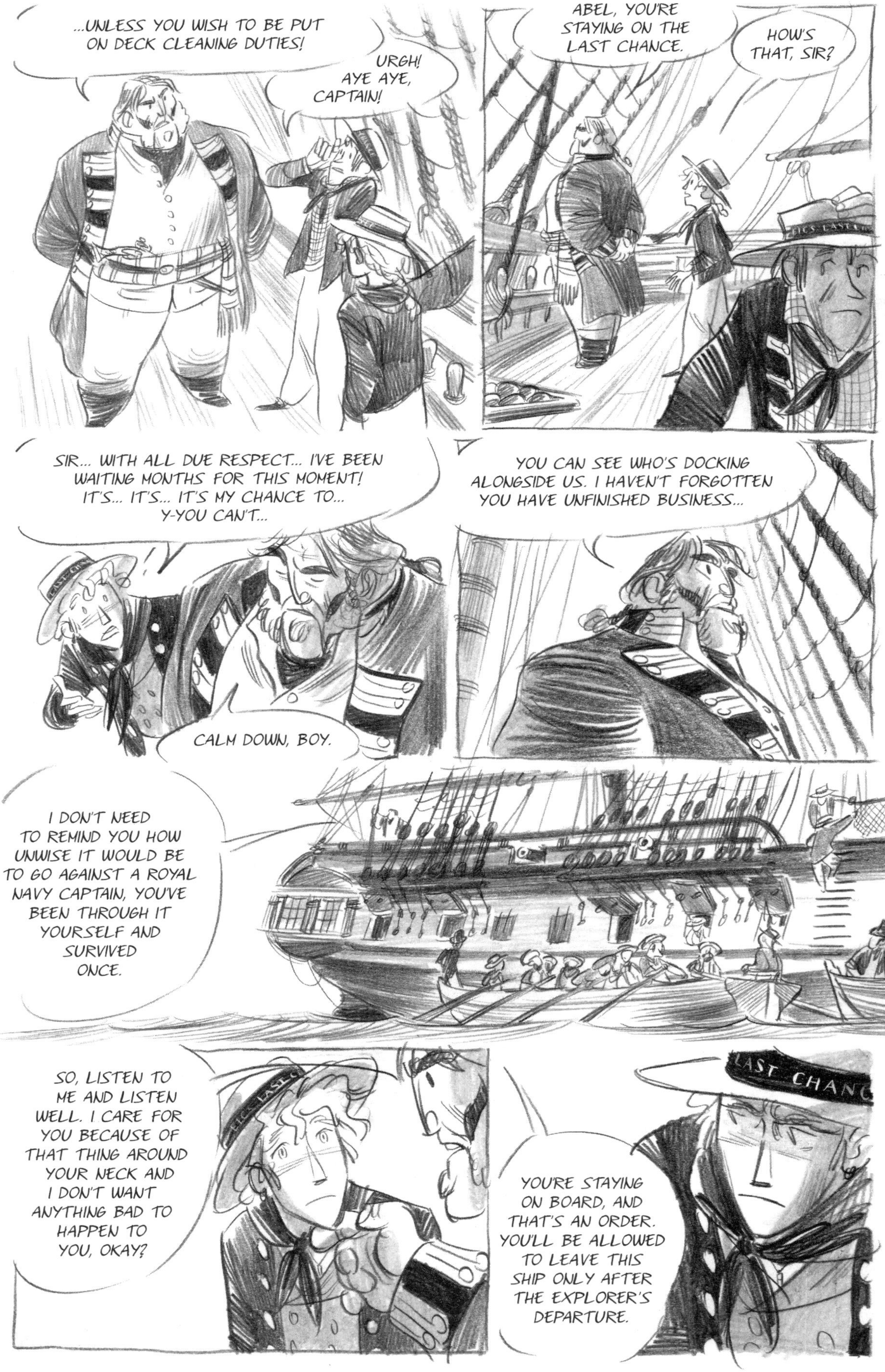
...UNLESS YOU WISH TO BE PUT ON DECK CLEANING DUTIES!
URGH! AYE AYE, CAPTAIN!
ABEL, YOU'RE STAYING ON THE LAST CHANCE.
HOW'S THAT, SIR?
SIR... WITH ALL DUE RESPECT... I'VE BEEN WAITING MONTHS FOR THIS MOMENT! IT'S... IT'S... IT'S MY CHANCE TO... Y-YOU CAN'T...
CALM DOWN, BOY.
YOU CAN SEE WHO'S DOCKING ALONGSIDE US. I HAVEN'T FORGOTTEN YOU HAVE UNFINISHED BUSINESS...
I DON'T NEED TO REMIND YOU HOW UNWISE IT WOULD BE TO GO AGAINST A ROYAL NAVY CAPTAIN, YOU'VE BEEN THROUGH IT YOURSELF AND SURVIVED ONCE.
SO, LISTEN TO ME AND LISTEN WELL. I CARE FOR YOU BECAUSE OF THAT THING AROUND YOUR NECK AND I DON'T WANT ANYTHING BAD TO HAPPEN TO YOU, OKAY?
LAST CHANC
YOU'RE STAYING ON BOARD, AND THAT'S AN ORDER. YOU'LL BE ALLOWED TO LEAVE THIS SHIP ONLY AFTER THE EXPLORER'S DEPARTURE.

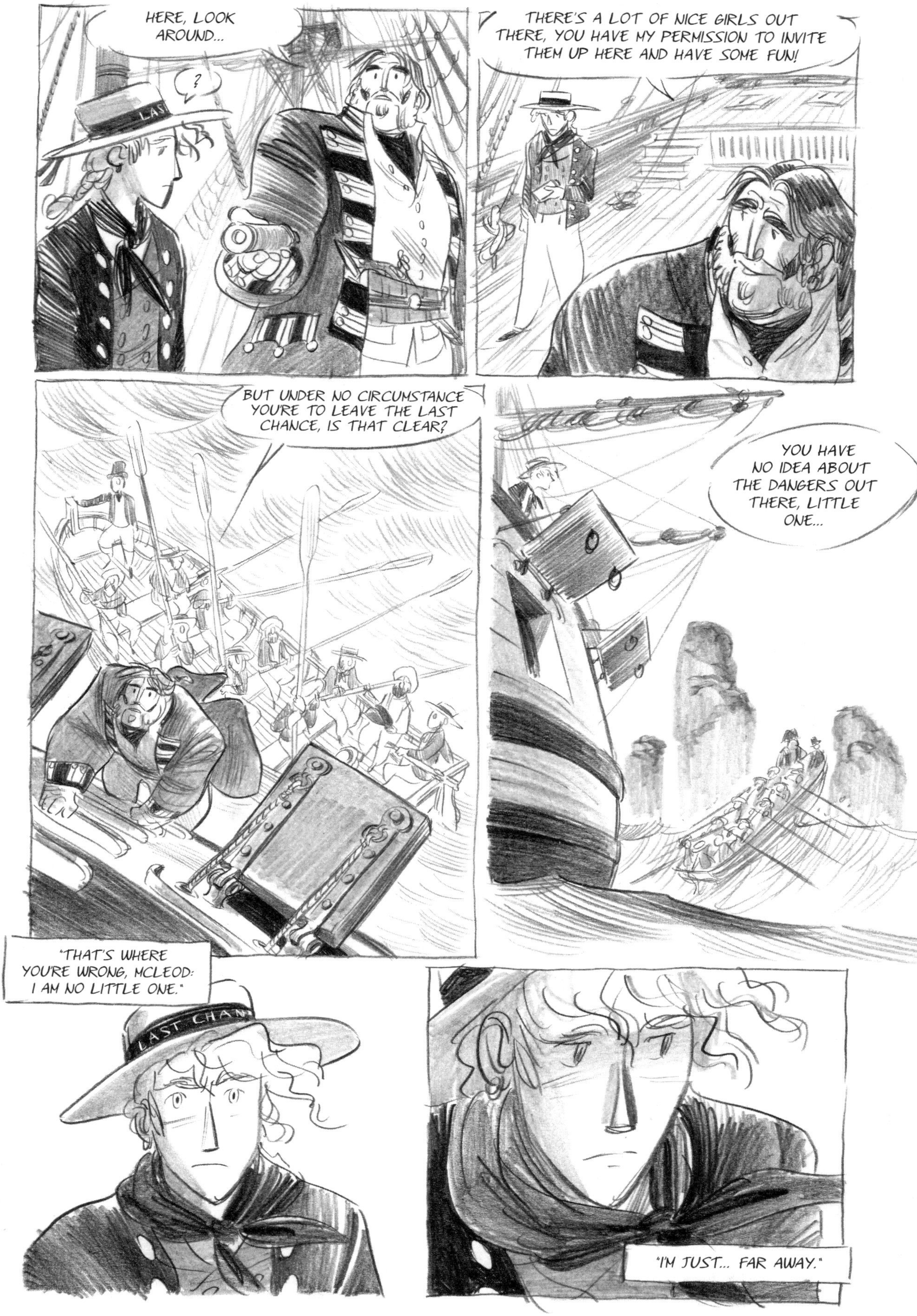
HERE, LOOK AROUND...
?
THERE'S A LOT OF NICE GIRLS OUT THERE, YOU HAVE MY PERMISSION TO INVITE THEM UP HERE AND HAVE SOME FUN!
BUT UNDER NO CIRCUMSTANCE YOU'RE TO LEAVE THE LAST CHANCE, IS THAT CLEAR?
YOU HAVE NO IDEA ABOUT THE DANGERS OUT THERE, LITTLE ONE...
"THAT'S WHERE YOU'RE WRONG, MCLEOD: I AM NO LITTLE ONE."
LAST CHAN
"I'M JUST... FAR AWAY."

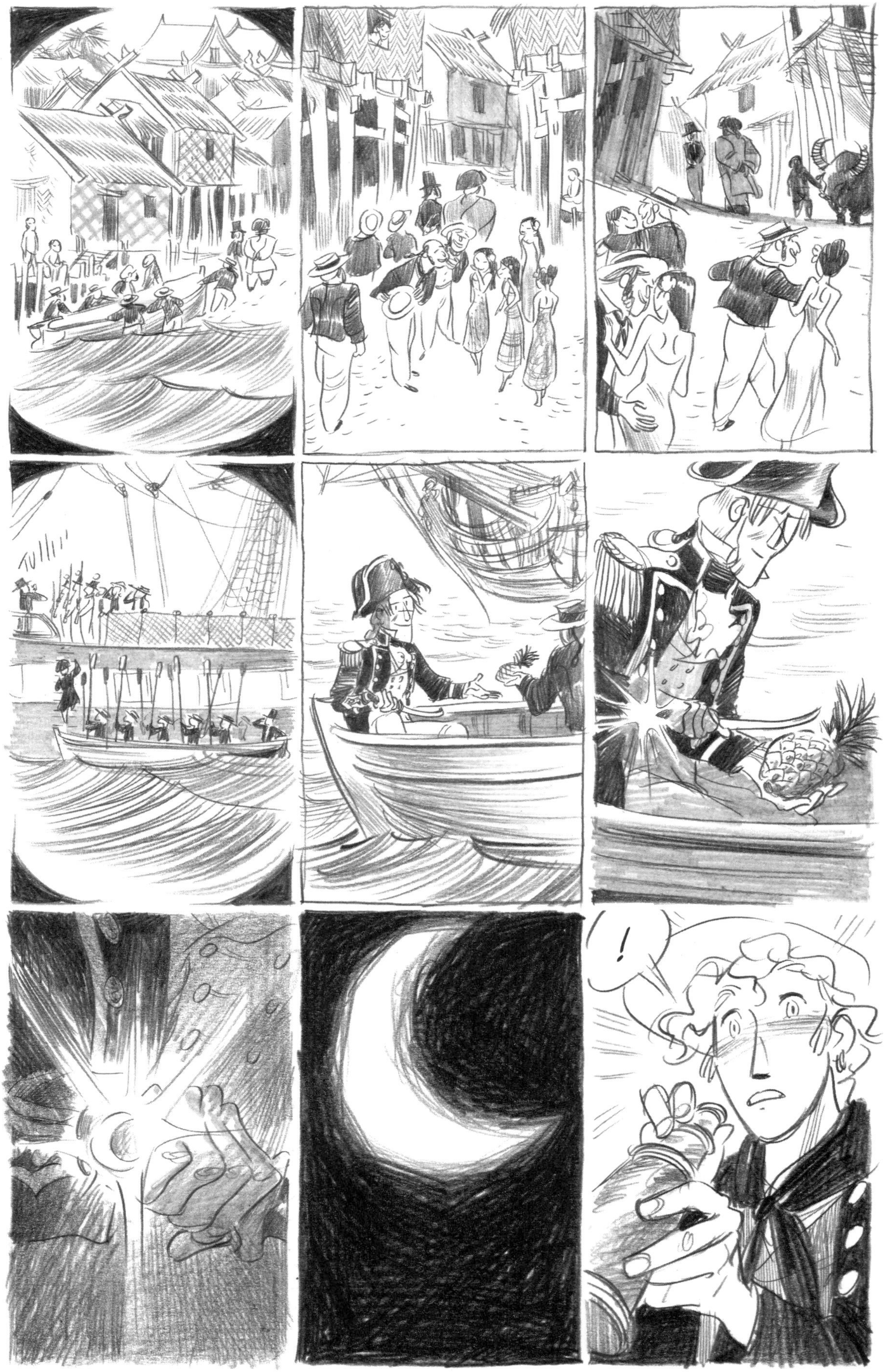
!

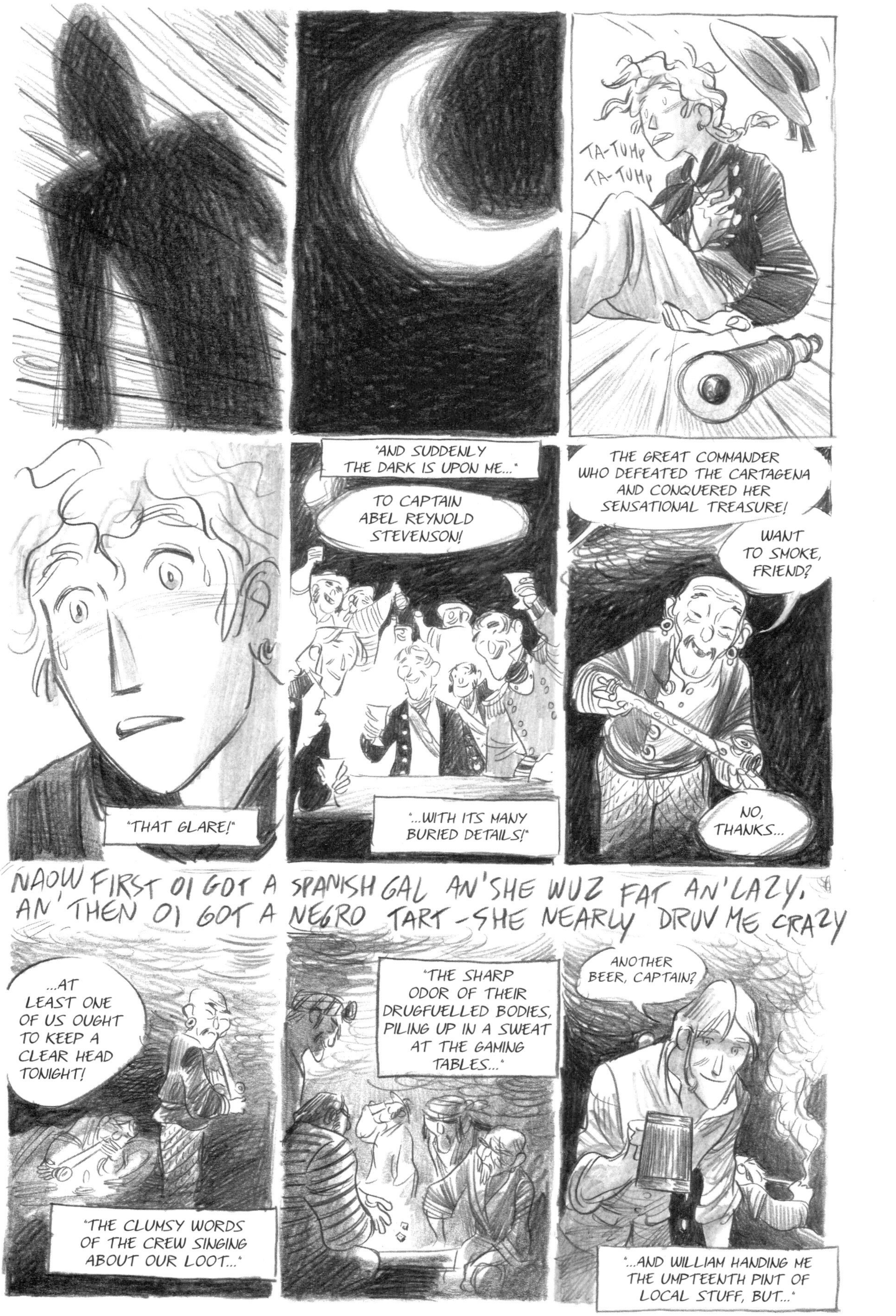

TA-TUMP
TA-TUMP
"THAT GLARE!"
"AND SUDDENLY THE DARK IS UPON ME..."
TO CAPTAIN ABEL REYNOLD STEVENSON!
"...WITH ITS MANY BURIED DETAILS!"
THE GREAT COMMANDER WHO DEFEATED THE CARTAGENA AND CONQUERED HER SENSATIONAL TREASURE!
WANT TO SMOKE, FRIEND?
NO, THANKS...
NAOW FIRST OI GOT A SPANISH GAL AN'SHE WUZ FAT AN'LAZY,
AN' THEN OI GOT A NEGRO TART - SHE NEARLY DRUV ME CRAZY
...AT LEAST ONE OF US OUGHT TO KEEP A CLEAR HEAD TONIGHT!
"THE CLUMSY WORDS OF THE CREW SINGING ABOUT OUR LOOT..."
"THE SHARP ODOR OF THEIR DRUGFUELLED BODIES, PILING UP IN A SWEAT AT THE GAMING TABLES..."
ANOTHER BEER, CAPTAIN?
"...AND WILLIAM HANDING ME THE UMPTEENTH PINT OF LOCAL STUFF, BUT..."

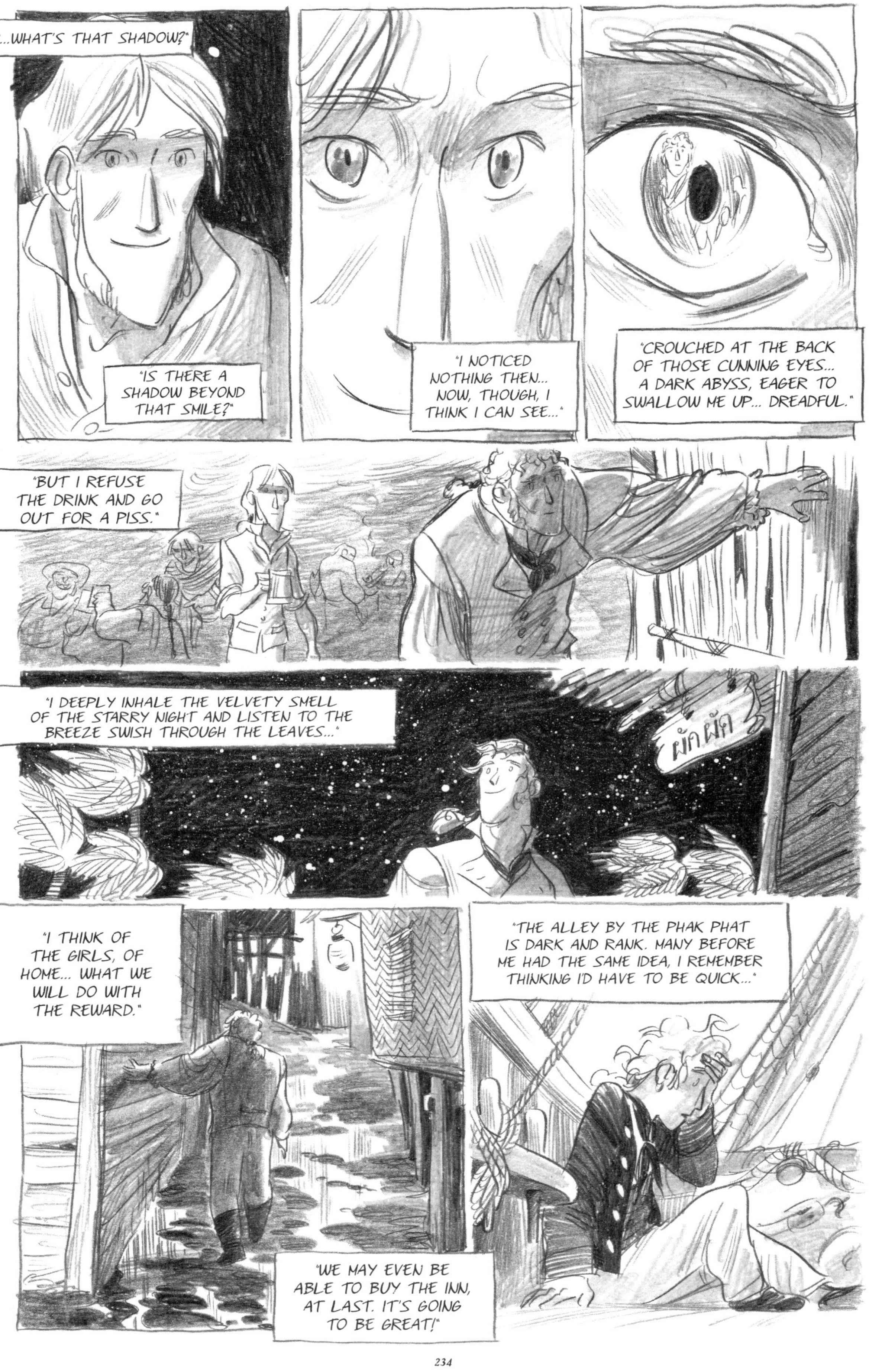
"...WHAT'S THAT SHADOW?"
"IS THERE A SHADOW BEYOND THAT SMILE?"
"I NOTICED NOTHING THEN... NOW, THOUGH, I THINK I CAN SEE..."
"CROUCHED AT THE BACK OF THOSE CUNNING EYES... A DARK ABYSS, EAGER TO SWALLOW ME UP... DREADFUL."
"BUT I REFUSE THE DRINK AND GO OUT FOR A PISS."
"I DEEPLY INHALE THE VELVETY SMELL OF THE STARRY NIGHT AND LISTEN TO THE BREEZE SWISH THROUGH THE LEAVES..."
"I THINK OF THE GIRLS, OF HOME... WHAT WE WILL DO WITH THE REWARD."
"WE MAY EVEN BE ABLE TO BUY THE INN, AT LAST. IT'S GOING TO BE GREAT!"
"THE ALLEY BY THE PHAK PHAT IS DARK AND RANK. MANY BEFORE ME HAD THE SAME IDEA, I REMEMBER THINKING I'D HAVE TO BE QUICK..."

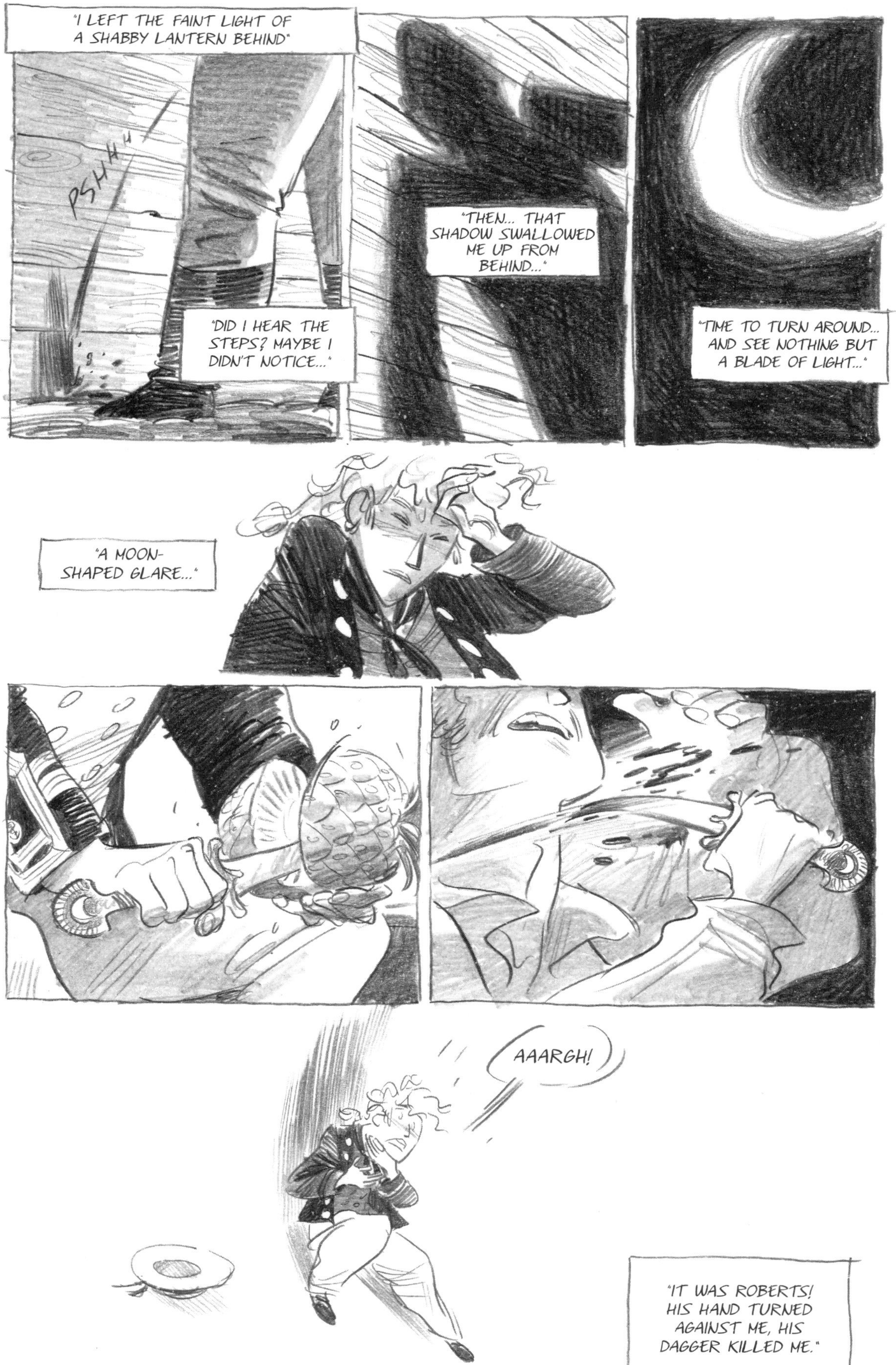
"I LEFT THE FAINT LIGHT OF A SHABBY LANTERN BEHIND"
PSHH
"DID I HEAR THE STEPS? MAYBE I DIDN'T NOTICE..."
"THEN... THAT SHADOW SWALLOWED ME UP FROM BEHIND..."
"TIME TO TURN AROUND... AND SEE NOTHING BUT A BLADE OF LIGHT..."
"A MOON-SHAPED GLARE..."
AAARGH!
"IT WAS ROBERTS! HIS HAND TURNED AGAINST ME, HIS DAGGER KILLED ME."

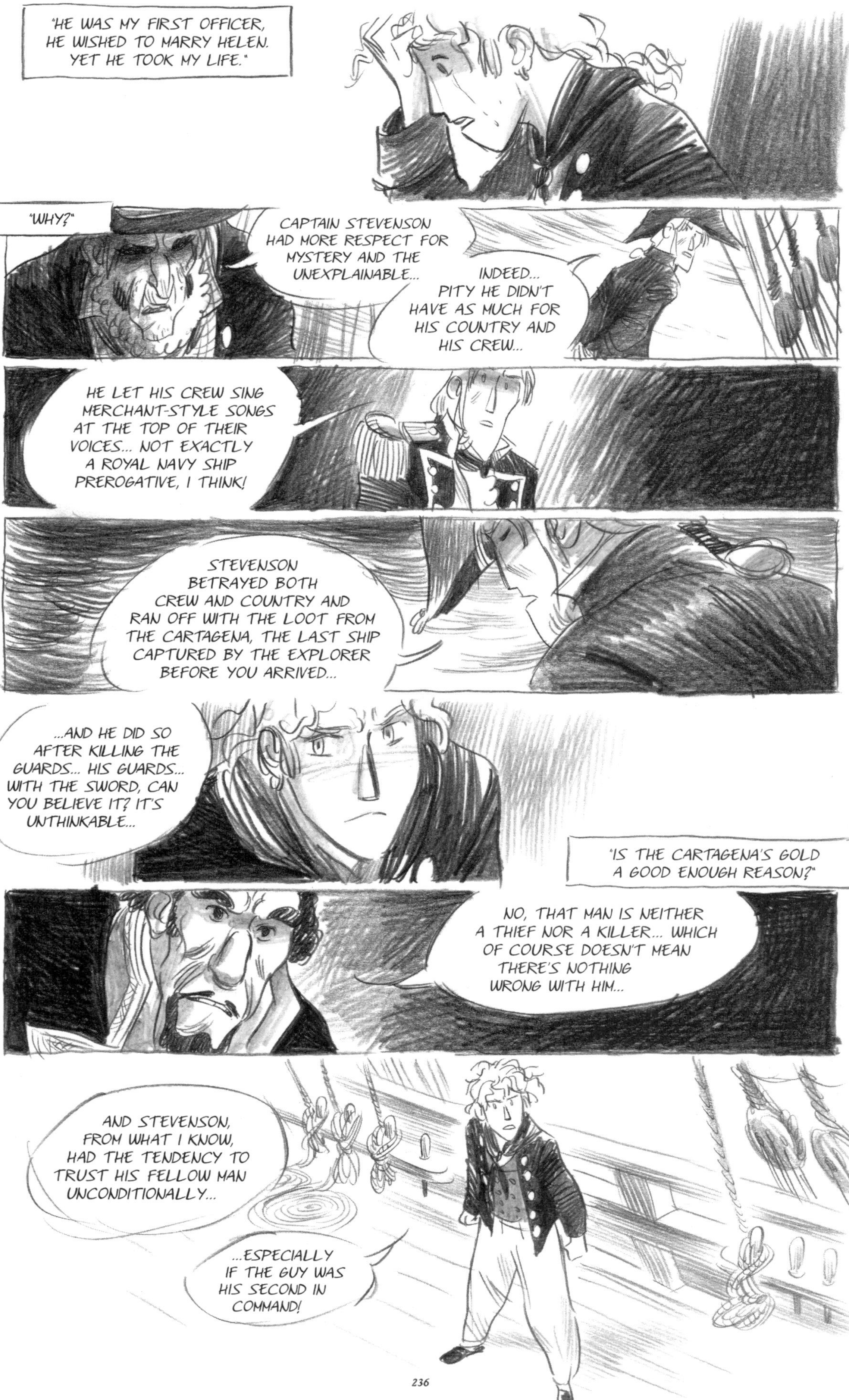
"HE WAS MY FIRST OFFICER, HE WISHED TO MARRY HELEN. YET HE TOOK MY LIFE."
"WHY?"
CAPTAIN STEVENSON HAD MORE RESPECT FOR MYSTERY AND THE UNEXPLAINABLE...
INDEED... PITY HE DIDN'T HAVE AS MUCH FOR HIS COUNTRY AND HIS CREW...
HE LET HIS CREW SING MERCHANT-STYLE SONGS AT THE TOP OF THEIR VOICES... NOT EXACTLY A ROYAL NAVY SHIP PREROGATIVE, I THINK!
STEVENSON BETRAYED BOTH CREW AND COUNTRY AND RAN OFF WITH THE LOOT FROM THE CARTAGENA, THE LAST SHIP CAPTURED BY THE EXPLORER BEFORE YOU ARRIVED...
...AND HE DID SO AFTER KILLING THE GUARDS... HIS GUARDS... WITH THE SWORD, CAN YOU BELIEVE IT? IT'S UNTHINKABLE...
"IS THE CARTAGENA'S GOLD A GOOD ENOUGH REASON?"
NO, THAT MAN IS NEITHER A THIEF NOR A KILLER... WHICH OF COURSE DOESN'T MEAN THERE'S NOTHING WRONG WITH HIM...
AND STEVENSON, FROM WHAT I KNOW, HAD THE TENDENCY TO TRUST HIS FELLOW MAN UNCONDITIONALLY...
...ESPECIALLY IF THE GUY WAS HIS SECOND IN COMMAND!

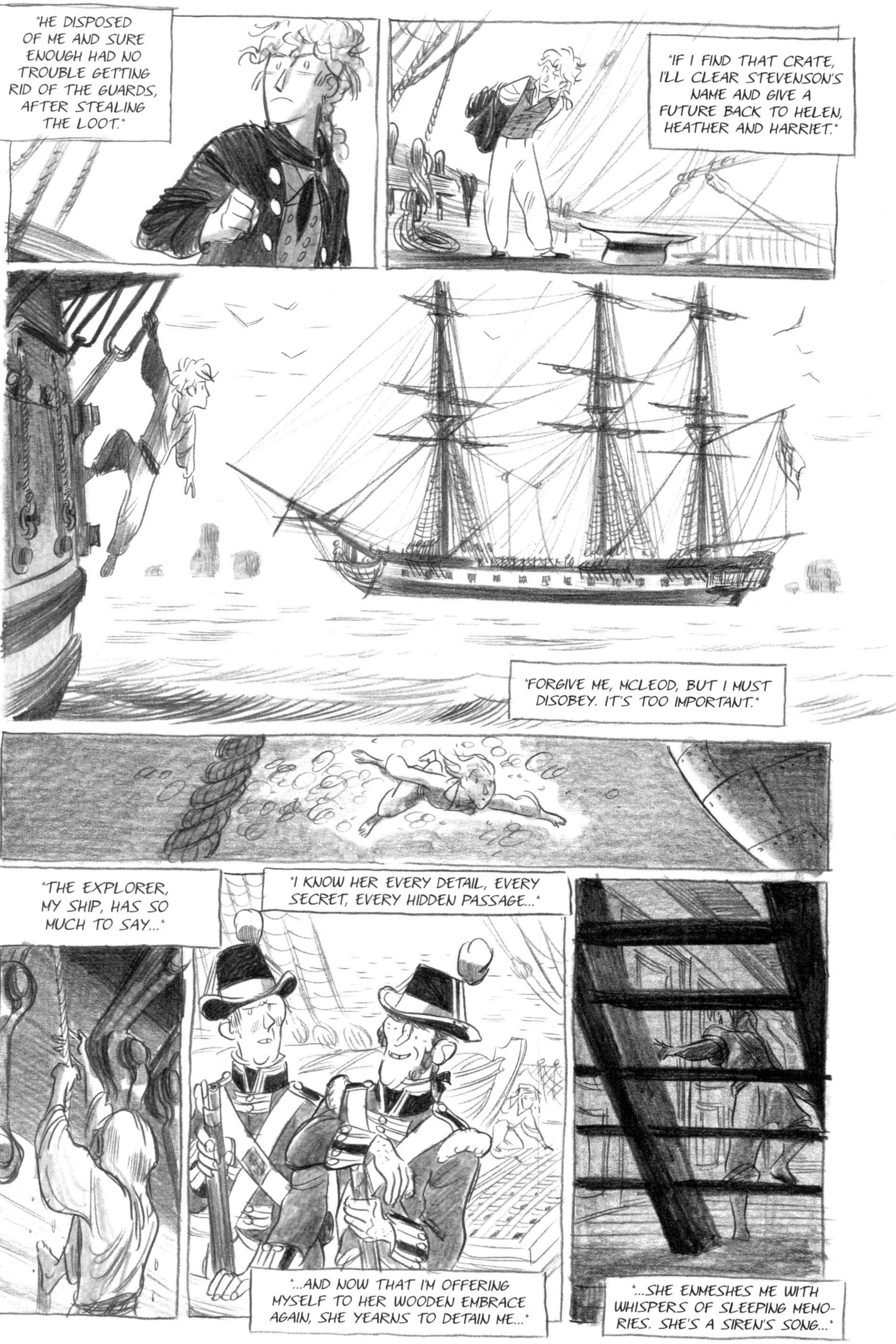
"HE DISPOSED OF ME AND SURE ENOUGH HAD NO TROUBLE GETTING RID OF THE GUARDS, AFTER STEALING THE LOOT."
"IF I FIND THAT CRATE, I'LL CLEAR STEVENSON'S NAME AND GIVE A FUTURE BACK TO HELEN, HEATHER AND HARRIET."
"FORGIVE ME, MCLEOD, BUT I MUST DISOBEY. IT'S TOO IMPORTANT."
"THE EXPLORER, MY SHIP, HAS SO MUCH TO SAY..."
"I KNOW HER EVERY DETAIL, EVERY SECRET, EVERY HIDDEN PASSAGE..."
"...AND NOW THAT I'M OFFERING MYSELF TO HER WOODEN EMBRACE AGAIN, SHE YEARNS TO DETAIN ME..."
"...SHE ENMESHES ME WITH WHISPERS OF SLEEPING MEMORIES. SHE'S A SIREN'S SONG..."

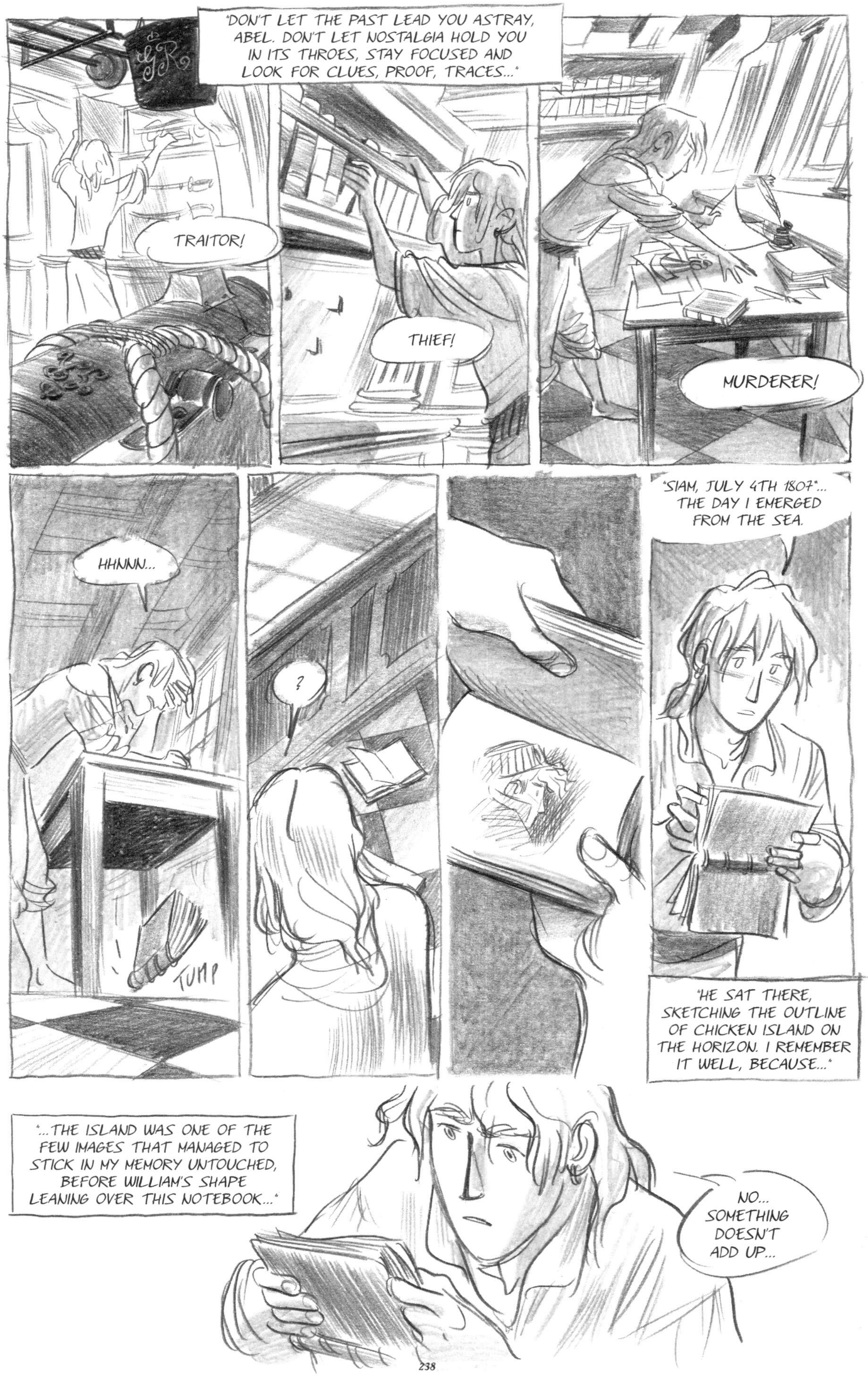
"DON'T LET THE PAST LEAD YOU ASTRAY, ABEL. DON'T LET NOSTALGIA HOLD YOU IN ITS THROES, STAY FOCUSED AND LOOK FOR CLUES, PROOF, TRACES..."
TRAITOR!
THIEF!
MURDERER!
HHNNN...
!
TUMP
?
"SIAM, JULY 4TH 1807"... THE DAY I EMERGED FROM THE SEA.
"HE SAT THERE, SKETCHING THE OUTLINE OF CHICKEN ISLAND ON THE HORIZON. I REMEMBER IT WELL, BECAUSE..."
"...THE ISLAND WAS ONE OF THE FEW IMAGES THAT MANAGED TO STICK IN MY MEMORY UNTOUCHED, BEFORE WILLIAM'S SHAPE LEANING OVER THIS NOTEBOOK..."
NO... SOMETHING DOESN'T ADD UP...

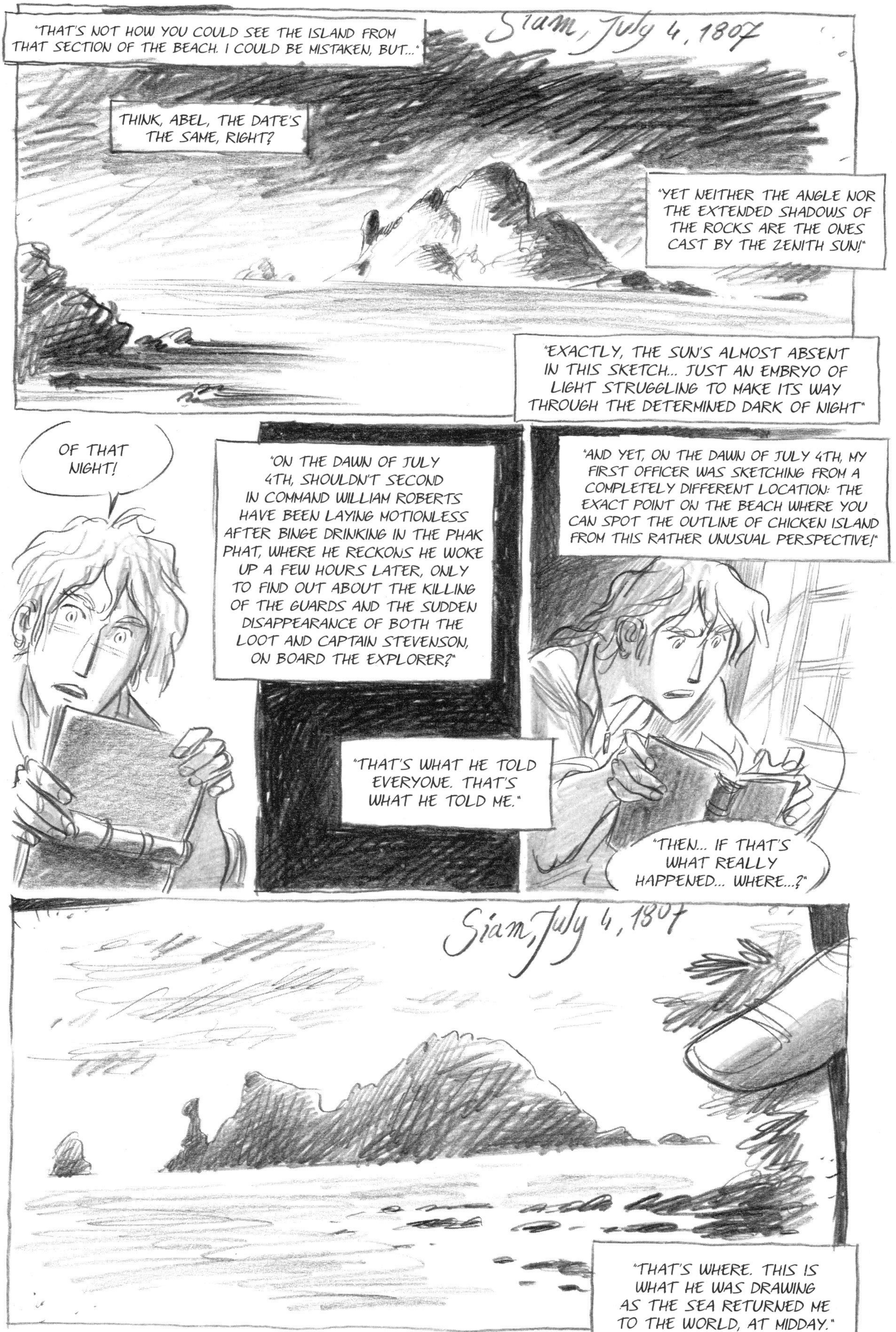
"THAT'S NOT HOW YOU COULD SEE THE ISLAND FROM THAT SECTION OF THE BEACH. I COULD BE MISTAKEN, BUT..."
Siam, July 4, 1807
THINK, ABEL, THE DATE'S THE SAME, RIGHT?
"YET NEITHER THE ANGLE NOR THE EXTENDED SHADOWS OF THE ROCKS ARE THE ONES CAST BY THE ZENITH SUN!"
"EXACTLY, THE SUN'S ALMOST ABSENT IN THIS SKETCH... JUST AN EMBRYO OF LIGHT STRUGGLING TO MAKE ITS WAY THROUGH THE DETERMINED DARK OF NIGHT"
OF THAT NIGHT!
"ON THE DAWN OF JULY 4TH, SHOULDN'T SECOND IN COMMAND WILLIAM ROBERTS HAVE BEEN LAYING MOTIONLESS AFTER BINGE DRINKING IN THE PHAK PHAT, WHERE HE RECKONS HE WOKE UP A FEW HOURS LATER, ONLY TO FIND OUT ABOUT THE KILLING OF THE GUARDS AND THE SUDDEN DISAPPEARANCE OF BOTH THE LOOT AND CAPTAIN STEVENSON, ON BOARD THE EXPLORER?"
"THAT'S WHAT HE TOLD EVERYONE. THAT'S WHAT HE TOLD ME."
"AND YET, ON THE DAWN OF JULY 4TH, MY FIRST OFFICER WAS SKETCHING FROM A COMPLETELY DIFFERENT LOCATION: THE EXACT POINT ON THE BEACH WHERE YOU CAN SPOT THE OUTLINE OF CHICKEN ISLAND FROM THIS RATHER UNUSUAL PERSPECTIVE!"
"THEN... IF THAT'S WHAT REALLY HAPPENED... WHERE...?"
Siam, July 4, 1807
"THAT'S WHERE. THIS IS WHAT HE WAS DRAWING AS THE SEA RETURNED ME TO THE WORLD, AT MIDDAY."

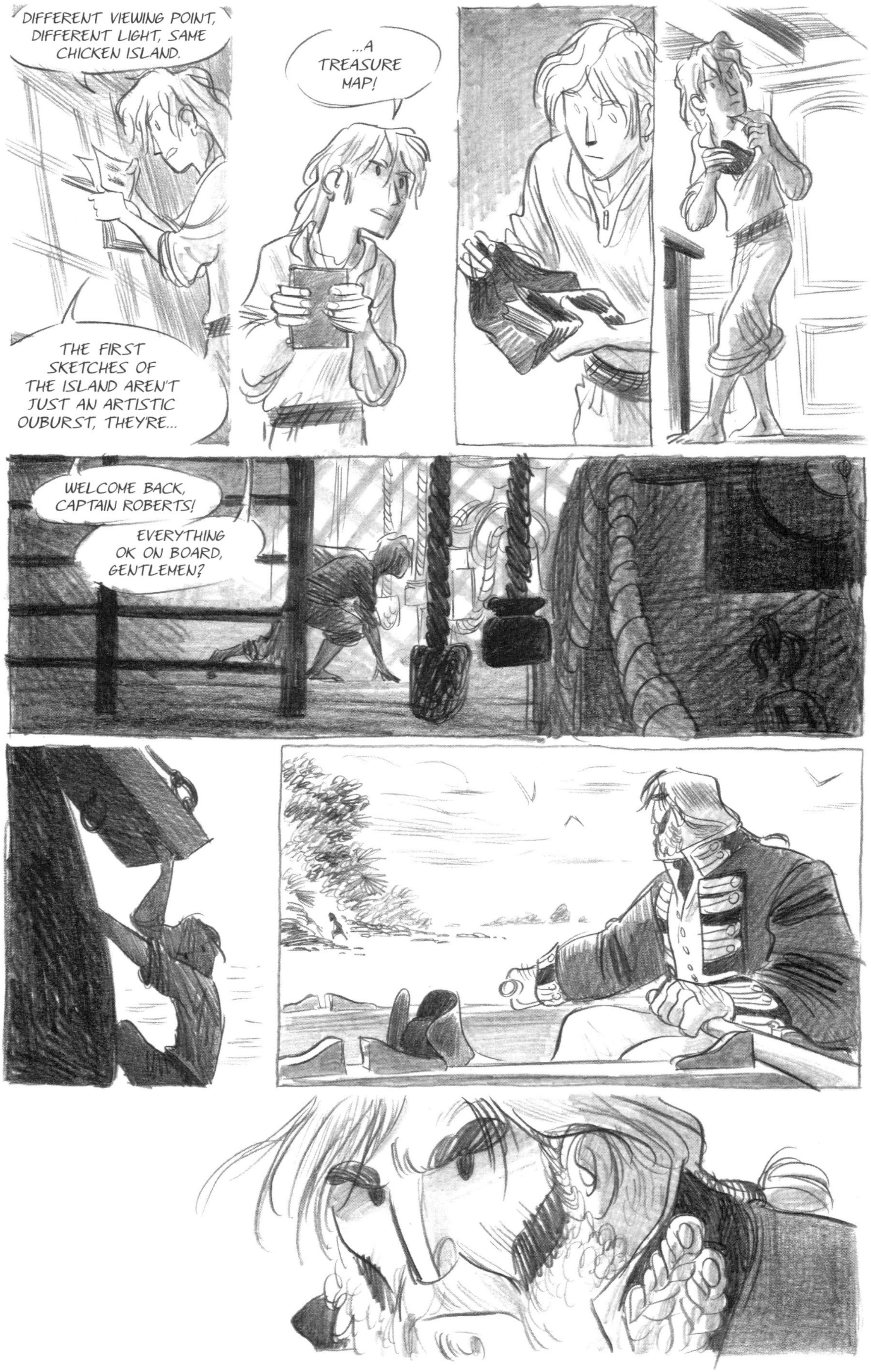
DIFFERENT VIEWING POINT, DIFFERENT LIGHT, SAME CHICKEN ISLAND.
THE FIRST SKETCHES OF THE ISLAND AREN'T JUST AN ARTISTIC OUBURST, THEY'RE...
...A TREASURE MAP!
WELCOME BACK, CAPTAIN ROBERTS!
EVERYTHING OK ON BOARD, GENTLEMEN?

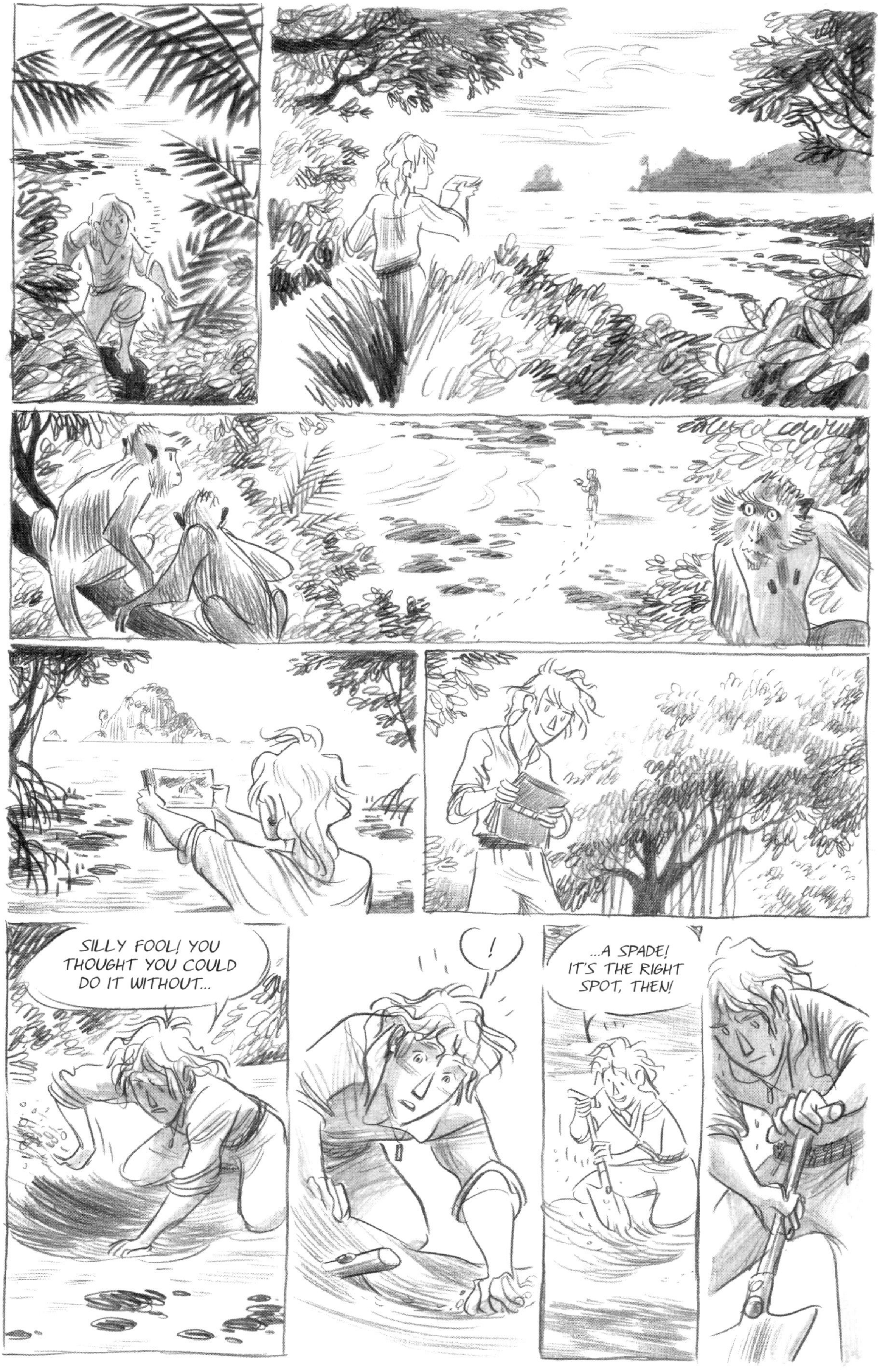

SILLY FOOL! YOU THOUGHT YOU COULD DO IT WITHOUT...
!
...A SPADE! IT'S THE RIGHT SPOT, THEN!

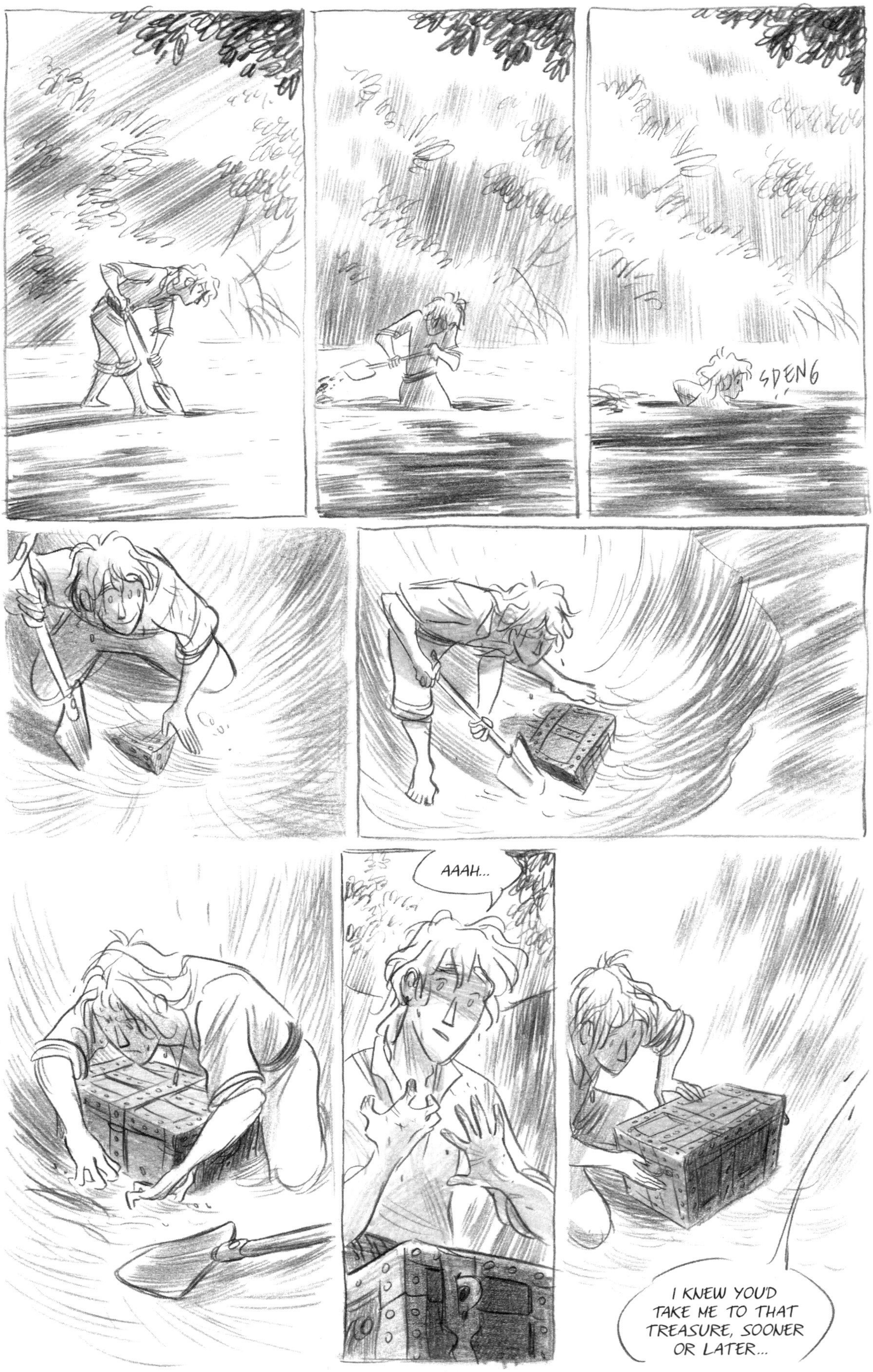
SDENG
AAAH...
I KNEW YOU'D TAKE ME TO THAT TREASURE, SOONER OR LATER...

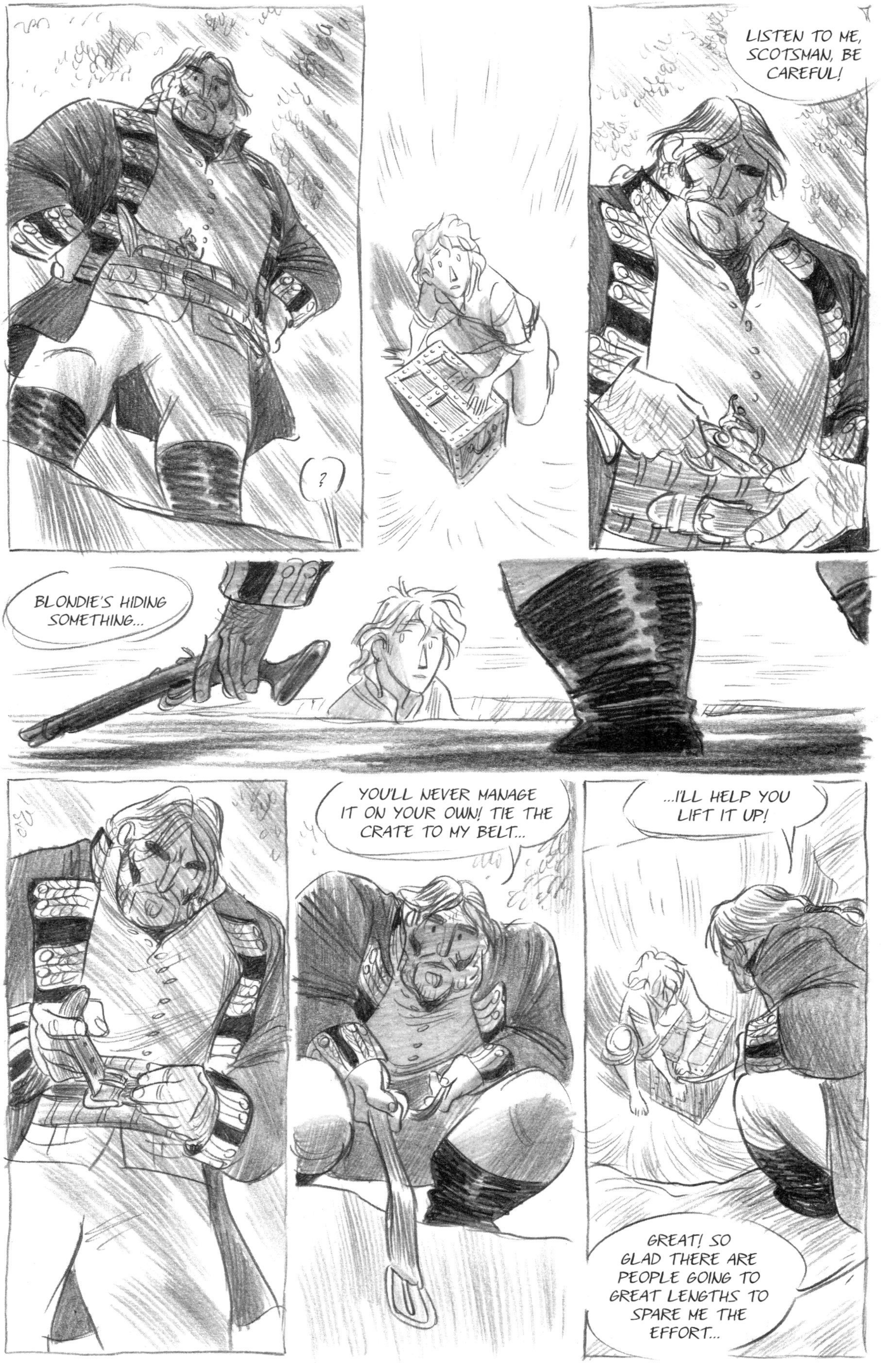
?
LISTEN TO ME, SCOTSMAN, BE CAREFUL!
BLONDIE'S HIDING SOMETHING...
YOU'LL NEVER MANAGE IT ON YOUR OWN! TIE THE CRATE TO MY BELT...
...I'LL HELP YOU LIFT IT UP!
GREAT! SO GLAD THERE ARE PEOPLE GOING TO GREAT LENGTHS TO SPARE ME THE EFFORT...

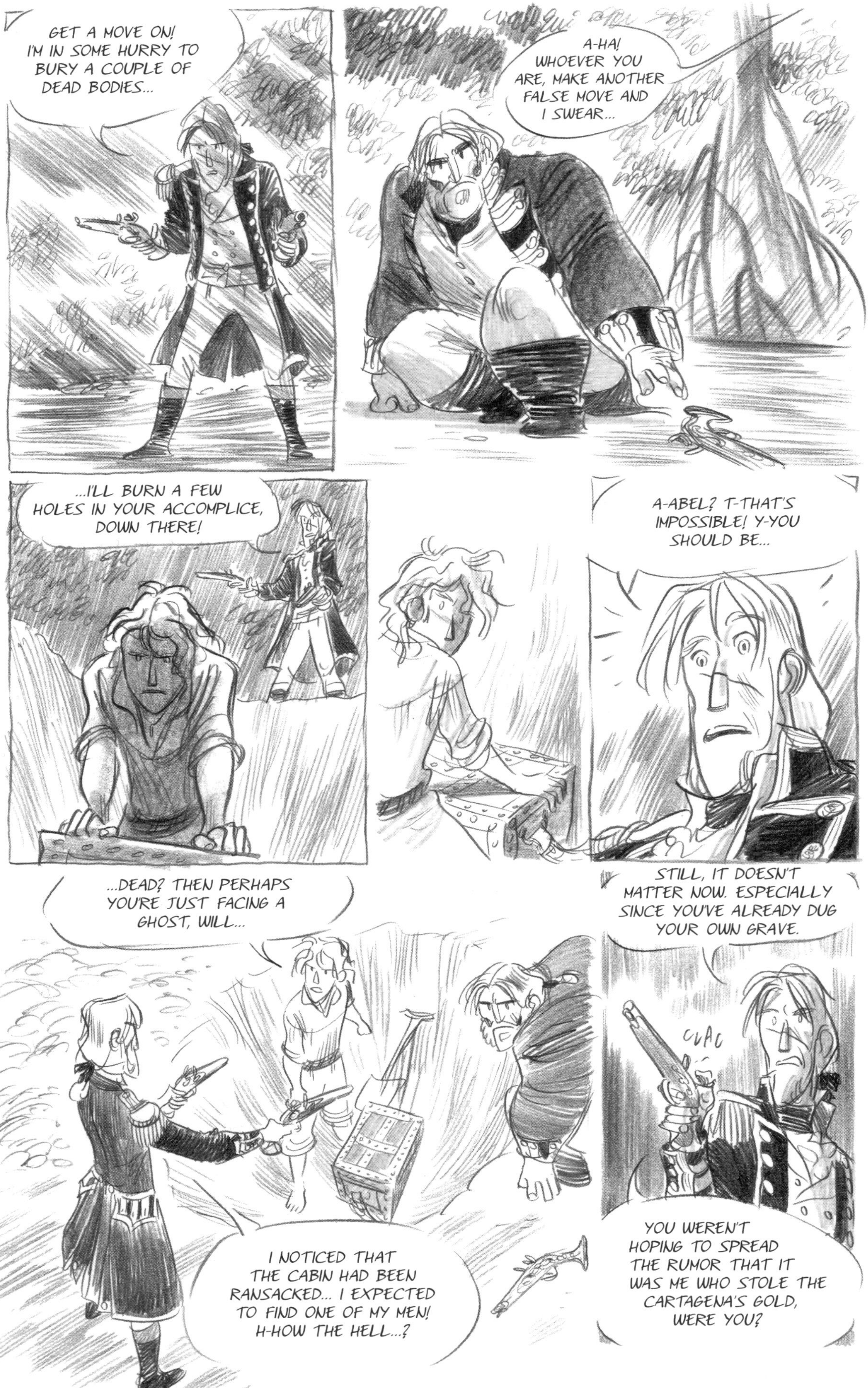
GET A MOVE ON! I'M IN SOME HURRY TO BURY A COUPLE OF DEAD BODIES...
A-HA! WHOEVER YOU ARE, MAKE ANOTHER FALSE MOVE AND I SWEAR...
...I'LL BURN A FEW HOLES IN YOUR ACCOMPLICE, DOWN THERE!
A-ABEL? T-THAT'S IMPOSSIBLE! Y-YOU SHOULD BE...
...DEAD? THEN PERHAPS YOU'RE JUST FACING A GHOST, WILL...
I NOTICED THAT THE CABIN HAD BEEN RANSACKED... I EXPECTED TO FIND ONE OF MY MEN! H-HOW THE HELL...?
STILL, IT DOESN'T MATTER NOW. ESPECIALLY SINCE YOU'VE ALREADY DUG YOUR OWN GRAVE.
CLAC
YOU WEREN'T HOPING TO SPREAD THE RUMOR THAT IT WAS ME WHO STOLE THE CARTAGENA'S GOLD, WERE YOU?

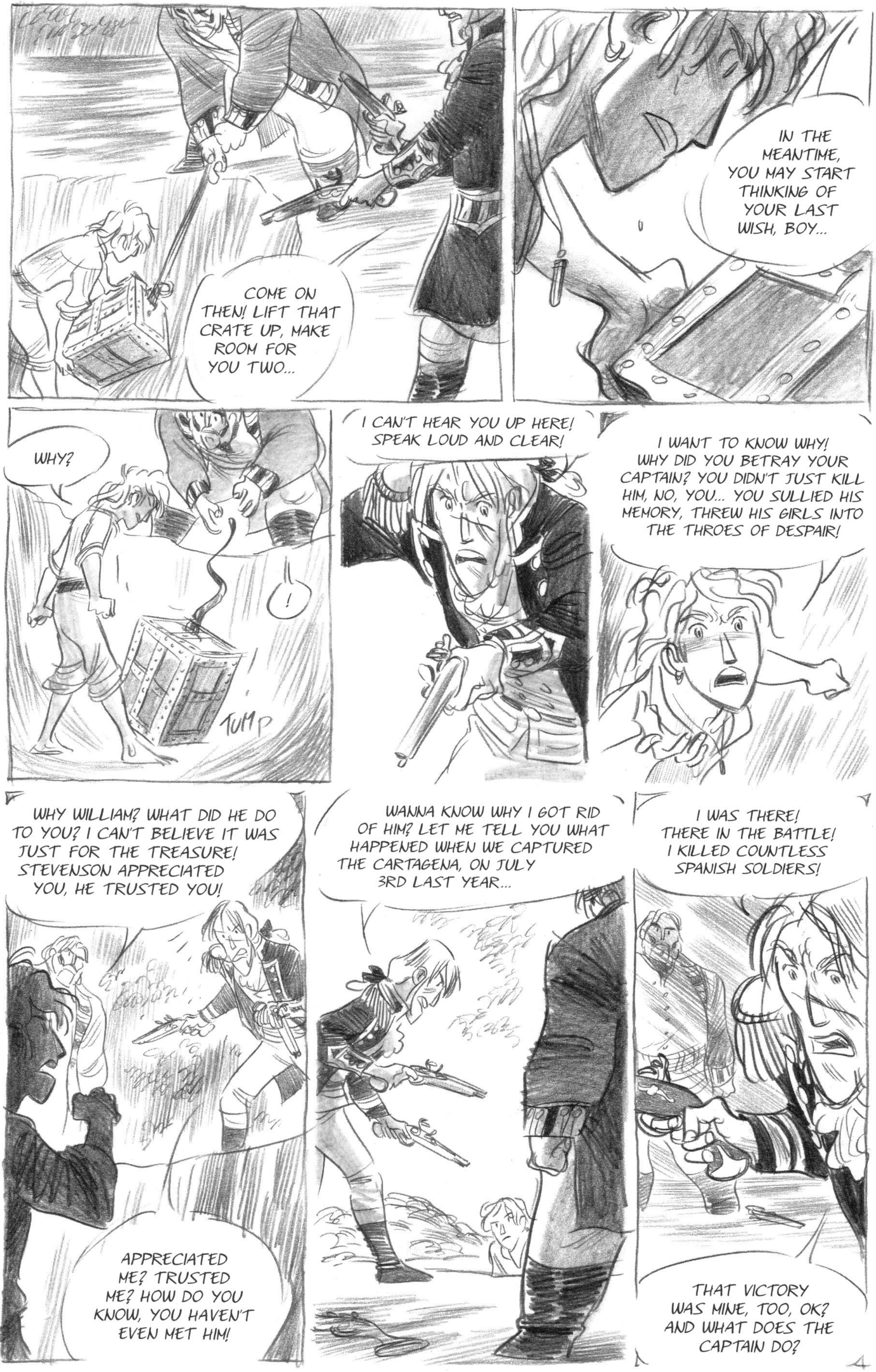

COME ON THEN! LIFT THAT CRATE UP, MAKE ROOM FOR YOU TWO...
IN THE MEANTIME, YOU MAY START THINKING OF YOUR LAST WISH, BOY...
WHY?
!
TUMP
I CAN'T HEAR YOU UP HERE! SPEAK LOUD AND CLEAR!
I WANT TO KNOW WHY! WHY DID YOU BETRAY YOUR CAPTAIN? YOU DIDN'T JUST KILL HIM, NO, YOU... YOU SULLIED HIS MEMORY, THREW HIS GIRLS INTO THE THROES OF DESPAIR!
WHY WILLIAM? WHAT DID HE DO TO YOU? I CAN'T BELIEVE IT WAS JUST FOR THE TREASURE! STEVENSON APPRECIATED YOU, HE TRUSTED YOU!
APPRECIATED ME? TRUSTED ME? HOW DO YOU KNOW, YOU HAVEN'T EVEN MET HIM!
WANNA KNOW WHY I GOT RID OF HIM? LET ME TELL YOU WHAT HAPPENED WHEN WE CAPTURED THE CARTAGENA, ON JULY 3RD LAST YEAR...
I WAS THERE! THERE IN THE BATTLE! I KILLED COUNTLESS SPANISH SOLDIERS!
THAT VICTORY WAS MINE, TOO, OK? AND WHAT DOES THE CAPTAIN DO?

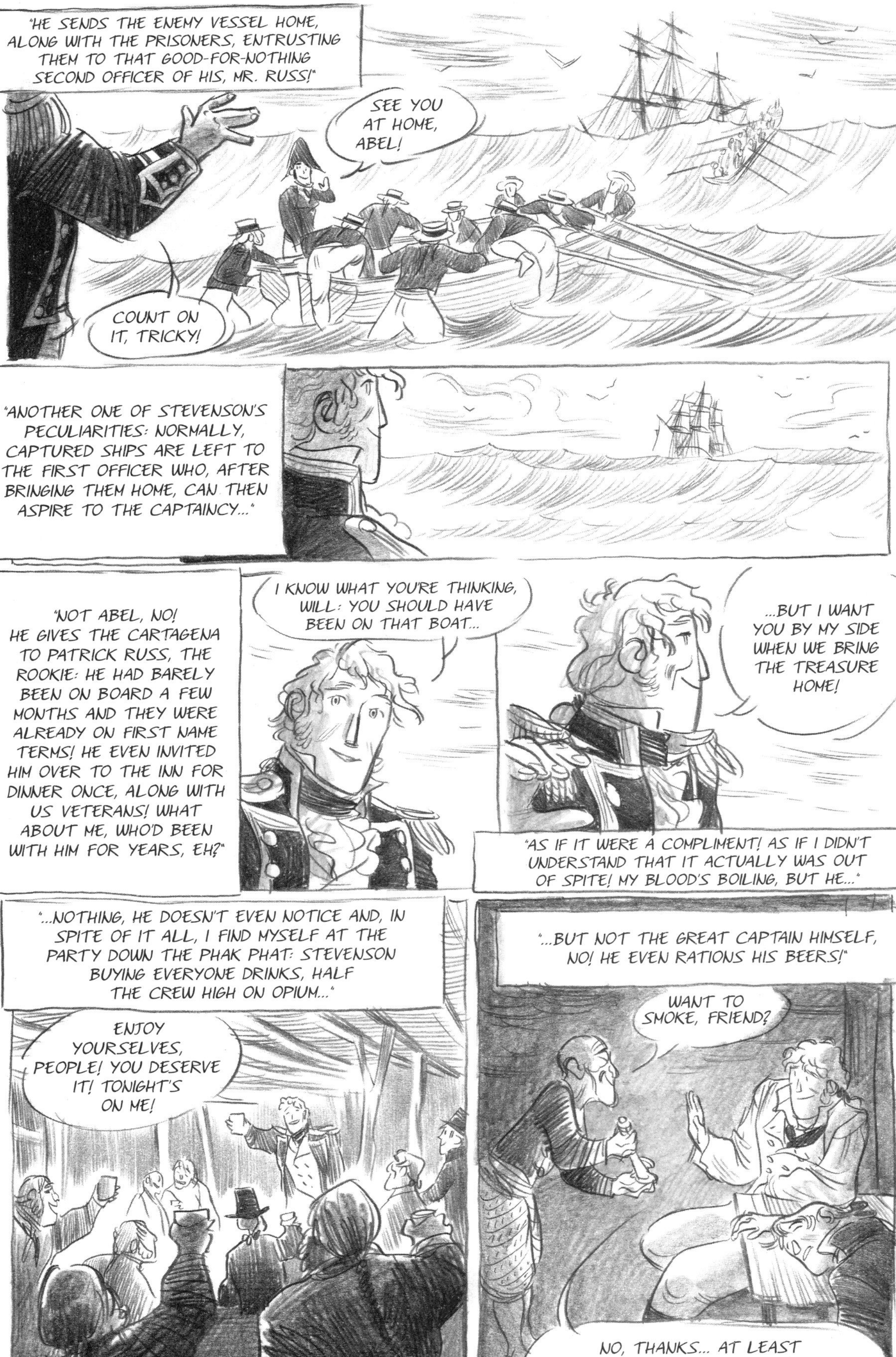
"HE SENDS THE ENEMY VESSEL HOME, ALONG WITH THE PRISONERS, ENTRUSTING THEM TO THAT GOOD-FOR-NOTHING SECOND OFFICER OF HIS, MR. RUSS!"
SEE YOU AT HOME, ABEL!
COUNT ON IT, TRICKY!
"ANOTHER ONE OF STEVENSON'S PECULIARITIES: NORMALLY, CAPTURED SHIPS ARE LEFT TO THE FIRST OFFICER WHO, AFTER BRINGING THEM HOME, CAN THEN ASPIRE TO THE CAPTAINCY..."
"NOT ABEL, NO! HE GIVES THE CARTAGENA TO PATRICK RUSS, THE ROOKIE: HE HAD BARELY BEEN ON BOARD A FEW MONTHS AND THEY WERE ALREADY ON FIRST NAME TERMS! HE EVEN INVITED HIM OVER TO THE INN FOR DINNER ONCE, ALONG WITH US VETERANS! WHAT ABOUT ME, WHO'D BEEN WITH HIM FOR YEARS, EH?"
I KNOW WHAT YOU'RE THINKING, WILL: YOU SHOULD HAVE BEEN ON THAT BOAT...
...BUT I WANT YOU BY MY SIDE WHEN WE BRING THE TREASURE HOME!
"AS IF IT WERE A COMPLIMENT! AS IF I DIDN'T UNDERSTAND THAT IT ACTUALLY WAS OUT OF SPITE! MY BLOOD'S BOILING, BUT HE..."
"...NOTHING, HE DOESN'T EVEN NOTICE AND, IN SPITE OF IT ALL, I FIND MYSELF AT THE PARTY DOWN THE PHAK PHAT: STEVENSON BUYING EVERYONE DRINKS, HALF THE CREW HIGH ON OPIUM..."
ENJOY YOURSELVES, PEOPLE! YOU DESERVE IT! TONIGHT'S ON ME!
"...BUT NOT THE GREAT CAPTAIN HIMSELF, NO! HE EVEN RATIONS HIS BEERS!"
WANT TO SMOKE, FRIEND?
NO, THANKS... AT LEAST ONE OF US OUGHT TO KEEP A CLEAR HEAD TONIGHT.

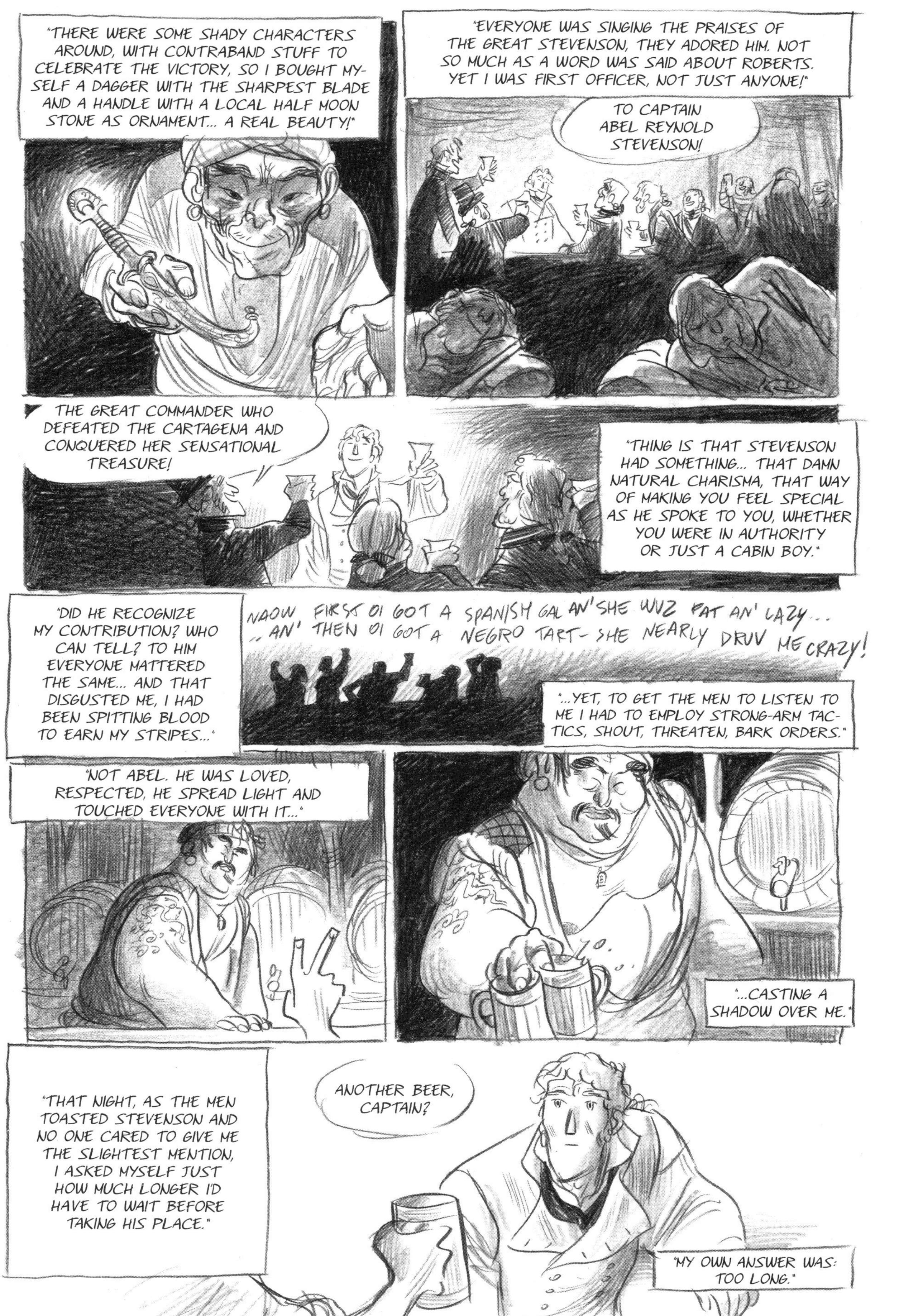
"THERE WERE SOME SHADY CHARACTERS AROUND, WITH CONTRABAND STUFF TO CELEBRATE THE VICTORY, SO I BOUGHT MY-SELF A DAGGER WITH THE SHARPEST BLADE AND A HANDLE WITH A LOCAL HALF MOON STONE AS ORNAMENT... A REAL BEAUTY!"
"EVERYONE WAS SINGING THE PRAISES OF THE GREAT STEVENSON, THEY ADORED HIM. NOT SO MUCH AS A WORD WAS SAID ABOUT ROBERTS. YET I WAS FIRST OFFICER, NOT JUST ANYONE!"
TO CAPTAIN ABEL REYNOLD STEVENSON!
THE GREAT COMMANDER WHO DEFEATED THE CARTAGENA AND CONQUERED HER SENSATIONAL TREASURE!
"THING IS THAT STEVENSON HAD SOMETHING... THAT DAMN NATURAL CHARISMA, THAT WAY OF MAKING YOU FEEL SPECIAL AS HE SPOKE TO YOU, WHETHER YOU WERE IN AUTHORITY OR JUST A CABIN BOY."
"DID HE RECOGNIZE MY CONTRIBUTION? WHO CAN TELL? TO HIM EVERYONE MATTERED THE SAME... AND THAT DISGUSTED ME, I HAD BEEN SPITTING BLOOD TO EARN MY STRIPES..."
NAOW, FIRST OI GOT A SPANISH GAL AN' SHE WUZ FAT AN' LAZY...
... AN' THEN OI GOT A NEGRO TART- SHE NEARLY DRUV ME CRAZY!
"...YET, TO GET THE MEN TO LISTEN TO ME I HAD TO EMPLOY STRONG-ARM TAC-TICS, SHOUT, THREATEN, BARK ORDERS."
"NOT ABEL. HE WAS LOVED, RESPECTED, HE SPREAD LIGHT AND TOUCHED EVERYONE WITH IT..."
"...CASTING A SHADOW OVER ME."
"THAT NIGHT, AS THE MEN TOASTED STEVENSON AND NO ONE CARED TO GIVE ME THE SLIGHTEST MENTION, I ASKED MYSELF JUST HOW MUCH LONGER I'D HAVE TO WAIT BEFORE TAKING HIS PLACE."
ANOTHER BEER, CAPTAIN?
"MY OWN ANSWER WAS: TOO LONG."

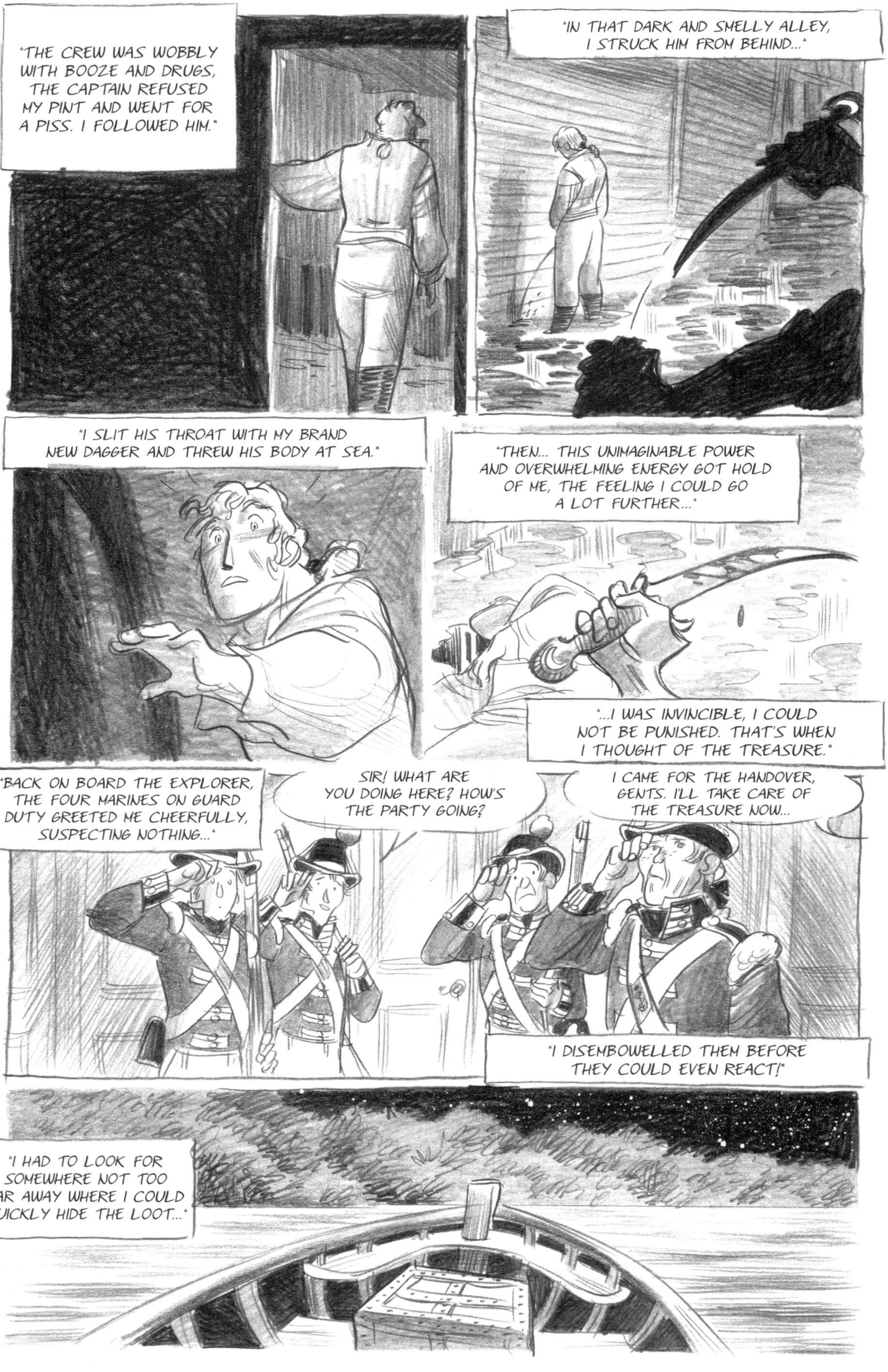
"THE CREW WAS WOBBLY WITH BOOZE AND DRUGS, THE CAPTAIN REFUSED MY PINT AND WENT FOR A PISS. I FOLLOWED HIM."
"IN THAT DARK AND SMELLY ALLEY, I STRUCK HIM FROM BEHIND..."
"I SLIT HIS THROAT WITH MY BRAND NEW DAGGER AND THREW HIS BODY AT SEA."
"THEN... THIS UNIMAGINABLE POWER AND OVERWHELMING ENERGY GOT HOLD OF ME, THE FEELING I COULD GO A LOT FURTHER..."
"...I WAS INVINCIBLE, I COULD NOT BE PUNISHED. THAT'S WHEN I THOUGHT OF THE TREASURE."
"BACK ON BOARD THE EXPLORER, THE FOUR MARINES ON GUARD DUTY GREETED ME CHEERFULLY, SUSPECTING NOTHING..."
SIR! WHAT ARE YOU DOING HERE? HOW'S THE PARTY GOING?
I CAME FOR THE HANDOVER, GENTS. I'LL TAKE CARE OF THE TREASURE NOW...
"I DISEMBOWELLED THEM BEFORE THEY COULD EVEN REACT!"
"I HAD TO LOOK FOR SOMEWHERE NOT TOO FAR AWAY WHERE I COULD QUICKLY HIDE THE LOOT..."

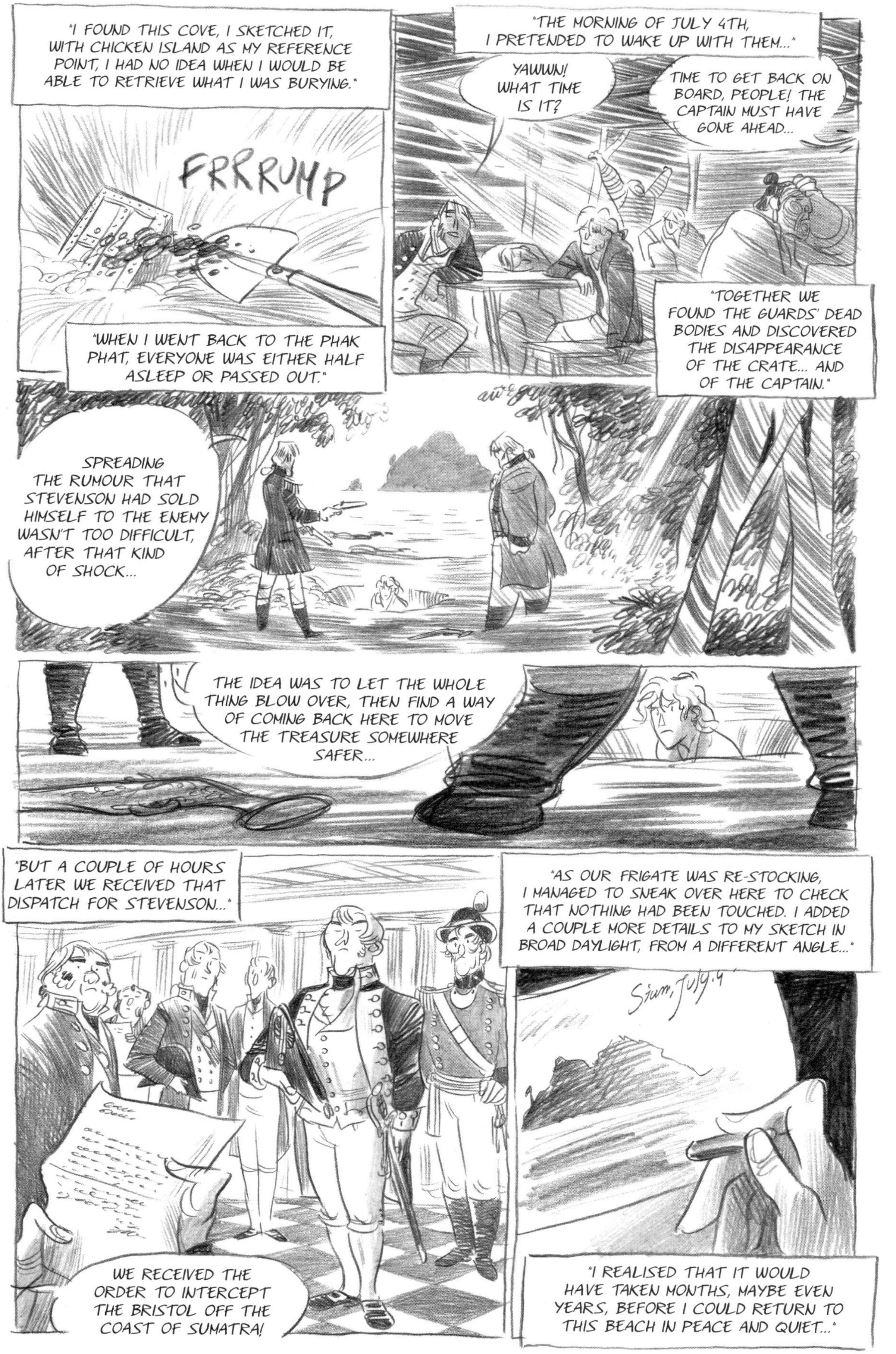
"I FOUND THIS COVE, I SKETCHED IT, WITH CHICKEN ISLAND AS MY REFERENCE POINT, I HAD NO IDEA WHEN I WOULD BE ABLE TO RETRIEVE WHAT I WAS BURYING."
FRRRUMP
"WHEN I WENT BACK TO THE PHAK PHAT, EVERYONE WAS EITHER HALF ASLEEP OR PASSED OUT."
"THE MORNING OF JULY 4TH, I PRETENDED TO WAKE UP WITH THEM..."
YAWWN! WHAT TIME IS IT?
TIME TO GET BACK ON BOARD, PEOPLE! THE CAPTAIN MUST HAVE GONE AHEAD...
"TOGETHER WE FOUND THE GUARDS' DEAD BODIES AND DISCOVERED THE DISAPPEARANCE OF THE CRATE... AND OF THE CAPTAIN."
SPREADING THE RUMOUR THAT STEVENSON HAD SOLD HIMSELF TO THE ENEMY WASN'T TOO DIFFICULT, AFTER THAT KIND OF SHOCK...
THE IDEA WAS TO LET THE WHOLE THING BLOW OVER, THEN FIND A WAY OF COMING BACK HERE TO MOVE THE TREASURE SOMEWHERE SAFER...
"BUT A COUPLE OF HOURS LATER WE RECEIVED THAT DISPATCH FOR STEVENSON..."
WE RECEIVED THE ORDER TO INTERCEPT THE BRISTOL OFF THE COAST OF SUMATRA!
"AS OUR FRIGATE WAS RE-STOCKING, I MANAGED TO SNEAK OVER HERE TO CHECK THAT NOTHING HAD BEEN TOUCHED. I ADDED A COUPLE MORE DETAILS TO MY SKETCH IN BROAD DAYLIGHT, FROM A DIFFERENT ANGLE..."
Siam, July 4
"I REALISED THAT IT WOULD HAVE TAKEN MONTHS, MAYBE EVEN YEARS, BEFORE I COULD RETURN TO THIS BEACH IN PEACE AND QUIET..."

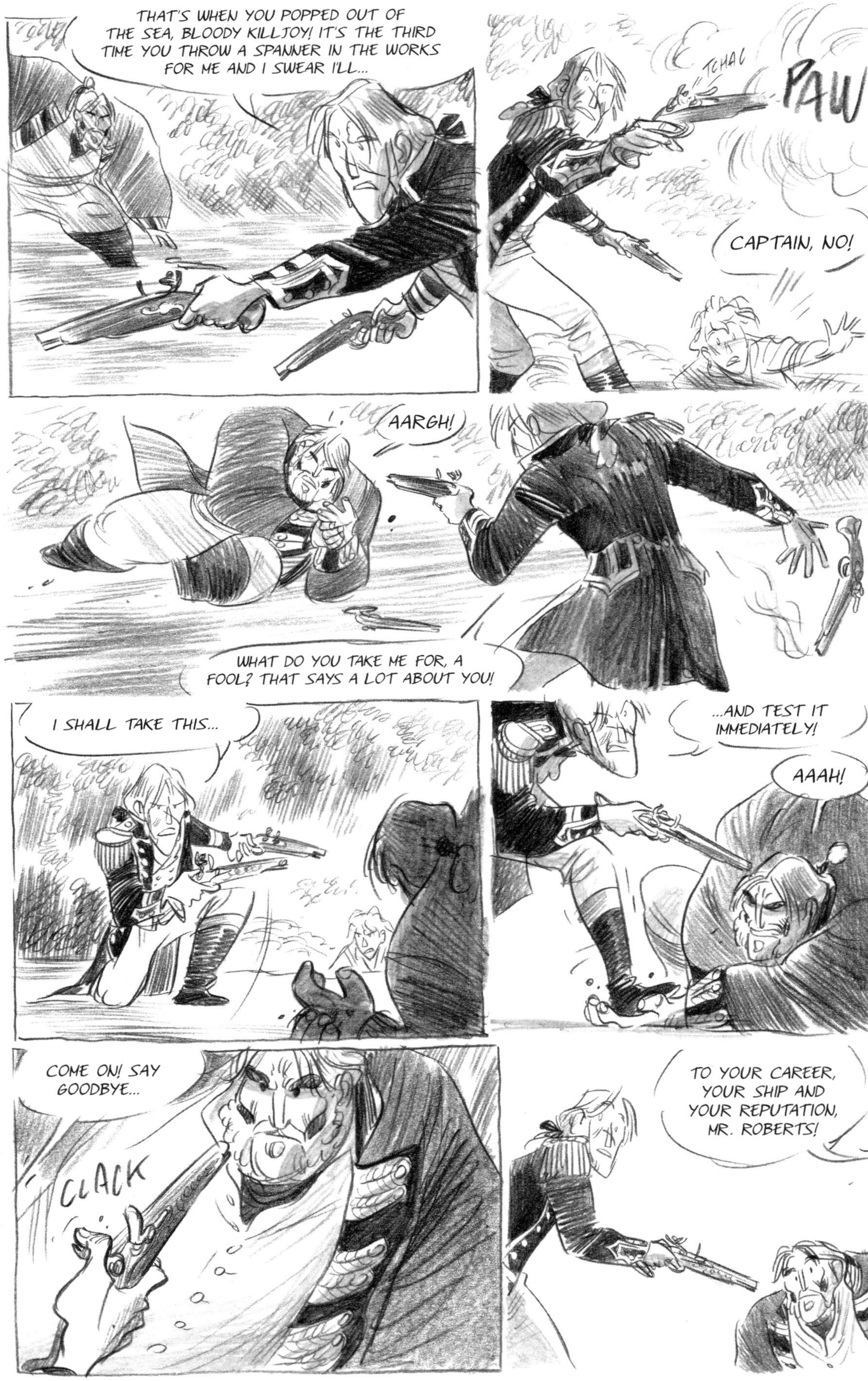
THAT'S WHEN YOU POPPED OUT OF THE SEA, BLOODY KILLJOY! IT'S THE THIRD TIME YOU THROW A SPANNER IN THE WORKS FOR ME AND I SWEAR I'LL...
TCHAC
PAW
CAPTAIN, NO!
AARGH!
WHAT DO YOU TAKE ME FOR, A FOOL? THAT SAYS A LOT ABOUT YOU!
I SHALL TAKE THIS...
...AND TEST IT IMMEDIATELY!
AAAH!
COME ON! SAY GOODBYE...
CLACK
TO YOUR CAREER, YOUR SHIP AND YOUR REPUTATION, MR. ROBERTS!

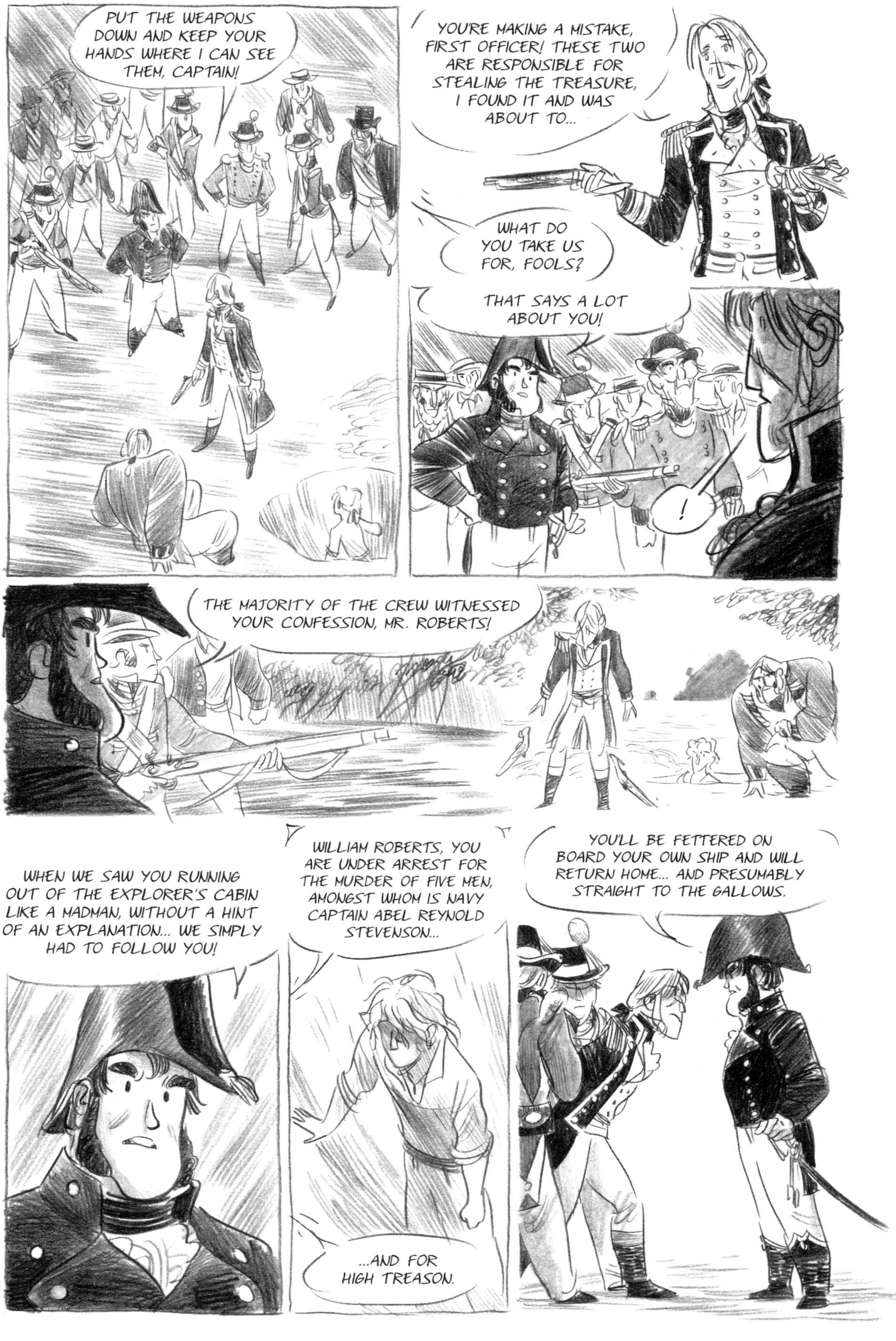
PUT THE WEAPONS DOWN AND KEEP YOUR HANDS WHERE I CAN SEE THEM, CAPTAIN!
YOU'RE MAKING A MISTAKE, FIRST OFFICER! THESE TWO ARE RESPONSIBLE FOR STEALING THE TREASURE, I FOUND IT AND WAS ABOUT TO...
WHAT DO YOU TAKE US FOR, FOOLS?
THAT SAYS A LOT ABOUT YOU!
!
THE MAJORITY OF THE CREW WITNESSED YOUR CONFESSION, MR. ROBERTS!
WHEN WE SAW YOU RUNNING OUT OF THE EXPLORER'S CABIN LIKE A MADMAN, WITHOUT A HINT OF AN EXPLANATION... WE SIMPLY HAD TO FOLLOW YOU!
WILLIAM ROBERTS, YOU ARE UNDER ARREST FOR THE MURDER OF FIVE MEN, AMONGST WHOM IS NAVY CAPTAIN ABEL REYNOLD STEVENSON...
...AND FOR HIGH TREASON.
YOU'LL BE FETTERED ON BOARD YOUR OWN SHIP AND WILL RETURN HOME... AND PRESUMABLY STRAIGHT TO THE GALLOWS.

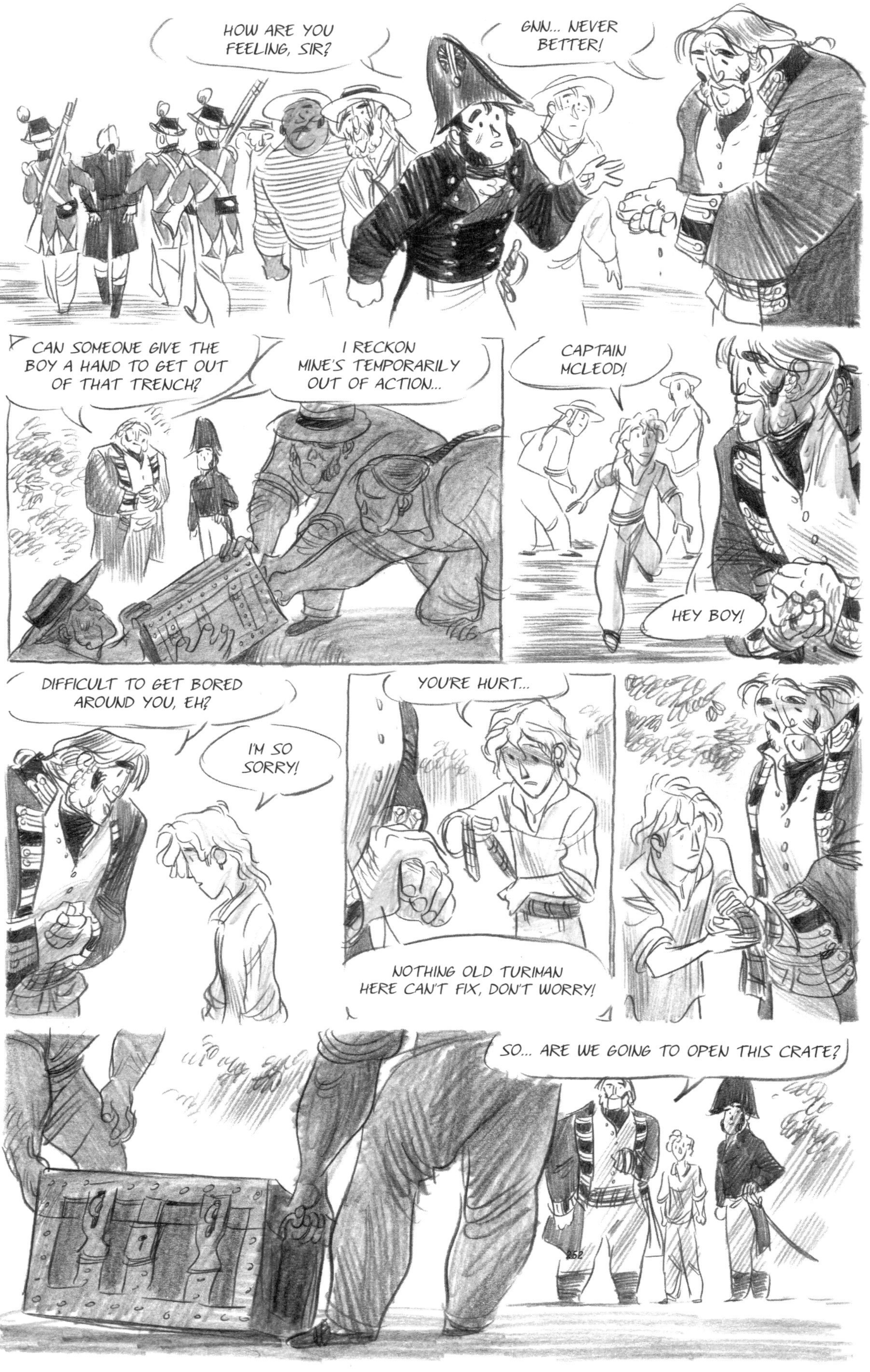
HOW ARE YOU FEELING, SIR?
GNN... NEVER BETTER!
CAN SOMEONE GIVE THE BOY A HAND TO GET OUT OF THAT TRENCH?
I RECKON MINE'S TEMPORARILY OUT OF ACTION...
CAPTAIN MCLEOD!
HEY BOY!
DIFFICULT TO GET BORED AROUND YOU, EH?
I'M SO SORRY!
YOU'RE HURT...
NOTHING OLD TURIMAN HERE CAN'T FIX, DON'T WORRY!
SO... ARE WE GOING TO OPEN THIS CRATE?

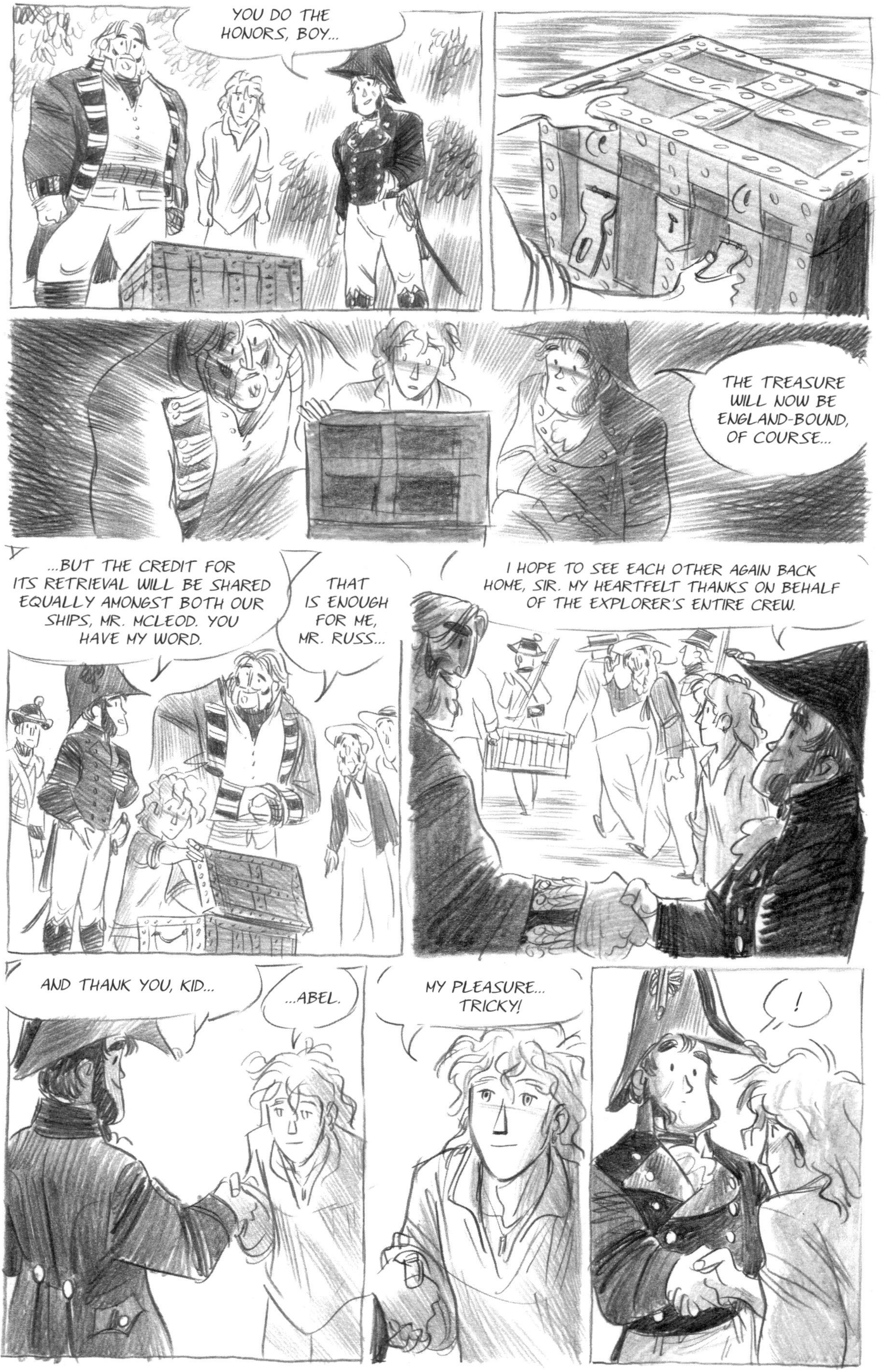
YOU DO THE HONORS, BOY...
THE TREASURE WILL NOW BE ENGLAND-BOUND, OF COURSE...
...BUT THE CREDIT FOR ITS RETRIEVAL WILL BE SHARED EQUALLY AMONGST BOTH OUR SHIPS, MR. MCLEOD. YOU HAVE MY WORD.
THAT IS ENOUGH FOR ME, MR. RUSS...
I HOPE TO SEE EACH OTHER AGAIN BACK HOME, SIR. MY HEARTFELT THANKS ON BEHALF OF THE EXPLORER'S ENTIRE CREW.
AND THANK YOU, KID...
...ABEL.
MY PLEASURE... TRICKY!
!

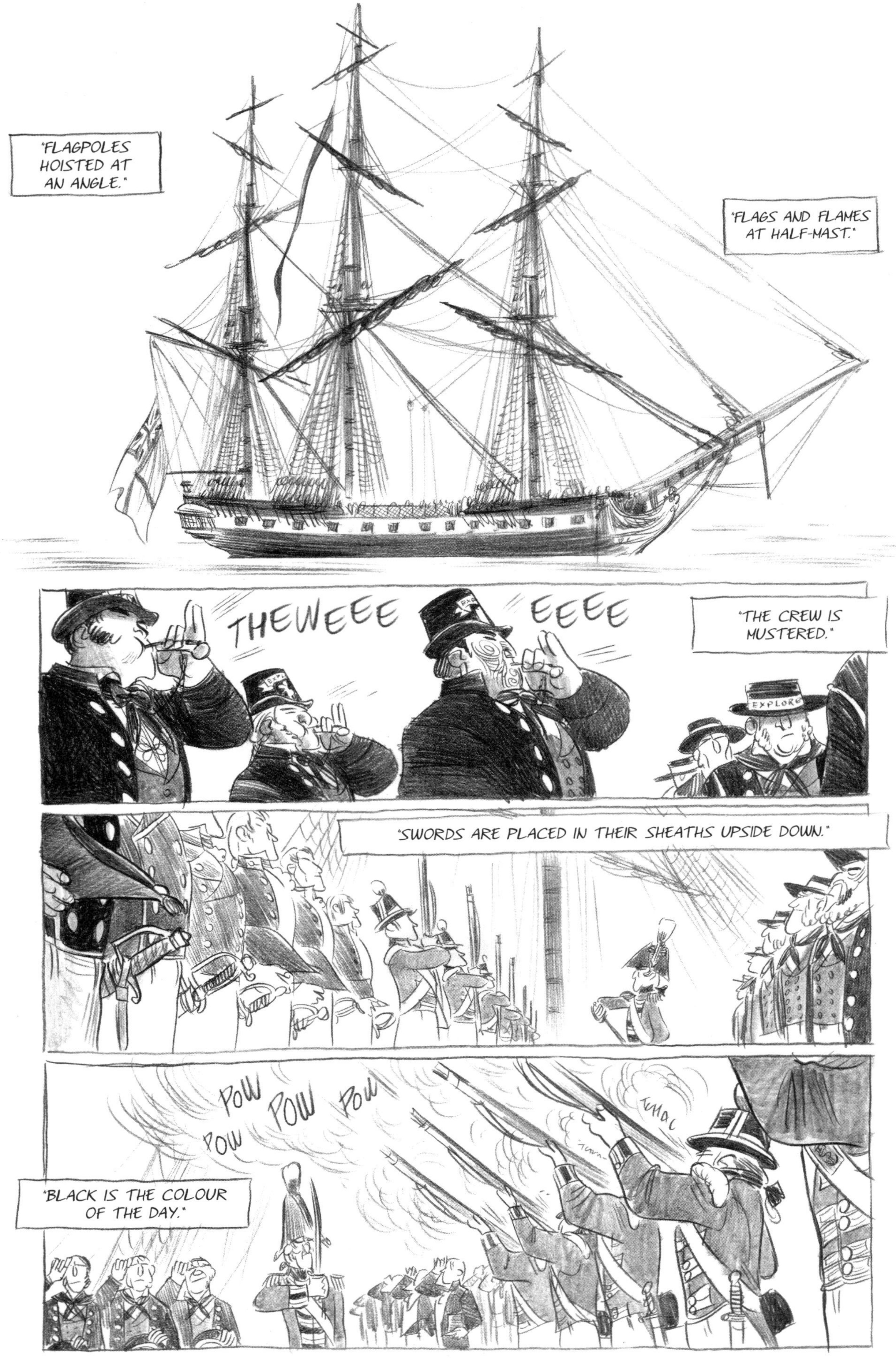
"FLAGPOLES HOISTED AT AN ANGLE."
"FLAGS AND FLAMES AT HALF-MAST."
THEWEEE EEEE
"THE CREW IS MUSTERED."
"SWORDS ARE PLACED IN THEIR SHEATHS UPSIDE DOWN."
POW POW POW POW
"BLACK IS THE COLOUR OF THE DAY."

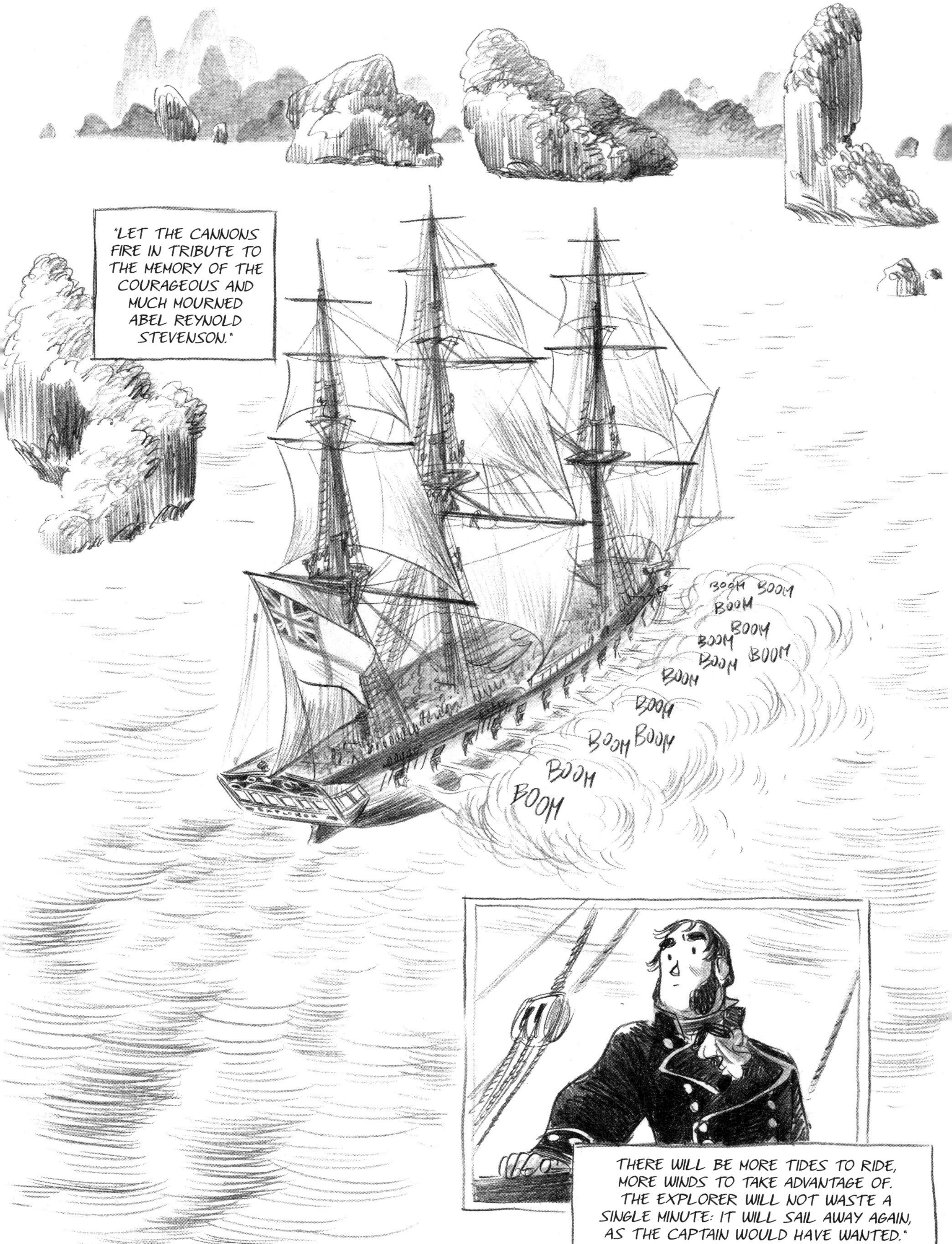
"LET THE CANNONS FIRE IN TRIBUTE TO THE MEMORY OF THE COURAGEOUS AND MUCH MOURNED ABEL REYNOLD STEVENSON."
BOOM BOOM BOOM BOOM BOOM BOOM BOOM BOOM BOOM BOOM BOOM BOOM BOOM
THERE WILL BE MORE TIDES TO RIDE, MORE WINDS TO TAKE ADVANTAGE OF. THE EXPLORER WILL NOT WASTE A SINGLE MINUTE: IT WILL SAIL AWAY AGAIN, AS THE CAPTAIN WOULD HAVE WANTED."

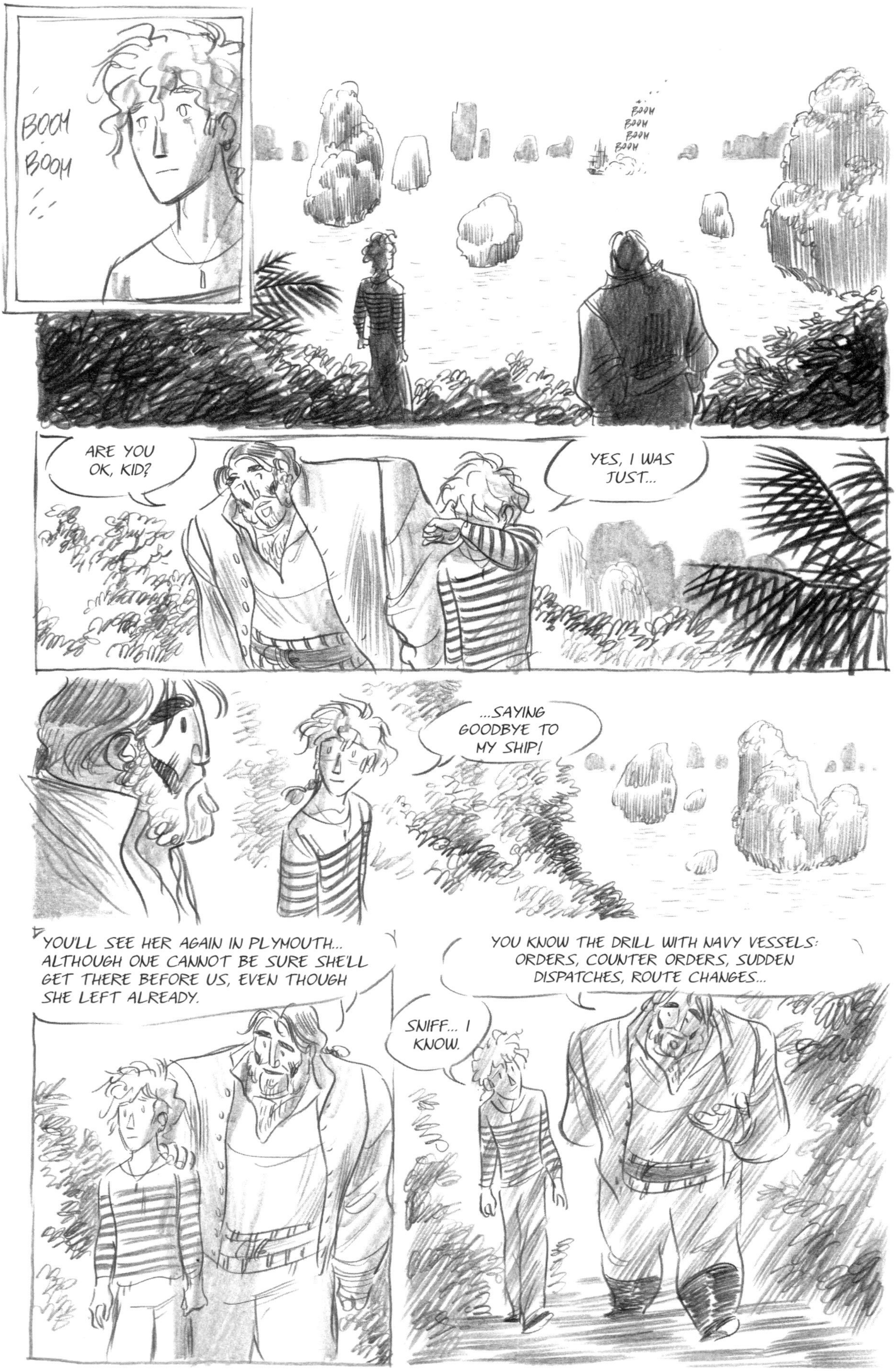
BOOM
BOOM
BOOM
BOOM
BOOM
BOOM
ARE YOU OK, KID?
YES, I WAS JUST...
...SAYING GOODBYE TO MY SHIP!
YOU'LL SEE HER AGAIN IN PLYMOUTH... ALTHOUGH ONE CANNOT BE SURE SHE'LL GET THERE BEFORE US, EVEN THOUGH SHE LEFT ALREADY.
YOU KNOW THE DRILL WITH NAVY VESSELS: ORDERS, COUNTER ORDERS, SUDDEN DISPATCHES, ROUTE CHANGES...
SNIFF... I KNOW.

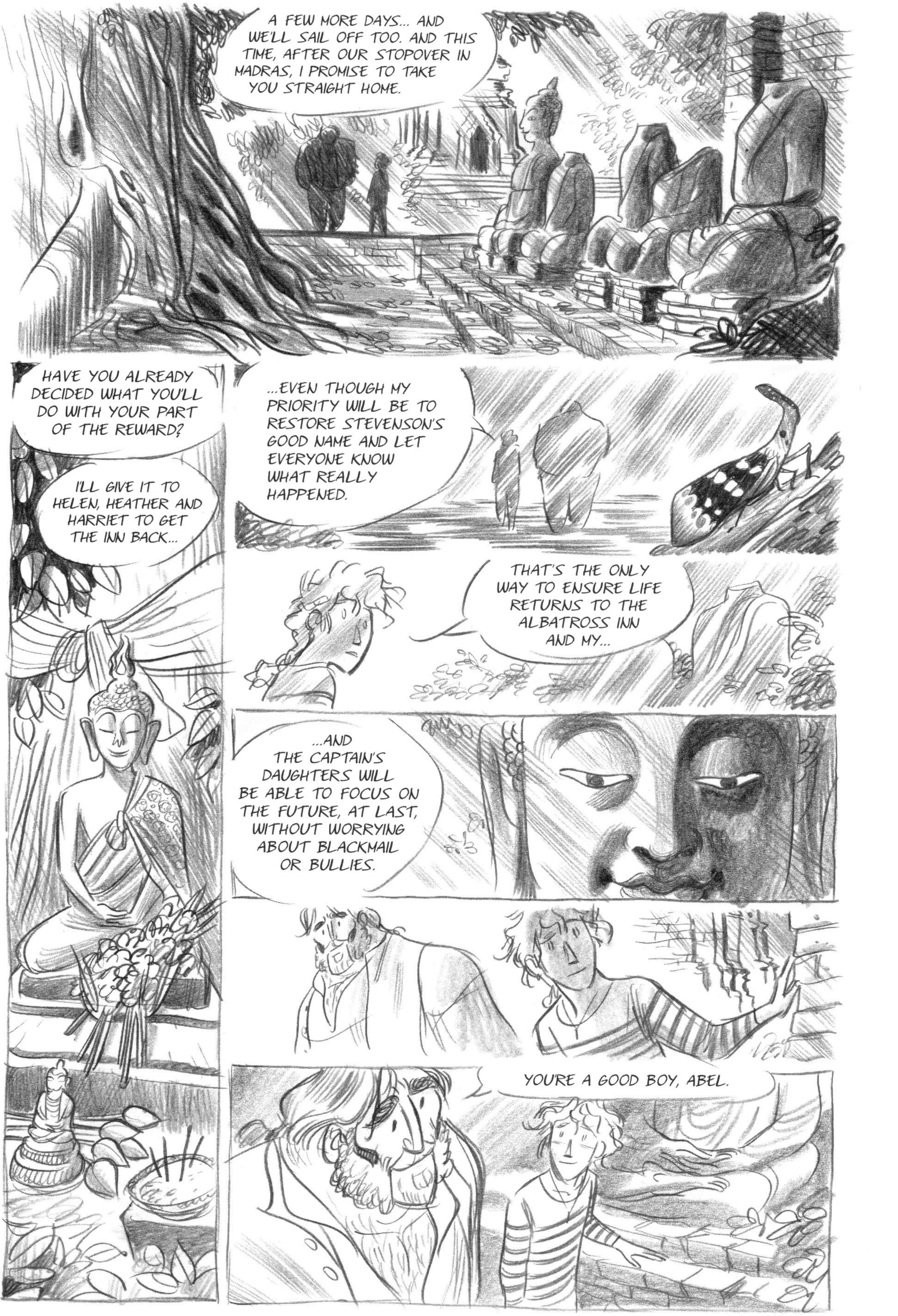
A FEW MORE DAYS... AND WE'LL SAIL OFF TOO. AND THIS TIME, AFTER OUR STOPOVER IN MADRAS, I PROMISE TO TAKE YOU STRAIGHT HOME.
HAVE YOU ALREADY DECIDED WHAT YOU'LL DO WITH YOUR PART OF THE REWARD?
I'LL GIVE IT TO HELEN, HEATHER AND HARRIET TO GET THE INN BACK...
...EVEN THOUGH MY PRIORITY WILL BE TO RESTORE STEVENSON'S GOOD NAME AND LET EVERYONE KNOW WHAT REALLY HAPPENED.
THAT'S THE ONLY WAY TO ENSURE LIFE RETURNS TO THE ALBATROSS INN AND MY...
...AND THE CAPTAIN'S DAUGHTERS WILL BE ABLE TO FOCUS ON THE FUTURE, AT LAST, WITHOUT WORRYING ABOUT BLACKMAIL OR BULLIES.
YOU'RE A GOOD BOY, ABEL.

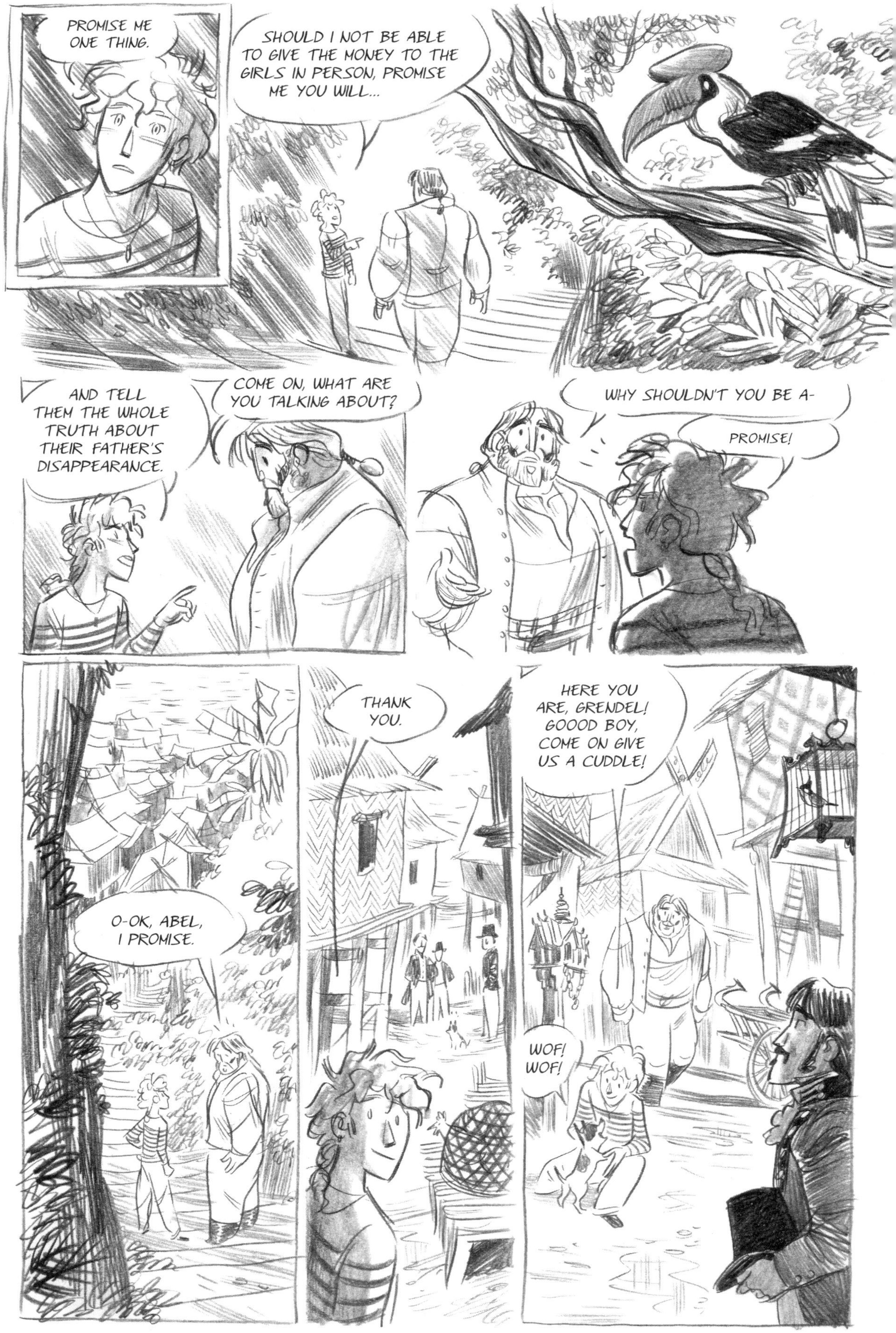
PROMISE ME ONE THING.
SHOULD I NOT BE ABLE TO GIVE THE MONEY TO THE GIRLS IN PERSON, PROMISE ME YOU WILL...
AND TELL THEM THE WHOLE TRUTH ABOUT THEIR FATHER'S DISAPPEARANCE.
COME ON, WHAT ARE YOU TALKING ABOUT?
WHY SHOULDN'T YOU BE A-
PROMISE!
O-OK, ABEL, I PROMISE.
THANK YOU.
HERE YOU ARE, GRENDEL! GOOOD BOY, COME ON GIVE US A CUDDLE!
WOF! WOF!

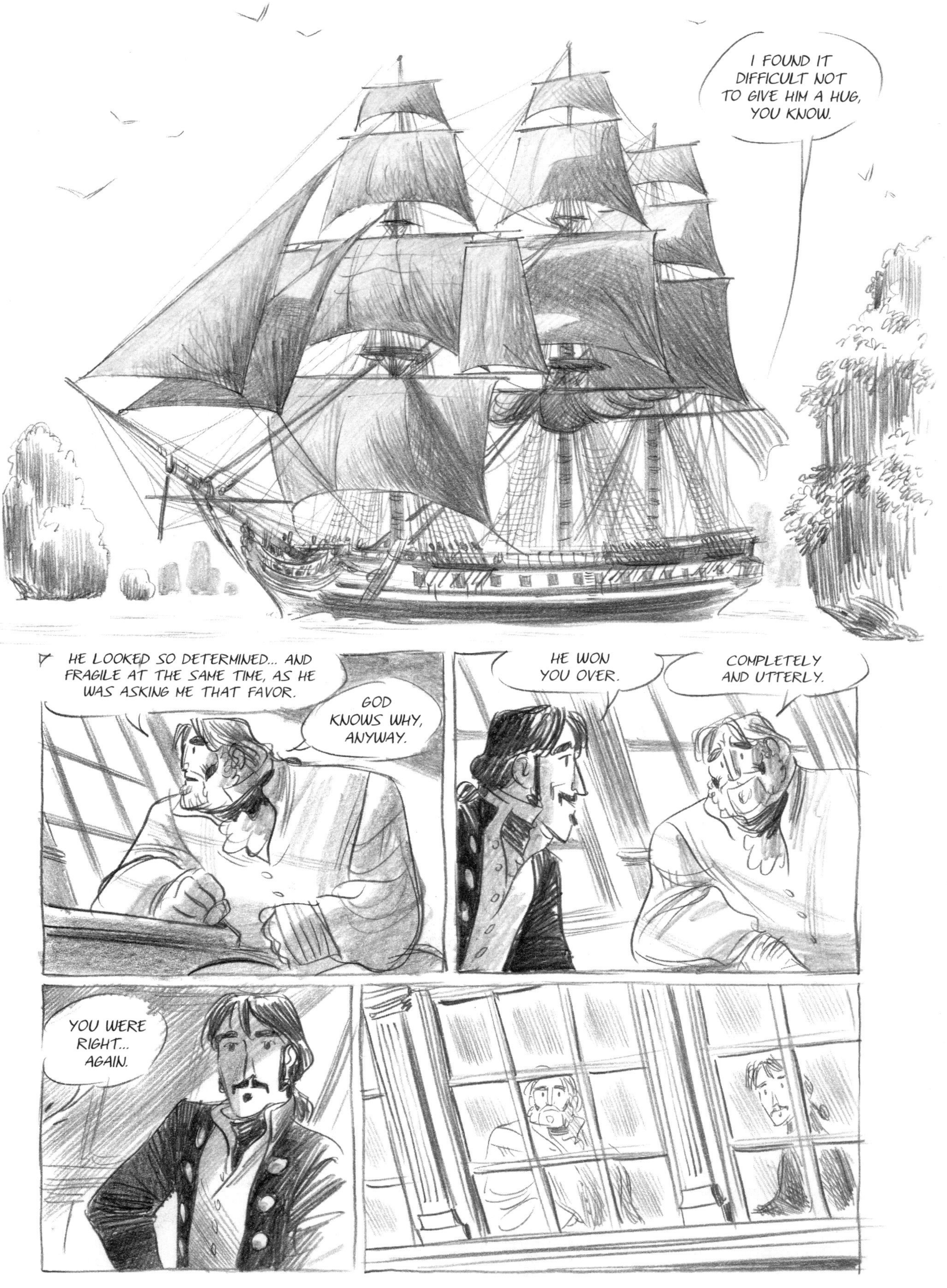
I FOUND IT DIFFICULT NOT TO GIVE HIM A HUG, YOU KNOW.
HE LOOKED SO DETERMINED... AND FRAGILE AT THE SAME TIME, AS HE WAS ASKING ME THAT FAVOR.
GOD KNOWS WHY, ANYWAY.
HE WON YOU OVER.
COMPLETELY AND UTTERLY.
YOU WERE RIGHT... AGAIN.

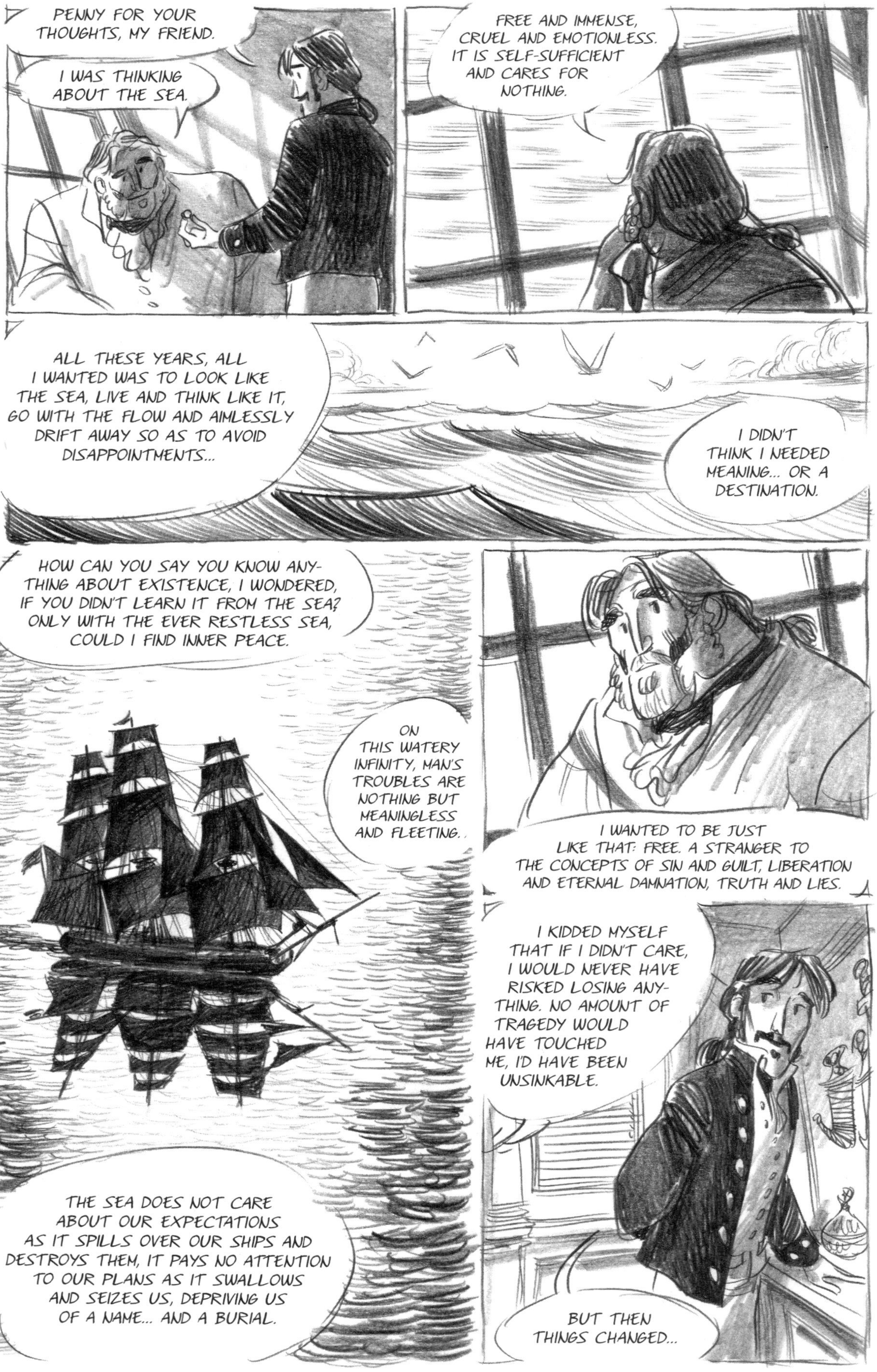
PENNY FOR YOUR THOUGHTS, MY FRIEND.
I WAS THINKING ABOUT THE SEA.
FREE AND IMMENSE, CRUEL AND EMOTIONLESS. IT IS SELF-SUFFICIENT AND CARES FOR NOTHING.
ALL THESE YEARS, ALL I WANTED WAS TO LOOK LIKE THE SEA, LIVE AND THINK LIKE IT, GO WITH THE FLOW AND AIMLESSLY DRIFT AWAY SO AS TO AVOID DISAPPOINTMENTS...
I DIDN'T THINK I NEEDED MEANING... OR A DESTINATION.
HOW CAN YOU SAY YOU KNOW ANYTHING ABOUT EXISTENCE, I WONDERED, IF YOU DIDN'T LEARN IT FROM THE SEA? ONLY WITH THE EVER RESTLESS SEA, COULD I FIND INNER PEACE.
ON THIS WATERY INFINITY, MAN'S TROUBLES ARE NOTHING BUT MEANINGLESS AND FLEETING.
THE SEA DOES NOT CARE ABOUT OUR EXPECTATIONS AS IT SPILLS OVER OUR SHIPS AND DESTROYS THEM, IT PAYS NO ATTENTION TO OUR PLANS AS IT SWALLOWS AND SEIZES US, DEPRIVING US OF A NAME... AND A BURIAL.
I WANTED TO BE JUST LIKE THAT: FREE. A STRANGER TO THE CONCEPTS OF SIN AND GUILT, LIBERATION AND ETERNAL DAMNATION, TRUTH AND LIES.
I KIDDED MYSELF THAT IF I DIDN'T CARE, I WOULD NEVER HAVE RISKED LOSING ANYTHING. NO AMOUNT OF TRAGEDY WOULD HAVE TOUCHED ME, I'D HAVE BEEN UNSINKABLE.
BUT THEN THINGS CHANGED...

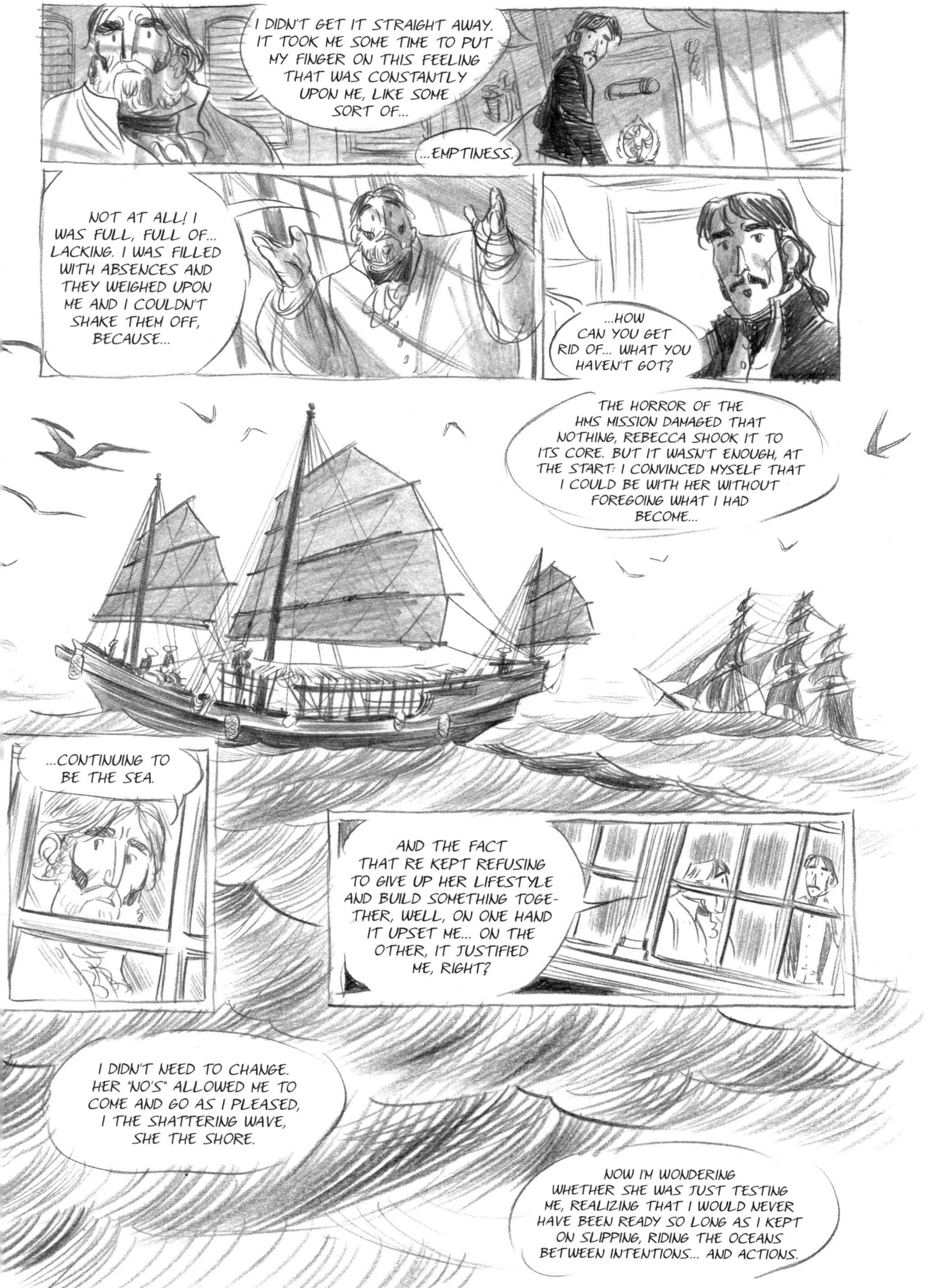
I DIDN'T GET IT STRAIGHT AWAY. IT TOOK ME SOME TIME TO PUT MY FINGER ON THIS FEELING THAT WAS CONSTANTLY UPON ME, LIKE SOME SORT OF...
...EMPTINESS.
NOT AT ALL! I WAS FULL, FULL OF... LACKING. I WAS FILLED WITH ABSENCES AND THEY WEIGHED UPON ME AND I COULDN'T SHAKE THEM OFF, BECAUSE...
...HOW CAN YOU GET RID OF... WHAT YOU HAVEN'T GOT?
THE HORROR OF THE HMS MISSION DAMAGED THAT NOTHING, REBECCA SHOOK IT TO ITS CORE. BUT IT WASN'T ENOUGH, AT THE START: I CONVINCED MYSELF THAT I COULD BE WITH HER WITHOUT FOREGOING WHAT I HAD BECOME...
...CONTINUING TO BE THE SEA.
AND THE FACT THAT RE KEPT REFUSING TO GIVE UP HER LIFESTYLE AND BUILD SOMETHING TOGE-THER, WELL, ON ONE HAND IT UPSET ME... ON THE OTHER, IT JUSTIFIED ME, RIGHT?
I DIDN'T NEED TO CHANGE. HER "NO'S" ALLOWED ME TO COME AND GO AS I PLEASED, I THE SHATTERING WAVE, SHE THE SHORE.
NOW I'M WONDERING WHETHER SHE WAS JUST TESTING ME, REALIZING THAT I WOULD NEVER HAVE BEEN READY SO LONG AS I KEPT ON SLIPPING, RIDING THE OCEANS BETWEEN INTENTIONS... AND ACTIONS.

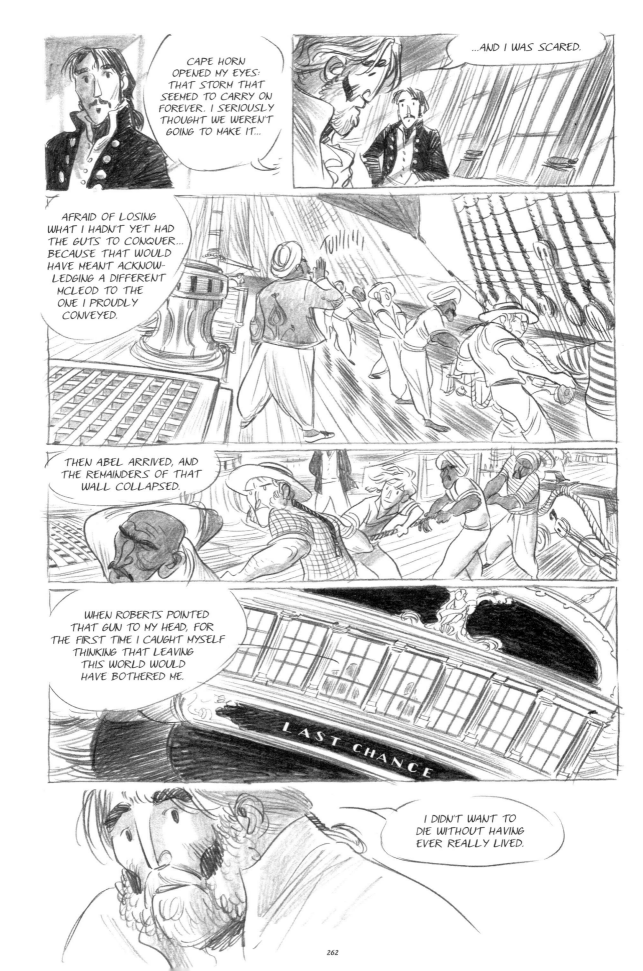

CAPE HORN OPENED MY EYES: THAT STORM THAT SEEMED TO CARRY ON FOREVER. I SERIOUSLY THOUGHT WE WEREN'T GOING TO MAKE IT...

...AND I WAS SCARED.

AFRAID OF LOSING WHAT I HADN'T YET HAD THE GUTS TO CONQUER... BECAUSE THAT WOULD HAVE MEANT ACKNOW- LEDGING A DIFFERENT MCLEOD TO THE ONE I PROUDLY CONVEYED.

THEN ABEL ARRIVED, AND THE REMAINDERS OF THAT WALL COLLAPSED.

WHEN ROBERTS POINTED THAT GUN TO MY HEAD, FOR THE FIRST TIME I CAUGHT MYSELF THINKING THAT LEAVING THIS WORLD WOULD HAVE BOTHERED ME.

LAST CHANCE

I DIDN'T WANT TO DIE WITHOUT HAVING EVER REALLY LIVED.

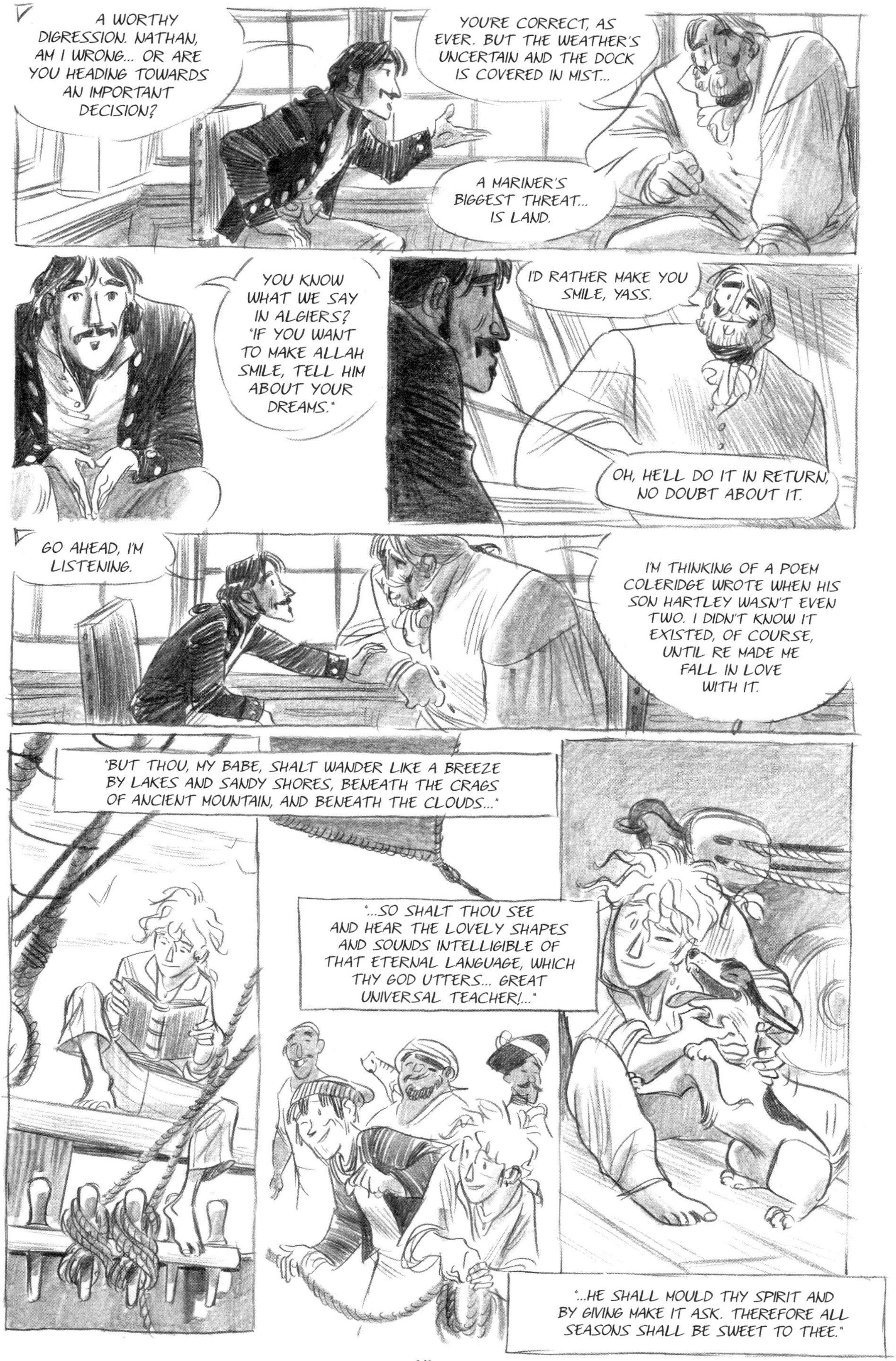
A WORTHY DIGRESSION. NATHAN, AM I WRONG... OR ARE YOU HEADING TOWARDS AN IMPORTANT DECISION?
YOU'RE CORRECT, AS EVER. BUT THE WEATHER'S UNCERTAIN AND THE DOCK IS COVERED IN MIST...
A MARINER'S BIGGEST THREAT... IS LAND.
YOU KNOW WHAT WE SAY IN ALGIERS? "IF YOU WANT TO MAKE ALLAH SMILE, TELL HIM ABOUT YOUR DREAMS."
I'D RATHER MAKE YOU SMILE, YASS.
OH, HE'LL DO IT IN RETURN, NO DOUBT ABOUT IT.
GO AHEAD, I'M LISTENING.
I'M THINKING OF A POEM COLERIDGE WROTE WHEN HIS SON HARTLEY WASN'T EVEN TWO. I DIDN'T KNOW IT EXISTED, OF COURSE, UNTIL RE MADE ME FALL IN LOVE WITH IT.
"BUT THOU, MY BABE, SHALT WANDER LIKE A BREEZE BY LAKES AND SANDY SHORES, BENEATH THE CRAGS OF ANCIENT MOUNTAIN, AND BENEATH THE CLOUDS..."
"...SO SHALT THOU SEE AND HEAR THE LOVELY SHAPES AND SOUNDS INTELLIGIBLE OF THAT ETERNAL LANGUAGE, WHICH THY GOD UTTERS... GREAT UNIVERSAL TEACHER!..."
"...HE SHALL MOULD THY SPIRIT AND BY GIVING MAKE IT ASK. THEREFORE ALL SEASONS SHALL BE SWEET TO THEE."

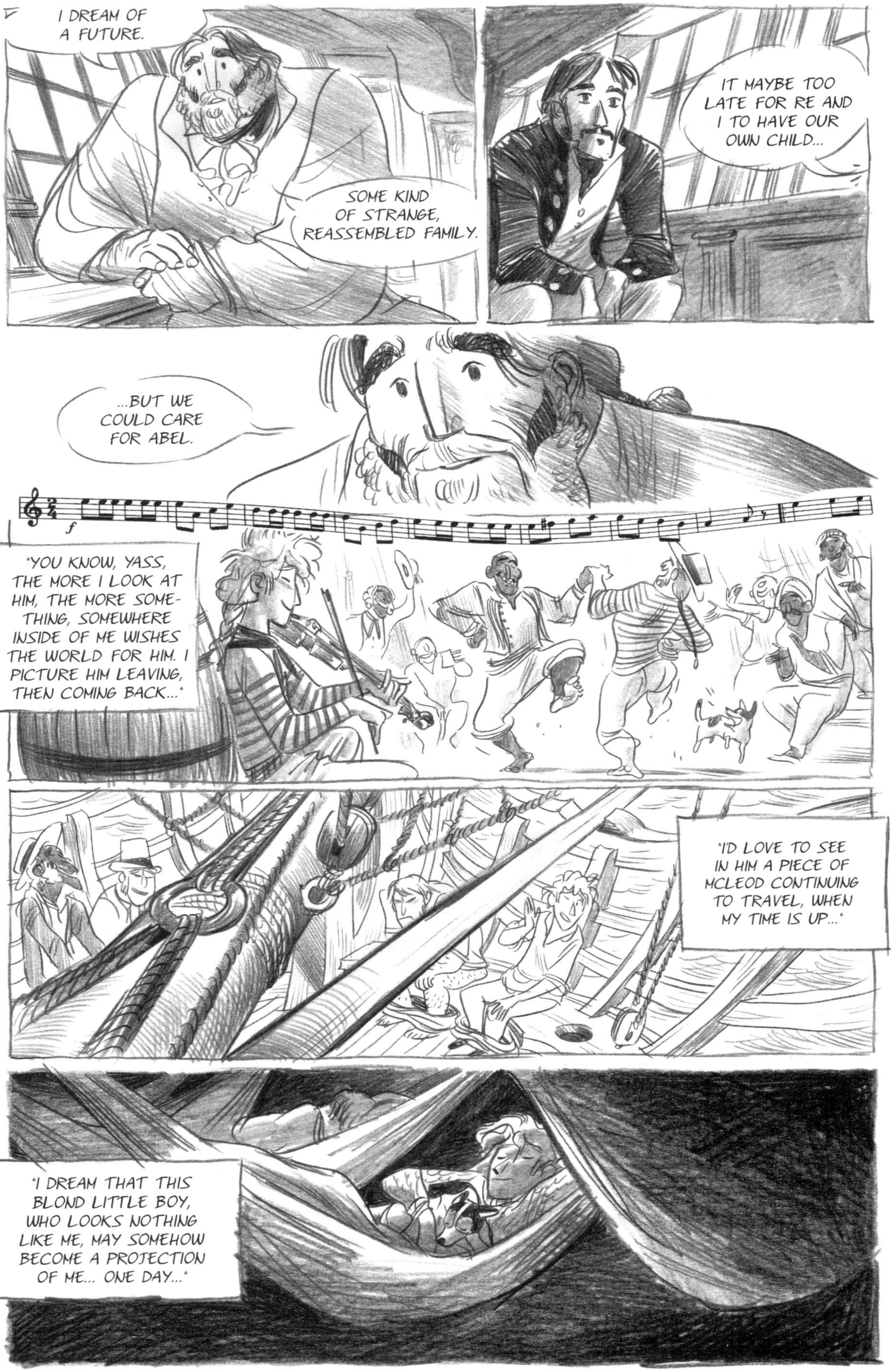
I DREAM OF A FUTURE.
SOME KIND OF STRANGE, REASSEMBLED FAMILY.
IT MAYBE TOO LATE FOR RE AND I TO HAVE OUR OWN CHILD...
...BUT WE COULD CARE FOR ABEL.
"YOU KNOW, YASS, THE MORE I LOOK AT HIM, THE MORE SOME-THING, SOMEWHERE INSIDE OF ME WISHES THE WORLD FOR HIM. I PICTURE HIM LEAVING, THEN COMING BACK..."
"I'D LOVE TO SEE IN HIM A PIECE OF MCLEOD CONTINUING TO TRAVEL, WHEN MY TIME IS UP..."
"I DREAM THAT THIS BLOND LITTLE BOY, WHO LOOKS NOTHING LIKE ME, MAY SOMEHOW BECOME A PROJECTION OF ME... ONE DAY..."

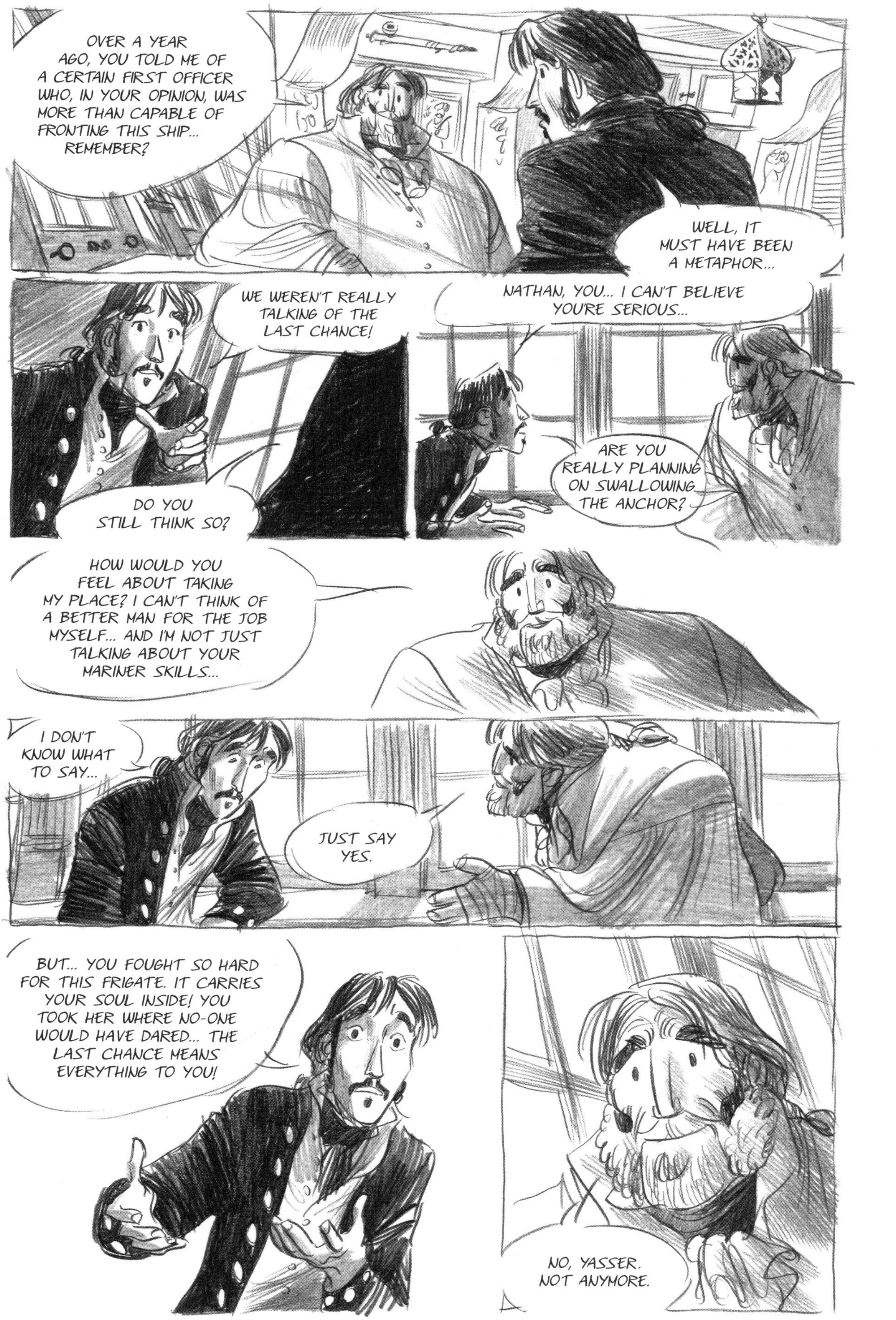

OVER A YEAR AGO, YOU TOLD ME OF A CERTAIN FIRST OFFICER WHO, IN YOUR OPINION, WAS MORE THAN CAPABLE OF FRONTING THIS SHIP... REMEMBER?
WELL, IT MUST HAVE BEEN A METAPHOR...
WE WEREN'T REALLY TALKING OF THE LAST CHANCE!
DO YOU STILL THINK SO?
NATHAN, YOU... I CAN'T BELIEVE YOU'RE SERIOUS...
ARE YOU REALLY PLANNING ON SWALLOWING THE ANCHOR?
HOW WOULD YOU FEEL ABOUT TAKING MY PLACE? I CAN'T THINK OF A BETTER MAN FOR THE JOB MYSELF... AND I'M NOT JUST TALKING ABOUT YOUR MARINER SKILLS...
I DON'T KNOW WHAT TO SAY...
JUST SAY YES.
BUT... YOU FOUGHT SO HARD FOR THIS FRIGATE. IT CARRIES YOUR SOUL INSIDE! YOU TOOK HER WHERE NO-ONE WOULD HAVE DARED... THE LAST CHANCE MEANS EVERYTHING TO YOU!
NO, YASSER. NOT ANYMORE.

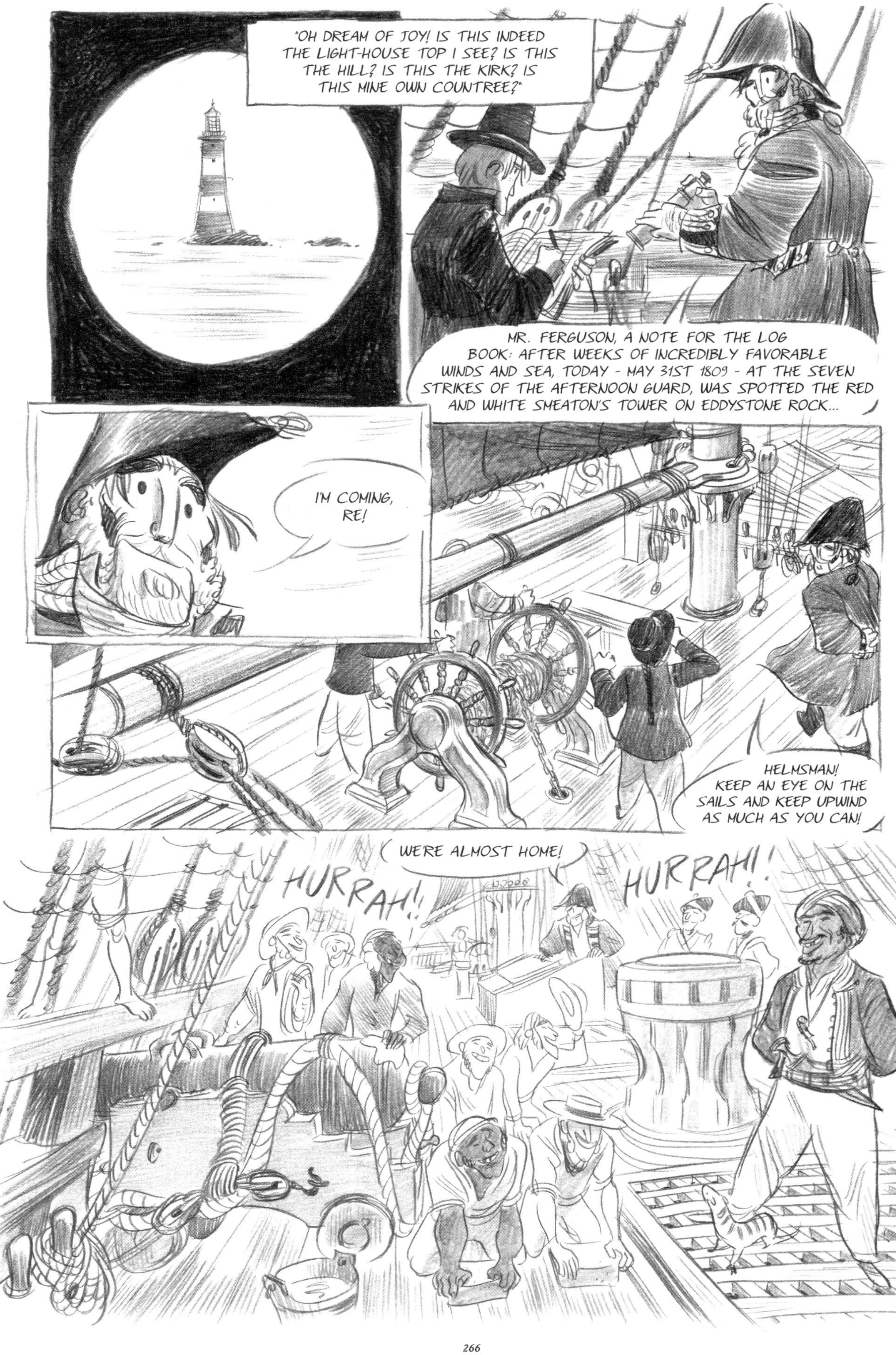
"OH DREAM OF JOY! IS THIS INDEED THE LIGHT-HOUSE TOP I SEE? IS THIS THE HILL? IS THIS THE KIRK? IS THIS MINE OWN COUNTREE?"
MR. FERGUSON, A NOTE FOR THE LOG BOOK: AFTER WEEKS OF INCREDIBLY FAVORABLE WINDS AND SEA, TODAY - MAY 31ST 1809 - AT THE SEVEN STRIKES OF THE AFTERNOON GUARD, WAS SPOTTED THE RED AND WHITE SMEATON'S TOWER ON EDDYSTONE ROCK...
I'M COMING, RE!
HELMSMAN! KEEP AN EYE ON THE SAILS AND KEEP UPWIND AS MUCH AS YOU CAN!
WE'RE ALMOST HOME!
HURRAH!!
HURRAH!

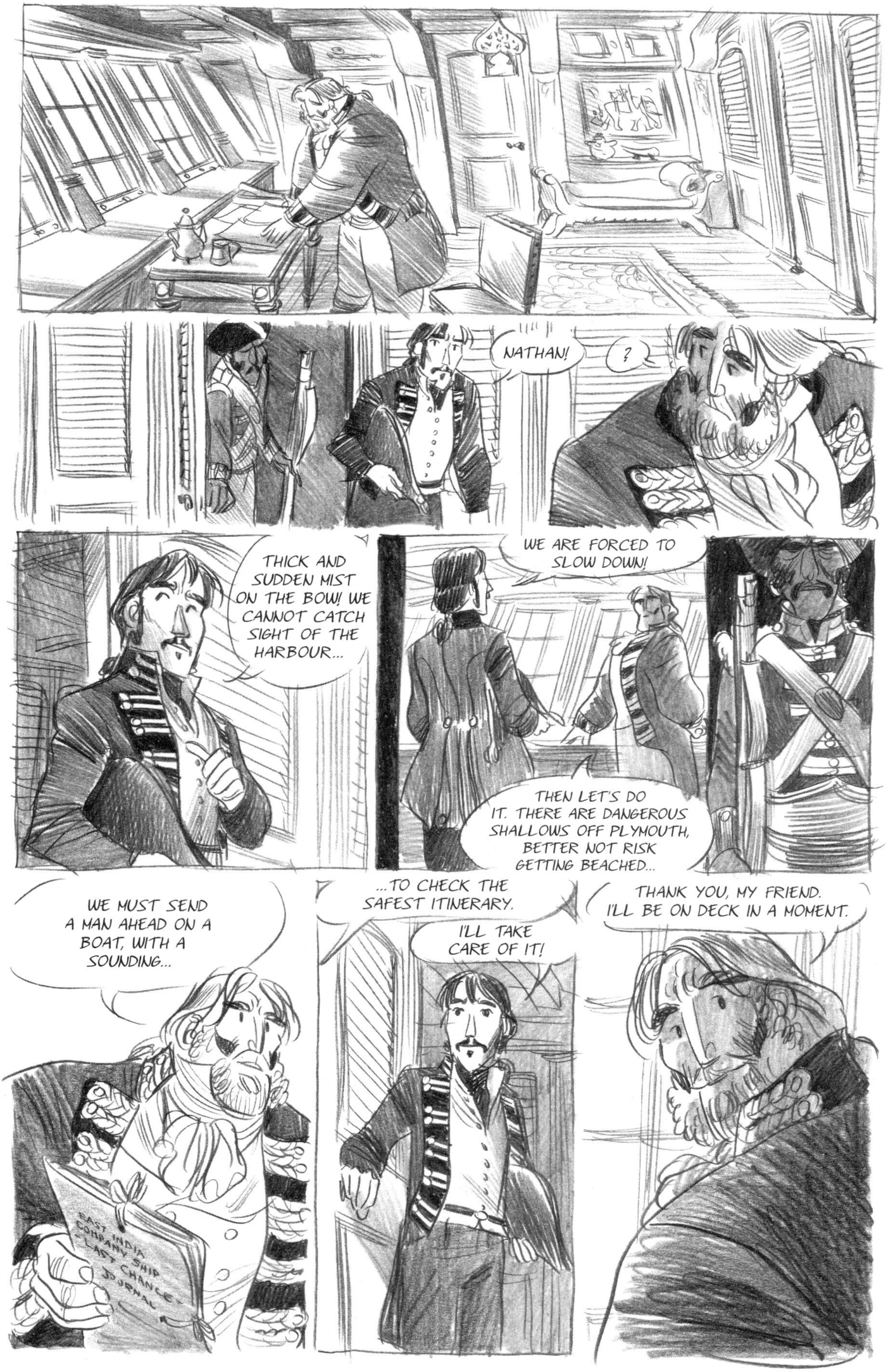
NATHAN!
?
THICK AND SUDDEN MIST ON THE BOW! WE CANNOT CATCH SIGHT OF THE HARBOUR...
WE ARE FORCED TO SLOW DOWN!
THEN LET'S DO IT. THERE ARE DANGEROUS SHALLOWS OFF PLYMOUTH, BETTER NOT RISK GETTING BEACHED...
WE MUST SEND A MAN AHEAD ON A BOAT, WITH A SOUNDING...
EAST INDIA COMPANY SHIP -LADY CHANCE- JOURNAL
...TO CHECK THE SAFEST ITINERARY.
I'LL TAKE CARE OF IT!
THANK YOU, MY FRIEND. I'LL BE ON DECK IN A MOMENT.

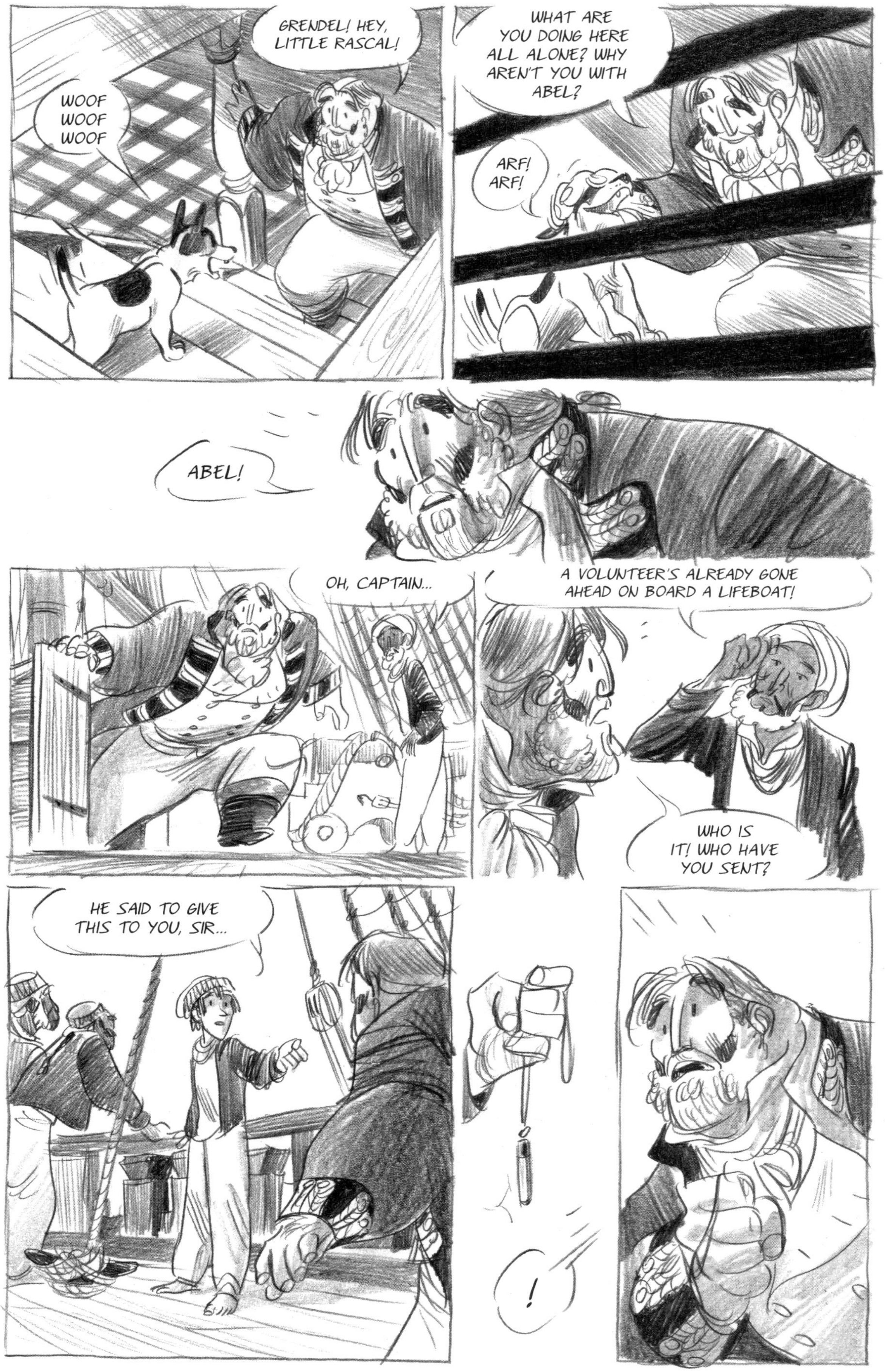

GRENDEL! HEY, LITTLE RASCAL!
WOOF WOOF WOOF
WHAT ARE YOU DOING HERE ALL ALONE? WHY AREN'T YOU WITH ABEL?
ARF! ARF!
ABEL!
OH, CAPTAIN...
A VOLUNTEER'S ALREADY GONE AHEAD ON BOARD A LIFEBOAT!
WHO IS IT! WHO HAVE YOU SENT?
HE SAID TO GIVE THIS TO YOU, SIR...
!

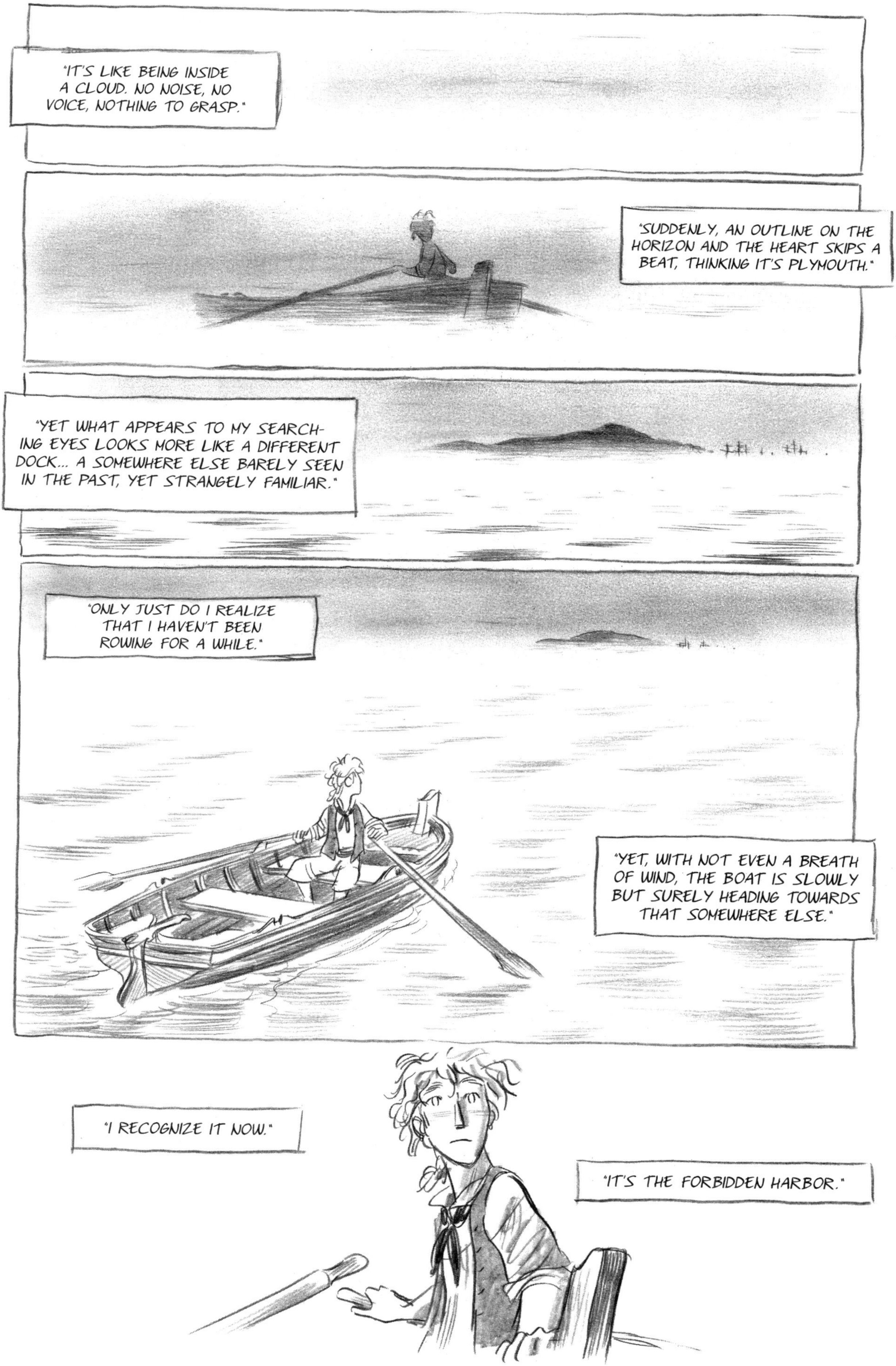
"IT'S LIKE BEING INSIDE A CLOUD. NO NOISE, NO VOICE, NOTHING TO GRASP."
"SUDDENLY, AN OUTLINE ON THE HORIZON AND THE HEART SKIPS A BEAT, THINKING IT'S PLYMOUTH."
"YET WHAT APPEARS TO MY SEARCHING EYES LOOKS MORE LIKE A DIFFERENT DOCK... A SOMEWHERE ELSE BARELY SEEN IN THE PAST, YET STRANGELY FAMILIAR."
"ONLY JUST DO I REALIZE THAT I HAVEN'T BEEN ROWING FOR A WHILE."
"YET, WITH NOT EVEN A BREATH OF WIND, THE BOAT IS SLOWLY BUT SURELY HEADING TOWARDS THAT SOMEWHERE ELSE."
"I RECOGNIZE IT NOW."
"IT'S THE FORBIDDEN HARBOR."

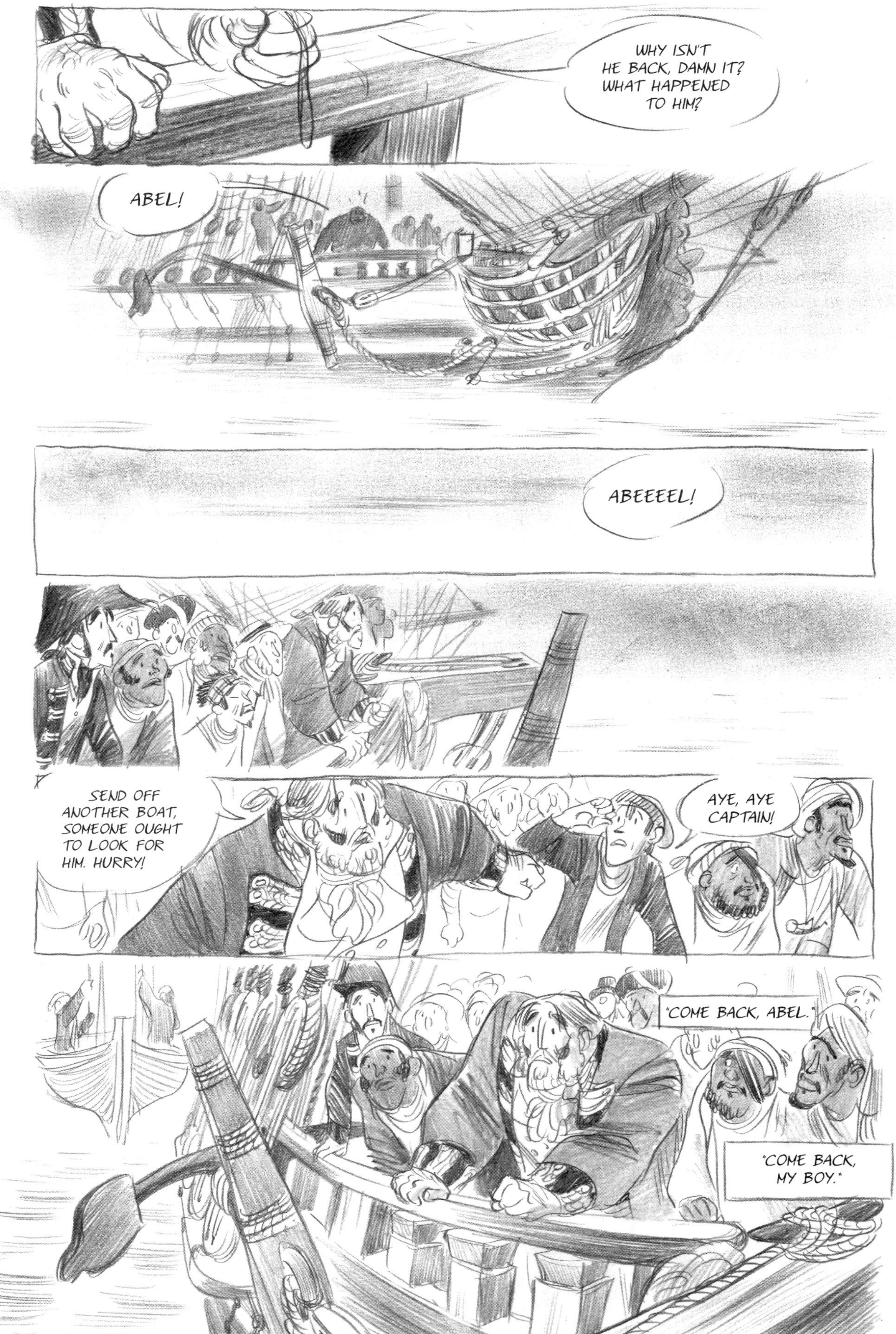

WHY ISN'T HE BACK, DAMN IT? WHAT HAPPENED TO HIM?
ABEL!
ABEEEEL!
SEND OFF ANOTHER BOAT, SOMEONE OUGHT TO LOOK FOR HIM. HURRY!
AYE, AYE CAPTAIN!
"COME BACK, ABEL."
"COME BACK, MY BOY."

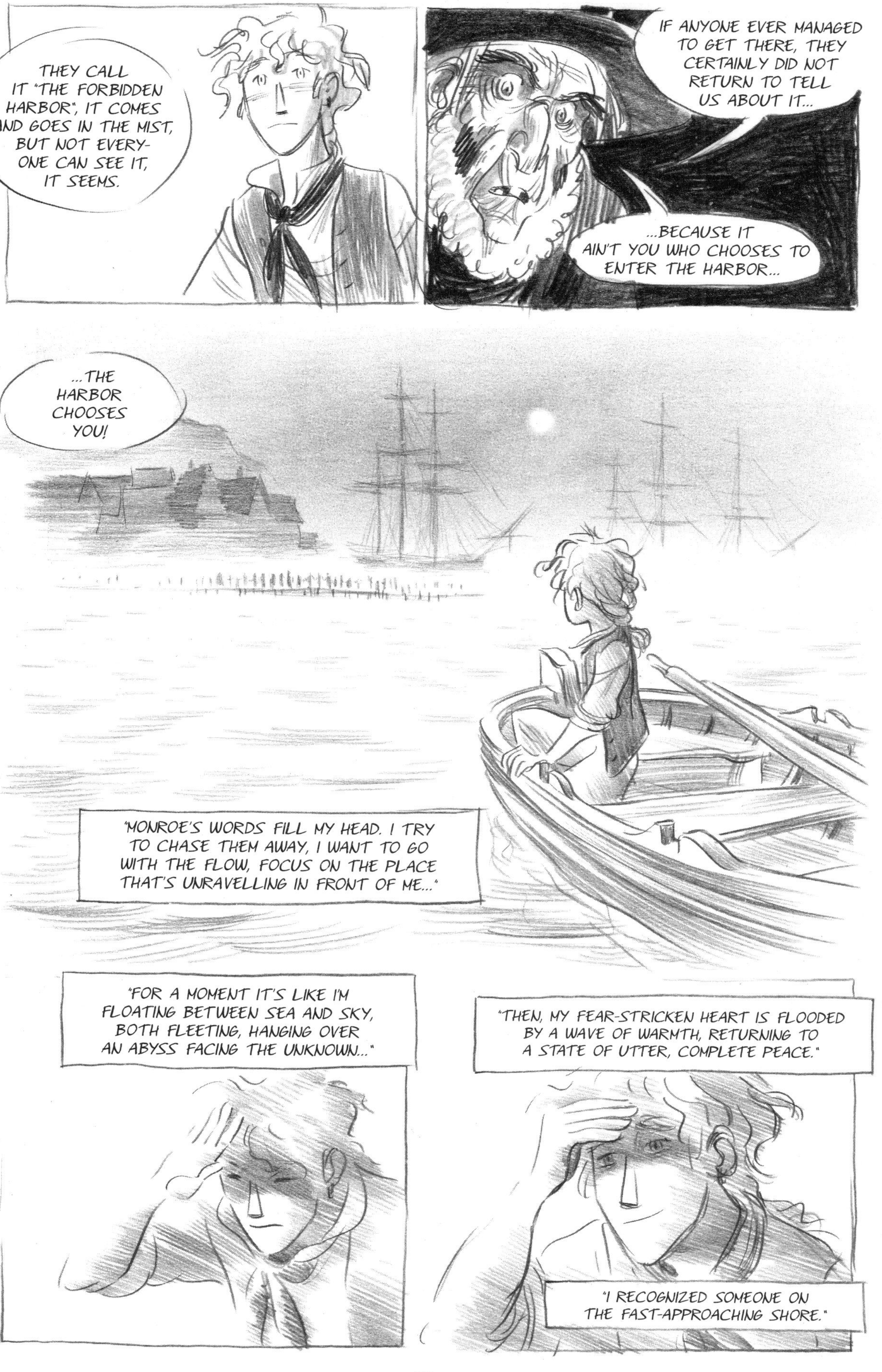

THEY CALL IT "THE FORBIDDEN HARBOR", IT COMES AND GOES IN THE MIST, BUT NOT EVERY-ONE CAN SEE IT, IT SEEMS.
IF ANYONE EVER MANAGED TO GET THERE, THEY CERTAINLY DID NOT RETURN TO TELL US ABOUT IT...
...BECAUSE IT AIN'T YOU WHO CHOOSES TO ENTER THE HARBOR...
...THE HARBOR CHOOSES YOU!
"MONROE'S WORDS FILL MY HEAD. I TRY TO CHASE THEM AWAY, I WANT TO GO WITH THE FLOW, FOCUS ON THE PLACE THAT'S UNRAVELLING IN FRONT OF ME..."
"FOR A MOMENT IT'S LIKE I'M FLOATING BETWEEN SEA AND SKY, BOTH FLEETING, HANGING OVER AN ABYSS FACING THE UNKNOWN..."
"THEN, MY FEAR-STRICKEN HEART IS FLOODED BY A WAVE OF WARMTH, RETURNING TO A STATE OF UTTER, COMPLETE PEACE."
"I RECOGNIZED SOMEONE ON THE FAST-APPROACHING SHORE."

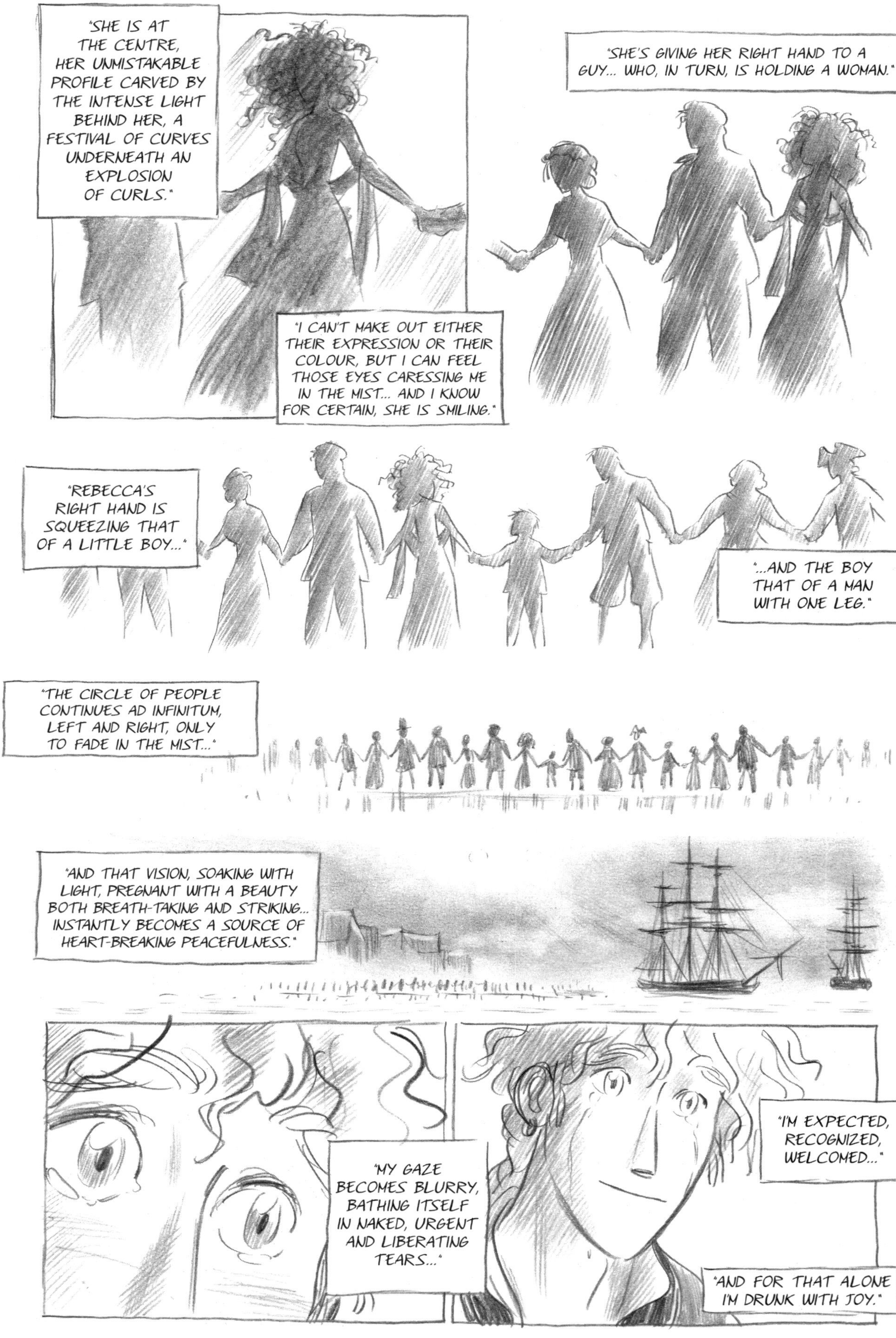
"SHE IS AT THE CENTRE, HER UNMISTAKABLE PROFILE CARVED BY THE INTENSE LIGHT BEHIND HER, A FESTIVAL OF CURVES UNDERNEATH AN EXPLOSION OF CURLS."
"I CAN'T MAKE OUT EITHER THEIR EXPRESSION OR THEIR COLOUR, BUT I CAN FEEL THOSE EYES CARESSING ME IN THE MIST... AND I KNOW FOR CERTAIN, SHE IS SMILING."
"SHE'S GIVING HER RIGHT HAND TO A GUY... WHO, IN TURN, IS HOLDING A WOMAN."
"REBECCA'S RIGHT HAND IS SQUEEZING THAT OF A LITTLE BOY..."
"...AND THE BOY THAT OF A MAN WITH ONE LEG."
"THE CIRCLE OF PEOPLE CONTINUES AD INFINITUM, LEFT AND RIGHT, ONLY TO FADE IN THE MIST..."
"AND THAT VISION, SOAKING WITH LIGHT, PREGNANT WITH A BEAUTY BOTH BREATH-TAKING AND STRIKING... INSTANTLY BECOMES A SOURCE OF HEART-BREAKING PEACEFULNESS."
"MY GAZE BECOMES BLURRY, BATHING ITSELF IN NAKED, URGENT AND LIBERATING TEARS..."
"I'M EXPECTED, RECOGNIZED, WELCOMED..."
"AND FOR THAT ALONE I'M DRUNK WITH JOY."

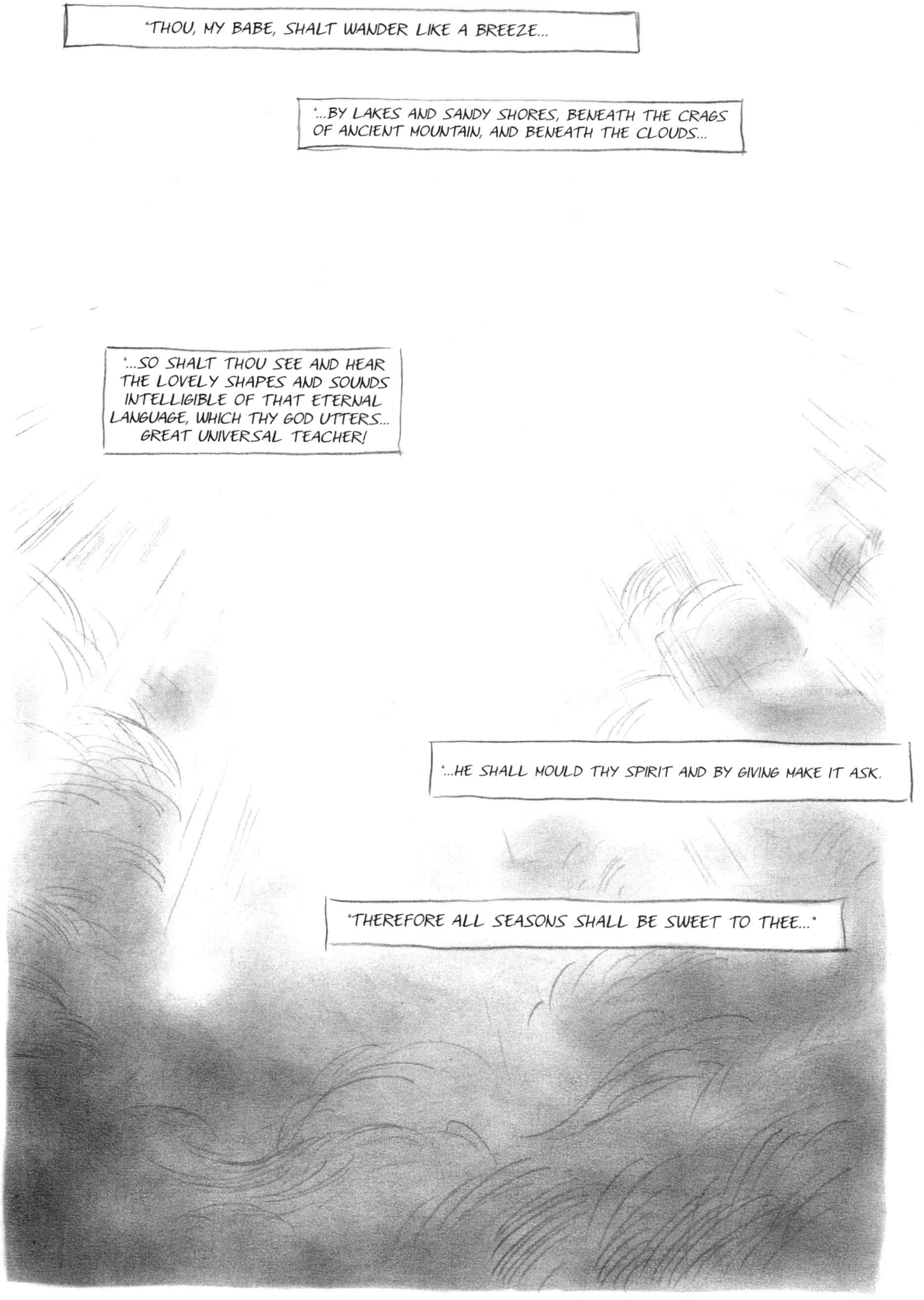
"THOU, MY BABE, SHALT WANDER LIKE A BREEZE...
"...BY LAKES AND SANDY SHORES, BENEATH THE CRAGS OF ANCIENT MOUNTAIN, AND BENEATH THE CLOUDS...
"...SO SHALT THOU SEE AND HEAR THE LOVELY SHAPES AND SOUNDS INTELLIGIBLE OF THAT ETERNAL LANGUAGE, WHICH THY GOD UTTERS... GREAT UNIVERSAL TEACHER!
"...HE SHALL MOULD THY SPIRIT AND BY GIVING MAKE IT ASK.
"THEREFORE ALL SEASONS SHALL BE SWEET TO THEE..."

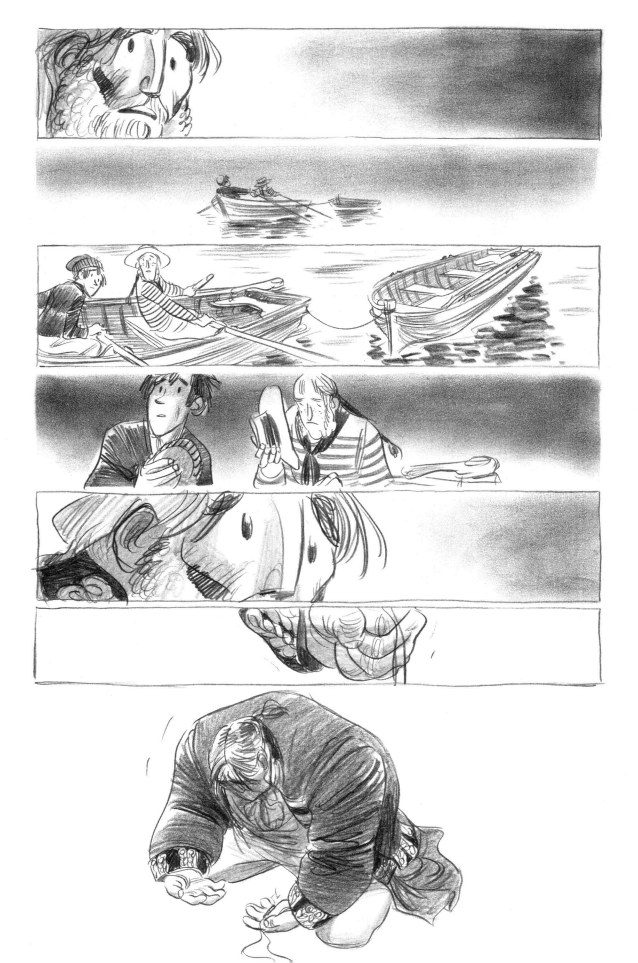

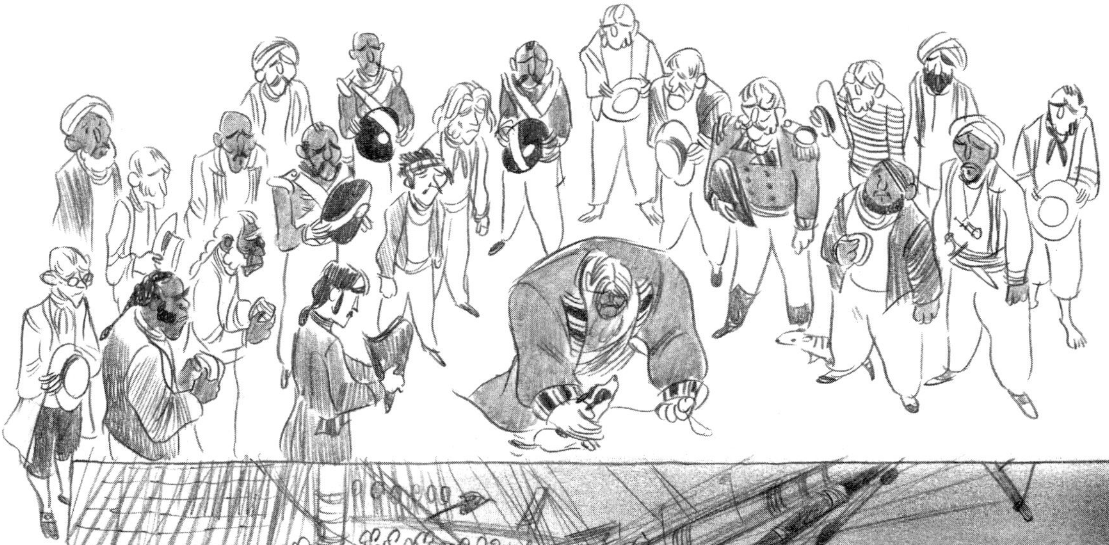

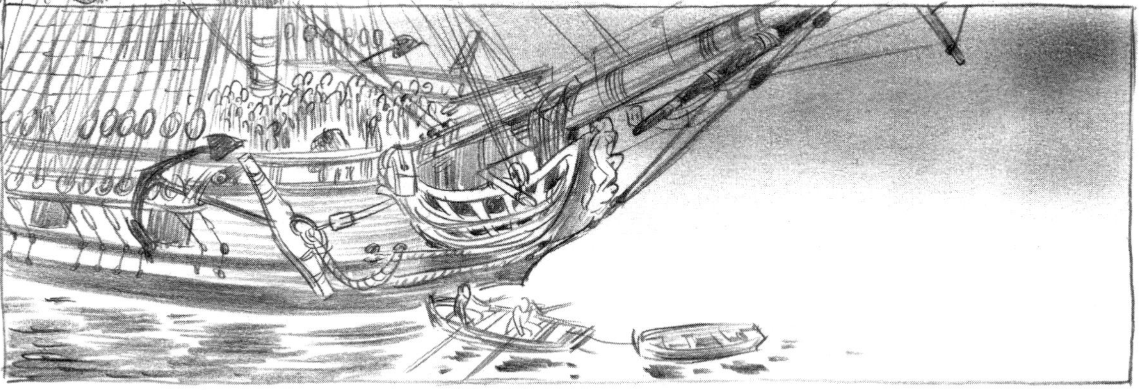

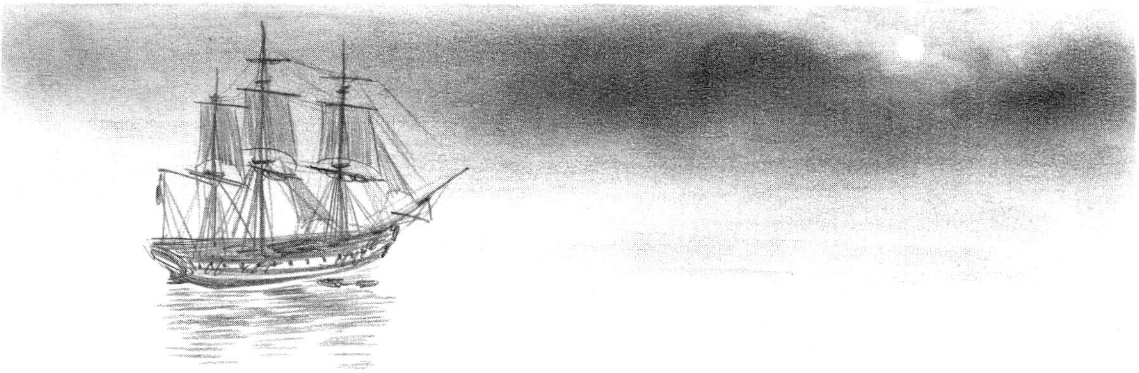

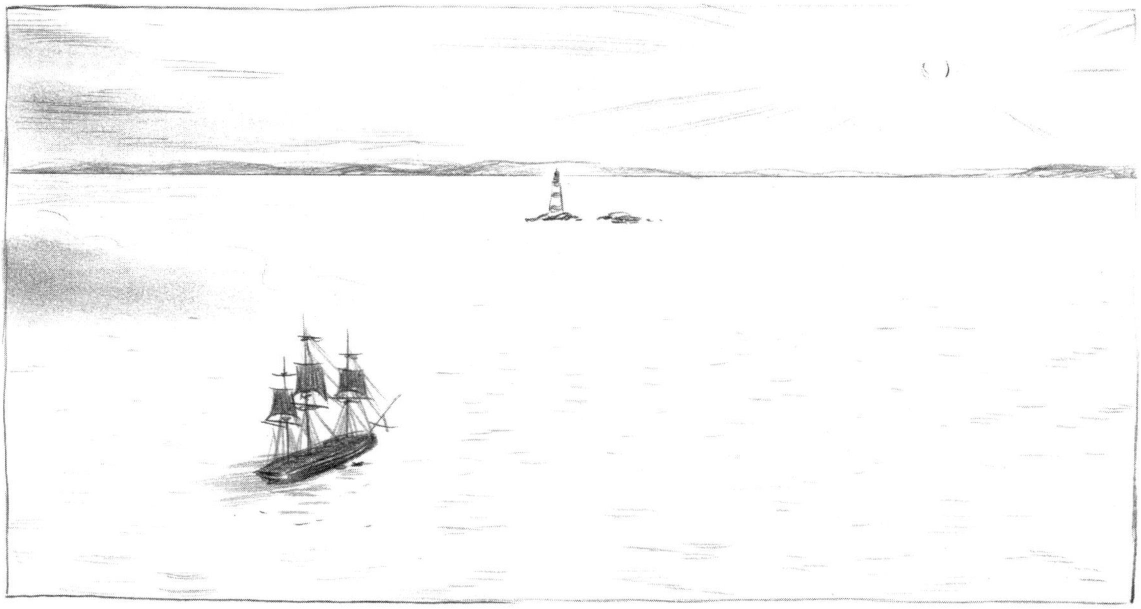

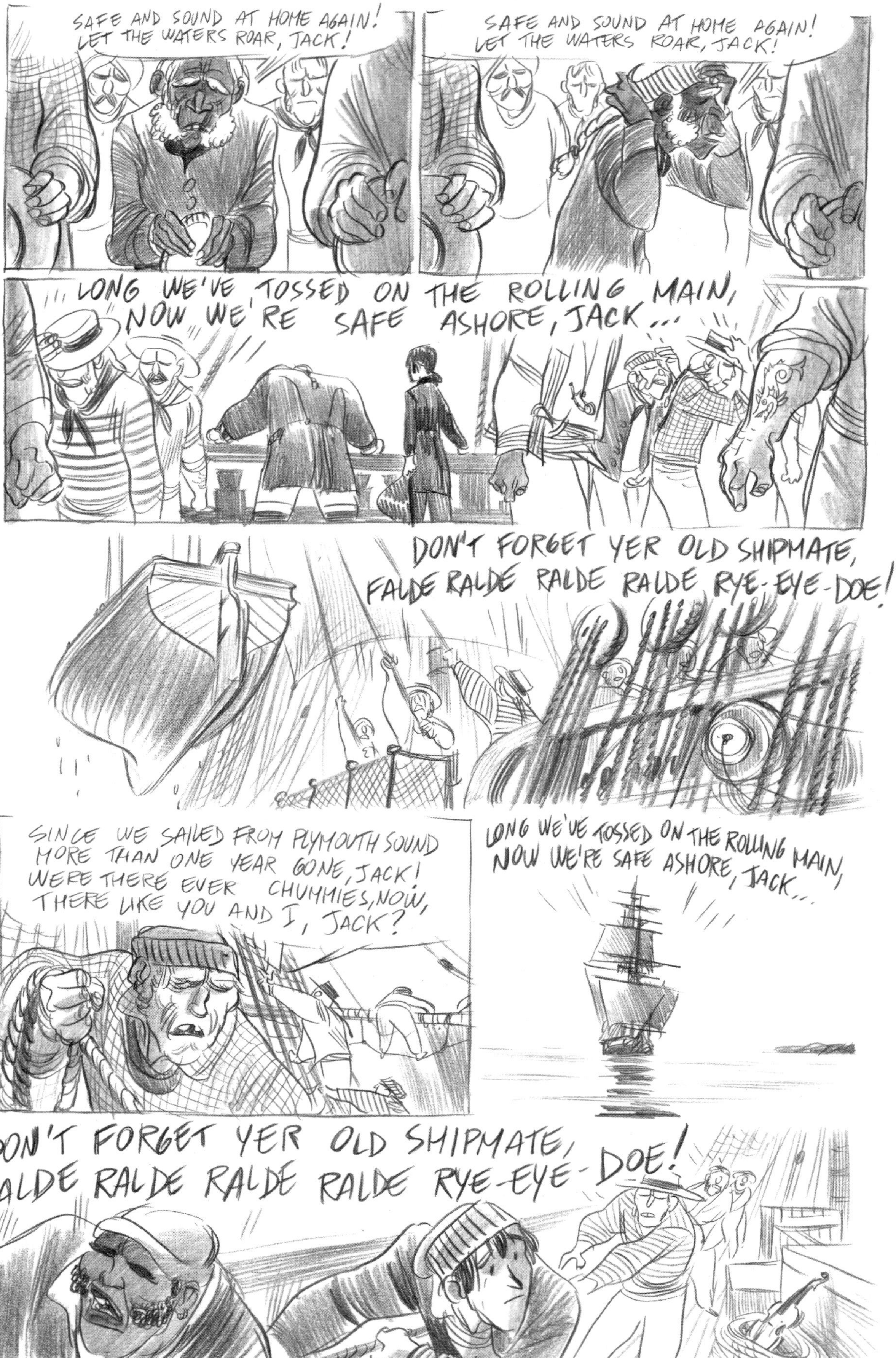
SAFE AND SOUND AT HOME AGAIN! LET THE WATERS ROAR, JACK!
SAFE AND SOUND AT HOME AGAIN! LET THE WATERS ROAR, JACK!
LONG WE'VE TOSSED ON THE ROLLING MAIN, NOW WE'RE SAFE ASHORE, JACK...
DON'T FORGET YER OLD SHIPMATE, FALDE RALDE RALDE RALDE RYE-EYE-DOE!
SINCE WE SAILED FROM PLYMOUTH SOUND MORE THAN ONE YEAR GONE, JACK! WERE THERE EVER CHUMMIES, NOW, THERE LIKE YOU AND I, JACK?
LONG WE'VE TOSSED ON THE ROLLING MAIN, NOW WE'RE SAFE ASHORE, JACK...
DON'T FORGET YER OLD SHIPMATE, FALDE RALDE RALDE RALDE RYE-EYE-DOE!

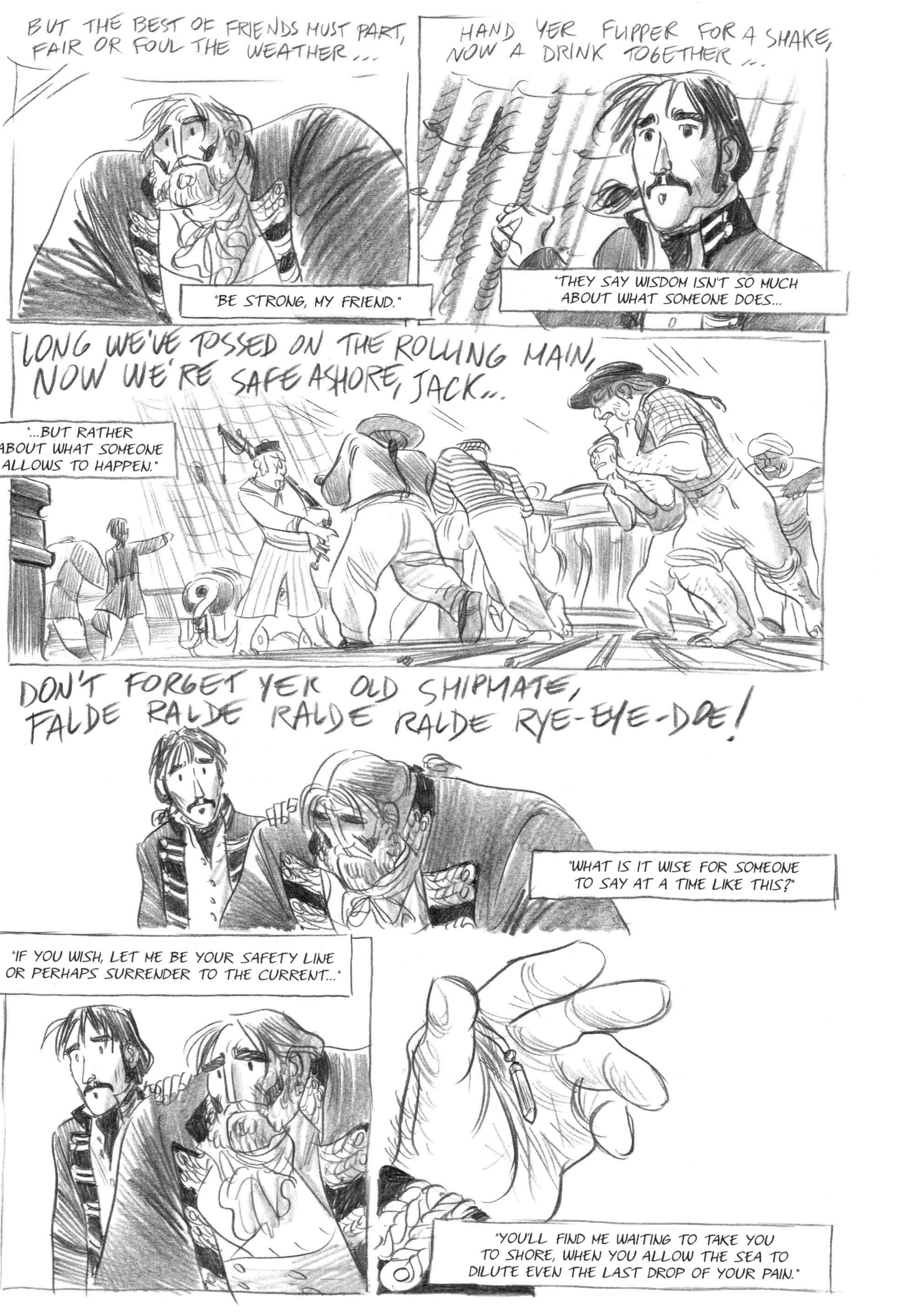
BUT THE BEST OF FRIENDS MUST PART, FAIR OR FOUL THE WEATHER...
"BE STRONG, MY FRIEND."
HAND YER FLIPPER FOR A SHAKE, NOW A DRINK TOGETHER...
"THEY SAY WISDOM ISN'T SO MUCH ABOUT WHAT SOMEONE DOES...
LONG WE'VE TOSSED ON THE ROLLING MAIN, NOW WE'RE SAFE ASHORE, JACK...
"...BUT RATHER ABOUT WHAT SOMEONE ALLOWS TO HAPPEN."
DON'T FORGET YER OLD SHIPMATE, FALDE RALDE RALDE RALDE RYE-EYE-DOE!
"WHAT IS IT WISE FOR SOMEONE TO SAY AT A TIME LIKE THIS?"
"IF YOU WISH, LET ME BE YOUR SAFETY LINE OR PERHAPS SURRENDER TO THE CURRENT..."
"YOU'LL FIND ME WAITING TO TAKE YOU TO SHORE, WHEN YOU ALLOW THE SEA TO DILUTE EVEN THE LAST DROP OF YOUR PAIN."

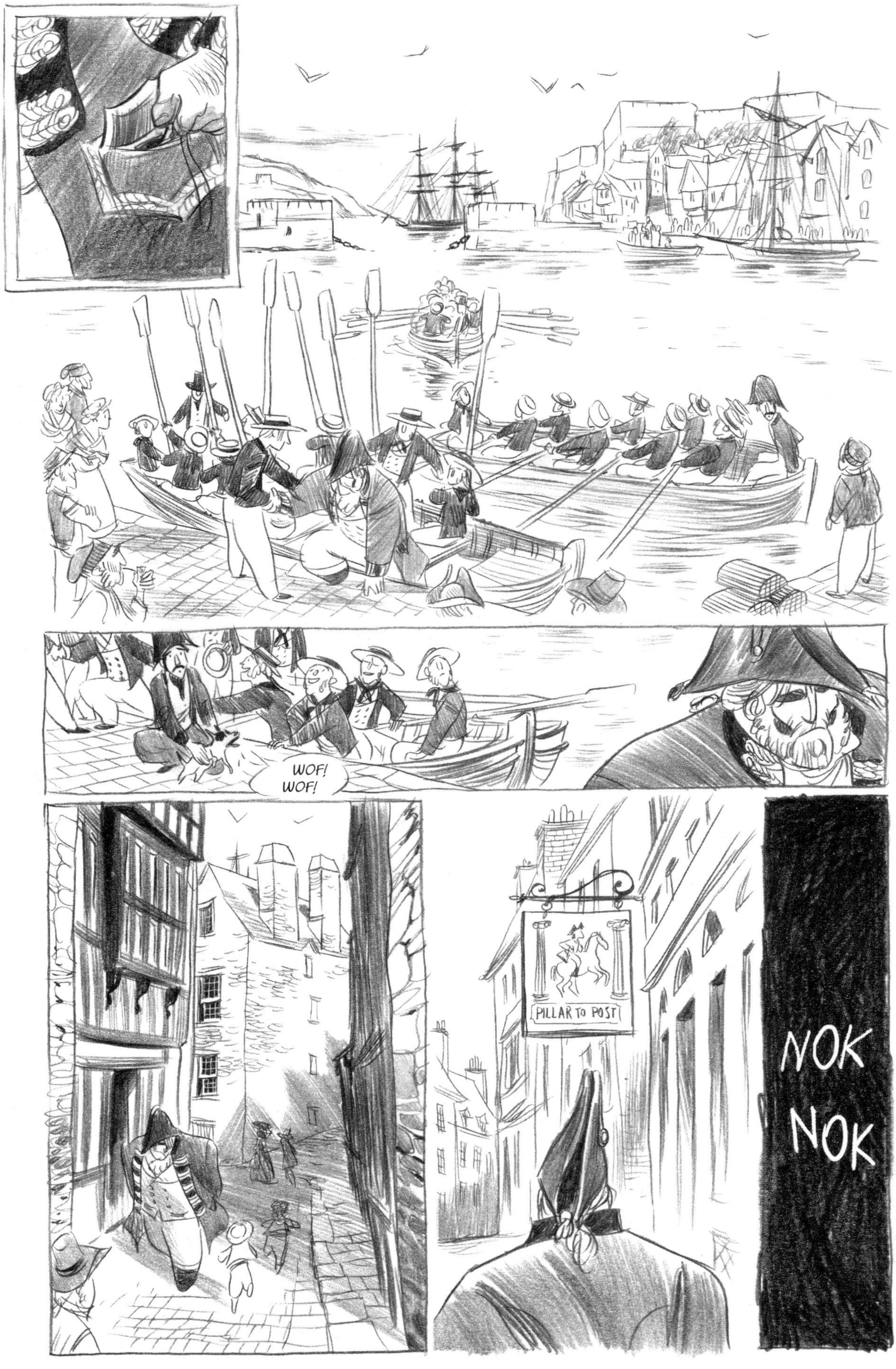
WOF! WOF!
PILLAR TO POST
NOK NOK

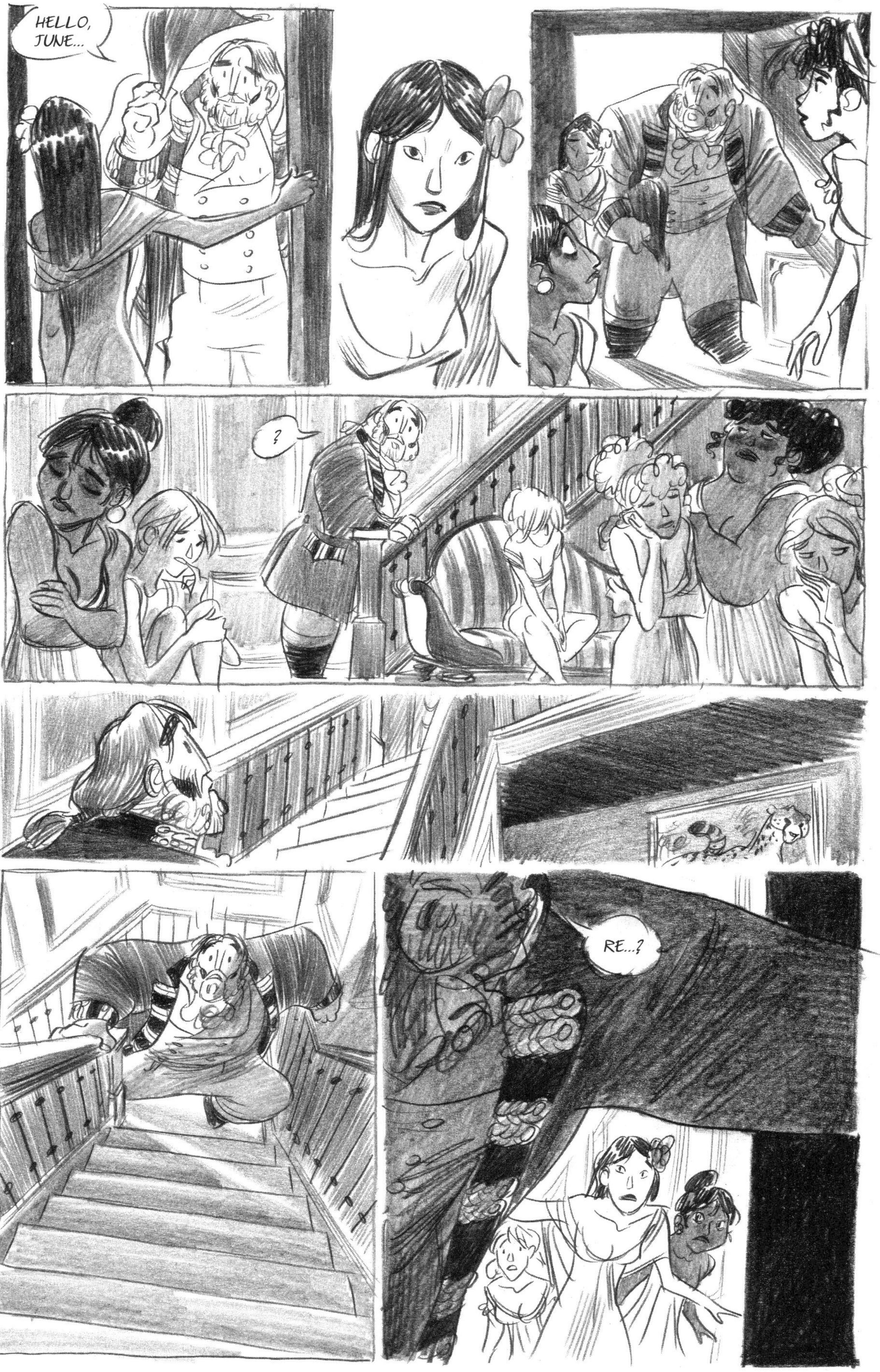
HELLO, JUNE...
?
RE...?

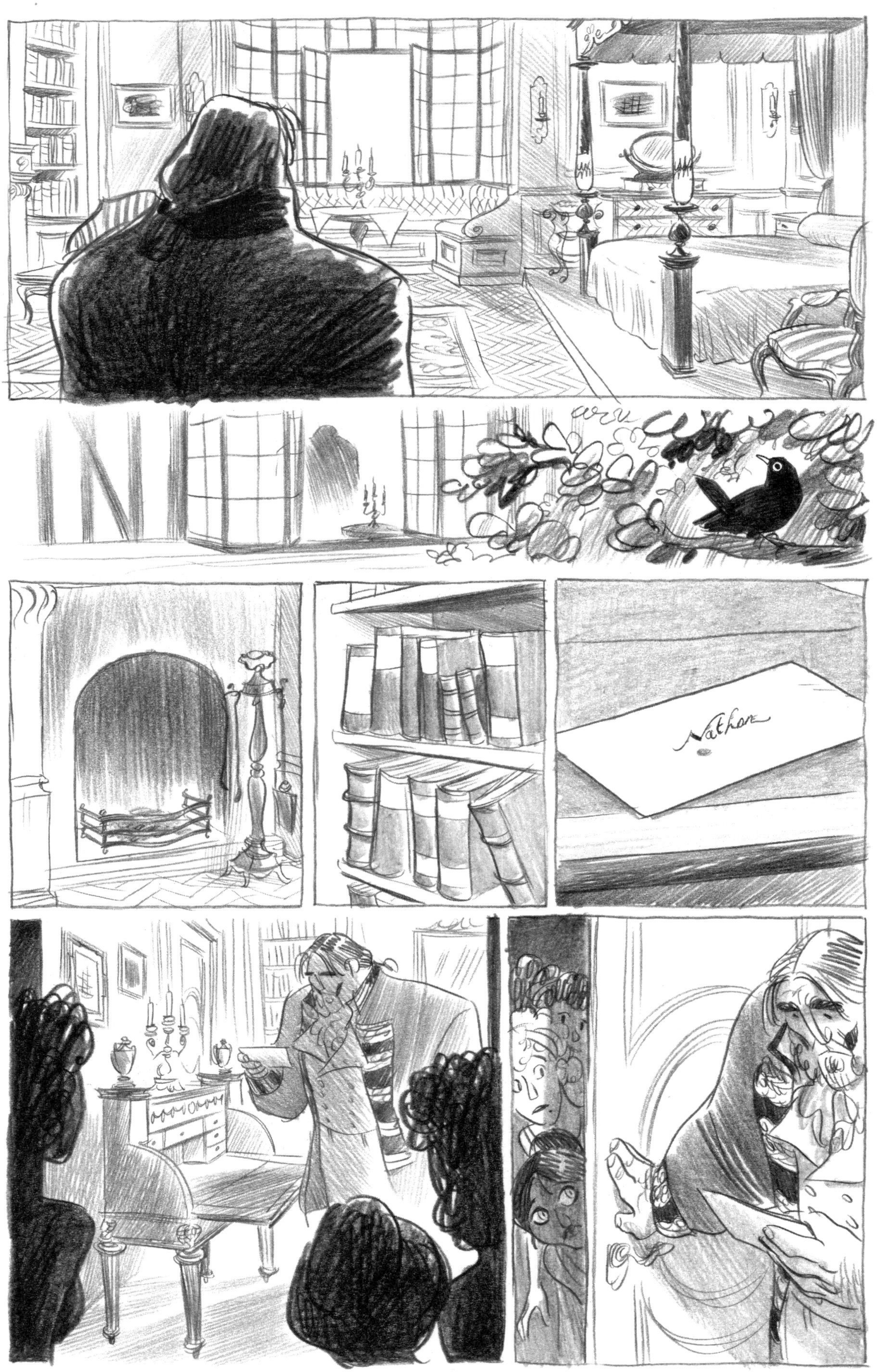
Nathan

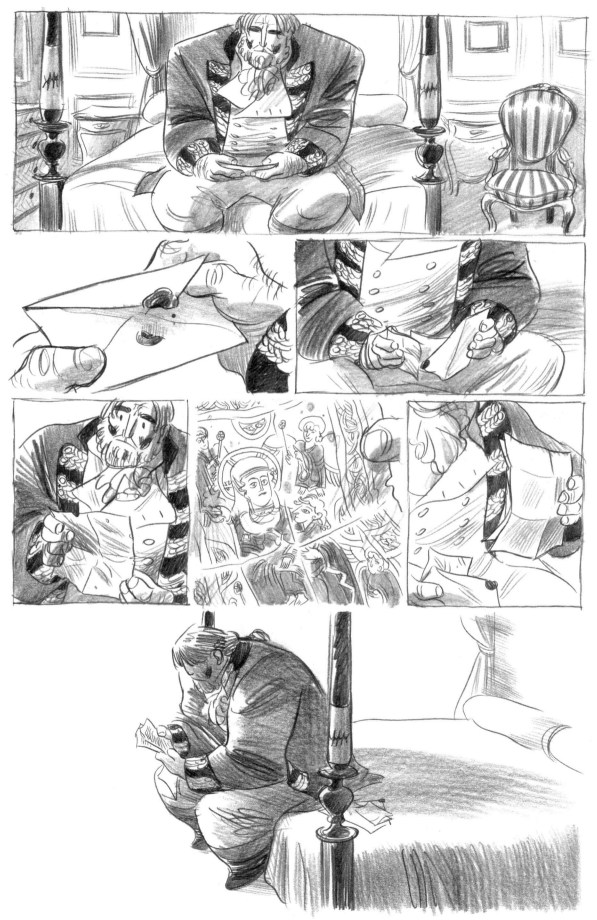

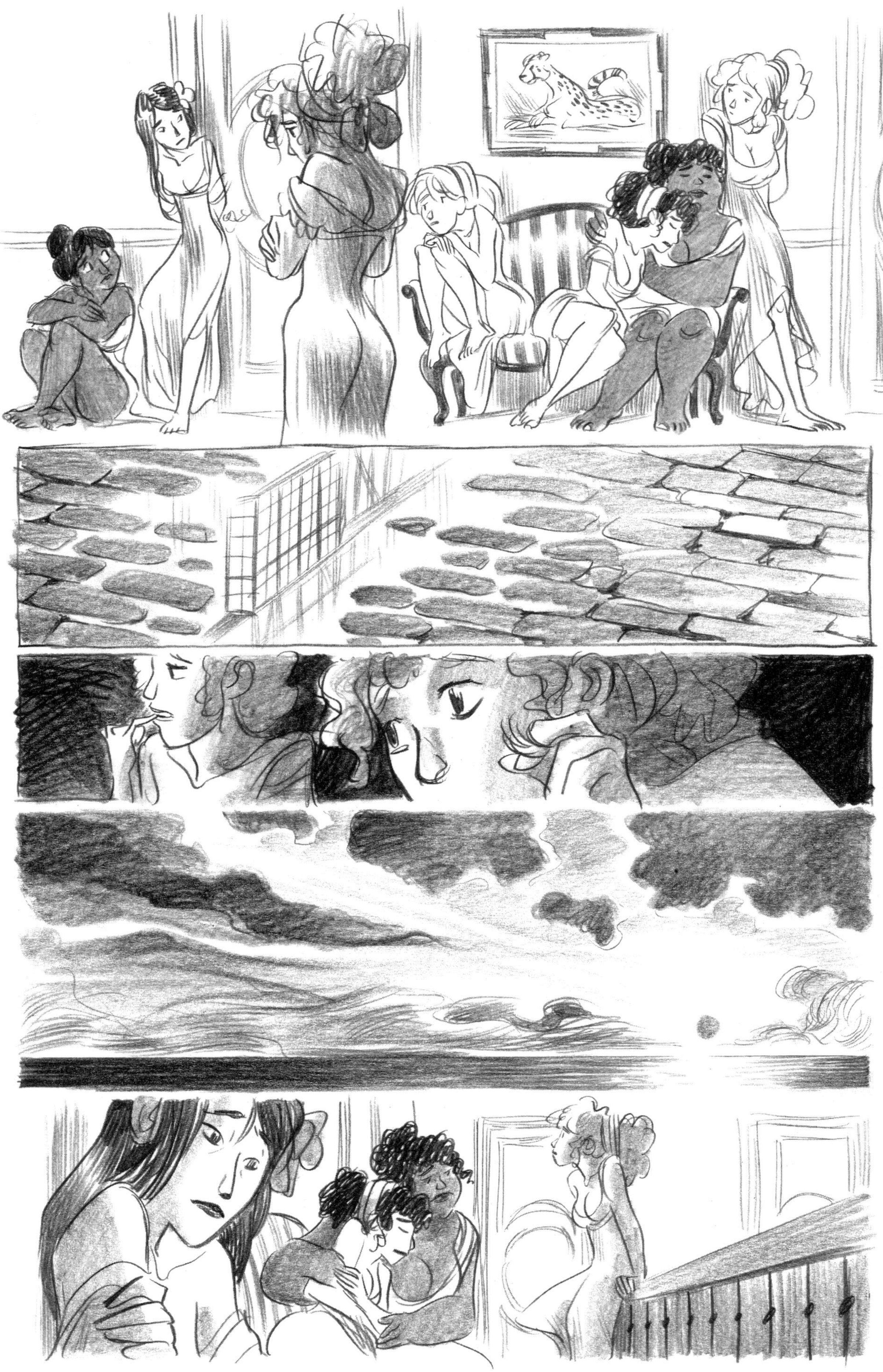

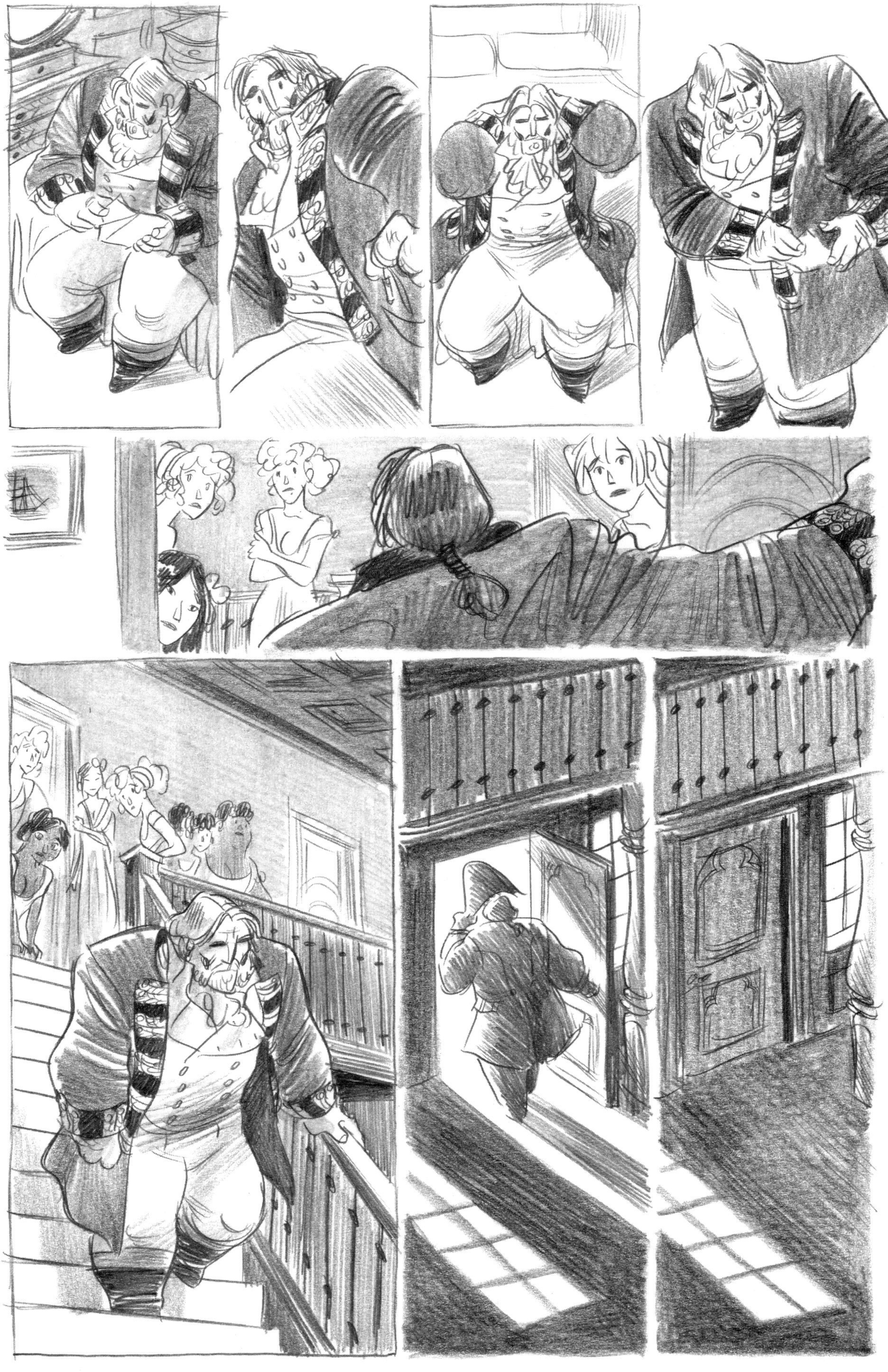

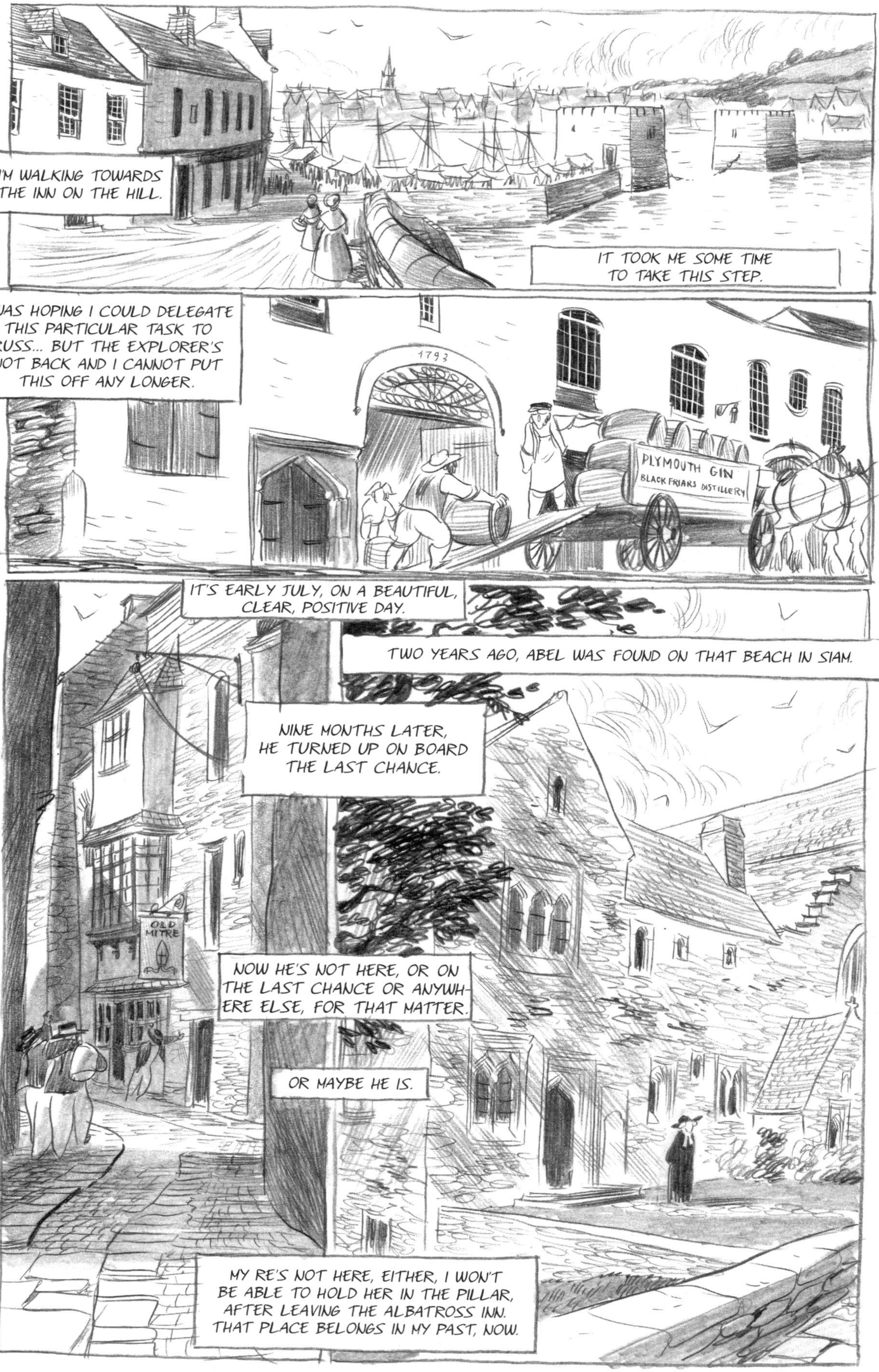
I'M WALKING TOWARDS THE INN ON THE HILL.
IT TOOK ME SOME TIME TO TAKE THIS STEP.
I WAS HOPING I COULD DELEGATE THIS PARTICULAR TASK TO RUSS... BUT THE EXPLORER'S NOT BACK AND I CANNOT PUT THIS OFF ANY LONGER.
1793
PLYMOUTH GIN
BLACK FRIARS DISTILLERY
IT'S EARLY JULY, ON A BEAUTIFUL, CLEAR, POSITIVE DAY.
TWO YEARS AGO, ABEL WAS FOUND ON THAT BEACH IN SIAM.
NINE MONTHS LATER, HE TURNED UP ON BOARD THE LAST CHANCE.
OLD MITRE
NOW HE'S NOT HERE, OR ON THE LAST CHANCE OR ANYWHERE ELSE, FOR THAT MATTER.
OR MAYBE HE IS.
MY RE'S NOT HERE, EITHER, I WON'T BE ABLE TO HOLD HER IN THE PILLAR, AFTER LEAVING THE ALBATROSS INN. THAT PLACE BELONGS IN MY PAST, NOW.

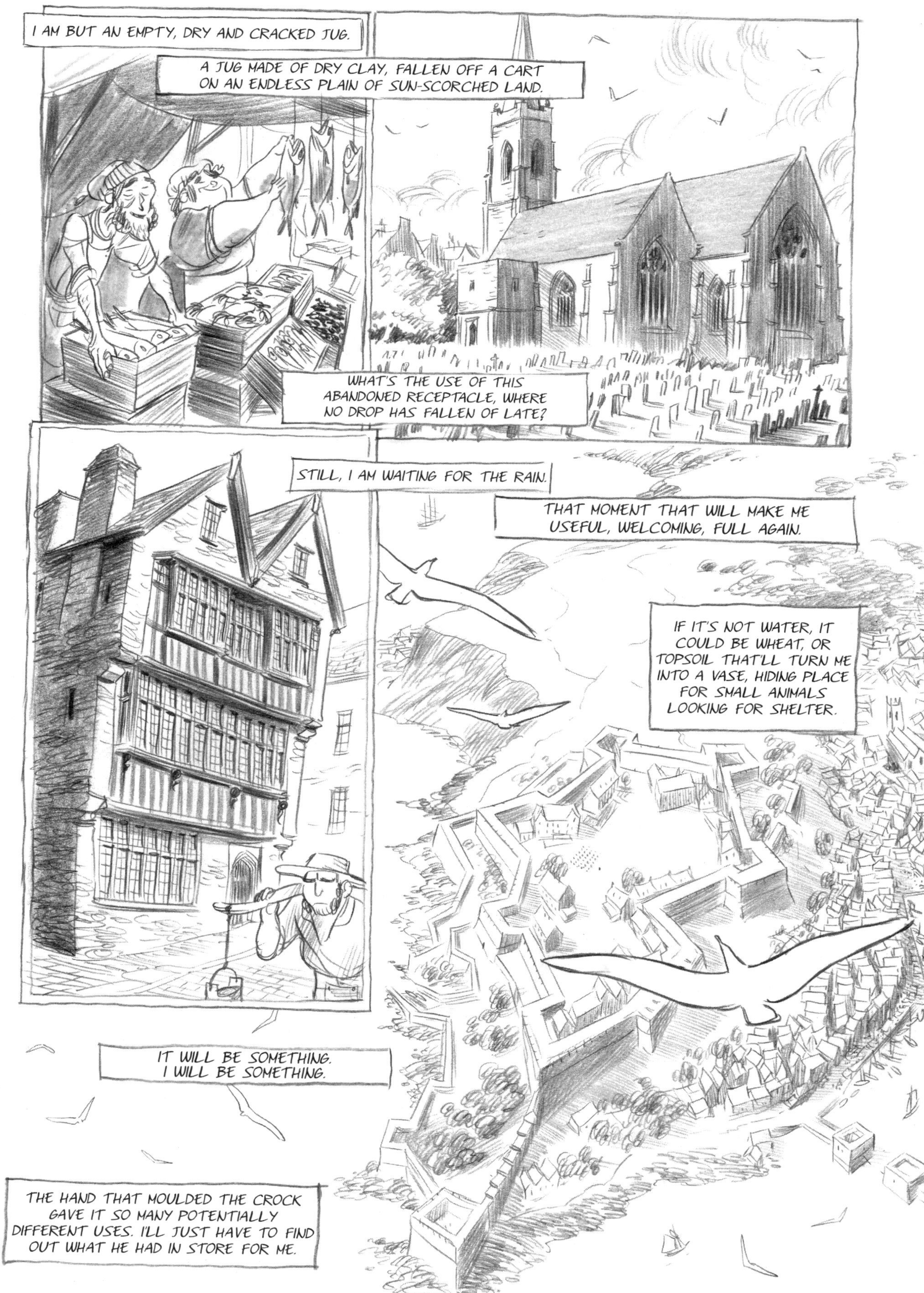
I AM BUT AN EMPTY, DRY AND CRACKED JUG.
A JUG MADE OF DRY CLAY, FALLEN OFF A CART ON AN ENDLESS PLAIN OF SUN-SCORCHED LAND.
WHAT'S THE USE OF THIS ABANDONED RECEPTACLE, WHERE NO DROP HAS FALLEN OF LATE?
STILL, I AM WAITING FOR THE RAIN.
THAT MOMENT THAT WILL MAKE ME USEFUL, WELCOMING, FULL AGAIN.
IF IT'S NOT WATER, IT COULD BE WHEAT, OR TOPSOIL THAT'LL TURN ME INTO A VASE, HIDING PLACE FOR SMALL ANIMALS LOOKING FOR SHELTER.
IT WILL BE SOMETHING. I WILL BE SOMETHING.
THE HAND THAT MOULDED THE CROCK GAVE IT SO MANY POTENTIALLY DIFFERENT USES. I'LL JUST HAVE TO FIND OUT WHAT HE HAD IN STORE FOR ME.

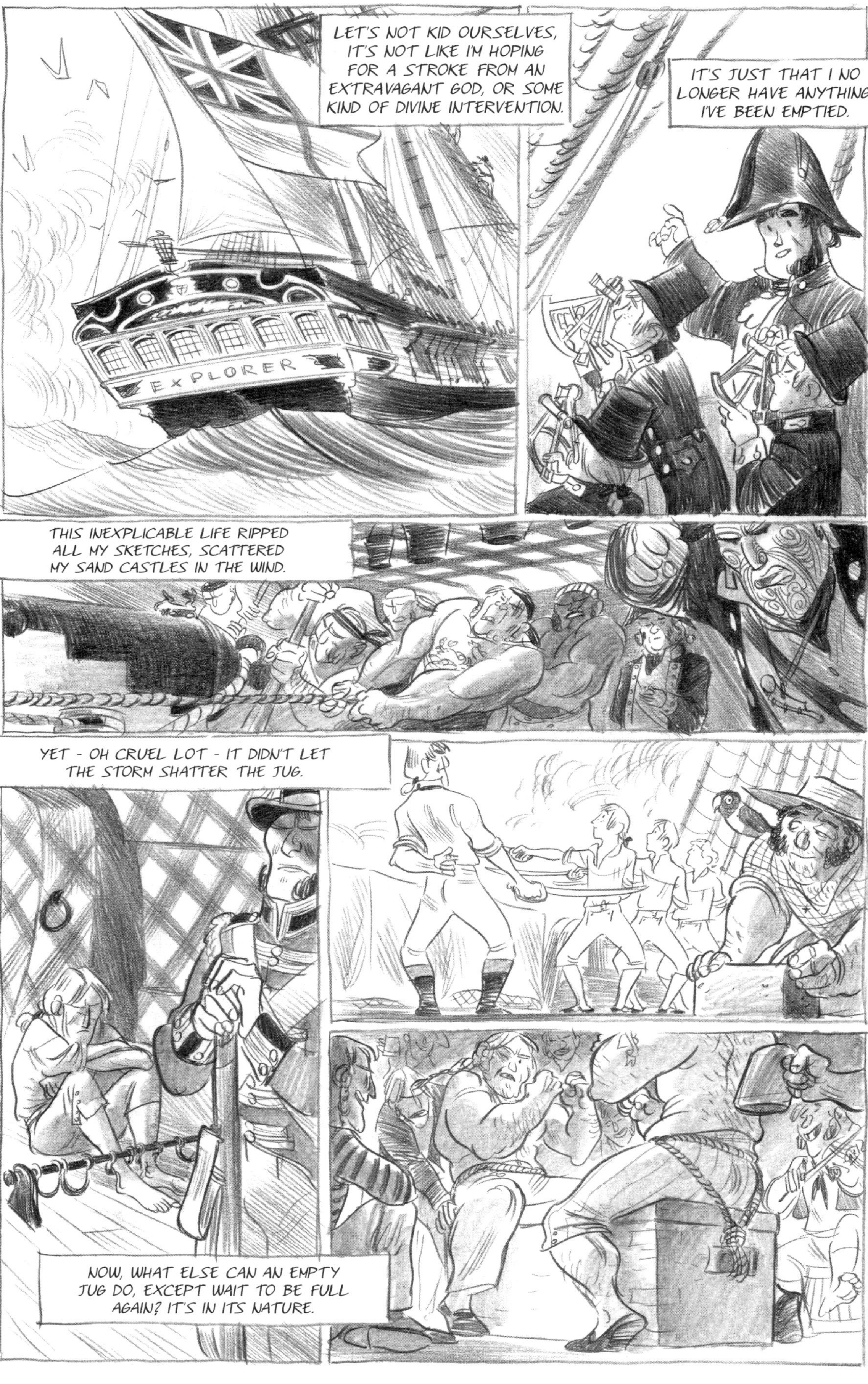

LET'S NOT KID OURSELVES, IT'S NOT LIKE I'M HOPING FOR A STROKE FROM AN EXTRAVAGANT GOD, OR SOME KIND OF DIVINE INTERVENTION.
EXPLORER
IT'S JUST THAT I NO LONGER HAVE ANYTHING. I'VE BEEN EMPTIED.
THIS INEXPLICABLE LIFE RIPPED ALL MY SKETCHES, SCATTERED MY SAND CASTLES IN THE WIND.
YET - OH CRUEL LOT - IT DIDN'T LET THE STORM SHATTER THE JUG.
NOW, WHAT ELSE CAN AN EMPTY JUG DO, EXCEPT WAIT TO BE FULL AGAIN? IT'S IN ITS NATURE.

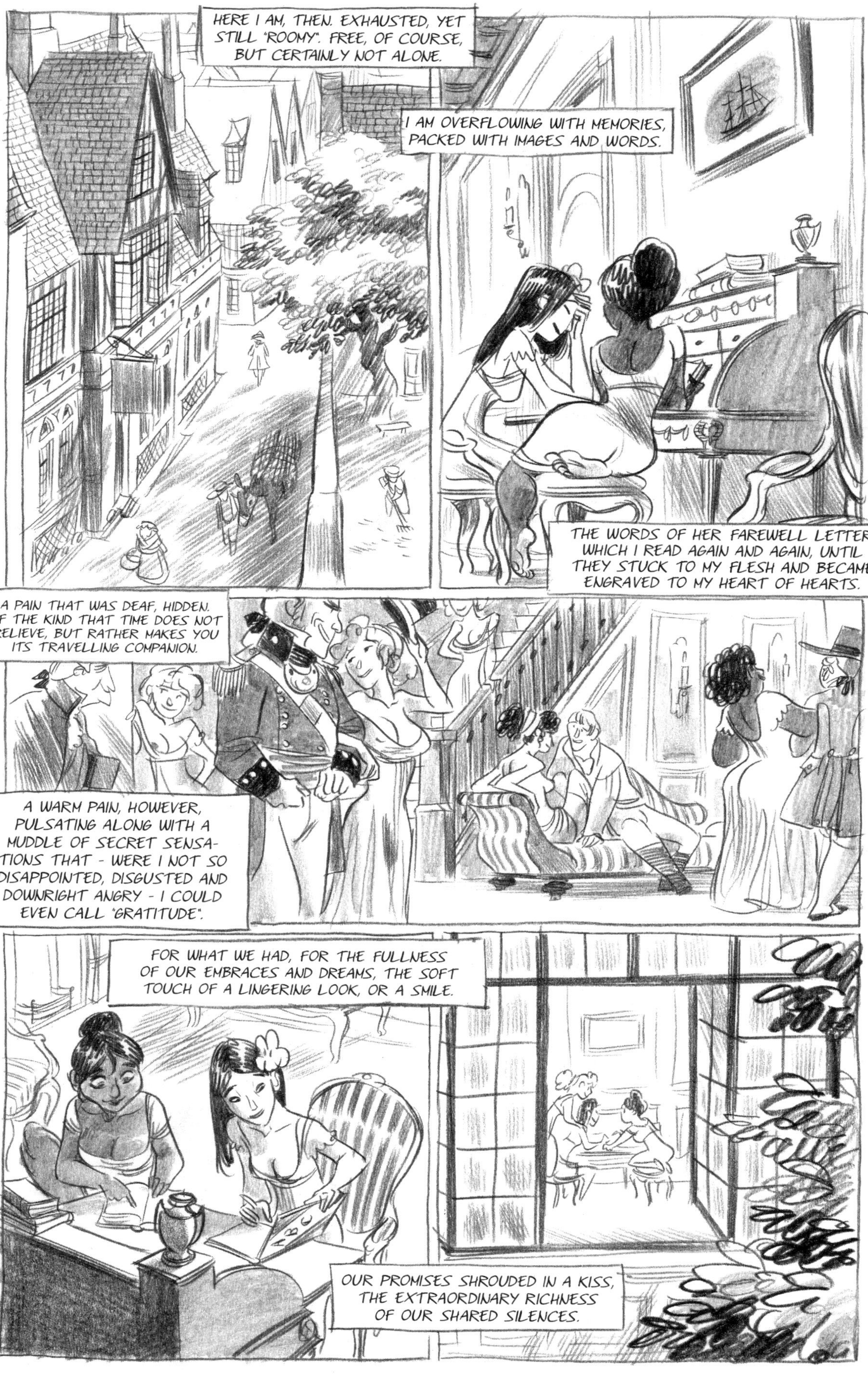
HERE I AM, THEN. EXHAUSTED, YET STILL "ROOMY". FREE, OF COURSE, BUT CERTAINLY NOT ALONE.
I AM OVERFLOWING WITH MEMORIES, PACKED WITH IMAGES AND WORDS.
THE WORDS OF HER FAREWELL LETTER, WHICH I READ AGAIN AND AGAIN, UNTIL THEY STUCK TO MY FLESH AND BECAME ENGRAVED TO MY HEART OF HEARTS.
A PAIN THAT WAS DEAF, HIDDEN. OF THE KIND THAT TIME DOES NOT RELIEVE, BUT RATHER MAKES YOU ITS TRAVELLING COMPANION.
A WARM PAIN, HOWEVER, PULSATING ALONG WITH A MUDDLE OF SECRET SENSATIONS THAT - WERE I NOT SO DISAPPOINTED, DISGUSTED AND DOWNRIGHT ANGRY - I COULD EVEN CALL "GRATITUDE".
FOR WHAT WE HAD, FOR THE FULLNESS OF OUR EMBRACES AND DREAMS, THE SOFT TOUCH OF A LINGERING LOOK, OR A SMILE.
OUR PROMISES SHROUDED IN A KISS, THE EXTRAORDINARY RICHNESS OF OUR SHARED SILENCES.

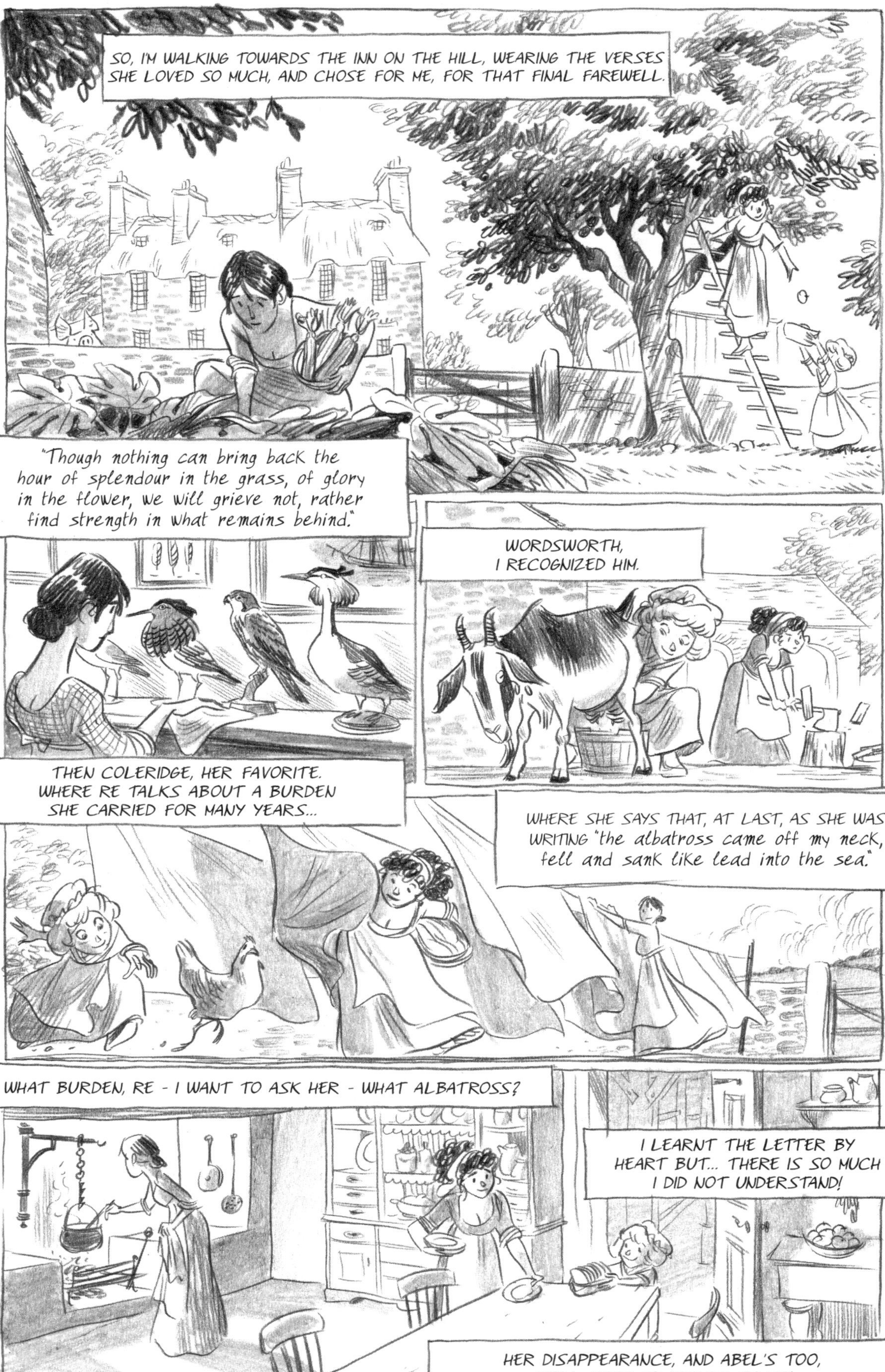
SO, I'M WALKING TOWARDS THE INN ON THE HILL, WEARING THE VERSES SHE LOVED SO MUCH, AND CHOSE FOR ME, FOR THAT FINAL FAREWELL.
"Though nothing can bring back the hour of splendour in the grass, of glory in the flower, we will grieve not, rather find strength in what remains behind."
WORDSWORTH, I RECOGNIZED HIM.
THEN COLERIDGE, HER FAVORITE. WHERE RE TALKS ABOUT A BURDEN SHE CARRIED FOR MANY YEARS...
WHERE SHE SAYS THAT, AT LAST, AS SHE WAS WRITING "the albatross came off my neck, fell and sank like lead into the sea."
WHAT BURDEN, RE - I WANT TO ASK HER - WHAT ALBATROSS?
I LEARNT THE LETTER BY HEART BUT... THERE IS SO MUCH I DID NOT UNDERSTAND!
HER DISAPPEARANCE, AND ABEL'S TOO, STILL SEEM SO ABSURD TO ME!

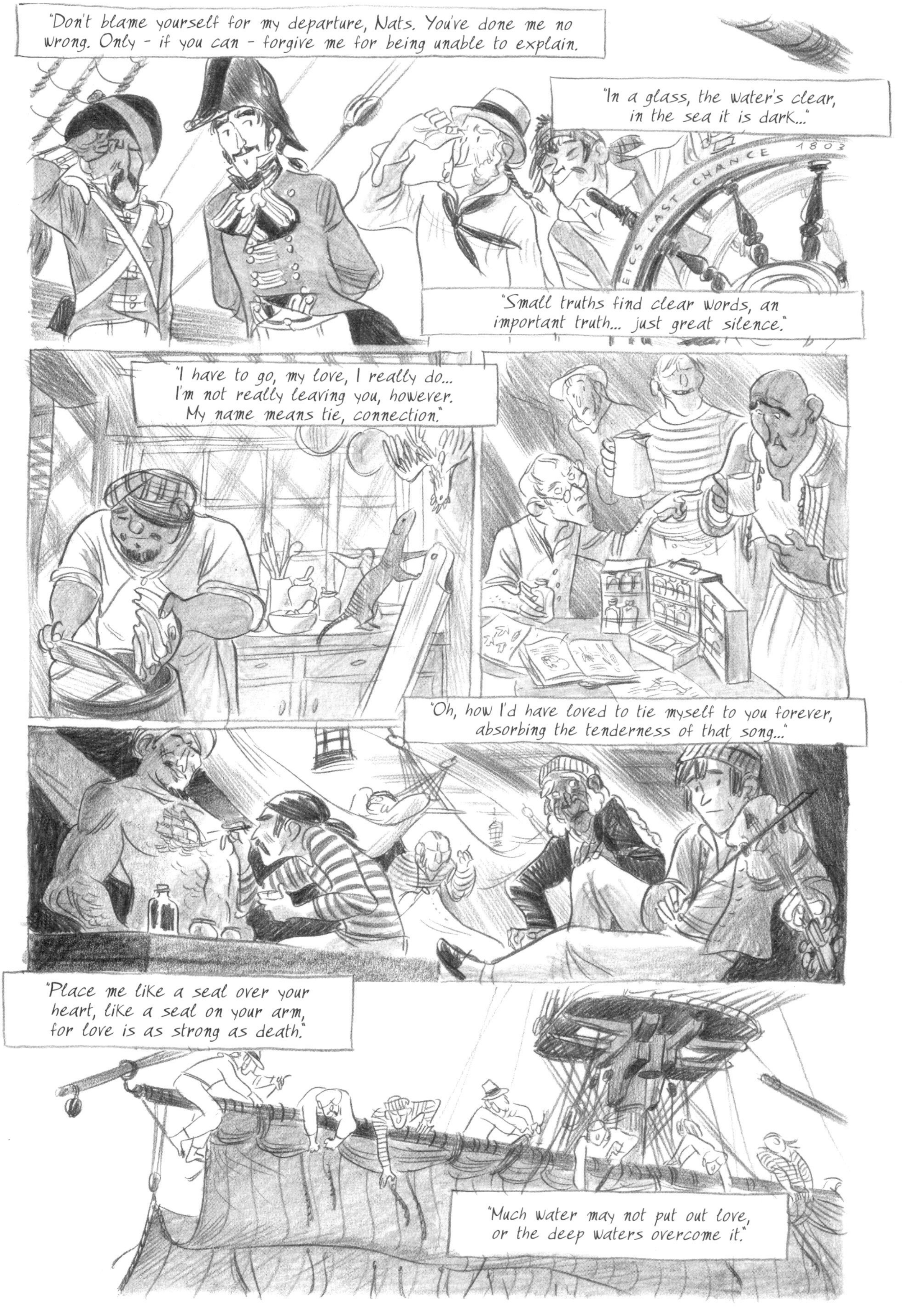
"Don't blame yourself for my departure, Nats. You've done me no wrong. Only - if you can - forgive me for being unable to explain.
"In a glass, the water's clear, in the sea it is dark..."
EICS LAST CHANCE 1803
"Small truths find clear words, an important truth... just great silence."
"I have to go, my love, I really do... I'm not really leaving you, however. My name means tie, connection."
"Oh, how I'd have loved to tie myself to you forever, absorbing the tenderness of that song..."
"Place me like a seal over your heart, like a seal on your arm, for love is as strong as death."
"Much water may not put out love, or the deep waters overcome it."

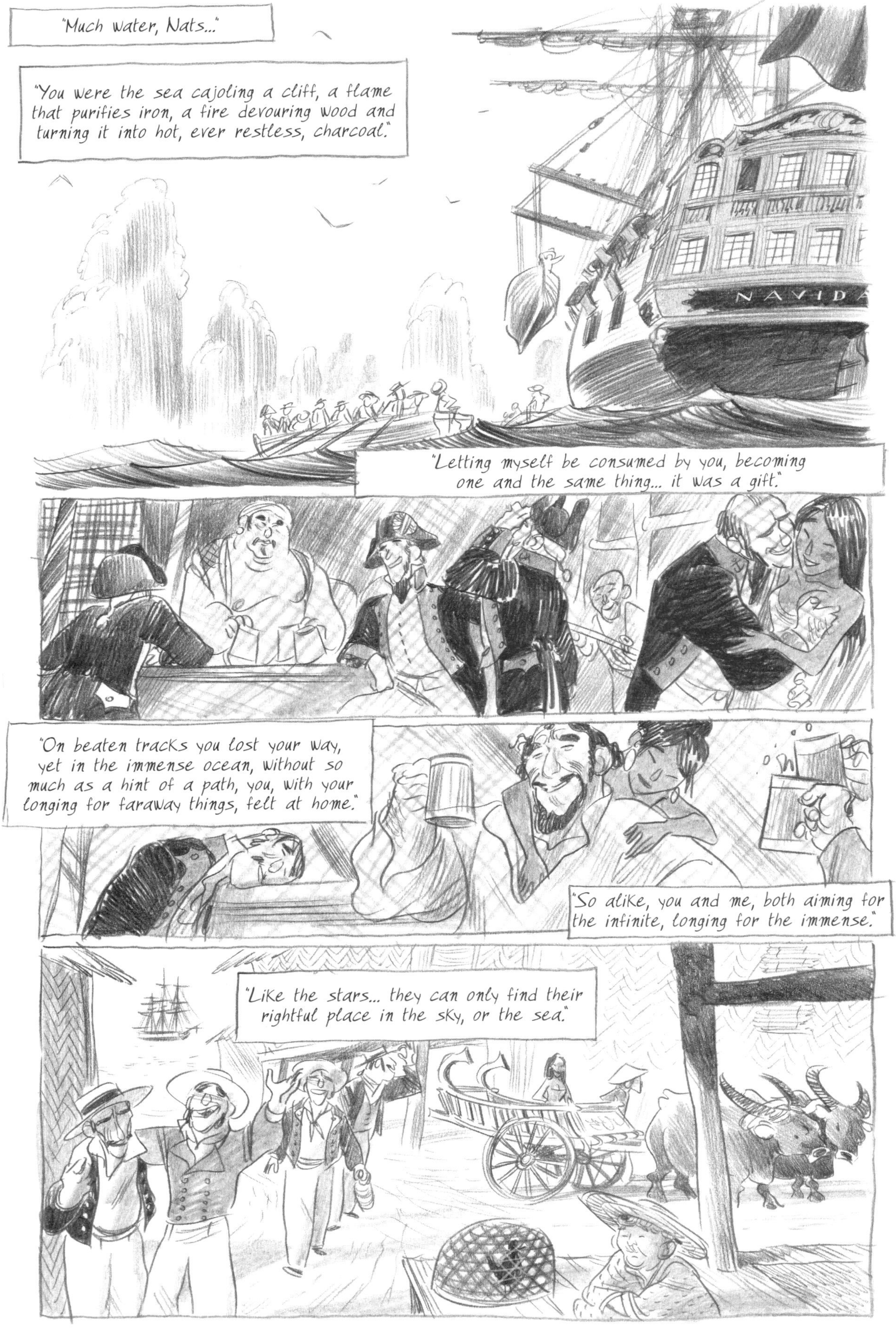
"Much water, Nats..."
"You were the sea cajoling a cliff, a flame that purifies iron, a fire devouring wood and turning it into hot, ever restless, charcoal."
NAVIDA
"Letting myself be consumed by you, becoming one and the same thing... it was a gift."
"On beaten tracks you lost your way, yet in the immense ocean, without so much as a hint of a path, you, with your longing for faraway things, felt at home."
"So alike, you and me, both aiming for the infinite, longing for the immense."
"Like the stars... they can only find their rightful place in the sky, or the sea."

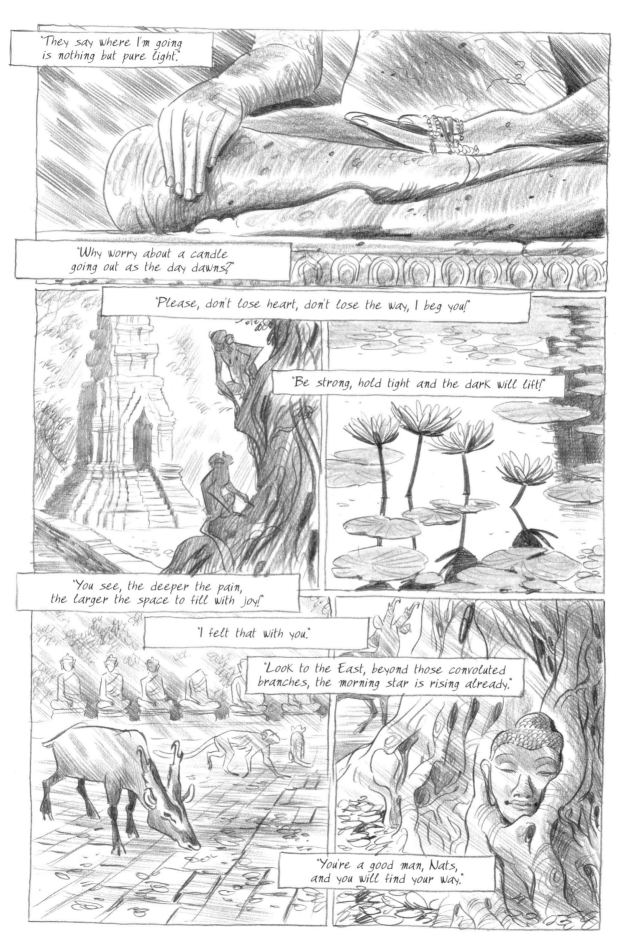

"They say where I'm going is nothing but pure light."

"Why worry about a candle going out as the day dawns?"

"Please, don't lose heart, don't lose the way, I beg you!"

"Be strong, hold tight and the dark will lift!"

"You see, the deeper the pain, the larger the space to fill with joy!"

"I felt that with you."

"Look to the East, beyond those convoluted branches, the morning star is rising already."

"You're a good man, Nats, and you will find your way."

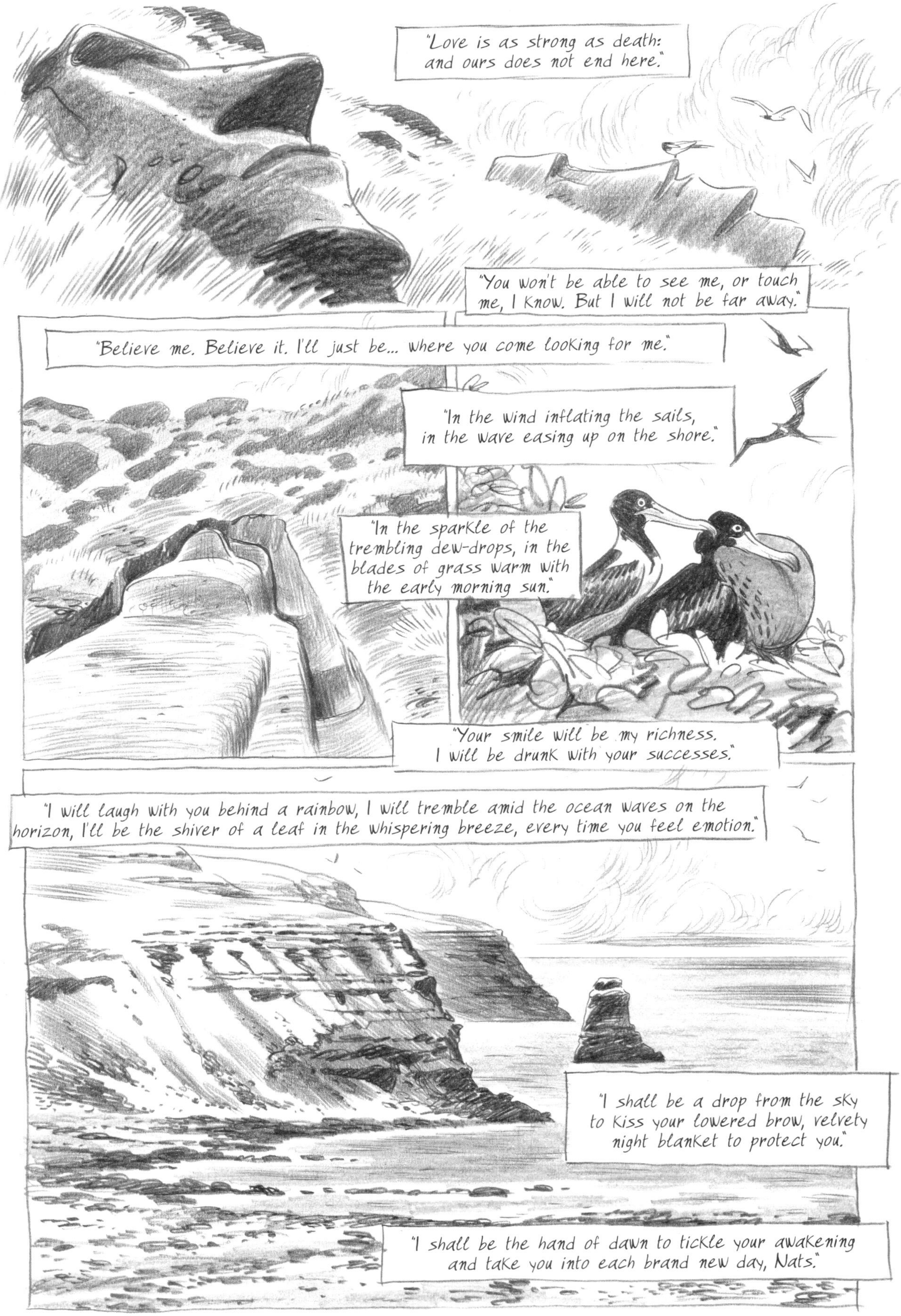
"Love is as strong as death: and ours does not end here."
"You won't be able to see me, or touch me, I know. But I will not be far away."
"Believe me. Believe it. I'll just be... where you come looking for me."
"In the wind inflating the sails, in the wave easing up on the shore."
"In the sparkle of the trembling dew-drops, in the blades of grass warm with the early morning sun."
"Your smile will be my richness. I will be drunk with your successes."
"I will laugh with you behind a rainbow, I will tremble amid the ocean waves on the horizon, I'll be the shiver of a leaf in the whispering breeze, every time you feel emotion."
"I shall be a drop from the sky to kiss your lowered brow, velvety night blanket to protect you."
"I shall be the hand of dawn to tickle your awakening and take you into each brand new day, Nats."

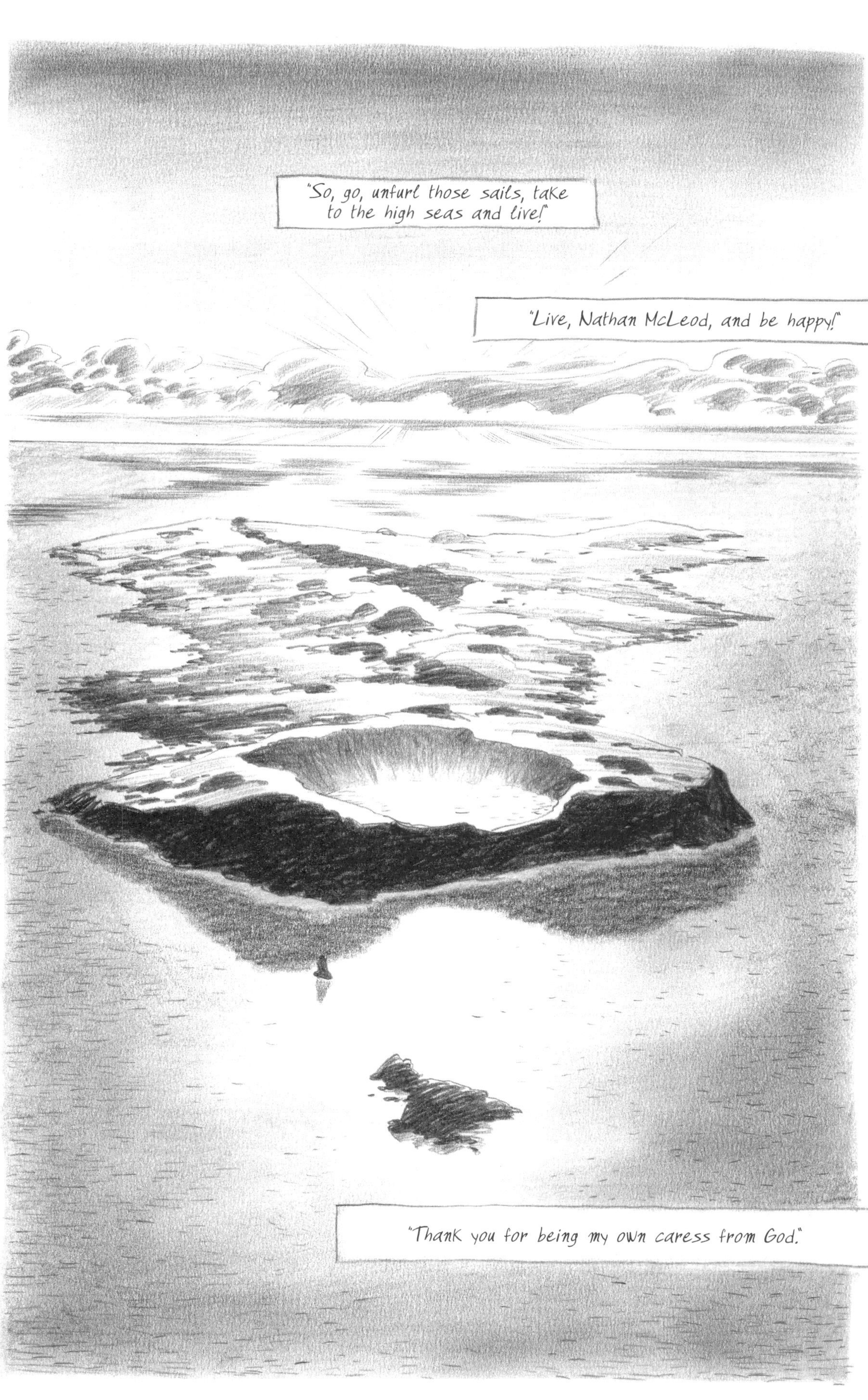
"So, go, unfurl those sails, take to the high seas and live!"
"Live, Nathan McLeod, and be happy!"
"Thank you for being my own caress from God."

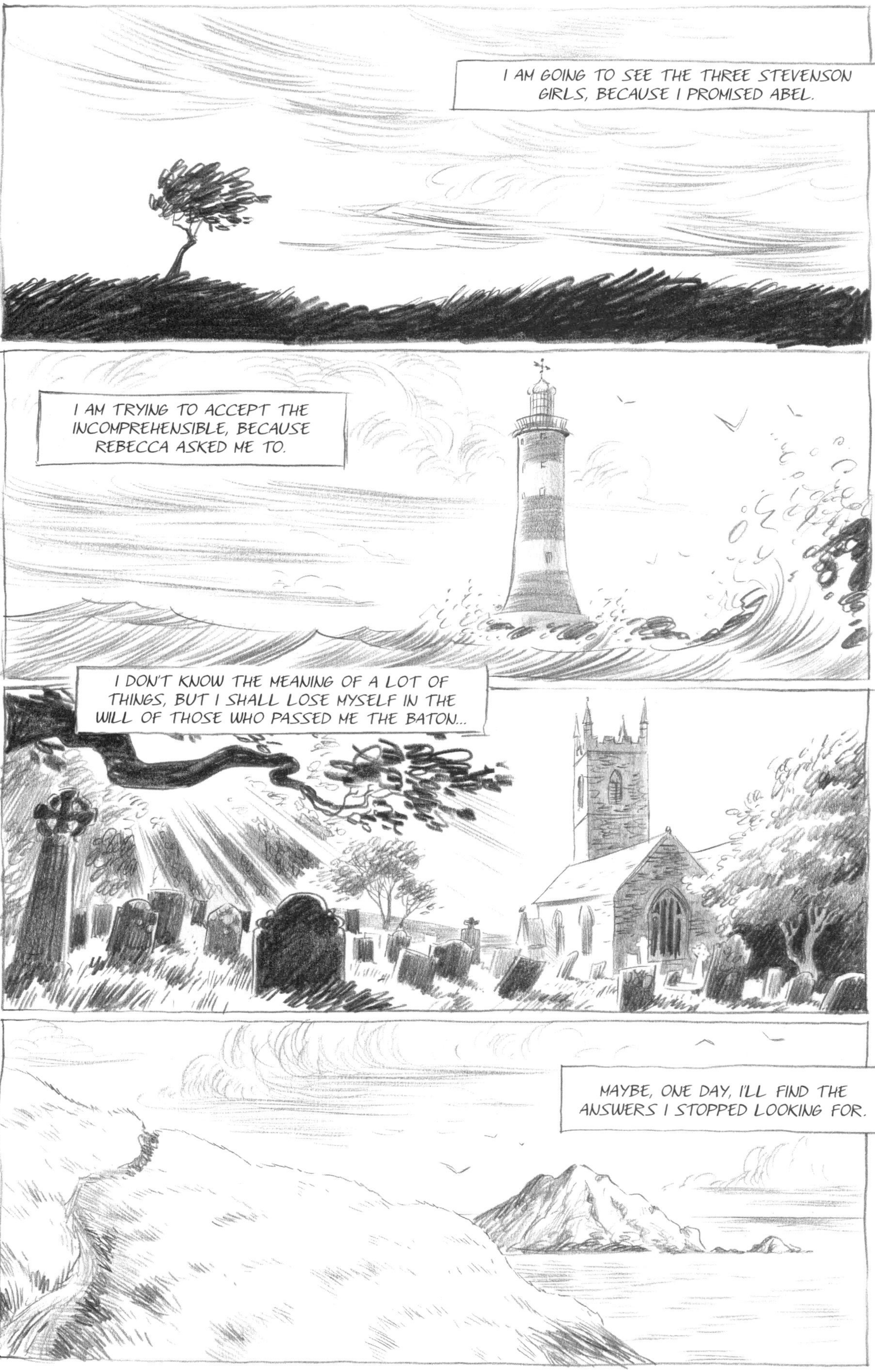
I AM GOING TO SEE THE THREE STEVENSON GIRLS, BECAUSE I PROMISED ABEL.
I AM TRYING TO ACCEPT THE INCOMPREHENSIBLE, BECAUSE REBECCA ASKED ME TO.
I DON'T KNOW THE MEANING OF A LOT OF THINGS, BUT I SHALL LOSE MYSELF IN THE WILL OF THOSE WHO PASSED ME THE BATON...
MAYBE, ONE DAY, I'LL FIND THE ANSWERS I STOPPED LOOKING FOR.

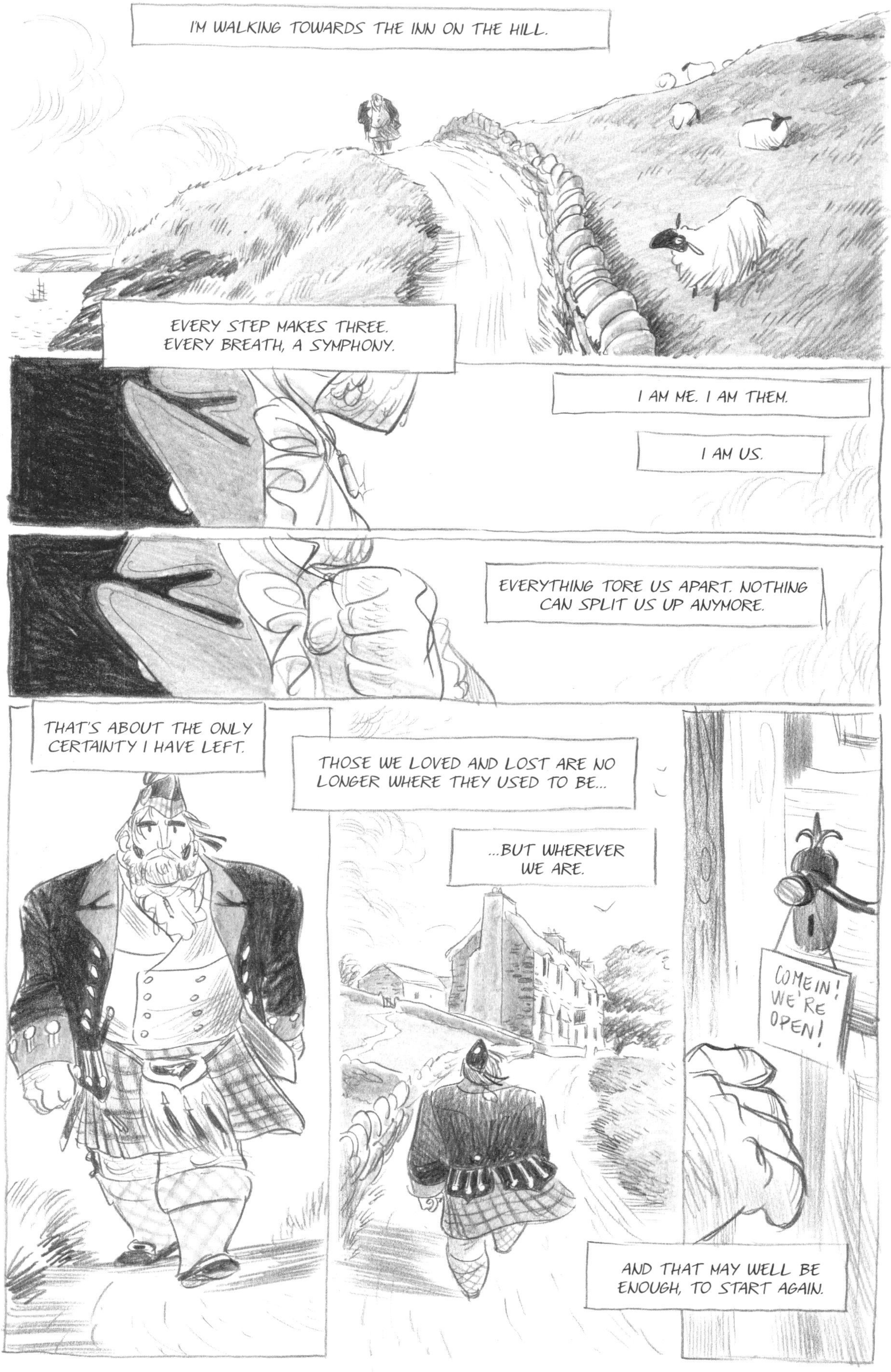
I'M WALKING TOWARDS THE INN ON THE HILL.
EVERY STEP MAKES THREE. EVERY BREATH, A SYMPHONY.
I AM ME. I AM THEM.
I AM US.
EVERYTHING TORE US APART. NOTHING CAN SPLIT US UP ANYMORE.
THAT'S ABOUT THE ONLY CERTAINTY I HAVE LEFT.
THOSE WE LOVED AND LOST ARE NO LONGER WHERE THEY USED TO BE...
...BUT WHEREVER WE ARE.
COME IN! WE'RE OPEN!
AND THAT MAY WELL BE ENOUGH, TO START AGAIN.

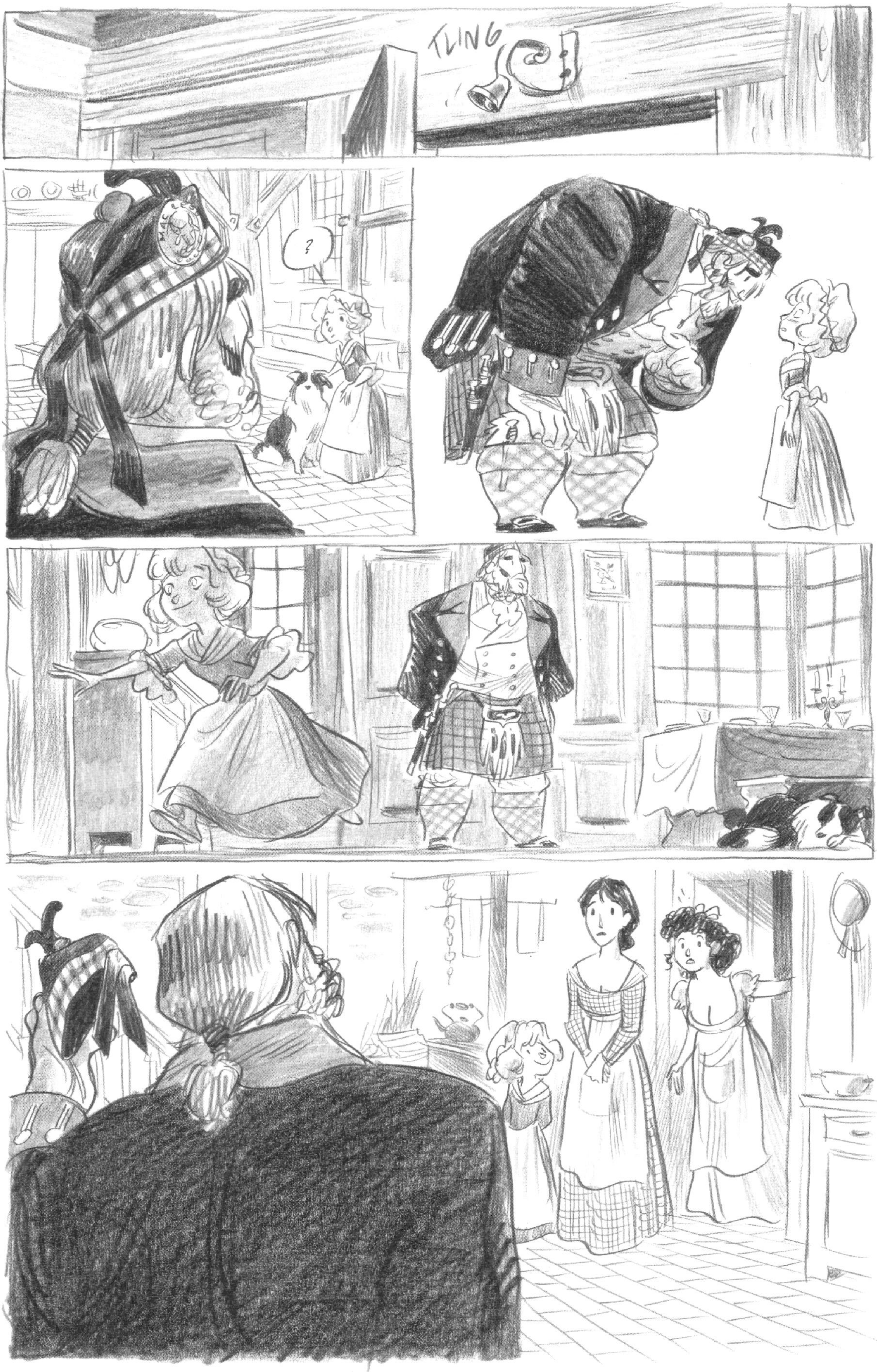
TLING
?

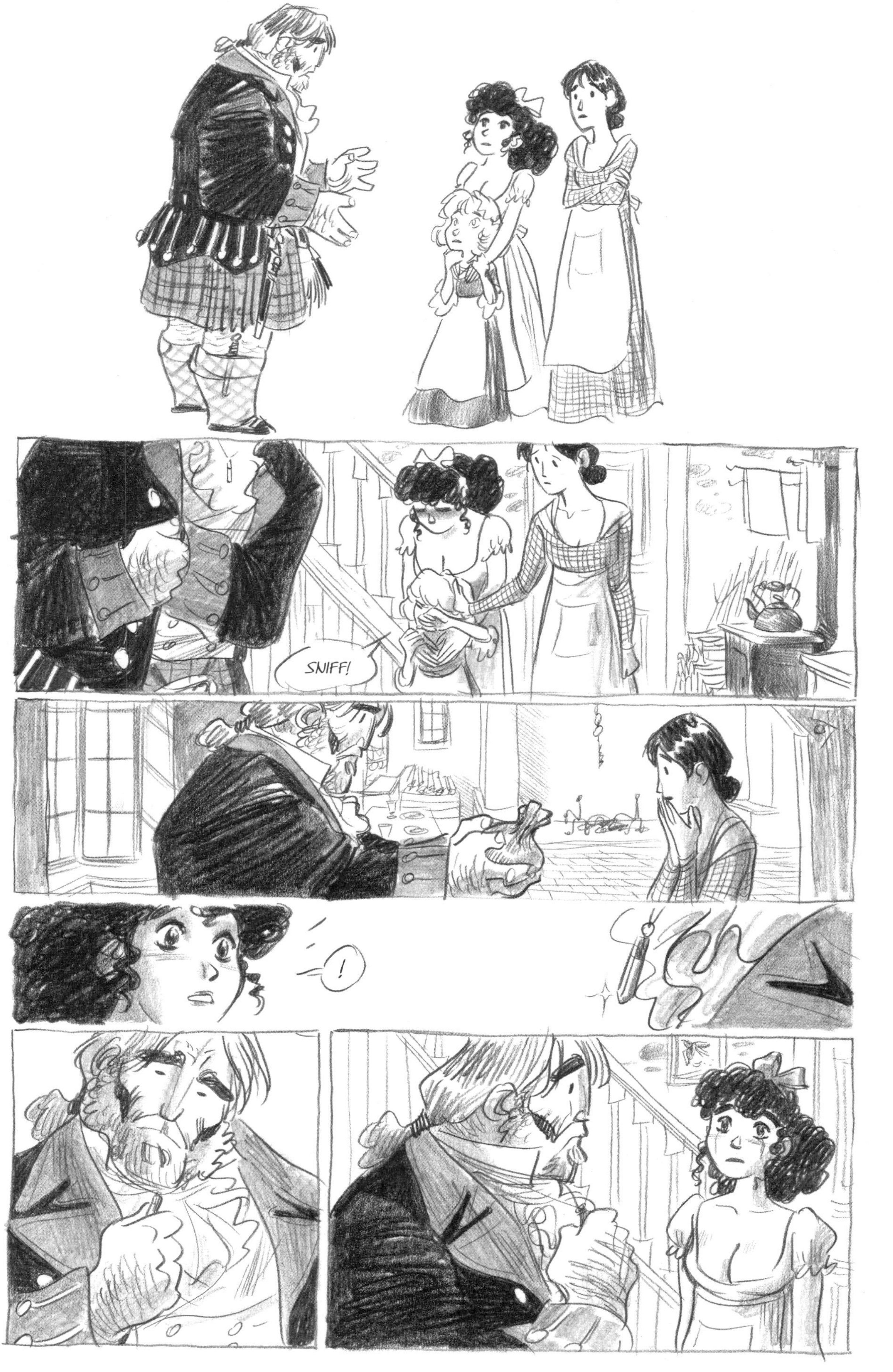
SNIFF!
!

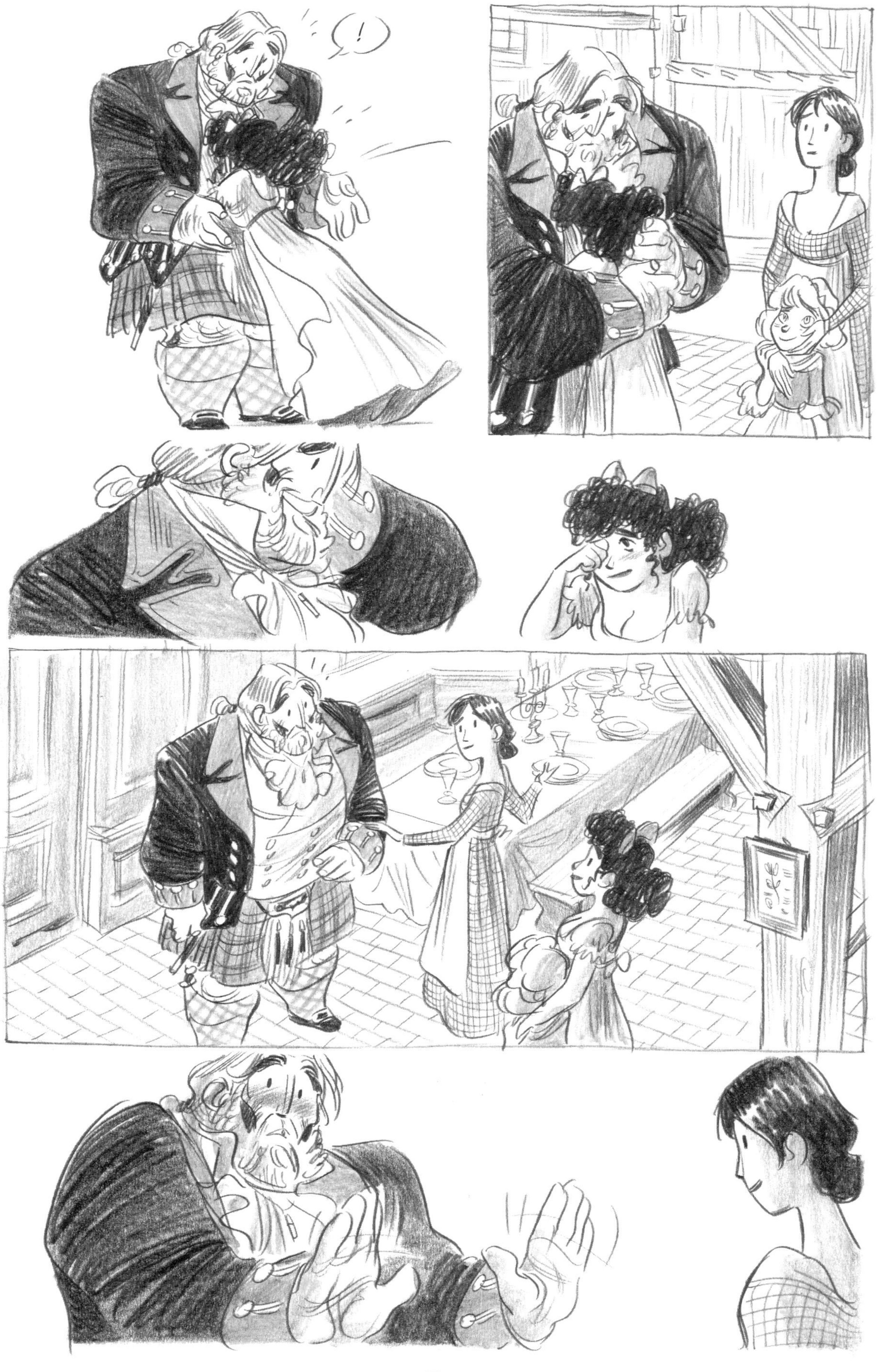
!

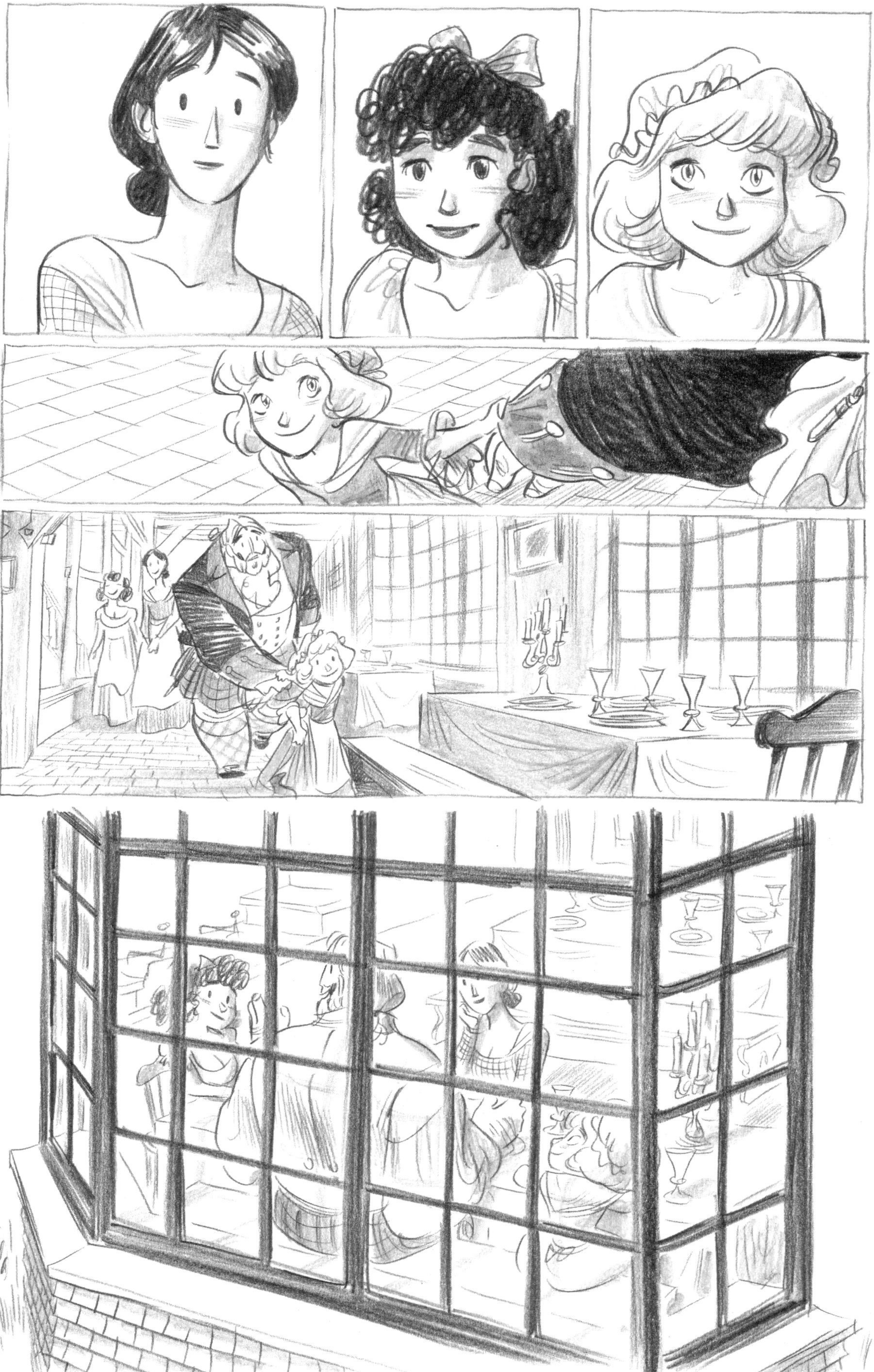

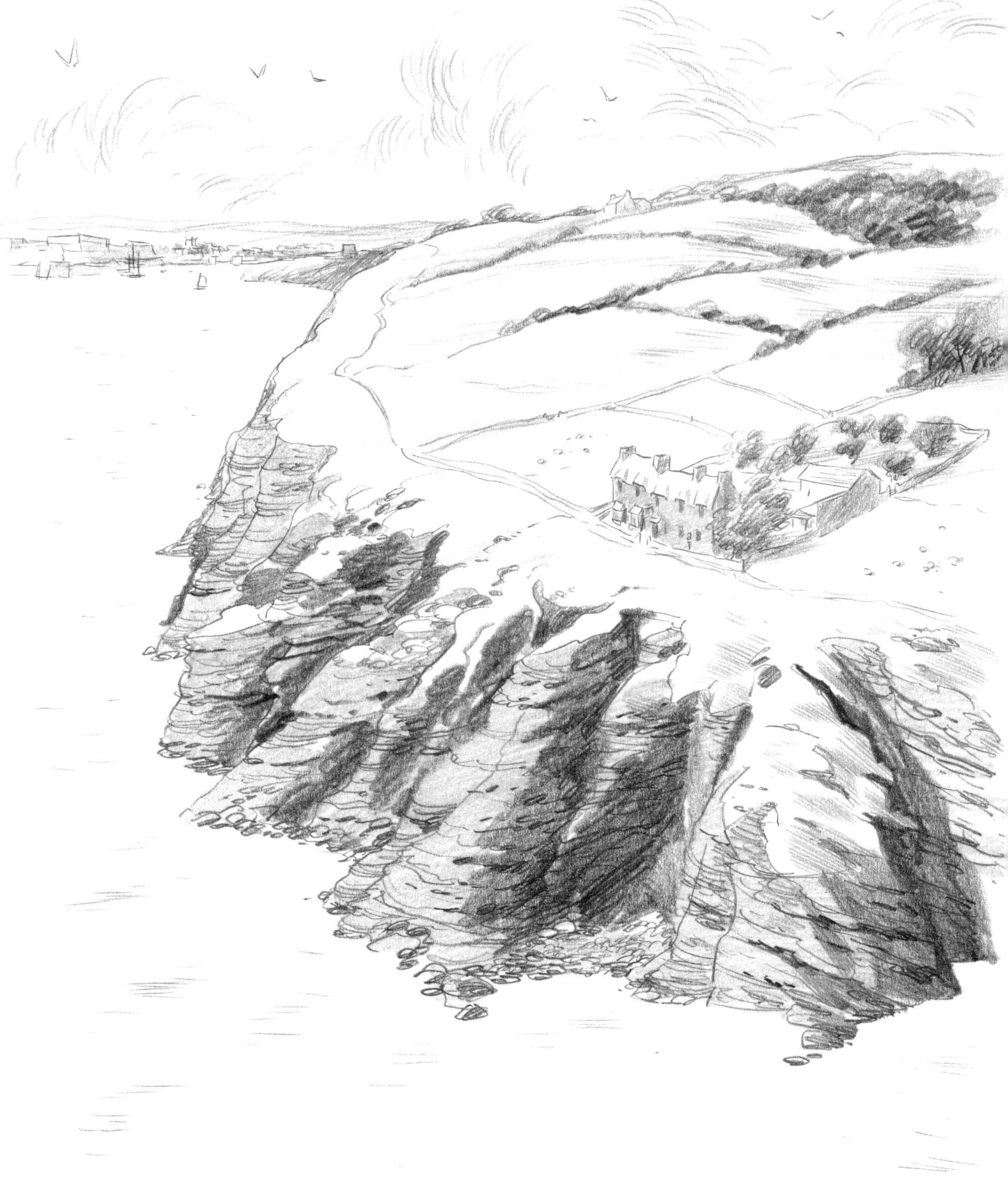

"THERE'S JOY IN THE MOUNTAINS,
THERE'S LIFE IN THE FOUNTAINS,
SMALL CLOUDS ARE SAILING,
BLUE SKY PREVAILING, THE
RAIN IS OVER AND GONE!"

Hasta luego invitado.
Buenos días.
Sucedió mi poema
para ti, para nadie,
para todos.

Voy a rogarte: dé jame intranquilo.
Vivo con el océano intratable
y me cuesta mucho el silencio.

Me muero con cada ola cada dia.
Me mureo con cada ida en cada ola.
Pero el día no muere
nunca.
No muere.
¿Y la ola?
No muere.

Gracias.

Aún

So long, vistor.
Good day.
My poem happened
for you, for nobody,
for everyone.

I beg you: leave me restless.
I live with the impossible ocean
and silence bleeds me dry.

I die with each wave each day.
I die with each day in each wave.
But the day does not die
not ever.
It does not die.
And the wave?
It does not die.

Gracias.

Still Another Day
translated from the Spanish by
Willam O'Daly

PABLO NERUDA

CURTAINS

WORDS

Dear reader who sailed with us so far, THANK YOU.

If you enjoyed the fragments of poetry in this book, may we suggest you read them in their entirety. They are, in order of appearance:

-Samuel Taylor Coleridge, *The Rime of the Ancient Mariner*,
pp. 65, 89, 89, 90, 120, 121, 122, 185, 203, 206, 288.

-William Wordsworth, *Ode: Intimations of Immortality*, pp. 89, 114.

-William Wordsworth, *My Heart Leaps up*, p. 90

-William Wordsworth, *Composed Upon Westminster Bridge, Sept. 3rd 1802*, p. 94

-William Wordsworth, *It is a Beauteous Evening*, p. 95

-William Wordsworth, *Lines Composed a Few Miles Above Tintern Abbey*, p. 126

-William Blake, *Infant Sorrow*, p. 148

-William Blake, *Infant Joy*, p. 150

-William Wordsworth, *I Wandered Lonely as a Cloud*, p. 174

- Samuel Taylor Coleridge, *Frost at Midnight*, pp. 263, 273

-William Wordsworth, *Written in March*, p. 300

Rebecca and Abel also recite a few verses from the Bible. They are:

Isaiah 21, II

Psalm 127, vv. 5-8

Matthew 18, 3

Jeremiah 20, 9

Isaiah 21, 4

Song of Songs 8: 6-7

Nathan uses William Shakespeare's words to describe the waves around Cape Horn
The Tempest, Act I, vv.16-17

Lastly, ok, we admit it, Mummy Gwen's song to little Rebecca
is no less than a fragment from Steve Cooney's "Island Girl",
played by Irish band Altan in their album Another Sky, in 2000.
It is so moving that it really felt like an old ballad and the verses
seemed perfect for those tender mother-daughter moments.

MUSIC

Music also makes its way into the book. With his violin Abel played:

Wolfgang Amadeus Mozart, Violin Concerto n.3 K216 (third movement).

The sea shanty "Drunken Sailor."

Antonio Vivaldi, The Four Seasons op. 8, Winter (first movement).

Many a sea shanty were sung on board the ships.

Here they are, in order of appearance:

ROLL AN' GO

ALL FOR ME GROG

BLOW, YE WINDS

DRUNKEN SAILOR

HAUL AWAY, JOE

RANDY DANDY-OH

DON'T FORGET YOUR OLD SHIPMATE

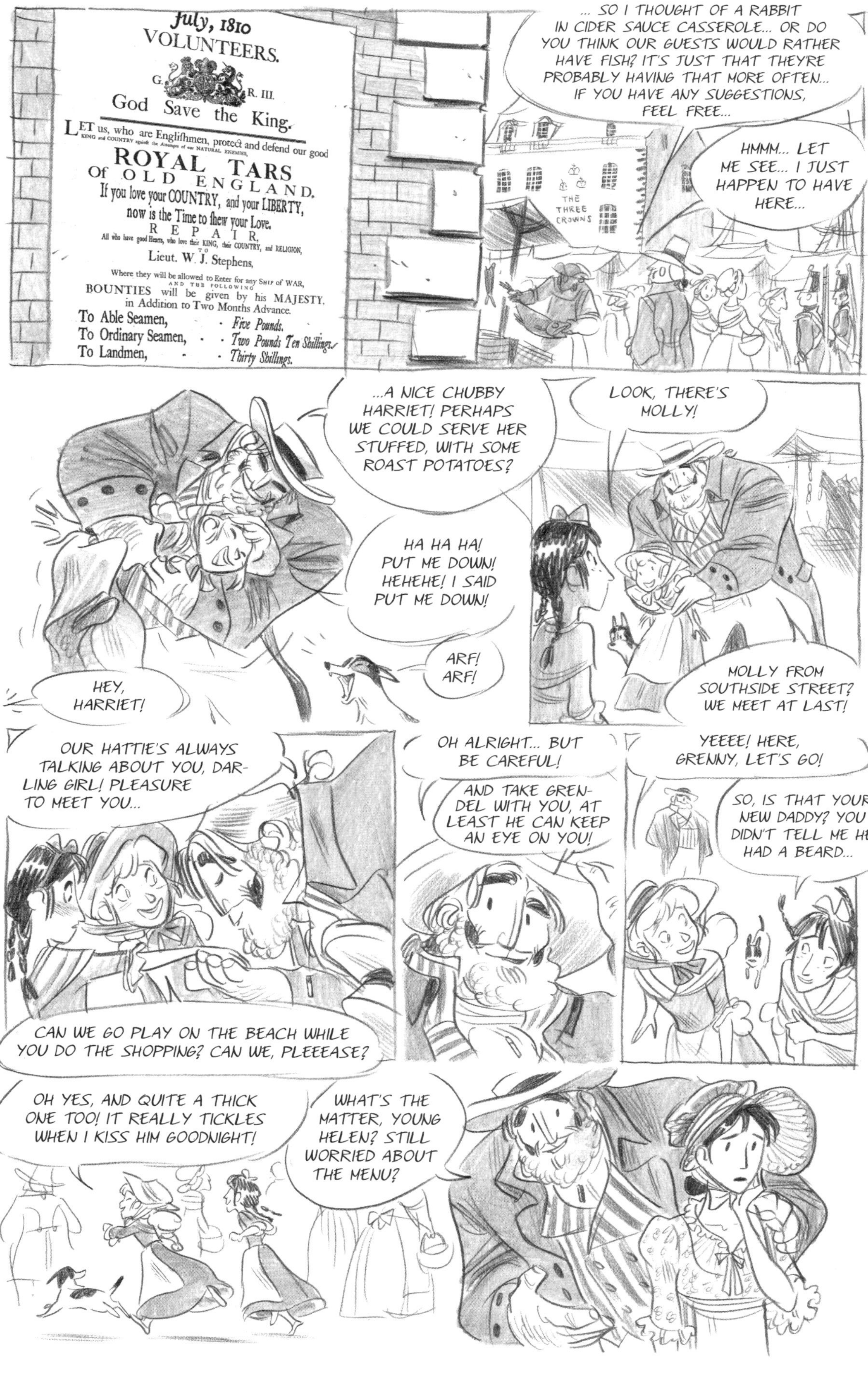
July, 1810
VOLUNTEERS.
G. R. III.
God Save the King.
LET us, who are Englishmen, protect and defend our good KING and COUNTRY against the Attempts of our NATURAL ENEMIES,
ROYAL TARS
Of OLD ENGLAND.
If you love your COUNTRY, and your LIBERTY,
now is the Time to shew your Love.
REPAIR,
All who have good Hearts, who love their KING, their COUNTRY, and RELIGION,
TO
Lieut. W. J. Stephens,
Where they will be allowed to Enter for any SHIP of WAR,
AND THE FOLLOWING
BOUNTIES will be given by his MAJESTY,
in Addition to Two Months Advance.
To Able Seamen, - Five Pounds.
To Ordinary Seamen, - Two Pounds Ten Shillings.
To Landmen, - Thirty Shillings.
... SO I THOUGHT OF A RABBIT IN CIDER SAUCE CASSEROLE... OR DO YOU THINK OUR GUESTS WOULD RATHER HAVE FISH? IT'S JUST THAT THEY'RE PROBABLY HAVING THAT MORE OFTEN... IF YOU HAVE ANY SUGGESTIONS, FEEL FREE...
THE THREE CROWNS
HMMM... LET ME SEE... I JUST HAPPEN TO HAVE HERE...
...A NICE CHUBBY HARRIET! PERHAPS WE COULD SERVE HER STUFFED, WITH SOME ROAST POTATOES?
HA HA HA! PUT ME DOWN! HEHEHE! I SAID PUT ME DOWN!
ARF! ARF!
HEY, HARRIET!
LOOK, THERE'S MOLLY!
MOLLY FROM SOUTHSIDE STREET? WE MEET AT LAST!
OUR HATTIE'S ALWAYS TALKING ABOUT YOU, DARLING GIRL! PLEASURE TO MEET YOU...
CAN WE GO PLAY ON THE BEACH WHILE YOU DO THE SHOPPING? CAN WE, PLEEEASE?
OH ALRIGHT... BUT BE CAREFUL!
AND TAKE GRENDEL WITH YOU, AT LEAST HE CAN KEEP AN EYE ON YOU!
YEEEE! HERE, GRENNY, LET'S GO!
SO, IS THAT YOUR NEW DADDY? YOU DIDN'T TELL ME HE HAD A BEARD...
OH YES, AND QUITE A THICK ONE TOO! IT REALLY TICKLES WHEN I KISS HIM GOODNIGHT!
WHAT'S THE MATTER, YOUNG HELEN? STILL WORRIED ABOUT THE MENU?

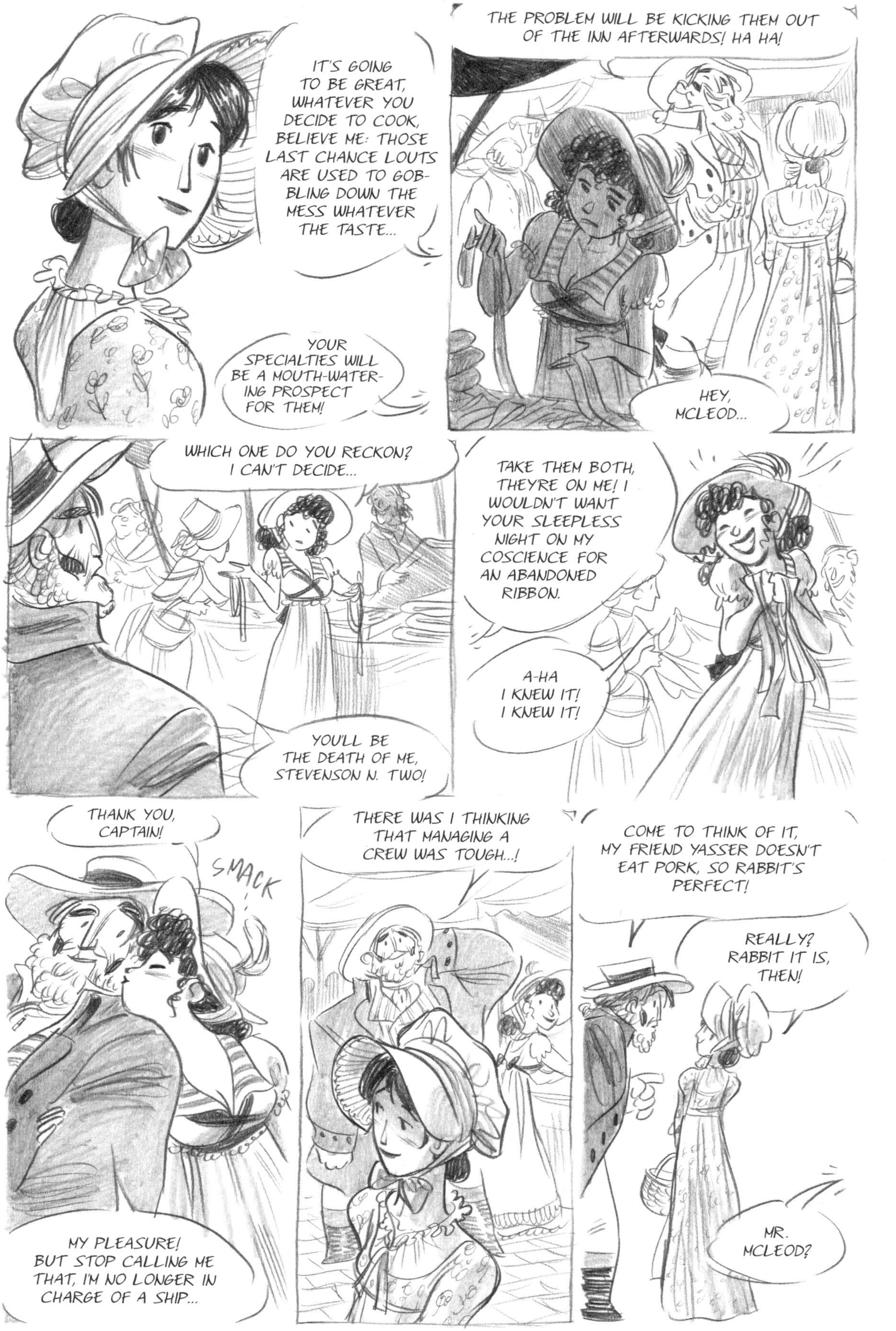
IT'S GOING TO BE GREAT, WHATEVER YOU DECIDE TO COOK, BELIEVE ME: THOSE LAST CHANCE LOUTS ARE USED TO GOB-BLING DOWN THE MESS WHATEVER THE TASTE...
YOUR SPECIALTIES WILL BE A MOUTH-WATER-ING PROSPECT FOR THEM!
THE PROBLEM WILL BE KICKING THEM OUT OF THE INN AFTERWARDS! HA HA!
HEY, MCLEOD...
WHICH ONE DO YOU RECKON? I CAN'T DECIDE...
YOU'LL BE THE DEATH OF ME, STEVENSON N. TWO!
TAKE THEM BOTH, THEY'RE ON ME! I WOULDN'T WANT YOUR SLEEPLESS NIGHT ON MY COSCIENCE FOR AN ABANDONED RIBBON.
A-HA I KNEW IT! I KNEW IT!
THANK YOU, CAPTAIN!
SMACK
MY PLEASURE! BUT STOP CALLING ME THAT, I'M NO LONGER IN CHARGE OF A SHIP...
THERE WAS I THINKING THAT MANAGING A CREW WAS TOUGH...!
COME TO THINK OF IT, MY FRIEND YASSER DOESN'T EAT PORK, SO RABBIT'S PERFECT!
REALLY? RABBIT IT IS, THEN!
MR. MCLEOD?

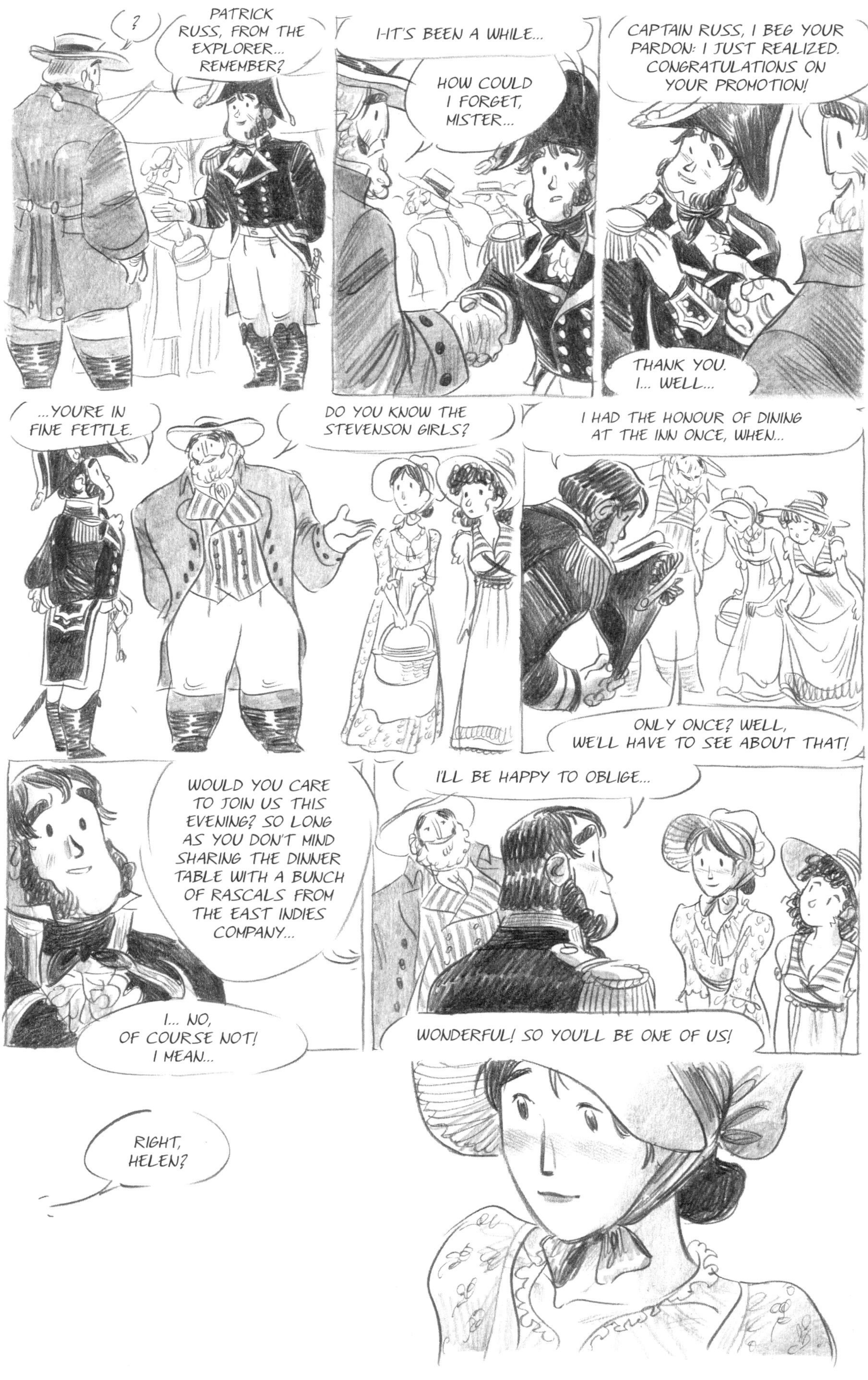
?
PATRICK RUSS, FROM THE EXPLORER... REMEMBER?
I-IT'S BEEN A WHILE...
HOW COULD I FORGET, MISTER...
CAPTAIN RUSS, I BEG YOUR PARDON: I JUST REALIZED. CONGRATULATIONS ON YOUR PROMOTION!
THANK YOU. I... WELL...
...YOU'RE IN FINE FETTLE.
DO YOU KNOW THE STEVENSON GIRLS?
I HAD THE HONOUR OF DINING AT THE INN ONCE, WHEN...
ONLY ONCE? WELL, WE'LL HAVE TO SEE ABOUT THAT!
WOULD YOU CARE TO JOIN US THIS EVENING? SO LONG AS YOU DON'T MIND SHARING THE DINNER TABLE WITH A BUNCH OF RASCALS FROM THE EAST INDIES COMPANY...
I... NO, OF COURSE NOT! I MEAN...
I'LL BE HAPPY TO OBLIGE...
WONDERFUL! SO YOU'LL BE ONE OF US!
RIGHT, HELEN?

For you, at last, Tata (1959-1994) and Abele (1963-2001),
true pirates; you left too early, but remained essential.
For the interrupted stories, the endings left to the imagination;
the reasons why I write. I miss you terribly, every new day.
I cannot stop looking for you in every precious encounter.
And I keep taking you with me: in a gesture, a look, a laugh...
In the stone of light that has breathed in the rythm of my
steps for over twenty years, and contains you both.
Perhaps from your Honey Valley, you already know all this.

And in memory of Grandad Natale (1918-2013) who,
as he walked down the steps, unknowingly,
towards boarding, would put on his hat.

The Authors

Teresa and Stefano were both born in the Grande Pianura, in the mid-'70's, but only met in 2004, thanks to a pan-eared mouse and a sucker-shooting pistol.

She writes stories for a living; he draws them. They like each other immediately and marry the following year.

Having discovered one another as curious travellers, avid readers and relentless dreamers, they travel around the world with nothing but boots and a rucksack. It wasn't long before, having walked together, they started telling stories together.

Their first four-hand adventures were for Disney's weekly "Topolino" (Mickey Mouse), with dozens of stories, amongst which a mousy adaptation of R.L. Stevenson's Treasure Island (2015).

In 2011, they move to the House with No North – a ten minute ride from the Farms, a twenty minute walk from the Wood, and a half-hour train journey from the Lake – and start planting their first trees.

In their Creative Den, their bottomless drawers are filled with plans and ideas, things to do, places to see, faces to meet.

The Forbidden Harbor has won The Gran Guinigi Award for Best Graphic Novel in 2015, the Micheluzzi Award for best Italian Graphic Novel in 2016 and the Prix Academie de Marine in 2017. A page from the book has been part of an exhibit at the Louvre museum in Paris.

The most original fruit of their collaboration have big eyes and heads full of stories already. Their names are Viola and Michele.

(Teresa and Stefano send their humble apologies to William Hogarth for abusing one of his paintings and hope to rely on the artist's British sense of humor.)

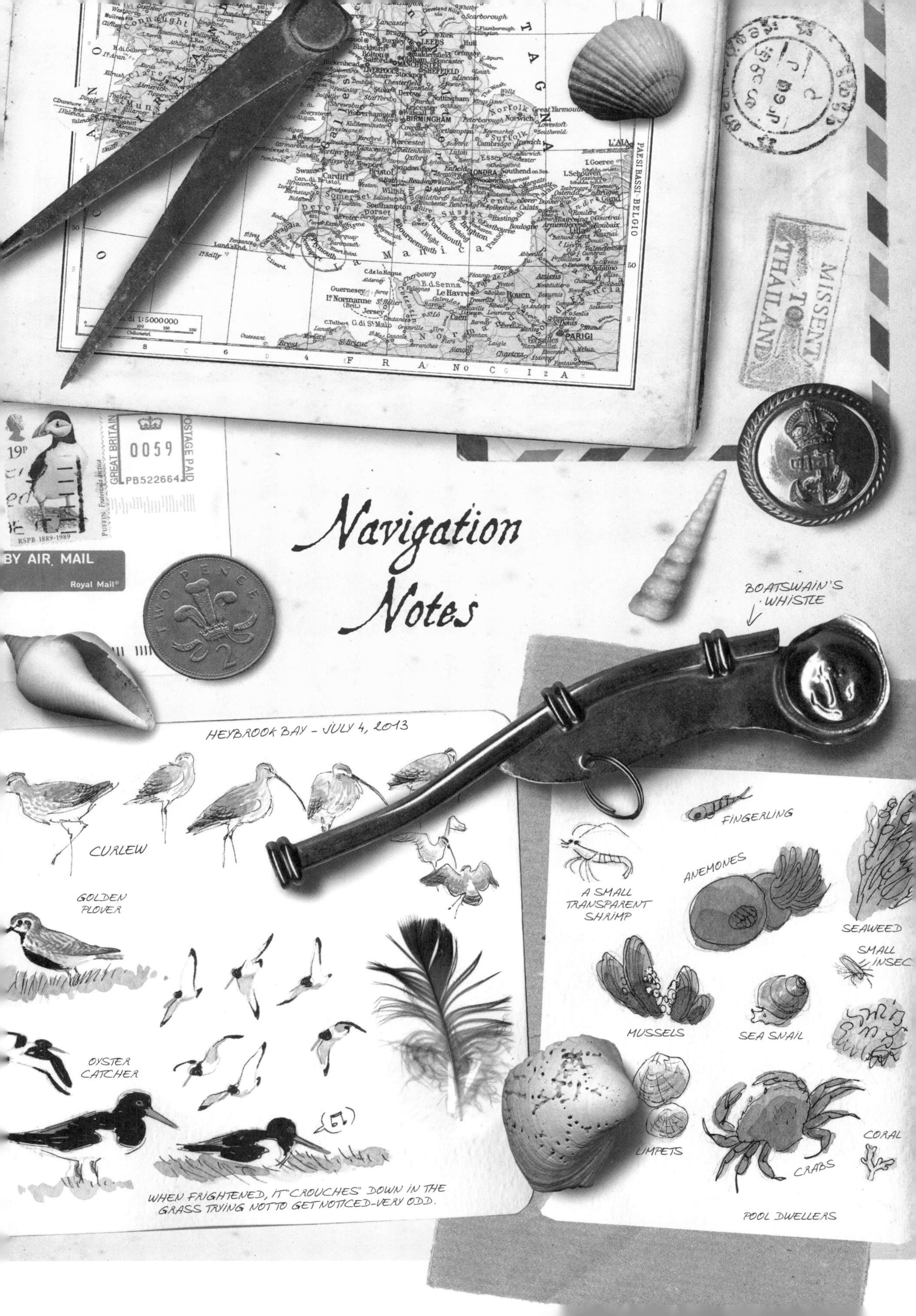

Navigation Notes
MISSENT TO THAILAND
19p
GREAT BRITAIN
0059
POSTAGE PAID
PB522664
PUFFIN Fratercula arctica
RSPB 1889-1989
BY AIR MAIL
Royal Mail®
TWO PENCE
2
BOATSWAIN'S WHISTLE
HEYBROOK BAY - JULY 4, 2013
CURLEW
GOLDEN PLOVER
OYSTER CATCHER
WHEN FRIGHTENED, IT "CROUCHES" DOWN IN THE GRASS TRYING NOT TO GET NOTICED-VERY ODD.
FINGERLING
A SMALL TRANSPARENT SHRIMP
ANEMONES
SEAWEED
SMALL INSEC
MUSSELS
SEA SNAIL
LIMPETS
CRABS
CORAL
POOL DWELLERS

Royal Navy Studies

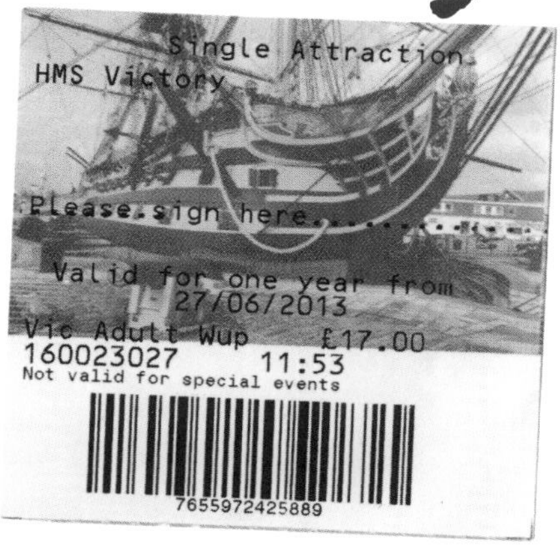

Single Attraction
HMS Victory
Please sign here........
Valid for one year from
27/06/2013
Vic Adult Wup £17.00
160023027 11:53
Not valid for special events
7655972425889

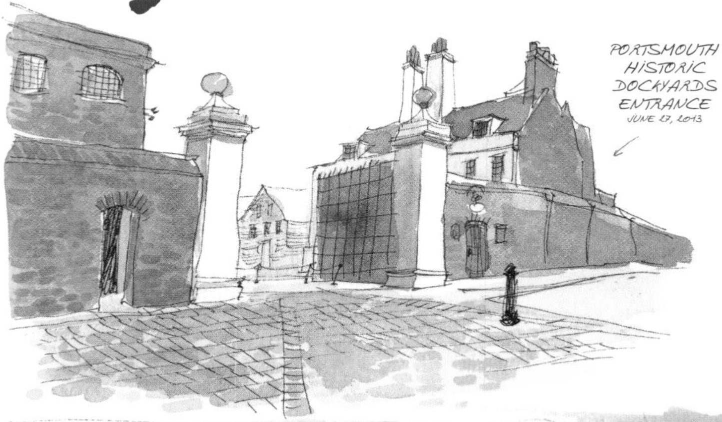

PORTSMOUTH HISTORIC DOCKYARDS ENTRANCE
JUNE 27, 2013

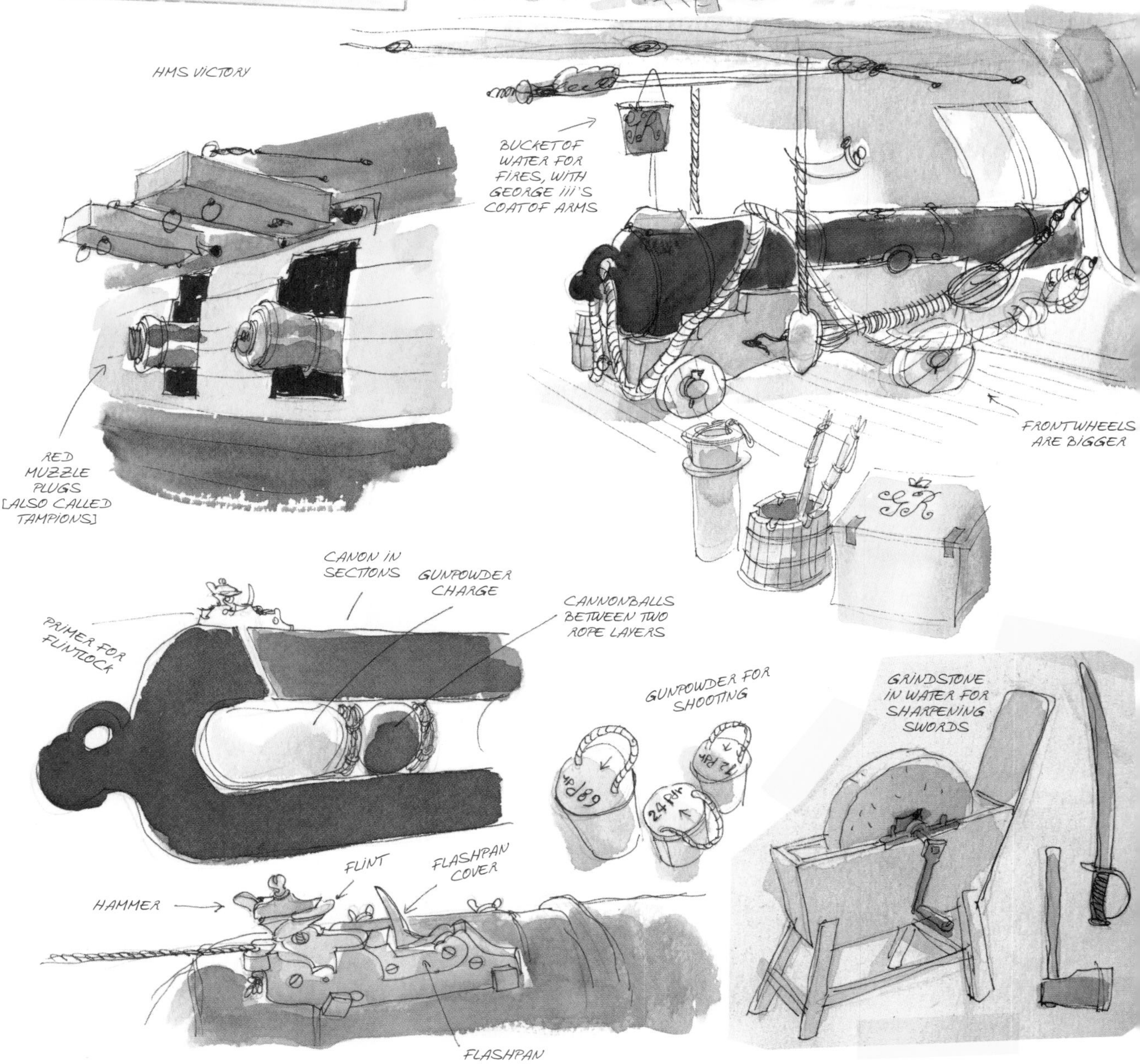

HMS VICTORY
BUCKET OF WATER FOR FIRES, WITH GEORGE III'S COAT OF ARMS
RED MUZZLE PLUGS [ALSO CALLED TAMPIONS]
FRONT WHEELS ARE BIGGER
CANON IN SECTIONS
GUNPOWDER CHARGE
CANNONBALLS BETWEEN TWO ROPE LAYERS
PRIMER FOR FLINTLOCK
GUNPOWDER FOR SHOOTING
68 Pdr
24 Pdr
12 Pdr
GRINDSTONE IN WATER FOR SHARPENING SWORDS
FLINT
FLASHPAN COVER
HAMMER
FLASHPAN

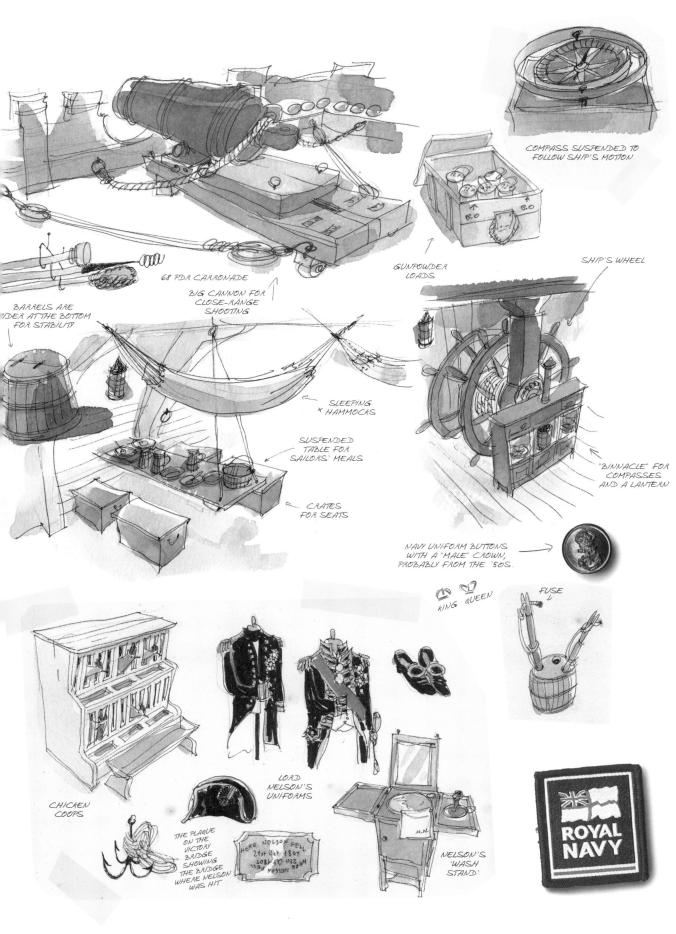

COMPASS SUSPENDED TO FOLLOW SHIP'S MOTION

GUNPOWDER LOADS

68 PDR CARRONADE

BIG CANNON FOR CLOSE-RANGE SHOOTING

BARRELS ARE WIDER AT THE BOTTOM FOR STABILITY

SHIP'S WHEEL

SLEEPING × HAMMOCKS

SUSPENDED TABLE FOR SAILORS' MEALS

CRATES FOR SEATS

"BINNACLE" FOR COMPASSES AND A LANTERN

NAVY UNIFORM BUTTONS WITH A "MALE" CROWN, PROBABLY FROM THE '50S.

KING   QUEEN

FUSE

CHICKEN COOPS

LORD NELSON'S UNIFORMS

THE PLAQUE ON THE VICTORY BRIDGE SHOWING THE BRIDGE WHERE NELSON WAS HIT

HERE NELSON FELL 21st Oct. 1805

NELSON'S 'WASH STAND'

ROYAL NAVY

Plymouth (Devon)

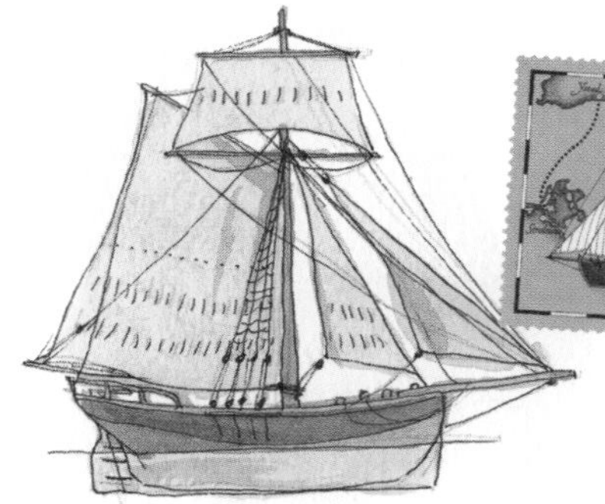

1780 FISHING VESSEL,
HARTLAND QUAY MUSEUM,
JULY 16, 2013

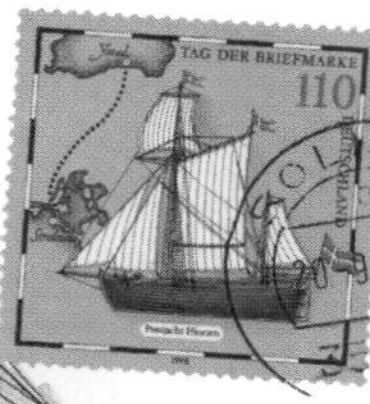
TAG DER BRIEFMARKE
110

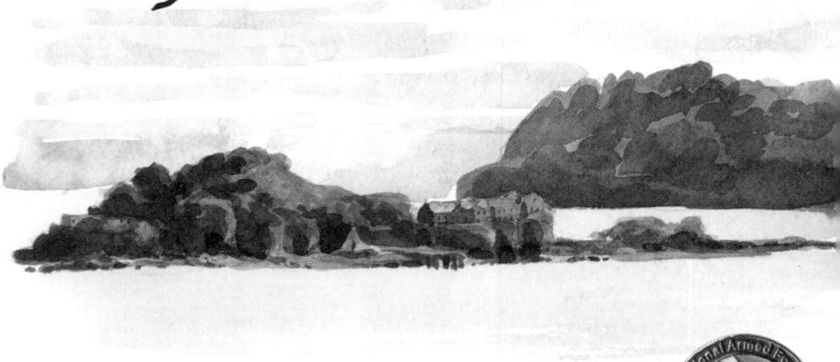

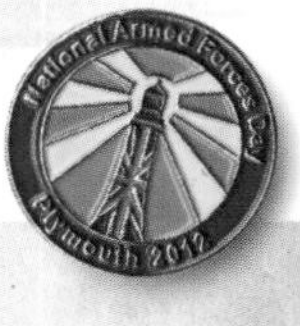
National Armed Forces Day
Plymouth 2012

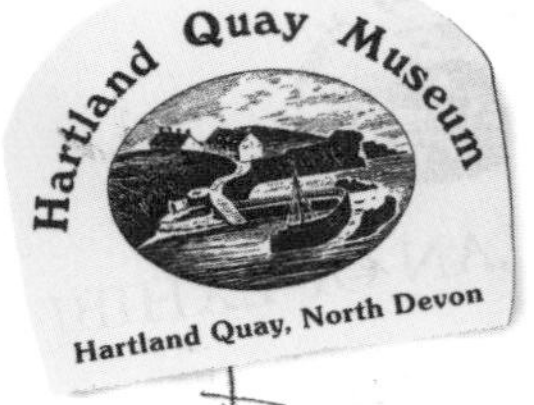
Hartland Quay Museum
Hartland Quay, North Devon

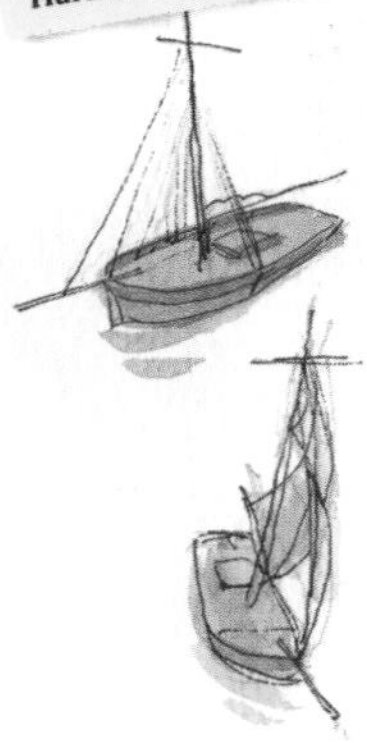

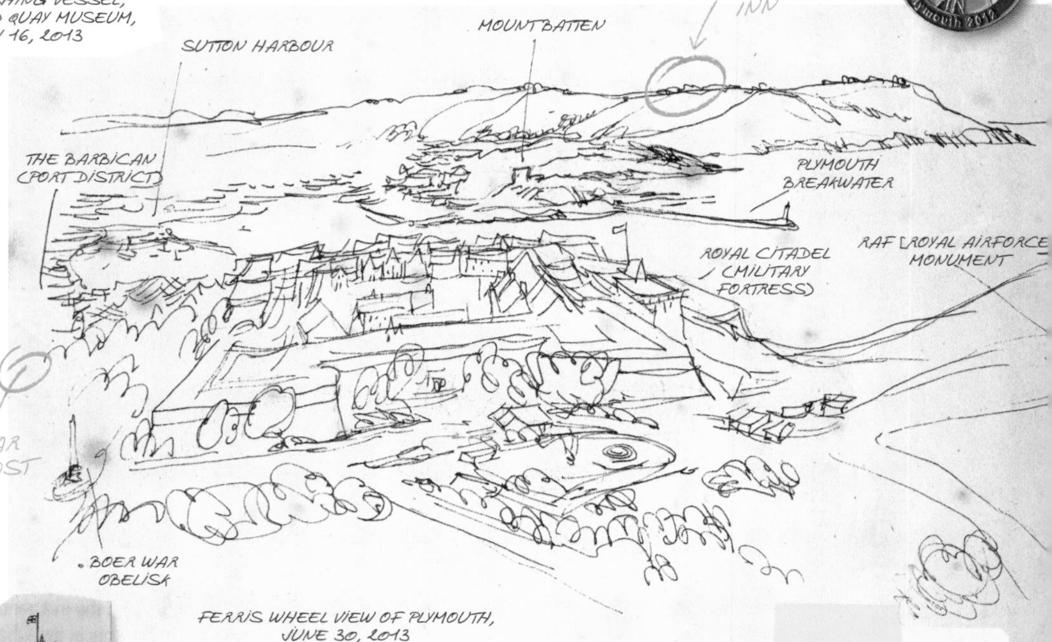
SUTTON HARBOUR
MOUNTBATTEN
ALBATROSS INN
THE BARBICAN (PORT DISTRICT)
PLYMOUTH BREAKWATER
ROYAL CITADEL (MILITARY FORTRESS)
RAF (ROYAL AIRFORCE MONUMENT
PILLAR TO POST
BOER WAR OBELISK

FERRIS WHEEL VIEW OF PLYMOUTH,
JUNE 30, 2013

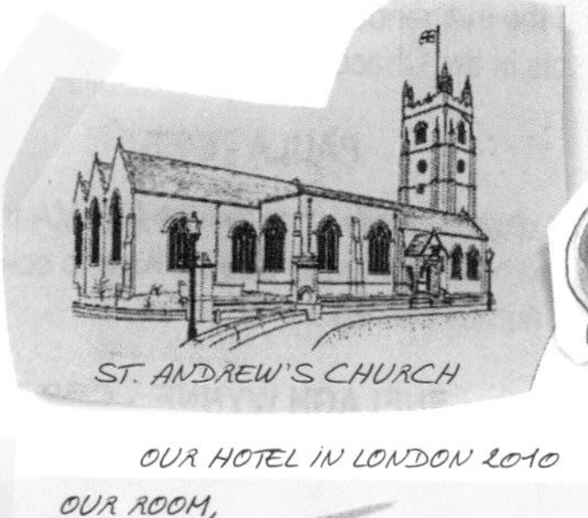
ST. ANDREW'S CHURCH

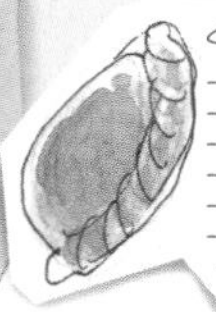

CORNISH PASTRY
- LAMB AND MINT
- BACON AND CHEESE
- MINCE BEEF
- STEAK
- WHOLE WHEAT VEGETABLE
- CHEESE & ONION
- PORK & APPLE
- RICOTTA & SPINACH

PUB SIGNS

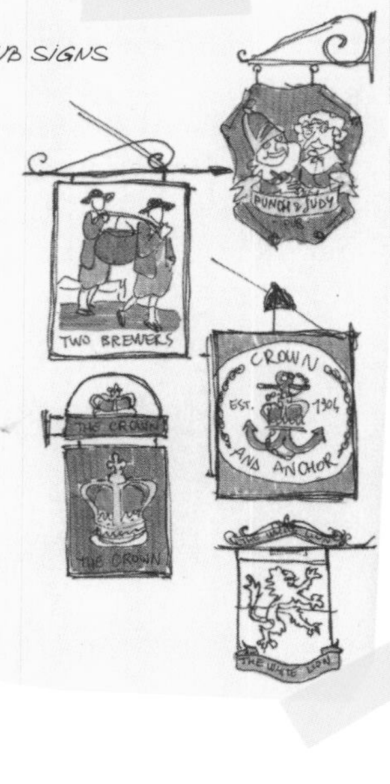
PUNCH & JUDY
TWO BREWERS
CROWN
EST. 1704
AND ANCHOR
THE CROWN
THE CROWN
THE WHITE LION

OUR HOTEL IN LONDON 2010

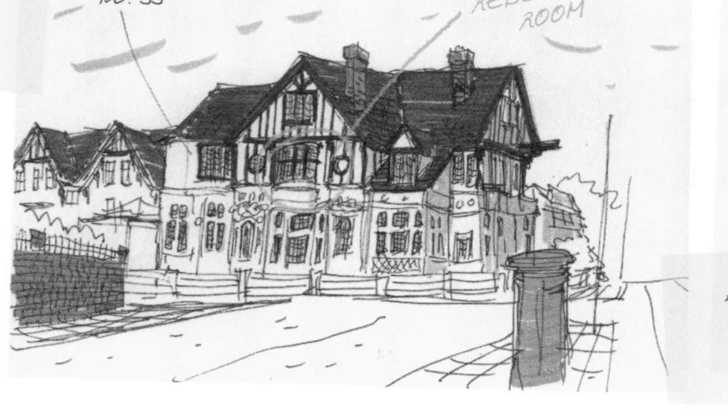
OUR ROOM, NO. 33
REBECCA'S ROOM

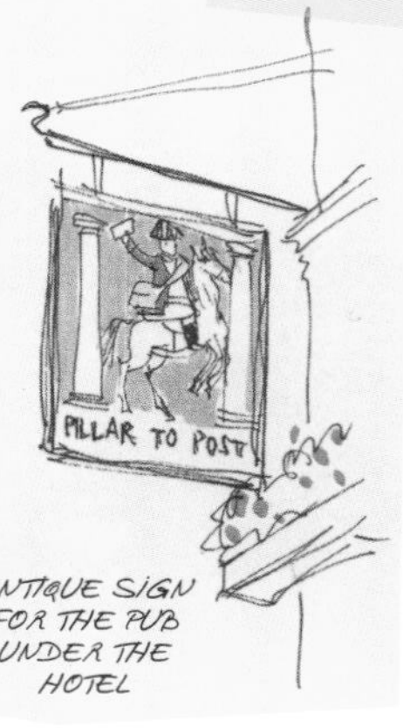
PILLAR TO POST

ANTIQUE SIGN
FOR THE PUB
UNDER THE
HOTEL

AKE'S
LAND

SMEATON'S TOWER, THE PLYMOUTH LIGHTHOUSE UNTIL 1881, WAS ON EDDYSTONE ROCK, 14 MILES OFFSHORE. DISMANTLED AND RECONSTRUCTED IN THE PLYMOUTH HOE, IT OPENED TO THE PUBLIC IN SEPTEMBER 1884. NOW EDDYSTONE LIGHTHOUSE STANDS IN ITS PLACE. JULY 3, 2013.

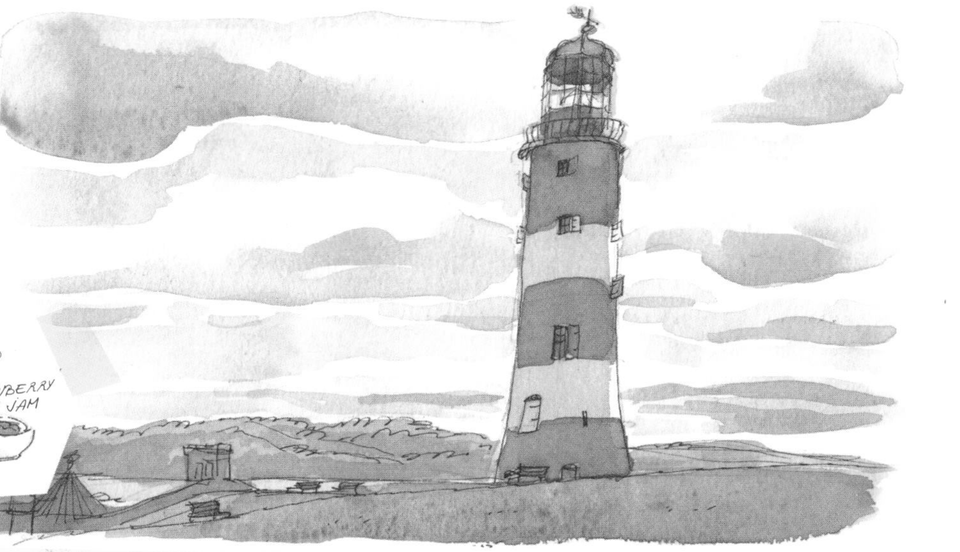

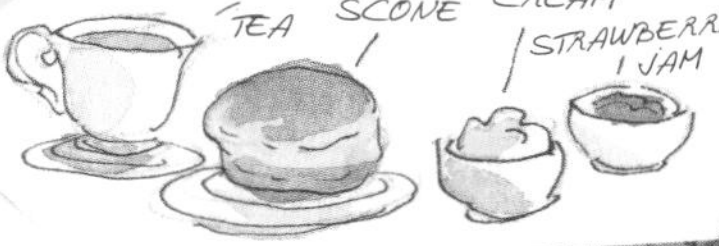

DEVON
CREAM TEA
TEA
SCONE
CLOTTED
CREAM
STRAWBERRY
JAM

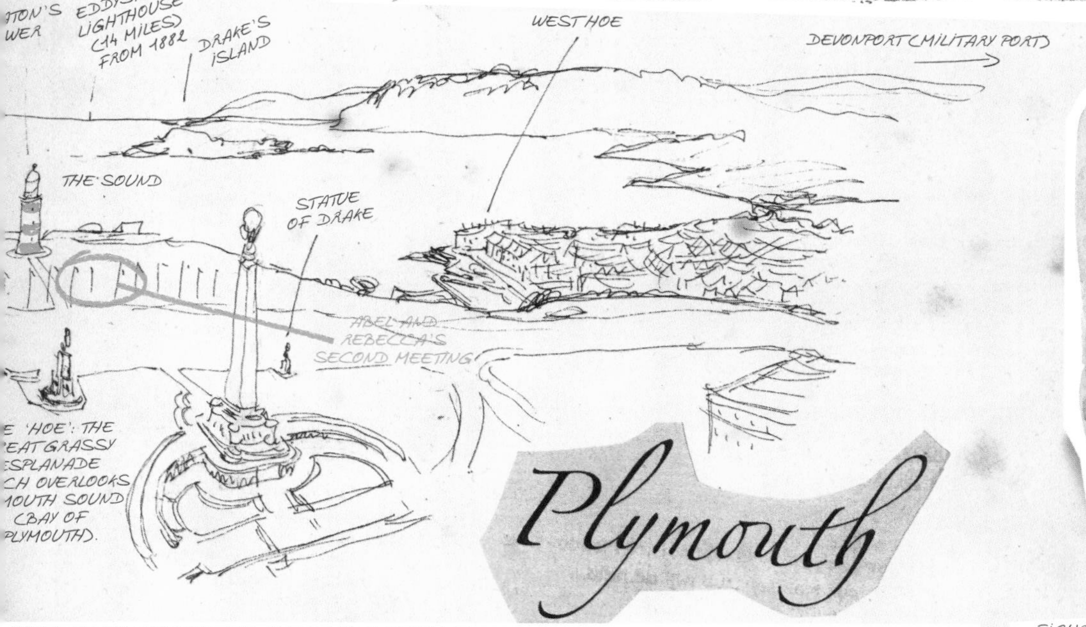

TON'S
WER
EDDYSTONE LIGHTHOUSE (14 MILES) FROM 1882
DRAKE'S ISLAND
WEST HOE
DEVONPORT (MILITARY PORT)
THE SOUND
STATUE OF DRAKE
ABEL AND REBECCA'S SECOND MEETING
E 'HOE': THE
EAT GRASSY
ESPLANADE
CH OVERLOOKS
MOUTH SOUND
(BAY OF
PLYMOUTH).

Plymouth

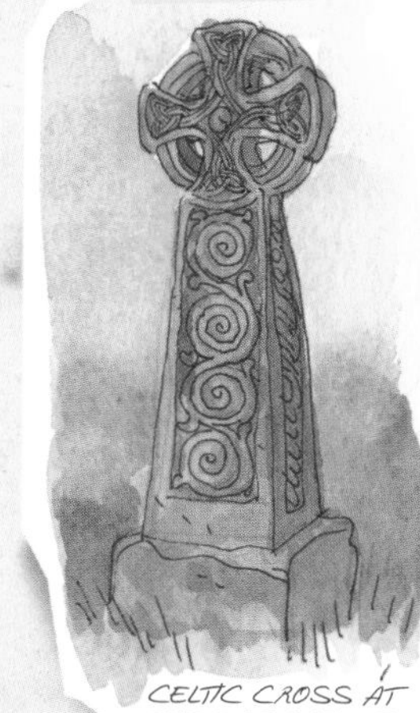

CELTIC CROSS AT THE ENTRANCE TO THE CEMETERY

MORWENSTOW CHURCH AND CEMETERY IN CORNWALL

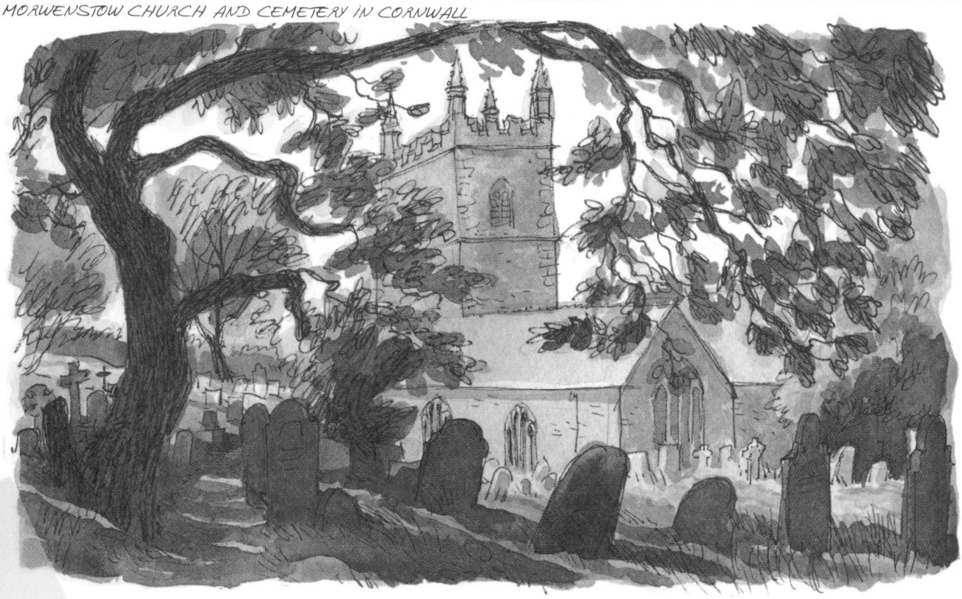

FIGUREHEAD FROM THE BRIG "CALEDONIA," OUT OF ARBROATH, WHICH SANK SEPTEMBER 7, 1842, SERVES AS A TOMBSTONE FOR THE CAPTAIN AND SAILORS WHO DIED IN THE SHIPWRECK AND WERE BURIED IN THE MORWENSTOW CEMETERY INSTEAD OF ALONG THE SHORE BY THE ORDER OF THE VICAR, POET AND OPIUM ADDICT ROBERT HAWKER

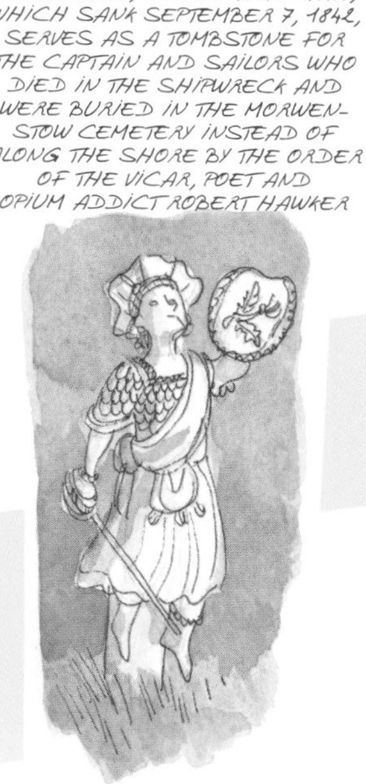

East India Company / Siam

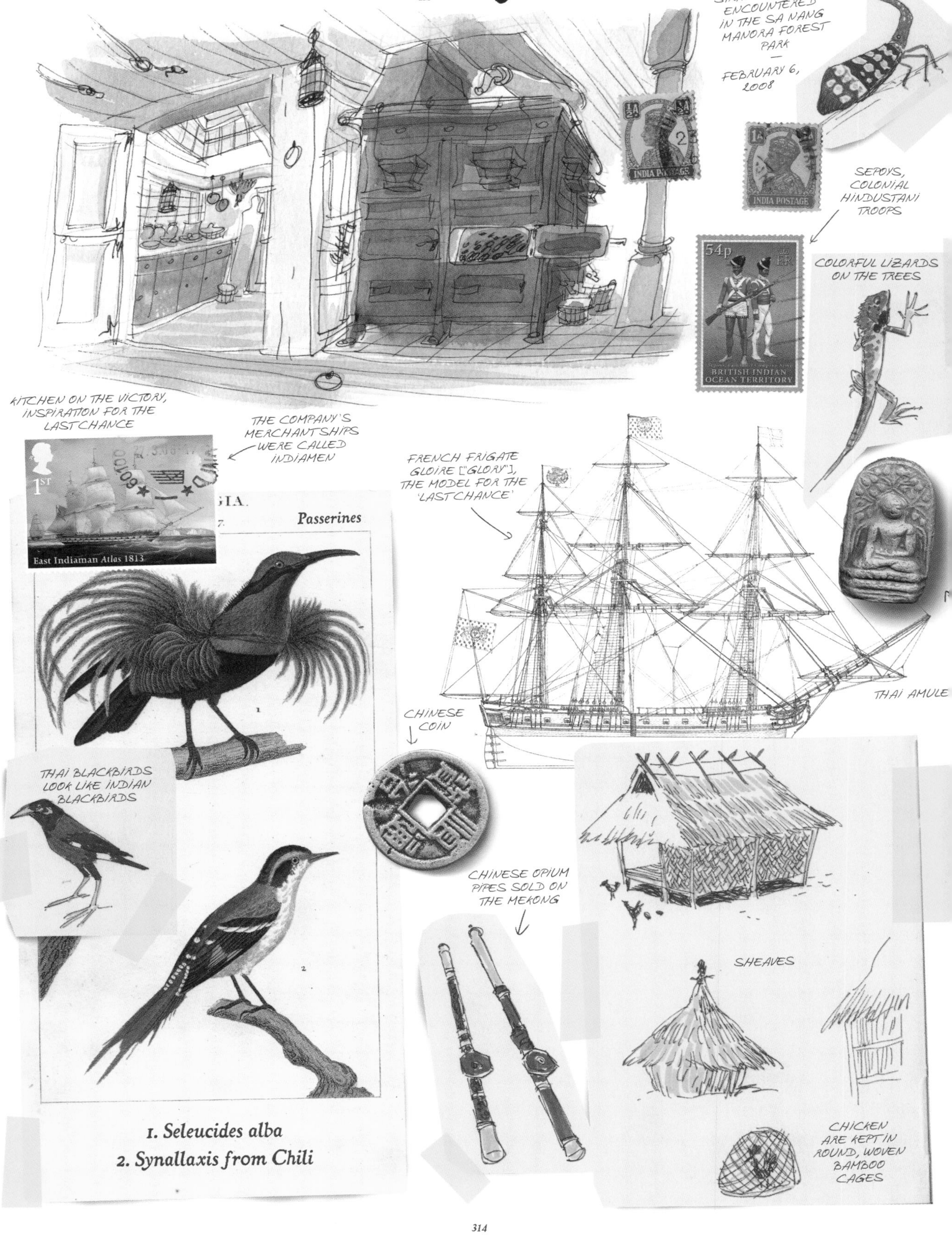
STRANGE INSECT ENCOUNTERED IN THE SA NANG MANORA FOREST PARK — FEBRUARY 6, 2008
INDIA POSTAGE
INDIA POSTAGE
SEPOYS, COLONIAL HINDUSTANI TROOPS
54p
BRITISH INDIAN OCEAN TERRITORY
COLORFUL LIZARDS ON THE TREES
KITCHEN ON THE VICTORY, INSPIRATION FOR THE LASTCHANCE
THE COMPANY'S MERCHANTSHIPS WERE CALLED INDIAMEN
1ST
East Indiaman Atlas 1813
FRENCH FRIGATE GLOIRE ["GLORY"], THE MODEL FOR THE 'LASTCHANCE'
GIA.
7.
Passerines
THAI AMULE
CHINESE COIN
THAI BLACKBIRDS LOOK LIKE INDIAN BLACKBIRDS
CHINESE OPIUM PIPES SOLD ON THE MEKONG
SHEAVES
CHICKEN ARE KEPT IN ROUND, WOVEN BAMBOO CAGES
1. Seleucides alba
2. Synallaxis from Chili

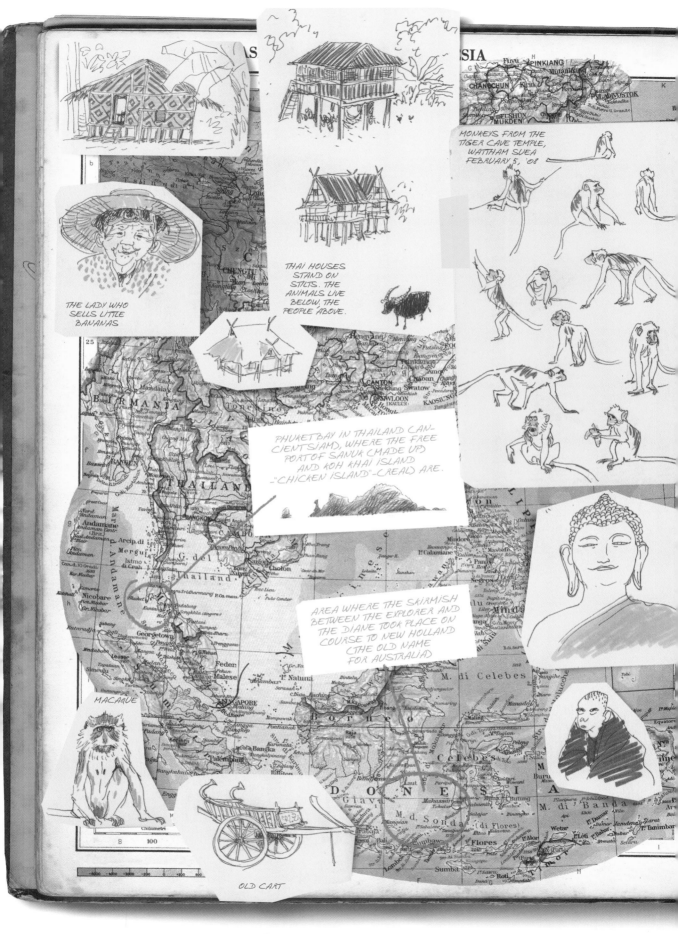

MONKEYS FROM THE TIGER CAVE TEMPLE, WATTHAM SUEA FEBRUARY 5, '08

THE LADY WHO SELLS LITTLE BANANAS

THAI HOUSES STAND ON STILTS. THE ANIMALS LIVE BELOW. THE PEOPLE ABOVE.

PHUKET BAY IN THAILAND CAN-CIENT SIAM), WHERE THE FREE PORT OF SANUK (MADE UP) AND KOH KHAI ISLAND "CHICKEN ISLAND"-(REAL) ARE.

AREA WHERE THE SKIRMISH BETWEEN THE EXPLORER AND THE DIANE TOOK PLACE ON COURSE TO NEW HOLLAND (THE OLD NAME FOR AUSTRALIA)

MACAQUE

OLD CART

HMS EXPLORER CREW - ROYAL NAVY

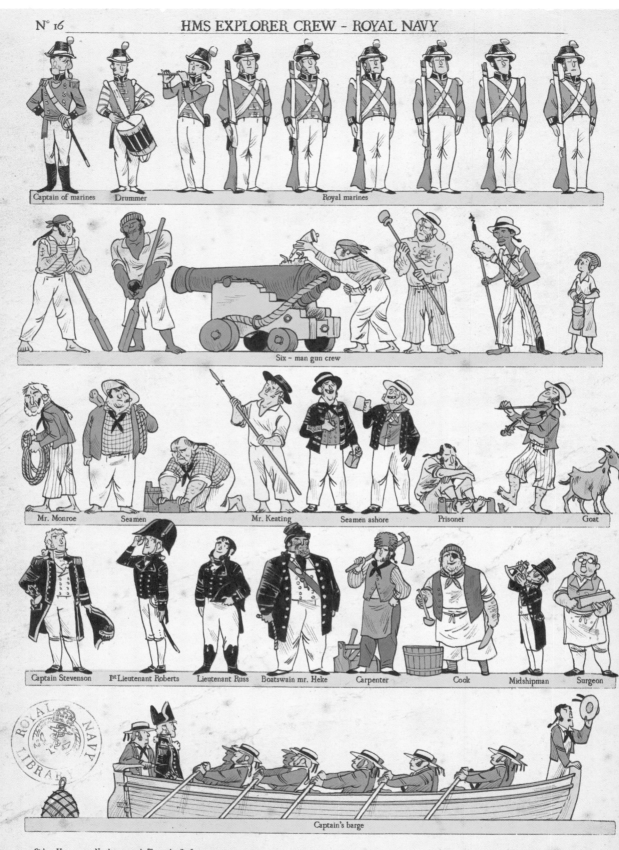

Captain of marines — Drummer — Royal marines

Six - man gun crew

Mr. Monroe — Seamen — Mr. Keating — Seamen ashore — Prisoner — Goat

Captain Stevenson — 1st Lieutenant Roberts — Lieutenant Russ — Boatswain mr. Heke — Carpenter — Cook — Midshipman — Surgeon

Captain's barge

Sidney House - 27, North-west road, Plymouth, 1806. - 10 pence

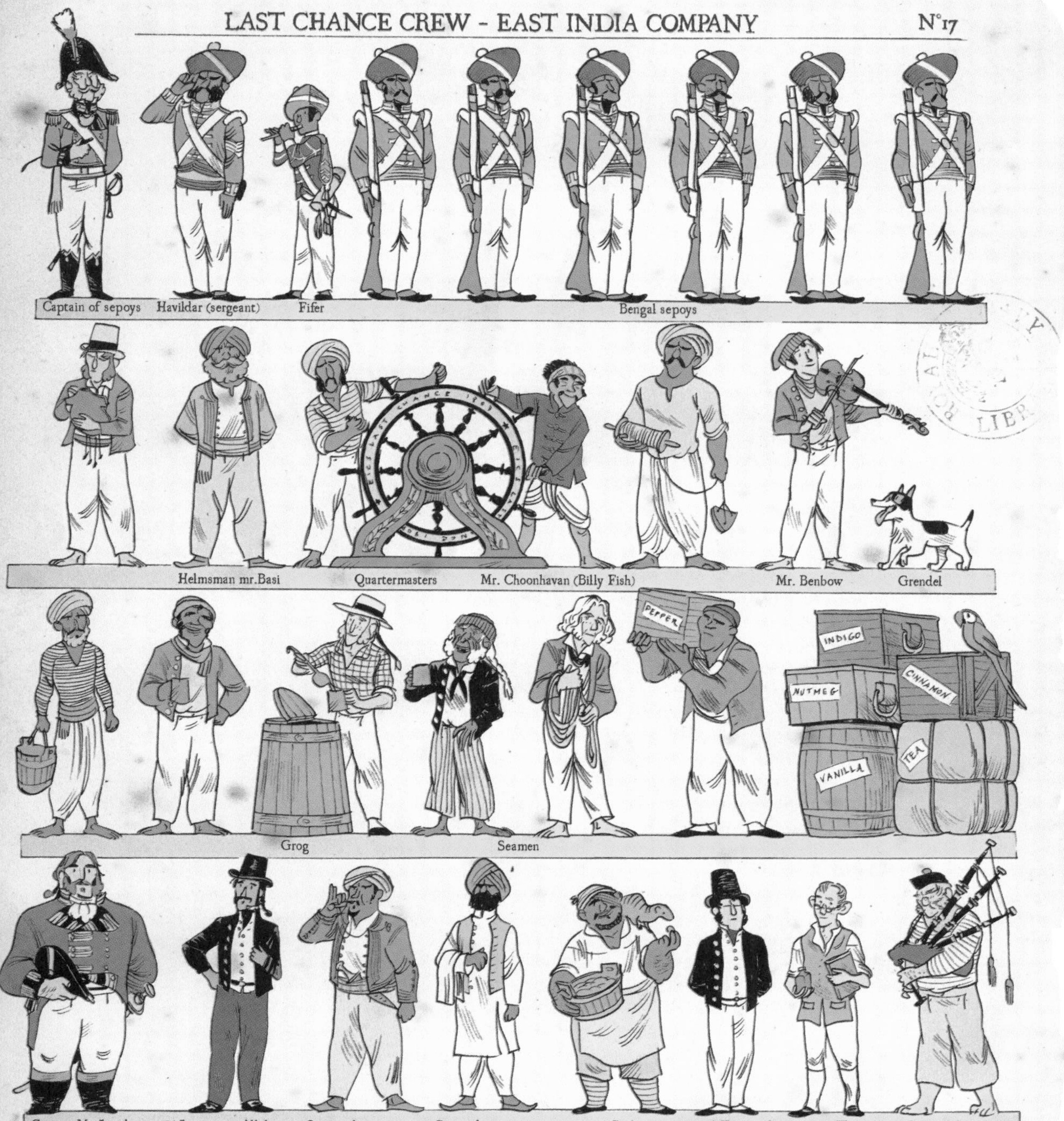
LAST CHANCE CREW - EAST INDIA COMPANY
N°17
Captain of sepoys
Havildar (sergeant)
Fifer
Bengal sepoys
Helmsman mr.Basi
Quartermasters
Mr. Choonhavan (Billy Fish)
Mr. Benbow
Grendel
PEPPER
INDIGO
NUTMEG
CINNAMON
VANILLA
TEA
Grog
Seamen
Captain MacLeod
1st Lieutenant Allali
Serang (boatswain)
Captain's servant
Cook
Officer
Surgeon mr. Turiman
Scottish bagpiper
Captain's barge
Sidney House - 27, North-west road, Plymouth, 1806. - 10 pence

East India Company Ship
Last Chance

*

Private Frigate in the service
of the Honorable East India Company
Built under the name of HMS Gannett at the
Chatham (London) Royal Shipyards in 1774.
Reactivated in 1803 under a new owner,
Captain Nathan MacLeod.
Current commander, Capt. Yassar Allali.

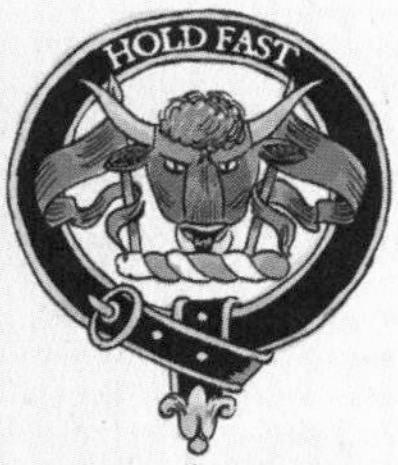
HOLD FAST

Clan MacLeod Emblem,
Skye Island,
Scottish Highlands.

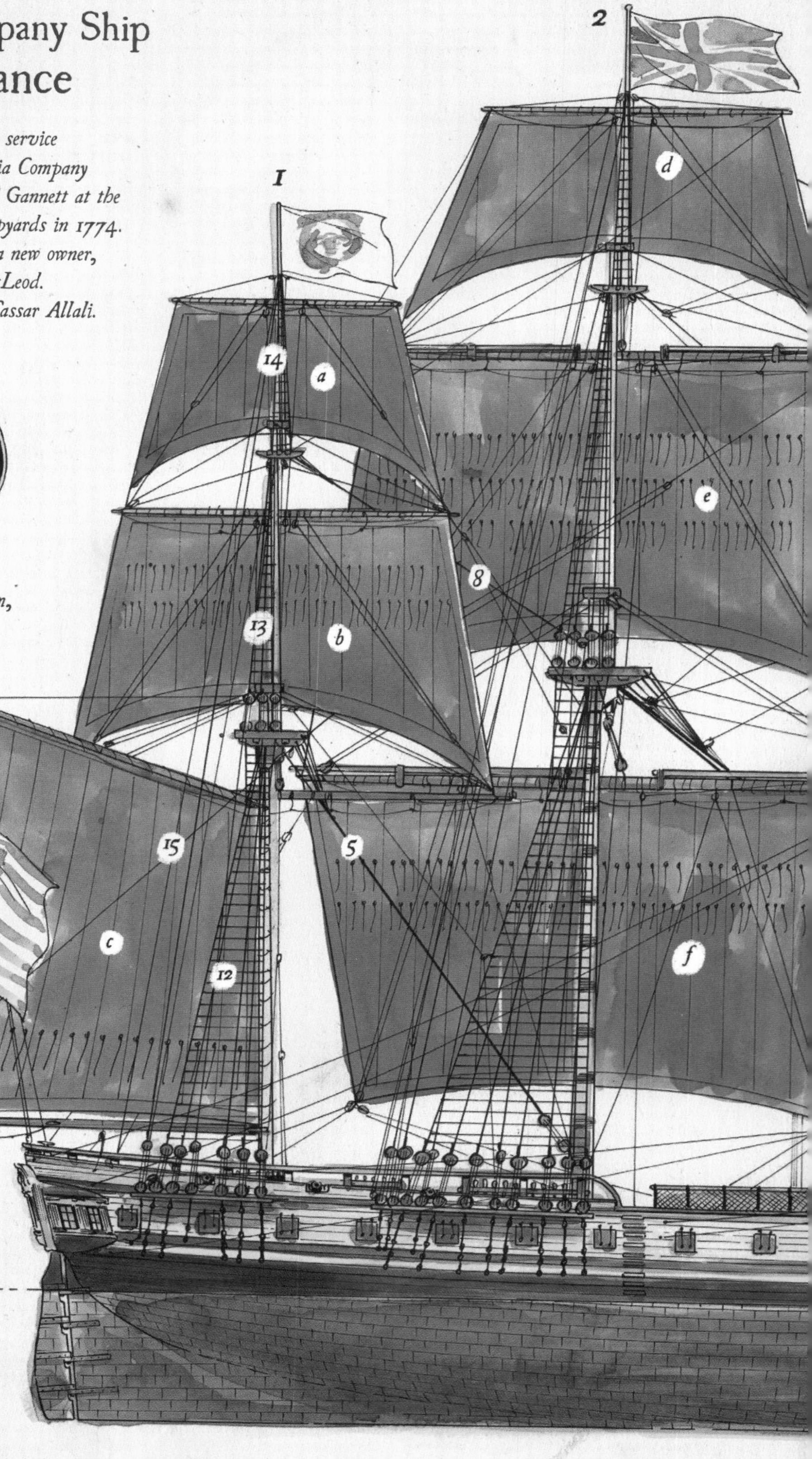
1
2
a
b
c
d
e
f
5
8
12
13
14
15